Using Microsoft® C/C++ 7

LEE ATKINSON
MARK ATKINSON
ED MITCHELL

PROGRAMMING
S E R I E S

ABOUT THE AUTHORS

LEE ATKINSON

Lee Atkinson is a 20-year veteran of the data processing industry. He has written code professionally in C, Pascal, COBOL, FORTRAN, PL/I, APL, and a number of assembly languages for machines ranging from the smallest micro-processors to IBM's top-of-the-line mainframes. He is currently an MVS systems programmer for a Mississippi-based regional retail company. He was coauthor for Que's *Using C* and *Using Borland C++ 3*. He can be contacted on CompuServe at 71641, 3122.

MARK ATKINSON

Mark Atkinson was introduced to computer programming in 1969 with a FORTRAN ballistics program that tracked the Saturn V rocket and astronauts to the moon. He has been involved with computing continuously since that time, including consulting and contract programming for IBM PCs and mainframes in a variety of languages. Based in Mississippi, he is currently a PC technician for one of the area's largest vendors of office systems. He was coauthor for Que's *Using C* and *Using Borland C++ 3*. He can be contacted on CompuServe at 73307, 252.

ED MITCHELL

Ed Mitchell has been developing PC software since before the introduction of the original IBM PC. He formerly worked for Software Publishing Corporation as an engineering manager where he was coauthor of the award-winning, best-selling PFS First Choice integrated software package. At SPC, he was also coauthor of one of the first word processors for the IBM PC, PFS Write (now known as Professional Write).

He is also the author of *Turbo Pascal Programmer's Reference* (Que, 1992), and *Software Construction Set for the IBM PC* (Hayden Books, 1984, under the pseudonym Eric Anderson). He has also written magazine articles on a variety of topics for many publications. He can be contacted on CompuServe at 73317, 2513.

TRADEMARK ACKNOWLEDGMENTS

Que Corporation has made every attempt to supply trademark information about company names, products, and services mentioned in the book. Trademarks indicated below were derived from various sources. Que Corporation cannot attest to the accuracy of this information.

ANSI is a registered trademark of American National Standards Institute.

AT&T and UNIX are registered trademarks of American Telephone & Telegraph.

EPSON is a registered trademark of Epson Corporation.

IBM is a registered trademark of International Business Machines Corporation.

Lotus is a registered trademark of Lotus Development Corporation.

CodeView, Microsoft, and MS-DOS are registered trademarks of Microsoft Corporation. Windows is a trademark of Microsoft Corporation.

WordStar is a registered trademark of MicroPro International Corporation.

OVERVIEW

Introduction 1

I Using Microsoft C/C++'s Basic Features

1 Getting Started with Microsoft C/C++ 11
2 Understanding the Foundations of C 61
3 Using C Functions 101
4 Using Pointers and Derived Types 139
5 Building, Compiling, and Testing
   Microsoft C/C++ Programs 187
6 Using the Microsoft C/C++ I/O Function Library 231
7 Using Memory Models 277
8 Using the Microsoft C/C++ Video Functions 311
9 Using CodeView and Profiler 355
10 Using Microsoft C/C++'s Advanced Features 385

II Using Microsoft C/C++'s Object-Oriented Features

11 Using C++ Classes 411
12 Creating C++ Objects 461
13 Accessing C++ Objects 507
14 Using Overloaded Functions and Operators in C++ 561
15 Using C++ Constructors and Destructors 611
16 Using C++ Streams 663
17 Using C++ Derived Classes 719
18 Object Control and Performance Issues 757

III Using Microsoft C/C++ with Windows

19 Introduction to Microsoft C/C++ Windows Programming 797
20 Designing Windows Applications 841
21 Writing Windows Applications with Microsoft C/C++ 885

A ASCII Charts...915
B Details on Using *printf()* and *scanf()* 919
C Details on Using *_exec...()* and *_spawn...()*............................927
D Program Listings for the *quad* Class 933
E Complete Listings of FCWIN Resources 947
   Index..961

TABLE OF CONTENTS

Introduction 1

What's New in Microsoft C/C++ 7.0...1
Who Should Read This Book 2
What This Book Is About 3
How This Book Is Organized 3
How To Use This Book 4
Conventions Used in This Book 4
A Note on Practicing C and C++ 7

I Using Microsoft C/C++'s Basic Features

1 Getting Started with Microsoft C/C++ 11

Understanding Your Microsoft C/C++ Disks 11
 Installing Microsoft C/C++ 12
 Running SETUP 12
 Using DOS Mode SETUP 13
 Using Windows-Based SETUP 14
 Installing Additional Libraries 16
 Selecting Memory Models 17
Using the Programmer's WorkBench (PWB) 19
 Starting the PWB 19
 Using the PWB's Menus and Windows 20
 The Menu System 21
 The Window System 22
Configuring Microsoft C/C++ 25
 Key Assignments 26
 Editor Settings 27
 Colors 28
 Build Options 29
 Set Project Template 29
 Language Options 30

LINK Options 31
NMAKE Options 31
Compiling and Executing Programs in the PWB 32
Compiling and Linking Outside the PWB 32
/Yc, /Yd, /Yu 35
Writing Your First C Program 36
Understanding C Program Structure 36
Preprocessor Directives 38
Global Declarations 40
The *main( )* Function 42
User-Defined Functions 43
Using the Editor To Write a Program 43
Introducing the Library Functions 49
Using Some Basic Input Functions 49
The *get...( )* Functions 50
The *scanf( )* Function 51
Using Some Basic Output Functions 53
The *put...( )* Functions 53
The *printf( )* Function 54
Using Some Format-Conversion Functions 55
The *atoi( )* Function 56
The *toupper( )* Function 57
Exercises 58
Summary 59

2 Understanding the Foundations of C 61

Laying the Foundations 61
Understanding Source, Object, and Load Modules 61
Understanding Program Logic and Execution Flow 64
Using Conditional Instructions 64
Using Loop Instructions 68
Using the Basic Data Types 72
Understanding C's Basic Data Types 72
Integers 72
Floating-Point Numbers 73
Character Data 74
Knowing Where To Define Data Objects 75
Writing C Expressions and Statements 79
Understanding Expressions and Statements 79
Introducing the C Operator Set 81
Controlling Type Conversions 85
Understanding Implicit Type Conversions 86

Using C Macros 89
    Defining Object-Like Macros 89
    Defining Function-Like Macros 93
Exercises 97
Summary 98

3 Using C Functions 101

Understanding the *main( )* Function and Library Functions .. 101
    Writing the *main( )* Function 102
    Using Library Functions 105
        Knowing What Library Functions Are Available 105
        Including Library Functions in Your Program 106
Writing Your Own Functions 108
    Writing Prototypes for Your Functions 109
    Passing Arguments to Your Functions 111
Returning Values from Functions 115
    Defining and Using Function Types 115
    Using Functions Like Objects 118
Understanding Storage Classes 119
    Determining a Variable's Scope 119
    Determining a Variable's Duration 121
    Determining a Variable's Linkage 122
Using Advanced Program Control Logic 123
    Writing Loop-Control Statements 123
        Using *goto* 124
        Using *break* 125
        Using *continue* 125
    Changing the Flow of Program Execution 126
        Using *exit( )* and *abort( )* 126
        Using the *system( )*, *exec...( )*,
            and *spawn...( )* Functions 128
Using Variable Argument Lists 130
    Designing Variable Argument Lists 130
    Using the *va_...( )* Functions 131
Exercises 136
Summary 136

4 Using Pointers and Derived Types 139

Understanding Standard C Derived Types 139
    Understanding C's Typing Scheme 140
    Creating New Types from Old 140
Understanding C Pointers 144
    Understanding Indirect Addressing 145
    Using C's Indirection and Address-of Operators 151

Using Arrays and Strings 155
    Declaring and Using Arrays of Objects 156
    Understanding C Strings 159
Using Structures and Unions 163
    Building Structures from Different Types 164
    Using Unions To Give Alternate Views of Structures
        and Objects 167
Using Pointers to Functions 170
    Declaring and Initializing Pointers to Functions 170
    Calling Functions with a Pointer Reference 171
Using Pointers with Dynamic Memory 175
    Your C Program and Dynamic Memory 176
    Using Dynamic Memory 178
Exercises 185
Summary 185

5 Building, Compiling, and Testing Microsoft C/C++ Programs 187

Using Several Source Files for One Program 188
    Deciding What To Put in a Source File 188
    Setting Up a Microsoft C/C++ Project File 208
    Creating Project Files 208
Understanding External References 210
    Using the *extern* Keyword 210
    Using External Functions 212
Writing Header Files for External Modules 213
    Deciding What Goes in the Header File 214
    Including User-Supplied Header Files 215
Using Conditional Compiler Directives in Header Files 216
Compiling and Running Programs with the PWB 219
    Compiling and Running Simple Programs 219
    Compiling and Running Complex Programs 220
The NMAKE Utility Program 221
    Example Use of NMAKE 222
    Explicit Rules 224
Important: List All Files 225
    Command Lines 225
    Inference Rules 226
    Macros 226
    Conditional Directives 227
Exercises 229
Summary 230

6 Using the Microsoft C/C++ I/O Function Library 231

Understanding I/O Concepts 231
    Understanding Files and Devices 232
    Understanding Files and Streams 234
    Understanding Text and Binary Streams 235
Using the Standard Streams for I/O 237
    Using Formatted I/O Functions 237
        Understanding *scanf( )* 241
        Understanding *printf( )* 244
    Using Character I/O Functions 247
Using the File Control Functions 253
    Opening, Closing, and Controlling Files 253
    Controlling File Buffers 257
Using the Direct File I/O Functions 259
    Understanding Direct I/O Concepts 260
    Reading and Writing Direct Files 261
Using the File-Positioning Functions 268
    Obtaining the Current File Position 269
    Setting a New File Position 270
Handling File I/O Errors 272
    Detecting File I/O Errors 272
    Displaying and Clearing File I/O Errors 273
Exercises 274
Summary 274

7 Using Memory Models 277

Introducing 80x86 Architecture 278
    Understanding Segments, Paragraphs, and Offsets 278
    Understanding CPU Addressing Registers 280
Understanding *near*, *far*, and *huge* Pointers 283
    Choosing the Pointer Size You Want 283
    Using the *near*, *far*, and *huge* Specifiers 286
Using the Six Microsoft C/C++ Memory Models 288
    Deciding Which Memory Model To Use 289
    Programming with Mixed Models 290
Creating .COM Executable Program Files 293
    Using .COM Files 293
Understanding the Microsoft Overlay Virtual Environment ...295
    Knowing What an Overlay Manager Does 295
    Understanding MOVE 296
Designing and Creating Overlay Programs 297
    Deciding What Modules To Overlay 297
    Compiling and Linking an Overlay Program 299

Using Virtual Memory 304
    Using _vlock() 307
    Freeing up a Virtual Memory Block 308
    Terminating Virtual Memory Usage 308
Exercises 308
Summary 309

8 Using the Microsoft C/C++ Video Functions 311

Understanding the IBM/PC Text Modes 311
    Surveying PC Video Adapters and Screens 312
    Understanding Memory-Mapped Screen I/O 313
Controlling the Text Screen 314
    Selecting a Video Mode 314
    Selecting Text Colors 315
    Displaying Text in Color 317
Using the Window Functions 318
    Placing Text at a Specific Screen Location 320
    Determining the Current Text-Mode Settings 321
    Determining the Current Text Color Settings....................321
    Determining the Current Text Window Boundaries 322
    Determining the Current Text Output Position 322
    Determining Other Screen Attributes 322
Understanding the IBM/PC Graphics Mode..............................323
    Understanding Pixels and Palettes 323
    Using Color Palettes 324
    Using CGA Color Palettes 325
    Selecting a Background Color 326
    Selecting Colors from the Current Palette 326
    Using CGA High-Resolution Mode....................................327
    Selecting EGA/VGA Video Mode Colors 327
    Custom Designing VGA Palette Colors 328
    Custom Designing MCGA Color Palettes 330
    Custom Designing EGA Palette Colors 330
Introducing the Graphics Drawing Functions 330
    Using _setvieworg() 331
    Using _setviewport()...332
    Using Window Coordinates 333
Using the Drawing and Filling Functions 334
    Drawing Filled Objects 339
    Controlling the Drawing Functions 341
    Using _getcurrentposition()..341
    Using _setlinestyle() 341
    Using _setfillmask() 343
    Clearing the Graphics Display Screen 345
    Controlling the Graphics Screen 346

Using Text in Graphics Mode 346
    Understanding Fonts 347
    Using the Graphics-Mode Text Functions 348
    Using Microsoft Windows Fonts 351
    Using Other Font Functions 351
Exercises 352
Summary 352

9 Using CodeView and Profiler 355

Setting Up for Debugging 356
    Understanding Bugs and Debuggers 356
    Preparing To Run CodeView from the PWB 358
Using CodeView 359
    Running a Program with CodeView 360
    Mixing Source and Assembly Language 364
    Using the Command Window 364
    Viewing Data 366
Setting Breakpoints 368
Using Microsoft Profiler 370
    Knowing What Profiling Is 370
    The Profiling Process 370
    Starting Microsoft Profiler 372
    Knowing Basic Profiling Information 372
    Improving ptest1 378
    Selecting a Profiling Mode 380
    Looking Toward Other Profiling Features 381
Exercises 382
Summary 382

10 Using Microsoft C/C++'s Advanced Features 385

Using Inline Assembly Language 386
    Understanding the Inline Assembly Environment 386
    Using the __asm Keyword 387
Using Interrupt Functions 391
    Understanding 80x86 Interrupt Architecture 391
    Using the Microsoft Interrupt Interfaces 393
Using Interrupt Handlers 396
    Declaring Interrupt Handler Functions 397
    Implementing a Timer Tick Interrupt Handler 398
Using Program Optimization Features 403
Using p-code 406
Exercises 407
Summary 407

II Using Microsoft C/C++'s Object-Oriented Features

11 Using C++ Classes 411

Important Features of C++ 412
How to Access C++ Features 412
Derived Types in C and C++..413
    Redefining "Derived" in C++......................................413
    Understanding C++ Encapsulation..............................415
    Declaring Classes with *struct* 417
Declaring C++ Classes..422
    Understanding the *class* Declaration 425
        Using Class Declaration Syntax 426
        Declaring Class Members 429
        Building a LIFO Stack Class 429
        Using the *this* Pointer 438
    Using the *public*, *private*, and *protected* Keywords 444
Writing Member Functions for a Class 445
    Associating Member Functions with a Class 446
        Compiling Member Functions Separately 446
        Declaring Inline Member Functions 447
        Specifying Default Arguments
            for Member Functions 449
    Providing Constructor and Destructor Functions 450
Using Friend Functions 455
    Including Friend Functions in a Class............................455
    Deciding When To Use a Friend Function 456
Exercises 457
Summary 458

12 Creating C++ Objects 461

Defining C++ Objects 461
    Assigning Storage Classes to Class Objects 462
    Defining Arbitrary-Duration Class Objects 464
    Defining Local (*auto*) Class Objects 482
    Defining Global (*static*) Class Objects 491
Initializing Class Objects 500
    Using Constructors To Initialize Class Objects 501
    Using Initializer Lists 503
Exercises 504
Summary 505

13 Accessing C++ Objects 507

Using the Scope Resolution Operator 507
   Using Scope Resolution In General 508
   Using Scope Resolution for Syntax Control 510
   Controlling Ambiguities with Scope Resolution 512
Understanding the C++ Scope Rules......................................517
   Understanding the Differences Between C
      and C++ Scope..517
   Examining the C++ Scope Rules 519
Communicating with C++ Objects..523
   Sending Messages to Objects 523
   Understanding *this 548
Using the Reference Operator 549
   Evolving the Reference Operator from
      the Address-Of Operator 549
   Understanding the Reference Operator 550
Using Objects as Function Parameters 551
   Passing Objects by Value and by Reference 551
   Accessing Other Objects from a Member Function 553
Using Pointers to Objects 555
   Understanding When Pointers Are Required 555
   Declaring Pointers and Arrays of Objects 557
Exercises 559
Summary 559

14 Using Overloaded Functions and Operators in C++ 561

Overloading Member Functions 561
   Understanding C++ Overloading 562
   Declaring Overloaded Member Functions 565
Overloading Friend and Nonmember Functions......................567
   Overloading Friends of a Class 568
   Overloading Nonmember Functions 573
Understanding Type-Safe Linkage 575
   Understanding Function Mangling......................................575
   Controlling Linkage Problems with Standard C
      Include Files 576
Overloading Operators with C++ 579
   Understanding Operator Overloading 580
   Declaring Overloaded Operator Functions 585
     Setting the Stage for Operator Functions 585
     Understanding Overloaded Operator
        Function Syntax 586
     Specifying Arguments for Overloaded
        Operator Functions 588

Specifying a Return Type for
    an Operator Function 589
    Overloading Operators with Friend Functions 591
    Defining Cast Operator Functions 594
  Overloading Binary and Unary Operators 595
Overloading the Subscript and Function Call Operators 598
  Using an Overloaded Subscript Operator 598
  Using an Overloaded Function Call Operator 603
Exercises 607
Summary 608

15 Using C++ Constructors and Destructors 611

Understanding Constructor and Destructor Calls 612
  Declaring Constructors and Destructors 612
    Declaring Constructor Functions 613
    Declaring Destructor Functions 618
  Using Constructor Initializers 620
  When Are Constructor Functions Called? 624
  When Are Destructor Functions Called? 632
Overloading Constructor Functions 636
Writing a Default Constructor Function 637
  Writing Other Constructors 640
  Deciding When You Need a Copy Constructor 642
Using operator *new( )* and operator *delete( )* 643
  Using *new* and *delete* in General 643
  Dynamically Creating and Deleting Class Objects 646
Overloading operator *new( )* and operator *delete( )* 648
  Overloading the Global Operators 649
  Overloading the Operators for a Class 657
Exercises 660
Summary 660

16 Using C++ Streams 663

Introducing C++ Streams 663
  Comparing C++ Streams to Standard Streams 664
  Using C++ Streams for Standard I/O 667
Handling C++ Stream Errors 678
  Detecting C++ Stream Error States 679
  Using the Stream State Member Functions 682
Controlling Data Formats with C++ Streams 684
  Using Inserters and Extractors for Built-In Types 684
  Overloading the << and >> Operators 690

Using C++ Stream Manipulators 694
    Understanding C++ Manipulators 695
    Using Manipulators To Change States and Attributes 696
Using C++ File I/O Streams 705
    Reading and Writing *fstream* Files 710
    File Positioning with C++ Streams 712
Exercises 714
Summary 715

17 Using C++ Derived Classes 719

Reusing Code Without Inheritance 719
    Understanding Code Reusability 720
    Reusing Code by Composition 721
Using Single Base Classes 725
    Understanding Inheritance 725
    Declaring Base Classes and Derived Classes 726
Using Virtual Functions 735
    Using Late Binding and Virtual Functions 735
    Using Scope Resolution To Control Member
        Function Access 740
Using Multiple Base Classes 741
    Deriving from More Than One Base Class 741
    Declaring and Using Virtual Base Classes 745
Deriving Classes from Abstract Classes 747
    Understanding Pure Virtual Functions 748
    Implementing Pure Virtual Functions 748
Using Constructors and Destructors with Inheritance 750
    Initialization Code Is Not Inherited 750
    Understanding the Order of Constructor
        and Destructor Calls with Inheritance 751
    Using Virtual Destructor Functions 751
Exercises 754
Summary 755

18 Object Control and Performance Issues 757

User-Defined Type Conversions 758
    Using Constructors to Convert Types 758
    Overloading Typecast Operators 760
Using Generic Classes 764
    Understanding Abstraction and Generic Class Design 765
    Building Generic Classes 769

Controlling Object Behavior and Performance 778
Using Friend Functions to Boost Efficiency 778
Using the *static* Storage Class
    to Avoid Repetitive Instantiation 779
Using References and Pointers 782
Using Inline Functions to Eliminate Function Calls 785
Using the Source Browser 786
Finding Unreferenced Symbols 789
Using the Call Tree...790
Exercises 792
Summary 793

III Using Microsoft C/C++ with Windows

19 Introduction to Microsoft C/C++ Windows Programming 797

Understanding the Windows Programming Environment 798
Understanding the QuickWin Library 799
Compiling the order.c Program 800
Running a QuickWin Application 803
Using the Special Features of QuickWin 803
Adding Multiple Windows 804
Another Approach to Creating Child Windows 807
Exiting from a Window 808
Using the About Box 808
Controlling a Window's Size and Location 808
Adding Scroll Bars to a Child Window 809
Accessing Menu Bar Functions 810
Programming in the Windows Applications
    Programming Interface 810
Understanding the Windows Multitasking Environment 811
Windows Is an Object-Oriented Environment 814
Compiling and Linking Windows Applications 822
Using the PWB to Compile and Link a
    Windows Application 823
Using the *cl* Command-Line Compiler 823
Using The Resource Compiler 824
Preparing Resource Files 824
Creating Resources 825
Resources Needed by the fcwin.c Sample Program 826
Creating and Editing Menus..827

Creating and Editing Dialog Boxes 829
Creating and Editing Icons 835
Compiling Resources Using the Resource Compiler 837
Exercises 838
Summary 839

20 Designing Windows Applications 841

Setting Up the Windows Application Environment 841
The WINSTUB.EXE Program 842
Windows Directory Usage 843
Learn by Doing: Designing fcwin.c 845
Creating Source Files for Windows Applications 876
Understanding the Windows 3.1
Programming Environment 877
Creating a Module-Definition File 878
Designing the Program's Header File 879
Creating a Project File for FCWIN 881
Exercises 882
Summary 882

21 Writing Windows Applications with Microsoft C/C++ 885

Designing Windows Interfaces 885
Registering the Window Class 886
Setting Up the Main Message Loop 889
Writing the *WndProc( )* Function 891
Setting Up Callback Functions for Dialogs 892
Creating Dialog Functions 893
Controlling the Dialog 894
Using *MessageBox( )* for Pop-Up Help
and Error Messages 896
Spooling Hard Copy to the Windows Print Manager 898
Using Dynamic-Link Libraries 906
Understanding DLLs 907
Writing a DLL Application 908
Exercises 912
Summary and Conclusion 913

A ASCII Charts 915

B Details on Using *printf( )* and *scanf( )* 919

xxiii

C Details on Using _exec...() and _spawn...() 927

D Program Listings for the *quad* Class 933

E Complete Listings of FCWIN Resources 947

Index..961

Introduction

Welcome to the exciting, changing world of C and C++ programming. The C language is evolving rapidly into one of the most popular and powerful programming languages in existence. Microsoft's C/C++ 7.0 compiler and development environment make available to personal computer programmers sophisticated programming tools especially geared to the creation of large software projects.

What's New in Microsoft C/C++ 7.0

Microsoft C/C++ 7.0 represents a major upgrade to Microsoft's C 6.0 product. The most important new feature is, of course, the introduction of ANSI 2.1 C++ compatibility, which provides a new world of object-oriented programming capabilities to Microsoft C developers. Of particular importance, Microsoft C++ strives to provide the most accurate interpretation of the ANSI 2.1 C++ language specification. Other popular C++ compilers contain a number of subtle C++ implementation errors that could cause a problem if your code must be compatible between different hardware platforms.

Microsoft C/C++ 7.0, however, includes many new and significantly enhanced features beyond the C++ language. Traditionally, by using Microsoft C, you could create .EXE or .COM executable program files containing 80x86 machine instructions. With C/C++ 7.0, you now have the option to generate *p-code*—or *packed-code*—instructions. The use of p-code can create programs that are 40- to 60-percent smaller than native code programs. Best of all, you can mix native code and p-code in the same program, using native code for time-critical program sections and p-code for areas in which speed is not as important.

Microsoft C/C++ 7.0 includes additional optimizations to reduce compile times and produce faster executables.

Lastly, Microsoft introduces the Microsoft Foundation Classes/Application Framework. These class libraries provide an object-oriented framework with which you can develop Microsoft Windows applications.

Who Should Read This Book

The present explosive growth in popularity of the C language and its successor language C++ is the continuation of a phenomenon that quietly began when C was the primary language used by UNIX systems programmers. Many people with desktop PCs and mainframe computers of all brands now also know and use C and C++. C is quickly becoming the language of choice for the serious programmer, whether for the individual or the professional software developer. C++ is also rapidly becoming quite popular. C++ is intimately related to C, yet there are enough differences between C and C++ to speak of two distinct languages. You will discover what those differences are in this book.

This book is for you if you belong to one or more of the following groups of people:

■ *People who want to learn more about C programming.* This group includes users who know nothing about C or C++, as well as users who have some experience with C or C++. This book has plenty of introductory material to get the beginner started. The book also contains enough intermediate and advanced material to add significantly to the experienced programmer's pool of knowledge.

■ *People who specifically want to use the Microsoft C/C++ programming environment.*

■ *People who want to gain an understanding of object-oriented programming.*

■ *People who want to learn the C++ language.*

■ *People who want to have an introduction to creating Microsoft Windows applications.*

What This Book Is About

Using Microsoft C/C++ 7 has two purposes: to help you learn C and C++, and to show you how to use the Microsoft C++ programming and development environment.

The primary focus of this book is on the C and C++ languages, particularly as they are implemented in Microsoft C++. You will probably be more interested in writing C and C++ programs than in reading about the text editor or debugger (although these are covered, also). *Using Microsoft C/C++ 7,* therefore, is primarily a comprehensive introduction to the C and C++ languages.

How This Book Is Organized

The Microsoft C++ package is well-documented—almost too well, in fact. With more than 8,000 pages of documentation provided by Microsoft, you need a book that begins with the basics, guides you through a jungle of information, and makes sure that you understand the important points—all in an orderly manner that is conducive to efficient learning. That's what *Using Microsoft C/C++ 7* does. It presents the essential material succinctly so that your first experience with Microsoft C/C++ is pleasant and productive.

This book is a learning tool rather than a reference manual. Your needs as a student have been considered, as well as your needs as a programmer. The book is specifically organized to ease your introduction to C and C++ and to the programming environment.

- *The book is divided into three parts.* Part I covers the basic Microsoft C++ programming environment and the C (non-object-oriented) language. Part II covers the C++ (object-oriented) language. Part III is a basic introduction to the world of Windows application programming.

- *The chapters are divided into carefully designed sections.* These sections contain just the right amount of material so that you can digest it easily.

- *The chapters appear in an order that does not require you to look ahead to comprehend what is being covered.* In general, each chapter stands alone. You do not need to read material in, for example, the next three chapters to understand the current chapter.

- *The order of presentation is designed to defer the more complicated aspects of C and C++.* The languages' foundations must come first, but this does not mean that you are deprived of the more powerful and technical features of Microsoft C++.

How To Use This Book

How you approach this book depends on your level of experience with C and C++. If you have little or no C programming experience, you should start at the beginning and work straight through to the end. That way, you can build your knowledge of C and C++ in the proper order and minimize your confusion. If, however, you already have some C and C++ programming experience, you may want to skip immediately to the topics that interest you. This second approach is recommended if you already have a solid understanding of C language structure.

Whether or not you have prior experience, you should read an entire section at a time. The sections within the chapters are short enough to be read in one sitting, and they are also sufficiently self-contained so that you do not need to read several sections to understand one point.

Conventions Used in This Book

To get the most out of this book, you need to know something about how it is designed. The chapters contain italicized text, bulleted lists, numbered lists, figures, program listings, code fragments, and tables of information. All these design features should help you understand the material being presented.

Italic type is used to emphasize an important word or phrase. You should pay close attention to italicized text. It is used also to introduce new technical terms. An italicized term is followed immediately by a definition or an explanation.

Bulleted lists have the following characteristics:

■ *Each item in a bulleted list is preceded by a black box (the bullet).* The bullet is a special flag that draws your attention to important material.

■ *The order of items in a bulleted list is not mandatory.* In other words, the items represent related points you should understand, but not in a special sequence.

■ *The text for items in a bulleted list is often longer than the text you see in other kinds of lists.* Items in bulleted lists contain explanations rather than simple actions.

Numbered lists contain actions you should perform, or lists of items that must be kept in a particular sequence. When you see a numbered list, you should do the following:

1. Start at the beginning of the list. Don't skip ahead to later items in the list. Order is important.

2. Make sure that you completely understand each item as you encounter it.

3. Read all the items in the list. Don't skip any of them—each item is important.

Figures are pictures or graphics that can help you understand the text. Each figure has a number that is comprised of the chapter number (or letter, in the case of the Introduction or Appendixes) and the number of the figure in its sequence within the chapter. Figure I.1, which is the first figure in the Introduction, shows how a figure will appear.

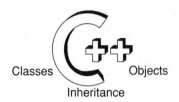

Figure I.1.

A sample illustration.

Program listings give the C or C++ source code for a complete program, or perhaps for a program module that can be compiled separately. In either case, you *can* compile source code shown in a program listing. Listing I.1, for example, shows the source code for a complete program. (Most complete programs are much longer than this short sample.)

Listing I.1. begin.c. A sample program listing.

```
1   #include <stdio.h>
2
3   void main()
4   {
5   puts( "------ My program works!! ------" );
6   }
```

You should notice a couple of things about listing I.1. As this listing shows, complete program listings have line numbers down the left side of the page. These line numbers are for reference only. *You should not type the line numbers if you want to enter and compile the program.* Program listings, like figures, are numbered (see the heading for listing I.1). However, the reference numbers for figures and program listings are numbered independently of each other. Note that this Introduction has a figure I.1 *and* a listing I.1.

A *code fragment* also shows C or C++ source code, but the code does not make up a complete program (you cannot compile the fragment). Code fragments appear directly in the text and do not have headings, reference numbers, or line numbers. Code fragments contain enough source code to illustrate a point, but they are short (usually only five or six lines long). Note that a special monospace typeface is used for C keywords, program listings, and code fragments.

Characters that you are asked to type appear in **bold**. Also in lines that you must type, ***bold italic*** is used for characters that hold the place of a drive or file name (such as *n:*) or anything else you must substitute.

The syntax form is a special kind of code fragment that shows you the general form used for writing a C statement or declaration. A syntax form looks like this:

```
struct ,tag_opt { member-list_opt } obj-name_opt ;
```

In a syntax form, the *italicized* characters are placeholders for names and labels of your own choosing, whereas you must write the regular monospace items exactly as you see them. Furthermore, the letters opt, when shown as a subscript following an item, indicate that the item is optional—it does not have to be present at all.

Tables appear where lists and columns of information are suitable. Tables also have their own headings and reference numbers—again, independent of the numbers for figures and program listings. Table I.1 shows how a table is presented in this book.

Table I.1. The formatting conventions used in *Using Microsoft C/C++ 7*.

Format Convention	Purpose
Italic	An eye-catching typestyle used to emphasize important words or phrases.
Bulleted list	A list of items with a bullet flagging each item. The sequence of these items is not usually important.
Numbered list	A list of items with numbers flagging each item. The sequence of these items is important.
Program listing	A complete program that you can compile.
Code fragment	A small number of C or C++ source code lines that illustrate a single point. You cannot compile a code fragment apart from other code.
Table	Information arranged in columnar format. A table may or may not contain explanations or descriptions.

A Note on Practicing C and C++

Many readers of this book already have some experience writing C programs. If you have such experience, you need no further explanation about how to learn C.

If, however, you are approaching C and C++ for the first time, you need to know an important point about learning C: It is impossible to learn C or C++ without writing code, compiling your programs, and observing the way they work (or possibly don't work).

Because practicing C programming is essential to learning C or C++, a section called "Exercises" appears at the end of each chapter. In that section, you can practice what you have just learned in the chapter. When appropriate, hints and tips about writing the exercise code are provided; it is up to you, however, to devise a program that does what it is supposed to do. You will know when you have the correct solution: The program will work, and you will have solved a problem on your own. After all, that is what C programming is all about—finding solutions to your problems.

PART

I

OUTLINE

1   Getting Started with Microsoft C/C++

2   Understanding the Foundations of C

3   Using C Functions

4   Using Pointers and Derived Types

5   Building, Compiling, and Testing Microsoft C/C++ Programs

6   Using the Microsoft C/C++ I/O Function Library

7   Using Memory Models

8   Using the Microsoft C/C++ Video Functions

9   Using CodeVeiw and Profiler

10   Using Microsoft C/C++'s Advanced Features

Using Microsoft C/C++'s Basic Features

Getting Started with Microsoft C/C++

T his chapter helps you install Microsoft C/C++ on your computer and
shows you how to start taking advantage of the powerful features of
Microsoft C/C++. First, you learn how to install Microsoft C/C++ and configure
it for your particular needs. Next, you explore some of the most useful features
of the Programmer's WorkBench (PWB). Finally, after becoming familiar with
the PWB, you learn how to write a simple C program.

Understanding Your Microsoft C/C++ Disks

When you get your Microsoft C/C++ package, you may be surprised by the
number of disks you receive. Fortunately, you don't have to worry about
keeping track of every file on these disks. The SETUP program does the hard
work for you.

Before you begin the installation, take a few minutes to make backup copies of
your distribution disks. Because Microsoft does not copy-protect its disks, you
can use the DOS DISKCOPY program to make backup copies.

Installing Microsoft C/C++

The Microsoft C/C++ package consists of a set of nine 3 1/2-inch disks or eleven 5 1/4-inch disks, plus a separate Microsoft Source Profiler disk. These disks contain everything you need to perform a complete installation of Microsoft C/C++.

To perform the installation, you must run the SETUP program that Microsoft provides on the Microsoft C/C++ Setup/Disk 1. SETUP automatically determines if Microsoft Windows is installed on your computer (you must have either Windows 3.0 or 3.1). If Windows is available, SETUP runs as a Windows application. If Windows is not available, SETUP runs as a DOS application.

If you wish to develop Windows applications, you must have Windows installed on your system. When SETUP is run as a DOS application, it installs only the DOS development tools.

If Windows is not already installed on your hard disk and you wish to develop Windows applications, install Windows before you install Microsoft C/C++ 7.0.

Depending on the options you select, Microsoft C/C++ requires between 10 and 20 megabytes of disk space. A standard installation—including the Windows development tools, class libraries, and sample files—falls in the 15- to 30-megabyte range. A minimal system containing the basic C/C++ compiler for developing DOS applications only, two memory model configurations, the Programmer's WorkBench, the CodeView debugger, and the online help files requires approximately 10 megabytes.

Running SETUP

Installing Microsoft C/C++ and its companion products is an easy task. Microsoft's SETUP program relieves you of the strain of installing a large package. Basically, all you have to do is tell the SETUP program which options you want, and then load each disk when prompted. The program does the rest of the work for you, except for inserting the appropriate disks!

The Microsoft Source Profiler is not installed by the Microsoft C/C++ SETUP program. To install the Profiler, you first should install the Microsoft C/C++ package. Then insert the Microsoft Source Profiler Setup disk into an appropriate disk drive and type:

n:setup

where *n*: is the floppy drive containing the Setup disk.

Before running SETUP, be sure that you have enough space available on your hard drive. A standard installation requires about 20 megabytes of disk space and takes one to two hours to complete.

To begin the installation process, put the disk labeled Microsoft C/C++ Setup/Disk 1 in a floppy disk drive and type

n:setup

where *n*: is the floppy drive that contains the Setup disk.

As SETUP starts executing, it automatically searches for Microsoft Windows and switches to a Windows SETUP application if Windows is already installed on your hard disk. If Windows is unavailable, SETUP runs as a DOS application and provides a somewhat different set of installation options.

Using DOS Mode SETUP

If you are using the DOS-based version of SETUP, read this section. If you are using the Windows versions of SETUP, skip to the next section "Using Windows-Based SETUP."

The DOS SETUP displays the screen shown in Figure 1.1. For the simplest installation process, use the arrow keys to move the highlight bar to *Install the MS C/C++ compiler using defaults* and press the Enter key.

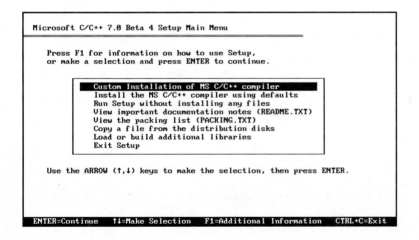

```
Microsoft C/C++ 7.0 Beta 4 Setup Main Menu
─────────────────────────────────────────────────────

   Press F1 for information on how to use Setup,
   or make a selection and press ENTER to continue.

        ┌──────────────────────────────────────────────┐
        │ Custom Installation of MS C/C++ compiler     │
        │ Install the MS C/C++ compiler using defaults │
        │ Run Setup without installing any files       │
        │ View important documentation notes (README.TXT)│
        │ View the packing list (PACKING.TXT)          │
        │ Copy a file from the distribution disks      │
        │ Load or build additional libraries           │
        │ Exit Setup                                   │
        └──────────────────────────────────────────────┘

   Use the ARROW (↑,↓) keys to make the selection, then press ENTER.



 ENTER=Continue    ↑↓=Make Selection   F1=Additional Information   CTRL+C=Exit
```

Figure 1.1.

The DOS SETUP Main Menu.

The default installation directory for the Microsoft C/C++ 7.0 packages is \C700. Throughout the examples in this book, the \C700 directory is assumed to contain the Microsoft C/C++ package. Feel free, however, to install the C/C++ compiler package in another directory.

To select a custom installation, choose Custom Installation of MS C/C++ compiler. This option displays a screen showing the current list of components to be installed (see Figure 1.2).

Figure 1.2.

The DOS SETUP custom installation screen.

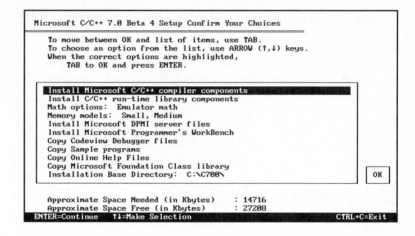

```
Microsoft C/C++ 7.0 Beta 4 Setup Confirm Your Choices

    To move between OK and list of items, use TAB.
    To choose an option from the list, use ARROW (↑,↓) keys.
    When the correct options are highlighted,
        TAB to OK and press ENTER.

  ┌─────────────────────────────────────────────────────┐
  │ Install Microsoft C/C++ compiler components          │      ┌────┐
  │ Install C/C++ run-time library components            │      │ OK │
  │ Math options:   Emulator math                        │      └────┘
  │ Memory models:  Small, Medium                        │
  │ Install Microsoft DPMI server files                  │
  │ Install Microsoft Programmer's WorkBench             │
  │ Copy Codeview Debugger files                         │
  │ Copy Sample programs                                 │
  │ Copy Online Help Files                               │
  │ Copy Microsoft Foundation Class library              │
  │ Installation Base Directory:  C:\C700\               │
  └─────────────────────────────────────────────────────┘

    Approximate Space Needed (in Kbytes)     : 14716
    Approximate Space Free  (in Kbytes)      : 27208
  ENTER=Continue   ↑↓=Make Selection                   CTRL+C=Exit
```

To change an option, use the cursor keys to move the highlight bar to the option you wish to change. Press the space bar to check or uncheck a check box item. For example, by default, SETUP installs the Sample Source Code files. If you do not want to install Microsoft's sample programs, move the highlight bar to the Sample Source Code item and press the space bar to toggle the check box setting. Use this feature to select only the options that you need to have in your installation. You may wish to select a different *memory model* configuration. Memory models are discussed later in this chapter under the heading "Memory Models."

After you select the type of installation you desire, the SETUP program copies the package to your hard disk and configures it according to your options. SETUP prompts you when it needs you to insert a particular disk in the floppy disk drive. When all the software has been copied to the hard disk, SETUP builds the libraries you need to support the various memory model configurations.

Using Windows-Based SETUP

When the Windows-based SETUP program begins execution, it displays the message Initializing Setup. Initialization takes several minutes, so do not be alarmed at the delay. During the initialization period, SETUP automatically detects the version of DOS that you are running, the location of Windows and its version, and so on. When SETUP completes initialization, it asks you to specify the name of the installation directory. The default directory for installing Microsoft C/C++ 7.0 is \C700; however, you can change it to another directory if you want.

Next, SETUP asks you to select Default Installation or Custom Installation. The default installation is the easiest to perform; however, be forewarned that the default configuration does not install the DOS Graphics Library files.

NOTE   If you want to write DOS applications that use graphics routines or other common text mode video functions that are available in the Graphics Library, you must select the Custom Installation option. The Graphics Library is required for many of the examples used in this book. I highly recommend that you use the Custom Installation option to ensure that the Graphics Libraries are installed.

To install the Graphics Libraries, choose Custom Installation. You are presented with a C/C++ 7.0 File Groups dialog box (see Figure 1.3). The default custom installation automatically includes the MS-DOS Graphics Libraries.

Custom Installation: C/C++ 7.0 File Groups

Select the file groups to install. Choose Libraries to specify library options. Choose Directory to change installation directory. Choose Target to choose target environment. Choose Help for explanations of all file groups.

☒ C/C++ 7.0 Compiler.................	3273 Kb	**Libraries...**
☒ Run-Time Libraries.................	2806 Kb	
☒ Microsoft Foundation Classes...	6358 Kb	**Directory...**
☒ Programmer's WorkBench.........	959 Kb	
☒ CodeView Debugger.................	1987 Kb	**Target...**
☒ Sample Source Code................	773 Kb	
☒ Online Help..........................	3423 Kb	
☒ MS-DOS Graphics Libraries......	248 Kb	**Continue**
		Back

Space Required:	20245 Kb
Space Available:	65256 Kb
Install Directory:	C:\C700\
Target	Both MS-DOS & Windows

Exit

Help

Figure 1.3.

The C/C++ 7.0 File Groups dialog box.

At this time, you can optionally choose to install additional support libraries. Some of the examples used later in *Using Microsoft C/C++ 7* require these libraries. If you want, you can skip this step now. Later, when the additional libraries are required, you can run the Microsoft C/C++ SETUP program again and choose the Build Libraries option from the SETUP menu. Using Build Libraries makes it easy to add libraries to your existing Microsoft C/C++ installation. If you want to skip adding additional libraries, click the Continue button on the File Groups dialog box.

Installing Additional Libraries

Both Default Installation and Custom Installation install the Small and Medium memory model libraries only (see the next section for information about memory models). These models are sufficient for most of the program examples in this book. Certain examples, however, require additional libraries. If you have sufficient disk space and you wish to compile all the program examples in *Using Microsoft C/C++ 7,* I recommend that you install as many memory model configurations as you can. The Compact model is used only in the Windows chapters; if you do not intend to program in Windows, you do not need to install the Compact memory model.

To install all the memory models, select the Libraries button from the File Groups dialog box. This displays a C Run-Time Customization dialog box (see Figure 1.4). Under the Memory Models heading, click the mouse on each memory model, or use the arrow keys to navigate to each item and press the space bar to check each option.

If you intend to program in Windows (see Chapters 19 through 21), you need also to install each of the Windows Targets. Check each of the Windows Targets options: Windows .EXE Files, Windows .DLL Files, and QuickWin .EXE Files. Click the mouse on the unchecked items, or press the Tab key to move from the Memory Models check boxes to the Windows Targets check boxes. Then use the arrow keys and the space bar to make your selections.

Figure 1.4.

The C Run-Time Customization dialog showing the MS-DOS Graphics Libraries option.

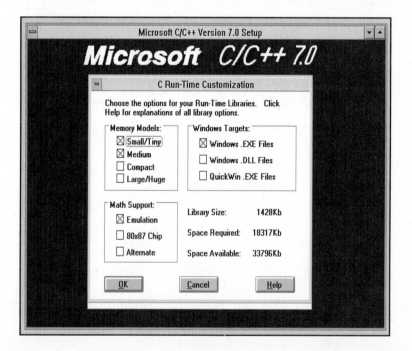

When the installation process is underway, SETUP prompts you when it needs another disk. Because SETUP runs as a Windows application, you can work on other tasks while the disks are copied (this can take up to 90 minutes). During the installation, SETUP thoughtfully displays the README icon. If you double-click this icon, you can read the README file during the installation.

Selecting Memory Models

One of the most important parts of the installation utility is the selection of the *memory models* you want to install. The Microsoft C/C++ 7.0 compiler produces programs for the Intel 80x86 family of microprocessors. For historical reasons, Intel's 80x86 processors initially were designed to support a similar memory layout to that used in the 8080 microprocessor, the precursor to the modern PC family. The 8080 CPU could only address a maximum of 64K of memory. Hence, the modern 80x86 family defines its vastly larger memory capacity in terms of 64K *memory segments*. The term *memory model* refers to how the available 64K memory segments are used in your application.

By convention, there are six different memory models. Table 1.1 summarizes the characteristics of each memory model. For each memory model, the SETUP program creates library files with each memory layout. When you use the Microsoft C/C++ compiler, options are available to select the memory model you wish to use. For most of the example programs in this book, you can compile your programs using the compiler's default Small memory model setting.

Table 1.1. Memory model specifications.

Memory Model	Characteristics
Tiny	64K is available for your code, data, and stack. Near pointers are always used.
Small	64K is available for your code, and 64K is available for your data and stack. Near pointers are always used.
Medium	1M is available for your code, and 64K is available for your data and stack. A far pointer can be used for your code, but the data and stack can use only a near pointer.
Compact	64K is available for your code, and 1M is available for your data and stack. A near pointer is used for the code, and a far pointer is used for the data.

continues

Table 1.1. Continued.

Memory Model	Characteristics
Large	1M is available for your code, and 1M is available for your data and stack. Far pointers are always used.
Huge	Far pointers are used for both code and data. The normal 64K limit for static data is bypassed.

The choice of memory model affects how the compiler translates your C or C++ source code into machine instructions. In particular, if you have a small application that has little data memory requirements, choosing the Small model enables the compiler to generate the most efficient set of machine instructions. This can result in slightly smaller and faster programs. To set the compiler's memory model option, see the section "Language Options" later in this chapter.

On the other hand, if your application is large or requires access to large amounts of data memory, you may have to use the Compact, Large, or Huge memory models. To access this additional memory requires twice as many machine instruction bytes, making your program slightly larger and slightly slower.

The default installation provides the Small and Medium models. If you have room on your hard disk, you can choose to have all the models installed at once. Installing support for all the memory models, however, takes extra room you may not want to use. In that case, you can specify the particular memory models you want to include.

Because of the similarities among the models, Microsoft combines some of the support libraries so that in some instances you get two for the price of one. Hence, if you choose to have support for different memory models than those provided in the default configuration, you can choose any of the following:

Small/Tiny

Compact

Medium

Large/Huge

Before Using the PWB or Command-Line Compiler

The Microsoft C/C++ 7.0 compiler must execute in 80386-protected mode. There are two ways to satisfy this requirement.

If you have Windows, you can run the compiler or Programmer's WorkBench (PWB) in a *DOS box* or as a Windows-launched DOS application. In this mode of operation, DOS is executing in protected mode.

If you do not have Windows, the Microsoft C/C++ package includes the 386MAX memory management utility program. To run the C/C++ compiler in DOS (without Windows), you must run the 386MAX INSTALL program. The 386MAX.SYS device driver will be installed into your CONFIG.SYS file and will replace your HIMEM.SYS driver that came with Windows. Once installed, 386MAX.SYS provides you with a protected mode DOS environment, yet it continues to provide a Windows-compatible HIMEM.SYS interface.

If you try to use the Microsoft C/C++ 7.0 compiler without running in a Windows DOS box or without the use of the 386MAX.SYS, you will receive an error message from the compiler saying that a protected mode interface is required.

Using the Programmer's WorkBench (PWB)

With the Programmer's WorkBench, or PWB, you can do all your programming work in one convenient environment. The PWB provides a text editor and project maintenance facilities. From within the PWB you can compile, make, execute, and debug your program. The PWB automatically calls NMAKE or CodeView, as needed, to give you direct access to the other development tools. This section introduces you to the Programmer's WorkBench and helps you start using its features immediately.

Starting the PWB

Starting Microsoft C/C++ is simple. You just change to your Microsoft C/C++ directory's BIN directory (for example: \C700\BIN) and type **PWB** at the DOS prompt. To begin editing an existing program, you can optionally specify the source filename as a command-line option, like this:

```
PWB source.c
```

Starting Microsoft C/C++ with this single command works well and takes care of most of your needs. The Programmer's WorkBench provides an integrated development environment. In essence, the PWB looks like a text-editing program that also includes commands for compiling and running your program, as well as a great variety of configuration options for customizing both the PWB itself and the resulting compiler output. The PWB also includes an integrated "source browser," a powerful utility to help you understand and monitor the structure of your program, locate definition and reference points for symbols, display class hierarchies, and display information about how your C functions call other C functions.

You do not have to use the PWB, however. Many programmers prefer to use their own text editor and to call the compiler and linker directly. Later in this chapter, the section "Compiling and Linking Outside the PWB" describes the use of the command-line compiler.

Using the PWB's Menus and Windows

With the Programmer's WorkBench, you have all the programming tools you need in a single, easy-to-use environment. In this section, you learn how to use the PWB's menus and windows. Figure 1.5 shows the main parts of the PWB.

Figure 1.5.

The Programmer's WorkBench (PWB).

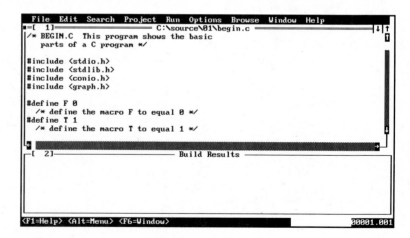

The PWB is composed of three main parts:

■ *The menu system.* The menu system gives you access to Microsoft C/C++'s powerful utilities and features. You use these utilities and features by selecting an option from the menu bar. As you can see in Figure 1.5, the menu bar is the first line on the screen. The commands on the menu bar access each of the major groups of utilities or features.

■ *The window system.* The window system—the most visible and most-used part of the PWB—offers a variety of windows. Windows are available for editing a program, debugging a program, and viewing a program's operation. Other windows enable you to select options for utilities or display important messages. Figure 1.5 shows an edit window, where you create and modify your programs. This window contains the file FIRST.C.

■ *The status bar.* At the bottom of the screen, the status bar displays the shortcut keys for the most commonly used commands, tells you what Microsoft C/C++ is doing, or gives you hints about the command you have chosen. In Figure 1.5, the status bar displays a list of shortcut keys.

The Menu System

The menu system contains the utilities and features necessary for managing your programming tasks efficiently. There are utilities and features for handling files, for editing your program, and for compiling, debugging, and running your own support programs. You can enter the menu system in three ways—two with the keyboard, and a third with the mouse:

■ *Move to the menu bar, highlight a command, and select it.* You can move to the menu bar from anywhere in the PWB by pressing the Alt key. When the cursor is on the menu bar, use the arrow keys to highlight a particular command. After the highlight is on the command you want, press Enter to pull down a menu. You can use the arrow keys to select a command or you can type the highlighted letter in the command name. When you finish selecting the command, press Enter to execute it. Figure 1.6 shows the pull-down menu for the **S**earch command.

■ *Use an Alt-key combination.* To select a command from the menu bar, hold down the Alt key and press the highlighted letter of the command. When a pull-down menu appears, use the arrow keys to move to the command you want, and then press Enter to select it. Selecting a command has three possible outcomes:

1. The command is carried out.

2. A submenu is displayed.

3. A dialog box is displayed that contains a menu offering other choices available for the command you picked. You must provide in the dialog box the necessary information before the command can be executed.

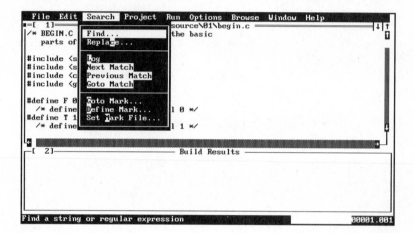

Figure 1.6.

A pull-down menu in the PWB.

■ *Click a command in the menu bar.* You can choose a command in the pull-down menus the same way: Using the mouse, point to the command and click. If the command you choose makes a dialog box pop up, you may need to type some information. You can still use the mouse, however, for many of the selections inside a dialog box. I discuss dialog boxes more thoroughly later in this section.

The Window System

When you use Microsoft C/C++, you do most of your work inside a window. Several kinds of windows are available in the PWB. They provide areas in which you can write your programs, see the program output and messages, display status information, and keep track of what is happening in your computer. Most of the windows have similar features (see Figure 1.5).

The following basic features are found in a Microsoft C/C++ window:

■ *Close box.* The close box is located in the upper-left corner of the window. Clicking the close box with the mouse closes the window. If you don't have a mouse, you can close a window with the **Close** command on the **Window** pull-down menu.

■ *Title bar.* The title bar, located at the top of the window, displays the window name. Dragging the title bar moves the window.

■ *Window number.* The window number helps you keep track of the open windows. When windows overlap, you can hide some windows behind others. To see a list of all active windows, choose the **W**indow menu option. The first four menus, numbered from 1 through 4, appear as options at the bottom of this menu. When more than four windows are active, an additional option, All **W**indows, appears as the last item on the Window menu. The All **W**indows option displays a dialog box with a list containing all of your active windows. You can select one of the windows from this dialog. You also can make a window active by using one of the following methods:

1. To access windows numbered 1 to 9, hold down the Alt key and type the number of the window you want to make active.

2. Select the **W**indow menu and then choose the window you want to make active. The first four windows are shown as the menu options 1 through 4. When there are more than four active windows, the All **W**indows selection appears at the bottom of the pull-down menu. Choosing this option displays the All **W**indows dialog box. Use this dialog to select from all available windows.

3. You can press F6 from any menu to automatically switch to the next menu in sequence.

4. Click the mouse anywhere in the window.

The active window appears on top of all the other windows and displays scroll bars on the bottom and the right side.

■ *Zoom box.* The zoom box, at the upper-right corner of the active window, allows you to zoom the window to its largest size. Clicking the zoom box activates the zoom command. If you don't have a mouse, you can select Ma**x**imize or Mini**m**ize from the **W**indow menu. If a window is already at its maximum size when you click the zoom box, the window returns to its former size.

■ *Scroll bars.* Vertical and horizontal scroll bars are on the bottom and the right side of the window. You use the scroll bars to scroll the contents of the window. At each end of the scroll bars are arrows. Clicking the arrows moves the screen one line at a time. Next to the arrows are shaded boxes. Clicking a shaded box moves the contents of the window one page at a time. You can also drag the scroll box to change the contents of the window quickly. The position of the scroll box indicates the location of the information in the window relative to the rest of the document.

■ *Resize box.* You can resize a window by clicking and holding down the mouse button when the mouse cursor is pointing to the lower-right corner of the window. Then, by dragging the mouse, you resize the window box. When the window box is the size you want, release the mouse button.

One window that you may not be familiar with is the *dialog box.* A dialog box "pops up" for some of the menu commands, enabling you to make several choices about the command you have selected. Any menu command that is followed by an ellipsis (...) generates a dialog box when you select it. Figure 1.7 shows the dialog box for the **Find** command on the **Search** menu.

Figure 1.7.

A typical dialog box.

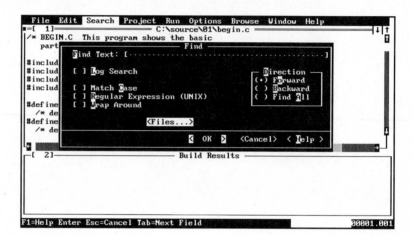

Most dialog boxes contain the following items:

■ *Input boxes.* You type text into an input box and use the basic editing keys to work with the text you enter. If you need to enter a control code in the input box, you must precede the code with ^P. If the input box is followed by a down-arrow symbol, a list of values is associated with the input box. The list contains alternative values for use in this field. You access the list by pressing the down-arrow or right-arrow key when you are in an input box, or by clicking the down-arrow symbol. Each time you press an arrow key, one of the other values in the list is cycled into the input box.

■ *List boxes.* A list box lets you select an item from a list without having to leave the dialog box. The displayed list can vary in length. An example of a list box is the file list that displays when you choose the **O**pen command from the **F**ile menu.

■ *Action buttons.* When you have made your selection from a dialog box or have typed the necessary information, you execute (or cancel) the command with the appropriate action button, which is a label surrounded by angle brackets, such as < OK >. The standard action buttons are OK, Cancel, and Help (see Figure 1.7). You activate an action button by clicking it with the mouse, or by holding down the Alt key and pressing the highlighted letter in the action box.

■ *Radio buttons.* You use the radio buttons to choose one—and only one—item from a group of mutually exclusive commands. To "push" a radio button, you can click it with the mouse or press the Alt key and the highlighted letter in the radio button you want. You also can use the Tab key to move to a group of radio buttons, and then use the arrow keys and the space bar to select a particular radio button. Figure 1.7 has radio buttons beneath the Direction heading at the right side of the dialog box.

■ *Check boxes.* You use a check box, which is an item surrounded by square brackets, to turn on or off an option. If the check box contains an ×, that option is turned on. If the check box does not contain an ×, that option is turned off. When several check boxes apply to one topic, they are grouped together. You can tab to a group of check boxes, use the arrow keys to pick a particular check box, and press the space bar to switch on or off the option. If you have a mouse, clicking a check box switches it on or off. The boxes beneath the Find Text input field in Figure 1.7 illustrate the appearance of check boxes.

Configuring Microsoft C/C++

Part of the power of Microsoft C/C++ is its versatility. With Microsoft C/C++, you are not constrained to a programming environment that Microsoft thought would be nice. Microsoft C/C++ lets you change the programming environment to suit your needs and interests. You can change the Microsoft C/C++ environment by using the **O**ptions menu. You can use the **O**ptions menu to customize the features with which you program. The **O**ptions menu also enables you to customize the keystrokes used to run the editor program. In the latter case, you can opt to redefine the editing command keystrokes so that they match an editor with which you are already familiar.

Generally, you can begin to use the PWB to write, compile, and execute programs without making any configuration changes. For this reason, you may wish to skip ahead to "Writing Your First C Program." You can return to this section later when you find it necessary to customize some of the PWB features.

You can make many changes to your programming environment from within the Programmer's WorkBench. The facilities to change the environment are in the menu system under the **O**ptions command. The **O**ptions menu is broken into five sections that deal with the PWB environment, project options, language-specific options (C or C++), linking and access to the CodeView debugger, and the object browser. Figure 1.8 shows the **O**ptions menu.

Figure 1.8.

The Microsoft C/C++
Options menu.

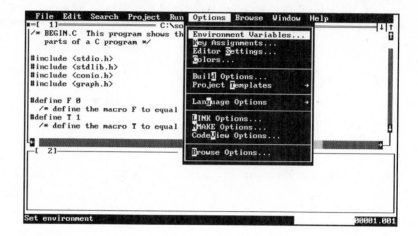

The first section of the **O**ptions menu controls the overall environment. You use the **E**nvironment Variables... selection to view or edit the set of DOS environment variables. The next three selections enable you to configure the appearance and operation of the PWB itself.

Key Assignments

Select **K**ey Assignments... if you wish to redefine the command keys the editor uses. The default settings include standard Common User Access (CUA) compatibility settings that many DOS and Windows applications use. Additionally, the editor supports the original WordStar word processor keystrokes that were once a widely adopted standard. This means that there are often two command keystrokes to access one feature. For instance, you can toggle between insert and overstrike typing modes by pressing either the Ins key or Ctrl-V.

To redefine a keystroke, select the desired command function from the Macro/Function List list box shown in the Key Assignments dialog box in Figure 1.9. For example, to modify the keystroke used to toggle between Ins and Overstrike typing modes, move the cursor to the insert mode item within the list box. Beneath the **C**urrent Keys: heading, you should see Ctrl-V and Ins. To define a new keystroke combination for accessing the function, select one of the unassigned keys from the **U**nassigned Keys list box. As you scroll through this list box, the current selection appears in the New **K**ey input field. When you have identified the desired keystroke, select the <**A**ssign> action command.

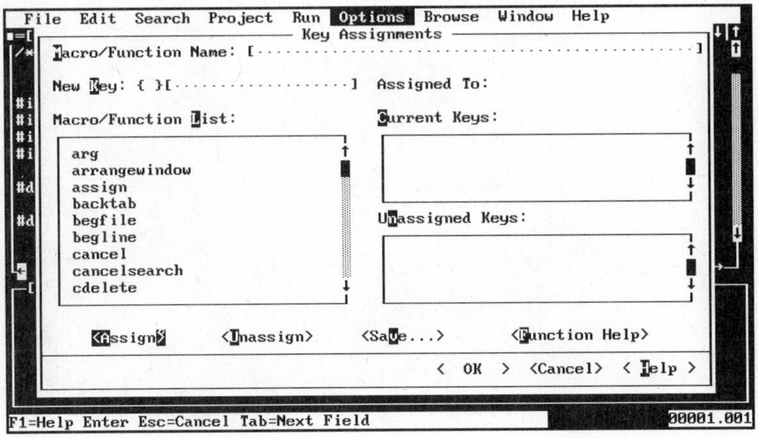

```
 File  Edit  Search  Project  Run  Options  Browse  Window  Help
                        ── Key Assignments ──────────────────────
   Macro/Function Name: [ ·····················································]
   New Key: { }[·················]  Assigned To:
   Macro/Function List:              Current Keys:
      arg
      arrangewindow
      assign
      backtab
      begfile
      begline
      cancel
      cancelsearch
      cdelete                       Unassigned Keys:


      <Assign>      <Unassign>     <Save...>        <Function Help>
                                        <  OK  >  <Cancel>  < Help >

 F1=Help Enter Esc=Cancel Tab=Next Field                     00001.001
```

Figure 1.9.

The Key Assignments
dialog box.

Repeat this procedure for the functions you wish to define. You can remove a keystroke-function association by selecting the current keystroke in the Current Keys list box and then choosing <Unassign>.

When you have finished making your keystroke changes, select <Save...>. This presents a list box showing all the keystroke changes you have made. If you want to remove any of the changes, position the list box cursor to the desired item and select <Delete>. When you are satisfied with the changes, select < OK > to save all your keystroke definitions. Your new keystroke definitions are now available for use in the editor.

Editor Settings

Use the Editor Settings dialog box to change the default values of a variety of editor operations. For instance, the editor normally does not perform word wrapping. However, you can change the setting of the editor's word wrap option using the Editor Settings dialog box, which is shown in Figure 1.10.

To change a specific option, use the Switch List list box to scroll to the option. Note that the editor settings appear in three separate groups. Figure 1.10 shows only the options that have a Boolean parameter. To see other settings, select Numeric or Text from the Switch Type radio buttons.

When you have located the option that you want to change, edit the parameter value in the Switch input field and then choose the <Set Switch> action button. When you are finished making changes, choose <Save...>.

If you are unsure if the cryptic textual title in the Switch List is the function that you wish to change, you can select <Switch Help>. This displays an explanatory message about the currently highlighted item in the Switch List.

Figure 1.10.

The Editor Settings
dialog box.

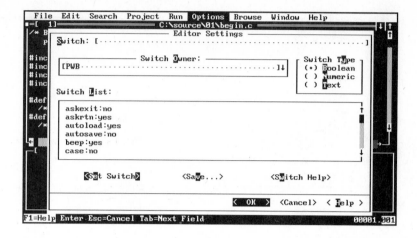

Colors

The PWB lets you create your own color scheme within the PWB. To access
the color selection dialog box, choose **Colors...** from the **O**ptions menu. This
displays the Colors dialog box shown in Figure 1.11.

Figure 1.11.

The Colors dialog box.

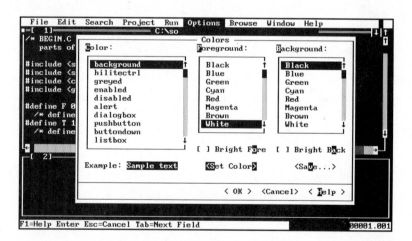

To change the colors of a specific item in the user interface, you must first find
the item in the list box labelled **C**olor:. As you scroll through this list box, the
corresponding current color selection is indicated in the **F**oreground and
Background boxes on the right. The default color scheme uses relatively few
colors, mostly black on white, white on black, or white on blue.

To change the color of one of the user interface elements, select the desired new foreground and background colors. A sample of how this color combination appears is shown in the Example area in the lower-left corner of the dialog box. When you are satisfied with your color selection, choose <Set Color>. When you are finished making your changes, choose <Save...>.

One problem you will soon encounter is that of selecting the correct user interface element. Some of the names in the Color: list box are relatively obvious, but many others are not. Undoubtedly, the names are meaningful to the authors of the PWB, but not necessarily to its users. You likely will find that you must experiment with your color changes. Make a change and then return to the PWB to see if you identified the correct user interface element. Repeat this process until you locate the desired interface component and successfully change its color.

Build Options

Build Options has a simple function: By making a simple selection you can set the compiler and linker options to generate a file suitable for debugging with CodeView, or you can choose to have a *releasable executable* built. The Release Options dialog item selects an appropriate set of compile and link options so that the resulting executable is small, fast, and doesn't include any codes or checks typically used during debugging. Once your program is finished and tested, you typically will compile the final version using the Release Options setting.

If you wish to use CodeView, always remember to select Use Debug Options. You can also access this selection by choosing one of two radio buttons on the Link Options dialog box.

Set Project Template

The project template specifies the type of runtime support and executable file to be produced. Using this dialog, you can elect to produce different types of executable files, such as DOS .EXE files, Windows .EXE files, or *p-code* executable files. P-code programs are new with Version 7.0 of the Microsoft C compiler, and provide a compact way of storing a compiled program at the expense of some reduction in execution speed. See the section "Using p-code" in Chapter 10, "Using Microsoft C/C++'s Advanced Features."

Select your desired language in the Runtime Support list box. Then choose the desired output file type in the Project Templates list box.

Language Options

The Language Options vary slightly, depending on whether you are programming in C or C++. Whichever language you select, the result is a display of
various compile options. Figure 1.12 illustrates the options using the C Compiler Options dialog box.

Figure 1.12.

The C Compiler Options
dialog box.

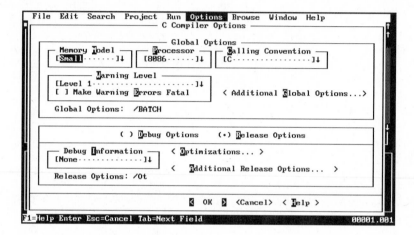

```
  File   Edit   Search   Project   Run  Options  Browse   Window   Help
 ┌──────────────────────── C Compiler Options ────────────────────────┐
 │                          ─ Global Options ─                          │
 │  ┌─ Memory Model ──┐  ┌─ Processor ──┐  ┌─ Calling Convention ─┐    │
 │  [Small ·······]↓     [8086·······]↓    [C ··············]↓         │
 │  ┌──── Warning Level ────┐                                           │
 │  [Level 1 ···············]↓                                          │
 │  [ ] Make Warning Errors Fatal        < Additional Global Options...>│
 │  Global Options:  /BATCH                                             │
 │                                                                      │
 │                 ( ) Debug Options    (·) Release Options             │
 │  ┌─ Debug Information ─┐   < Optimizations... >                      │
 │  [None ··············]↓   <  Additional Release Options...  >        │
 │  Release Options: /Ot                                                │
 │                                                                      │
 │                    ◄  OK  ►  <Cancel>  < Help >                      │
 └──────────────────────────────────────────────────────────────────────┘
 F1=Help Enter Esc=Cancel Tab=Next Field                    00001.001
```

The Memory **M**odel field selects the appropriate memory model: Small,
Medium, Compact, Large, Huge, or a custom memory model. Use the
Processor field to specify which type of processor the executable program will
run on. The 8086 selection results in programs that run on all types of 80x86
processors. However, if you know that your executable will be run on an
80286, for example, selecting 80286 will cause the compiler to generate machine instructions that exist only on the 80286 or better CPUs. This can result
in tighter, faster code.

To select a warning level, use the Warning Level item on the C Compiler
Options dialog. A *warning* is issued when the compiler finds a questionable—
but not necessarily wrong—condition in your source code. The various levels
range from Level 0 (turn off all warning message generation) to Level 4 (generate all possible warning messages). Level 1 is the default setting and identifies
only potentially severe conditions. Level 2 adds warnings for more conditions
and many less-serious situations. Level 3 adds warnings for even less-serious
situations. Finally, Level 4 provides the most warning messages possible,
including warnings for using nonportable features of the Microsoft C/C++
language.

The <Additional **G**lobal Options...> button accesses some additional compiler
settings. From this dialog box (which is not shown), you select protected
mode Windows application compatibility, use of the ANSI C versus Microsoft C
language extensions, and other features.

The <Optimizations...> action button displays the set of radio buttons and check boxes shown in Figure 1.13.

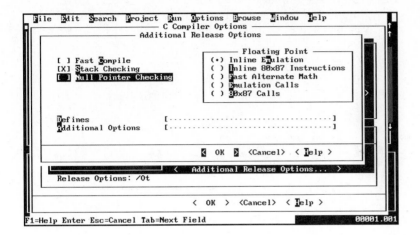

Figure 1.13.

The Additional Release Options dialog box.

This dialog box controls the level and type of optimization that the compiler will perform.

The <Additional Release Options...> button provides access to Floating Point control features. On this dialog box, you can request code generation for 80x87 compatibility.

LINK Options

Use the LINK Options selection to select a number of items related to the linking step. Here you can specify additional libraries, incremental linking (which is faster than regular linking), and CodeView compatibility. Assuming that your program files were compiled with the debug options turned on (see "Build Options"), the Linker incorporates the debugging code from the object modules into the final executable files. If you wish to produce a map file showing the addresses where the various public symbols have been placed in the code file, select <Additional Release Options...> from the LINK Options dialog and choose one of the Map File options on that subdialog.

NMAKE Options

NMAKE is the Microsoft project make utility. NMAKE manages large projects by determining which source files have changed and which must be recompiled. When a source file has changed, NMAKE automatically invokes the compiler (or Microsoft Assembler for assembly files if you have installed the assembler). By default, if NMAKE encounters any errors while it is running, it halts the project build. If you are making a project that contains several source files, NMAKE halts the compilation as soon as it encounters a single error and does not compile any remaining files. If you wish to have NMAKE skip to the next file, you can select **C**ontinue Building Unrelated Targets on Error from the NMAKE Options dialog.

If your computer has available Expanded Memory (EMS) or Extended Memory (XMS), you can use this memory during the compilation and linking process. By default, NMAKE tries to use EMS or XMS if they are available.

Compiling and Executing Programs in the PWB

To compile programs that fit into a single source file, select **C**ompile File on the **P**roject menu. This compiles your source program, producing an .OBJ object module. To compile and link your program, select the **B**uild function instead. (See Chapter 5, "Building, Compiling, and Testing Microsoft C/C++ Programs," to learn how to build programs that are split into multiple files.)

To run your compiled and linked program, choose **E**xecute: from the **R**un menu. Your program will load and execute. When the program's execution finishes, control returns to the PWB. In this way, you can edit, compile, and run your programs entirely within the PWB.

You can also launch the CodeView debugger from within the PWB. Chapter 9, "Using CodeView and Profiler," describes use of the debugger.

Compiling and Linking Outside the PWB

You also can edit, compile, and link your programs outside of the PWB environment. Use your own text editor to type and edit your program source. Then run the compiler directly from the DOS command line by typing

```
cl source.c
```

The compiler compiles and links your program, hence the compiler name `cl`, producing an executable file with the name source.exe. You then can run your program as you run any other DOS application: by typing the program's name at the command line.

When relying on the command-line interface to the Microsoft C/C++ tools, you may wish to have access to online help. You can do so by typing the command QH at the DOS command prompt. This runs the Microsoft quick help utility, providing access to comprehensive online help.

If your program has multiple source files, you can add the additional files on the command line, as in

```
cl source.c source1.c source2.c
```

cl compiles each of the source files and invokes the linker to link the three object modules into an executable program file. If you need to access non-standard libraries or object modules that you may have previously compiled, you can specify these also on the command line, like this:

```
cl source.c source1.obj graphics.lib
```

To assist with managing large projects that are split across multiple files, you may wish to use the NMAKE program. The use of NMAKE is described in Chapter 5, "Building, Compiling, and Testing Microsoft C/C++ Programs."

A large number of options for controlling the operation of the compiler can be specified as command-line *switches*. Each switch turns on or off a compiler feature. A switch is specified with a slash character followed by one or more letters, such as /AM or /qc. Switches can appear anywhere in the command line (except that the /f, /qc, or /Oq options must appear first, at the beginning of the command). By tradition, compiler switches are usually placed before the name of the file to be compiled, as in this example:

```
cl /AM begin.c
```

Some of the most common switches are shown in Table 1.2. The compiler is case-sensitive with all of the switches, except for /HELP. For information about other switches, you can consult the quick help utility or refer to the Microsoft reference manuals.

To produce the fastest executing code, compile your program using these switches:

```
/Oxaz /Ob2 /Gr
```

For the smallest code generation, you may wish to use Microsoft C/C++'s *p-code*—or *packed-code*—representation. In this form, the compiler generates specially compressed executable code, and the Microsoft Linker attaches a 9K p-code interpreter to your code file. For this reason, p-code does not provide an advantage to short programs. Additionally, because p-code runs more slowly than normal compiler output, you should use p-code in program areas where speed is not critical. To compile a module into p-code, place the following switch at the beginning of your command-line switches:

```
/Oq
```

The following are some of the `cl` compiler command-line switches. Note that these commands are case-sensitive. For instance, `/c` should always be written with a lowercase letter *c*.

Table 1.2. Commonly used `cl` command-line switches.

Switch	Purpose
/AT	Selects the Tiny memory model.
/AS	Selects the Small memory model.
/AM	Selects the Medium memory model.
/AC	Selects the Compact memory model.
/AL	Selects the Large memory model.
/AH	Selects the Huge memory model.
/B1	Runs the C1L compile instead of `cl`. Use this switch if the compiler generates the error `the compiler is out of near heap`.
/c	Compiles and creates an object module but does not link.
/f	Selects the `fast compile` option of the compiler, disabling all optimizations. In this mode, the compiler compiles your programs faster but produces larger programs. The /f switch is intended for use during development to speed the compilation process. /f is selected by default if you do not specify any compiler optimizations. To disable the fast compile feature, use /f-.
/FPa	Selects the alternate math library for floating-point operations.
/FPc	Selects the emulator library. The emulator simulates an 80x87 if a math coprocessor is not present. If a coprocessor is available, it will be used to achieve the fastest performance possible.
/FPc87	Generates code for the 80x87 coprocessor. The 80x87 must be present on the system that runs the compiled program.
/GA /GEf	These options are required when compiling programs for Microsoft Windows. They cause the compiler to generate special entry and exit code for each __far function in a Windows program. /GA and /GEf replace Microsoft C 6.0's /Gw switch for compiling Windows programs.

Switch	Purpose
/G0	This default selection generates code that is compatible with the 8088 and 8086 CPUs.
/G1	Compiler uses 80188/80186 instructions.
/G2	Compiler generates 80286 instructions.
/Gi	Performs an incremental compile, recompiling only the functions that have changed since a previous compile. You must also select the /qc option.
/Oopt_codes	/O controls the level of optimization employed by the compiler. For maximum optimization, select /Oxaz, in which x maximizes all available optimizations, a assumes no aliasing, and z enables maximum loop optimization. /Osae maximizes code reduction rather than speed. The s option requests optimization for small code size, and e enables global register optimization. /Oq enables p-code generation.
/qc	Invokes the *quick compile* mode of the compiler. In this mode, the compiler reduces its optimizations and performs a fast compile. A number of compiler features cannot be used when you perform a quick compile. With Version 7.0 of the Microsoft C/C++ compiler, the /qc options has been replaced with /f (for fast compile). You may, however, continue to use /qc with Version 7.0.

/Yc, /Yd, /Yu

Microsoft C/C++ 7.0 has a new *precompiled headers* feature. This feature lets you precompile a portion of your program—especially large header files such as windows.h—so that on subsequent compiles the precompiled information is already available and does not need to be recompiled. The use of precompiled headers can drastically speed the compilation of large programs.

Use /Yc to create a precompiled header for the current source file. If you compile the program source.c, the /Yc option generates a source.pch file containing the precompiled header. If you want, you can write the precompiled header information to a different file by typing **/Ycfilename** (with no spaces between the /Yc and the filename).

To use the precompiled header on subsequent compilations, use the /Yu option with an optional filename (**/Yufilename**).

If you are using the CodeView Debugger, you need to use the /Yd and /Zi switches when you initially create the precompiled header using /Yc. In that situation, use /Yc, /Yu, and /Zi together in your command-line switches.

/W*n*	*n* varies from 0 to 4 with a default of 1. The /W switch selects the level of warning messages provided by the compiler. /W0 suppresses the display of all warning messages.
/Zi	Stores special symbol table information in the object file. This switch must be enabled before you can use CodeView. See Chapter 9 for additional information regarding the use of CodeView for debugging your programs.
/Zs	Scans the source file, producing only a syntax check.

Writing Your First C Program

Now that you have installed Microsoft C/C++ and are familiar with the basic layout of the Programmer's WorkBench, you are ready to start programming in C. You need to know what components are necessary to create a C program, and how to enter and run a program in Microsoft C/C++.

Understanding C Program Structure

This section shows you the basic components necessary to create a C program: preprocessor directives, global declarations, the main() function, and user-defined functions. When you finish the section, you will be able to look at a C program and know what its parts do. Subsequent chapters describe in greater detail the features introduced here. Listing 1.1 shows all the major parts of a C program.

Listing 1.1. begin.c. A sample C program.

```
1   /* BEGIN.C  This program shows the basic
2      parts of a C program */
3
4   #include <stdio.h>
5   #include <stdlib.h>
6   #include <conio.h>
7   #include <graph.h>
8
9   #define F 0
10     /* define the macro F to equal 0 */
```

```
11   #define T 1
12     /* define the macro T to equal 1 */
13
14   int i = 0;
15
16   void put_msg( void );
17
18   main()
19   {
20     int answer;
21
22     _clearscreen( _GCLEARSCREEN );
23     printf( "Do you want to see the message?\n" );
24     printf( "Enter 0 for NO, 1 for YES ==> " );
25     scanf( "%d", &answer );
26     if( answer == T )
27       put_msg();
28       else
29       puts( "Goodbye for now." );
30   }
31
32   void put_msg( void )
33   {
34     _clearscreen( _GCLEARSCREEN );
35     for( i = 0; i <=10; i++ )
36       printf( "Test string # %d.\n", i );
37   }
```

The first time you see a C program, it may seem cryptic and confusing. C's syntax is brief, and brevity is what helps make C so powerful, flexible, and efficient. After you have studied a few C programs, the meaning of most C statements will be obvious. Soon you will see how C's tight syntax speeds program development. The syntax lets you spend more time developing the logic of your program and less time typing program statements. As for C being confusing, good programming practices take care of that problem. Laying out your program in a neat and orderly manner prevents confusion.

All C programs follow the same basic structure. Even a large, complex C program generally has the same layout as a short program. Figure 1.14 shows the main parts of a C program.

Figure 1.14.

The basic structure of a
C program.

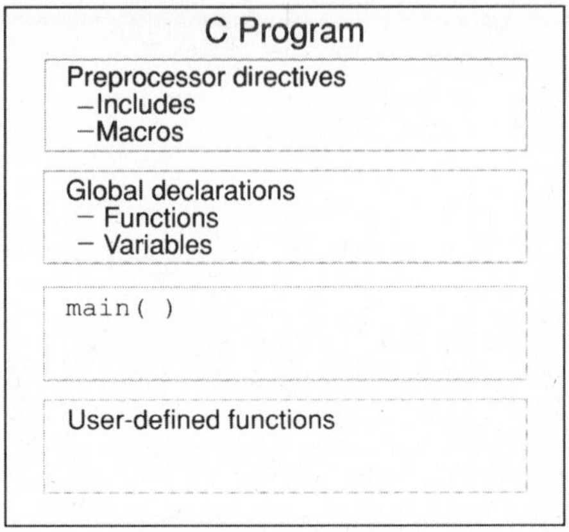

```
                    C Program
  ┌─────────────────────────────────────────┐
  │ Preprocessor directives                 │
  │  −Includes                              │
  │  −Macros                                │
  ├─────────────────────────────────────────┤
  │ Global declarations                     │
  │  − Functions                            │
  │  − Variables                            │
  ├─────────────────────────────────────────┤
  │ main( )                                 │
  │                                         │
  ├─────────────────────────────────────────┤
  │ User-defined functions                  │
  │                                         │
  └─────────────────────────────────────────┘
```

The following discussion examines, in turn, the four major parts of a C program. You learn what each part is and how it works. In the discussion, refer to both Listing 1.1 and Figure 1.14. The program listing shows you actual C code, and the figure shows you how that code fits in the program. Later in the chapter, you learn how all the parts work together in a sample program.

The first two lines of Listing 1.1 are a comment, which is included to tell you about the program. A comment is not a required part of the program, nor does a comment perform a programming task. Comments are simply an aid to you, the programmer. A C comment begins with the characters /*, followed by one or more lines of explanatory text, and terminated with the characters */. The compiler ignores everything between /* and */, so you can put anything you want here.

While not really part of the C language, judicious use of indenting, extra spaces, and blank lines can make C programs much easier to read. The compiler ignores all extra spaces and blank lines, and their use for all practical purposes has no impact on the compile process.

Preprocessor Directives

The first part of a C program that performs a task consists of the *preprocessor directives.* In Listing 1.1, the preprocessor directives are in lines 4 through 11. These directives instruct the compiler to perform certain tasks before program compilation begins. The most common preprocessor directive is the #include directive. This preprocessor directive instructs the compiler to include another C source file before compilation begins. Another common preprocessor directive is the #define directive, which is a macro definition. A macro definition in a C program functions much like one in a word processor.

The `#include` preprocessor directive tells the preprocessor to include another C source file during the program compilation process. The most common use of the `#include` directive is seen in lines 4 through 7, where `#include` is used to include a header file. It may be best to place this in a text box.

The `#include` directive has two forms:

```
#include <filename.ext>
```

and

```
#include "filename.ext"
```

In the form using quotes around the filename, Microsoft C/C++ searches for the file first by looking in the directory where the "parent" file was found. For example, if begin.c contains an `#include "begin.h"` statement, Microsoft C/C++ looks for begin.h in the same directory where it found begin.c. If that fails, and if begin.c was `#included` in some other file, the compiler checks that directory, and so on, tracking back as far as is necessary. If the file is not located, Microsoft C/C++ proceeds to its next alternative: treating the filename as if it were surrounded by angle brackets.

When the `#include` filename is inside paired <...> angle brackets, Microsoft C/C++ looks for the indicated file by searching through a predetermined set of directories. The directories to search are specified by setting a DOS environment variable named INCLUDE, like this:

```
SET INCLUDE=C:\C700\INCLUDE;C:\C700\MFC\INCLUDE
```

Now the compiler looks in the C:\C700\INCLUDE directory, and if it fails to find the file there, proceeds to check C:\C700\MFC\INCLUDE. At this point, if the `#include` file has still not been found, the compiler stops and issues an error message.

Generally, you should place angle brackets around `#include` filenames when you are including library interface files provided by Microsoft, such as `<graphics.h>` or `<stdio.h>`. Use double quotes when including files that you created, such as `"myprog.h"` or `"game.h"`.

Header files are composed mainly of function declarations, variable declarations, and macro definitions. A function declaration tells the compiler about a function that will be used but has not been coded at that point in the program. The compiler needs this information about functions that have not been written in order to determine whether the function calls that you made were made correctly. Variable declarations let the compiler know what variables you will be using. Macro definitions supply the replacement text for the macros you use. When you use a macro in your program, the preprocessor replaces the macro you entered with the replacement text found in the macro definition. The following discussion about `#define` directives explains macros more thoroughly.

#define signals the start of a macro definition, which lets you substitute one string for another. Lines 9 and 11 in Listing 1.1 are macro definition statements. These lines tell the preprocessor to replace every occurrence of the word TRUE with 1 and every occurrence of FALSE with 0. In line 26, the preprocessor replaces the macro TRUE with 1. Therefore, when the compiler encounters line 26, the line of code will look like this:

```
if( answer == 1 )
```

You can use macros in other ways, also. Note the following lines:

```
#define FALSE 0
#define SALESTAX 0.06
```

These two macro definitions cause every occurrence of FALSE and SALESTAX in your program to be replaced with 0 and 0.06, respectively. Here, the macros FALSE and SALESTAX are sometimes referred to as *constants* because they hold a constant numeric value. If the sales tax is increased, you need only change this single definition rather than searching for every occurrence of 0.06 in your program. You can even include C statements in macro definitions, like this:

```
#define STALL for( i = 1; i < 10000; i++ )
...
STALL;    /* Make program pause */
```

This macro definition substitutes a for() loop for the word STALL. Whenever the word STALL is encountered in the program, the for() loop is substituted.

Global Declarations

The second major part of a C program consists of global declarations. Global declarations tell the compiler about user-defined functions and variables that are common to all functions in a source file. The global declarations in Listing 1.1 are in lines 14 and 16.

As indicated earlier, function declarations, called *prototypes,* tell the compiler about your functions. Specifically, a function declaration tells the compiler what type of data your function requires and what type of answer your function will return. The only function declaration in Listing 1.1 is in line 16. This function declaration tells the compiler that the function is not passed a value and that the function does not return a value. Here is a function declaration that requires arguments and returns a value:

```
int sum( int a, int b );
```

This function declaration declares a function named sum(). The sum() function requires two arguments, each of which must be an integer. The function declaration indicates also that sum() returns a value. The type of the return value for `sum()` is `int`, which means that the function returns an answer that is an integer.

The compiler uses the information in the function declaration to verify that function calls are made correctly. After the compiler has passed the function declaration, the compiler checks the function calls to see whether the data types match correctly. The compiler checks the arguments you pass to a function to verify that the function can accept the arguments. In addition, the compiler checks to see whether the value returned by a function is used correctly.

Function Declarations, Definitions, and Calls

The first time you come across the terms *function declaration* and *function definition,* you may not realize the distinction between the two. However, each has a special purpose in a C program.

A function declaration tells the compiler about the function, whereas a function definition tells the compiler what is in the function. The function declaration is usually found near the top of the program, and the function definition is usually found near the bottom.

The function declaration tells the compiler what type of data the function requires and what type of return value it generates. This information is all the compiler needs to start compiling the program. Look at the following function declaration:

```
int product( int a, int b );
```

This function declaration tells the compiler that you will be using a function that requires two integer arguments and returns an integer value.

When the compiler encounters a function call, the compiler uses the information from the function declaration to determine whether the variables passed to the function are the correct type and if the return value is used correctly. The next example shows a function call:

```
c = product( 3, 5 );
```

The compiler verifies that the values passed to `product()` are integers and that the variable assigned the return value of `product()` is an integer.

Notice that function declarations always end with a semicolon. The semicolon informs the compiler that the function declaration is complete.

continues

A function definition contains the same information as a function declaration and more. Also included in the function definition is the C code that performs the work of the function. Programming for the function is done in the function definition. The following example shows the body of the `product()` function definition:

```
int product( int a, int b )
  {
    int c;
    c = a * b;
    return c;
  }
```

Notice that function definitions are not followed by a semicolon. Because the first line of a function definition is followed by the body of the function, you cannot use a terminating semicolon.

It is possible to skip the function declarations. You simply *define* the function at the top of the source file before any calls are made to the function. If you define the function before it is called, a function declaration is not needed because the compiler already has all the necessary information to verify that function calls are made correctly. Defining functions at the beginning of a program is legal, but the program may be harder to read.

The global declarations portion of your program can include variable declarations in addition to function declarations. A global variable declaration makes that variable available for use to all the functions in the source file. In Listing 1.1, line 14 is a global variable declaration for the integer variable i. Notice that i is used in the `put_msg()` function (line 35) even though i is not declared in `put_msg()`.

Global variable declarations can cause trouble. In larger programs, you may depend on the value of a global variable but forget that you've changed the value of that variable in another function. Because you easily can lose track of a global variable's value, use as few global variables as possible. If you use a global variable only when you need one, you are less likely to have trouble remembering its value.

The *main()* Function

The third major part of a C program is the `main()` function. Every C program must have a `main()` function. Program execution begins in the `main()` function. In a well-structured program, execution ends in the `main()` function. In Listing 1.1, the `main()` function begins on line 18 and ends on line 30.

In a well-structured program, execution ends in the main () function. In listing 1.1, the main () function begins on line 18 and ends on line 30.

Some programs may have only one function—the main() function. In a short program, the entire program may fit easily inside the main() function. A large program, however, has too much code to fit inside this function. The main() function in a large program may consist almost entirely of calls to user-defined functions. Listing 1.1 falls between these two extremes. In begin.c, some of the program's tasks are performed in main(), and some are performed in the put_msg() function. In similar programs, some tasks are carried out in main(), and longer, logically separate steps are made into user-defined functions.

User-Defined Functions

The fourth part of a C program consists of *user-defined functions*—groups of statements you design to accomplish your programming tasks. User-defined functions can do anything you want them to do. Their only limit is the extent of your imagination.

In Listing 1.1, lines 32 through 37 are the user-defined function put_msg(). This is a short function that writes a series of messages to the video screen. Notice several points about put_msg():

■ *The function name is preceded by the type of the function's return value.* This tells the compiler what kind of value the function will return. The return value can be an integer, a character, or some other data type. In Listing 1.1, put_msg() has no return value, so the return type is specified as void.

■ *The function name is followed by a list of arguments that will be passed to the function.* The argument list is enclosed in the parentheses that follow the function name. This list tells the compiler how many and what kind of arguments the function requires. In Listing 1.1, put_msg() does not require any arguments; the argument list is therefore void.

■ *The body of the function is enclosed in a set of braces.* In Listing 1.1, the body begins with the opening brace in line 33 and ends with the closing brace in line 37. If you forget a brace, the compiler catches your mistake and generates an error message.

Using the Editor To Write a Program

You are now ready to see how a real program is put together. First, you use Microsoft C/C++ to enter the sample program, named order.c. Second, you compile and run the program. Practicing with a real program enables you to see what each part of the program does and how all the parts work together.

Listing 1.2 shows the order.c program. The numbers on the left are not part of the program, so don't type these numbers when you type the program. They are only an aid in the discussion that follows.

Listing 1.2. order.c. A sample program.

```
1   /* ORDER.C  An illustration of the basic parts of a
2      C program. */
3
4   #include <stdio.h>
5   #include <stdlib.h>
6   #include <graph.h>
7
8   float calc_sub_total( int quantity, float price );
9   float calc_tax( float sub_total );
10
11  main()
12  {
13    char name[30];
14    char product[30];
15    int quantity;
16    float price;
17    float sub_total;
18    float tax;
19
20    _clearscreen( _GCLEARSCREEN );
21    printf( "\n\nEnter your last name => " );
22    scanf( "%s", name );
23    printf( "\n\nEnter the name of the product => " );
24    scanf( "%s", product );
25    printf( "\n\n Enter the quantity and price => " );
26    scanf( "%d %f", &quantity, &price );
27
28    sub_total = calc_sub_total( quantity, price );
29    tax = calc_tax( sub_total );
30
31    _clearscreen( _GCLEARSCREEN );
32    printf( "\n\nOrder Information\n\n" );
33    printf( "Name: %s\n", name );
34    printf( "Product ordered: %s\n\n", product );
35    printf( "Quantity ordered: %d\n\n", quantity );
36    printf( "Price per unit: $%3.2f\n", price );
```

```
37    printf( "Sub total:     $%3.2f\n", sub_total );
38    printf( "Tax:           $%3.2f\n", tax );
39    printf( "Total:         $%3.2f\n", ( sub_total + tax ) );
40  }
41
42  float calc_sub_total( int quantity, float price )
43  {
44    float sub_total;
45
46    sub_total = price * quantity;
47    return sub_total;
48  }
49
50  float calc_tax( float sub_total )
51  {
52    const float tax_rate = 0.06;
53
54    float tax;
55
56    tax = sub_total * tax_rate;
57    return tax;
58  }
```

Writing a program in the Programmer's WorkBench is easy. After you start Microsoft C/C++, you need to type the program, save the program, compile it, and run it.

If you start Microsoft C/C++ and you don't have an edit screen, you should create one. Use the **New** command from the **F**ile menu to create a new edit screen. Your cursor is then placed at the top of the screen.

Microsoft C/C++ has many handy editing features built into its program editor. You do not, however, have to learn all these features to get started quickly. When you are entering your program, you will find that the cursor-movement and text-editing keys work the way you expect. These basic editing keys are all you need to enter the program quickly and correctly.

As you type the order.c program, be sure to save it frequently. If you used **F**ile **New** to create a new edit screen, you will need to assign a name to your program file. When you are ready to save the program, select **S**ave from the **F**ile menu to bring up the Save dialog box. Type the name of the file and press Enter. Be sure to type the full name: **order.c**. Microsoft C/C++ does not make any assumptions about the file extension.

Now that you have typed and saved your program, you are ready to compile and run it. Microsoft C/C++ enables you to compile and run a program from within the PWB.

NOTE

Because the order.c program, like many programs in this book, references the Graphics Library routine _clearscreen(), it's important that you tell the linker to link in the Graphics Library. So, before compiling any program that needs to use the Graphics Library, select the **LINK** Options item from the **O**ptions menu. Enter graphics.lib in the Additional Global Libraries input file of the Link Options dialog box.

If you are using the command-line compiler cl, you can compile this program by typing at the DOS command prompt:

```
cl order.c graphics.lib
```

By adding graphics.lib to the command line, cl ensures that the linker incorporates the Graphics Library routines.

The Graphics Library contains a great variety of graphics functions used for drawing pictures on the computer screen. The Graphics Library also contains a number of general purpose video or screen input/output functions, including the _clearscreen() function used here. So even though your program does not draw pretty pictures, there are many instances where you will choose to use routines from the Graphics Library. For more information about the Graphics Library, see Chapter 8, "Using the Microsoft C/C++ Video Functions."

To compile and link the order.c program, select **B**uild: order.exe from the **P**roject menu. You see a status box that tells how much progress the compiler has made on the program. When the compiler is finished, select **E**xecute: order.exe from the **R**un menu. The *user screen* appears. This is where your program is displayed as Microsoft C/C++ executes it. You can interact with the program just as if you were running it from the DOS prompt. When the program ends, the PWB editor screen becomes active again.

The user screen is one of the features that make Microsoft C/C++ productive. The screen enables you to see your program run without leaving the programming environment. Your program works just as it would from the DOS prompt, even though the program is running under the control of the PWB. Facilities like the user screen make programming in the PWB more efficient than programming with stand-alone editors, compilers, and debuggers.

Now that you know how to use the PWB to enter and compile a program, it's time to see how the program works. Refer to Listing 1.2 as I discuss the order.c program. Keep in mind that you do not need to understand all of the program details yet. This example program should give you an overview of C program structure. The features introduced here are covered more thoroughly in subsequent chapters.

In Listing 1.2, lines 1 and 2 are a brief comment about what the program does. Comments help other people understand what you are trying to do, and also jog your memory if you haven't looked at the program for a while. In addition to comments, blank lines can make your program easier to read. Blank lines help you separate the program into logical units. You do not have to worry about the blank lines causing problems, because the compiler ignores these lines.

Lines 4 and 5 tell the preprocessor to include the stdio.h and stdlib.h header files. These two header files contain declarations for the standard input/output and library functions. Because these two header files contain declarations for so many basic functions, they are included in most C programs.

Line 6 includes the graph.h library header file. Whenever you see this `#include` file in the example programs in this book, you need to ensure that you link in the graphics.lib library.

Lines 8 and 9 are the global declarations for the program. Global declarations declare variables and functions that can be used anywhere in the source file. Notice that this program uses only function declarations; there are no global variable declarations.

Each of the function declarations in lines 8 and 9 can be broken into three parts: the return type, the name of the function, and the argument list. The declaration for `calc_sub_total` is on line 8. The first item in line 8, the word `float`, indicates that the `calc_sub_total` function returns a floating-point number. The second item is, of course, the name of the function. The third part of the `calc_sub_total` declaration is the argument list. This list indicates that `calc_sub_total` requires two arguments, one an integer number and the other a floating-point number. The function in line 9, `calc_tax`, returns a floating-point number and requires only one floating-point argument. Notice that each of the declarations ends with a semicolon.

The `main()` function begins in line 11. The empty parentheses following the word `main` indicate that no arguments are passed to this function. The braces in lines 12 and 40 show where the `main()` function begins and ends.

Lines 13 through 18 are declarations for six variables used in the `main()` function. The first two variables, `name` and `product`, are character arrays. A character array is a *string* of characters that are stored together. Both `name` and `product` are composed of 30 characters. The third variable, in line 15, is the integer variable `quantity`. An integer variable stores a whole number. The last three variables—`price`, `sub_total`, and `tax`—are floating-point variables. Each of the floating-point variables can hold a number that has a fractional part. All the variables declared in lines 13 through 18 are local to the `main()` function. In other words, the variables declared in lines 13 through 18 can be used only inside the `main()` function, as opposed to global variables that are not limited to `main()`.

Lines 20 through 26 contain the C code that clears the screen, prompts you for information, and retrieves the information. Each of the statements on these lines is a function call. Each statement calls a function that performs a special task. The `_clearscreen()` statement is a function call to a function that clears the video screen. The `printf()` statement is a function call that prints formatted information. In this case, the `printf()` statement prints a string on the monitor. The characters `\n` in the `printf()` statement instruct `printf()` to generate a carriage return/line feed signal. The `scanf()` statement is a call to a function that retrieves information. In the `scanf()` statement, the characters `%s`, `%d`, and `%f` tell `scanf()` to retrieve a string, an integer, and a floating-point number, respectively. The values retrieved by `scanf()` are stored in the variables found in the last part of the `scanf()` statement.

Lines 28 and 29 are calls to user-defined functions, which are functions you create and include in your programs. In a function call, the values of the argument variables are passed to the user-defined function. The values are then used in the user-defined function, and another value is passed back. Look at the following statement:

```
answer = my_func( arg1, arg2 );
```

The user-defined function `my_func()` is passed the values of the arguments `arg1` and `arg2`. `my_func` performs its calculations and returns a value, which is then assigned to the variable answer. The function calls in lines 28 and 29 work the same way.

Lines 31 through 39 print the results of all the calculations. Line 31 clears the screen, and lines 32 through 39 print the report, using the `printf()` function. `printf()` lets you easily format and display data.

Lines 42 through 48 list the function definition for the user-defined function `calc_sub_total()`. Notice that the first line of the function definition looks just like a function declaration, but without a semicolon. The missing semicolon tells the compiler that the code that follows defines what the function is supposed to do. The compiler looks for opening and closing braces to define what is contained in the function.

The variables in the user-defined function `calc_sub_total()` have the same names as the variables in the `main()` function. The variables in these two functions, however, are completely separate. Only the *values* of the variables are passed from `main()` to `calc_sub_total()`. Passing the values of variables from one function to another is called, naturally, *passing by value* (see the section "Passing Arguments to Your Function" in Chapter 3, "Using C Functions," for more information).

Line 47 contains a `return` statement, which passes the value of its argument back to the calling function. In other words, the `return` statement in `calc_sub_total()` passes a value back to the `main()` function.

Lines 50 through 58 contain another user-defined function. At the last matched brace, the compiler knows that it has come to the end of the program. If you do not have opening and closing braces properly matched, your program may not do what you want it to do.

Introducing the Library Functions

The purpose of any computer program is the manipulation of data. A program inputs data, processes the data, and then outputs the results. In C, each of these steps is accomplished with the built-in library functions.

Microsoft C/C++ comes with an extensive set of built-in library functions that help you input, process, and output data. This section shows you how to start using some of the most helpful library functions. First, you see how to get data into your program. Second, you learn how to output the results of your program. Third, you are introduced to functions that let you manipulate the data read into your program.

Using Some Basic Input Functions

For the programs you write to be useful, they must enable the user to input data. Even a program as simple as the DOS CHKDSK program has provisions for the user to specify options. This section introduces you to the C input functions. You learn how to use two of the most popular groups of input functions.

C has two main families of input functions: the `get...()` functions and the `scanf()` functions. The `get...()` functions read character data—either a single character or an entire string. The `scanf()` functions input formatted information, which can include numbers and text.

Before you learn about the I/O functions, you need to learn about *streams*. As you start using the I/O functions, you will see that, generally, you are controlling streams instead of files. You will see also that controlling a stream is easier than controlling a file.

Simply put, a stream is a representation of a file. Opening a file associates a stream with that file. After the file is opened, you can use I/O functions that control the stream. When you control the stream, you are indirectly controlling the file.

The concept of streams was developed to enable programmers to write programs that can be used on different kinds of computers. Streams let programmers write device-independent programs. A device-independent program is one that can be compiled and run on almost any computer. The reason that a program can be compiled on different computers is that the stream type function calls are usually made the same way in every compiler. The compiler maker gives you a standard stream type I/O function and does the hard work of controlling the I/O hardware for you.

The hiding of the actual control of the I/O hardware is what makes stream type I/O functions so easy to use. The next few sections show you how to start controlling your data by using Microsoft C/C++'s stream type I/O functions.

The *get...()* Functions

The first group of input functions includes two functions that read single characters: getc() and getche(). Another function, gets(), reads an entire string. This section covers all three functions.

getc() is a function-like macro that reads a single character from a stream you specify. You use the following syntax for getc():

```
int getc( FILE *stream );
```

This statement simply means that getc() returns an integer value from the stream you specify. The integer value that is returned is the value of the character that was read. The stream argument is a *pointer* to a stream.

Take a look at this example:

```
int char_in;
...
char_in = getc( stdin );
printf( "The input character was %d", char_in );
```

Here getc() has an argument that points to the stream associated with the standard input device stdin, which is the keyboard. getc() reads a character from the keyboard and stores the integer value of that character in the char_in variable. The printf() statement just prints a short message and the character you entered.

Other functions in the get...() family, such as getche(), do not require a stream argument. Note the following syntax for getche():

```
int getche( void );
```

Notice that the argument list for getche() is void. In other words, getche() does not require any arguments at all. getche() is written so that it always reads a character from the keyboard.

The value returned by getche() is the integer value of the character that was read. The return value is the same as that returned by the getc() function.

The getc() and getche() functions have two important differences. First, the getche() function does not require a stream argument. getche() reads directly from the keyboard. Second, the getche() function bypasses the normal C streams and echoes the input character directly to the screen, using a BIOS (Basic Input/Ouput System) call. The BIOS is a hidden software component of your PC that manages input and output operations to the disk drives, from the keyboard, to the screen, and so on. For the purposes of this book you only need to know that the BIOS exists.

Some functions in the get...() family work with strings instead of characters. In C, a string is simply an array of characters, such as a name or text stored in a file. By using strings, you can work with groups of characters instead of single characters. gets() is a good example of an input function that works with strings.

The gets() function reads a string from the standard input device, stdin. You use the following syntax for gets():

```
char *gets( char *buffer );
```

gets() reads a string from the standard input device and stores that string in the character array pointed to in the function's argument list.

The following example shows how you can use the gets() function:

```
char name[30];

printf( "Enter your name => " );
gets( name );
printf( "Hello %s.", name );
```

Here gets() inputs your name and stores it in the character array name. gets() stores the string it reads in the array *pointed to* in the argument list. Notice that the argument list consists of the variable name. At first, you might not think that name is a pointer, but remember that the name of an array is a pointer to the first character in that array.

The *scanf( )* Function

The other group of input functions is the scanf() family of functions. The scanf() function has several varieties, but only the basic version is introduced here.

The scanf() function performs formatted input. In other words, scanf() inputs data in a predefined, or formatted, sequence. You determine the sequence in which data will be input.

Listing 1.3 shows a simple program that uses the scanf() function to input integer and string data at the same time.

Listing 1.3. scandemo.c. A program that demonstrates the scanf() function.

```
1   /* SCANDEMO.C - This program demonstrates scanf(). */
2   #include <stdio.h>
3   #include <stdlib.h>
4   #include <string.h>
5
6   main()
7   {
8     int num1;
9     int num2;
10    char operation[4];
11    int comp_result;
12
13    printf( "This program lets you input two numbers and\n" );
14    printf( "the type of mathematical operation \n" );
15    printf( "for the numbers. At the INPUT > prompt,\n" );
16    printf( "enter two numbers and the operation to be\n" );
17    printf( "performed. ADD for addition, SUB for\n" );
18    printf( "subtraction.\n\n" );
19
20    printf( "INPUT > " );
21    scanf( "%d %d %s", &num1, &num2, operation );
22
23    comp_result = strcmp( "ADD", operation );
24    if( comp_result == 0 )
25      printf( "The sum equals %d\n", num1 + num2 );
26    else
27      printf( "The difference is %d\n", num1 - num2 );
28
29    return 0;
30  }
```

In Listing 1.3, lines 8 through 11 declare the variables to be used in the program. Lines 13 through 20 print the program instructions and the prompt. In line 21, scanf() reads two integers and a string. In the scanf() function, the string in quotation marks is called the *format string*. This string tells scanf() what kind of data to input. The rest of the arguments in the scanf() function call are variables in which the input data will be stored.

scanf() requires that you list the address of each variable in which data will be stored, which is why the variables num1 and num2 are preceded by the ampersand (&). The & indicates that the address of the variable is being used and not the variable itself. Notice that the character-array variable, operation, is not preceded by the &. The name of a character array is equivalent to the address of the first character of the array. Therefore, you do not have to precede the character array's name with the & to get the address of the array.

> **WARNING:** You should not use scanf("%s...."...) to read an entire line because scanf() will only read up to the first blank in the line. Instead, use the gets() function.

In line 23, the string-comparison function, strcmp(), compares the input string with the string ADD. If the two strings match, the strcmp() function returns a value of zero. The value returned by strcmp() determines which branch of the if() statement, in lines 24 through 27, will be executed. If the value returned by strcmp() is 0, the first branch in the if() statement, line 25, will be executed. If the value returned by strcmp() is not 0, the second branch of the if() statement, line 27, will be executed.

In summary, the scanf() function is used to input data. The data that scanf() retrieves do not have to be a specific type. You determine the type of data input with scanf(). The arguments for the scanf() function consist of a format string and a list of addresses of variables. The format string determines what kind of data will be input, and the addresses determine where the data will be stored.

Using Some Basic Output Functions

After your program has processed its data, the program must be able to output the results. You need not only input functions but also output functions. The output functions covered in this section include functions that output characters, strings, and formatted data.

Like the input functions, the output functions are grouped in two families. One family of functions, the put...() functions, outputs character and string data. The other family of functions, the printf() functions, outputs formatted data.

The *put...()* Functions

This section introduces two put...() functions: putc() and puts(). The putc() function writes one character at a time, whereas the puts() function writes an entire string.

putc() is a function-like macro that writes a single character to the stream you specify. putc() requires two arguments: The first argument tells putc() what character it will write and the second argument tells `putc()` where to write the character. You use the following syntax for `putc()`:

```
int putc( int c, FILE *stream );
```

The first argument in the argument list is the integer value of the character to be output. The second argument is a pointer to the stream where the character will be written. The stream is just a pointer associated with a particular file or device. `putc()` does return an integer value. If `putc()` successfully writes the character, the value of the character is returned. If `putc()` is unsuccessful, the value of `EOF` is returned.

The following example shows how you can use `putc()`:

```
int c;
...
for( c = 65; c <= 90; c++ ) putc( c, stdout );
```

`putc()` is called with two arguments, `c` and `stdout`. The argument `c` is an integer variable used as a loop counter in the `for()` statement. On each loop of the `for()` statement, `putc()` writes the character value of `c`, the loop counter. `putc()` writes the character to the device pointed to by `stdout`, which is a pointer to the standard output device, usually the video screen.

Sometimes, writing a single character is not enough. You may need to write a complete string at one time. In that case, you can use the `puts()` function.

The following example shows how `puts()` can write a string to the screen:

```
char my_string[] = "This is a test!"
...
puts( my_string );
```

You can see that the `puts()` function requires an argument that points to a string. In this case, `puts()` writes the string that is pointed to by `my_string`. On the first line of the example, `my_string` is declared as a character array, which is a string, and assigned an initial value. The `puts()` function sends the string to `stdout` and appends a new-line character to the end of the string.

The *printf()* Function

The character and string output functions do a good job when you need to output only character-based information. At times, however, you may need to write all kinds of data rather than just character data. You then use the `printf()` function. `printf()` is just one of the functions found in the `printf()` family of functions. Although all the functions in the `printf()` family output formatted data, the functions differ in their arguments and in where the output is sent. See Chapter 6, "Using the Microsoft C/C++ I/O Function Library," for more information about the other functions in the `printf()` family.

With `printf()`, you can generate formatted output. The function enables you to control the appearance, or *format*, of your output data.

The syntax for the `printf()` function looks like this:

```
int printf( const char *format [,argument, ...] );
```

You can see that the argument list for `printf()` is composed of two parts. The first part is the format string, which controls the appearance of the output data. The second part consists of the data that `printf()` will output.

The format string controls how the `printf()` function formats and displays its arguments. This string contains plain text and conversion specifiers. These specifiers determine what kind of data is to be output and in what format that data will appear. The argument list must contain enough variables to match each of the conversion specifiers. If there are not enough variables, the results are unpredictable.

The next example shows a `printf()` function with a format string that contains regular text and conversion specifiers:

```
printf( "The answer is: %d", sum );
```

In a `printf()` function, the format string is the first argument in the list, and the string is enclosed in quotation marks. Note that this format string contains text information and one conversion specifier. The text in the format string will be printed just as it appears in the `printf()` function call. The conversion specifier, which is preceded by the `%` character, will be replaced before it is printed. In this example, the conversion specifier will be replaced by the integer value stored in the variable `sum`.

You may have noticed `\n` in some of the `printf()` format strings. `\n` (the new-line character) is a special character that tells `printf()` to include the carriage return and line-feed characters when the string is printed. Whenever you need to go to a new line, you can use `\n` (see the section "Understanding `printf()`" in Chapter 6).

Using Some Format-Conversion Functions

Format-conversion functions convert a value from one data type to another. The `atof()` function, for example, converts a string to a floating-point number. Another example is the `atoi()` function, which converts a string to an integer.

At first, such functions may not seem useful. Suppose, however, that you have just logged off your favorite bulletin board, and you've got a disk full of financial figures. You probably downloaded the information as some form of text file, and you now have a disk containing information in character format. You can read the information, but you can't add it, subtract it, or perform any computations on it. In this case, you need to read your text file and convert all the character-based numeric information to regular C numeric data types. Microsoft C/C++ provides 16 functions and macros to help solve your conversion needs. See Section 2.3, "Data Conversion," in your *Microsoft C/C++ Run-Time Library Reference* for a complete list.

The following sections introduce the atoi() andtoupper() functions and show how useful they can be in your programs.

The *atoi()* Function

The atoi() function converts a string value to an integer value. The syntax for atoi() looks like this:

```
int atoi( const char *string );
```

You can see from this declaration that the atoi() function requires a pointer to a string as an argument and that the function returns an integer value. The data that atoi() accepts has some limitations. When scanning a string, atoi() looks for the following characters:

- *A whitespace character.* Whitespace is composed of space and tab characters; its presence is optional.

- *A sign character.* The sign character is optional.

- *A string of digit characters.* The string of digit characters ends when a nondigit character is encountered.

The value returned by atoi() is a regular integer value. If atoi() is able to convert the string, it returns the integer value of the converted string. If atoi() is unsuccessful, it returns the value 0.

Listing 1.4 shows how the atoi() function is used in a simple program. strtoint.c reads a string, converts the string to an integer, and then prints the integer value.

Listing 1.4. strtoint.c. A program that converts a string to an integer.

```
1   /*  STRTOINT.C  Converting a string value to an integer
2       value.  */
3
4   #include <stdio.h>
5   #include <stdlib.h>
6   #include <conio.h>
7   #include <graph.h>
8
```

```
 9   main()
10   {
11     char num_str[6];
12     int  num_int;
13
14     _clearscreen( _GCLEARSCREEN );
15     printf( "Enter an integer number => " );
16     gets( num_str );
17     num_int = atoi( num_str );
18     printf( "\n\nYour integer was %d", num_int );
19   }
```

In Listing 1.4, lines 11 and 12 are the variable declarations for the program. Line 11 declares a character array that is six characters long. This array actually holds only five characters; the last space is used for the terminating null character. Line 12 declares a simple integer variable.

In line 17, the gets() function reads a string from the stdin stream. The string is stored in the num_str character array. In line 17, the atoi() function converts the string value to an integer value. atoi() takes the string in num_str and converts it to an integer value that will be stored in num_int. Line 18 uses the printf() function to print the results of the conversion.

The *toupper()* Function

The toupper() function converts lowercase alphabetic characters to uppercase. One use of the toupper() function is to convert to uppercase the lowercase letters input by a program's user. Converting input to a uniform pattern can save you much programming time and effort.

Although toupper() converts lowercase characters to uppercase, the function works with *integer* values. The integer values that toupper() uses are the ASCII character values. Note the syntax for the toupper() function declaration:

```
int toupper( int c );
```

You can see that toupper() requires an integer argument and returns an integer value. The argument passed to toupper() is the ASCII value of any character between *a* and *z*. The return value is the ASCII value of the corresponding uppercase letter. If the argument is not a lowercase letter between *a* and *z*, toupper() does not perform a conversion and returns the value of the argument passed to it.

Listing 1.5 shows one way you can use toupper() in a program. The program upperc.c reads a character from the keyboard, converts it to an uppercase letter, and displays the result.

Listing 1.5. upperc.c. A program that uses the `toupper()` function to convert lowercase letters to uppercase.

```
1   /* UPPERC.C  Convert a lowercase letter to an upper case
2       letter using the toupper() function.  */
3
4   #include <stdio.h>
5   #include <stdlib.h>
6   #include <conio.h>
7   #include <graph.h>
8
9   main()
10  {
11      int in_char;
12      int out_char;
13
14      _clearscreen( _GCLEARSCREEN );
15      printf( "Enter a single character => " );
16      in_char = getche();
17      out_char = toupper( in_char );
18      printf( "\n\nThe uppercase character is: %c",
19              out_char );
20  }
```

In Listing 1.5, lines 11 and 12 set up two variables to hold the integer values of the input character and the converted character.

In line 16, the `getche()` function reads a character from the keyboard and echoes that character to the screen. In line 17, the `toupper()` function converts the input character to an uppercase letter if possible. `toupper()` stores the result of its conversion in the `out_char` variable. Lines 18 and 19 are a `printf()` statement that displays the converted value.

Exercises

The following exercises give you practice in installing, configuring, and using the PWB:

1. Install the Microsoft C/C++ package with all of its memory models.

2. Use the **Options** menu's **Colors...** selection to create a set of custom colors for the user interface.

3. If your monitor supports more than 25 display lines, select 43- or 50-line modes, as appropriate for your hardware.

4. Write a program that compares the getc() and getche() functions. Use the putc() function to display the result.

5. Write a program that uses the puts() and printf() functions to display messages.

6. Write a program that uses the scanf() function to read name and age data. Also include gets() to read a comment string. Use printf() to print the results.

7. Write a program that demonstrates the use of the toupper() function.

Summary

In this chapter, you learned how to install, configure, and run Microsoft C/C++. You learned some basic C programming concepts, and you became acquainted with many useful functions. The following important points were covered:

■ *Installing and configuring Microsoft C/C++ is easy.* You install Microsoft C/C++ using the SETUP program. After Microsoft C/C++ is installed, you can use the **O**ptions menu program to modify and configure many of Microsoft C/C++'s features.

■ *The PWB contains all the programming tools you need in one easy-to-use package.* This includes utilities for writing, testing, debugging, and managing your programming projects.

■ *The two main parts of the PWB are the menu system and the window system.* The menu system gives you access to Microsoft C/C++'s programming tools. The window system is where you write your program and get information about the program from Microsoft C/C++.

■ *The command-line compiler, cl, enables you to use your favorite text editor.* The command-line compiler is invoked from the DOS command line and is controlled using options specified on the command line. cl can both compile and link your program.

■ *There are four basic parts of a C program: preprocessor directives, global declarations, the main() function, and user-defined functions.* Preprocessor directives are used to include other source files and to define macros. Global declarations define functions and data that will be used throughout your program. main() is the only required function. Program execution always begins with main().

■ *User-defined functions are functions you create.* A user-defined function is a group of C statements you put together to perform a task. Generally, a user-defined function has a single purpose, and all the statements in the function help accomplish that purpose.

■ *Some functions input characters, strings, and formatted data.* The `getche()` function reads a single character at a time, whereas `gets()` reads an entire string. If you need to retrieve data of different types, you can use the `scanf()` function. `scanf()` is composed of two parts: the format string and the argument list. The format string lets you specify the kind of data to be retrieved and the order in which the data will be retrieved. The argument list is a list of addresses where retrieved data will be stored.

■ *Microsoft C/C++ has many useful functions to output data.* The `putc()` function writes a single character at a time, and the `puts()` function outputs an entire string. One of the most useful functions in C is the `print()` function, which enables you to write many different types of data. Like `scanf()`, `printf()` is composed of two parts: a format string and a variable argument list. The format string specifies what kind of data is to be output and the format in which the data will be output. The variable argument list specifies the data to be output.

■ *Some functions convert data from one format to another.* You saw how the `atoi()` function works, converting a string of ASCII digits to an integer value. You saw also how the `toupper()` function converts lowercase alphabetic characters to uppercase.

Understanding the Foundations of C

In the first chapter, you learned how to use the command-line compiler and the Programmer's WorkBench (PWB) and how to write basic C programs. This chapter focuses on the foundations of the C language: You learn how your program is compiled and executed, how the data in your program is handled, how to write C statements, and how to use macros.

Laying the Foundations

This section helps you understand two important programming concepts: the generation of executable programs from your source code and the flow of execution in your program. You first see how your program is transformed as its source code is compiled to an executable program. You then see how the flow of execution in your program can be controlled.

Understanding Source, Object, and Load Modules

When you sit down at your computer and type a program, you are creating a *source file* (the source module)—a program in an English-like language you can understand. At this point, you cannot run the program because the computer does not understand your source file. Processing must be performed to convert the source file to a language the computer can understand. This section explains the process of converting your C program into an executable program the computer can run.

Figure 2.1 illustrates the program-creation process and the type of file created at each step.

Figure 2.1.

The creation of source, object, and load modules.

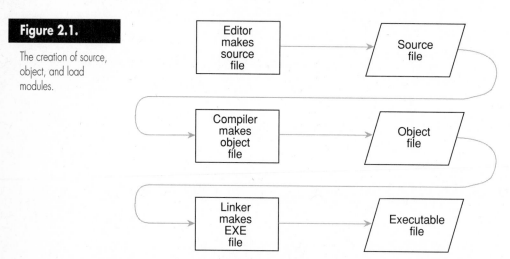

The first step in the program-creation process is to use your text editor—or the text editor that is built-in to the Programmer's WorkBench—to write a C source file (a list of instructions for the computer to follow). The source file is written in C, an English-like language that emulates the way the computer works. The computer, however, cannot understand the English-like instructions you have written.

For the computer to understand the instructions you give it, you must convert your program from an English-like language to one the computer can understand. This is the job of the compiler. It converts your C language source file into an object module composed of machine-language instructions.

The compiler performs the following actions to convert your C language program into a machine-language program:

1. *Your source file is read and converted to a series of preprocessing tokens and whitespace characters.* In this phase, special characters are converted, and individual statements occupying two or more lines are spliced together. The preprocessing tokens are simply elements with which the compiler can work. For example, operators, constants, and keywords are tokens. Whitespace characters include space characters, tab characters, and comments. At this point, comments are deleted and replaced by a single space.

2. *Preprocessing directives are executed.* These directives include instructions like `#include` and `#define`. The `#include` directive instructs the compiler to read in source code from another file. The source code is then put through the same initial processing your program received. Any macros that were defined are expanded at this time.

3. *Further character and string processing is performed.* Your program is analyzed for correct syntax and semantics. During this phase of compilation, any illegal coding mistakes are caught.

4. *If no serious errors are found, an object file is created.*

The preprocessor's `#include` directive enables you to compile more than one source file at a time. The `#include` directive causes the preprocessor to stop processing your source file and to merge into it the file specified in `#include`.

The following directive, for example, instructs the preprocessor to halt temporarily the processing of your program:

```
#include <stdio.h>
```

The preprocessor reads the stdio.h header file and includes the C code in that file with your source code. `#include` is not limited to using header files, but can include any file you specify. In Chapter 3, "Using C Functions," the section "Including Library Functions in Your Program" explores the `#include` directive in more detail.

At this point, you have your source file, which you can understand, and an object module (a translation of the source file), which the computer can understand. Although the compiler has created a machine-language object module, the computer still cannot execute the object module. One more step must be performed before an executable program is created.

The last step in creating an executable program is to process your object module with the *linker*. The linker combines the object module that the compiler created with special object modules that came with the compiler. The result is an executable program, or a *load module*. The special object modules that are combined with your object module contain an extra set of machine-language instructions. These instructions cause the computer to perform a setup routine that is necessary before your program can be run.

Microsoft C/C++ has automated the process of creating executable programs. You don't have to worry about the intermediate steps involved in creating an executable program. For example, if your program's source has been saved to the file begin.c, to compile using the command-line compiler, type

```
cl begin.c
```

This single command invokes both the compiler and linker to create an executable .EXE program file.

If you are using the Programmer's WorkBench, select the **B**uild option from the **P**roject menu to compile and link your program. If your project contains multiple source files and nonstandard libraries, you may need to create a project file, using **N**ew project or **O**pen project from the **P**roject menu. The project file specifies which files and libraries are required when you compile and link your application.

Understanding Program Logic and Execution Flow

Usually, your program is executed one line at a time and in sequence. Executing one line after another is fine most of the time. Your program does not always operate in a vacuum, however. When things change, the program needs to adjust to those changes. You can then use conditional instructions (`if`, `if-else`, and `switch`). To perform certain tasks repeatedly, you can use loop instructions (`do-while`, `while`, and `for`).

Using Conditional Instructions

When you are dealing with changing situations, you need to execute different groups of code based on some condition. Two tools can help you handle changing conditions: `if` and `switch`. The `if` statement handles one or two conditions, and the `switch` statement deals with multiple conditions.

The basic form of the `if` statement is this:

```
if( expression is true )
  execute statement or group of statements;
```

This pattern indicates that if the expression inside the parentheses is true, the following statement or group of statements is executed. To see how the `if` statement works, look at an example:

```
if( a > b )
  printf( "A is greater than B" );
```

The expression being evaluated is `a > b`. If a really is greater than b, the following `printf()` statement is executed. If a is not greater than b, `printf()` is not executed.

The question now is, "What tools can you use to evaluate expressions?" Two basic groups of tools are available. The first group is the relational operators (see Table 2.1), and the second group is the logical operators (see Table 2.2).

Table 2.1. Relational operators.

Operator	Explanation	Example
>	Greater than	2 > 1
<	Less than	1 < 2
==	Equal to	1 == 1
!=	Not equal to	1 != 2
>=	Greater than or equal to	2 >= x
<=	Less than or equal to	1 <= x

The relational operators compare two values. If the values compare correctly according to the relational operator, the expression is true. For example, the expression 2 > 1 yields a true value. If the values do not compare correctly, the expression is false. The expression 1 > 2 yields a false value because 1 is not greater than 2.

Table 2.2. Logical operators.

Operator	Explanation
&& (AND)	Yields true if both expressions are true
¦¦ (OR)	Yields true if either expression is true
! (NOT)	Reverses the true or false condition of an expression

When you use logical operators, you can evaluate more than one condition at a time. Each expression is evaluated, and the results of the expressions are logically compared. The following example demonstrates the OR operator:

```
if( ( 2 > 1 ) ¦¦ ( 2 > 3 ) )
 printf( "The final result was true." );
```

The first expression evaluates as true because 2 is greater than 1. The second expression evaluates as false because 2 is not greater than 3. The entire if statement evaluates as true, however, because one of the two expressions ORed together is true. You can also use another form of the if statement: if-else. The syntax of an if-else statement is this:

```
if( expression is true )
  execute the first statement or group of statements;
else
  execute the second statement or group of statements;
```

Like the first type of `if`, the `if-else` statement evaluates the expression in parentheses. If the expression is true, the statement or group of statements following the `if` is executed. Unlike `if`, however, `if-else` adds another piece. If the expression in parentheses evaluates as false, the second statement or group of statements is executed.

The `if-else` statement can be more flexible than the `if` statement. Note the following use of `if-else`:

```
if( line_count < 66 )
   line_count = line_count + 1;
else:
   line_count = 0;
```

In this code fragment, the value of the variable `line_count` is checked. If the value of `line_count` is less than 66, the value of `line_count` is incremented by 1. If the value of `line_count` is 66 or greater, however, the value of `line_count` is reset to 0. In that case, `if-else` is more flexible than `if` because `if-else` provides different responses for two different instances.

You may have noticed from this discussion that after an expression is evaluated, the next statement or group of statements is executed. To execute more than one statement, you need to be aware of one thing: If you have multiple statements, you must enclose the group of statements in a set of braces. The reason is that after the `if` statement evaluates an expression, `if` looks to execute only *one* statement.

The following statements illustrate the use of braces to execute multiple statements:

```
if( line_count >= 66 )
{
   line_count = 0;
   if( page_count >= 100 )
      printf( "Maximum allowed page is number 100." );
}:
else
   line_count = line_count + 1;
```

If the value of `line_count` exceeds 66, two C statements are executed. The first resets `line_count` to 0 and the other is a nested `if` statement to check the value of a variable named `page_count`.

When you are dealing with more than two conditions, an `if-else` construction will not meet your needs. In that case, you have two alternatives: either write a set of nested `if-else` statements or use a `switch` statement.

Writing a series of nested `if-else` statements is legal in C. The compiler won't flag a nested `if-else` as an error or even a warning. Writing a nested `if-else` statement is difficult, however. With many levels, you can easily lose track of what is happening. Instead of using a nested `if-else` statement, you usually can use a `switch` statement, which is easier both to program and to read.

Here is the general form of the `switch` statement:

```
switch( value )
{
   case value: statement or group of statements;
   ...
   default: statement or group of statements;
}
```

The `switch` statement is composed of several parts. The value at the top of the statement represents the value of the variable condition you will evaluate. The word `case` is required; it signals the beginning of the code that handles a particular condition. `default` indicates the beginning of the code that is executed if no case value matches the conditional value. The default selection is optional.

When the `switch` statement finds a case that matches the condition, `switch` starts executing the statement immediately following that case. Execution continues until the end of the `switch` statement is reached or until a `break` is encountered. Listing 2.1 demonstrates the use of `switch`.

Listing 2.1. swdemo.c. A program that uses a `switch` statement.

```
1   /* SWDEMO.C   A demonstration of the switch statement */
2
3   #include <stdio.h>
4   #include <stdlib.h>
5   #include <conio.h>
6   #include <graph.h>
7
8   main()
9   {
10     char char_in;
11
12     _clearscreen( _GCLEARSCREEN );
13
14     printf( "----- Diagnostic Menu -----\n\n" );
15     printf( "A: System Tests\n" );
16     printf( "B: Video Tests\n" );
17     printf( "C: Hard Drive Tests\n" );
18     printf( "D: Keyboard Tests\n\n" );
```

Listing 2.1. Continued.

```
19    printf( "Enter a letter to select the tests => " );
20
21    char_in = getche();
22    printf( "\n\n\n");
23    char_in = toupper( char_in );
24
25    switch( char_in )
26    {
27      case 'A': printf( "You chose the system tests.\n" );
28              break;
29      case 'B': printf( "You chose the video tests.\n" );
30              break;
31      case 'C': printf( "You chose the drive tests.\n" );
32              break;
33      case 'D': printf( "You chose the keyboard tests.\n" );
34              break;
35      default : printf( "You did not choose a test.\n" );
36    }
37  }
```

Listing 2.1 is a simple menu program. Using a switch statement instead of a series of nested if-else statements makes this code much easier to follow.

Lines 14 through 19 print the main menu screen. Lines 21 through 23 read the menu selection and convert it to an uppercase letter if needed. Converting the selection to uppercase lets the switch statement use half the space it would otherwise need.

Lines 25 through 36 are the switch statement. Line 25 contains the variable to be checked: char_in. Lines 27 through 33 select the right action for the menu selection. Notice that each case is followed by a break. The break tells the switch statement to stop executing instructions and to jump just past the end of the switch statement. Line 35 is the default selection. The statements following default are executed if the value of the char_in variable does not match any of the cases.

Using Loop Instructions

Some operations need to be repeated over and over. A loop defines a block of code that is repeatedly executed. Depending on the kind of loop you use, the block of code could be executed a set number of times or until a certain condition is met.

Microsoft C/C++ provides three loop structures: do-while, while, and for.

The do-while loop is a *postchecked* loop. This loop executes a block of code as long as a specified condition is true. do-while is a postchecked loop because it checks the controlling condition *after* the code is executed. You use the following general form for do-while:

```
do statement or group of statements
   while expression is true
```

The do-while loop is useful when you have a condition that you do not, or cannot, check before the body of the loop is processed. Consider the following example:

```
do{
   printf( "\n\nEnter a letter => " );
   c = getche();
   c = toupper( c );
   printf( "\nYour uppercase letter is: %c", c);
} while( c != 'X' );
```

Here you are prompted to enter a letter that will be converted to uppercase and displayed. The value of the input character controls the loop. Because the input character is read during the middle of the loop, that character's value cannot be checked until the end of the loop.

The while loop is a *prechecked* loop. Like do-while, while executes a block of code as long as a certain condition is true. The while loop checks the conditional expression at the beginning of the loop, however, and not at the end. The while loop takes the following form:

```
while expression is true
   execute statement or group of statements
```

The while loop is useful when the state of the controlling expression could adversely affect the function of the loop. Listing 2.2 shows how you can use the while loop to dump the contents of a file.

Listing 2.2. fdump.c. A program that uses the while loop.

```
1   /*  FDUMP.C  File dump utility using a while loop */
2   #include <stdio.h>
3   #include <stdlib.h>
4
5   main()
6   {
7      FILE *f_in;
8      char c;
```

Listing 2.2. Continued.

```
 9
10    if( ( f_in = fopen( "\\test.txt", "rt" ) ) == NULL )
11    {
12      printf( "Unable to open file. Aborting.\n" );
13      return 1;
14    }
15
16    while( !feof( f_in ) ) {
17      c = fgetc( f_in );
18      putchar( c );
19    }
20  }
```

Listing 2.2 shows how a while loop drives a routine that reads a disk file and prints its contents on the screen. Line 7 declares a FILE object that points to a stream. In line 10, this stream pointer is assigned a value that points to the stream associated with the file TEST.TXT. The fopen() function tries to open the file. If fopen() is successful, it returns a pointer to the file's stream; if fopen() is unsuccessful, it returns NULL. If the fopen() function in line 10 returns NULL, an error message is printed and the program ends.

Lines 16 through 19 contain the entire while loop that reads and writes the data file. Line 16 contains the expression that controls the operation of the loop. The feof() function in line 16 checks for the end-of-file indicator on the stream pointed to by f_in. The while loop runs as long as the end of the file is not encountered. In lines 17 and 18, the body of the loop reads a character from the data file and prints that character on the screen. Finally, the brace in line 19 closes the body of the loop.

If you want to execute the loop a certain number of times and the execution does not depend on another condition, you can use a for loop. Here is its structure:

```
for( starting value; condition; changes )
   execute a statement or a group of statements
```

The three values in the control section of a for loop determine how many times the loop will be executed. You can specify these values in many different ways. This discussion focuses on the most common way to control a for loop.

The starting value specifies a value at which counting will begin. The condition expression limits the for loop to a certain number of iterations, and the changes expression indicates how much the starting value will be incremented or decremented on each pass of the loop. Note the following typical for loop:

```
for( i = 48; i <= 122; i = i + 1 )
  printf( "\c\n", i );
```

Here the `for` loop uses the variable `i` to count from 48 (the starting value) to 122 (the value specified in the `condition` expression). The `changes` expression increments the value of `i` by 1 on each pass through the loop. If you run this sample code, you will see that the `printf()` statement uses the value of `i` to print the ASCII characters from *1* to *z*.

Because the process of incrementing a variable is so common, C provides a special syntax using the ++ increment operator. Instead of writing

```
i = i + 1;
```

you can write

```
i++;
```

This shorthand format is convenient and widely used in C programming, especially in the `for` statement. The preceding example `for` statement can be changed, using the increment operator, to read as follows:

```
for( i = 48; i <= 122; i++ )
```

As you have probably guessed, C also provides the decrement operator - -, so that

```
i--;
```

is equivalent to

```
i = i - 1;
```

You learn more about C's operators in the section "Introducing the C Operator Set" later in this chapter.

The next example shows no arguments in the control section of the `for` loop:

```
for( ; ; )
  printf( "Infinite loop" );
```

If no arguments are present, there is no condition to be met. The loop, therefore, will continue to run forever, or at least until you turn off your computer.

The `break` statement enables you to break out of a `switch` statement or a loop without completing the rest of the `switch` or loop. The `continue` statement enables you to start a loop over without executing the statements following the `continue` statement. These two statements—break and continue—give you extra flexibility in dealing with uncertain events that can occur during loop processing. Both statements are covered in greater detail in the section "Writing Loop-Control Statements" in Chapter 3, "Using C Functions."

Using the Basic Data Types

The information, or data, used by a C program is categorized by its *type*. The type of a variable tells you what kind of data the variable can contain, as well as the range of values the variable can store. This section examines the basic data types and shows you where and how they are used.

Understanding C's Basic Data Types

Any program you write manipulates some kind of data. The data your program works with comes in different sizes and types. Each type of data requires a different amount of memory for storage. To provide correct answers, your program must therefore know what type of data you expect it to process.

The C programming language has three basic types of data: integer numbers, floating-point numbers, and character data. Each of these basic data types comes in many varieties, giving you a wide range of values.

Integers

The most basic data type is the *integer*, which is a numeric data type that represents whole numbers. Whole numbers do not have a fractional part.

When you want to use an integer in a program, you need to declare a variable of type int. Here are some examples of integer variable declarations:

```
int loop_counter;
int cookies, cakes;
int cars = 5;
```

To declare an integer, you first list the reserved word int and then list the name of the variable you want to use. The word int signals your program to set aside enough space for the integer and to assign the name following int— in this first declaration, loop_counter—to represent that memory space.

The second integer declaration lists two variables, cookies and cakes. In C, it is legal to declare multiple variables on one line. Such a declaration saves space and typing time. Use your judgment. If you try to put too many declarations on one line, your program may become unreadable.

The third declaration sets up a variable named cars and assigns it an initial value. Assigning an initial value to a variable is legal and often useful.

You can use three different modifiers with the reserved word int to change the range of values that can be stored in an integer variable. These modifiers are unsigned, long, and short. Table 2.3 lists the various integer types, the number of bytes of memory required, and the range of values each type can store.

Table 2.3. Integer data types, sizes, and ranges.

Type	Size	Range of Values
int	2 bytes	–32,768 to 32,767
unsigned int	2 bytes	0 to 65,535
short int	2 bytes	–32,768 to 32,767
long	4 bytes	–2,147,483,648 to 2,147,483,647
unsigned long	4 bytes	0 to 4,294,967,295

Floating-Point Numbers

The second C numeric data type is the *floating-point number*. Unlike an integer, a floating-point number can have a fractional part. Floating-point numbers are also known as *real* numbers.

You use floating-point numbers when you need to express an exact mathematical quantity. Because floating-point numbers are exact, they are routinely used in scientific and financial calculations. In addition to being more precise than integers, floating-point numbers can represent values of greater or lesser magnitude. In other words, floating-point numbers can represent larger or smaller values than integer numbers.

Declaring a floating-point variable is simple. You just type the reserved word float and the variable name. When your program encounters the reserved word float, the program sets aside enough memory to hold a floating-point number and assigns the variable name (following the word float) to represent that number.

The next code fragment demonstrates some basic ways to declare floating-point numbers:

```
float radius;
float principal, interest;
float mileage = 5.25;
```

The first declaration is the simplest. It declares a single variable with no initial value. The second declaration shows how you can declare multiple variables on a single line. Again, use discretion when declaring several variables on one line. Cramming too much on the line will make your program hard to follow. The third declaration shows the assignment of an initial value.

Floating-point variables come in different sizes. The larger floating-point types give better precision and range, but they also use more memory. The floating-point types are `float`, `double`, and `long double`. Table 2.4 summarizes the floating-point types, size (byte) requirements, and ranges.

Table 2.4. Floating-point types, sizes, and ranges.

Type	Size	Range
float	4 bytes	1.2×10^{-38} to 3.4×10^{38}
double	8 bytes	2.2×10^{-308} to 1.8×10^{308}
long double	10 bytes	3.4×10^{-4932} to 1.2×10^{4932}

As you can see from the table, floating-point variables can represent very large numbers. The trade-off for using large numbers is the amount of space required to store them. For example, every floating-point variable of type `long double` requires 10 bytes of memory. If your application is limited to a small memory space, be careful about using many large floating-point variables.

Besides providing a greater magnitude of values, `double` and `long double` provide more precise values. Table 2.5 indicates the floating-point types and their precisions.

Table 2.5. Floating-point types and their approximate precisions.

Type	Precision
float	6 digits of precision
double	15 digits of precision
long double	18 digits of precision

Character Data

As you have seen, C provides two good sets of data types for handling numerical data. Numbers are not, however, the only type of data with which your programs work. Most C programs also use *character data*. Because character data is important to programming, C provides another data type to handle your character information.

The basic data type for character information is denoted by the reserved word char. A variable of type char can hold a value that represents a single letter.

Recall that your computer stores information in binary code. It is impossible, therefore, to store a letter directly. To get around this problem, the computer uses a numeric value to represent each letter. A variable of type char, then, actually stores a numeric value associated with a particular letter.

Your PC, as well as all PCs like it, uses the ASCII code to represent character data. ASCII, which refers to the American Standard Code for Information Interchange, is a widely recognized code that represents 128 different character values.

You use a char type variable to store a value representing any of the ASCII characters. An object of type char uses one byte of memory. An object of type char, however, needs only seven bits of the byte to represent any character. The remaining bit is used as a sign bit. An object of type char is therefore equivalent to an object of type signed char..

Your PC also uses an extended character set that contains another 128 characters. In all, your computer can use 256 characters. One byte can hold 256 different values if the sign bit is not used. To use both the ASCII and extended character sets, then, you must use an object of type unsigned char.

In summary, a char type object can represent the ASCII character set. An unsigned char type object can represent the ASCII character set and the extended character set.

You should notice that some of the library routines that work with characters actually require you to use an int to store the values. For example, the gtche() function reads a character from the keyboard and returns the value of the character read. The type of the return value is not char; it is int. char and int type objects are similar and can usually be interchanged with little trouble.

Knowing Where To Define Data Objects

Now that you know what basic data types are available, you need to know where you can use them. Otherwise, your data will not be useful. This section shows you where you can declare data objects and introduces the concepts of scope and duration. Chapter 3, "Using C Functions," covers these topics in more detail.

One place that you can declare a data object is at the top of the source file, before the main() function. An object declared there becomes a *global variable*—a data object that can be used anywhere in the program. Listing 2.3 shows an example of a global variable.

Listing 2.3. gvar.c. A program that contains a global variable.

```
1   /*  GVAR.C  Using a global variable */
2
3   #include <stdio.h>
4   #include <stdlib.h>
5
6   int gvar;
7   void funct_1( void );
8
9   main()
10  {
11     gvar = 2;
12     funct_1();
13     printf( "In main()\n" );
14     printf( "gvar = %d\n\n", gvar );
15  }
16
17  void funct_1( void )
18  {
19     printf( "In funct1()\n" );
20     printf( "gvar = %d\n\n", gvar );
21     gvar = gvar * 2;
22  }
```

In Listing 2.3, the only variable, gvar, is declared in line 6—above main() and funct_1(). Because gvar is above and outside both these functions, it can be accessed by both functions. gvar is assigned a value of 2 in line 11. Line 12 calls funct_1(). When the report in funct_1() is executed, you can see that gvar still has a value of 2. In line 21, the value of gvar is multiplied by 2, and control is then passed back to main(). When the report in main() is executed, you can see on-screen that gvar has the value it was assigned in funct_1().

The example in Listing 2.3 shows that a global variable has global scope. The variable can therefore be accessed and used anywhere in that source file. A global variable also has *static duration,* meaning the variable is always available. In fact, room is created for global variables in your object module at compile time.

Global variables are not used much in C programming for two reasons. First, global variables make inefficient use of memory space; they are always available, even when you don't need them. Second, you can easily lose track of their values. A common mistake is to change the value of a global variable and forget that you made the change. The next time you use the global variable, it contains an unexpected value! Mistakes like this can be hard to track.

Most programs use only *local variables*. A local variable, which is declared and used inside a single function, can be accessed only by that function. Even when you call another function that uses a variable with the same name, the value of the variable in the original function remains unchanged. Listing 2.4 shows how you can use—and misuse—local variables.

Listing 2.4. lvar.c. A program that contains local variables.

```
1   /* LVAR.C  Using local variables */
2
3   #include <stdio.h>
4   #include <stdlib.h>
5
6   #define PI 3.1416
7   void square_1( void );
8   float square_2( float );
9
10  main()
11  {
12    float radius_1 = 5.0; /* Declare local variables */
13    float radius_2 = 7.0;
14    float area_1;
15    float area_2;
16
17    square_1();
18    radius_2 = square_2( radius_2 );
19
20    area_1 = PI * radius_1;
21    area_2 = PI * radius_2;
22
23    printf( "Area 1 = %f\n", area_1 );
24    printf( "Area 2 = %f\n", area_2 );
25
26  }
27
28  void square_1( void )
29  {
30    float radius_1;
31
32    radius_1 = radius_1 * radius_1;
33  }
```

Listing 2.4. Continued.

```
34
35  float square_2( float   radius_2 )
36  {
37    radius_2 = radius_2 * radius_2;
38    return radius_2;
39  }
```

Listing 2.4, which calculates the area of two circles, demonstrates two ways to use local variables. The area of the first circle is calculated the wrong way, and the area of the second circle is calculated the right way.

Because the radius of the first circle is declared in line 12 in the `main()` function, the variable can be accessed in `main()` only. When the `square_1()` function is called, the value of `radius_1` is unchanged, even though `square_1()` manipulates a `radius_1` variable. The `radius_1` variables in `main()` and `square_1()` are completely separate although they have the same name. The result is that the variable `radius_1` in `main()` was never squared, and the value of `area_1` is therefore incorrect.

The handling of the variable values for `radius_2` is performed correctly. Notice that two `radius_2` variables are declared. One variable is declared in `main()` and the other is declared in `square_2()`. These are completely different variables. The value of `radius_2` in `main()` is correctly calculated because the value of `radius_2` was passed to `square_2` properly.

Note the sequence of events in line 18. The function `square_2()` is called. `square_2()` is passed a *copy* of the value of `radius_2` in `main()`. `square_2()` then assigns the passed value to its own `radius_2` variable. The calculation is performed, and a value is finally returned. When the call to `square_2()` is completed, the value returned is assigned to `main()`'s copy of `radius_2`. Because the values of the variables were passed and returned correctly, the value of `area_2` is correct.

Local variables have *local scope,* which means that a local variable can be used only in the function in which it was declared. Local scope is the reason why two functions can have variables with the same name. Furthermore, local variables have *automatic duration.* This means that when a function is called, space is automatically allocated for the variables the function will use. When the function ends, the space for the variables is deallocated automatically. A local variable, therefore, does not retain its value from one function call to the next.

If you want a local variable in one function to have the same value as a variable in another function, you must pass a value to the variable in the called function. You saw this done in line 18 of Listing 2.4. The function call to `square_2()`

passed the value of main()'s variable radius_2 to the function square_2(). Inside the function square_2(), the value passed to the function was assigned to the radius_2 variable that is local to square_2().

Writing C Expressions and Statements

Expressions and statements are the building blocks for your C functions and programs. This section explains what expressions and statements are and how you can use them. After you learn about expressions and statements, you learn how to use the C operator set.

Understanding Expressions and Statements

The terms *expression* and *statement* are used throughout this book. In most instances, these terms may seem to be synonymous. This is not the case, however. Expressions and statements have some important differences.

Basically, expressions are the pieces from which statements are made. An expression can be a group of operators and operands that computes a value, or an expression can simply refer to a data object or function.

An expression can contain three parts: operators, operands, and punctuators. *Operators* are symbols that tell the program to perform some type of computation. *Operands* are the arguments that operators require to perform a computation. *Punctuators* help define and organize the relationships of operands and operators.

Expressions can range from simple to complex. A simple expression might consist of just a single operand, and a complex expression might contain several operators and operands. A complex expression might even be composed of subexpressions. The next few lines of code are examples of expressions:

```
a
15
i + 1
j++
x * y + 4 * z
( 1 + j ) * ( x / ( 28 - y ) )
sum( a, b )
```

Notice that expressions can use constants and variables, which can be mixed freely.

The way Microsoft C/C++ evaluates the operands in an expression may not correspond to the way the operands are written. Microsoft C/C++ tries to rearrange the expression to produce better code. If an operator specifies an evaluation order for the operands, however, Microsoft C/C++ will not rearrange those operands.

You can use parentheses to force Microsoft C/C++ to evaluate an expression in a certain order. Note this example:

```
x = y + ( 2 + 3 )
```

Because of the parentheses, the expression 2 + 3 is evaluated first, and the result is then added to y.

The main difference between expressions and statements is that an expression produces a value. A statement does not generate a value, but rather completes an operation. Expressions are used for the values they generate; statements are used for the effects they cause. Examine these examples:

```
2 + 3
x = 2 + 3
```

Both lines of code are expressions. The first expression's value, 5, is obvious. Notice that the second line of code is also an expression, but what value does it have? This value is also 5, which is assigned to both the variable x and the expression as a whole. The reason that the second line of code is not a statement is that this line does not complete an operation. For the second line of code to become a statement, the line would have to be terminated with a semicolon. The semicolon indicates that an action has been completed and that the effect caused by the expression has occurred.

Now look at these logical operations:

```
10 < 15
result = 10 < 15
```

The value of the first line of code is 1. If the expression were false, its value would be 0. Because the logical operation in the second line of code is true, that subexpression yields a value of 1 also. The value of 1 is assigned to both the variable result and the expression as a whole.

A C statement is terminated by a semicolon. When the compiler encounters the semicolon, it knows that the preceding statement has ended and that another statement is beginning.

If a group of statements is enclosed in a set of braces, the group is treated as a single statement. When encountering an opening brace, the compiler scans the source code for the matching brace that closes the group of statements. Using braces is handy when you need to perform several actions but only one statement is possible—for example, after an if statement. Only one statement following the if will be executed when the if is true. To execute a group of statements, just enclose the entire group in a set of braces.

Microsoft C/C++ uses eight different types of statements. They are summarized in Table 2.6.

Table 2.6. Statement types.

Type	Explanation
Compound	A group of statements enclosed in a set of braces and treated as a single statement.
Expression	A statement terminated with a semicolon. Any side effects of the expression are completed before any other statements are executed.
Labeled	An identification of a location to jump to for goto and switch statements.
Selection	A flow-control statement; the selection statements are if, else, and switch.
Iteration	A loop-control statement; the iteration statements are while, do, and for.
Jump	A statement that causes an unconditional change in execution flow. The jump statements are break, continue, goto, and return.
asm	A statement used to include inline assembler code.
Declaration	A statement that sets up and possibly initializes data objects.

Introducing the C Operator Set

The operator set is a group of tokens defining the basic operations that can be performed on your data objects. Microsoft C/C++ provides an extensive set of operators that enhance the speed and ease of programming.

This section covers all the Microsoft C/C++ operators and introduces you to operator precedence—the set of rules governing the order in which operators are evaluated. Understanding operator precedence is extremely important in C programming. To produce accurate answers, you have to know how the operators manipulate your data.

The first group of operators is the *unary operators*. A unary operator requires only one operand. Table 2.7 lists the unary operators and their functions.

Table 2.7. Unary operators.

Operator	Meaning
+	Unary plus.
-	Unary minus.
!	NOT operator (or logical negation).
&	Address operator.
*	Indirection operator.
++	Increment operator. If the operator is prefixed to an operand, a preincrement is performed. If the operator is postfixed to an operand, a postincrement is performed.
- -	Decrement operator. If the operator is prefixed to an operand, a predecrement is performed. If the operator is postfixed to an operand, a postdecrement is performed.
~	Bitwise (1's) complement.

The second group of operators is the *binary operators*. A binary operator, as the name suggests, requires two operators. Table 2.8 lists the binary operators and their functions.

Table 2.8. Binary operators.

Operator	Meaning
	Mathematical Operators
+	Addition
-	Subtraction
*	Multiplication
/	Division
%	Modulus
	Assignment Operators
=	Assignment
+=	Assign sum

Operator	Meaning
-=	Assign difference
*=	Assign product
/=	Assign quotient
%=	Assign remainder
&=	Assign bitwise AND
!=	Assign bitwise OR
^=	Assign bitwise XOR
<<=	Assign bitwise left-shift
>>=	Assign bitwise right-shift

Logical Operators

&&	Logical AND
!!	Logical OR

Equality and Relational Operators

==	Equal to
!=	Not equal to
<	Less than
>	Greater than
<=	Less than or equal to
>=	Greater than or equal to

Shift and Bitwise Operators

<<	Shift left
>>	Shift right
&	Bitwise AND
!	Bitwise OR
^	Bitwise XOR

Component Selection Operators

.	Direct component selector
->	Indirect component selector

continues

Table 2.8. Continued.

Operator	Meaning
Conditional Operator	
a?b:c	if a then b; else c
Comma Operator	
,	Forces evaluation from left to right
Class Member Operators	
::	Scope access/resolution
.*	Dereference a pointer to a class member
->*	Dereference a pointer to a class member

As indicated earlier, operator precedence is the set of rules determining the order in which operators are evaluated. If you have only one operator in a statement, you don't have to worry about the precedence rules. When you use two or more operators in a statement, however, operator precedence becomes important. Consider this example:

```
x = 1 + 2 * 3;
```

Notice the two operators, + and *. If there were no precedence rules, this simple formula could have two answers. If the addition operator is evaluated first, x equals 9. If the multiplication operator is evaluated first, x equals 7. As you can see from this example, knowing the precedence rules is vital to producing accurate and reliable programs.

Table 2.9 shows the precedence of the Microsoft C/C++ operators. The operators at the top of the table have a greater precedence than those at the bottom. In other words, an operator higher in the table is executed before an operator lower in the table.

Each group of operators in the table has a certain associativity. The operators are evaluated from left to right, or from right to left.

Table 2.9. Precedence of Microsoft C/C++ operators.

Operator(s)	Associativity
() [] -> .	Left to right
! ++ -- +	Right to left
- * & (typecast) sizeof	Right to left
* / %	Left to right
+ -	Left to right
<< >>	Left to right
< <= > >=	Left to right
== !=	Left to right
&	Left to right
^	Left to right
¦	Left to right
&&	Left to right
¦¦	Left to right
?:	Right to left
= += -= *= /= %=	Right to left
&= ^= ¦= <<= >>=	Left to right

Controlling Type Conversions

As you learned earlier in the chapter, each piece of data that your program uses has a certain *type* associated with that data. The type determines what kind of data it is. Data of type int is integer data, and data of type char is character data. A type conversion occurs when data of one type is changed to a different type. Sometimes these conversions are automatic, but at other times you may need to force a type conversion. In this section, you learn how type conversions work and how to control them.

Understanding Implicit Type Conversions

A *type conversion* is simply the conversion of an object's type, such as `char`, to a different type, such as `int`. Another example occurs when an object of integer type is changed so that it is handled as a floating-point type.

Although you can explicitly cause a type conversion, many type conversions are made automatically by Microsoft C/C++. When Microsoft C/C++ is responsible for a type conversion, it is called an *implicit type conversion.*

Implicit type conversions occur in arithmetic operations using two different types of objects. Such type conversions cause objects of a lower, or less precise, type to be converted to a higher, or more precise, type. Automatic type conversion results in mathematical operations that are more precise. Another benefit of automatic type conversion is the consistent evaluation of mathematical expressions.

Microsoft C/C++ has a set of rules governing the automatic type conversion process. When a type conversion is required, the basic integer types are converted in one phase, and any other conversions are handled in a second phase.

Table 2.10 summarizes the type-conversion process for integer type objects.

Table 2.10. Implicit conversion of integer types.

Original Type	Converted Type	Conversion Method
char	int	High byte set to zero or sign extended, depending on default char type
unsigned char	int	High byte zero filled
signed char	int	Sign extended
short	int	Same value
unsigned short	unsigned int	Same value
enum	int	Same value

An object of type `char` consists of a single byte. When a `char` type object is converted to an `int` type object, however, two bytes are used. When the conversion takes place, the value of the low-order byte of the new `int` is the same as for the original `char`. The value of the high-order byte depends on whether the `char` object is signed or unsigned. An `unsigned char` causes the high-order byte of the `int` to be zero. A `signed char` causes the high-order byte of the `int` to be –1. If the original object is of type `char`, the conversion process depends on the Microsoft C/C++ setup. Microsoft C/C++ can define a `char` type object to be signed or unsigned by default.

Before evaluating a mathematical expression, Microsoft C/C++ performs several steps in a type-conversion process. The first step is to convert `char`, `short`, or `enum` type to integers; Table 2.10 summarizes the conversions. The rest of the steps in the type-conversion process are explained in the following list:

1. The expression is checked for an operand of type `long double`. If either operand is a `long double`, the other operand is converted to a `long double`. If neither operand is a `long double`, the next step in the process is performed.

2. The expression is checked for an operand of type `double`. If either operand is a `double`, the other operand is converted to a `double`. If neither operand is a `double`, the next step in the process is performed.

3. The expression is checked for an operand of type `float`. If either operand is a `float`, the other operand is converted to a `float`. If neither operand is a `float`, the next step in the process is performed.

4. The expression is checked for an operand of type `unsigned long`. If either operand is an `unsigned long`, the other operand is converted to an `unsigned long`. If neither operand is an `unsigned long`, the next step of the process is performed.

5. The expression is checked for an operand of type `long`. If either operand is a `long`, the other operand is converted to a `long`. If neither operand is a `long`, the next step of the process is performed.

6. The expression is checked for an operand of type `unsigned int`. If either operand is an `unsigned int`, the other operand is converted to an `unsigned int`. If neither operand is an `unsigned int`, both operands must be of type `int`.

Arithmetic expressions are not the only places implicit type conversions can occur. Automatic type conversion also occurs during assignments and function calls. When an assignment is made, the value type on the right side is converted to the type on the left side. In a function call, the argument to the function call is an expression; therefore, an implicit type conversion can occur just as a conversion can occur for any expression.

Using Explicit Type Conversions

Automatic type-conversion routines handle many of the type-conversion tasks you will encounter. At times, however, you will want to take control of the type conversions yourself. When you issue a command that causes a type conversion to occur, you have performed an *explicit* type conversion. The explicit type-conversion process is known as *type casting*. The format of an explicit type cast is the following:

```
( type-name ) expression
```

As you can see, any valid C expression can be type cast. To perform the type cast, simply precede the expression with a unary *cast* operator. This operator is made by enclosing the type-name in a set of parentheses. The result of the expression appears in the type you specified.

The following code fragment shows a `float` being type cast to an `int`:

```
int i;
float x = 5.9876;
i = ( int ) x;
printf( "i = %d, x = %f", i, x );
```

This code fragment contains two variables: an integer variable and a floating-point variable. The `float` is assigned a value in the second line. On the third line, `i` is assigned the value of the `float` after it has been typecast. The `printf()` statement shows that the fractional part of the `float` was dropped in the type conversion.

The next code fragment shows how a type conversion can provide a function with the proper arguments:

```
int a = 2, b = 4;
double x;
x = pow( ( double ) a, ( double ) b );
printf( "x = %f", x );
```

In this example, a function that requires two `double` arguments is called with two `int` arguments. The two type-cast operators on the third line convert the integer arguments to floating-point arguments. The `pow()` function works correctly with two arguments of type `double`. Here `pow()` returns the value 16.0 as it should.

You should be aware that the values of your variables can change during a type-cast operation. The change in value is obvious when a `float` is converted to an `int`. The `int` cannot hold the fractional part of the `float`. When a `float` is converted to an `int`, the fractional part of the number is lost. The change in value may not be as obvious when an `int` is converted to a `float`. Even though the range of a `float` is large, a `float` cannot store an exact value for every number. Therefore, when an `int` is converted to a `float`, the new value may not equal the value before the typecast occurred. The new value will be as close as possible to the original value, but the two values may not be equal.

From these brief examples, you can see that explicit type conversions offer a great deal of flexibility in acquiring and processing data. One of the most useful functions of the type-cast operator is to cast arguments for functions.

Using C Macros

Like macros in a word processor, macros in your C programs can save you time and effort. Macros can also be versatile. You can use a macro, for example, to represent an often-used variable or to work like a function. This section shows you how to start using macros productively in your own programs.

In Microsoft C/C++, you can create two kinds of macros: *object-like* macros and *function-like* macros. When the preprocessor encounters an object-like macro in your source file, a value you defined at the beginning of your program replaces the macro. The replacement value can be any C data type, a character, an integer, or a floating-point number. In an object-like macro, a data object replaces the macro. When the preprocessor encounters a function-like macro, a piece of code that performs an action replaces the macro name. You can even use function-like macros with arguments. As the name suggests, a function-like macro works similarly to a function.

Defining Object-Like Macros

A macro is a string-replacement utility. When the preprocessor encounters a macro name, another string that was previously defined replaces it. You use the following form for an object-like macro definition:

```
#define identifier replacement-list
```

The #define directive tells the preprocessor that a macro definition is about to begin. The *identifier* is the name of the macro; it is the name that is found in your program. The *replacement-list* replaces the macro name when the preprocessor encounters it in your program.

Note the following object-like macro definition:

```
#define SALES_TAX 0.06
...
total = sales * SALES_TAX;
```

#define signals that a macro definition is about to start. SALES_TAX is the macro name, and 0.06 is the replacement-list. The last line of the example shows how the macro is used. When you want to use the value of sales tax, simply type the macro name **SALES_TAX**. When the preprocessor scans the program, every occurrence of SALES_TAX is replaced with 0.06.

Follow these simple rules when you create macros:

- *A #define preprocessor directive signals the beginning of the macro definition.*

- *The macro follows the #define directive.* When you name a macro, use the guidelines for naming any other C variable. The macro name cannot contain any spaces. Although uppercase letters are not required, the common practice is to enter the macro in uppercase.

- *The replacement string follows the macro name.*

- *The macro definition is not terminated by a semicolon.* If you terminate the definition with a semicolon, the preprocessor treats it as part of the replacement string.

- *The backslash character (\) enables you to extend the macro definition to more than one line.*

Note that the C compiler is not responsible for handling macros. The C preprocessor does all the necessary work of translating a macro into a form the compiler can accept and use. The preprocessor treats your program as a data file. When scanning the text of your program, the preprocessor replaces each occurrence of a macro name with the predefined replacement text.

Using macros to define constant values can enhance the performance of your program. Consider this reconstruction of the preceding example:

```
double sales_tax = 0.06;
...
total = sales * sales_tax;
```

Here sales_tax is not a macro, but is instead a double variable that has been assigned the value 0.06. Because sales_tax is now a variable, the program must look up the value of sales_tax each time it is encountered. Before, when SALES_TAX was a macro, the preprocessor replaced it with the value 0.06. The sales tax amount was therefore coded into the program whenever the amount was used. When the program needed the sales tax amount, the value was already there. Using a macro saved you the time required to look up the value of the variable each time it was used.

The time a macro saves may not be significant in straight line code. When you have calculations inside a loop, however, the savings can be substantial.

Using macros can save you time in other ways. First, macros can save you valuable coding time by making it easy to change constant values. If you use macros to define constants, you have to change only one macro definition to change the value of the constant throughout the program. Second, macros can speed the debugging process. When you use a macro, you enter a value once instead of many times. Because you make fewer keystrokes, you are likely to make fewer errors.

Macros also make your program easier to read. Instead of scattering obscure values throughout the program, you can use descriptive names that make more sense to your readers.

The first example in this section showed you how to use a macro to represent a numeric value. In some cases, you may need to use a macro to represent a character or a string instead of a numeric value. Listing 2.5 defines macros that use characters and strings.

Listing 2.5. objmac.c. A program that uses characters and strings in macros.

```
1   /* OBJMAC.C  This program demonstrates the use of object-
2       like macros that work with characters and strings. */
3
4   #include <stdio.h>
5   #include <stdlib.h>
6
7   #define FIRST_CHAR 'H'
8   #define SECOND_CHAR 'i'
9   #define COMMA ','
10  #define STRING " this is a macro example."
11
12  main()
13  {
14    putchar( FIRST_CHAR );
15    putchar( SECOND_CHAR );
16    putchar( COMMA );
17    puts( STRING );
18  }
```

Listing 2.5 shows that object-like macros are not restricted to working with numeric information. Lines 7 through 9 are macro definitions for a group of characters. Notice that each macro's substitution text is enclosed in quotation marks. When the macro substitution takes place, the entire substitution text replaces the macro name. Thus, the character and the quotation marks replace the macro name. For example, in the macro expression

```
putchar( FIRST_CHAR );
```

the macro symbol FIRST_CHAR expands to

```
putchar( 'H' );
```

You can see that every occurrence of the macro name is replaced with a *character constant*. This replacement works correctly in this example because the macro was used in a function call that required a character-constant argument. When you use a single character in a macro replacement-list, make sure that you include the quotation marks only if it is necessary.

Line 10 is a macro definition that expands to a string constant. Notice in the replacement-list that the string is enclosed in quotation marks. The macro will therefore be replaced with a string literal. Again, when you use a string in a macro replacement-list, be sure to include quotation marks only when you need them.

Lines 14 through 17 are a simple series of statements that print all the macro definitions.

You have to keep track of your quotation marks carefully when you are defining strings for macros. Remember that anything in the replacement-list is copied during the macro expansion. If you include quotation marks in the replacement string, they will be copied during the expansion. Also remember that in a program, any string in quotation marks is treated as a string literal. Note the following code fragment:

```
#define STRING "This is my string."
...
printf( "%s", "STRING" );
```

This example does not work as you might expect. Instead of printing the replacement string found in the macro definition, printf() prints the word STRING instead. The reason is that "STRING" in the printf() statement is treated as a string literal. Therefore, the preprocessor won't treat it as a macro. When you use a macro as an argument to a function, be sure to pay attention to the quotation marks and how they will be interpreted.

After expanding a macro, the preprocessor rescans the result to look for other macros. Because macros are rescanned, one macro can be made of other macros. The next example demonstrates the rescanning feature of the preprocessor:

```
#define NUM_1 10
#define NUM_2 15
#define SUM NUM_1 + NUM_2
...
printf( "SUM is equal to %d", SUM );
```

Here three macros are defined. The first two macro definitions are simple, and the third references the first two. When scanning the program, the preprocessor changes the printf() statement to the following:

```
printf( "SUM is equal to %d", NUM_1 + NUM_2 );
```

The preprocessor then rescans the expanded macro to look for any new macros. In this case, the preprocessor finds two new macros. After the second macro expansion, the `printf()` statement looks like this:

```
printf( "SUM is equal to %d", 10 + 15 );
```

When you are through with a macro or you want to use the macro name for something else, you can *undefine* the macro. To remove a macro definition, you use the `#undef` preprocessor directive, which requires the following form:

```
#undef identifier
```

Note this example of the `#undef` directive:

```
#define MY_MACRO 1
....
#undef MY_MACRO
```

Here the `#undef` preprocessing directive undefines, or removes, the macro definition for `MY_MACRO`. After encountering the `#undef` directive, the preprocessor no longer recognizes `MY_MACRO` as a valid macro.

Defining Function-Like Macros

Macros can have more sophisticated uses than just supplying constant values. You can write a macro so that it looks and works much like a function. A function-like macro definition contains more pieces than an object-like macro definition. The function-like macro definition also contains a formal argument list. This list enables you to supply values that can change or control the substituted text.

You use the following general form for a function-like macro:

```
#define identifier(identifier-list) replacement-list
```

The `#define` directive signals the preprocessor that the rest of the information on the line is a macro definition. The *identifier* is the name of the macro. When the preprocessor encounters the *identifier* in your program, a macro expansion occurs, and the *identifier* is replaced with the *replacement-list*. The *identifier-list* is a formal argument list. When you use a function-like macro in a program, you should follow the macro name with a number of arguments that correspond to the *identifier-list*. When the macro is expanded, the arguments you supplied are copied into the *replacement-list*.

The next code fragment shows a function-like macro that requires a single argument:

```
#define MTOK(m) m * ( 8.0 / 5.0 )
...
```

```
double miles, kilometers;
miles = 62.0;
kilometers = MTOK(miles);
```

Here the macro roughly translates `miles` to `kilometers`. The macro definition is different from the definition for an object-like macro because of the formal argument list following the macro name. The argument list must start with a left parenthesis and *immediately* follow the macro name. When the macro is expanded, the argument in the replacement-list is replaced with the value of the argument in the identifier-list. The preprocessor expands the last line of this code fragment to

```
kilometers = miles * ( 8.0 / 5.0 );
```

The `MTOK()` macro was invoked with an argument of `miles`. As you can see, the preprocessor expanded the macro and replaced the formal argument, `m`, with the variable `miles`.

You can use more than one argument in a function-like macro definition. To invoke the macro with more than one argument, all you have to do is separate the arguments with commas. Consider this example:

```
#define WATTS(v,a) v * a
...
int voltage = 120;
int amperage = 5;
int wattage;
wattage = WATTS(voltage,amperage);
printf( "Power consumption = %d", wattage );
```

Notice that both arguments in the formal argument list are used in the replacement-list. The number of arguments in the argument list must always match the number of arguments in the replacement-list.

One useful feature of function-like macros is that they can work with arguments of any data type. Now look at the following example:

```
#define CUBE(x) x * x * x
...
int i;
float y;
i = CUBE(2);
y = CUBE(1.5);
```

The last two lines expand to

```
i = 2 * 2 * 2;
y = 1.5 * 1.5 * 1.5;
```

In this example, a single function-like macro calculates the cube of an integer *and* a floating-point number. Without a macro, you would need two functions to accomplish this same task. The reason that a function is not as versatile is that it can accept arguments of only a certain data type. A macro, however, does not care what argument types are passed to it. As you can see from this example, the macro's arguments are simply copied into the expanded replacement-list expression. Each time the macro is used, the macro is expanded to a new expression. Because a new expression is created, you can supply the macro with arguments of different types each time you use the macro.

When you use function-like macros, you can reference the formal arguments in the replacement-list in three different ways. The first way to reference a formal argument is for it to appear by itself. So far, this is the only way you have seen the formal argument referenced. The second way is to precede the formal argument with the string literal operator (#). The third way is to precede the formal argument with the string concatenation operator (##). The following paragraphs examine the various ways that formal arguments can be used.

In the preceding examples, the argument in the replacement-list appeared by itself. That is why no special character processing occurred during macro expansion. The formal argument in the replacement-list was replaced with the argument you supplied. Review this example of a function-like macro:

```
#define SUM(a,b) a + b
```

The SUM() macro requires two arguments. The arguments in the macro definition, a and b, are the formal arguments. Now examine the expression that uses the SUM() macro:

```
SUM(1,2)
```

This expression uses the SUM() macro and supplies the macro with actual arguments. The actual arguments in this example are the integers 1 and 2. When the macro is expanded, the actual arguments will be copied into the replacement-list. The SUM() macro is therefore expanded to

```
1 + 2
```

This expression is the actual expansion that is placed in your program. The preprocessor removes the macro name and replaces it with the replacement-list. As you can see, the preprocessor uses the actual arguments when inserting the replacement-list.

The second way to reference a formal argument in the replacement-list is to precede the formal argument with the string literal operator (#). This operator causes the actual argument to appear in quotation marks in the expanded macro. The next code fragment shows one way to use the string literal operator in a printf() statement:

```
#define QUOTE(s) #s
...
printf( "%s\n", "He said " QUOTE("Hi, my name is Joe.") );
```

In this example, the QUOTE() macro is replaced with the macro's argument, which is enclosed in quotation marks. The funny-looking printf() statement therefore prints as

```
He said "Hi, my name is Joe."
```

When scanning the program, the preprocessor converts the QUOTE() macro to a regular string the printf() statement can use. At first glance, you might think that the preprocessor will expand the QUOTE() macro to this:

```
""Hi, my name is Joe.""
```

The two quotation marks in a row, however, would cause the compiler to generate an error. The string literal preprocessor command is designed to prevent such an error. Instead of generating the preceding string, the preprocessor generates the following:

```
"\"Hi, my name is Joe.\""
```

The backslash characters tell the compiler that you want to print the actual quotation marks and not delimit another string. Because the backslashes indicate that actual quotation marks will be printed, this string will not generate any errors.

You may have noticed that the argument list for the printf() statement is composed of two *data* strings. When the printf() was executed, it printed *both* data strings. The reason for both strings being printed is that the data strings were not separated by a comma. The compiler therefore treated both strings as a single string literal. This way of generating a string literal wherever one is required is perfectly acceptable.

The third way to reference a formal argument in a macro replacement-list is to use the argument with the string concatenation operator (##). This operator joins two tokens in a macro replacement-list to form a new, larger token. Unlike the string literal operator, the string concatenation operator does not put quotation marks around the expanded macro.

The next code fragment shows how to use the string concatenation operator:

```
#define CAT(a,b) a ## b
...
printf( "%s\n", CAT("my_","macro" );
```

The printf() statement prints as

```
my_macro
```

The macro definition for CAT() is similar to macro definitions you have seen before—except for ##, the string concatenation operator. This operator causes the actual arguments for CAT() to be concatenated, or joined together. In this example, the arguments "my_" and "macro" are concatenated into one string.

The result is `my_macro`.

After the preprocessor expands a macro with a string concatenation operator, the preprocessor rescans to look for any new macros. Study the next example:

```
#define STR_1 "This is a test!"
#define CAT(a,b) a ## b
...
printf( "%s\n", CAT(STR_1,) );
```

Here the `CAT()` macro is scanned and replaced with `STR_1`. After the `CAT()` macro is expanded, the preprocessor rescans the line, looking for new macros. When the preprocessor finds the new macro `STR_1`, it is expanded also. The `printf()` statement then looks like this:

```
printf( "%s\n", "This is a test!" );
```

Again, the preprocessor rescans the line. Because it finds no more macros, the processing is finished.

The next example shows a string concatenation operator that does not produce the result you want:

```
#define STR_1 "This is "
#define STR_2 "a test"
#define CAT(a,b) a ## b
...
printf( "%s\n", CAT(STR_1,STR_2);
```

This piece of code produces an error when compiled. The intended effect of this code fragment is to combine the *expanded* macros `STR_1` and `STR_2` and to produce the following printed message:

```
"This is a test"
```

The code fragment, however, cannot generate this message. The preprocessor instead replaces the `CAT()` macro with

```
STR_1STR_2
```

The preprocessor properly expanded the `CAT()` macro, but the expansion of the `CAT()` macro resulted in a meaningless string. When compilation starts, `STR_1STR_2` is flagged as an error and compilation is aborted so that you can fix the error.

Exercises

These exercises give you practice in using the C operators, controlling program execution flow, controlling data types and conversions, and using macros.

1. Write a short program and compile it using the **B**uild option. As the program is compiling, watch the message windows and notice the status of the compile and link procedures.

2. Write a program that uses an `if` statement to demonstrate at least three of the relational operators.

3. Write a program that generates a *truth table* for the logical operators `&&` and `¦¦`. A truth table lists the outcomes of using a logical operator with all possible combinations of operands.

4. Write the beginning of a menu program that uses the `switch` statement.

5. Demonstrate the `while`, `do-while`, and `for` loops.

6. Show that a global variable can be accessed anywhere in a source file and that a local variable can be accessed only in the function in which it was declared.

7. Write an `if` statement that, when true, causes a group of statements to be executed.

8. Write two identical expressions. For one expression, use parentheses to change the order of evaluation.

9. Write several statements that will result in an implicit type conversion for each statement. Notice the change in precision as the type conversions occur.

10. Create a function-like macro that converts temperatures expressed in degrees Fahrenheit to degrees Centigrade. Use the expression `C = ( F - 32 ) * ( 5 / 9 )` to convert from Fahrenheit to Centigrade, or `F = ( 9 / 5 ) * C + 32` to convert from Centigrade to Fahrenheit, where `F` is degrees Fahrenheit and `C` is degrees Centigrade.

Summary

This chapter discussed the generation of executable modules, program execution flow, data types and how they are used, C expressions and statements, C operators, and the use of macros. You learned the following important points:

■ *A source file is the file you create when you write a C program.* An object file is created when the source file is compiled. Although the object file is a machine-language file, it is not an executable file. A load module, or executable file, is created when the object module is processed by the linker. The linker links the object module to other machine-code instructions. The machine code linked to the object module performs the setup necessary to make the object module executable.

■ *Your program executes one line of code after another until it encounters a statement that changes execution flow.*

■ *An `if` statement evaluates an expression and can execute one or two different sets of instructions, depending on the evaluation of the expression.*

■ *You use a `switch` statement when the evaluation of an expression has several possible results.*

■ *The `do-while` loop is a postchecked loop.* It executes the body of the loop and checks the controlling condition at the end of the loop.

■ *The `while` loop is a prechecked loop.* It checks the controlling condition before beginning to process the body of the loop.

■ *The `for` loop executes a loop a certain number of times.* The controlling structure of a `for` loop has three parts:

> A beginning condition
>
> A conditional expression that determines when the loop will terminate
>
> An expression that can change a controlling value on each pass of the loop

■ *Three basic data types are available in the C language.* The `char` data type represents characters. The `int` data type represents integer, or whole numbers. The `float` data type represents real or floating-point numbers.

■ *You can declare a data object as either global or local.* A global variable is always accessible anywhere in the source file. A local variable is accessible only in the function in which it is declared. A local variable can be used, therefore, only when the function in which it was created is active.

■ *An expression represents a value.* The expression can result in a value or can refer to a data object or a function. Furthermore, the expression can contain several operators and operands.

■ *A statement is composed of expressions, but does not represent a value.* A statement is executed only for its effect.

■ *The C language contains a rich set of operators.* The secret to mastering the operators is to learn operator precedence—the set of rules governing the order in which operators are executed.

■ *A type conversion occurs when a data object is converted from one data type to another data type.* The compiler automatically performs an implicit type conversion. An explicit type conversion occurs when you perform a typecast.

■ *C has two types of macros: object-like macros and function-like macros.* An object-like macro contains an identifier and a replacement-list. When encountering an identifier in your source file, the preprocessor replaces the identifier with the replacement-list. A function-like macro contains an identifier, an identifier-list, and a replacement-list. The identifier is the macro name that is replaced in your source file and the identifier-list is a list of arguments used in the replacement-list. The replacement-list is the text that is substituted for the identifier. A function-like macro works much like a regular function.

Using C Functions

I n the first two chapters, you learned how to lay the foundation of a C
program. This chapter shows you how to build the walls that support the
structure of your program: You learn how to use C functions.

Functions are an important part of the C language because they bring together
all the components necessary to complete a task. A *function* is an organized
package of data and instructions that performs a specific job. Functions are
useful because they hide the complexity associated with performing tasks.
Consider, for example, printf(). It's an easy-to-use function that generates
formatted output. Using printf() saves you the tedious work often associated
with generating formatted output.

In this chapter, you learn what functions are and how to use them. More
important, you learn how to design and write your own functions. The chapter
shows you how to set up a function, pass data to the function, and get answers
back from the function.

Understanding the *main()* Function and Library Functions

Every C program has at least one function. A program that does much of
anything contains several functions. In this section, you learn how to use the
function every program *must* have: the main() function. You also become
familiar with the extensive set of library functions supplied with Microsoft C/
C++, and you see ways to use them in your programs.

In C, a function is simply a group of statements. In a well-written program, each group of statements performs a specific task. Ideally, all the statements in a function work together to accomplish a single objective. A good function is easy to design, understand, and maintain.

The C language is built around the modularity of functions. Almost any programming task that requires more than a few lines of code will likely be written as a function. Dividing your program into modular functions enables you to build complex programs quickly and easily.

The functions used in a C program can be broken into three groups: the main() function, the library functions, and the user-defined functions. The main() function is a special function required in *every* C program. You create the contents of the main() function. The library functions are included in the Microsoft C/C++ package. Generally, they handle basic programming tasks and the low-level control of your computer hardware. The user-defined functions are ones you create. They are as varied as the programming projects you tackle. This section covers the main() function and the library functions. User-defined functions are discussed in the section "Writing Your Own Functions" later in this chapter.

Writing the *main()* Function

The purpose of the main() function is to serve as an entry point for your program. As you saw in Chapter 2, the linker adds a special segment of code to your program when it is converted to an executable file. The added code performs the setup necessary for the program to be loaded and executed. When the setup code has completed its tasks, the main() function is automatically called. Because main() is automatically executed whenever your program is run, main() has to be included in your program. Although the rules of the C language require that you have a main() function, they do not require any special code to be included in main(). In fact, main() can include as much or as little code as you want. Listing 3.1 shows a C program with a very short main() function.

Listing 3.1. blank.c. A program with a short main() function.

```
1   /* BLANK.C   A program that doesn't do a thing! */
2   main()
3   {
4   }
```

The program in Listing 3.1 has a main() function, as the rules require, but main() includes nothing else. The program is perfectly legal even though it doesn't do anything!

The main() functions in most programs are much larger than main() in Listing 3.1. The size of your program determines how much code should be included in main(). In a short program, you may want to put the code for the entire program in the main() function. In a large program, however, placing all the code in the main() function would be confusing. In many large programs, the only purpose of the main() function is to call the user-defined functions as they are needed.

Every C function—including main(), library functions, and user-defined functions—has the same basic structure. Figure 3.1 shows the structure of a typical function.

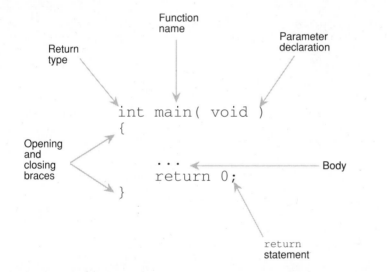

Function name

Parameter declaration

Return type

```
int main( void )
{

    ...
    return 0;
}
```

Opening and closing braces

Body

return statement

Figure 3.1.

The structure of a C function.

For every function you write, you should specify a return type. The return type indicates the *data type* of the value returned by the function. The compiler uses the return type information to verify that the value returned from a function is used correctly.

You use the function name to refer to the function. This name is the identifier in a function call.

The parameter declaration list declares variables that accept values passed to the function. The variables declared in this list are used to store values passed to the function when it is called. Any other variables used by the function are declared inside the body of the function.

The opening and closing braces define the body of the function. In other words, the braces indicate where the function begins and ends.

The body of the function is a group of C statements. In a well-written function, all the statements in the function body work toward accomplishing a single task. The body of the function can contain variable declarations, regular C statements, and even other function calls.

A special statement contained in the body of a function is the return statement. This statement has a dual purpose. First, when the return statement is encountered, it indicates that the function has completed its processing. Second, when a function calculates a value, the return statement returns the value calculated by the function. The value passed back by the return statement should be compatible with the return type of the function.

The following code fragment shows the typical use of a return statement:

```
float speed( float size, float rpm )
{
   /* Calculate the speed of a tooth on a saw blade
      rotating at a given speed. The calculated speed
      is expressed in units per second */

   float tooth_speed;

   tooth_speed = ( ( size * 3.1416 ) * ( rpm / 60.0 ) );
   return( tooth_speed );
}
```

The return statement returns the value of the variable tooth_speed. Notice that the data type of the function matches the data type of the variable tooth_speed. When the function is completed, program execution resumes at the point where the function was called. The function call is replaced by the value passed back by the return statement.

Many functions are called for the effects they produce. A function executed for a certain effect may not return a value. If a function does not have a return statement, function execution terminates at the closing brace. When a function without a return statement is compiled, the compiler generates a warning message. The compiler does not generate an error that halts compilation, but simply warns you that the function has no return statement.

A function that doesn't return a value can be declared with a void type. This type tells the compiler that a return value is not expected. Such a function does not have to contain a return statement. If a function declared with a `void` type does have a `return` statement, it has this form:

```
return;
```

Using Library Functions

The Microsoft C/C++ function libraries boost your productivity by providing hundreds of ready-to-use functions. These functions are designed to handle basic programming chores and to provide a convenient interface to the computer's facilities. The library functions relieve you of the burden of creating functions that handle low-level programming and interface tasks.

The graphics library, for example, illustrates the convenience of the function libraries. Microsoft C/C++ has an extensive library of graphics functions that do the tedious work of controlling your video hardware, and they create most of the images you need. When you use these functions, you can concentrate on your programming project and not worry about basic video programming.

Knowing What Library Functions Are Available

As noted before, there are hundreds of functions in the Microsoft C/C++ libraries. Here are the major groups of functions and their general purposes:

- *Standard functions.* The standard functions are a group of basic C programming utilities.

- *I/O functions.* The I/O functions handle the tasks of moving data in and out of your program. Microsoft C/C++ has two different types of I/O functions. One type of function uses C streams to handle data. The other type of function uses the DOS I/O utilities to handle data.

- *Classification functions.* Known as the `is...()` family of functions, these functions classify characters. Characters can be classified into various categories, such as uppercase, lowercase, and hexadecimal.

- *Conversion functions.* The conversion functions convert data from one format to another.

- *Directory-control functions.* These functions enable you to work with DOS directories and paths.

- *Diagnostic functions.* With the diagnostic functions, you can troubleshoot bugs in your program.

- *Graphics functions.* The graphics functions control the video hardware in your computer and create many basic graphic images.

■ *Interface functions.* With the interface functions, you can directly use the DOS and BIOS functions.

■ *Manipulation functions.* The manipulation functions work with strings and blocks of memory.

■ *Math functions.* These functions handle almost any calculation you need to perform.

■ *Memory functions.* The memory functions handle dynamic memory allocation for the small and large data memory models.

■ *Miscellaneous functions.* These functions handle a variety of programming tasks.

■ *Process-control functions.* These functions handle the creation and termination of processes that originate inside other processes.

■ *Standard functions.* These are the general-purpose functions from the stdlib.h header file.

■ *Text-window functions.* The text-window functions are used to send text information to the video display.

■ *Time and date functions.* These functions handle time and date information.

■ *Variable argument list functions.* These functions process the variable-length arguments passed to a function.

You can find specific information about the library functions in two ways. The first way is to use the Microsoft C/C++ online help facility. This facility has a complete list of the library functions. The listing for each function contains a brief description of the function, information about the function declaration, example code, and cross-references to related functions. The second way to find out more about a function is to use the *Microsoft C/C++ Run-Time Library Reference,* which contains all the information you need to use every library function.

Including Library Functions in Your Program

Now that you know what kinds of library functions are available, you need to learn how to use them in your program. Using the library functions is simple. When you find a function you want to use, you include the appropriate header file in your source code and make sure that you pass any needed arguments to the function.

When you use a library function in your program, you must include the header file associated with that function. A library function's header file contains the declarations of variables, macros, and functions necessary to use the function in your program. The statement that includes a header file looks like the following:

```
#include <stdio.h>
```

`#include` is a preprocessor directive that tells the compiler to merge the specified file into your source file during compilation. The included file is not permanently copied into your source file but is referenced during the compilation of the source file. The angle brackets surrounding the filename tell the compiler to look in the standard library directories for the file of that name. During compilation, the file is included with your source file. In this example, the included file is the stdio.h header file.

Listing 3.2 shows how you can use some of the library functions in a program.

Listing 3.2. txt_demo.c. A program that uses text-window functions.

```
1   /* TXT_DEMO   This program uses the text window functions
2                 to demonstrate the use of the library
3                 functions. */
4
5   #include <stdio.h>
6   #include <stdlib.h>
7   #include <conio.h>
8   #include <graph.h>
9
10  main()
11  {
12    int i, j;
13    char buffer[80];
14
15    _clearscreen( _GCLEARSCREEN );
16    _setvideomode ( _TEXTC80 );
17
18    while( !kbhit() ) {
19      for( i = 0; i <=15; i++ ) {
20        _settextcolor( i );
21        for( j = 48; j <= 90; j++) {
22          sprintf( buffer, "%c", j );
23          _outtext( buffer );
24        }
25      }
26    }
27  }
```

The program in Listing 3.2 uses the text-window functions to generate a multicolor, rolling ASCII display. The program is composed of three loops. The outermost loop waits for you to press a key to terminate the test. The next loop (the i loop) cycles through the 16 text-mode foreground colors. The innermost loop prints the ASCII characters from *0* (zero) to *Z*.

The main feature of this program is not its loop structures, however, but its library functions. In line 15, the _clearscreen() function clears the screen. _clearscreen() is defined in graph.h and is part of the graphics library. Its single parameter specifies that the region to clear is equal to the entire screen. _setvideomode(_TEXTC80) puts the display into color text mode (this works for all displays except the Monochrome display type). The use of _setvideomode() is described in Chapter 8, "Using the Microsoft C/C++ Video Functions."

Inside the loops, the _settextcolor() function is called. Notice that the argument passed to _settextcolor() is the loop-index variable i. The loop index is used with _settextcolor() so that all 16 text-mode colors can be displayed. Also inside the loops is the sprintf() function. sprintf() has a format string and a variable argument list. The arguments passed to sprintf() cause the function to format the ASCII value of variable j for printing, and to store the result in the array buffer. Finally, _outtext() copies the contents of buffer to the display. As you will learn in Chapter 8, the text video functions do not work in conjunction with printf(), putch(), and so on. To set text color or position on the screen you must use the _outtext() function for output. Chapter 8 describes all of this.

To use these special text-window functions, you must include the correct header file in your source file. You can see in line 8 that the graph.h header was included in the source file. The text video functions are defined in graph.h and contained in the graphics library, graph.lib. If you did not include graph.h, the program would not compile correctly. To compile and link this program using the command-line compiler, you must type

```
cl txt_demo.c graphics.lib
```

You must specify the special library file graphics.lib so that the linker knows where to find the text functions.

Writing Your Own Functions

The Microsoft C/C++ libraries provide a wide range of useful, specialized utility functions. Still, these functions cannot do everything. By their nature, the library functions perform specialized tasks. For general programming, you need to create your own functions. This section shows you how to create your own user-defined functions and transfer data to those functions.

Writing Prototypes for Your Functions

Function prototypes, or function declarations, tell the compiler about the functions you write. A function prototype contains the name of the function, the number and type of arguments passed to the function, and the type of the value returned by the function. The function prototype differs from a function definition in that the prototype does not contain any information about the body of the function—only information about the data passed to and from the function. A typical function prototype looks like this:

```
int my_sum( int a, int b, int c );
```

This function prototype declares the function my_sum(), which requires three integer arguments when it is called. After my_sum() has performed its calculations, it returns an integer value as an answer.

Why do you need to include function prototypes in your program? The answer is that the compiler needs to know what type of data your functions require to verify that they are used correctly.

Figure 3.2 shows how the user-defined function declarations and function definitions are arranged in a typical C program. The accepted programming practice is to place function declarations at the top of the program, along with global declarations. Function definitions appear at the bottom of the program.

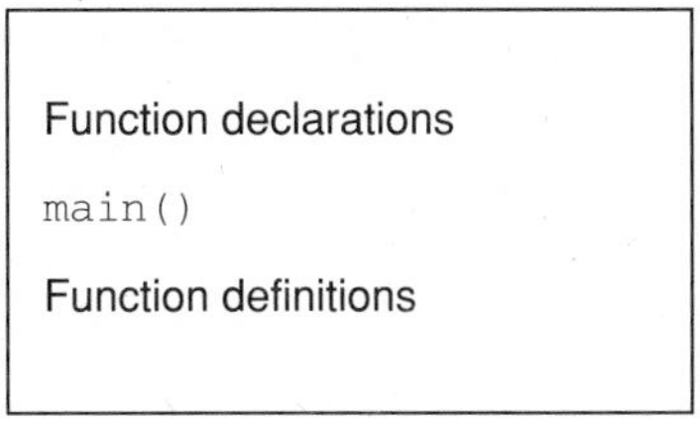

```
Function declarations

main()

Function definitions
```

Figure 3.2.

Typical placement of user-defined function declarations and function definitions.

Placing the function declaration at the top of the program enables the compiler to learn what type of information the function requires before it is called. If a function call occurs before a function declaration, the compiler is not able to determine whether the function call is made correctly. There is a way to get around the need for function declarations. You can avoid writing a function declaration if you define the function at the beginning of the program. The function definition contains not only the information about the data passed to and from the function, but also the complete body of the function. With the function definition at the top of the program, the compiler knows what kind of data the function uses and what the body of the function does.

Defining a function at the beginning of a program has two drawbacks, however. The first drawback is that the program is harder to read. You may have difficulty following the flow of a program when the first function you see is one of the most detailed functions in the program. A program with the most general functions at the beginning is much easier to understand than a program with the most specific functions listed first. The second drawback is that you must be sure to define the most detailed functions first. Defining a function that calls an undefined function will generate an error. Using function prototypes is easier than trying to determine which function you must declare first.

Figure 3.3 shows the steps in designing and writing a user-defined function.

Figure 3.3.

The function-creation process.

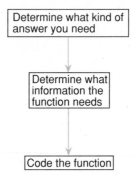

The first step in the function-creation process is to decide what kind of answer you need. Do you need a function that calculates an integer value, returns a character, or generates an answer of some other type? When you decide what type of answer the function should generate, you know what type of data the function will return. The type of answer that the function returns is the type of the function.

The second step is to determine what data the function requires. You need to decide which values the function needs to calculate an answer, and you need to know the data type of the values passed to the function. The argument list in the function declaration contains the information about the type of data passed to the function.

The last step is writing the function. In this step, you create the function definition. It contains the body of the function—the group of C statements that form the function. The information you gathered in the first two steps of the function-creation process is used in the function prototype (function declaration). Here is the exact format of the function prototype:

```
return_type function_name( argument-type argument-name ... );
```

The *return_type* specifies the type of the answer that the function returns. The type can be an int, a double, or any of the other data types. The *function_name* is simply the name you use to call the function. This name can contain up to 32 characters, including letters, numbers, and the underscore character. The only restriction on the function name is that it must begin with a letter or an underscore. The variables in the argument list are those to which data passes when the function is called. Finally, the *argument-type* specifies the data type of an element in the argument list.

 NOTE Avoid function names that start with an underscore, because Microsoft C/C++ uses identifiers that begin with the underscore character for many of its library functions.

Now look at the following code fragment:

```
double cube( double x );
```

The function `cube()` has a return type specified as a `double`. This means that the value calculated by `cube()` can be assigned to any variable declared as type `double`. The argument list for `cube()` contains a variable of type `double`. Therefore, any function calls to `cube()` should pass to it a value that is a `double` floating-point number.

As noted earlier, you can use a special data type, `void`, in function declarations. Declaring a function with a `void` return type signals that the function does not return any kind of value. Look at this example:

```
void show_logo( void );
```

The function declaration for `show_logo()` indicates that it neither requires an argument nor returns a value.

If you write a function prototype and do not include a return type, the compiler assumes that the function returns a value of the default, or integer, type. Note the following code fragment:

```
sum( int a, int b );
```

The compiler assumes that the value returned by the function `sum()` is an integer.

Passing Arguments to Your Functions

In the preceding section, you learned how to create prototypes for your functions. In those function prototypes, you declared variables used to store values that are passed to the functions. In this section, you learn how to pass information to your functions and how to use the variables declared in function prototypes.

The most important concept to remember when you use C functions is that arguments are passed to functions *by value,* not *by reference.* Passing arguments by value means that when you call a function, the called function works with *copies* of the arguments in the function call.

Some programming languages (including C++, but not C) enable you to pass arguments by reference. When an argument is passed by reference, the function receives the memory address of the argument instead of the argument's value. This feature enables the function to access the argument directly, even to change the original argument to a new value. Although C only passes function parameters by value, the use of pointers enables you to pass arguments by reference. This will be explained in this section. For more information about pointers, see Chapter 4, "Using Pointers and Derived Types."

Listing 3.3 shows how arguments are passed by value.

Listing 3.3. loopcnt.c. A program that passes arguments by value.

```
1   /* LOOPCNT.C  This program demonstrates how arguments are
2                 passed by value. */
3
4   #include <stdio.h>
5   #include <stdlib.h>
6
7   void loop_count( int i );
8
9   main()
10  {
11    int i = 2;
12
13    loop_count( i );
14    printf( "In main, i = %d.\n", i );
15  }
16
17  void loop_count( int i )
18  {
19    for( ; i < 10; i++ )
20      printf( "In loop_count, i = %d.\n", i );
21  }
```

In Listing 3.3, a function is passed a value that is modified inside the body of the function. Although the value of the argument is changed in the function's body, the value of the variable in the function call is not changed. The function modifies a *copy* of the variable used in the function call. In line 11, the integer variable i is declared and assigned a value of 2. The loop_count() function is called with the variable i. Immediately after the function call, the value of the variable i is printed. The value of i still equals 2.

The variable i in main() has a value of 2 both before and after the call to loop_count(). This variable has the same value before and after the function call, although loop_count() modifies another i variable in the body of the loop. Notice the for statement in line 19. In the for loop, the first statement—the one that specifies an initial condition for the loop—is blank. This statement is left blank because the variable used to control the loop—the variable i—has already been assigned a value. The value of i in loop_count() is equal to the value of i in main(). Although loop_count() modifies the value of i, the value of i in main() remains the same. Figure 3.4 shows how arguments are passed by value and by reference.

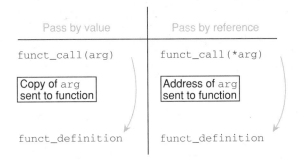

Figure 3.4.

Passing arguments by value and by reference.

From Listing 3.3, you can see that passing arguments by value protects the original values of the variables. Most of the time, you will want to leave the original values of the variables unchanged. Passing arguments by value helps prevent program errors caused by unrecognized changes in an argument's original value. Although this method of passing arguments is usually better, you may at times need to change the original value of an argument. In those cases, you can pass arguments by reference.

In C, the way to pass arguments by reference is to pass a pointer to the argument. A pointer contains the memory address of the argument. Because the called function has the address of the original argument, the function can change the value of that argument. Listing 3.4 shows the preceding program rewritten to use pointers.

Listing 3.4. loopref.c. A program that shows how to pass arguments by reference.

```
1   /* LOOPCNT.C  This program demonstrates how arguments are
2                 passed by value. */
3
4   #include <stdio.h>
5   #include <stdlib.h>
6
```

Listing 3.4. Continued.

```
7   void loop_count( int *i );
8
9   main()
10  {
11    int i = 2;
12
13    loop_count( &i );
14    printf( "In main, i = %d.\n", i );
15  }
16
17  void loop_count( int *i )
18  {
19    for( ; *i < 10; (*i)++ )
20      printf( "In loop_count, i = %d.\n", *i );
21  }
```

In Listing 3.4, the value of the variable used in the function call changes when the function is executed. Notice that the function prototype in line 7 is different. In Listing 3.3, the function prototype declares an integer. In Listing 3.4, the function prototype declares a *pointer* to an integer. The symbol * in the function declaration indicates that the variable being declared is a pointer to an integer.

Because the function is declared with a pointer as an argument, the argument passed to loop_count() must be an address. In line 13, you can see how the address of main()'s i variable is passed to loop_count(). The symbol & in the function call indicates that the address of the specified variable is being passed to loop_count().

The version of loop_count() in Listing 3.4 modifies the value of the variable in main(). In main(), the address of the variable i is passed to loop_count() during the function call. Because loop_count() is passed an address, loop_count() modifies the information stored at that address.

In loop_count(), the value stored in the variable i is a pointer. In other words, the value stored in i is an address. If you looked at the value stored in the variable i in loop_count(), you would find the address of the variable i in main(). The for statement in loop_count() works with an integer value, however, not an address. The for statement works correctly because the *indirection operator* is used. This operator is specified by the symbol * and causes the value stored at the address indicated by the pointer to be used.

Notice the last part of the for statement in line 19. The indirection operator and the pointer variable are enclosed by parentheses. The parentheses force the indirection operator to execute before the increment operator. Without the parentheses, the increment operator tries to increment the *pointer* value instead of the value to which the pointer points. Incrementing the pointer value instead of the data value can produce strange results.

Type promotions can occur when the argument passed to a function has a less precise type than the function parameters specify. Note the following example:

```
char c;
int d;
...
d = toupper( c );
```

The variable c is declared as type char. The toupper() function, however, requires an int argument. The type of c in the function call is promoted just as it would be if c were assigned to an integer variable.

Returning Values from Functions

C functions are designed so that a value is usually returned when a function completes its processing. Like any other value in a C program, the value returned by a function has a data type. It can be any of the valid C data types, such as int, char, or double.

Because functions return values, you can use a function wherever a value is required. A function can return a value for use, for example, as part of a calculation, in an assignment, or even in a function call.

This section shows you how to specify a function's return type when you write the function prototype. You also learn how a function's data type can change the value of the data returned by the function. Finally, you see how functions can be used like data objects.

Defining and Using Function Types

In the C language, every function has a data type. The compiler uses the information about a function's data type to verify that the values returned by the function are used in a legal manner. Usually, the compiler gets its information about the type of a function's return value from the function prototype. Examine this function prototype:

```
int my_calc( int a, int b );
```

The keyword int at the beginning of the function prototype specifies the return type of the function. Here int indicates that the function returns an integer value.

In many cases, a function returns a value that is one of the fundamental types, such as char or int. However, a function is not limited to returning values of only the basic types; a function can return any type of value you can legally declare in your program. For example, when you are working with arrays, it is more efficient for your function to return a pointer to an array. You can even return data objects that have data types you create, such as structures.

Listing 3.5 shows a function that works with strings. Because strings are arrays of characters, the function has a return type that is a pointer to a character array.

Listing 3.5. name_cmp.c. A program containing a function that returns a pointer.

```
1   /* NAME_CMP.C  This program shows a function that returns
2       a pointer to a string. */
3
4   #include <stdio.h>
5   #include <stdlib.h>
6   #include <graph.h>
7
8   char *long_name( char *first, char *second );
9
10  main()
11  {
12    char *first = "Joe";
13    char *second = "John";
14
15    _clearscreen( _GCLEARSCREEN );
16    printf( "The longest name is %s\n",
17            long_name( first, second ) );
18
19    return 0;
20  }
21
22  char *long_name( char *first, char *second )
23  {
24    if( strlen( first ) >= strlen( second ) )
25      return first;
26    else
27      return second;
28  }
```

The program in Listing 3.5 uses a function that returns a pointer to a string. The function long_name() compares two strings passed to it. After comparing the strings, long_name() returns a pointer to the longer of the two strings.

In line 8 of Listing 3.5, the long_name() function is declared to have a return value that is a pointer to a character array. The compiler knows that long_name() returns a pointer to a string because of the char * type declaration for the function. Because the long_name() function returns a pointer to a string, you can use long_name() anywhere you can use a string. The pointer returned by long_name() is used in the printf() statement in lines 16 and 17. In that statement, the value returned by long_name() points to the string that printf() prints.

Notice in Listing 3.5 that both the function declaration and the function definition (lines 8 and 22) specify the same return type for the function. If they do not specify the same return type, the compiler generates an error message.

As noted earlier, a function that does not return a value has a void type. The long_name() function in Listing 3.5 could be rewritten so that it has a void type. The function declaration and function definition for long_name() would then look like this:

```
void long_name( char *first, char *second )
...
void long_name( char *first, char *second )
{
  if( strlen( first ) >= strlen( second ) )
    printf( "The longest name is %s.\n", first );
  else
    printf( "The longest name is %s.\n", second );
}
```

Both the function declaration and the function definition begin with the keyword void, indicating that the function does not return a value. Because a void function does not return a value, the function does not need to contain a return statement. A function of any other data type should contain a return statement, however, even if the function does not generate a useful value.

In the program examples earlier in this book, the main() functions do not contain return statements. When compiled, each program would generate a warning message. As noted before, this warning does not cause compilation to abort, nor does the warning cause any error in the program. The warning just lets you know that the compiler was expecting a return statement.

The main() function in Listing 3.5 has a return statement and does not, therefore, generate a warning when the program is compiled. By default, the value returned in Listing 3.5 is an integer. If you do not specify the type of a function, the compiler automatically assumes that the function returns an integer.

Even if a function returns a value, you may not want to use that value. When you call a function, you don't have to use the value returned by the function. In that case, the value is simply ignored.

Notice that the long_name() function in Listing 3.5 has two return statements. Multiple return statements, which are legal, do not cause problems because the first return that is encountered ends processing in the function. You can use as many return statements as you like. The first return, however, causes program execution to resume immediately following the call to the current function.

A type cast can occur during the execution of a return statement. For example, if a function is declared to have a return type of double and the return statement returns integers, the integers are promoted to doubles. The following code fragment shows how to cast a function's return value:

```
double sum_it( int a, int b )
{
    return a + b;
}
```

In this example, the function sum_it() is declared to return a double floating-point value. In the function, however, the return statement returns an integer value. Declaring the function's return value as a double causes the value passed back by the return statement to be type cast from an integer to a double. An implicit type cast of a function's return value can cause errors that are difficult to debug. Be careful when you use implicit type casts.

Using Functions Like Objects

When a function call is encountered in a C statement, the called function is executed and a value from the function is passed back. The program considers the value passed back from the function to be a regular data object that it can use like a variable or constant.

If your program has a statement that uses an integer value, the program won't care whether that integer value is stored in an integer variable or comes from a function with an integer return type. The program treats a function call just like any data object.

The following example shows how a function can be used as a data object:

```
int a, b, c;
int answer;
...
a = 10;
b = 2;
c = 3;
answer = a / ( sum_it( b + c );
```

The sum_it() function is used in place of a regular data object. The variable a is divided by an integer value. This value is not a variable or a constant, but the value returned by a function.

Generally, whenever you need a data object, you instead can use a function that returns a value of the correct type. When the function completes its processing, the value returned by the function occupies the same spot in the C statement that the call to the function occupied.

Understanding Storage Classes

In C, a variable has two main attributes. The first attribute is the variable's type. You have already learned that the type of a variable determines what kind of object the variable is and how much space it uses. Some of the most common data types are integer, character, and floating-point. The second attribute is the variable's storage class, which determines when and where a variable can be used.

The term *storage class* covers several specific aspects of variable availability and longevity. In this section, you become familiar with storage classes. You learn what scope, duration, and linkage are and how they affect your data. In addition, you learn how to use the different storage classes to your advantage when you create your own functions.

Although *scope, duration,* and *linkage* are interdependent, each describes a different characteristic. Scope determines where a variable can be used in a source file, and duration determines when a variable can be used in a source file. Linkage is important when you have multiple source files to be compiled into one program. Linkage determines whether the same name in different source files refers to the same data object.

Determining a Variable's Scope

Scope indicates where in a program you can use a variable. The C language has four different types of scope:

■ *File scope.* If a variable has file scope, you can use the variable anywhere in the source file. File scope is equivalent to the global scope you have already seen. Any function in a source file can use a variable that has file scope. You can create a variable that has file scope by declaring the variable outside any function. The declarations for variables with file scope generally appear before the main() function.

■ *Function scope.* If a variable has function scope, you can use the variable only in the function in which you declared the variable. Therefore, only one function in a program has access to a variable declared with function scope. A variable with function scope is declared at the top of a function definition.

■ *Block scope.* Block scope, also known as local scope, is slightly different from function scope. A variable declared with block scope can be used only in the block in which the variable was declared. Block scope covers only a block of code, but it doesn't have to be an entire function. The following code fragment shows how you can use block scope:

```
main()
{
  int i = 10;
  int cnt;

  for( cnt = 0; cnt <=20; cnt++ ) {
    int j = 1;
    printf( "In loop, j = %d.\n", j );
  }

  printf( "Out of loop, i = %d.\n", i );
}
```

Notice the variables i and j. The variable i is declared with function scope and can be used anywhere in the program. The variable j is declared with block scope and can be used only in the for loop in which j is declared. If you try to access j outside the for loop, an error is generated.

■ *Function prototype scope.* Function prototype scope is a scope you use all the time but never notice. This scope applies to the variables in a function declaration's parameter list. A variable with function prototype scope is accessible only until the end of the function prototype. Thus, variables in a function declaration's parameter list can be used only in that parameter list.

Scope and visibility are similar concepts. Usually, they mean the same thing. In some instances, however, a variable is in scope but is not visible. Note the following variation of the preceding code fragment, showing how scope and visibility can differ:

```
main()
{
  int i = 10;
  int cnt;
```

```
for( cnt = 0; cnt <=20; cnt++ ) {
   int i = 1;
   printf( "In loop, i = %d.\n", i );
}

   printf( "Out of loop, i = %d.\n", i );
}
```

This code fragment declares two distinct i variables. The first i variable has function scope. The second i variable—the i in the for loop—has block scope. When execution is in the for loop, the i declared at the top of the function is in scope, but the variable is not visible. Only the i variable declared in the for loop is in scope and visible during the execution of the loop. Therefore, although a variable is in scope, the variable may not be visible.

Determining a Variable's Duration

Duration refers to the time a variable is available. A variable's duration determines when memory is allocated for the variable.

In a large program, allocating memory for all the variables for the entire length of the program would be wasteful. C gets around this space problem by allocating memory for a variable only when the variable is used. When a function is called, memory is allocated for the variables in the function. When the function ends, the memory allocated for the function's variables is freed. Note that there are two kinds of duration:

■ *auto duration.* This is the default duration of variables declared in a function. When a function is called, memory is allocated for the auto variables. When the function ends, the memory allocated for the auto variables is freed. auto variables make the most efficient use of memory.

■ *static duration.* This is the default duration of variables with file scope. A static variable is always available because the memory allocated for it is not freed until the program ends. You can even declare the variables in your function to have static duration. You just precede the variable declaration with the static keyword. Look at the following example:

```
void my_func( void )
{
   static int i;
   ...
}
```

The variable i in my_func() has static duration. Even after my_func() ends, the variable i still has a section of memory allocated. Thus, the variable i retains its value from one function call to the next. i has static duration but still has function scope. Having function scope means that i can be accessed only from my_func(); no other function has access to i. The variable i is stored in memory between function calls, but i can be accessed only from my_func() when that function is called.

Determining a Variable's Linkage

The linkage of a variable indicates whether it can be accessed from another source file. Three different types of linkage are available:

- *Internal linkage.* A variable with internal linkage is visible to all parts of a single source file. Because the variable is visible to the entire file, the variable also has file scope. Variables with internal linkage are declared outside any functions in the source file.

- *External linkage.* Like a variable with internal linkage, one with external linkage is visible to all parts of a source file. However, a variable with external linkage is visible also in other source files; such a variable can be accessed in more than one source file. An external variable has file scope. Because of this scope, the variable must be declared outside any functions. To access a variable in another file, you must redeclare the variable and precede the declaration with the extern keyword.

- *No linkage.* If a variable has no linkage, it is visible only in the block in which the variable was declared. It cannot be accessed by more than one function.

A variable declared outside any functions has both internal and external linkage by default. Look at the following code fragment:

```
#include <stdio.h>
#include <stdlib.h>

int global_int;

main()
{
...
```

The variable global_int can be used anywhere in the source file because the variable is declared with file scope. global_int can be used in other source files also, if it is declared correctly. For another source file to have access to global_int, that source file must include the following declaration:

```
extern int global_int;
```

If you changed the preceding code fragment to

```
#include <stdio.h>
#include <stdlib.h>

static int global_int;

main()
{
...
```

the variable global_int would have only internal linkage. The static keyword modifies the declaration so that the variable can be used in just one source file.

Using Advanced Program Control Logic

In Chapter 2, "Understanding the Foundations of C," you learned how to use C loops to change the flow of execution in your program. You learned how to use the do-while, while, and for loop-control structures. This section shows you some new tools for more precise control of these structures. After you learn better control of your loops, you learn some new ways to change the flow of execution in a program. Finally, you learn a new way to end program execution and a way to start another program from inside your program.

Writing Loop-Control Statements

You have already seen how useful loop-control structures are. They provide a way for you to execute a group of instructions as many times as you want. With loop structures, your program can follow a circular execution path instead of a linear execution path.

All loops have the same basic parts. Each loop contains a section of code that performs setup functions, a section that does the main work of the loop, a section that updates a limiting condition, and a section that checks a limiting condition. Figure 3.5 shows each step in the execution of a loop.

Figure 3.5.

A basic loop structure.

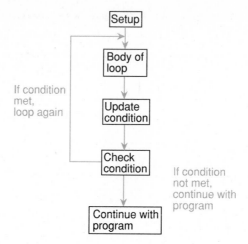

Each of the three C loops—do-while, while, and for—contains the parts of the loop structure shown in Figure 3.5. The parts of the loop, however, may be in different order.

The do-while, while, and for loops add a great deal of versatility to a program. These loops can handle almost any repetitive task you have. If the standard loop structure cannot handle a particular task, C provides additional statements you can use: goto, break, and continue. With these statements, you can change the flow of control inside your loop structures.

Using *goto*

The goto statement causes an unconditional transfer of control. This statement takes the following form:

goto *label*

The *label* in the goto statement specifies the location where program execution continues. The following code fragment shows how you can use a goto statement:

```
for( i = 0; i < 10; i++ ) {
  if( i = 5 ) goto label1;
  printf( "In the for loop, i = %d.\n", i );
  label1: ;
}
```

Although this code fragment does not do much, it clearly shows the use of goto. On the first line, in the body of the for statement, an if statement checks the variable i. If i is equal to 5, the goto statement is executed and the program resumes execution at the label1 statement.

In a well-designed program, you seldom need a goto statement. Note, however, that you can use goto anywhere in a program, not just in loop-control structures.

Using *break*

You use the break statement in loop structures and in switch statements. In switch statements, break causes program execution to jump to the end of the switch statement. In loop structures, break causes program execution to break out of the loop. You saw in Chapter 2, "Understanding the Foundations of C," how to use break with switch. The next code fragment shows how to use break in a loop structure:

```c
int no_of_cust, i, status;
...
for( i = 1; i <= no_of_cust; i++ ) {
  status = process_cust( no_of_cust );
  if( status == -1 ) break;
}
if( status == -1 )
  printf( "An error occurred during customer processing." );
```

In this code fragment, the for loop executes as many times as there are customers. In the body of the loop, the customer-processing function process_cust() is called. It returns a –1 if an error occurs during process_cust(). If an error occurs, the for loop does not need to continue. The if statement checks the value returned by process_cust(). If the value returned by that function indicates that an error occurred, the break statement causes program flow to break out of the for loop.

Using *continue*

The continue statement causes program execution to resume at the top of the loop. Any statements following the continue statement are skipped. The next code fragment shows how you can use continue to print the multiples of 5 from 1 to 100:

```c
int i;
...
for( i = 1; i <= 100, i++ ) {
  if( i % 5 != 0 ) continue
  printf( "%d is a multiple of 5!\n", i );
}
```

The for loop is used to count from 1 to 100. In the body of the loop, the if statement determines whether the variable i is a multiple of 5. If i is not a multiple of 5, the continue statement is executed. The continue statement causes the printf() statement to be skipped and execution to resume at the top of the loop.

The do-while, while, and for loops can handle most repetitive tasks. When you combine the goto, break, and continue statements with these loop structures, you have tools that are even more versatile.

Changing the Flow of Program Execution

When you think of changing the flow of execution in a program, you usually think of using the iteration statements or the conditional statements (if and switch). These tools, however, are not the only ones available for changing the flow of execution. You can also use a number of *functions*.

The functions that change the flow of execution in a program can be divided into two groups. The functions in the first group handle the early termination of a program. This group includes the exit() and abort() functions. The functions in the second group cause a program to be suspended while another program is executed. This group includes the spawn...() family of functions, the exec...() family of functions, and the system() function.

Using *exit()* and *abort()*

You use the exit() and abort() functions to terminate a program early. The exit() function terminates a program normally, and the abort() function terminates a program abnormally.

The exit() function causes any open buffers to be written, closes open files, and executes any specified shut-down functions. Although the exit() function terminates a program normally, exit() is not used unless a serious error is encountered. In that case, the exit() function shuts down the program in as orderly a manner as possible. This function has the following format:

```
exit( status );
```

In the exit() function call, the *status* parameter indicates whether the program is terminating normally or abnormally. If the program is to terminate normally, the *status* argument is EXIT_SUCCESS, a macro that has a value of 0. If the program is to terminate abnormally, the *status* argument is EXIT_FAILURE, a macro with a nonzero value. The *status* argument is passed to the process that called the program, letting the calling process know the condition of the program at termination.

You can use the atexit() function with the exit() function to provide a series of up to 32 functions that can be called when the program terminates. When the exit() function is called, any functions *registered* by the atexit() function are executed before the program terminates. The functions registered by atexit() are called on a last-in-first-out basis. Listing 3.6 demonstrates the exit() and atexit() functions.

Listing 3.6. term.c. A program that uses the exit() and atexit() functions to terminate a program.

```
1   /* TERM.C  Using the exit() and atexit() functions to
2               terminate a program. */
3
4   #include <stdio.h>
5   #include <stdlib.h>
6
7   void term_1( void );
8   void term_2( void );
9
10  main()
11  {
12    atexit( term_2 );
13    atexit( term_1 );
14
15    printf( "In main, processing normally.\n" );
16    printf( "Beginning termination.\n" );
17    exit( EXIT_SUCCESS );
18    printf( "This statement is never executed.\n" );
19    return( 0 );
20  }
21
22  void term_1( void )
23  {
24    printf( "Program termination eminent.\n" );
25    printf( "In function term_1.\n" );
26  }
27
28  void term_2( void )
29  {
30    printf( "Program termination proceeding.\n" );
31    printf( "In function term_2.\n" );
32  }
```

In lines 12 and 13 of Listing 3.6, the atexit() function registers two functions. The registered functions are executed when the exit() function is called. Notice the order in which the functions are registered. The last function to be executed is registered first, and the first function to be executed is registered last.

In line 17, the exit() function is called. This function halts program execution after the registered functions are executed. When the program terminates, the parameter passed to exit() is a result code returned to DOS to indicate whether your program succeeded or failed in its task. EXIT_SUCCESS is a symbol predefined in stdlib.h used to indicate that your program terminated normally. Use EXIT_FAILURE to indicate abnormal program termination.

The registered functions term_1() and term_2() are called before the program ends. In addition, the exit() function closes any open files and writes any open output buffers. This program has no files or buffers to close. Note that the statements following the exit() function are never executed.

Like exit(), the abort() function causes a program to terminate. However, abort() does not perform any cleanup before halting the program. The abort() function simply causes the program to crash. This function is most often used when a catastrophic error has occurred and the only thing you can do is to bomb out of your program. abort() is a messy but effective way to end a program.

The following code fragment shows the use of abort() in a program:

```
printf( "Catastrophic errors have occurred.\n" );
printf( "Terminating program.\n" );
abort();
```

As you can see, calling the abort() function is simple. When abort() is executed, it causes an exit code of 3 to be returned to the parent process or to DOS.

Using the *system()*, *exec...()*, and *spawn...()* Functions

The abort() and exit() functions are two useful functions Microsoft C/C++ provides for handling extraordinary circumstances. Microsoft C/C++ has a second group of functions you can use to change your program execution. The functions in this group, however, are not as severe as abort() and exit(). You use the functions in this second group to run other programs under your application. Running other programs from within your program is a handy feature of Microsoft C/C++. You have available the utility of the other program without having to rewrite that program yourself.

This section introduces the system(), exec...(), and spawn...() functions. The system() function lets you run programs or DOS commands from within your program. You use the `exec...()` and `spawn...()` functions only to execute programs. The `exec...()` and `spawn...()` functions are more versatile than the `system()` function.

The `system()` function starts COMMAND.COM and executes a normal DOS command. The function has this form:

```
system( const char *command )
```

The `const` keyword in the argument list for `system()` indicates that the function does not change the value of the parameter. When writing your own functions, you can use the `const` keyword before any function argument. Within the body of your function, you should only use or read the value of the argument and should make no attempt to change the argument's value. The compiler checks to ensure that your function does not alter the argument.

The `command` in the `system()` parameter list can be any valid DOS command or the name of an executable or batch file. In the following line of code, the `system()` function calls the DOS CHKDSK.COM program:

```
system( "CHKDSK" );
```

You use the `exec...()` and `spawn...()` families of functions to run other programs. The programs run by `exec...()` and `spawn...()` are known as *child processes*.

The difference between `exec...()` and `spawn...()` is that `spawn...()` accepts an extra argument: the `mode` argument. This argument specifies how `spawn...()` behaves when a child process is called. The three possible values for the `mode` argument are these:

■ `P_WAIT`

The `P_WAIT` argument specifies that your program will be temporarily stopped while the child process is executed.

■ `P_OVERLAY`

The `P_OVERLAY` argument specifies that the child process will overlay the memory location of the calling process. Using the `P_OVERLAY` option with `spawn...()` works the same as with `exec...()`.

■ `P_NOWAIT`

This argument is currently unavailable. If `P_NOWAIT` were available, it would let your process continue while the child process runs.

Except for `mode`, the arguments for the `spawn...()` and `exec...()` functions are the same. Both families of functions have a `path` argument and an argument list that will be passed to the child process. The `path` argument is the location and name of the child process. `spawn...()` and `exec...()` use the standard DOS procedures when searching for the child process specified in the `path` argument. Here is a typical `spawn...()` function call:

```
spawnl( P_WAIT, "my_prog", NULL );
```

The spawn...() function executes the program my_prog. spawn...() searches first for MY_PROG.COM; if it doesn't exist, spawn...() looks for MY_PROG.EXE. The calling—or parent—process is suspended while the my_prog child process is executed. In this example, no arguments are passed to my_prog.

See Appendix C to learn more about the exec...() and spawn...() functions. You can also find information about these functions in the *Microsoft C/C++ Run-Time Library Reference*.

Using Variable Argument Lists

Many of the functions you write require a fixed number of arguments. Passing arguments to one of these functions is simple because the function always uses the same number and type of arguments. All functions are not this simple, however. Consider the printf() function. Each call to printf() could have different types and numbers of arguments. The printf() function has a variable argument list.

In this section, you learn how to use variable argument lists in your functions. Variable argument lists can enhance the utility and compactness of the functions you write. The utility of your functions is enhanced because they can handle more data as well as different kinds of data. Your functions will be more compact because, with variable argument lists, you can write one function instead of several.

Designing Variable Argument Lists

Although a variable argument list is more complicated than a standard argument list, a variable argument list is still easy to use. It requires more planning than a regular argument list because a variable argument list has to determine how many and what kind of arguments are passed to the function.

To access the arguments in a variable argument list, you use a pointer that points to the arguments in the list. The first step in pulling arguments from the variable argument list is to initialize a pointer to the first argument in the list. After the argument pointer is initialized, each item in the list can be read as the argument pointer is "bumped down" the argument list. When designing a variable argument list, keep in mind two important points so that the argument pointer points correctly to the arguments in the list:

- *You have to specify how long the variable argument list will be.*

- *You have to specify what type of data will be contained in the variable argument list.*

Providing such specific information at first may seem to contradict the idea of a variable argument list. You can use one of three ways to provide this information, however, and still use a *variable* argument list.

The first and most common way to indicate how much and what kind of data you have is to use a *format string*. A format string uses a set of symbols to indicate the type and number of arguments that follow in the variable argument list. Note the use of a format string in this `printf()` function:

```
printf( "i = %d, x = %f", i, x );
```

`printf()` prints two variables of different types. This function knows what kind of information to print because of the format string

```
"i = %d, x = %f"
```

The two characters preceded by the % sign are called *conversion specification characters*. These characters let the `printf()` function know how many and what type of variables follow in the variable argument list.

The second way to keep track of the variables in a variable argument list is to include a *terminating value*. This value is not used in the function but is placed at the end of the variable argument list to signal that all data has been read. Look at this line of code:

```
sum( num_type, 2, 39, 56, 0 );
```

The value 0 (zero) is the terminating value. Because this example contains a `sum()` function, the 0 value is not needed. Therefore, when you encounter a 0 in the variable argument list, you know that you have read all the numbers you need. The 0 tells you that you can stop fetching numbers to `sum()`.

The drawback to using a terminating value is that all the numbers have to be a fixed type. If you use a terminating value, you cannot mix data types. The computer has to know what data type you want so that the computer can read the proper number of bytes from memory. (Remember that each data type uses a different number of bytes for storage.)

The third way to track the arguments in a variable argument list is to include a variable that tells the function how many data items to read. This method suffers from the same drawback as using a terminating value. All the items in the variable argument list must be the same type.

Using the va_...() Functions

In the preceding section, you learned what a variable argument list is, and you saw how to use a pointer to move down the list and point to the next data item to be retrieved. This section presents the tools you can use with variable argument lists. Microsoft C/C++ provides three macros and one data type for manipulating a variable argument list. These tools belong to the va_...() family of functions.

The data type defined is va_list. It is used to declare an *argument pointer* that points to the data items in the variable argument list. The macros in the va_...() family have the following syntax:

```
void va_start( va_list arg_ptr, prev_param );
type va_arg( va_list arg_ptr, type );
void va_end( va_list arg_ptr );
```

va_start() sets up the argument pointer to point to the first variable argument in the list. The *arg_ptr* parameter tells va_start() which pointer will be used to access the variable argument list, and the *prev_param* parameter specifies the last fixed argument in the variable argument list. The va_start() macro causes *arg_ptr* to point just beyond the argument specified by *prev_param*. This macro must be executed before either va_arg() or va_end() can be used.

va_arg() has a twofold purpose. First, va_arg() returns the value of the object pointed to by the argument pointer *arg_ptr*. Second, va_arg() updates the argument pointer to point to the next item in the list. The type specified in the va_arg() parameter list tells va_arg() what type of data is being read. The *type* argument tells va_arg() whether the data pointed to is an integer, a double, or some other type. The *type* argument also provides va_arg() with the information necessary to update the argument pointer correctly.

va_end() performs the housekeeping chores necessary for the called function to return correctly. If va_end() is not called after all the variable arguments have been read, your program can suffer from strange and undefined errors.

The next two program listings, Listing 3.7 and Listing 3.8, show how you can use the va_...() family of functions. The first program contains a variable argument list that has the number of arguments specified when the function is called. The second program, which is a variation of the first program, uses a special value to indicate the end of the list.

Listing 3.7. v_list1.c. A program that uses a variable argument list.

```
 1   /*  V_LIST1.C  This program uses a variable argument list
 2                  that specifies the number of arguments in
 3                  the list when the function is called. */
 4
 5   #include <stdio.h>
 6   #include <stdlib.h>
 7   #include <stdarg.h>
 8   #include <graph.h>
 9
10   int sum( int no_args, ... );
11
12   main()
```

```
13  {
14      int no_args;
15      int result;
16
17      _clearscreen( _GCLEARSCREEN );
18      printf( "This program calculates the sum of a \n" );
19      printf( "group of numbers. You will supply the \n" );
20      printf( "sum function with the number of items to \n" );
21      printf( "sum and a list of integer values. \n\n" );
22
23      no_args = 5;
24      result = sum( no_args, 3, 5, 18, 57, 66 );
25      printf( "The value of result = %d\n", result );
26
27      return 0;
28  }
29
30  int sum( int no_args, ... )
31  {
32      va_list ap;
33      int result = 0;
34      int number, i;
35
36      va_start( ap, no_args );
37
38      for( i = 1; i <= no_args; i++ ) {
39          result += va_arg( ap, int );
40      }
41
42      return result;
43  }
```

Listing 3.7 shows a sum() function that uses a variable argument list. The sum() function uses a variable that stores the number of arguments to be passed to the function.

As you have seen, a variable argument list requires a method of detecting the end of the argument list. In Listing 3.7, an extra variable stores a value that equals the number of arguments passed to the function. This extra variable lets you read all the arguments passed to the function without going past the end of the argument list.

Line 10 contains the function prototype for the sum() function. This function returns an integer value, which is equal to the sum of the arguments passed to the function. Two specifications are in the argument list for sum(). The first argument, no_args, is the variable indicating the number of items in the variable argument list. You supply the value of the no_args variable each time you call the function. The second argument is the ellipsis (...). It indicates that a variable number of arguments will be passed to the function.

An example of a function call to sum() is shown in line 24. Notice in line 23 that the no_args variable is assigned a value that equals the number of arguments passed to sum() in line 24. The sum() function is defined in lines 30 through 43. An argument pointer, with a va_list data type, is declared in line 32. The argument pointer points to an argument in the variable argument list. In line 36, the va_start() macro loads the argument pointer ap with the address of the first variable argument.

In lines 38 through 40 of Listing 3.7, the for loop steps through the items in the variable argument list. The va_arg() macro returns the value of an item in the variable argument list and increments the argument pointer to the next item in the list. The result variable accumulates the values returned by the va_arg() macro. When the for loop finishes, the value of the result variable is returned to the calling function.

The program in Listing 3.8 does not require a variable indicating the number of arguments passed to the function. Instead, the function checks the variable argument list for a terminating value. When one is encountered, the function stops processing arguments.

Listing 3.8. v_list2.c. Another function with a variable argument list.

```
1   /*  V_LIST2.C   This program uses a variable argument list
2                   that contains a terminating value. */
3
4   #include <stdio.h>
5   #include <stdlib.h>
6   #include <stdarg.h>
7   #include <graph.h>
8
9   int sum( int first_num, ... );
10
11  main()
12  {
13    int result;
14
15    _clearscreen( _GCLEARSCREEN );
16    printf( "This program calculates the sum of a \n" );
```

```
17    printf( "group of numbers. You will supply the \n" );
18    printf( "sum function with a list of values. \n" );
19    printf( "You must have at least one value, and the \n" );
20    printf( "last value must be zero. \n\n" );
21
22    result = sum( 43, 56, 1, 19, 3 ,0 );
23    printf( "The value of result = %d\n", result );
24
25    return 0;
26  }
27
28  int sum( int first_num, ... )
29  {
30    va_list ap;
31    int result;
32    int number;
33
34    va_start( ap, first_num );
35
36    result = first_num;
37
38    while( ( number = va_arg( ap, int ) ) != 0 ) {
39      result += number;
40    }
41
42    return result;
43  }
```

The program in Listing 3.8 is similar to the program in Listing 3.7. This program, however, does not require a value to be passed to the sum() function indicating how many arguments will be in the variable argument list.

Notice the function declaration in line 9 of Listing 3.8. Every function with a variable argument list requires that you have at least one fixed argument. In sum(), the fixed argument stores the first item in the list of items to be summed. In line 36, you can see that the fixed variable is processed separately. In Listing 3.8, the loop that reads the values in the variable argument list is different from the loop in Listing 3.7. To loop through the variable argument list, the for loop in Listing 3.7 uses the variable that indicates the number of items in the list. In Listing 3.8, the while loop gets values from the variable argument list until the terminating value is encountered.

In line 38, the va_arg() macro reads a value from the variable argument list and the value is assigned to the variable number. The value assigned to number is then checked to determine whether the terminating value was read. When the terminating value is read, the while loop ends.

Exercises

These exercises give you practice in creating your own functions, passing and returning values from functions, controlling loops, handling errors, and using variable argument lists:

1. Write a program containing functions that return int, double, and char values.

2. Design and write a function that gets two letters from the keyboard, compares the letters, and tells you which letter has the greater value. Use the function-creation process described in the section "Writing Prototypes for Your Function."

3. Write a function with arguments passed by value. Then write a similar function with arguments passed by reference.

4. Write a function to demonstrate the use of a static variable.

5. Design a loop that uses the continue statement.

6. Write a program that uses exit() to handle a simulated error.

7. Define a function that uses a variable argument list. Use a terminating character to detect the end of the variable argument list.

Summary

In this chapter, you learned more about the use and design of C functions. The following important points were covered:

- *The main() function is required in every C program.*

- *Microsoft C/C++ has an extensive set of library functions.* To use a function from the Microsoft C/C++ libraries, you must include the appropriate header file in your program.

- *A function prototype, or function declaration, tells the compiler about the data sent to and from a function.* This information helps the compiler catch errors that result from the improper use of a function.

- *You can pass arguments to a function either by value or by reference.* Passing by value means that a copy of the argument is sent to the function. Passing by reference means that the address of the data variable is sent to the calling function.

■ *A variable's storage class determines where and when the variable can be accessed.* The three parts that make up a variable's storage class are scope, duration, and linkage. Scope refers to the parts of the program that can be accessed by a variable. Duration indicates the length of time a variable exists. Linkage refers to the accessibility of your data from another source file.

■ *You use the va_...() family of functions to process variable argument lists.*

Using Pointers and Derived Types

N ow that you have learned the basic features of C programming, you can write moderately useful programs. This chapter covers some of the most powerful features of the C language and enables you to write advanced programs. You learn more about C's data types, and you learn how to use the derived and aggregate data types. Perhaps most important, you see how pointers can provide new ways to access functions and data in your applications. A pointer is, strictly speaking, a derived type. Pointers are so special and useful in C programs, however, that they occupy a category by themselves.

Understanding Standard C Derived Types

This section introduces C's derived types. So far, all you have seen are the basic data types, which declare the fundamental data objects used in C. An object declared with a basic type represents only a single piece of data. An object declared with a derived type, however, can represent several pieces of data, or it can represent a new use for an already familiar type.

Understanding derived types involves expanding your view of how C categorizes and controls data objects. Therefore, in this section, you first learn about C's data typing scheme. With that conceptual foundation in place, you then learn what the derived types are and how your computer uses them.

Understanding C's Typing Scheme

Only three broad categories of types are at the apex of the C typing scheme: *object types,* which describe variables and more complex data objects, *function types,* which are associated with all C functions, and *incomplete types,* which identify the kind of object being used but lack sufficient information to determine the object's size. It is important to know these categories of C types, because derived types can cut across the boundaries of type categories.

Beginning students of C are generally surprised to learn that C, at the most fundamental level, knows about only two kinds of data: integers and floating-point numbers. All other basic data types are qualified or derived versions of these two. Some groups of type versions overlap other groups. C recognizes the following broad categories of object types:

- *Integral types.* These are the most fundamental to C. The integral types include characters, integers, and enumerations. The integral types also include both the signed and unsigned character and integer types.

- *Arithmetic types.* This more general group of types overlaps the integral types. The arithmetic types include all the integral types plus the floating-point types.

- *Scalar types.* These comprise an even more general grouping of types. The scalar types include both the arithmetic types and the pointer types. Because a pointer is a derived type, the scalar types include both basic and derived object types.

C creates the derived types from the categories of types just listed.

Creating New Types from Old

A *derived type* is a modified form of a basic data type. Microsoft C/C++ follows the ANSI standard for C in providing two derived object types and a function type, as follows:

- *Array type.* An array is a collection of many objects, all of which have the same basic type. You can define an array of `int`, an array of `char`, and so on for all the basic C types. You can also declare an array of the aggregate type `struct` (`struct` is described shortly), resulting in an array of `struct`.

- *Function type.* From the perspective of C's typing scheme, a function is a special type of object that returns a value having a type that you define. A function that returns an integer, for example, has a *function type* returning `int`. You might also declare a function with type function returning `char*` (a pointer to `char`), function returning `void*` (a void pointer), or simply function returning `void` (a function returning nothing).

■ *Pointer type.* The pointer is a special object in C. A pointer is an object having a value that is the memory address of another object. A pointer type may be derived from a function type, a basic type, or an incomplete type (see the following sidebar, "What Is an Incomplete Type?"). The kind of object being pointed to is called the *reference type* of the pointer. For example, if you define a pointer to `int`, the reference type is `int`. C pointers give you tremendous power and flexibility in managing and manipulating data and functions.

What Is an Incomplete Type?

An *incomplete type* describes instance objects (particular, defined objects) but lacks enough information to determine an object's size. You can take the address of such an object, but you cannot access the object. Only arrays and structures can have incomplete type, as described in the following paragraphs.

An array with a missing size value (subscript bound) has incomplete type. The declaration `extern int ages[]` has incomplete array type, for instance. You can use such a declaration to describe an array of unknown size residing in another source file, or to pass an array of variable size to a function. For multidimensional arrays, only the leftmost subscript bound can be omitted (for example, `extern int stats[][2]` is a list of pairs of statistics, but the length of the list is unknown). An incomplete array type is completed when you initialize the array, like this:

```
int numbers[] = { 1, 2, 3, 4 };
```

If the leftmost bound (or the only bound) is omitted, you can use the array normally—but be sure that you do not refer to elements beyond the end of the array.

A structure declaration with a tag but no member list has incomplete type. In other words, a structure declared without its contents has incomplete type. You might want to write such a declaration if all you need to do at the moment is reserve the structure's name for use in a `typedef`, defining the structure's contents later. For example:

```
struct bigrec;              /* Incomplete struct type */
...
typedef struct bigrec REC;  /* Here's the typedef */
...
struct bigrec {       /* Now complete struct definition */
  double data1, data2, data3, data4;
};
...
REC averages;         /* Finally, use struct via typedef */
```

Note that you cannot use an incomplete struct type as a function parameter.

As you have seen, a function is a collection of C statements that performs some task. When a function completes its processing, it generally returns a value to its caller. The kind of value returned is determined by the declaration of the function's type. The type of the value returned by the function determines the function's precise type.

The type of a pointer is determined by the type of the object referenced by the pointer (that is, by the reference type). Microsoft C/C++ uses the pointer's reference type when the pointer is used for processing array-like objects. The pointer's reference type determines how much the pointer must be incremented to advance to the next object.

Arrays are a hybrid object type, spanning the boundaries of both derived and aggregate types. Arrays are collections of objects that have the same data type. An array is a derived type because it represents a new use for its element type. An array is considered also an aggregate type because it is a collection of similar objects.

Many arrays contain objects declared only as basic data types, but you can declare an array of pointers to objects, an array of pointers to functions, and even an array of structures. Figure 4.1 shows how an integer array is stored in your computer's memory.

Figure 4.1.

How an array is stored in memory.

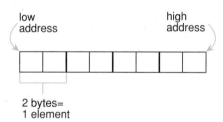

A 4=element integer array uses 8 bytes of memory.

low address   high address

2 bytes=
1 element

As you can see from Figure 4.1, an array occupies a contiguous block of memory. The amount of memory used is determined by the number of elements in the array and the space required to store each element. A 10-element int array, for instance, occupies less space than a 10-element double array. You can find the sizes (and value ranges) of the basic types in Chapter 2, "Understanding the Foundations of C."

You can declare an array also with multiple dimensions. You can think of a two-dimensional array as a grid of elements. Each item in the two-dimensional array can be accessed by its row-and-column number. Even though a two-dimensional array is like a grid, the computer stores the elements of the array in a one-dimensional sequence of memory locations in row order—that is, one row after another—as shown in Figure 4.2.

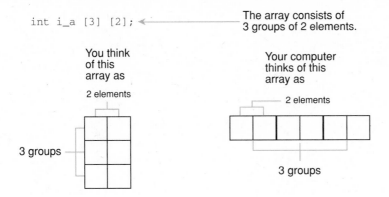

Figure 4.2.

How a two-dimensional array is stored in memory.

From Figure 4.2, you can see that the two-dimensional array occupies six contiguous memory locations. Your program treats these six locations as three groups of two elements instead of as a grid of objects.

You can declare arrays with more than two dimensions. Think of the elements in the arrays as being stored in groups and subgroups. Memory is allocated for an array so that all the elements indexed by the rightmost subscript are in contiguous memory locations.

An *enumeration* is a special integer type, and not really a derived type. I mention the enumeration here simply because it is syntactically similar to derived type declarations. An enumeration lets you assign mnemonic identifiers to integer values. The classic example is the assignment of values to the days of the week:

```
enum wk_days{ sun, mon, tue, wed, thu, fri, sat };
int day_no;
for( day_no = sun; day_no <= sat; day_no++ )
  printf( "The day number is: %d\n", day_no );
```

On the first line of this code fragment, the enum statement assigns an integer value to the name of each weekday. After the enumeration statement, whenever the name of a weekday is used, that name is replaced with the integer value assigned to it in the enumeration. Here, the symbol sun is set to 0, mon to 1, tue to 2, and so on. Because each weekday name is assigned an integer value, the assignment expressions in the last two lines do not generate errors. By default, the first identifier in an enumeration statement is assigned a value of 0. Subsequent identifiers received the value of the previous identifier plus 1. You can optionally set the first identifier to a different value, by writing a statement such as:

```
enum wk_days{ sun = 1, mon, tue, wed, thu, fri, sat };
```

If you want, you can explicitly assign arbitrary values to any or all of the identifiers in the enumeration list:

```
enum wk_days{ sun = 10, mon = 20, tue = 30, wed = 40, thu = 50, fri = 60,
sat = 70 };
```

Understanding C Pointers

The pointer may be the most flexible feature of C—and it may be the most widely misunderstood as well. Programmers familiar with other languages may have found pointers difficult to use. In C, however, you can easily include pointers in your programs after you master the underlying concept. Of all derived types, the pointer is discussed first because almost all significant C programs heavily use pointers.

The basic concept of a C pointer is easy to understand. A pointer is a data object that holds the memory address of another object. Thus, you can deal directly with the pointer or you can deal with the object addressed by the pointer. You can change the value of a pointer, thus changing the location in memory to which it is pointing. You also can change the value of the object pointed to, accessing the object by means of the pointer.

Now here is a statement that should give you pause for thought: The size of a pointer object is not necessarily the same as the size of the object to which it is pointing. Hang in there for just a minute. It is important to sort out the ideas of a pointer as an object, and a pointer as a locator for another object.

To highlight that difference, think for a moment about a pointer to a function in a small model Microsoft C/C++ program. Because the small model is being used, the pointer requires only two bytes of memory to hold the address of the function. But how big is the function? A function's executable code could occupy thousands of bytes of memory. You can see that there is a considerable difference between the size of the function and the size of the pointer to the function.

Pointers can sometimes speed up the handling of data. You can move the address of a complex data structure more quickly than you can move the data structure itself, simply because pointers are typically much smaller than the object they point to. Pointers also give you more control over your data: With a pointer, you can access data that does not even reside in the boundaries of your program!

This section explains how you can use pointers. You learn how Microsoft C/C++ implements pointers by using the indirection and address-of operators to control indirect addressing.

Understanding Indirect Addressing

Understanding indirect addressing requires that you first understand how *any* object is stored in RAM. A computer's random-access memory (RAM) is arranged as a contiguous series of storage locations. Each location contains enough bits to hold the smallest recognizable object for the machine. On the 80x86 CPU, the smallest addressable location is an eight-bit byte, which is sufficient to store one C character. (On some machines, the smallest addressable unit is a *word,* which may be able to hold more than one byte.)

RAM Addresses and the System Loader

Addresses of program variables are known relative to the beginning of the memory segments used during compilation and link editing. For example, `function_a()` might be 256 bytes beyond the start of the code segment, and the integer counter might be 16 bytes beyond the start of the data segment.

Actual memory addresses are determined by the DOS loader when the program is run. The process of computing true function and variable addresses at run-time is called *address relocation.*

Each RAM location is associated with a number called its *address.* Each data object therefore has a specific address in your computer's memory. When the Microsoft C/C++ compiler encounters the variables you declare, it sets aside storage for the variables and keeps track of where the variables were placed in memory. In other words, the address of the variable is recorded in the compiler's symbol table (see the preceding sidebar "RAM Addresses and the System Loader"). Later references to the same function or variable cause the compiler to use the address stored in the symbol table to access the object. Figure 4.3 illustrates how data objects are stored and accessed directly.

As noted, a pointer is a data object that contains the memory address of another object. A pointer to an integer, for instance, contains the address (that is, the RAM location) of the integer variable. To access the variable being pointed to, the compiler must generate code in two steps. First, the pointer object must be fetched to get the address of the target variable. Second, the address from the first step is used to access the variable. This process is called *indirect addressing,* and is the method Microsoft C/C++ uses to implement pointers in your program. Figure 4.4 shows how a variable can be accessed using indirect addressing (that is, by using a pointer). Listing 4.1 shows how an integer variable can be accessed indirectly, through a pointer.

Figure 4.3.

Accessing an object
through direct addressing.

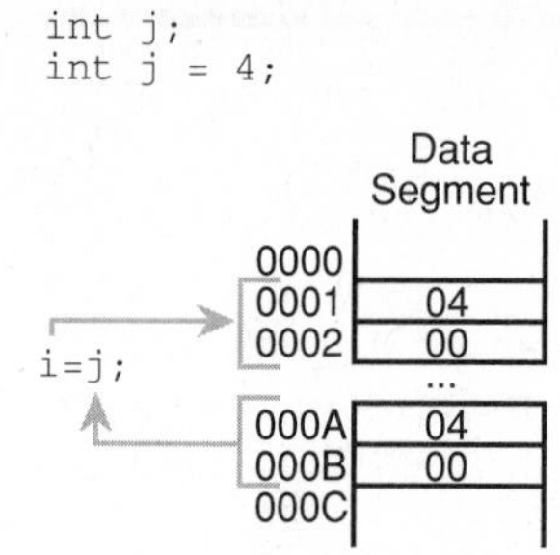

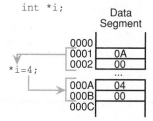

Figure 4.4.

Accessing an object
through indirect
addressing.

Listing 4.1. p_intro.c. A program that uses indirect addressing.

```
1   /* P_INTRO.C   This program demonstrates the use of
2                  pointers and indirect addressing. */
3
4   #include <stdio.h>
5   #include <stdlib.h>
6
7   main()
8   {
9     int i, j;
10    int *i_ptr;
11
12    i = 34;
13    i_ptr = &i;
14    j = *i_ptr;
15
16    printf( "i = %d\n", i );
17    printf( "j = %d\n", j );
18    printf( "i_ptr = %p\n", i_ptr );
19
20    return 0;
21  }
```

In Listing 4.1, two integer variables are declared. In line 12, the first integer, i, is assigned the value 34. In line 14, the second integer, j, is assigned, by indirection, the value stored in the first integer. Before the second integer can be assigned a value, however, a pointer must be declared and initialized, as shown in line 13.

In line 10, a pointer to int is declared. The indirection operator (*) indicates that the object being declared is a pointer and not a regular variable. In line 13, the integer pointer i_ptr is assigned the address of the integer variable i. Note that the address-of operator (&) is used to get the address of the i variable. (The * and & operators are discussed in the next section.)

Next, in line 14, the value stored in i is assigned to j by indirection—that is, through the pointer. Now the * indirection operator prefixed to i_ptr indicates that the value stored in the object pointed to by i_ptr will be assigned to j. Think about this carefully: An object's value, not the pointer's value, is assigned.

The output produced by lines 16 and 17 shows that the values of i and j are identical. Line 18 uses the %p print format specifier to output the memory address contained in i_ptr. A memory address is displayed in the form xxxx:yyyy, where x and y are hexadecimal digits. The x values correspond to the memory segment address and the y values are the offset address (see Chapter 7, "Using Memory Models," to learn more about memory addressing). To learn more about the printf() format type specifiers, see "Using Formatted I/O Functions" in Chapter 6, "Using the Microsoft C/C++ I/O Function Library."

The purpose of Listing 4.1 is to introduce you to the concept of indirection; this program is only a limited demonstration of pointers and indirection. Using pointers to refer to objects of the basic data types has little value. Pointers are most useful when they refer to complex data structures and when they are used to manage dynamically controlled data.

You can use a single pointer to flexibly select different data objects. There are many applications of this idea. A common example is "stepping through" the characters in a string quickly, without using array subscripts. Listing 4.2 shows a program that does this.

Listing 4.2. exchange.c. A program that uses a pointer to step through a string.

```
1   #include <stddef.h>
2   #include <stdlib.h>
3   #include <stdio.h>
4   #include <string.h>
5   #include <graph.h>
6
```

Listing 4.2. Continued.

```
 7   /* +-----------------------------------------------------+
 8      + Exchange two areas of memory with no auxiliary
 9      +    storage used.
10      +
11      + Calling Sequence:
12      +
13      + mem_exchange( void *s1, void *s2, size_t n );
14      +
15      +    where s1 and s2 can be of any type (using
16      +    the appropriate casts). Two areas of
17      +    storage each "n" bytes long are exchanged in
18      +    place.
19      +-----------------------------------------------------+
20   */
21   void mem_exchange( void *s1, void *s2, size_t n )
22   {
23     unsigned char *p1, *p2;
24
25     p1 = s1;
26     p2 = s2;
27     for ( ; n>0; n-- ) {
28       *p1 ^= *p2;
29       *p2 ^= *p1;
30       *p1++ ^= *p2++;
31     }
32   }
33
34   void main()
35   {
36     char s1[40] = "This is the FIRST string. ";
37     char s2[40] = "This is the SECOND string.";
38     int i1 = 255;
39     int i2 = 127;
40
41     _clearscreen( _GCLEARSCREEN );
42     printf( "%s\n%s\n", s1, s2 );
43     mem_exchange( (void *)s1, (void *)s2, strlen( s1 ) );
44     printf( "%s\n%s\n\n", s1, s2 );
45
46     printf( "%d\n%d\n", i1, i2 );
```

```
47     mem_exchange( (void *)&i1, (void *)&i2, sizeof( int ) );
48     printf( "%d\n%d\n\n", i1, i2 );
49  }
```

The exchange.c program shown in Listing 4.2 demonstrates using pointers to step through strings. It shows you also how to swap the contents of two memory locations without using an intermediate holding area.

The mem_exchange() function in lines 21 through 31 does all the work. The first two arguments to this function are void pointers so that callers of this function can use any pointer type. size_t is a predefined type equivalent to an unsigned int. void pointers have the following characteristics:

- *void pointers have the same internal representation and address alignment requirements as character pointers.*

- *You can assign any pointer to a void pointer without worrying about pointer types.* Pointer typecasting is not required when assigning to or from a void pointer.

- *Pointers are implicitly converted to and from void* in four circumstances.* A pointer is implicitly converted to or from void* in assignments, function prototypes, comparisons, and conditional expressions. The implicit conversion only occurs if there is a clash between the pointer type used and void*.

  The program in Listing 4.2 takes advantage of this rule. The first two arguments for mem_exchange() have type void* (see line 21), but you can call the function using any pointer type, as long as you recast the parameters to type void*. This recast is shown in lines 43 and 47.

- *A void pointer cannot be dereferenced.* That is, you can manipulate address values with a void pointer, but you cannot use it to access a data object (dereferencing a pointer is discussed in the next section).

Because a void pointer cannot be dereferenced, mem_exchange() declares two local pointer variables with type unsigned char* (line 23) and uses them to step through the strings. (This function treats everything as if it were a string.)

mem_exchange() swaps the contents of the two memory locations addressed by the void pointers s1 and s2 by applying to every byte in each area a series of three exclusive OR operations. The order in which the exclusive ORs are performed and the order of the operands for each operation are crucial to the success of the technique.

Suppose, for example, that you have two objects—A and B—and you want to exchange their contents. Using an algebra-like pseudocode, the sequence of operations is as follows:

```
A = A XOR B
B = B XOR A
A = A XOR B
```

To understand how the XOR operator works, you must understand the exclusive-OR process. When two bits have the exclusive-OR operator applied between them, the result is as follows:

Bit 1	XOR	Bit 2	=	Result
0		0		0
0		1		1
1		0		1
1		1		0

The XOR operator is normally applied to integer or byte quantities. The result is that each bit in the first operand (such as A in the preceding) is exclusive-ORed with the corresponding bit in the second operand (such as B). Consider the example where A contains the decimal value 100 and B contains the decimal value 200. Translated to binary, A contains 01100100 and B contains 11001000. The statement

```
A = A XOR B
```

sets A to 10101100. You may wish to write these bit values on a piece of paper and manually perform the exclusive-or operation for each bit in A and B to help you understand the process.

The statement

```
B = B XOR A
```

now sets B to 01100100, which, interestingly, is the original value of A, or decimal 100.

Finally

```
A = A XOR B
```

sets A to 11001000, the original value of B, or decimal 200.

In mem_exchange(), the same effect as this sequence of steps is achieved by using the powerful C exclusive-OR-and-assign compound operator (^=). The series of XORs is seen in lines 28 through 30. The syntax of line 30 is particularly interesting. Here it is again:

```
*p1++ ^= *p2++;
```

If you just keep operator precedence in mind, this line is not as complicated as it may seem. Recall that the indirection operator (*) has higher precedence than the postfix increment operator (++). (Operator precedence was shown in Chapter 2, Table 2.9.) Thus, the right side of the assignment is interpreted as meaning that the object pointed to by p2 is fetched for use first, and only then is the pointer incremented. The same rule applies to the p1 pointer on the left side. Therefore, the XOR operation is logically completed before the pointers are adjusted to the next byte location.

Because a character string is an array of characters, the technique used in Listing 4.2 should apply to arrays in general. It does—you can use pointers to step through any array in the manner illustrated in Listing 4.2. Figure 4.5 shows how a pointer can be used to step through the elements of an array.

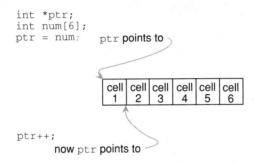

```
int *ptr;
int num[6];
ptr = num;
```

Figure 4.5.

Using a pointer to access array elements.

The integer array in Figure 4.5 has six cells. Two bytes are required to store each integer in the array. When the array is declared, it is assigned a contiguous block of memory that starts, in this case, at the address FF00. Referencing the array name without a subscript returns the starting address of the array. You can see how this works when ptr is assigned the value of num. The ptr pointer is assigned the address of the first element in the array.

If the ptr pointer is incremented by 1, ptr points to the next element in the array. Now ptr holds the address FF02. Note that ptr was incremented by 1, but the address value in ptr was incremented by 2. When you increment a pointer, the new value stored in the pointer always points to the next data object. It does not matter whether the data object takes 2 or 20 bytes; when the pointer is incremented, the pointer points to the next data object. Microsoft C/C++ uses the size of the pointer's reference type to determine how many byte locations to add when incrementing a pointer by 1.

Using C's Indirection and Address-of Operators

Microsoft C/C++ has two special unary operators for working with pointers and address values. You have already seen them, because it is impossible to use a pointer without them. These operators are the *indirection operator* and the *address-of operator.* The indirection operator is represented by the * symbol, and the address-of operator is represented by the & symbol. Now I discuss these operators in more detail.

The indirection operator has a twofold purpose. First, the indirection operator is used to *declare a pointer.* Second, the indirection operator is used to *dereference a pointer.* Dereferencing a pointer means accessing (fetching or storing) the value of the object pointed to.

Note how the indirection operator (*) is used in the following examples of pointer declarations for most of C's basic data types:

```
int *int_ptr;        \* Declare a pointer to int *\
char *char_ptr;      \* Declare a pointer to char *\
double *flt_ptr;     \* Declare a pointer to double *\
const int *ci_ptr;   \* Declare a pointer to const int *\
void *any_ptr;       \* Declare a pointer to anything *\
```

As you can see, you can declare a pointer for any type of data object. Some of these declarations can even point to arrays. Look at this example:

```
char *char_ptr;
```

char_ptr is obviously a pointer to a character type object. However, char_ptr can be used also as a pointer to a character array. You can use any pointer to a basic data type as a pointer to an array of the same type.

The next code fragment shows how a pointer is dereferenced:

```
int *int_ptr;
int i = 6;
int_ptr = &i;
printf( "i = %d", *int_ptr );
```

In this example, a pointer is assigned the address of an integer variable. The pointer is dereferenced in the printf() statement, and printf() displays the value stored in the integer variable. The pointer is dereferenced (the object is accessed) by the expression *int_ptr.

The second unary operator, the address-of operator (&), returns the memory address of its operand. This memory address can be assigned directly to a pointer variable of the correct type. You have seen the address-of operator used several times before. Look at the examples in the following code fragment:

```
char *char_ptr;      /* Declare a pointer       */
char c = 'A';        /* Declare a variable      */
char str[30]         /* Declare an array        */
char_ptr = &c;       /* Get address of variable */
char_ptr = str;      /* Get address of array    */
```

These examples show when the address-of operator is and is not needed. In the fourth line, the & operator takes the address of the variable c. The address is then assigned to the character pointer variable char_ptr. The address-of operator is needed when you want to take the address of a basic data object. In the fifth line, however, the address-of operator is not needed because the address of an array is assigned to a character pointer. Remember that when you reference an array name and you do not supply a subscript, the value returned is the address of the first element in the array. Because you have the address of the first element, you do not need to use the address-of operator. Function names without the function call parentheses also yield the address of the function without using the address-of operator.

The address-of operator cannot be used with a bit-field object or a *register variable.* A bit-field occurs only in a structure, and is discussed later in this chapter.

Using the *register* Keyword

A register variable is an auto variable that you've asked to have placed in a CPU hardware register whenever possible. (To learn more about CPU registers, see the section titled "Understanding CPU Addressing Registers" in Chapter 7, "Using Memory Models.")

You can suggest that the compiler place an integer type variable into a CPU register by prefacing the variable's definition with the register keyword, like this:

```
register int i;
```

The register keyword tells the compiler that this variable will be used and referenced extensively; as such, it may make sense to place the variable in one of the CPU registers rather than a memory location. Values stored in a CPU register can be accessed much more quickly than those stored in a standard memory location.

Only two CPU registers are available on the 80x86 CPU for use by register variables, so you will gain little by placing register in front of all of your variable declarations. Additionally, because the Microsoft C/C++ compiler automatically (depending on compiler option settings) places variables into registers, by suggesting that a particular variable be placed in a register, you may interfere with the compiler's built-in optimization strategies. Because of these limitations, use of the register keyword is not common in most Microsoft C/C++ programs.

You should exercise some care to be sure that you properly initialize any pointer you declare before you use it. The compiler will not stop you from using an uninitialized pointer, but the results are unpredictable.

The value you assign to a pointer can be any valid data address, as well as the NULL value. NULL is a predefined symbol in the various header files, such as stdio.h, stdlib.h, and so on. The NULL value has some interesting features. First, NULL is guaranteed to be unequal to any pointer to an object or function. Therefore, the NULL value will never compare as equal to any valid pointer value in your program. Second, any two NULL values are guaranteed to compare as equal. The NULL values are guaranteed to be equal even if the pointers in which the values are stored are of different types.

Only three arithmetic operations are legal on pointers: You can add integers to pointers, subtract integers from pointers, or subtract pointers from pointers. All other mathematical operations are illegal and pointless. The following list explains the three legal operations:

- *Adding an integer value to a pointer.* Adding an integer to a pointer increases the pointer value by the specified number of data objects. For example, if you add 3 to an integer pointer, you will point to the third integer from your current location. You will *not* point to the third byte from your location. Microsoft C/C++ always increments by data objects, not by bytes.

- *Subtracting an integer value from a pointer.* Subtraction is similar to addition. Subtracting 2 from a double pointer causes the pointer to point to a preceding double variable. You will *not* point to a location two bytes in front of your current location. When you perform integer arithmetic on a pointer, Microsoft C/C++ makes sure that you move by the specified number of data objects, not by bytes.

- *Subtracting one pointer from another.* Subtracting one pointer from another returns the number of data objects between the pointers. You do *not* get the number of bytes between the objects. When you subtract two pointers, Microsoft C/C++ automatically takes the difference in bytes and divides it by the size of the data object. The result of subtracting two pointers can be stored in a variable with the type ptrdiff_t.

You can also cast a pointer from one type to another in an expression. A *pointer cast* simply tells the compiler to assume that a different reference type is now being used—the data pointed to does not change, but the compiler handles the data as if it has another type. Pointer casts can be useful when manipulating data in sophisticated ways that are not ordinarily allowed. Listing 4.3 demonstrates a pointer cast.

Listing 4.3. uitoh.c. A program that prints an unsigned int, byte by byte.

```
1   /* UITOH.C  This program takes an unsigned integer
2              number and uses a typecast to print
3              each byte of the number in hexadecimal.  */
```

```
4
5    #include <stdio.h>
6    #include <stdlib.h>
7
8    main()
9    {
10     unsigned long x = 4096;
11     char *dump;
12     int i;
13
14     dump = ( char * ) &x;
15     for( i = 1; i <= 4; i++ )
16       printf( "Byte %d = %.2x\n", i, *dump++ );
17
18     return 0;
19   }
```

Listing 4.3 uses a pointer cast to print each byte of a multibyte data object—in this case, an unsigned long integer. The unsigned long is declared and initialized in line 10. A character pointer is declared in line 11. An unsigned long integer requires four bytes of memory. The unsigned long is printed, however, with a char pointer that points to one byte at a time. Before the dump character pointer can access the data stored in the variable x, a type cast must be performed. The type cast is executed in line 14, where the address of the unsigned long integer is obtained. Then the address is type cast to a character pointer, which enables you to access the data in the variable one byte at a time. Because the dump pointer points to one byte at a time, printf() must be called four times to print the complete value of the x variable.

Using Arrays and Strings

An *aggregate type* is a special derived type. An aggregate is an object that is composed of simpler objects having various other types. Types that can be included in an aggregate object include the basic types, derived types (except for functions), and even other aggregate types. C's aggregate data objects are useful because they can group and control collections of objects as a unit while still permitting access to individual member objects.

There are two kinds of aggregate data objects in C: arrays and structures. Although a union is not an aggregate type, it has some similarities to structures. Thus, unions are discussed together with structures a little later, in the "Using Structures and Unions" section.

Arrays belong to both the derived and aggregate categories of object types. In this section, you learn how to declare, initialize, and use arrays.

This section shows you also how to use C strings. In C, a string is an array of characters. In fact, the terms *character array* and *string* are synonymous. You learn how to determine the size of an array for a given string, how to initialize a string, and how to assign values to the string.

Declaring and Using Arrays of Objects

An *array* is a collection of data objects, called *array elements,* that all have the same base data type and occupy a contiguous area of memory. Array elements can have any valid data type. An array declaration has the following form:

```
typename identifier[ size-constant-expression ]
```

typename specifies the type of the array's elements. For example, if the element type is `double`, every element in the array is a `double` floating-point number.

The *identifier* is the name of the array. You use this name when you refer to the array in your program. The standard rules for creating a variable name apply to creating a name for the array.

The square brackets enclosing the *size-constant-expression* are called the *array declarator,* and they must be coded as shown. The *size-constant-expression* is an expression that evaluates to a positive integer value and determines how many elements the array has. If the *size-constant-expression* evaluates to 25, for example, the array has 25 elements. The *size-constant-expression* can be an expression, but it must yield a constant value. You cannot use a variable as the *size-constant-expression*.

Now examine the following declaration:

```
int my_array[100];
```

`int` is the element type of the array, specifying that the elements in the array are integer objects. `my_array` is the identifier of the array. The value 100 indicates how many elements are in the array—it is the array size. In this case, `my_array` has 100 integer elements.

Later, when you want to access an element in the array, you use an array index: the array name `my_array` followed by a number enclosed in square brackets. The brackets in a reference to an array element are called the *array subscript operator.* Note that the array declarator previously mentioned is, in fact, an array subscript operator (it is just used to indicate size in the declaration) and has the same operator precedence as the subscript operator.

The array index is an expression that evaluates to an integer value, indicating which array element will be accessed. The array index is known also as the *array subscript.* It is important to remember that arrays use a *zero-origin array index.* This means that the first element in the array is element 0, not element 1. When looping through an array, be sure that you start at array element 0.

The following code fragment declares, initializes, and prints an array of integers:

```
int i;
int my_array[100];

for( i = 0; i <= 99; i++ )
  my_array[i] = 100 - i;

for( i = 0; i <= 99; i++ )
  printf( "my_array[%d] = %d\n", i, my_array[i] );
```

In the second line of this code fragment, `my_array` is declared as an integer array that holds 100 integer values.

The first `for` statement in the code fragment initializes the array. Note that the array subscript starts with a value of 0. The `for` loop loops from 0 to 99, or once for every element in the array. As the subscript increases, the corresponding element values in `my_array` are decreased. The last `for` loop in the preceding code fragment prints the value of each element in `my_array`.

Note in the preceding code fragment that a variable can be used as an array subscript. Only the array size must be a constant expression.

Using a multidimensional array is as easy as using a one-dimensional array. The declaration of the array changes only a little—you can declare an array *of array.* You can declare a two-dimensional array, for example, in this way:

```
int my_array[10][3];
```

This array has 10 groups of three elements. This declaration is interpreted to mean an array containing 10 arrays. Each array element is an array that happens to contain three integers (in other words, the element type is still `int`). Each group of three integers is stored together in memory. Thus, when stepping through an array sequentially, the rightmost subscript is exhausted first.

To access a member in a multidimensional array, you use a statement like this:

```
int *i;
...
i = my_array[5][2];
```

You can initialize an array during its declaration, by providing an *initializer list.* An initializer list is a list of values separated by commas and enclosed in braces, as shown in the following line of code:

```
int even_int[5] = { 2, 4, 6, 8, 10 };
```

The values in an initializer list are assigned to corresponding array elements from left to right. The leftmost value in the string is assigned to `even_int[0]` and the second value in the string is assigned to `even_int[1]`. The process continues until all the values are assigned. If you do not supply enough initial values, the remaining elements of the array will be initialized to 0.

If you initialize an array during its declaration, you can optionally omit the *size* of the array (the size expression inside square brackets is also called the *subscript bound*). If you omit the array size expression when declaring an array, the compiler counts the number of elements in the initializer list and automatically allocates enough memory to store the values you provided. You could therefore rewrite the preceding declaration as follows:

```
int even_int[] = { 2, 4, 6, 8, 10 };
```

Although you did not specify the size of the array, you can still use the array subscript to access any element in the array. Just be sure to note how many elements you assign to the array. Trying to read a value past the end of the array will produce strange results, because the data values will be unpredictable.

You can also use an initializer list with a multidimensional array declaration. Multidimensional array initializer lists can optionally use interior braces to group elements belonging to different indexes. For example, the following code fragment shows two equivalent methods of initializing an array containing three pairs of screen coordinates:

```
    /* Declare the array with fully bracketed syntax */
int screenxy[3][2] = {
  { 0, 0, },
  { 40, 40, },
  { 80, 25, },
};
    /* Declare the array without interior bracketing */
int screenxy[3][2] = { 0, 0, 40, 40, 80, 25, };
```

Notice in the preceding declarations that the initial values are written in the order needed to accommodate the left-to-right assignment of values used. You could also have omitted the array bound values because the initializer list is given.

Using array subscripts is not the only way you can access array elements. You can also use a *pointer*. Using the name of the array without an array subscript yields the address of the first element in the array. The expression `my_array` gives the address of the first element in `my_array`. To access a specific element in the array, you simply add the number of the element you want to the address returned by the array name. The next line of code shows how you can get the value stored in the second element in `my_array`:

```
i = *( my_array + 1 );
```

`my_array` written without the subscript operator gives the address of the first element in the array. Adding 1 (remember zero origins) to `my_array` gives the address of the second element in the array. You do not have to specify the number of bytes to add to `my_array`. The number of bytes needed for the offset you specify is calculated automatically. The indirection operator, `*`, returns the value stored at the address calculated in the parentheses.

To get to the fifth element of `my_array`, you use the expression `*( my_array + 4 )`. This expression is equivalent to the expression `my_array[4]`. Array subscript notation is always equivalent to pointer notation in C.

Understanding C Strings

A string is stored in a character array. You can declare a character array to hold a string in the following ways:

```
char str_1[31];
char str_2[] = "This is a demonstration string.";
```

The first declaration, for `str_1`, sets up a character array that can hold 31 elements. This character array is long enough to hold a 30-character string. `str_1` can hold only a 30-character string because every string in C is terminated by the null character. The null character, `\0`, acts as a *fence* that indicates the end of the string.

The second declaration, for `str_2`, sets up a character array long enough to hold the string assigned to `str_2` plus a null character. As you can see from this declaration, the initializer in a string declaration is a string literal, not a list of characters in curly braces. Note that you cannot assign a string literal to a string in an ordinary assignment statement.

Figure 4.6 shows how Microsoft C/C++ stores a string in your computer's memory.

You don't have to declare strings just barely large enough to hold the initial value. You can declare the string to be considerably longer, and you should if the string will be manipulated in some of the ways shown later in this section.

To get the address of the beginning of the string, you use the name of the string without the braces or an element number. You need to be able to specify the beginning address of the string when you use functions like `printf()`. When you print a string, `printf()` requires that you supply only the address of the string. Passing the address of the string increases the speed of your program because only the string's address (not its contents) is passed as an argument. The next line of code prints the contents of str_2:

```
printf( "str_2 = %s\n", str_2 );
```

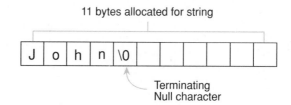

Figure 4.6.

How strings are stored.

```
char f_name[11] = "John";
```

11 bytes allocated for string

| J | o | h | n | \0 | | | | | | |

Terminating
Null character

You can initialize a string outside the string declaration by using the strcpy() function. This function copies the contents of one string into another string. Here is the syntax of strcpy():

```
*strcpy( char *string1, const char *string2 );
```

To use the strcpy function and other string functions, you must #include <string.h> in your source files.

The contents of the character array pointed to by *string2* are copied into the character array pointed to by *string1*. strcpy() returns a pointer to the string *string1* (the location of string1 is not changed). It is up to you, the programmer, to arrange matters so that there is enough room in the receiving string. The compiler cannot and will not stop you from copying in a string that is too long (destroying the variables stored just beyond the end of the string).

Actual arguments to the strcpy() function can be either string literals or string names (the receiving string, of course, cannot be a string literal). The following code fragment demonstrates the use of strcpy():

```
char s1[30];
char s2[30] = "This is a demonstration.";
...
strcpy( s1, s2 );
printf( "s1 = %s\n", s1 );
```

This code fragment copies the string in the s2 character array into the s1 character array. Notice that the arguments for the strcpy() function are pointers to the strings being processed. After the strcpy() is completed, the printf() statement prints the contents of the s1 string.

Two other useful string-handling functions are strcat() and strlen(). The strcat() function concatenates two strings, and the strlen() function calculates the length of the string. Note the format for the strcat() function:

```
*strcat( char *string1, const char *string2 )
```

strcat() concatenates, or appends, *string2* to the end of *string1*. The terminating null character at the end of *string1* is removed so that the only terminating character will be at the end of the new string. Like strcpy(), strcat() requires arguments that point to strings. strcat() returns a pointer to *string1* when the concatenation is complete.

The following code fragment shows the use of strcat():

```
char first_name[81] = "Bob";
char last_name[20]= "Johnson";
...
strcat( first_name, " " );
strcat( first_name, last_name );
printf( "The name is: %s\n", first_name );
```

The first strcat() function adds a blank character to the first_name string so that the first and last names are separated correctly. The second strcat() function adds the last_name string to the first_name string. The printf() function prints the final result of the concatenation operations.

When you use the strcat() function, make sure that the string into which you are copying can hold the entire string. You can use the strlen() function to check the lengths of the strings. Listing 4.4 shows how you can use strlen() and strcat() together.

Listing 4.4. name.c. A program that uses string functions.

```
1   /* NAME.C  This program demonstrates the strlen() and
2                  strcat() functions. */
3
4   #include <stdio.h>
5   #include <stdlib.h>
6   #include <string.h>
7
8   #define LONG_STR 81
9   #define SHORT_STR 31
10
11  main()
12  {
13    char first_name[LONG_STR] = "Bob ";
14    char last_name[SHORT_STR] = "Johnson";
15    int i;
16
17    i = strlen( first_name ) + strlen( last_name );
```

Listing 4.4. Continued.

```
18    if( i <= LONG_STR ) {
19       strcat( first_name, last_name );
20       printf( "string length = %d\n", i );
21       printf( "%s\n", first_name );
22    }
23    else
24       printf( "Strings too long.\n" );
25
26    return 0;
27  }
```

In line 17, `strlen()` calculates the lengths of the `first_name` and `last_name` strings. The results of `strlen()` are stored in the variable `i`. In line 18, the value stored in `i` is compared with the maximum string-length value. If the length of both strings is less than the maximum string length, the statements in lines 19 through 21 are executed. The two strings are concatenated, and the results are displayed.

The `strlen()` function requires an argument that is a pointer to the string, the length of which is to be calculated. The value returned by `strlen()` has the data type `size_t`. The value returned by `strlen()` can be stored in a regular integer, however, as in line 17.

You can use the `strlen()` function—and take advantage of the fact that strings are arrays—to insert individual characters anywhere in the string. The following code fragment contains a function that performs this task:

```
#include <string.h>
...
void cinsert( char ccode,char *anystring,int spos )
{
  int p;

  p = strlen(anystring);
  spos = ( spos < 0 ) ? 0 : spos;
  spos = ( spos >= p ) ? p : spos;
  for ( ; p>=spos; p--) anystring[p+1]=anystring[p];
  anystring[spos]=ccode;
}
```

The `cinsert()` function will insert a character anywhere within a string: at the beginning, in the middle, or at the end. The character to be inserted, `ccode`, will be placed at the insertion point, defined by the argument `spos`. Note that `spos` should have the sense of a subscript: To insert a character at the beginning of the string, set spos to zero. The inserted character will appear in the string preceding the character originally in that same position.

To make room for the new character, all the characters at the insertion point and to the right of it are moved out of the way (by moving them one position to the right). The terminating null character is moved also. Because character movement proceeds from right to left, it is easier to use array subscript notation than pointer notation to access characters in the string. Here is how the function works:

1. The length of the target string is computed first and stored in the local variable p. Note that p used as a subscript at this time would index to the position of the terminating null character. That is exactly right, because the null character should "move out of the way" also.

2. The first conditional assignment statement determines whether the requested insertion point is to the left of the string (that is, whether spos is negative). If it is, the insertion point is set to the beginning of the string.

3. The second conditional assignment statement determines whether the requested insertion point is to the right of the string (beyond the null terminating character). If it is, the insertion point is positioned to the right end of the string.

4. The for loop now moves the right fragment of the string one position to the right to make room for the new character. This is accomplished quite easily, by successively assigning the [p+1] character in the string the value of the [p] character. The string is treated just like any other array by the for loop, subscripting to the desired locations. Many string functions use only pointer notation, but that is only a matter of convenience and suitability for a specific task.

5. Finally, the new character is placed in the string at the insertion point.

The string functions presented here are just a few of those that Microsoft C/C++ provides. An extensive library of string functions is accessible when you include the string.h header file in your programs.

Using Structures and Unions

Structures and unions enable you to keep related data together in one object. This section shows you how to create structures and unions, and how to implement them in your programs. Although a structure and a union may look similar, they are handled differently.

Building Structures from Different Types

Like an array, a *structure* stores a group of data. However, the member objects in a structure do not have to be of the same type. A structure can contain members that are either basic, derived, or aggregate data types. Thus, unlike arrays, structures do not overlap the categories of derived and aggregate types—a structure is strictly an aggregate object.

Although the member objects of a structure may have different types, member objects are usually related functionally. A medical record is a good example of a structure. Such a record contains character arrays for the patient's name, integers for age, and floating-point numbers for weight, as well as many other kinds of information. Structures provide a way to keep all the information together where it is needed. Figure 4.7 shows a typical structure.

Figure 4.7.

A structure data type object.

```
struct med_rec {
    char name [30];
    int age;
    double weight;
};
```

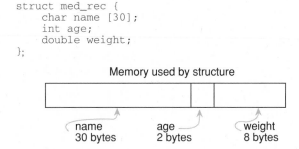

Memory used by structure

name
30 bytes

age
2 bytes

weight
8 bytes

The structure object in Figure 4.7 contains three member objects. One member in the structure has an aggregate data type, and the other two members have basic data types. The structure member with an aggregate type is name, which is a character array. The other objects, age and weight, have basic data types.

A structure type declaration has the following basic form:

struct *tag-name*_{opt} {
  *member-list*_{opt}
} *identifier-list*_{opt} ;

In the first line, the struct keyword signals the compiler that a structure declaration is about to begin. The *tag-name* gives the structure type a name and makes it possible for you to declare a structure type object later in the program. The *tag-name* is optional; you do not have to supply one, but omitting it will prevent declaring later structure objects with this specific structure type. The *member-list* contains the data types and names of the member objects that are included in the structure. The *member-list* is also optional, but the structure type is incomplete until a member list is declared to complete the declaration (see the sidebar "What Is an Incomplete Type?" earlier in this chapter). Finally, the optional *identifier-list* can define one or more structure objects to be used in your program.

The following code fragment is a typical structure declaration that includes a tag name:

```
struct cars{
  char make[31];
  int year;
  double miles;
  double cost;
};
...
struct cars car1, car2;
```

Here `struct` tells the compiler that a structure is being declared. `cars` is the tag name used to declare other objects with this same structure type. The declarations between the braces are the member list, containing the data objects in which the structure's information is stored. Any structure objects defined with this type will have type `struct cars`.

Notice on the last line of this code fragment that the `cars` tag name defines two structure type data objects. The data objects defined each contain all the member variables listed in the structure declaration.

If a structure does not use a tag name, all the data objects of that structure type must be declared immediately following the structure declaration. Without a tag name, the preceding structure declaration would look like this:

```
struct {
  char make[31];
  int year;
  double miles;
  double cost;
} car1, car2;
```

You can create a type definition by using the `typedef` keyword with your structure declaration. `typedef` works like a tag name, but its purpose is to define a synonym for any existing type name. Here, using a `typedef` enables you to create another name for your structure type. If you rewrote this structure declaration with a `typedef`, you would have the following form:

```
typedef struct {
  char make[31];
  int year;
  double miles;
  double cost;
}  CAR_TYPE;
...
CAR_TYPE car1, car2;
```

You can even use a tag name with the `typedef` statement if you like, but using both is redundant.

You use the structure member operator (.) to access a member of a structure. To get the `miles` member of the `car1` object, for example, you use this statement:

```
x = car1.miles
```

Here the value stored in the `miles` member of the `car1` object is assigned to the variable x.

If you have two objects with the same structure type, you can assign all the values in one structure to the other structure with one statement:

```
car1 = car2;
```

The value of each member in `car2` is assigned to the corresponding member in `car1`. This kind of assignment can be handy for initializing structures from existing structures.

When you are using pointers to locate and control structures, accessing a member object is a little different. To access a member through a pointer to `struct`, you must use the structure pointer operator (`->`). The following code fragment demonstrates the use of the structure pointer operator:

```
struct demo_s {
  char d_str[20];
  int d_int;
  double d_flt;
};
struct demo_s d_struct1;
struct demo_s *d_ptr;
d_ptr = & d_struct1;
...
i = d_ptr -> d_int;
```

In the first five lines, a structure is declared. On the sixth line, an object of type `struct demo_s` is declared. This structure type object is `d_struct1`, and the seventh and eighth lines set up a pointer to the `d_struct1` data object. On the last line of the code fragment, the `->` operator is used to fetch the value stored in the `d_int` member of the `d_struct1` structure type object. The value stored in this instance of `d_int` is assigned to the variable i.

To determine the size of a structure object, you use the `sizeof` operator. The value returned by `sizeof` may be different from the value you calculate by summing the sizes of the members of the structure. The reason for the discrepancy is that the compiler may insert empty space in your structure to control the alignment of member objects.

Bit-fields are data formats you can use only inside a structure. A bit-field lets you declare signed or unsigned integers from 1 to 16 bits wide. A bit-field also can store multiple values in one byte of information. The declaration of a bit-field variable has this form:

```
type-specifier bitfield-id : width
```

The `type-specifier` determines what type of value is stored in the bit-field. The possible data types are char, unsigned char, int, and unsigned int. `bitfield-id` specifies the name of the bit-field. If the bit field name is left blank, space for the bit-field is allocated but is inaccessible. This feature helps you match hardware registers in which all the available bits are not used. The `width` specifies the size (as a number of bits) of the bit-field. The colon must be coded as shown; it signals that the declaration is a bit-field.

Bit-fields are allocated memory from the low-order bit to the high-order bit within a word of memory. A word of memory is 2 bytes, or 16 bits. Thus, bit-fields are allocated bit sequences from right to left within a word.

Signed integers in a bit-field are stored in *2's-complement* form. The leftmost bit of a 2's-complement number is used as the *sign bit*. (A sign bit is 0 if the number is positive, and 1 if the number is negative.) Therefore, if the bit-field type is int, the leftmost bit is a sign bit. If the data type is unsigned, the leftmost bit is a normal bit. For most applications, you will not need to concern yourself with the internal details of 2's complement numbers.

Using Unions To Give Alternate Views of Structures and Objects

A *union* is a derived type, not an aggregate type. Unions exhibit many of the syntactical and functional characteristics of structures but use memory differently. Like a structure, a union can declare a group of different data objects, but in a union only one member is active at a time. The effect is much like overlaying several transparencies on a slide-projector at once. Every union member thus has an offset of zero from the beginning of the union.

A union type object is allocated enough memory to hold only the largest member found in the union declaration. If a smaller member is active, the remaining space is *padding* (wasted space). Figure 4.8 shows memory allocation for a typical union object.

Figure 4.8.

How a union uses memory space.

```
union demo_u
{
    int i;
    double d;
} d_u;
```

Eight bytes of memory are allocated for a demo_u **type** object.

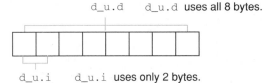

d_u.d   d_u.d **uses all 8 bytes.**

d_u.i   d_u.i **uses only 2 bytes.**

You can see from Figure 4.8 that only enough memory to hold only the d member is allocated. Because d is declared as a double, eight bytes of memory are allocated. These eight bytes are the total memory allocated for the union. Remember that a union declaration allocates memory only for the largest object in the union—in this case, d.

Unions are declared using syntax almost identical to that for structures. The only difference is the union keyword itself, as follows:

union *tag-name*_{opt} {
   *member-list*_{opt}
} *identifier-list*_{opt} ;

The same rules for tag names, member lists, and member identifier lists apply to union declarations as apply to structures.

Union members can be accessed with the structure member operator (.) and structure pointer operator (->), the same as for structures. You must be aware, however, of which member is active at the moment—the compiler makes no effort to keep track of an active member for you.

You can even access a union using two different member names without reinitializing the union. This action results in the overlay appearance of unions. You can look at the same object in different ways, just by using a different member name. Always remember, however, that the data does not change when you do this; only your perspective changes.

Perhaps the most common use of the ability to view data in multiple concurrent ways with a union is to describe the system registers as both a set of word (integer) objects and a set of byte (character) objects. Microsoft C/C++ provides such a union, named _REGS, in the dos.h header file. _REGS is the union of two structures, _WORDREGS and _BYTEREGS. Thus, all the required declarations look like this:

```
struct _WORDREGS {
    unsigned int  ax, bx, cx, dx, si, di, cflag, flags;
```

```
};

struct _BYTEREGS {
    unsigned char  al, ah, bl, bh, cl, ch, dl, dh;
};

union      _REGS {
    struct    _WORDREGS x;
    struct    _BYTEREGS h;
};
```

As you can see in the _REGS declaration, the x member is a structure describing the word registers, and h is a structure describing the byte registers. The following code fragment illustrates how to use the _REGS union to set up a call to the BIOS write-characters video routine (with Microsoft C/C++'s int86() built-in function):

```
unsigned ch = '*';
int attr = 7;
int  count = 20;
...
REGS reg;
...
reg.h.ah=9; reg.h.al=ch; reg.x.cx=count; reg.x.bx=attr;
int86(0x10,&reg,&reg);
```

Note in this code fragment that the AX register is set up one byte at a time (using AH and AL). The CX register, however, is initialized with an integer (word) with the expression reg.x.cx = count.

You can write an initializer list with a union declaration, but you must remember that only the first member of the union will be initialized. Consider, for example, the following code fragment:

```
struct itype {
  int a, b;
};
struct dtype {
  double c, d;
};
...
union alltype {
  struct itype;
  struct dtype;
};
```

Given the preceding `union` declaration, the following lines illustrate valid and invalid uses of a union initializer list:

```
union alltype = { 1, 2 };                /* Okay: First member init */
union alltype = { 3.1316, 6.28 };        /* Invalid: Not first member */
union alltype = { 1, 2, 3.1416, 6.28 };    /* Invalid: 2 members */
```

Using Pointers to Functions

You already know how easily you can call C functions. You simply write the function's name followed by a list of arguments enclosed in parentheses. Calling a function this way is fine for almost all your programming tasks. C provides a more versatile way to call functions, however, that gives you greater control of your program. You can use a pointer to call a function. A pointer to a function is like any other pointer: It stores the address of the function. When the pointer is dereferenced, the function is executed.

Declaring and Initializing Pointers to Functions

Using pointers with functions differs from using pointers with data objects when the pointer is dereferenced. When you dereference a pointer to a data object, you get the value addressed by the pointer. Dereferencing a pointer to a function does not retrieve a value. Instead, the function is called.

Before a pointer to a function can be initialized or used, it must be declared, as is true for any other pointer type. The declaration of a pointer to a function has the following form:

```
type ( *function-pointer ) ( parameter-list_opt );
```

`type` specifies the data type of the value returned by the function. The compiler requires the return type of the function to carry out its type checking tasks, and particularly to determine whether the pointer is valid for the function to which it is pointing.

The `function-pointer` specifies the name of the function pointer you will use. The `*` is the indirection operator, and indicates that a pointer is being declared and must be present. The function-pointer name is enclosed in parentheses because the function call parentheses (the ones enclosing the argument list) have a higher operator precedence than the indirection operator. Therefore, if the function-pointer name is not enclosed in parentheses, you declare a function returning a pointer to type. Look at the next two declarations:

```
int ( *f_ptr ) ( ... );  /* Pointer to a function
                             returning int */
```

```
int *f_ptr ( ... );      /* Function returning a pointer
                               to an integer */
```

The first declaration properly declares a pointer to a function, but the second declaration declares a function that returns a pointer to an integer value. The parentheses in the first declaration force f_ptr to be evaluated as a function pointer.

The *parameter-list* is an optional part of the function-pointer declaration. Omitting a function parameter list, when declaring functions or pointers to functions, means that the function does not expect any arguments (not that they do not matter). If the function does accept arguments, you must specify the type of each argument to satisfy type-checking requirements. (Remember that formal parameter names can be omitted from a prototype, but type names cannot.)

You can declare an array of function pointers by including an array declarator in the function-pointer declaration. Use the following syntax:

```
type ( *function-pointer[bound] ) ( parameter-list );
```

This function-pointer declaration is like a regular function-pointer declaration, but with one difference: The *bound* value specifies how many elements are in the array of pointers to functions. The square brackets are the array declarator and must be coded as shown.

After you declare the function pointer, you still have to initialize the pointer before you can use it. To initialize the pointer, you must assign the address of the function to the pointer. Using the function's name by itself (without the function-call parentheses and argument list that normally follow a function name) yields the address of the function. You can then assign the address to the function pointer. The next line of code initializes a function pointer:

```
f_ptr = printf;
```

The address of the printf() function is assigned to the function pointer f_ptr. Because printf is a function name, the address-of operator (&) is not needed to take its address.

Calling Functions with a Pointer Reference

Using a pointer to a function to call a function is as easy as dereferencing the pointer. You can call a function through a pointer in two ways. First, when you dereference a pointer to a function, the function is called. Second, you can call the function with normal function call syntax, thanks to the new requirements of the ANSI standard for C. The following code fragment shows how to call a function through a pointer:

```
void (__far *my_clr ) ( short area );
my_clr = &_clearscreen;
...
( *my_clr ) ();  /* Old way, but still valid */
...
my_clr( _GCLEARSCREEN );        /* New ANSI way, sometimes preferred */
```

The first line of this code fragment declares a function pointer, my_clr, as a
_far pointer to the library routine _clearscreen(), having a single parameter.
On the second line, the function pointer my_clr is assigned the address of the
_clearscreen() function. Because my_clr has the address of _clearscreen(),
that function is executed when my_clr is dereferenced. The last line uses the
new ANSI method of calling a function through a pointer. This method is
preferred for its simplicity and clarity. You will often want to use the old
syntax, however, to highlight the fact that a pointer is being used to call a
function (especially if there are many pointers to functions in the program).

Listing 4.5 demonstrates the use of pointers to functions in the context of an
entire program.

Listing 4.5. car.c. A program that uses pointers to functions.

```
1   /* CAR.C  Using pointers to functions. Declaring,
2              initializing, and dereferencing function
3              pointers. */
4
5   #include <stdio.h>
6   #include <stdlib.h>
7   #include <graph.h>
8
9   void calc_mileage( void );
10  void maint_schedule( void );
11  void calc_cost( void );
12
13  main()
14  {
15    void ( *car_ptr[3] ) ( void );
16    int i = 0;
17
18    car_ptr[0] = calc_mileage;
19    car_ptr[1] = maint_schedule;
20    car_ptr[2] = calc_cost;
21
22    while( ( i < 1 ) || ( i > 3 ) ) {
```

```
23      _clearscreen( _GCLEARSCREEN );
24      printf( "Car Utilities\n\n" );
25      printf( "1. Gas mileage calculations.\n" );
26      printf( "2. Preventive maintenance schedule.\n" );
27      printf( "3. Calculate cost per mile.\n " );
28      printf( "\n\nEnter option => " );
29      scanf( "%d", &i );
30    }
31    ( *car_ptr[i-1]) ();
32
33    return 0;
34  }
35  void calc_mileage( void )
36  {
37    double begin;
38    double end;
39    double gallons;
40
41    _clearscreen( _GCLEARSCREEN );
42    printf( "-- Calculate mileage --\n" );
43    printf( "\n\n" );
44    printf( "\nEnter your beginning mileage => " );
45    scanf( "%lf", &begin );
46    printf( "\nEnter your ending mileage => " );
47    scanf( "%lf", &end );
48    printf( "\nEnter gallons of gas used => " );
49    scanf( "%lf", &gallons );
50    printf( "\n\n\n" );
51    printf( "Your mileage was %f miles per gallon.\n",
52            ( ( end - begin ) / gallons ) );
53    return;
54  }
55
56  void maint_schedule( void )
57  {
58    int miles;
59    int result;
60
61    _clearscreen( _GCLEARSCREEN );
62    printf( "-- Maintenance Scheduler --\n" );
63    printf ( "\n\n\n" );
64    printf( "Enter your mileage to the nearest thousand "
```

Listing 4.5. Continued.

```
65              "miles => " );
66     scanf( "%d", &miles );
67     printf( "\n\n\n" );
68     if( ( miles % 3000 ) == 0 )
69       printf( "Time to change the oil.\n\n" );
70     if( ( miles % 5000 ) == 0 )
71       printf( "Time to rotate the tires.\n\n" );
72     if( ( miles % 10000 ) == 0 )
73       printf( "Time for a tune up.\n\n" );
74     return;
75
76   }
77
78   void calc_cost( void )
79   {
80     double begin;
81     double end;
82     double allowance = 0.25;
83
84     _clearscreen( _GCLEARSCREEN );
85     printf( "-- Calculate Cost --\n" );
86     printf( "\n\n\n" );
87     printf( "\nEnter your beginning mileage => " );
88     scanf( "%lf", &begin );
89     printf( "\nEnter your ending mileage => " );
90     scanf( "%lf", &end );
91     printf( "\n\n\n" );
92     printf( "Your cost of operation is %6.2f",
93             ( ( end - begin ) * allowance ) );
94     return;
95   }
```

In Listing 4.5, an array of pointers is used to store the address of each function. The declaration for the array of pointers is in line 15. Notice there that the type of the function and the type of the function's arguments are used in the declaration of the function pointers. This information is necessary for the compiler to check the values passed to and from the function. Even though the parameter list and return type are void here, they must still be coded in the function-pointer declaration.

In lines 18 through 20, the addresses of the functions are assigned to the function pointers. To get the address of a function, you just reference the name without the function-call parentheses.

In line 31, the appropriate function is called. The expression i-1 converts the menu selection to a zero-origin array index. For the function to be called, its pointer must be dereferenced. To ensure that the function call is made correctly, enclose the dereferenced pointer in parentheses (the reason is again operator precedence). Be sure also to include an argument list. Without it, the function cannot be called. Even though the functions in this program do not expect arguments, the void (empty) argument list must be included in the function call.

Using Pointers with Dynamic Memory

You have seen how memory is allocated for constants, variables, and data structures. When you declare any of these objects, your program automatically allocates the memory needed to store these data items. In particular, these declarations set aside space for variables *in the bounds* of your program. Thus, your .EXE file on disk will be larger, for one thing.

Further, internal variables are useful, but they do not enable you to handle a changing amount of data. To handle more data, you can use arrays. In fact, you can declare an array that will hold more items than you plan to use. Declaring an array larger than you need, however, wastes memory space. As programs and data take more room, you have to be careful of the amount of memory you use. Modern PCs may be bigger and more powerful, but so are the applications. Always be aware of the amount of memory space you use.

The best way to deal with varying amounts of data is to use *dynamic allocation*. Dynamically allocated objects enable you to allocate memory for your data while your program is running. They are dynamic because the amount of space they require can be determined at run time. Dynamic objects are more efficient because you allocate and use memory space only when you need it. When a dynamic object is not needed, the space used by the object can be deallocated. The deallocated space is then available for other uses.

This section shows you how to set up and use dynamic objects. You learn how to declare pointers that can be used to access dynamic objects, how to allocate memory for dynamic objects, and how to free the memory so that it is available for other uses.

Your C Program and Dynamic Memory

When you allocate memory dynamically, your computer's memory resources are used more efficiently. Using memory more efficiently sounds like a good idea, but the following example shows just how much difference dynamic memory can make.

A program that handles customer-account information could have a structure like this:

```
typedef struct {
  char first_name[30];
  char last_name[30];
  char cust_street[30];
  char cust_city[30];
  char cust_state[3];
  int cust_zip;
  char account_num[10];
  double account_bal;
  double account_limit;
  int overdue;
}  cust_type;
...
cust_type c_array[100];
```

Each character in the structure requires one byte, each integer requires two bytes, and each `double` requires eight bytes. An object with this structure type requires 154 bytes of memory. (A byte is wasted aligning the integer `cust_zip` on a word boundary.) If you have ever kept track of customer information, you know that the structure in this example lacks fields for much of the information you need. Even this small structure, however, shows how much space can be used in your program when the array of 100 structures is declared—if you do not use dynamic memory.

The program that contains the preceding structure has more than 15K of memory for the array of structures. That much data space is set aside in your program whether or not you use the entire array. If you use only 30 of the array elements, you are left with 11K of wasted memory space. The 15K array takes up space on disk in your .EXE file, too.

To avoid wasting so much of your memory resources, you can allocate space for your data dynamically—on the C heap. This memory is not contained in your program. When your program begins execution, the program is given a certain amount of memory. The memory outside your program—the heap—is *dynamic memory,* which is available to you if you use the proper memory-allocation functions. Figure 4.9 shows how a typical program uses memory.

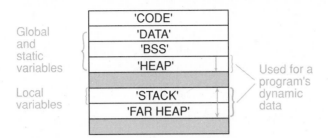

Figure 4.9.

How a C program uses memory.

In Figure 4.9, the amount of memory allocated to each section depends on the memory model used to compile the program. Although the actual amounts of memory can change from one memory model to another, all Microsoft C/C++ programs use memory in the same basic way.

Your program stores the data it uses in three areas: in the program itself, on the system stack, and on the heap. Global and static variables are stored in the program itself. The space taken up by these variables is a permanent part of your program. You can change the allocation of global and static variables only by recompiling the program.

Local variables (variables local to a function or an interior block of a function) are stored on the system stack. These variables are created, and space is allocated for them, only when the function or block of code begins execution. They are destroyed (and the space is released) when execution exits the function or block. In a sense, local variables are dynamically allocated and destroyed, but this is not what the term *dynamic memory* really means.

The *heap* is the area of memory reserved for use by your program's dynamically created variables. From the heap, you acquire the dynamic memory for the program. To acquire this space, you use the Microsoft C/C++ memory-allocation functions.

When you use the heap to store data, you specify exactly how much memory you want. By using dynamic memory, you avoid wasting space and thus save room for other data. Using the heap saves room on your disk, too, because dynamic memory is not contained in your program.

If you acquire memory from the heap, be sure to release the memory when you are through with it. If you do not deallocate the acquired memory, you could run out of memory. Using dynamic memory is more efficient, but only if you use it correctly.

An advantage of using dynamic data is that you don't have to determine how much memory you need when you write your program. You can design the program so that it calculates the amount of memory needed while the program runs. That way, you let the program make the most efficient use of the memory resources available.

Using Dynamic Memory

To use dynamic memory, follow these four steps:

1. Determine how much memory you need.

2. Allocate the memory.

3. Store (and use) a pointer to the acquired memory space.

4. Deallocate the memory when you are through with it.

You can allocate memory space in two ways. First, you can allocate memory for a specified number of objects. Microsoft C/C++ determines the size of the objects. All you have to do is calculate the number of objects you will use. Second, you can allocate a specified number of bytes of memory. For this method, you have to calculate the allocation amount as a product of how much space each object will require and how many objects will be used. Each method is covered here with its corresponding allocation function.

The first function is the `calloc()` function. It requires two arguments: one to specify the number of objects for which you will acquire memory and the other to tell `calloc()` what *type* of object you will be storing. `calloc()` performs all the calculations necessary to determine exactly how much memory is required. The other function for allocating memory is the `malloc()` function. This function allocates a specified amount of memory. With `malloc()`, you are responsible for determining how much memory is required. Usually, you code a formula that determines how much memory you need.

The function prototype for the `calloc()` function is as follows:

```
void *calloc( size_t nmemb, size_t size );
```

Notice that the declaration for this function does not declare a pointer to a function, but declares a function that returns a pointer. `calloc()` returns a `void` pointer to the allocated memory in the heap. The function returns a `NULL` pointer if the memory could not be allocated.

The *nmemb* argument specifies the number of members for which space will be allocated. You must provide a way for your program to determine how many members need allocated memory. The *size* argument specifies the size of the data object for which you are allocating space.

Microsoft C/C++ has an operator you can use to supply a value for the size argument of the `calloc()` function. The `sizeof` operator calculates the size of any data object given to it as an operand. The following code fragment shows how the `sizeof` operator works:

```
int i;
char c_a[] = "This is a string.";
float x;
double y = 4;
```

```
printf( "i occupies %d bytes.\n", sizeof( i ) );
printf( "c_a occupies %d bytes.\n", sizeof( c_a ) );
printf( "x occupies %d bytes.\n", sizeof( x ) );
printf( "y occupies %d bytes.\n", sizeof( y ) );
printf( "A long double requires %d bytes.\n",
        sizeof( long double ) );
```

The calloc() function and the sizeof operator are useful tools that can handle most of your dynamic-memory allocation needs. Usually, you will want to allocate memory for a number of data items. The easiest way is to use the calloc() function along with the sizeof operator to supply the size of the object.

You can also compute the number of bytes required for the dynamic data and request that amount of memory in bytes. This is done using malloc(), the second memory-allocation function. Note the following function prototype for malloc():

```
void *malloc( size_t size );
```

The malloc() function allocates a block of memory from the heap, and the size of the block in bytes is specified by the size argument. Like calloc(), malloc() returns a void pointer to the beginning of the allocated block of memory. malloc() returns NULL if the memory could not be allocated.

After you allocate a block of memory, be sure to test the value returned by either calloc() or malloc() to determine whether the allocation was successful. You need to provide a routine in your program that handles an unsuccessful allocation attempt.

After you allocate a block of memory, you need to assign the block's address to a pointer variable of the correct type. This assignment enables you to keep track of where your data is located, and to free the block of memory when you are through with it. (Freeing the block is especially important; if you do not, you can fill up the heap.) The following code fragment shows how you can store the address for an integer array:

```
int *int_ptr;
...
if( NULL == ( int_ptr = calloc( 500, sizeof( int ) ) ) ) {
  printf( "Could not allocate memory, aborting program. " );
  abort();
}
```

The first line of this code fragment declares a pointer to an integer. The pointer is used to keep track of the beginning address of the allocated block of memory. Inside the if block, the calloc() statement allocates space for an array of 500 integers. The value returned by calloc() is assigned to int_ptr. If the returned value is NULL, calloc() was unable to allocate the block of memory successfully. If calloc() was unsuccessful, the rest of the if block is executed and the program is aborted.

The `realloc()` function can resize an allocated block of memory. Note the function prototype of `realloc()`:

```
void *realloc( void *block, size_t size );
```

The value returned from `realloc()` is a pointer to the reallocated block of memory. The address of the new block of memory can be different from the address of the old block. If `realloc()` returns NULL, the original block still exists, but could not be reallocated.

The `block` argument is a pointer to the block to be reallocated. (Because the argument type is `void*`, you can call this function with any pointer type.) The `size` argument tells `realloc()` how much space is to be used for the reallocated block of memory. The amount of space used for the new block can be more or less than the amount of space used for the old block of memory. If the new size is less than the old size, as much of the old block as will fit is copied to the new block of memory (the block is truncated). If the new size is greater than the old size, the extra space in the new block should be considered uninitialized. `realloc()` is very inefficient, however, if called many times for small amounts of RAM.

`realloc()` has two more interesting and very useful features. First, if you call `realloc()` with the block pointer set to NULL, it acts just like `malloc()` and allocates the block (if possible). Second, if the `size` argument is zero but the block pointer is not NULL, the block is freed just as if `free()` had been called.

Perhaps the most important part of managing the heap is releasing old allocations. If you never release acquired dynamic memory during program execution, you may fill up the heap. Being inconsistent about releasing dynamic memory can be just as bad. If you free only some heap objects, you may *fragment the heap*. This means that dynamic data objects are scattered throughout the heap, with relatively small free areas between them. You may find, however, that not one of those smaller free areas is sufficient for the next allocation request.

Therefore, when you are through with a dynamic memory block, you need to free that memory for other uses. The `free()` function deallocates a block of memory allocated with the `calloc()`, `malloc()`, or `realloc()` function. Here is the function prototype for the `free()` function:

```
void free( void *block );
```

The `block` argument is a pointer to the beginning address of the allocated block of memory. This argument is declared as a `void` pointer so that any type of pointer can be passed to `free()` as an argument. Because the `free()` function does not need to return a value, `free()` is declared as a `void` function.

Listing 4.6 shows a program that uses the heap to store a two-dimensional array. The unique thing about this array is that the program prompts you to enter the number of elements in the array. This array is truly dynamic because the space for it is allocated during the execution of the program.

Listing 4.6. dyna.c. A program that uses dynamic memory and arrays.

```
1   /* DYNA.C  This program uses dynamic memory to simulate a
2               two-dimensional array. The number of elements
3               in the array is specified by the user at
4               run time. */
5
6   #include <stdio.h>
7   #include <stdlib.h>
8   #include <malloc.h>
9   #include <graph.h>
10
11  main()
12  {
13    int *i_ptr;
14    int row;
15    int column;
16    size_t nmemb;
17    int i, j, k = 0;
18
19    _clearscreen( _GCLEARSCREEN );
20    printf( "\n\nThis program simulates a two "
21            "dimensional array of integers." );
22    printf( "\n\nEnter the number of rows => " );
23    scanf( "%d", &row );
24    printf( "\n\nEnter the number of columns => " );
25    scanf( "%d", &column );
26
27    nmemb = row * column;
28    if( NULL == ( i_ptr = calloc( nmemb, sizeof( int ) ) ) ){
29      printf( "Not able to allocate memory.\n" );
30      printf( "Aborting program." );
31      abort();
32    }
33
34    for( i = 0; i < row; i++ ) {
35      for( j = 0; j < column; j++ ) {
36        i_ptr[ ( i * column + j ) ] = k;
37        k++;
38      }
39    }
40
```

Listing 4.6. Continued.

```
41    for( i = 0; i < row; i++ ) {
42      for( j = 0; j < column; j++ ) {
43        printf( "%4d  ", i_ptr[ ( i * column + j ) ]  );
44      }
45      printf( "\n" );
46    }
47
48    free( i_ptr );
49
50    return 0;
51  }
```

In line 8 of Listing 4.6, the malloc.h header file is included. This header file contains the declarations for the memory-management functions. The alloc.h header file is required if you want to use the calloc(), malloc(), realloc(), and free() functions.

In line 13, the integer pointer i_ptr is declared, which points to the beginning of the block of allocated memory. An integer pointer is used so that indexes into the block of allocated memory can be performed correctly.

Lines 19 through 25 are a routine that prompts the user for the number of elements to include in the array. The ability to specify (or compute) the number of elements at run time is one of the important benefits of using dynamic allocation. Because the array is allocated dynamically, the user can enter a different size for the array each time the program is run.

Line 27 calculates the number of elements in the array and stores the value in nmemb. The value stored in nmemb determines how much space will be allocated for the array when calloc() is called in line 28. If the calloc() call in line 28 is unsuccessful, the if statement falls through and the program terminates abnormally.

The allocated memory is initialized with the values of the array elements in lines 34 through 39. The elements in the array are initialized on a row-by-row basis, starting at the left of each row and moving to the right. The outer loop is used to step down the array row by row. The inner loop moves across the array column by column.

Because the memory is allocated dynamically, a regular two-dimensional array subscript cannot be used directly (hold that thought for a moment). Instead, the address for each element in the array has to be calculated. Line 36 shows the formula that calculates the correct array index. The expression i * column calculates the current row position. column is the number of columns in each row, and i is the number of the current row. Multiplying i by column gives the offset of the beginning of the current row. Adding j to the offset of the current row gives the offset of the current element. This expression calculates the offset of the current element from the beginning of the allocated memory block. The offset of the current array element can be used with the pointer i_ptr to determine the exact memory location of the current array element.

When the exact location of an array element is known, a data value can be stored in, or read from, the array element. In line 36, the value of the variable k is assigned to an array element. In the loop in lines 41 through 44, the printf() function in line 43 displays the value of each of the array elements.

Finally, notice the statement in line 48. The free() function deallocates the memory used to store the array. When you are through with a block of memory, be sure to deallocate that memory. Deallocating portions of memory that you no longer need frees the memory for other uses.

Now return to the idea of using array subscripts on a dynamically allocated array. It is true that you cannot use subscripts directly, but you can use subscript notation with a dynamically allocated array. You will, however, have to use enclosing parentheses and the indirection operator to access the array. Listing 4.7 shows how to do this.

Listing 4.7. newdyna.c. Using array subscripts with a dynamically allocated array.

```
1   #include <stdio.h>
2   #include <stdlib.h>
3   #include <malloc.h>
4   #include <graph.h>
5
6   #define MAXX 8
7   #define MAXY 8
8
9   main()
10  {
11    int (*iarray)[MAXX][MAXY];
12    size_t nmemb;
13    int i, j, k = 0;
14
15    _clearscreen( _GCLEARSCREEN );
16
17    nmemb = MAXX * MAXY;
18    if( NULL == ( iarray = calloc( nmemb, sizeof( int ) ) ) ){
19      printf( "Not able to allocate memory.\n" );
```

Listing 4.7. Continued.

```
20        printf( "Aborting program." );
21        abort();
22    }
23
24    for( i = 0; i < MAXX; i++ ) {
25      for( j = 0; j < MAXY; j++ ) {
26        (*iarray)[i][j] = k++;
27      }
28    }
29
30    for( i = 0; i < MAXX; i++ ) {
31      for( j = 0; j < MAXY; j++ ) {
32        printf( "%4d   ", (*iarray)[i][j]  );
33      }
34      printf( "\n" );
35    }
36
37    free( iarray );
38
39    return 0;
40  }
```

The MAXX and MAXY macros are provided (in lines 6 and 7) to control the array bounds (and to simplify the example a little). Note how the pointer to the dynamic array is declared in line 11. This pointer is no longer a simple pointer to int; it is now a pointer to a multidimensional array.

Note carefully that parentheses are used in line 11 to surround the pointer name: (*iarray). The parentheses are required because the subscript operator ([ ]) has higher precedence than the indirection operator. Therefore, omitting the parentheses would cause the declaration to be interpreted as an array of pointers to int, rather than the desired pointer to an array of int.

Now that the pointer is properly declared as a pointer to an array of int, reference can be made to array elements using the subscript operator, as shown in lines 26 and 32. Note again, however, that you must still use the surrounding parentheses to force the grouping of operators.

Exercises

The following exercises let you practice using arrays, strings, and structures:

1. Write a program that declares and initializes an integer array. After the array is initialized, add a different value to each element in the array. For element 0, add the value 1; for element 1, add the value 2; and so on.

2. Use the `strlen()` function to calculate the length of a string you enter. Use the `strcat()` function to concatenate at least three strings you enter.

3. Create an array of structures with any kind of members you want. Initialize and print the array of structures.

4. Write a program that uses an array of pointers to functions instead of a `switch` statement.

5. Modify the program you created in exercise 3 to place the array of structures on the heap. Here is a thought-provoking question: How are you going to access a member of a structure that is both an array element and is located by a pointer? Experiment until you have the method down pat.

Summary

This chapter discussed some of the most important topics in C programming: derived types, aggregate types, and most of all, pointers. The following important points were covered:

- *A pointer is a data object that contains the address of another object.* Accessing an object through a pointer is called *address indirection.*

- *In a declaration, the indirection operator * declares a pointer type object.* In the rest of your program, the indirection operator * dereferences a pointer.

- *When you dereference a pointer, you obtain the value stored at the address pointed to.* It is important to remember the distinction between a pointer used as an object itself (that happens to contain an address) and a pointer used as a locator for another data object (when it is dereferenced).

- *The & symbol yields the address of an object.* This symbol is not needed to take the address of arrays and functions. Referencing an array or function by name alone yields the address of the array or function.

- *An array is a data object that contains several members.* All members of an array have the same data type. Arrays can be accessed using subscript notation or using pointer notation; the two methods are equivalent.

■ *A string is simply stored in a character array.* A string does, however, contain a special terminating character: the null character, \0.

■ *A structure is a data object that contains several members.* The members of a structure can have different data types.

■ *A union is a structure-like object in which only one member is active at a given time.* Unions are most frequently used to give an alternate view of an object.

■ *A function can be referenced and called with a pointer to the function.* Dereferencing a pointer to a function invokes that function. The new ANSI standards permit the function pointer to be used with normal function-call syntax, as well.

■ *To make more efficient use of your computer's memory, you can use dynamic memory—the C heap.* Memory is then allocated outside your program while it runs. `calloc()` and `free()` are two of the most commonly used functions that handle dynamic memory.

Building, Compiling, and Testing Microsoft C/C++ Programs

This chapter shows you how to create larger and more useful programs with Microsoft C/C++'s project-management facilities. In earlier chapters, you learned how to use functions to organize and group related C statements. In this chapter, you see how to organize and group related functions into separate source files.

As you create larger, more powerful projects, you will find it difficult to keep all the functions in a single source file. You can keep track of what your project is doing by combining related functions into separate source files. You can then compile these source files separately to create your project. Another benefit of combining related functions into separate source files is that you can easily reuse the groups of functions in other projects.

In this chapter, you learn how to create projects that use several source files. You learn also how to create source files that are composed of groups of related functions. You then see how to combine the source files into powerful projects.

Using Several Source Files for One Program

As your programming projects get larger and more involved, you will want to package them in several source files or modules. Dividing a project into smaller pieces has the following advantages:

- *Following your program's logic is easier.* If all the code for a large project were contained in a single source file, the size of the file would make the program hard to follow. Breaking the program into smaller, logically re-lated pieces makes it easier to see the overall design of the program.

- *The process of debugging and modifying your program is easier.* Having your program divided into source files makes isolating a problem easier. You can quickly find which group of functions is causing the problem.

- *You can develop libraries of functions.* As you develop large projects, you will probably create functions that can be used extensively. Grouping the useful functions that you write into source files makes it easy to use those functions in other projects.

Deciding What To Put in a Source File

When you have a project that is large enough, you need to decide how to divide your functions into separate source files. You need also to consider how you can easily debug, modify, and reuse those source files. All good engineering is modular.

When you start dividing your functions into source files, be sure to keep related functions in one source file. If, for example, you keep all your data input functions in one source file, you will have only one source file to debug when you have an input problem. With all the related functions in one source file, you do not have to search through pages of listings to find the function you need to fix. Also, keep the data a function needs in the same source file as the function. This strategy helps prevent unintentional changes to data values.

Create groups of functions you can modify easily. For instance, if all the sorting functions for a database project are in one source file, you can make changes to these functions without disturbing other parts of the project. Organize your functions so that all the modifications to a function can be made in one source file.

Divide your functions so that you have groups of functions that can easily be included in other programs. As you develop bigger and more powerful pro-grams, you are likely to create functions that are useful in a number of other programs. Breaking these functions into groups makes it easier to reuse the functions in other programming projects.

However you divide your programs, just remember that you can have only one source file with a main() function. You can place any other functions you want in that source file, but one—and only one—source file can contain a main() function. Some projects are made so that the primary source file contains a main() function that has the sole purpose of calling all the other functions as they are needed.

Other projects are designed so that the main source file contains all the specialized code for that project. Any other source files are included as needed. The CW program is an example of this kind of design. CW comprises one main source file plus two other source files to handle the keyboard-input functions. CW is a program that helps you develop your Morse code skills. The program is designed primarily to help you learn Morse code for a ham radio license. In this chapter, however, the CW program is included to illustrate the features of a programming project that uses separate source files.

Listings 5.1, 5.2, 5.3, and 5.4 present the code for the CW program project. Listing 5.1 is the source code for the cw.c program itself. Listing 5.2 shows source code for the cinsdel.c program. Listing 5.3 shows the source code for stredit.c. Finally, Listing 5.4 shows the source code for utility.c. Detailed explanations of these listings appear at the end of the entire group.

Listing 5.1. cw.c. A Morse code practice program.

```
 1   /*
 2        ---------------------------------------------------------
 3        Program CW.C — Morse code generation and practice
 4        ---------------------------------------------------------
 5   */
 6
 7   #include <stdlib.h>
 8   #include <stdio.h>
 9   #include <conio.h>
10   #include <string.h>
11   #include <dos.h>
12   #include <math.h>
13   #include <time.h>
14   #include <graph.h>
15
16   #include "utility.h"
17   #include "cinsdel.h"
18   #include "stredit.h"
```

Listing 5.1. Continued.

```
19
20   #define maxc 44          /* Maximum number of Morse characters */
21   #define FALSE 0
22   #define TRUE 1
23    /* Define Morse code dots/dashes for each letter */
24   char *codes[] = {
25    "a.-",        "b-...",     "c-.-.",     "d-..",
26    "e.",         "f..-.",     "g--.",      "h....",     "i..",
27    "j.---",      "k-.-",      "l.-..",     "m--",       "n-.",
28    "o---",       "p.--.",     "q--.-",     "r.-.",      "s...",
29    "t-",         "u..-",      "v...-",     "w.--",      "x-..-",
30    "y-.--",      "z--..",     "0-----",    "1.----",    "2..---",
31    "3...--",     "4....-",    "5.....",    "6-....",    "7--...",
32    "8---..",     "9----.",    "..--.-",    ",--..--",   "?..--..",
33    "--....-",    ":---...",   ";-.-.-.",   "(-.--.-",   ")-.--.-"
34   };
35
36   int i,j,k;      /* Globally used subscripts */
37   int ewait;      /* Wait between elements */
38   int lwait;      /* Wait between letters */
39   int wwait;      /* Wait between words */
40   unsigned char keystroke;
41   unsigned char port_data;
42   char fname[80];
43   char workstr[255];
44
45
46   void fancy_box(int x1, int y1, int x2, int y2)
47   { /* Draws a box on screen--upper left = (x1,y1), lower right = (x2,y2) */
48     int i;
49
50     putch_at(x1,y1,201);
51     for ( i = x1+1; i < x2; i++ ) outch(205);
52     outch(187);
53     for ( i = y1+1; i < y2; i++ ) {
54       putch_at( x1,i,186 );
55       putch_at( x2, i, 186 );
56     }
57     putch_at( x1, y2, 200);
58     for ( i = x1+1; i < x2; i ++ ) outch(205);
```

```
59    outch(188);
60  }
61
62  void box_it(int x1, int y1, int x2, int y2)
63  { /* Like preceding, draws a box */
64    int i;
65
66    putch_at( x1, y1, 218 );
67    for ( i = x1+1; i < x2; i++ ) outch(196);
68    outch(191);
69    for ( i = y1+1; i < y2; i++ ) {
70      putch_at( x1, i, 179 );
71      putch_at( x2, i, 179 );
72    }
73    putch_at( x1, y2, 192 );
74    for ( i = x1+1; i < x2; i++ ) outch(196);
75    outch(217);
76  }
77
78  void dash()
79  { /* Send a dash through PC's speaker */
80    soundon(900); delay(150); nosound(); delay(55);
81  }
82
83  void dot()
84  { /* Send a dot through PC's speaker */
85    soundon(900); delay(45); nosound(); delay(55);
86  }
87
88  void find_letter()
89  {
90    i = 0;
91    while ( i < maxc && codes[i][0] != keystroke ) i += 1;
92  }
93
94  void send_letter()
95  { /* Send an individual letter in Morse code */
96    if ( i < maxc ) {
97      for ( j = 1; j < strlen(codes[i]); j++ ) {
98        if ( codes[i][j] == '.' ) dot(); else dash();
99        delay(ewait*5);
100
```

Listing 5.1. Continued.

```
101      delay(lwait*10);
102    }
103  }
104
105  void single_chars()
106  {
107    clearregion(2,12,79,23);
108    cputs_at(2, 12, "Strike \\ to Return to Menu.");
109    cputs_at(2, 13, "Strike Other Keys to Hear Code.");
110    keystroke = ' ';
111    while ( keystroke != '\\' ) {
112      gotoxy (2, 14);
113      keystroke = getch();
114      switch ( keystroke ) {
115        case 32: delay(1000); break;
116        case 13: move_to_next_line(); break;
117        default:
118            if ( keystroke != 27 && keystroke != '\\' ) {
119              find_letter();
120                if (i <= maxc) {
121                   gotoxy( 2, 15);
122                   outch( (short) codes[i][0]);
123                   eraseol();
124                   send_letter();
125                }
126            }
127      }
128    }
129  }
130
131  void show_chars()
132  {
133    clearregion(2,12,79,23);
134    cputs_at(2, 12, "Strike \\ to Return to Menu.");
135    cputs_at(2, 13, "Strike Other Keys to See Code.");
136    keystroke = ' ';
137    while ( keystroke != '\\' ) {
138      gotoxy( 2, 14 );
139      keystroke = getch();
140      switch ( keystroke ) {
```

```
141        case 13: move_to_next_line(); break;
142        default:
143            if ( keystroke != 27 && keystroke != '\\') {
144                find_letter();
145                if ( i <= maxc ) {
146                        cprintf_at( 2, 15, "%s", codes[i] );
147                    eraseol();
148                }
149            }
150        }
151    }
152 }
153
154 void set_stretch()
155 {
156    clearregion(2,12,79,23);
157    cputs_at(2, 12, "  Setting this parameter will \"stretch\" "
158        "the amount of time waited");
159    cputs_at(2, 13, "between the dots and dashes. The startup "
160        "value is 5, which will wait");
161    cputs_at(2, 14, "an extra 25 msecs. Set it to 0 for a "
162        "[mathematically] normal fist.");
163    cputs_at(2, 15, "You may specify a value from 0 to 50.");
164    cputs_at(2, 17, "Enter \"stretch\" parameter: " );
165    cscanf( "%d", &ewait );
166    if ( ewait < 0 ) ewait = 0;
167    if ( ewait > 20 ) ewait = 50;
168 }
169
170 void set_wwait()
171 {
172    clearregion(2,12,79,23);
173    cputs_at(2, 12, "  Setting this parameter will wait an "
174        "extra number of milliseconds");
175    cputs_at(2, 13, "between whole words. The startup value "
176        "is 1000, which will wait");
177    cputs_at(2, 14, "an extra 1 second. Set it to 0 for a "
178        "[mathematically] normal fist.");
179    cputs_at(2, 15,"You may specify a value from 0 to 1000.");
180    cputs_at(2, 17, "Enter Word-Wait parameter: " );
181    cscanf( "%d", &wwait );
182    if ( wwait < 0 ) wwait = 0;
```

Listing 5.1. Continued.

```
183    if ( wwait > 20 ) wwait = 1000;
184  }
185
186  void set_speed()
187  {
188    clearregion(2,12,79,23);
189    cputs_at(2, 12, "  This parameter sets the number of words "
190         "per minute that will be");
191    cputs_at(2, 13, "transmitted for random code groups, lines, "
192         "and text files.");
193    cputs_at(2, 14, "Default set to 3 WPM. If \"stretch\" > 0, "
194         "this will be inaccurate.");
195    cputs_at(2, 15, "Likewise, if word-wait time > 0, "
196         "this will be inaccurate.");
197    cputs_at(2, 16, "You may specify a value from 1 to 25.");
198    cputs_at(2, 17, "Enter Words Per Minute: " );
199    cscanf( "%d", &j );
200    if ( j < 1 ) j = 1;
201    if ( j > 25 ) j = 25;
202    lwait = floor(12000.0 / (25.0*j) - 10.0);   /* was 6000*/
203    if ( lwait < 0 ) lwait = 0;
204  }
205
206  void speed_menu()
207  {
208    while ( 1 ) {
209      clearregion(2,12,79,23);
210      cputs_at(2, 12, "Strike a NUMBER Key To:\r\n");
211      cputs_at(2, 13, "  1-Set Words Per Minute\r\n");
212      cputs_at(2, 14, "  2-Set Character Duration\r\n");
213      cputs_at(2, 15, "  3-Set Word Wait Time\r\n");
214      cputs_at(2, 16, "  x-Go Back to MAIN MENU\r\n");
215      keystroke = getch();
216      switch ( keystroke ) {
217        case '1': set_speed(); break;
218        case '2': set_stretch(); break;
219        case '3': set_wwait(); break;
220        case 'x':
221        case 'X': return;
222      }
```

```
223     }
224   }
225
226   void random_chars()
227   {
228     int again;
229     char buffer[79];
230
231     clearregion(2,12,79,23);
232     cputs_at(2, 12, "I will select a code at random and send it.");
233     cputs_at(2, 13, "You type the letter or character you "
234         "think matches it.");
235     cputs_at(2, 14, "If you miss one, type + to repeat, "
236         "anything else to go on.");
237     cputs_at(2, 15, "Type a \\ to end the random character session.");
238     keystroke = ' '; k = 0;
239     while ( keystroke != '\\' ) {
240       k = random(maxc);
241       again = TRUE;
242       while ( again ) {
243         keystroke = codes[k][0]; i = k; send_letter();
244         cputs_at( 2, 17, "? " );
245         keystroke = getch();
246         if ( keystroke == '\\' ) return;
247         if ( keystroke == codes[k][0] ) {
248           sprintf( buffer, "%c is CORRECT.", keystroke );
249       cputs_at( 2, 18, buffer ); eraseol();
250       again = FALSE;
251         }
252         else {
253           sprintf( buffer, "INCORRECT. That was %s "
254                   "Type + to repeat. ", codes[k] );
255       cputs_at( 2, 18, buffer ); eraseol();
256       keystroke = getch();
257           if ( keystroke != '+' ) again = FALSE;
258         }
259       }
260     }
261   }
262
263   void random_groups()
264   {
```

Listing 5.1. Continued.

```
265    int n;
266    char buffer[79];
267
268    clearregion(2,12,79,23);
269    cputs_at(2, 12, "I will send groups of 5 random codes.");
270    cputs_at(2, 13, "I will also display the codes as they are sent.");
271    cputs_at(2, 14, "You copy the codes until a group is finished, "
272        "and then check the screen.");
273    cputs_at(2, 15, "Strike Enter to go to the next group.");
274    cputs_at(2, 16, "Type a \\ to end the random group session.");
275    keystroke = ' '; k = 0;
276    while ( keystroke != '\\' ) {
277      for ( n = 0; n < 5; n++ ) {
278        k = random(maxc);
279        keystroke = codes[k][0]; i = k;
280        send_letter();
281        sprintf( buffer, "%s", codes[k] );
282        cputs_at( 2 + n * 10, 18, buffer );
283      }
284      keystroke = getch();
285    }
286  }
287
288  void with_edit()
289  {
290    clearregion(2,12,79,23);
291    cputs_at(2, 12, "Type in a line of characters; "
292        "strike Return to send.");
293    cputs_at(2, 13, "Type a line with only \\ in it to quit.");
294    cputs_at(2, 14, "? ");
295    strcpy( workstr, "" );
296    while ( workstr[0] != '\\' ) {
297      strcpy( workstr, "" );
298      edit_text( workstr, 4, 14, 60, 0, 0 );
299      if ( workstr[0] != '\\' ) {
300        delay(500); /* Pause before starting */
301        for ( k = 0; k < strlen(workstr); k++ ) {
302          keystroke = workstr[k];
303          if ( keystroke == ' ' ) delay(lwait*20);
304        find_letter();
```

```
305        if (i <= maxc) send_letter();
306        }
307        soundon(1200); delay(1000); nosound();
308      }
309    }
310  }
311
312  void send_file()
313  {
314    int slen;
315    char *temp = 0;
316    FILE *fspec;
317
318    clearregion(2,12,79,23);
319    cputs_at( 2, 12, "What File Name? " );
320    cscanf( "%s", fname );
321    while (kbhit()) getch(); /* Clear keyboard buffer */
322    if ( NULL != ( fspec = fopen( fname, "r+t" ) ) ) {
323      cputs_at( 2, 13, " *** Press any key to stop ***" );
324      while ( !feof(fspec) && !kbhit() ) {
325        fgets(workstr, 255, fspec );
326        if ( NULL != ( temp = strchr( workstr, '\n' ) ) )
327          *temp = '\0';
328        cputs_at( 2, 15, workstr ); eraseol();
329        slen = strlen( workstr );
330        for ( k = 0; k < slen; k++ ) {
331        if (kbhit()) break;
332        keystroke = workstr[k];
333          if ( keystroke == ' ' ) delay(lwait*20);
334        find_letter();
335        if (i <= maxc) send_letter();
336        }
337      }
338      fclose(fspec);
339    }
340    else
341      {cputs_at( 2, 17, "Unable to open file" ); getche();}
342  }
343
344  void MAIN_MENU()
345  {
346    while( 1 ) {
```

Listing 5.1. Continued.

```
347       clearregion(2,12,79,23);
348       cputs_at(2, 13, "Strike a Function Key.");
349       gotoxy(2, 14);
350       keystroke = getch();
351       if ( keystroke == 0 ) keystroke = getch();
352       switch ( keystroke ) {
353         case 59: single_chars(); break;
354         case 60: show_chars(); break;
355         case 61: random_chars(); break;
356         case 62: random_groups(); break;
357         case 63: with_edit(); break;
358         case 64: send_file(); break;
359         case 65: speed_menu(); break;
360         case 66: _clearscreen( _GCLEARSCREEN );
361                exit( 0 );
362       }
363     }
364 }
365
366 /* ----------------- MAIN PROGRAM BODY ----------------- */
367 void main()
368 {
369   time_t the_time;
370   ewait = 5; lwait = 140; wwait = 500;
371   _clearscreen( _GCLEARSCREEN );
372   /* Initialize the random number seed */
373   srand( (unsigned int) (time( &the_time ) % 0xFFFF ) );
374   fancy_box(1,1,80,10);
375   box_it(1,11,80,24);
376   clearregion(2, 2, 79, 9);
377   cputs_at(2, 2, "                              CW Practice");
378   cputs_at(2, 4, "            F1-Sound Single Characters    "
379       "F2-See Single Characters");
380   cputs_at(2, 5, "            F3-TX Random Characters    "
381       "F4-TX Random Code Groups");
382   cputs_at(2, 6, "            F5-TX Lines From Keyboard    "
383       "F6-TX An ASCII Text File");
384   cputs_at(2, 7, "            F7-Control TX Speed    "
385       "F8-QUIT");
386   MAIN_MENU();
387 }
```

Listing 5.2. cinsdel.c. A C program that handles keyboard insert and delete functions.

```
1   /*
2    Module CINSDEL.C
3   */
4   #include <string.h>
5   #include <ctype.h>
6
7   void cinsert( char ccode,char *anystring,int spos )
8   {
9     int p;
10
11    p = strlen(anystring);
12    spos=( spos < 0 ) ? 0 : spos;
13    spos=( spos >= p ) ? p : spos;
14    for ( ; p>=spos; p--) anystring[p+1]=anystring[p];
15    anystring[spos]=ccode;
16  }
17
18  void cdelete( char *anystring,int spos )
19  {
20    int p;
21
22    p=strlen(anystring);
23    if ( p>0 && spos>=0 && spos<=p) {
24      while ( spos < p ) {
25        anystring[spos]=anystring[spos+1]; spos++;
26      }
27    }
28  }
29
```

Listing 5.3. stredit.c. A keyboard-input program.

```
1   /*
2    Module STREDIT.C
3   */
4   #include <stdio.h>
5   #include <string.h>
6   #include <memory.h>
7   #include <conio.h>
```

Listing 5.3. Continued.

```
 8  #include <ctype.h>
 9
10  int inserton = 1;
11
12  #include "utility.h"
13  #include "cinsdel.h"
14
15
16  void edit_text( char *anystring,
17                  int colno,
18                  int lineno,
19                  int maxlen,
20                  int offset,
21                  int upcase
22                )
23  {
24    int X,x,y;
25    int x2,y2;
26    int oldlen, newlen;
27    char extcode,exitcode,ch;
28
29    extcode=0; exitcode=0;
30    X=0;
31    y=lineno; x=colno;
32    cprintf_at( x, y, "%s",anystring);
33    eraseol();
34    X=(offset > 0)?offset:0;
35    x=X+colno;
36    gotoxy( x, y );
37    do {              /* MAIN EDIT LOOP */
38      extcode=0;
39      ch=getch();
40      if (ch==0) { extcode=1; ch=getch(); }
41      if (!exitcode) {
42        if (extcode) {
43          switch ( ch ) {
44            case 60:    /* F2 = Erase EOL */
45                eraseol();
46                    anystring[X] = '\0';
47                    break;
```

```
48              case 61:    /* F3 = Kill Line */
49                      X=0; x=X+colno;
50                      gotoxy( x, y );
51                  eraseol();
52                      *anystring='\0';
53                      break;
54              case 71:    /* HOME */
55                      X=0;
56                      x=colno;
57                      gotoxy( x, y );
58                      break;
59              case 75:    /* LEFT */
60                      if (X>0) {
61                          X--; x--; gotoxy( x, y );
62                      }
63                      break;
64              case 77:    /* RIGHT */
65                      if (X<strlen(anystring)) {
66                          X++; x++; gotoxy( x, y );
67                      }
68                      break;
69              case 79:    /* END */
70                      X=strlen(anystring);
71                      x=X+colno;
72                      gotoxy( x, y );
73                      break;
74              case 82:    /* INSERT */
75                      inserton = !inserton;
76                      break;
77              case 83:    /* DELETE */
78                      if (X<strlen(anystring) && X>=0) {
79                          cdelete(anystring,X);
80                  eraseol();
81                          cprintf_at( x, y, "%s",anystring/*+X*/);
82                  }
83                      break;
84              case 115:   /* CTL LEFT = Prev. Word */
85                      while (X>0 && anystring[X] != 32) {
86                          X--; x--;
87                      }
88                      while (X>0 && anystring[X] == 32) {
89                          X--; x--;
```

Listing 5.3. Continued.

```
 90                        }
 91                        gotoxy( x, y );
 92                        break;
 93          case 116:    /* CTL RIGHT = Next Word */
 94                        while (X<strlen(anystring)
 95                              && anystring[X] != 32) {
 96                          X++; x++;
 97                        }
 98                        while (X<strlen(anystring)
 99                              && anystring[X] == 32) {
100                          X++; x++;
101                        }
102                        gotoxy( x, y );
103                        break;
104              }
105          }             /* end extcode */
106          else {
107            switch ( ch ) {
108              case 13: return;
109                        break;
110              case 4:    /* CTL-D = Erase EOL */
111                        anystring[X] = '\0';
112                eraseol();
113                        break;
114              case 8:    /* CTL-H or BACKSPACE */
115                        if (X>0) {
116                            X--; x--; gotoxy( x, y );
117                        }
118                        if (X<strlen(anystring) && X>=0) {
119                            cdelete(anystring,X);
120                    eraseol();
121                            cprintf_at( x, y, "%s",anystring+X);
122                            gotoxy( x, y );
123                        }
124                        break;
125              default:
126                        if (strlen(anystring)<maxlen) {
127                          if ( upcase && islower(ch) )
128                            ch = toupper(ch);
129                          if (inserton) {
```

```
130                        cinsert(ch,anystring,X);
131                    }
132                    else {
133                        if ( X >= strlen(anystring) )
134                            cinsert(ch,anystring,X);
135                        else anystring[X] = ch;
136                    }
137                    cprintf_at(x, y, "%s",anystring+X);
138                    X++; x++;
139                gotoxy( x, y );
140                    }
141                    break;
142            }
143          }
144        }
145    } while (!exitcode);
146  }
```

Listing 5.4. utility.c. Input/Output support routines for the Morse code program.

```
1   /*
2         Module UTILITY.C
3   */
4   #include <stdlib.h>
5   #include <stdio.h>
6   #include <graph.h>
7   #include <dos.h>
8   #include <time.h>
9
10  short    wherex, wherey; /* Keeps track of current cursor location */
11
12
13  static void movex( int amount)
14  /* Move the cursor 'amount' spaces to the right */
15  {
16    wherex = wherex + amount;
17    if(wherex > 80){
18      wherey++;
19      wherex -= 80;
```

Listing 5.4. Continued.

```
20        }
21   }
22
23
24   void gotoxy( short x, short y )
25   /* Position the cursor to (x, y) */
26   {
27     _settextposition( y, x );
28     wherex = x;
29     wherey = y;
30   }
31
32
33   void outch( short ch )
34   /* Output one (char) byte at current cursor location */
35   {
36     char buffer[2] = {0, 0};
37     buffer[0] = (char)ch;
38     _outtext( buffer );
39     movex( 1 );
40   }
41
42
43   void putch_at( short x, short y, short ch )
44   /* Output one (char) byte at (x, y) */
45   {
46     gotoxy( x, y );
47     outch( ch );
48   }
49
50
51   void cprintf_at( short x, short y, char * format, char * textbuf )
52   /* Equivalent to sprintf() followed by cputs_at(); outputs
53      textbuf at (x, y) */
54   {
55     char buffer[79];
56
57     gotoxy( x, y );
58     sprintf( buffer, format, textbuf );
59     _outtext( buffer );
```

```
 60    movex( strlen(buffer) );
 61  }
 62
 63
 64  void move_to_next_line()
 65  /* Moves to start of next lower line on the screen */
 66  {
 67    gotoxy( 2, wherey+1 );
 68  }
 69
 70
 71  void cputs_at(short x, short y, char * buffer )
 72  /* Writes buffer to screen location (x, y) */
 73  {
 74    gotoxy ( x, y );
 75    _outtext( buffer );
 76    movex( strlen(buffer) );
 77  }
 78
 79
 80  void eraseol(void)
 81  /* Erases from the current cursor location to the right
 82     edge of the line */
 83  {
 84    char empty[80];
 85    int tempx, tempy;
 86
 87    sprintf( empty,"%*c",80-wherex,' ' );
 88    tempx = wherex; tempy = wherey;
 89    cputs_at( wherex, wherey, empty );
 90    gotoxy( tempx, tempy );
 91  }
 92
 93
 94  void delay ( unsigned int ms )
 95  /* Pauses the program for ms milliseconds. Note that this uses the
 96     clock() function which has approximately 50ms accuracy. */
 97  {
 98    clock_t start_clock;
 99
100    start_clock = clock();
101    do {
```

Listing 5.4. Continued.

```
102      } while ( clock() < (start_clock + ms) );
103      return;
104  }
105
106  void soundon( unsigned int freq )
107  /* Turns on the speaker, using the 8253 timer */
108  {
109    unsigned int al;
110
111    freq = 0x1234DD / freq;
112
113    al = inp( 0x61 ) ¦ 3;
114    outp( 0x61, al );
115    outp( 0x43, 0xB6 );
116    outp( 0x42, freq && 255 );   /* Low byte of freq */
117    outp( 0x42, freq >> 8 );     /* High byte of freq */
118  }
119
120  void nosound( void )
121  /* Turns off speaker */
122  {
123    outp( 0x61, inp( 0x61) && 0xFC );
124  }
125
126
127  void clearregion (short x1, short y1, short x2, short y2)
128  /* Performs a clearscreen operation on the region bounded by
129     (x1,y1)...(x2,y2).
130     On input x1, y1, x2, and y2 are 1-relative and are converted
131     to 0-relative prior to calling the BIOS INT 0x10 */
132  {
133    union REGS regs;
134    regs.h.ah = 0x06;
135    regs.h.al = y2 - y1 + 1;
136    regs.h.bh = 7;
137    regs.h.ch = y1 - 1;
138    regs.h.cl = x1 - 1;
139    regs.h.dh = y2 - 1;
140    regs.h.dl = x2 - 1;
141    int86( 0x10, &regs, &regs );
```

```
142  }
143
144  unsigned int random( unsigned int maxvalue )
145  /* Returns a pseudo random value from 0 to maxvalue */
146  {
147    return rand() / (float)RAND_MAX * maxvalue;
148  }
```

The following discussion is a brief description of the CW program. As a program that helps you learn how to send and receive Morse code messages, CW has routines that let you practice receiving codes for single letters or a random group of characters. Another routine lets you practice transmitting characters from your keyboard. Other functions enable you to change the speed at which characters are sent to you.

Listing 5.1 is the source code for the cw.c source file. Lines 7 through 18 contain the #include directives for the program. Notice in lines 16 through 18 that three user-supplied header files are merged into the program. These three header files contain the declarations needed to support the cinsdel.c, stredit.c, and utility.c source files. Lines 20 through 43 contain the macro definitions and global variable declarations.

In Listing 5.1, the function definitions begin in line 46 and continue through line 364. These definitions are for all the functions except main(). Notice that this source file does not use function prototype declarations, because all the functions are defined before they are called.

In lines 78 through 86 of Listing 5.1, you can see the functions used to sound the Morse code dots and dashes. Lines 154 through 204 contain the functions for changing the way the Morse codes sound.

The main() function for the CW program is in lines 367 through 387 of Listing 5.1. The main() function blocks in the main screen and displays the program's menu. Control is then passed to the MAIN_MENU function defined in lines 344 through 364. MAIN_MENU scans keyboard input for a menu selection and transfers control to the appropriate function.

Notice that the MAIN_MENU function is locked in an endless loop caused by the while() statement in line 346. Because the while() statement is always true, the menu routine does not end until the exit() function is called in line 361. When exit() is called, the program terminates normally.

Listing 5.2 shows the source code for the cinsdel.c source file. This short file contains the cinsert() and cdelete() support functions used by stredit().

Listing 5.3 presents the source code for another user-supplied support source file: stredit.c. The edit_text() function in this source file provides text string data entry for the CW program. You can inspect the source code for `edit_text()` to determine what keystrokes are permitted during text string editing. The `edit_text()` function is powerful enough to meet most keyboard input needs.

Listing 5.4 contains the source code for important display routines and the special procedures needed to turn on and off the speaker. The display routines provide functions to display text at specific locations on the screen. These routines are a bit easier to use than the graph.h routines supplied by Microsoft.

Setting Up a Microsoft C/C++ Project File

When you have a programming project that uses more than one source file, you need to create a project file. The project file is a special list of the source files needed in your project. The project file contains not only a list of the files used in the project, but also information needed to create an executable file.

If you use the Programmer's WorkBench, you will create a project file. If you choose to use your own editor and the command-line compiler and utility programs, you will create a special command file known as a *make file* that is used to *make* your program. Both methods for building applications from multiple files are shown in this chapter.

Creating Project Files

A project file includes the following information:

- *The location of the source files on disk.* The location of the resulting executable file can also be specified.

- *Source file dependencies.* In other words, information is included about which file must be compiled before other files can be compiled.

- *A project template specifying the type of executable file to create.* The type can be a DOS .EXE or .COM file, an overlaid .EXE file, a special executable containing p-code, or various types of Windows code files.

You can create and maintain projects using options on the Project menu. Creating a project requires three basic steps. The first step is to create a new project file. The second step is to add source files to the project file. The third step is to build the project (make the .EXE file).

To access the Microsoft C/C++ project-management functions, you use the **P**roject option from the main menu of the PWB. To create a new project file, select **N**ew Project from the Project menu. With the **O**pen command, you can open an existing project or assign a name to a new project. After selecting **N**ew

Project, the New Project dialog box appears. In the dialog box, type the name and path of the new project file.

After you select the OK button, you are presented with the Set Project Template dialog options as shown in Figure 5.1. Select None for Runtime Support and select DOS EXE for the Project Template.

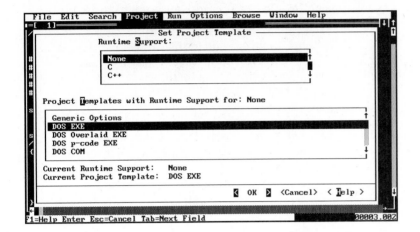

Figure 5.1.

The Set Project Template dialog specifies additional information about the executable file.

Next, you arrive at the Edit Project window. At this point, you have completed the first step in the creation of a project: You have created the new project file. Next, you need to add the source files to be used in the project. Figure 5.2 shows the project file screen for the cw.mak project file.

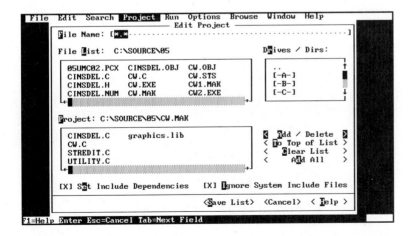

Figure 5.2.

The cw.mak project screen.

At the File Name field, you can type the name of a file used by your program. To add the file to the **Project** file list, select the < **A**dd / Delete > button. Your file now appears in the list box beneath the **Project** heading. Repeat this step for each of the .C source files used in your project.

Optionally, you can use the File Name field to select the directory containing your source files. Then, using the mouse or keyboard, you can select each source file, one at a time, from the File List box and add each to the **Project** list.

You also need to add the graphics.lib library file to the project list. To add graphics.lib, move to the File Name field, type **\C700\LIB\graphics.lib** (in which **\C700\LIB** is the name of the directory containing the Microsoft C/C++ library files), and select < **A**dd / Delete >.

When you are finished creating the Project file, select <**S**ave List>.

To delete files from the Project list, select the desired file from the Project list box and choose < **A**dd / Delete >. This removes the selected file from the **Project** list.

You have now created the project file and added the source files to the project list. The final step, compiling the project, is covered in the section "Compiling and Running Programs with the PWB" later in this chapter. Next, you see how to use functions and variables that are contained in separate source files.

Understanding External References

When you are using multiple source files, the concept of *external reference* becomes important. External reference has to do with functions in one source file accessing the data and functions in another source file. Without the external reference features of Microsoft C/C++, using multiple source files would be impossible.

The referencing of an external object has two parts. First, the object must be defined properly in one file. Second, the object must be declared in each file that references the external object. This section shows you how to set up and use external objects in your programs.

Using the *extern* Keyword

extern is a special keyword used in the declaration of objects that are referenced externally. The extern keyword tells the compiler that the data object you are declaring is an object defined in another source file. extern lets you use objects that were created in other source files. The next line of code shows a variable declared as an external variable:

```
extern double sales;
```

This code declares a double floating-point number. The declaration is different because the variable sales is actually defined in another source file.

Declaring an object and defining an object have a subtle difference. A *declaration* tells the compiler what kind of data an object works with. A declaration does not necessarily reserve storage for the object, however. A *definition* is the special declaration that sets aside memory for an object. A definition lets you create an object, whereas a declaration gives you access to that object.

An object can be defined in only one source file. The definition of the object causes space in your computer's memory to be allocated for that object. Because storage space is set aside for the object, it makes sense that the compiler allows only one definition of an object. After the definition is made, the object can be used in other source files.

Figure 5.3 shows how an external object is defined and declared.

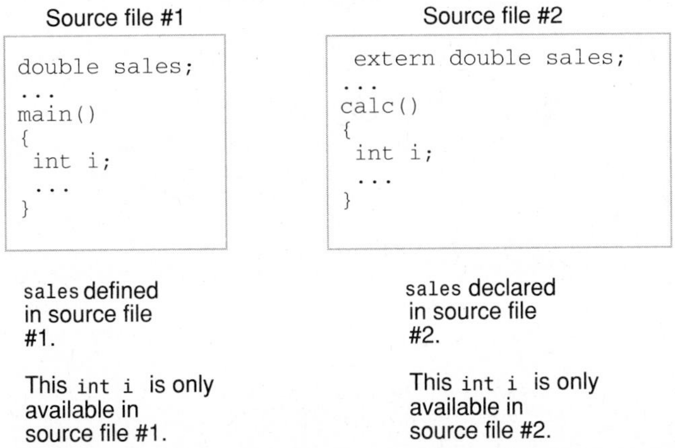

Source file #1

```
double sales;
...
main()
{
 int i;
 ...
}
```

sales defined
in source file
#1.

This int i is only
available in
source file #1.

Source file #2

```
 extern double sales;
 ...
calc()
{
 int i;
 ...
}
```

sales declared
in source file
#2.

This int i is only
available in
source file #2.

Figure 5.3.

How an external variable
operates.

Figure 5.3 graphically shows two source files. In the first source file, a global variable, sales, is defined. The definition in the first source file causes memory to be allocated for the double variable. In the second source file, the sales variable is declared as an external variable. The keyword extern signals that the actual data object is defined in another source file. The extern keyword indicates that space is not to be allocated for the sales variable again.

Also notice that an i variable is declared in both source files in Figure 5.3. The i variable declared in each source file is unique to that source file. In other words, the i variable in one source file cannot be referenced in the other source file. In fact, the i variable in each source file can be referenced only in the function in which it is declared, because i is an auto variable. i comes into existence when the function begins execution, and i is destroyed when the function ends.

A declaration for a variable with the extern storage class specifier references a data object that has external linkage. An object having external linkage can be accessed by functions in other source files.

Variables that need to be accessed by functions in other source files are usually declared as global variables. Recall that global variables are declared outside any functions in a source file. By default, global variables have external linkage and are therefore easily accessed by functions in other source files. You declare the variable in the other source file with the extern storage class specifier.

Using External Functions

The point of creating a project file is to separate your functions into logical and manageable files. This section shows you how to call and use the functions and external data objects in separate files.

In the preceding section, you saw how to share a variable across several separate source files. A variable with external linkage in one source file can be accessed in another source file if you declare the variable with the extern keyword. The extern keyword lets the compiler know that the variable was created in a different source file.

Calling functions that exist in other source files is similar to using variables from different source files. Using external functions requires you to perform two steps: You first define the function in one source file and then declare the function in the other source files.

You do not have to do anything special to define a function for callers to use in multiple source files. Because a function has external linkage by default, the function automatically is available for use by functions in other source files. Just don't forget to write a prototype declaration for the function in the other source files.

The declaration of a function found in another source file does not require the use of extern, as the declaration of a variable does. To use a function residing in another source file, write a normal function prototype declaration that includes the following information:

- *The return type of the function.*
- *The name of the function.*

■ *An argument list that includes declarations for all the arguments passed to the function.* The argument list must specify the data type for each of the arguments; specifying a variable name is optional.

Figure 5.4 shows how a function defined in one source file can be declared and used in another source file.

First source file	Second source file

```
#include <stdio.h>
...
int func1( int i);
...
main()
{
  ...
}
...
int func1( int i )
{
  ...
}
```

```
#include <stdio.h>
...
int func1( int i );
...
main()
{
  ...
  j = func1( 2 );
  ...
}
```

Figure 5.4.

How to reference an external function.

func1 is defined in the first source file.

func1 is declared and used in the second source file.

Two source files are shown in Figure 5.4. The first source file defines a function that can be called from either the first source file or another source file compiled with it. The function func1 in the first source file is declared and defined just like any other function. By default, func1 in the first source file has external linkage and can thus be called by functions in other source files.

The second source file shown in Figure 5.4 uses the func1 function defined in the first source file. Once func1 is declared in the second source file, function calls to the func1 function can be made in the usual manner.

Writing Header Files for External Modules

You have seen that using functions and variables residing in another source file requires that you declare those functions and variables in your source file. If you used many separate source files, keying all those extra declarations would be tedious. With header files, you can avoid all that extra typing.

A *header file* is a special file that contains all the declarations you need in order to use the functions and variables found in another source file. When you want to use functions or variables found in one of the other source files, you use the #include macro to merge the declarations for the other source file into the current source file.

Two of the benefits of using header files are speed and accuracy. Including a header file is much faster than typing all the necessary declarations for the functions and variables in another source file. Header files also prevent errors, because you have to type the declaration just one time. After you create a good header file, you do not have to worry about errors caused by typing.

You already are familiar with using the header files for Microsoft C/C++'s built-in library functions. The following section shows you how to create your own header files that work like the built-in header files supplied by Microsoft C/C++.

Deciding What Goes in the Header File

Deciding what to put in a header file is a simple task. The header file for a source file should include any objects you want to reference externally. In other words, a header file should contain declarations for any variables or functions to be accessed from other source files.

When you write declarations in a header for variables that will be used by other source files, do not forget to add the extern storage class specifier to the declarations. This is not necessary for function prototype declarations, because functions always have external linkage (unless you qualify the function definition with static).

Figure 5.5 shows how a basic header file is used.

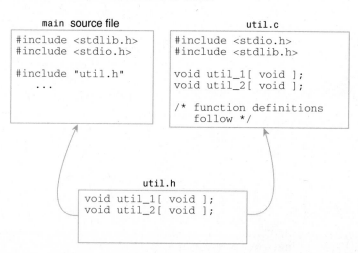

Figure 5.5.

Header files and object declarations.

```
main source file

#include <stdlib.h>
#include <stdio.h>

#include "util.h"
    ...
```

```
util.c

#include <stdio.h>
#include <stdlib.h>

void util_1[ void ];
void util_2[ void ];

/* function definitions
   follow */
```

```
util.h

void util_1[ void ];
void util_2[ void ];
```

The main source file in Figure 5.5 uses the `#include` macro to merge in the util.h header file. The util.h header file contains declarations for the `util_1` and `util_2` functions that are defined in the util.c source file. The util.h header file contains declarations for all the external objects that are to be referenced in the util.c source file.

If the util.c source file in Figure 5.5 had variables to be externally referenced, util.h would include declarations for the variables.

In addition to containing declarations for functions and variables, a header file can contain macro definitions. If macros make your external functions easier to use, include the macros in the header file. When the main source file includes the header file, the macros are ready to use.

Including User-Supplied Header Files

To pull in the header files you create, all you need is the `#include` macro. The following statement merges the file my_hdr.h into your source file:

```
#include "my_hdr.h"
```

Everything in the my_hdr.h file is included in your source file.

In line 16 of Listing 5.1, the cw.c source file uses the `#include` macro to merge the stredit.h header file into cw.c. Listing 5.5 shows the stredit.h header file.

Listing 5.5. stredit.h. The header file for stredit.c.

```
1   extern int inserton;
2
3   void eraeol(void);
4   void edit_text( char *anystring,
5                   int colno,
6                   int lineno,
7                   int maxlen,
8                   int offset,
9                   int upcase
10                  );
```

When you merge the code in Listing 5.5 into cw.c, the cw.c source file is able to use the `eraeol()` and `edit_text()` functions defined in the cinsdel.c source file. cw.c also can reference the `inserton` variable.

`#include` directives can be *nested*. This means that you can place `#include` inside files that are themselves included. When the preprocessor expands an `#include` directive, the resulting source code is rescanned to look for more `#include` directives (and macros).

Take another look at line 16 in Listing 5.1. Notice that the `#include` directive does not surround the filename with the less-than (<) and greater-than (>) symbols you have seen before. Instead, the `#include` directive encloses the filename in quotation marks.

The quotation marks in the `#include` directive tell the preprocessor that a user-supplied header file is being used. The quotation marks signal the preprocessor to modify its searching algorithm so that the user-supplied header file can be found. The preprocessor searches the current directory first. Usually, that is where the source file is located. If the header file is not found in the current directory, the preprocessor searches each of the `include` directories.

Using Conditional Compiler Directives in Header Files

Large projects often require that many header files be included during program compilation. When you include several header files, you can declare the same object several times. You can make many of the declarations more than once without any problems. A better practice, however, is to make sure that you only make the declarations once. Microsoft C/C++'s set of conditional compiler directives can help you ensure that declarations are made only one time.

The conditional compilation directives are also called the *conditional inclusion directives*. The purpose of these preprocessor directives is to enable you to include or exclude certain sections of code before compilation takes place. Using the preprocessor's `#if` directive, you can decide which sections of code to include or exclude. The various forms of the `#if` directive let you perform logical tests before compilation starts.

Note the syntax for the conditional compilation directives:

```
#if [!]constant-expression
#elif [!]constant-expression
#else
#if [!] defined identifier
#if [!] defined ( identifier )
#ifdef identifier
#ifndef identifier
#endif
```

The symbol ! indicates that the logical NOT can be used in the expression. The brackets surrounding the ! symbol are to indicate that use of ! is optional; if you use the ! symbol, don't type the bracket characters.

In the list of conditional compilation directives, the `constant-expression` can be any expression that evaluates to an integer value. The `constant-expression` can contain arithmetic operators, logical operators, and even other macro expressions. A `constant-expression` that evaluates to a nonzero value is considered to be true. If the `constant-expression` evaluates to zero, however, the expression is considered false.

In the preceding list, the identifier used in the `#if defined` series of directives is a symbol you create. The `#if defined` directives determine whether the symbol indicated by `identifier` has been previously defined in your source code. `identifier` can optionally be enclosed in parentheses.

With the `#if`, `#elif`, `#else`, and `#endif` directives, you can create a logical construct that includes or excludes code based on a certain condition. You must be able to express the condition that is to be evaluated as an integer value. A typical `#if` construct looks like this:

```
#if condition_1
   first code section
#elif condition_2
   second code section
#else
   default code section
#endif
```

When the preprocessor scans the preceding group of `#if` directives, it evaluates `condition_1` first. If `condition_1` evaluates to a nonzero integer value, the first code section is included for compilation. The other code sections are not included in the compilation of the program.

If `condition_1` yields a zero (false) value, the preprocessor then evaluates `condition_2`. The second code section is included in the program's compilation if `condition_2` evaluates to a nonzero (true) value.

If neither `condition_1` nor `condition_2` evaluates as true, the default code section following the `#else` directive is included during program compilation.

You don't necessarily have to include code in any of these code sections. At times, you may need to create a conditional compilation structure, but you will not want to include any code for some conditions.

The `#endif` signals the end of the `#if` structure. You must include an `#endif` directive for every `#if` directive you use.

Listing 5.6 shows the use of an `#if defined` directive. The code is the cinsdel.h header file that is included by the cw.c program found in Listing 5.1.

Listing 5.6. cinsdel.h. The cinsdel.c header file.

```
1   #if !defined _CINSDEL
2   #define _CINSDEL
3   #include <string.h>
4   #include <ctype.h>
5
6   cinsert( char ccode,char *anystring,int spos );
7   cdelete( char *anystring,int spos );
8   #endif
```

In line 1 of Listing 5.6, the #if defined directive is combined with the logical NOT symbol. The #if !defined directive causes the code section that follows to be included only if _CINSDEL has *not* been previously defined.

The #if defined directive determines whether the specified identifier has been previously defined in your source code. In Listing 5.6, the identifier that is checked is _CINSDEL. In Listing 5.6, the first action taken if _CINSDEL has not been defined is to define it. Once the identifier _CINSDEL is defined, the declarations in cinsdel.h will not be made if the cinsdel.h header file is included again.

Listing 5.6 illustrates another point. You can control the inclusion of header files by placing the #include directives inside an #if directive. In that listing, the inclusion of the string.h and ctype.h header files is controlled by the presence of the _CINSDEL identifier. Using an #if construct like the one in Listing 5.6 ensures that your header files include other header files only one time.

The directive

```
#if defined TEST_OBJ
```

is equivalent to the directive

```
#ifdef TEST_OBJ
```

You can use the #if defined directive anywhere you would use the #ifdef directive. The next two directives are equivalent also:

```
#if !defined TEST_OBJ
#ifndef TEST_OBJ
```

Compiling and Running Programs with the PWB

Once you create the source, header, and project files, you are ready to compile your program. Without the advanced project-management features of Microsoft C/C++, compiling a large project could be a complicated task. But the PWB's project-management functions make building programs easy, whether they are simple or complex.

After you compile your program, Microsoft C/C++ can even run it without leaving the Programmer's WorkBench. Running your program in the PWB can save you much time because you can make modifications quickly, and recompiling takes only a few keystrokes.

This section shows you how to use Microsoft C/C++ to compile and run your program. The instructions work for small C programs as well as large projects.

Compiling and Running Simple Programs

You have already used the Microsoft C/C++ compiler to compile your single source file programs. Compiling these programs is simple; all you do is select the Project menu's **B**uild command. This causes Microsoft C/C++ to compile your program and generate an .EXE file.

Compiling your project files is just as easy. To compile a project file, be sure that the project has been opened (using **O**pen Project... from the **P**roject menu) and then choose **B**uild or **R**ebuild All from the **P**roject menu. Microsoft C/C++ compiles all the files in your project, calls the LINK program linker, and creates an executable file.

If Microsoft C/C++ detects any errors or questionable conditions during the compilation of your code, Microsoft C/C++ creates a message window to inform you of these conditions. Select <View> to see any generated messages. This lets you view compiler- or linker-generated warning or error messages.

To obtain additional information about a specific warning or error condition, use the mouse to select the error number within the Build Results window, and then choose **T**opic from the **H**elp menu. This presents a help message that describes the error condition and possible solutions. For example, suppose you see the following warning in the Build Results window:

```
C4051: type conversion; possible loss of data
```

To obtain additional information about this warning, highlight or select the warning number C4051, and then choose **T**opic from the **H**elp menu.

When you are through with the message window, you can remove it in one of two ways: You can click the close box if you are using a mouse, or you can close the box using the keyboard. Assuming that Build Results is the active window, choose Close from the Window menu, or press Ctrl+F4.

Microsoft C/C++ lets you run your program without leaving the PWB environment. To run the program, select the Execute command from the Run menu. When you run the program, Microsoft C/C++ creates a user screen in which the program executes. While the program is running, the user screen is active by default. When the program ends, Microsoft C/C++ switches back to the current PWB window.

Microsoft C/C++ automatically saves the project you are working on when you exit the PWB. When you exit, Microsoft C/C++ generates two files: the project file (with a .MAK file extension) and a Programmer's WorkBench status file (with an .STS file extension). The project file contains all the information about your project. The status file contains information about the state of the PWB.

Compiling and Running Complex Programs

Microsoft C/C++ provides additional features to help you work with the more complex programs you create. In this section, you learn how to use some of these advanced features.

With the Project menu, you can do more than just create an executable file. Figure 5.6 shows the additional options on the Project menu.

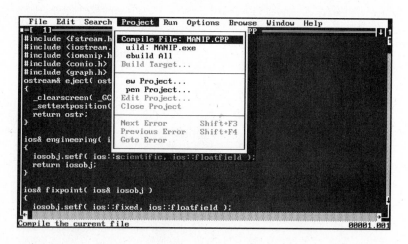

Figure 5.6.

The Microsoft C/C++ Project menu.

On the Project menu, the Compile File option generates an object file. Recall that an object file is a form of your program that has been converted to machine-language instructions. An object file is still not an executable file, however. The object file must be linked with other files before it can be run. With the **C**ompile File command, you can create an object file that will be linked at a later time. Use **B**uild to link together the object files specified in the current project file.

The **R**ebuild All option causes all the files in the project to be rebuilt. This command builds all files, even if they are up-to-date.

If your program requires command-line arguments to operate properly, you can pass them to your program with the **P**rogram Arguments command from the **R**un menu. The program receives the arguments you specify just as if you had started it from the DOS command prompt.

The purpose of a project file is to separate your program into manageable pieces. When you need to modify or correct a piece of code, you need to work with only one source file of your project. Having your code separated into smaller pieces makes it easier to maintain and upgrade your programs.

In a large project, recompiling and relinking the entire project when you make changes in the individual program modules takes too much time. It's also hard to keep track of files that need recompiling after you make several changes. The Microsoft C/C++ Project manager takes care of both these problems for you.

When you elect to build a project, the PWB automatically determines which files have changed and need compiling. Further, the PWB determines if any of the changed files affect other files. For example, if you update an `include` file, you must also recompile the modules that include that file. The PWB, through use of the project make features, automatically takes care of tracking the program source changes and ensuring that all files are recompiled as needed.

The PWB compares each file's date and time information stored in the disk directory to its .OBJ object module. If the source file is newer than the object module, the object module will be recompiled.

Make certain that the date and time are set correctly on your computer. If you are using an older computer that does not have a clock, be sure to set the date and time when you start the computer. If the date and time are not set, autodependency checking won't work correctly.

The NMAKE Utility Program

Many programmers prefer to use their own editors rather than the Programmer's WorkBench. When programming in this fashion, you still have a need to build entire projects. The NMAKE program performs the same function as the **P**roject menu's **B**uild option. Indeed, the PWB automatically creates a *make file* and invokes NMAKE to build your application.

When you use NMAKE as a standalone utility, you must prepare a separate make file, describing the dependencies between the files that cause them to be recompiled or reassembled. After you have created a make file for your application, NMAKE scans the file and compares each listed file's date and time. If any source file is newer than its corresponding object file, NMAKE ensures that each object file is recompiled or reassembled to incorporate the latest changes. The make file describes the dependencies between the source files and the object modules, and specifies which commands should be issued to recompile or reassemble the source.

Example Use of NMAKE

To invoke NMAKE, type the NMAKE command followed by the name of the make command file. For example, if you have created a make command file, cw.mak, you invoke NMAKE by typing

`NMAKE cw.mak`

The basic structure of the make file consists of dependency statements followed by commands. Each dependency statement specifies a target or destination file followed by a colon character and a list of source files (or object files) from which the destination file is constructed. NMAKE checks each of the source files; if any of the source files are newer than an existing copy of the destination file, NMAKE executes the subsequent command lines to bring the destination up-to-date. Listing 5.7 shows an example make command file for creating CW.EXE.

Listing 5.7. A sample make file for use with NMAKE.

```
# NMAKE command file to create CW.EXE, the
# Morse code practice program.
cw.exe: cw.obj cinsdel.obj stredit.obj utility.obj
  cl cw.obj cinsdel.obj stredit.obj utility.obj graphics.lib
cw.obj : cw.c
  cl /c /qc cw.c
cinsdel.obj : cinsdel.c cinsdel.h
  cl /c /qc cinsdel.c
stredit.obj : stredit.c stredit.h utility.h
  cl /c /qc stredit.c
utility.obj : utility.c utility.h
  cl /c /qc utility.c
```

The first few statements, which are preceded by the # symbol, are comments. Comments can appear anywhere in the file.

Lines beginning in the first column, other than comments, specify dependent relationships. For example, the statement

```
cw.obj : cw.c
  cl /c /qc cw.c
```

says that cw.obj is dependent on cw.c

Following the dependent condition, on a line beginning with one or more spaces or tab characters, is a command that NMAKE should execute if the preceding conditional test requires the destination file to be rebuilt.

The conditional test instructs NMAKE to compare the date and time stamps of the source files to the destination file. If changes have occurred to the source files, then and only then does NMAKE execute the next line containing the commands for recompiling cw.c.

The first dependency relationship in this make file is a little more complicated:

```
cw.exe: cw.obj cinsdel.obj stredit.obj utility.obj
  cl cw.obj cinsdel.obj stredit.obj utility.obj graphics.lib
```

If any of the .obj files shown to the right of the colon are newer than the cw.exe file, NMAKE executes the following command line, which invokes the cl command-line compiler to relink all the object modules.

Any number of commands can be executed as a consequence of a dependent test, provided that each command is indented by at least one space or tab. The next statement starting in column one of the make file is interpreted as a new dependency condition.

Command lines may invoke any .COM, .EXE, or .BAT file and may also use any DOS command. As such, the make file can do much more than merely invoke compilers and assemblers. NMAKE becomes a general-purpose automation utility that can perform functions such as copying source code to back up subdirectories when changes are made to the program.

Because most NMAKE files contain a large number of dependencies, NMAKE initially scans through the entire NMAKE file, identifying which files are dependent on other source files. If any of the source files are themselves listed as destination files in other dependency relationships shown elsewhere in the file, NMAKE ensures that those files are brought up-to-date first.

> **CAUTION:** A common problem encountered sooner or later by all users of NMAKE occurs when the system clock is changed, intentionally or unintentionally. Because NMAKE compares the date and time of the destination file to the source files, if for some reason the clock has changed so that an incorrect date or time is associated with a source file, strange problems can crop up. Clock changes can occur intentionally, such as when manually setting the system time (and sometimes we make errors when doing that), or unintentionally, as the result of running a program that fiddles with the clock, or even due to serious software errors.
>
> If you are using NMAKE to build a large application with a large number of modules, its easy not to notice if an incorrect time stamp has been placed on a file. As a result, you may make a project and find that no matter how hard you try, your latest changes are not showing up in the .EXE file. Thinking your code is wrong, you probably keep rewriting the errant section over and over. Then all of sudden, you notice that the system clock got reset, the file's time stamp is incorrect, and none of your changes made it into the .EXE file.
>
> If your changes do not appear to be included in a successful NMAKE, be sure to examine carefully the time and date stamps on the files.

Explicit Rules

NMAKE provides two kinds of dependent relationship statements: *explicit rules* and *inference rules.*

An explicit rule lists the file to be created and the source files that it depends on, in the following format:

```
destination-file : source-file-1 source-file-2 ...
    command

    ...
```

For example:

```
cw.exe: cw.obj cinsdel.obj stredit.obj utility.obj
  cl cw.obj cinsdel.obj stredit.obj utility.obj graphics.lib
```

Here, cw.exe is the resulting file, and it is dependent on each of the other files. If any of the dependent files have changed since the last time that cw.exe was built, NMAKE issues the following command to rebuild cw.exe:

```
cl cw.obj cinsdel.obj stredit.obj utility.obj graphics.lib
```

Any number of commands can follow the dependency relationship, provided that each is indented by at least one space or tab character. At least one of the commands should construct a new destination file.

If a dependent relationship contains only a destination file and no source files, as in

```
cw.exe:
  cl cw.obj cinsdel.obj stredit.obj utility.obj graphics.lib
```

the command line is executed directly.

Important: List All Files

When you build the make file, it's important that you ensure that every dependency for each file is completely specified. For example, in the dependency relationship

```
stredit.obj : stredit.c stredit.h utility.h
  cl stredit.c /c /qc
```

if utility.h is not specified and utility.h has changed some important definitions, the compilation of stredit.obj may fail.

For this reason, you should check the dependant relationship statements carefully and ensure that the make file can successfully build the project. To test, delete all unit and .obj files and then run NMAKE. If any dependencies are missing, NMAKE should stop with a compile or link error. If the dependencies are listed correctly, units that are required by other modules will be compiled or assembled before compiling the module that uses them.

Command Lines

Each command line or group of command lines follows a dependency statement and is indented by at least one blank or tab character. Normally, NMAKE displays each command as it is executed. If the command is prefixed with the @ symbol, however, NMAKE does not display the command when it is executed.

In most cases, if a command executed from NMAKE returns a nonzero exit code, NMAKE aborts the make file. You can restrict the abort process by prefacing each command line with a hyphen followed by an optional number. If no number is specified, NMAKE ignores all exit codes.

Inference Rules

Inference rules provide a way of specifying wildcards for filenames that need compiling or assembling. The syntax for an implicit rule references the file extensions rather than complete target and source filenames. The inference rule

```
.c.obj:
    cl $<
```

is a rule that means .obj files are created from .c files having the same filename. For example, utility.obj is created from utility.c. By placing this inference rule into the make file, you do not need to specify each of the modules as separate dependencies. The symbol $< is a special macro symbol, defined in the next section.

Macros

Macros provide text substitution by inserting a special symbol into the make file that is translated, when used, into actual text parameters. You assign macro symbols at the beginning of the make file by writing the symbol name, followed by an equals sign, followed by the substitution text. For example:

```
source=C:\RADIO
```

Consider the situation of sharing a single make file among a team of software developers. Each team member may wish to store some of the source and unit files in different directories than those used by other team members. Without macro symbols, each team member needs to edit the make file and change each subdirectory name to his or her subdirectory. With macro symbols, the problem is much easier to resolve. The macro file uses the first few lines to define macro symbols that are set equal to the subdirectory names. Each user changes only the symbol definitions, rather than the entire file. For example, in the following make file, the two symbols `source` and `modules` specify the respective subdirectories:

```
source=C:\RADIO
modules=C:\RADIO\OBJS
($modules)cw.exe:    $(source)cw.c \
        $(modules)cinsdel.obj \
        $(modules)stredit.obj \
        $(modules)utility.obj
    cl $(source)cw.c $(modules)cinsdel.obj \
        $(modules)stredit.obj ($modules)utility.obj \
        graphics.lib
```

Macro symbols may be defined or redefined anywhere in the make file. When a symbol is redefined, the old definition is thrown out.

NMAKE provides a set of predefined macros, as follows:

`$*`	Returns the `filename` part of the target's `filename.extension`.
`$<`	Returns the full filename, including path and extension.
`$@`	Contains the name of the current target file.
`$**`	Contains the list of all dependent files.
`$?`	Contains a list of files that are out of date relative to the target file.
`$$@`	Contains the target filename that is currently being evaluated (in other words, the name to the left of the colon in a dependency statement).
`$(CC)`	Equivalent to the name of the C/C++ compiler `cl`.
`$(AS)`	Equivalent to the name of the Microsoft Assembler `masm`.
`$(MAKE)`	Equivalent to the NMAKE program name. If used as a command line in a make file, this will run NMAKE recursively.
`$(MAKEDIR)`	Defined as the directory from which NMAKE was invoked.

Conditional Directives

The following make file directives can be embedded in the make file:

`!if`

The `!if` directive is a conditional statement, adding flexibility to the make file's design. `!if` has the following syntax:

```
!if expression
  make file lines
!endif
```

When an `else` part is added, `!if` takes the form:

```
!if expression
  make file lines
!else
  make file lines
!endif
```

The `else` part can be extended indefinitely into an `if-then-else-if` statement type:

```
!if expression
  make file lines
!elif expressione
  make file lines
!endif
```

The *expression* can reference macro symbols as well as constant values and basic arithmetic operators (see Table 5.1).

`!error text`

`!error` outputs the value of *text* to the display and halts the make file.

`!undef symbol`

`!undef` induces forgetfulness; specifically, `!undef` causes the definition for *symbol* to go away. Note the following example:

`!undef UNITDIRECTORY`

`!include <filename>`

`!include "filename"`

`!include` incorporates the contents of *filename* into the current make file. The *filename* string is surrounded by angle brackets or double quotation marks in this directive (for example, `<DIR.MAK>` or `"DIR.MAK"`). Included files can be nested, provided that you avoid recursive `includes`.

Table 5.1. NMAKE Expression Operators.

Operator	Description
-	unary negation
~	unary bitwise complement
!	unary logical NOT
+	addition
-	subtraction
*	multiplication
/	division
%	remainder
>>	right shift
<<	left shift
&	bitwise AND
¦	bitwise OR
^	bitwise exclusive OR
&&	logical AND
¦¦	logical OR
>	greater than
>=	greater than or equal
<	less than
<=	less than or equal
==	exactly equal
!=	not equal
()	Parentheses may group expression elements.

Exercises

The following exercises give you practice in designing multisource file programs, managing projects, and using the integrated debugger:

1. Design a book-cataloging program. In the program, use an array of structures to hold information about a book title, author, and publisher. Make this program a project by separating the functions that input data and the functions that print a report.

2. Write the support functions for the cataloging program. When you are through with a source file, go ahead and write the header file that will be used for the source file.

3. Create the project file for your cataloging program.

4. Compile and test your program.

Summary

This chapter covered complex project design. You learned the following important points:

■ *As your programs get larger, you will want to divide them into modules of related functions.* Dividing your large programs into smaller modules makes maintaining and modifying your programs easier.

■ *The Microsoft C/C++ Project manager simplifies the task of creating multiple source file projects.* The Project manager keeps track of the dependencies among your source files. This autodependency feature lets you concentrate on your C code instead of trying to remember which source file you last changed.

■ *The* extern *keyword signals the compiler that the object you are declaring was defined in another source file.* The extern keyword tells the compiler not to allocate space for the object again.

■ *You do not have to use the* extern *keyword when you declare functions defined in other source files.* Functions are created with external linkage by default. This means that a function is automatically available for use in other source files.

■ *When you create a source file that will be compiled with other programs, you need to create a header file for that source file.* The header file is a collection of all the declarations needed to access the functions and variables in the source file you created. The header file is included by other programs that will use the functions and variables in your source file.

■ *Microsoft C/C++ provides a group of conditional compilation preprocessor directives.* One purpose of these directives is to prevent multiple declarations of the same objects. The #if defined and #ifdef are two of the conditional compilation directives.

■ *Compiling and running complex programs is almost as easy as compiling and running simple programs—thanks to the PWB's project-management facilities.* To compile most programs or projects, you can use the **B**uild command from the **P**roject menu. To run a program in the PWB, use the **E**xecute command from the **R**un menu.

Using the Microsoft C/C++ I/O Function Library

So far, you have been using basic C input and output functions. These functions read data from the keyboard and send results to the screen. The functions are useful, but they cannot access or record permanent data. Without the ability to store data permanently, you have to enter the data manually each time you run your program. The usefulness of a program that cannot permanently store data is, as you might imagine, sharply limited.

This chapter shows you how to use the Microsoft C/C++ functions that enable you to access any of your computer's I/O devices—not just the screen and keyboard. You learn first how C handles data and then how to use the Microsoft C/C++ I/O library functions. With these functions, you can access the mass storage and other I/O devices on your computer. Using the disk drives and other devices on the computer opens up new worlds of programming possibilities.

Understanding I/O Concepts

Before you start using the Microsoft C/C++ I/O functions, you need to know how C handles input and output data. Microsoft C/C++ uses *streams* to represent the data that moves in and out of your program. Microsoft C/C++ streams let you use your computer's I/O devices without worrying about low-level control of your computer. A file contains arbitrary data bytes, whereas a stream, which is associated with a file, enables you to access the file in logical pieces, such as text lines. Think of a file as the physical data on a disk and the stream as the pipeline or buffer that transfers the data to or from your program.

This section introduces the primary I/O devices that are available on your computer. After you learn how your computer handles data, you see how Microsoft C/C++ associates streams with the devices and files on your system. Finally, you learn about the two basic types of files that Microsoft C/C++ uses: binary files and text files.

Understanding Files and Devices

Usually, when you work with large amounts of data, the data is stored in a file. A *file* is simply a group of related data. Depending on the type of file you are using, you can read data from the file or write data to the file, and sometimes you can do both.

Every file is associated with some type of *device*. A device is a piece of computer hardware that either stores or transfers information. One device that you are already familiar with is the *hard disk* in your computer. The hard disk is a mass storage device that permanently stores large amounts of information.

Devices can be divided into two groups: *permanent devices* and *interactive devices*. As you know, the hard disk in your computer is a permanent device. Permanent devices store data for a long time. Examples of other permanent devices are disk drives, tape drives, and CD-ROM drives. Each of these devices has its particular advantages and disadvantages, but all are designed to retain data for extended periods of time.

Interactive devices are generally used to transfer data to or from your computer. Unlike permanent devices, interactive devices store data for only a short period of time. Your video card and display monitor make up an interactive device. Data is sent to your video card, which produces an image on the monitor. The image on the monitor stays there as long as you have power and as long as you don't send other data that erases the screen. The monitor does not store data permanently; after the data on the screen is lost, the data is gone forever (or at least until you re-create it). Some of the other interactive devices attached to your computer are the mouse, the keyboard, and the modem.

One of the biggest problems with the devices that your computer uses is that they are slow. Even a fast hard disk transfers data much more slowly than the computer can process the data. Because the devices attached to your computer are slow compared to the CPU, many of the devices are *buffered*. A buffer is a special area of memory set aside to store the data being sent to or received from a device.

If the device is sending data to the computer, the buffer stores the information until it is convenient for the CPU to process the data. If the device is receiving data from the computer, the buffer stores the data sent by the CPU until the device is able to accept the data. Using a buffer correctly can greatly improve the performance of your programs.

Generally, an I/O buffer serves a similar purpose to that of the tank on an air compressor. The air compressor stores highly pressurized air in a tank. When a tool needs air, the tank has a large volume of high-pressure air readily available. Figure 6.1 uses the air compressor metaphor to illustrate how a buffer works.

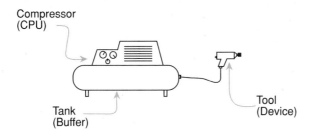

Compressor
(CPU)

Tank
(Buffer)

Tool
(Device)

Figure 6.1.

How a buffer works with the CPU and devices.

Because the tool remains idle much of the time, continuously running the air compressor would be inefficient. The compressor runs only when the pressure in the tank drops to a specified level. When the compressor does operate, it runs at full speed and efficiency.

An I/O buffer works similarly to the air tank. The I/O buffer stores data until the I/O device is ready to receive the data. When the device is ready, the buffer supplies the device with all the data the device can handle.

The compressor in this example is like the CPU in your computer. Because I/O devices are slow, it would be inefficient for the CPU to send data to the I/O device all the time. Without an I/O buffer, the CPU would be tied up for long periods of time. The buffer enables the CPU to send data in larger blocks, thereby increasing the efficiency of the CPU.

In the compressor example, the air tank represents only an output buffer. Your programs use *output* and *input buffers*. An input buffer stores the data sent from a device until the CPU is ready to process the data. An output buffer temporarily stores the outgoing data before writing the data to disk.

Understanding Files and Streams

For many operations, Microsoft C/C++ accesses data files through streams. A stream represents a file and is used to transfer the data to and from the file.

Streams are also a portable way to handle your I/O tasks. Microsoft C/C++ has several functions that enable you to manipulate your files directly through DOS interfaces. These functions, however, are not portable to other compilers. But many of the functions that use streams can be ported to other compilers without source code changes. If you need to write portable code, use the I/O functions that control data files through streams.

To associate a stream with a file, all you need to do is open the file. Functions like fopen() automatically associate a stream with a file. fopen() and the other file-access functions are declared in the stdio.h header file. The following example shows how to use the fopen() function:

```
#include <stdio.h>
FILE *my_file;
...
if ( ( my_file = fopen ( "text.tst", "w" ) ) == NULL ) {
  printf( "Could not open file.\n" );
  printf( "Exiting program.\n" );
  exit( 0 );
}
...
fclose( my_file );
```

In this code fragment, the fopen() function opens the test.txt file and prepares to write to the file. fopen() returns NULL if an error occurred when trying to open the file. Although fopen() automatically associates a stream with the test.txt file, you do not manipulate the my_file stream object directly. To control the stream, and therefore control the file, you must use the library functions—printf(), in this example—that control the FILE type data object pointed to by my_file.

my_file is a pointer to a special data object that holds information about a particular stream. The data object pointed to by my_file has the data type FILE, defined in stdio.h. To control a stream, you have to use functions that can access and use the data contained in a FILE type data object.

A FILE type data object contains several pieces of information about a particular stream. Some of the items contained in the FILE type data object are the following:

- Information about the I/O buffer associated with the file

- The size of the stream

- An indicator signaling that an I/O error has occurred

■ A file position indicator that marks the current position in the file

■ An indicator signaling that the end of the file has been encountered

When you are through with a file, you need to disassociate the stream from the file and close the file. The `fclose()` function performs both tasks. The last line in the preceding code fragment shows how `fclose()` is used.

Standard Microsoft C/C++ Streams

Microsoft C/C++ provides five standard streams for your program. Whenever you write a C program, you automatically have access to the following five streams:

Stream	Purpose	Default I/O Device
stdin	Input stream	Keyboard
stdout	Output stream	Video monitor
stdprn	Printer stream	Printer port
stdaux	Auxiliary output	Serial port
stderr	Error stream	Video monitor

`stdin` is the basic standard input stream that handles keyboard input. `stdaux`, which can be used for either input or output, enables you to send and receive data from the serial port. The serial port enables you to connect your computer to a modem or even to another computer.

Four of the five streams supplied by Microsoft C/C++ are standard output streams. `stdout` is the output stream that sends data to your screen, `stdprn` is the output stream that sends output data to the printer port, and `stdaux` is the stream that sends data to the serial or COM port. `stderr` is the standard error stream, which sends error messages to the screen.

Understanding Text and Binary Streams

Opening a file associates a stream with that file. The way you open a file, however, determines what *type* of stream will be associated with the file. Microsoft C/C++ has two types of streams you can use with your files: *text streams* and *binary streams*.

The type of stream used for a file determines the way the data in the file will be translated. Functions that work with text streams change, or translate, some of the special characters in the file. Functions that work with binary files do not translate any characters in the file.

When a text stream is read, special characters in the file are converted to an internal format. For example, when a carriage-return character and a line-feed character are read from a file, the two characters are converted to the new-line character (\n). Furthermore, when a file is treated as a text stream, a tab character is changed to a series of space characters.

No conversions take place when a file is processed as a binary stream. The data in a binary stream matches the data in the file bit-for-bit. When a binary stream reads a carriage-return character and a line-feed character, each of the control characters is included in the stream. A binary stream does not convert carriage-return/line-feed characters to a new-line character as a text stream does. Figure 6.2 shows how a text stream and a binary stream represent the information in a file.

Figure 6.2.

Data representation in binary and text streams.

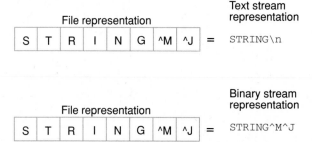

In Figure 6.2, you can see how data in a file is represented when the file is opened first as a text stream and then as a binary stream. The file consists of several characters. The first six characters spell the word *string*. The last two characters in the file represent the carriage-return character (^M) and the line-feed character (^J).

When the file in Figure 6.2 is opened as a text stream, the carriage-return/line-feed characters are converted to a single character by the functions that work with text streams. A new-line character (\n) in the stream replaces the carriage-return/line-feed characters in the file. When the same file is opened as a binary stream, no character conversion takes place. The carriage-return/line-feed characters are treated as separate characters in binary streams.

Text streams are useful for files containing information that can be read directly by people. Binary streams are often used when files are processed by the computer. For example, an object file is opened as a binary stream before the object is linked. Binary streams are used also in reading and writing files that contain numbers stored in the computer's internal format.

Using the Standard Streams for I/O

Microsoft C/C++ automatically opens five standard I/O streams for your program. Using these standard streams is easy because you do not have to open any files for the streams. Microsoft C/C++ automatically opens the standard streams and makes them available for your use. These standard streams are listed in the preceding section.

In this section, you learn about two groups of powerful I/O functions that you can use with the standard streams. First, you see how to use formatted I/O functions to input and output any of the standard data types. Next, you see how to use character I/O functions to input and output character-based information.

Using Formatted I/O Functions

Microsoft C/C++ has two main families of formatted I/O functions: the scanf() input functions and the printf() output functions. Chapter 1 introduced you to these families of functions. You learn more about using scanf() and printf() in this section.

The scanf() and printf() functions are similar in that both work with formatted data—data arranged in any order you specify. When you use the scanf() function, you specify what type of data will be read and the order in which it will be input. For printf(), you specify the type and order of the data that will be output. Both scanf() and printf() work with any of C's basic data types. For example, scanf() can be used to input floating-point numbers as easily as characters or integers, and printf() can print any of the basic data types in the sequence you want.

Listing 6.1 shows a rudimentary inventory-database program that uses functions from both the scanf() and printf() families to retrieve and display data. This program shows you how to use the formatted I/O functions to create, update, and display a simple inventory database.

Listing 6.1. fdata.c. A program that uses formatted I/O functions for terminal and file I/O.

```
1   /* FDATA.C  This program demonstrates the use of the
2              formatted I/O functions. Formatted I/O
3              functions are used for both terminal and
4              file I/O.  */
5
6   #include <stdlib.h>
```

Listing 6.1. Continued.

```
 7  #include <stdio.h>
 8  #include <conio.h>
 9  #include <io.h>
10  #include <graph.h>
11
12  #define DATA_FILE "data.fil"
13
14  int menu( void );
15  int add( void );
16  int display( void );
17
18  /* main() - The main() function calls functions based on
19              the value returned by the menu() function.
20
21              If main() executes correctly a value of 0 is
22              returned. */
23
24  main() {
25    int return_value;
26
27    while( ( return_value = menu() ) != 0 ) {
28      switch( return_value ) {
29        case 1:   add();
30                  break;
31        case 2:   display();
32                  break;
33        case 3:   _clearscreen( _GCLEARSCREEN );
34                  printf( "Enter a correct menu value.\n" );
35                  printf( "Press a key to continue.\n" );
36                  while( !kbhit() );
37                  break;
38      }
39    }
40    return 0;
41  }
42
43  /* menu() - The menu function displays a menu screen and
44             prompts the user to select a menu item. The
45             user's character input is converted to an
46             integer value.
```

```
47
48                menu() returns an integer value that represents
49                a menu selection. */
50
51   int menu() {
52     char char_in[2];
53     int i;
54
55     _clearscreen( _GCLEARSCREEN );
56     printf( "\n\n\n\n\n" );
57     printf( "1.  Add data to the data file.\n" );
58     printf( "2.  Display the data file.\n" );
59     printf( "0.  Quit.\n" );
60
61     printf( "\n\nEnter your selection ==> " );
62     gets( char_in );
63     i = atoi( char_in );
64     if( i >= 0 && i <= 3 )
65       return( i );
66     else
67       return( 3 );
68   }
69
70   /* add() - The add() function opens a data file, prompts
71                the user for the product information, and adds
72                the product information to the data file. When
73                all the new items are added to the file, add()
74                closes the data file.
75
76                If add() executes correctly, a value of 0 is
77                returned. */
78
79   int add() {
80     FILE    *fp;
81     char    more = 'Y';
82     char    name[30];
83     int     count;
84     float   weight;
85
86     _clearscreen( _GCLEARSCREEN );
87
88     if( ( fp = fopen( DATA_FILE, "ab" ) ) == NULL ) {
```

Listing 6.1. Continued.

```
 89      _clearscreen( _GCLEARSCREEN );
 90      printf( "\n\nData file could not be opened.\n" );
 91      exit( 0 );
 92    }
 93
 94    while( more == 'Y' ) {
 95      _clearscreen( _GCLEARSCREEN );
 96      printf( "\n\nEnter product name ==> " );
 97      scanf( "%s", name );
 98      printf( "\nEnter number of items ==> " );
 99      scanf( "%d", &count );
100      printf( "\nEnter product weight ==> " );
101      scanf( "%f", &weight );
102      fflush( stdin );
103
104      fprintf( fp, "%s %d %f", name, count, weight );
105
106      printf( "\n\n\nEnter another product? Y/N ==> " );
107      more = getche();
108      if( more == 'y' ) more = 'Y';
109    }
110
111    fclose( fp );
112    return 0;
113  }
114
115  /* display() - The display function displays the contents
116                 of the data file that was created or
117                 appended by the add() function.
118
119                 A value of 0 is returned if display()
120                 executes correctly. */
121
122  int display() {
123    FILE    *fp;
124    char    name[30];
125    int     count;
126    float   weight;
127
128    _clearscreen( _GCLEARSCREEN );
```

```
129    if( ( fp = fopen( DATA_FILE, "rb" ) ) == NULL ) {
130      _clearscreen( _GCLEARSCREEN );
131      printf( "\n\nData file could not be opened.\n" );
132      exit( 0 );
133    }
134
135    while( !feof( fp ) ) {
136      fscanf( fp, "%s %d %f", name, &count, &weight );
137      printf( "\n\n" );
138      printf( "Product name: %s\n", name );
139      printf( "Product count = %d\n", count );
140      printf( "Product weight = %4.2f\n", weight );
141    }
142
143    printf( "\n\nPress any key to continue." );
144    while( !kbhit() );
145
146    fclose( fp );
147    return 0;
148  }
```

Program execution in Listing 6.1 starts in the main() function (line 24). The while statement in line 27 repeatedly calls the main() function until a value of 0 is returned by main(). If main() returns a value of 1 or 2, the corresponding function is called. If main() returns a value of 3, an error message is displayed and execution continues.

In the add() function (lines 79 through 113), scanf() is used to store the inventory data input by the user. After the inventory data is input and stored in the proper variables, fprintf() writes the data to the disk file.

The display() function (lines 122 through 148) uses fscanf() to get the product data from the disk file, and uses printf() to display the data on the screen.

Understanding *scanf()*

This section discusses the use of the scanf() function in Listing 6.1. You learn how to format and use the functions in the scanf() family, and you also see what other scanf() functions are available.

The statement in line 99 of Listing 6.1 shows a typical use of scanf():

```
scanf( "%d", &count );
```

The `scanf()` function call consists of two parts: the *format string* and the *variable argument list*. In this line of code, the format string is the expression `"%d"`. This string tells `scanf()` the order and type of data that you want to read. Here the `%d` specification tells `scanf()` to read an integer value. As you can see, the format string is enclosed in parentheses.

The second part of the `scanf()` function call is the variable argument list. This is a list of addresses where input data is stored. Each item in the format string should have a matching address in the variable argument list. In the preceding line of code, for example, the integer value extracted from the `inout` stream will be stored at the address `&count` (in other words, in the variable `count`).

When you use any of the functions in the `scanf()` family, remember the following requirements:

■ *Every format specification in the format string requires an address in the variable argument list.*

■ *The data type of the conversion specifier in the format string and the data type at the address specified in the variable argument list should match.*

■ *The variable argument list is a list of addresses.* Each item in the variable argument list should be an address rather than a variable.

Look at the next two statements from Listing 6.1. The first statement is the `scanf()` function call in line 97, and the second statement is the `scanf()` function call in line 99:

```
scanf( "%s", name );
...
scanf( "%d", &count );
```

The `%s` conversion specifier in the first `scanf()` function call causes a string to be input. The string that is read is stored in the address specified by the variable `name`. Recall that when you use the name of an array without a subscript, you get the address of the array. In the first `scanf()` statement, `name` gives the address where the input string is stored.

The second `scanf()` statement is slightly different from the first in that the address-of operator (`&`) is used in the variable argument list. When the unary address-of operator is used with a variable, the address of that variable is returned. In the second `scanf()` function call, the address-of operator causes the address of the `count` variable to be returned. Whenever you use a variable with a basic data type in a `scanf()` statement, you must use the address-of operator to get the address of the variable.

The format string in the `scanf()` function can contain the following three types of objects:

- *Whitespace character.* The valid whitespace characters are the blank, tab, and new-line characters. A whitespace character in the format string instructs `scanf()` to read and ignore all the whitespace characters in the input until a non-whitespace character is encountered.

- *Non-whitespace character.* Non-whitespace characters are any ASCII characters except the percent sign (%). A non-whitespace character in the format string causes the `scanf()` function to read and discard a matching non-whitespace character in the input.

- *Conversion specifier.* A conversion specifier causes the `scanf()` function to read a data item of the specified type from the input stream. The data item that is read is stored at an address specified in the variable argument list. All conversion specifiers start with the percent sign (%).

In the following statement, the first conversion specifier tells `scanf()` to read and store an integer value:

```
scanf( "%d %d", &i, &j );
```

The blank character following the first conversion specifier instructs `scanf()` to ignore all whitespace characters until a non-whitespace character is encountered. Then the second conversion specifier causes `scanf()` to read and store another integer value. Refer to Appendix B for a complete list of the conversion specifiers and options that you can use with the `scanf()` function.

Table 6.1 lists the `scanf()` family of input functions and indicates their uses.

Table 6.1. The `scanf()` family of input functions.

Function	Description
`scanf()`	Used with the standard input stream `stdin`.
`cscanf()`	Reads data directly from the console.
`fscanf()`	Scans data from the stream you specify.
`sscanf()`	Reads data from a string.

All the functions in the `scanf()` family are alike in that they are used to input formatted data. Although all the `scanf()` functions have the same basic purpose, there are different functions for the different streams from which you input data.

The `scanf()` and `fscanf()` functions are the simplest members of this family of formatted input functions. The `display()` function in Listing 6.1 uses the `fscanf()` function. Like `scanf()`, `fscanf()` reads and stores data. However, `fscanf()` can input data from any stream you specify. Notice line 136 of Listing 6.1:

```
fscanf( fp, "%s %d %f", name, &count, &weight );
```

The first argument in the `fscanf()` function call specifies the stream from which data is to be read. In this example, `fscanf()` reads data from the stream pointed to by the `FILE` type variable `fp`. In Listing 6.1, `fp` is a variable that holds a pointer to the stream associated with the disk file data.fil (see the macro in line 11). It is from this disk file that `fscanf()` inputs all the data for the `display()` function.

Understanding *printf()*

Like the `scanf()` function, the `printf()` function consists of two main parts: a format string and a variable argument list. The format string specifies what type of data will be output by the `printf()` function. The variable argument list supplies the data to be output.

The variable argument list for the `printf()` function is optional. It is perfectly legal to use `printf()` without specifying a variable argument list. Line 34 of Listing 6.1 shows the use of `printf()` without a variable argument list:

```
printf( "Enter a correct menu value.\n" );
```

This line of code uses the `printf()` function to print a message.

If you do use conversion specifications and a variable argument list, you should make sure that the conversion specifications match the variables you provide. A mismatch between the format string and the variable argument list causes odd program behavior. You can have more arguments than conversion specifiers, however, without causing any errors.

The `printf()` format string can contain the following two types of objects:

- *Plain character.* Plain characters are any ASCII characters. Any plain characters you include in the format string are copied to the output stream.

- *Conversion specifier.* Conversion specifiers are instructions to the `printf()` function to output a data item of the specified type. Every conversion specification begins with the percent sign (%). A complete list of conversion specifications and options is in Appendix B.

The `printf()` family of functions consists of several output functions. Table 6.2 shows the different functions in the `printf()` family and explains how each function is used.

Table 6.2. The printf() family of functions.

Function	Description
printf()	Sends output to the stdout stream.
cprintf()	Sends output data to the current text window. Note that cprintf() does not translate the new-line character (\n) to carriage-return/line-feed characters.
fprintf()	Works like the printf() function with one exception: With fprintf(), you specify the stream to which output will be sent.
sprintf()	Sends output to a string instead of to a stream.
vprintf()	Like printf(), vprintf() sends formatted data to the standard output stream. vprintf() is called with a pointer to a variable argument list, however, instead of with the argument list itself.
vfprintf()	Called with a pointer to a variable argument list. vfprintf() sends output to the stream you specify.
vsprintf()	Sends formatted output to a string. vsprintf() is given a pointer to a variable argument list as a pointer.

Note how the fprintf() function is used in line 104 of Listing 6.1:

```
fprintf( fp, "%s %d %f", name, count, weight );
```

fprintf() sends a string, an integer, and a floating-point number to a stream pointed to by the FILE pointer variable fp. In Listing 6.1, fp points to the stream associated with the disk file DATA.FIL.

Each argument in the variable argument list for a printf() type function is an expression that yields a value compatible with the matching conversion specification in the format string. The arguments in the variable argument list are not limited to variable identifiers. Note the following example:

```
printf( "%d", 2+3 );
```

This is a valid printf() function call. The expression 2+3 is an integer expression that can be matched to the %d conversion specification. This line of code prints the integer value 5.

Listing 6.2 shows how the vprintf() function, which uses a pointer to a variable argument list, is called in a program.

Listing 6.2. varprint.c. A demonstration of `vprintf()`.

```
1   /* VARPRINT.C   This sample program shows how the vprintf()
2                   function can be used to print a program's
3                   error messages. */
4
5   #include <stdio.h>
6   #include <stdlib.h>
7   #include <stdarg.h>
8   #include <conio.h>
9   #include <graph.h>
10
11  void msg_print( char *format, ... )
12  {
13    va_list arg_ptr;
14
15    _clearscreen( _GCLEARSCREEN );
16    printf( "An error has occured.\n\n" );
17    va_start( arg_ptr, format );
18    vprintf( format, arg_ptr );
19    va_end( arg_ptr );
20  }
21
22  main()
23  {
24    int i = 50;
25
26    _clearscreen( _GCLEARSCREEN );
27    printf( "This is a demonstration of an error message "
28            "report function.\n" );
29    printf( "\n\nPress any key to continue." );
30    while( !_kbhit() );
31
32    msg_print( "Testing message utility i = %d\n", i );
33
34    return 0;
35  }
```

The program in Listing 6.2 shows how the `vprintf()` function makes it easy to display error messages. Listing 6.2 has a routine called `msg_print()` that clears the screen, informs you that an error has occurred, and then prints any information you pass to `msg_print()`. Usually, performing all three of these message-display tasks would take two function calls. The first function call would clear the screen and tell you that an error has occurred. The second function call would call printf() to print the diagnostic message. With vprintf(), however, you can perform all three tasks with one function call.

When msg_print() is called, it is passed an argument list just like the arguments passed to the printf() function. First, msg_print() uses the _clearscreen() function to clear the screen. Second, printf() prints a message telling you that an error has occurred. Finally, vprintf() prints the information that was passed to msg_print(). vprintf() performs this task easily because vprintf() needs only pointers to the data to be output. The arguments passed to vprintf() are pointers to the arguments that were passed to the msg_print() function.

Before you can call the vprintf() function, some set-up is required. First, you need a pointer that can point to the arguments passed to msg_print(). Line 11 declares the va_list type pointer arg_ptr. This pointer can point to the arguments in a variable argument list. Second, the argument list pointer must be initialized to the beginning of the variable argument list. The va_start() macro in line 17 correctly sets up the argument pointer arg_ptr. va_start() needs two arguments—the argument pointer and the name of the *last fixed argument*. The last fixed argument is the last argument before the variable argument list begins.

After va_start() has been called and the argument pointer is initialized, the vprintf() function can be called. Notice that the first argument passed to vprintf() in line 18 is the format argument that was passed to msg_print(). The second argument passed to vprintf() is the pointer to the variable argument list that was initialized by va_start(). When vprintf() has the arguments it needs, it outputs data just as the printf() function does.

When you are through using vprintf(), make sure that you call the va_end() macro, which ends access to the variable argument list. Failure to call the va_end() macro when you are through with the variable argument list pointer can cause your program to behave in strange and undefined ways.

Line 30 calls the _kbhit() function, defined in conio.h. _kbhit() checks the keyboard to see if a key has been pressed. The function returns a nonzero result if a key has been pressed, or zero if no key has been pressed. By placing _kbhit() in a while loop, as shown, you can suspend program execution until a key is pressed.

Using Character I/O Functions

This section shows you how to use the Microsoft C/C++ character I/O functions. The two groups of functions covered are those that input and output only one character at a time and those that work with strings. Table 6.3 summarizes the character I/O functions and describes what they do.

Table 6.3. The character I/O functions.

Function	Description
fgetc()	The basic character-input function that reads one character at a time from the stream you specify.
fputc()	The basic character output function that lets you specify the stream to which character data will be written. fputc() writes one character at a time.
fgetchar()	A version of fgetc() that automatically reads data from the stdin stream.
fputchar()	A function that works like fputc() except that fputchar() writes all data to the stdout stream.
fgets()	A function that reads a *string* from the stream you specify.
fputs()	The string output function that requires an argument specifying the stream to which data will be output.

The fgetc() function reads a single character from the stream you specify. Here is the format for the fgetc() function declaration:

```
int fgetc( FILE *stream );
```

The value returned by fgetc() is the integer value of the character that was read. Although the value returned is an integer value, it is legal (and common) to assign the returned value to a char type variable. Note, for example, the fgetc() statement in the following code fragment:

```
char c_in;
...
c_in = fgetc( my_stream );
```

This is a perfectly acceptable way to read a character from my_stream and assign the character value to c_in.

The only argument to fgetc() is a pointer to a stream. The stream that is pointed to is where fgetc() will read data. The stream must be open before the fgetc() function is called.

fputc() is the mirror-image function of fgetc(). Whereas fgetc() reads a single character from a stream, fputc() writes a single character to a stream. Note the format for the fputc() function declaration:

```
int fputc( int c, FILE *stream );
```

The fputc() function requires two arguments: the character that will be output and the stream where the character will be written. The first argument in the `fputc()` function call is the integer value of the character that will be output. You can pass `fputc()` a char type object as an argument with no problem. A char type argument is simply promoted to an int type argument.

The second argument in the `fputc()` function call is a pointer to the stream where data will be written. The stream should be opened in write or append mode before `fputc()` is called.

Listing 6.3 shows how the `fgetc()` and `fputc()` functions can be used together to read a disk file and display the file on the video screen.

Listing 6.3. chario.c. A program that uses `fgetc()` and `fputc()`.

```
1   /*  CHARIO.C  This program demonstrates the use of the
2                 character I/O functions fgetc() and fputc().
3                 This program opens a text file and uses the
4                 character I/O function to read and display
5                 the file. */
6
7   #include <stdio.h>
8   #include <stdlib.h>
9   #include <graph.h>
10
11  main()
12  {
13    FILE *file_ptr;
14    char xfer_char;
15
16    if( ( file_ptr = fopen( "text.dat", "rt" ) ) == NULL ) {
17      _clearscreen( _GCLEARSCREEN );
18      printf( "Could not open data file.\n" );
19      printf( "Calling the exit() function.\n" );
20      exit( 0 );
21    }
22
23    _clearscreen( _GCLEARSCREEN );
24    do{
25      fputc( ( xfer_char = fgetc( file_ptr ) ), stdout);
26    } while ( xfer_char != EOF );
27
28    fclose( file_ptr );
29    return 0;
30  }
```

The heart of the program in Listing 6.3 is the do-while loop in lines 24 through 26. The do-while loop calls the fputc() function as long as the xfer_char variable does not contain an EOF value.

Only one statement—the fputc() function call—is in the loop. At first glance, the fputc() function call in line 25 may look complicated. A closer examination, however, shows how simple this fputc() call is.

Every fputc() call requires two arguments—the integer value of the character to output and a pointer to the stream where the output character will be sent. In line 25, the second argument to the fputc() function call is a pointer to the standard output stream. The stdout stream pointer indicates that fputc() will write data to the screen one character at a time.

The first argument for the fputc() function call is another function call—a call to the fgetc() function. Remember that fgetc() reads a character and returns its integer value. The integer value returned by fgetc() is the same value that is output by fputc().

In line 25, the assignment of the value returned by fgetc() to the variable xfer_char is made so that the do-while loop can determine when to stop. When the value returned by fgetc() is the end-of-file character, the do-while loop stops.

fgetchar() is a special version of the fgetc() function. fgetc() requires an argument that indicates from which stream data will be read, whereas fgetchar() automatically reads data from the stdin stream. Thus, fgetchar() normally reads data from the keyboard. Note the following example:

```
char in;
...
in = fgetchar();
```

In this code fragment, the fgetchar() function reads a character from the keyboard and assigns the character to the char type variable in.

fputchar() works like fputc() except that fputchar() sends data to the stdout stream by default. Here is the format of the fputchar() function definition:

```
int fputchar( int c );
```

The integer value passed to fputchar() is the value of the character that will be output. The value returned by fputchar() is equal to the value of the output character if fputchar() wrote the character successfully. If the fputchar() function was not successful, it returns the value EOF (defined in stdio.h).

In line 25 of Listing 6.3, you could use the fputchar() function instead of the fputc() function. If you used fputchar(), the statement would look like this:

```
fputchar( xfer_char = fgetc( file_ptr ) );
```

The program in Listing 6.3 would work exactly the same. The `fputchar()` function call would use `fgetc()` to read a character, and would then output the value returned by `fgetc()`.

The last two functions discussed in this section, `fgets()` and `fputs()`, work with strings instead of characters. `fgets()` reads a string from a stream you specify, and `fputs()` writes a string to the stream you choose.

You use the following format for the `fgets()` function:

```
char *fgets( char *string, int n, FILE *stream );
```

The first argument in the `fgets()` function call is a pointer to the string where `fgets()` stores the string that is read. Note the following code fragment:

```
char c_array[81];
...
fgets( c_array, 81, my_stream );
```

The `c_array` argument in the `fgets()` call points to the character array `c_array`. Notice that it is the programmer's responsibility to ensure that the integer parameter (81 in this example) does not exceed the bounds of the array.

The second argument in the `fgets()` function call tells `fgets()` when to stop reading characters from the input stream. This second argument, n, tells `fgets()` to stop reading characters from the input stream when n − 1 characters have been read. `fgets()` stops reading before n − 1 characters are input if a new-line character is encountered. It's up to you to ensure that n is less than or equal to the size of the buffer, otherwise `fgets()` may overwrite memory outside the limits of the array.

The third and last argument to the `fgets()` function is a pointer to the stream where `fgets()` will read data. The stream pointer has a FILE data type.

The value returned by `fgets()` is either a pointer to a string or the null value. If `fgets()` reads a string successfully, `fgets()` returns a pointer to the string (character array) where the input string is stored. If `fgets()` encounters the end of the file, a null value is returned.

The `fputs()` function is the reciprocal function to `fgets()`. `fputs()` writes a string to any stream you choose. You use the following format for the `fputs()` function:

```
fputs( const char *string, FILE stream );
```

The first argument is a pointer to a character array, which contains the string that will be output. The second argument is a pointer to the stream where the output will be sent. Listing 6.4 shows how you can use the `fgets()` and `fputs()` functions.

Listing 6.4. strio.c. A program that uses the `fgets()` and `fputs()` string I/O functions.

```
1   /*   STRIO.C   This program demonstrates the use of the
2                  string I/O functions fgets() and fputs().
3                  This program opens a text file and uses the
4                  string I/O function to read and display
5                  the file. */
6
7   #include <stdio.h>
8   #include <stdlib.h>
9   #include <graph.h>
10
11  main()
12  {
13    FILE *file_ptr;
14    char store[256];
15
16    if( ( file_ptr = fopen( "strio.c", "rt" ) ) == NULL ) {
17      _clearscreen( _GCLEARSCREEN );
18      printf( "Could not open data file.\n" );
19      printf( "Calling the exit() function.\n" );
20      exit( 0 );
21    }
22
23    _clearscreen( _GCLEARSCREEN );
24    while( NULL != fgets( store, 256, file_ptr ) )
25      fputs( store, stdout );
26
27    fclose( file_ptr );
28    file_ptr = tmpfile();
29    if( file_ptr != NULL )
30      printf( "File created \n" );
31    fcloseall();
32    return 0;
33  }
```

Listing 6.4 is a variation of the program in Listing 6.3. The program in Listing 6.4 reads and writes an entire string with one function call, whereas the program in Listing 6.3 inputs and outputs data one character at a time.

The controlling statements for Listing 6.4 are found in lines 24 and 25. These two lines make a loop statement that reads one string at a time from the disk file pointed to by file_ptr. After a string is read, it is sent to the stdout stream for display on the video screen.

In line 24 of Listing 6.4, fgets() reads up to 255 (256 – 1 = 255) characters from the stream pointed to by file_ptr. The characters that are read are placed in the array pointed to by store.

If the fgets() function does not reach the end-of-file marker, the fputs() statement in line 25 is executed. The fputs() function writes to the stdout stream the string pointed to by store.

Using the File Control Functions

Before you use the file I/O functions discussed in this chapter, you need to make sure that the file you are using is opened properly. Otherwise, you will not be able to perform the desired I/O functions. This section shows you how to use the functions that enable you to open and access files on disk drives. It shows you also how to close the files and delete them when they are no longer necessary.

The last part of this section shows you how to control the buffers associated with your files. You can then better control the use of your system resources and the performance of your I/O functions.

Opening, Closing, and Controlling Files

Before you can access a file, you must open it. Opening a file performs two basic services. First, opening a file determines what kind of I/O can be performed on the file. In other words, the way a file is opened determines whether you can read or write data to the file. Second, opening a file associates a stream with the file. The stream is used to represent the file and to transfer data to and from the file.

In the programs in this chapter, you have seen that the data files are always opened before a file I/O function is called. The function used to open the files is fopen(). The prototype for the fopen() function looks like this:

```
FILE *fopen( const char *filename, const char *mode );
```

The fopen() function has two arguments that specify the file's name and the access mode for the file. The file's name is the regular DOS filename with which you are familiar. The mode argument tells fopen() whether the file can be read from, written to, or both. The file mode also determines whether the file is treated as a binary file or a text file.

The following `fopen()` statement attempts to open the file DATA.FIL:

```
file_ptr = fopen( "DATA.FIL", "r+" );
```

Because no path is specified in the filename, `fopen()` attempts to open DATA.FIL in the current directory. However, if the preceding `fopen()` statement were

```
file_ptr = fopen( "C:\\DATA.FIL", "r+" );
```

the `fopen()` statement would attempt to open the DATA.FIL file in the root directory of the C: drive. Notice that the first argument, the filename, is enclosed in quotation marks in the `fopen()` function call. Quotation marks are used because `fopen()` expects a string for the filename argument (a string variable identifier can also be used here—the compiler generates an address value for the argument either way). Notice also that two backslash characters (\\) are used to indicate the path to the root directory. Because the backslash character is a special editing character, you must use two backslashes in a row so that the actual backslash character is included in your string.

The second argument, `"r+"`, is the mode argument, which determines the way in which the file can be accessed. As for the filename string, you can define a mode string variable and use its identifier here, too. Table 6.4 lists the values you can use for the mode argument.

Table 6.4. Mode argument values for the `fopen()` function.

Mode Value	Access
r	File opened for reading only.
w	File opened for writing only.
a	File opened in append mode. The file is created if it does not exist. If the file does exist, the file is opened for updating at the end of the file.
r+	File opened in update mode. Update mode opens an existing file for read or write operations.
w+	A new file is created in update mode. Data can be read from or written to the file. If the file already exists, the old file is overwritten.
a+	File opened in append mode. An update can be performed at the end of the file. If the file does not exist, one is created.
t	If a t is appended to the previous mode strings, the file is opened in text mode.
b	If a b is appended to the previous mode strings, the file is opened in binary mode.

The value returned by the fopen() function is a pointer to the stream that fopen() associated with the file. The pointer to the stream is used by the I/O functions to access the file. The following code fragment calls fopen() and assigns the return value to a pointer that the other I/O functions will use:

```
FILE *file_ptr;
...
if( ( file_ptr = fopen( "myfile.txt", "rt" ) ) == NULL )
  printf( "Could not open file\n" );
```

The first line of this code fragment declares a pointer that can point to a stream. The second line calls the fopen() function. The value returned by the fopen() function is assigned to the variable file_ptr. file_ptr now points to the stream associated with myfile.txt. On the second line of the code fragment, the value returned by fopen() is compared to the value NULL. If fopen() is unable to open the file successfully, fopen() returns a null value. If a null value is returned, the printf() statement on the third line of the code fragment is executed. The printf() statement tells the user that the file was not opened.

The freopen() function is used to associate another file with an open stream. The declaration for the freopen() function looks like the declaration for fopen(), except that freopen() has one extra argument, as you can see in the function prototype:

```
FILE *freopen( const char *filename, const char *mode, FILE *stream );
```

Here the filename and mode arguments follow the same rules as for the fopen() function. The stream argument is a pointer to a currently open stream.

freopen() associates the file specified by the filename argument with the currently open stream pointed to by the stream argument. When freopen() is called, the stream listed by the stream argument will be closed. All subsequent stream access goes through the file specified by the filename argument.

You use the freopen() function to redirect the stdin, stdout, and stderr streams. The following code fragment shows how the stderr stream can be redirected to the disk file error.dat:

```
if( freopen( "ERROR.DAT", "w", stderr ) == NULL )
  printf( "Could not redirect stderr.\n" );
```

When you are through with a file, you should always close it. Closing the file properly helps prevent data loss. If you get out of your program without closing the files you use, you have no guarantee that those files will be there when you come back.

Microsoft C/C++ offers two useful functions for closing your files: fclose() and fcloseall(). The fclose() function closes a single stream and requires an argument indicating which stream you want to close. The following statement closes the stream pointed to by file_ptr:

```
flose( file_ptr );
```

When `fcloseall()` is called, all open streams (except the standard streams `stdin`, `stdout`, `stdprn`, `stdaux`, and `stderr`) are closed. `fcloseall()` does not require any arguments. The following statement closes any streams you have opened:

```
fcloseall();
```

The only streams left open are the standard streams that Microsoft C/C++ opened before your program began.

As your programs become larger and more complex, you will probably find that you need to create temporary disk files to store data. Microsoft C/C++ provides a function that makes the task of creating temporary files safe and easy. The `tmpnam()` function ensures that the temporary file that is created will have a unique name and will not, therefore, overlay any of your files.

The `tmpnam()` function creates a unique filename. `tmpnam()` can generate up to 65,535 different filenames. The `fopen()` function can use the generated filename to create a temporary data file.

`tmpnam()` can have either a null argument or a pointer to a character array that can hold the temporary filename. If the argument is a pointer to a character array, the array must be at least `L_tmpnam` characters long. `L_tmpnam` is a value that is defined in the stdio.h header file. If `tmpnam()` has an argument that is a pointer to a string, `tmpnam()` stores the unique filename in that string. If `tmpnam()` has a null argument, `tmpnam()` stores the filename in an internal static object and returns a pointer to the name. The following code fragment demonstrates the use of the `tmpnam()` function:

```
char file_name[L_tmpnam];
int i;
...
for( i = 0; i <= 50; i++ ) {
  tmpnam( file_name );
  printf( "%s\n", file_name );
}
```

This code fragment is a `for` loop that calls the `tmpnam()` function 51 times. Each time the `tmpnam()` function is called, the filename is stored in the array `file_name`. On every pass through the loop, the new value of `file_name` is displayed.

The `remove()` function deletes a file from your disk drive. All that `remove()` needs is a character string that is the name of the file you want to remove. When `remove()` is called with a valid filename, the file is erased. Note this example:

```
remove( "MYTEXT.DAT" );
```

This `remove()` function deletes the file MYTEXT.DAT from the current disk drive.

The `rename()` function, which renames a file, needs to know both the old filename and the new filename. Both arguments are passed to `rename()` as character strings. For example, the statement

```
rename( "C:\\AUTOEXEC.BAT", "C:\\AUTOEXEC.OLD" );
```

changes the name of your AUTOEXEC.BAT file to AUTOEXEC.OLD.

If drive specifiers are given in the `rename()` argument list, the drive specifiers must match. Directory specifiers in the old filename argument, however, do not have to match the directory specifiers in the new filename argument. If the directory specifiers are different, the file is moved from the directory listed in the old filename argument to the directory listed in the new filename argument.

Controlling File Buffers

In the earlier section "Understanding Devices and Files," you were introduced to buffers. You learned that a buffer is a section of memory set aside for data to be sent to or received from a device. A buffer can improve the performance of your program because the buffer provides a speed-matching service between the slow devices hooked to your computer and the fast memory your program uses. This section shows you how to use the Microsoft C/C++ functions that control the I/O buffers.

The first I/O buffer function is the `setbuf()` function. Note the syntax of the `setbuf()` declaration:

```
void setbuf( FILE *stream, char *buffer );
```

The `stream` argument is a pointer to the stream to which I/O buffering will be assigned, and the `buffer` argument is a pointer to the character array to be used as a buffer for the stream. If the `buffer` argument is null, the stream will be unbuffered. If the `buffer` argument points to a character array, the character array must be at least `BUFSIZ` bytes long. `BUFSIZ` is defined in the stdio.h header file.

The `setbuf()` function can be called immediately after any of the following instances has occurred:

■ The stream is created.

■ A call to `fseek()` is made.

■ The stream has been unbuffered.

Now note the following code fragment:

```
char io_buf[BUFSIZ];
FILE *file_ptr;
char in_char;

if( ( file_ptr = fopen( "C:\\AUTOEXEC.BAT", "rt" ) ) == NULL )
  printf( "Could not open file.\n" );

setbuf( file_ptr, io_buf );

do{
  fputchar( in_char = fgetc( file_ptr ) );
} while( in_char != EOF );
```

This code fragment shows how to set up and use the setbuf() function. The first line declares a character array to be used as a buffer. The character array is declared to be BUFSIZE characters long. Immediately after the stream is opened, the setbuf() function is called. After the setbuf() function is called, the data that is being read will be fully buffered.

The setvbuf() function is the second I/O buffer function Microsoft C/C++ provides. setvbuf() gives you more control over the type of buffer you use and the space allocated to the buffer. The setvbuf() function has the following prototype declaration:

```
int setvbuf( FILE *stream, char *buffer, int mode, size_t size );
```

The *stream* argument is a pointer to the stream you want to buffer, and the *buffer* argument is a pointer to the buffer to be used for the stream. If the *buffer* argument is null, the malloc() function is called, and a buffer is allocated for you. The *size* argument tells malloc() how much space to allocate for the buffer.

The *mode* argument indicates the type of buffering to use. This argument can be one of the following values:

_IOFBF	This value causes the file to be fully buffered.
_IOLBF	This value indicates that the file will be line-buffered (an entire text line is gathered, until the end-of-line character is encountered).
_IONBF	The file will be unbuffered.

The *size* argument specifies the size of the buffer to be used to buffer the file. This argument should be greater than 0 and less than or equal to 32,767. If type is _IONBF, the *size* argument is ignored.

Now look at the following code fragment:

```
FILE *file_ptr;
char in_char;

if( ( file_ptr = fopen( "C:\\AUTOEXEC.BAT", "rt" ) ) == NULL )
  printf( "Could not open file.\n" );

setvbuf( file_ptr, NULL, _IOLBF, 256 );

do{
  fputchar( in_char = fgetc( file_ptr ) );
} while( in_char != EOF );
```

This code fragment shows the setbuf() code fragment modified to use the setvbuf() file-buffering function instead. Notice that the buffer pointer argument has been set to NULL. A null buffer pointer causes setvbuf() to automatically call the malloc() function to allocate the buffer space (256 bytes here). In this code fragment, the setvbuf() function has created a 256-byte line buffer for the stream pointed to by file_ptr.

The fflush() function is the third I/O buffer function. fflush() is used with streams that have buffered output. When fflush() is called, all remaining data in the buffer is written to the file. fflush() requires a FILE type argument that points to the stream to be flushed.

Using the Direct File I/O Functions

The I/O functions that have been introduced in this chapter so far have been easy to use. These I/O functions enable you to write programs quickly and easily. These simple functions, however, don't give you as much control over I/O events and performance as do the *direct file I/O functions*.

What is direct file I/O? Direct file I/O (or simply *direct I/O*) is file input and output in which you can position directly to the part of the file you want to work with, skipping any intervening file data. Thus, the direct file I/O class of functions provides support for file positioning, and reading and writing chunks of data (usually referred to as *file records*).

Because direct I/O usually deals with fixed-length chunks of data, or records, direct I/O is also usually performed using a binary file-access mode. It is possible, however, to use the direct I/O functions in text mode. Direct I/O is often referred to as *random access file I/O* because of its ability to position to random locations or records within the file.

The direct I/O functions give you more precise control of the data you read and write. Using direct I/O functions can also increase file I/O performance. This section shows you what the direct I/O functions are and how to use them.

Understanding Direct I/O Concepts

When you start using the direct I/O functions, you will develop a better appreciation for the work your computer does for you. Soon you will realize what kinds of information you need to keep track of when working with a file:

■ *The beginning-of-file position.* Microsoft C/C++ (and all other ANSI standard C compilers) record locations within a file as a relative offset from the beginning of the file (also called the *file origin*). Thus, the relative position of the origin is zero.

■ *The current file position.* The current file position is the location in the file where the next read or write activity will take place. You can record the current file position at any time, using one of the position-reporting functions discussed later in this chapter.

■ *The end-of-file position.* The end-of-file position is the location just beyond the last byte actually used in the file. When reading or writing has progressed to the end-of-file position, an end-of-file indicator is turned on in the stream object. It is meaningless to read beyond the end-of-file, but you can position to the end-of-file and continue writing to extend the file (to append data to the file).

■ *Details about the sizes of the Microsoft C/C++ data types.* As you saw earlier in this book, each data type can occupy a different amount of memory. You need to know the type of the data you are using so that you can determine the number of bytes to read or write (especially in binary mode).

■ *The location and sizes of the buffer or buffers being used.* It is not necessary to "manually" keep track of buffer locations and sizes—unless you take over buffer allocation as explained earlier in this chapter.

■ *The stream associated with the data file.* The stream (in other words, the type FILE object) is where much of the control information mentioned in this list is stored.

The I/O functions covered earlier in this chapter kept track of most of this information for you. But with the direct I/O functions, you have to be able to access this information in order to make direct I/O function calls effectively. Although using the direct I/O functions means that you have to be more aware of the way your program works, these functions give you precise control of the input and output of your data.

Consider what happens when you write character data to a disk file. Opening the file requests the operating system (DOS, UNIX, or another system) to set aside some space on the disk (that is, to allocate space for the file). The beginning of the allocated space on disk is also the beginning of the file, but your program doesn't have to know the physical disk address. All the program does is begin writing at the file's origin (zero bytes from the beginning); the operating system handles translation of relative addresses into physical addresses.

When your program writes a character of data (one byte of data) to the file, the output library function automatically increments the file position indicator, which is just a number recorded in the FILE stream object noting the current relative address in the file. If your program requests that multiple bytes be written, the file position indicator is adjusted accordingly.

When your program has finished writing data to the file, it must call the file close function. The close function causes any data still in memory to be written out, and requests that the operating system make a record of how much data the file contains (in the file's directory entry and the disk's file allocation tables). Now, when your program terminates, nothing is lost. All the data just written is still there, waiting for you to use it again.

You can, of course, open the file just created and read and write in it using the functions already described in this chapter. But what if you want to read only the first 10 bytes and the last 10 bytes in the file? Reading the first 10 bytes is easy: Open the file as usual and read 10 bytes. To read the last 10 bytes, however, you must use one of the file-positioning functions to set the file position indicator 10 bytes before the end-of-file position. Then you can read the last 10 bytes. If your program attempts to read more data, the input library function returns only an end-of-file indicator. There is a macro for the end-of-file indicator, named EOF, supplied in the stdio.h header. In Microsoft C/C++, as in most systems, the value of EOF is –1 (0xFFFF), so that it will not likely be confused with a valid return value (direct I/O functions return the number of bytes read or written).

When a program reads and writes in a file directly in the manner just described, the file is commonly referred to as a *direct file.* This term is really a shorthand term for *direct access file,* meaning that you can read and write any part of the file without having to read or write data located earlier in the file. You can skip parts of the file, processing only the parts that are necessary at a given time. Note, too, that although one program may treat the file as a direct file, another program may treat it as a normal text file. That is perfectly acceptable, as long as the internal structure of the file is that of a text file.

Now that you have some idea of what sort of tasks the direct I/O functions can handle, you need to know how to use the functions in your programs.

Reading and Writing Direct Files

The fread() and fwrite() functions are a fast way to move chunks of data to and from your disk drive. fread() reads data from the file and places the data in an area of memory. The fread() function automatically increments the file position indicator (in other words, it updates the current file position) by the number of bytes just read. Thus, the next read operation inputs the next sequential data bytes from the file, unless you use the file-positioning functions to change the current position. fwrite() works similarly, but takes data from an area of memory and writes the data to the disk file. `fwrite()` also increments the file position indicator automatically.

Listing 6.5 shows the `fwrite()` and `fread()` functions in the context of a program. Refer to this program listing as you read this section.

Listing 6.5. dirio.c. A program that uses the `fwrite()` and `fread()` direct I/O functions.

```
1   /* DIRIO.C  This program uses the fread() and fwrite()
2                functions to create a file that holds an
3                array of double floating-point numbers,
4                write the array to disk, and then read
5                the array back to memory. */
6
7   #include <stdio.h>
8   #include <stdlib.h>
9   #include <conio.h>
10  #include <graph.h>
11
12  main()
13  {
14    FILE *file_ptr;
15    double x[3] = { 12.3, 45.6, 78.9 };
16    double y[3];
17
18    _clearscreen( _GCLEARSCREEN );
19    if( ( file_ptr = fopen( "mynum.dat", "w+b" ) ) == NULL ) {
20      printf( "Could not open file.\n" );
21      printf( "Exiting program.\n" );
22      exit( 0 );
23    }
24
25    if( fwrite( x, sizeof( x ), 1, file_ptr ) == 1 )
26      printf( "Successful write.\n" );
27    else
28      printf( "Unsuccessful write.\n" );
29
30    rewind( file_ptr );
31
32    fread( y, sizeof( y ), 1, file_ptr );
33
34    printf( "%6.3f, %6.3f, %6.3f\n", y[0], y[1], y[2] );
```

```
35      fclose( file_ptr );
36      remove( "mynum.dat" );
37      return(0);
38  }
```

The actual I/O functions in Listing 6.5 take only two lines. All the code from lines 7 through 23 is setup code for the variables and files. The fwrite() call that writes the entire x[] array to a disk file is in line 25 (notice how the sizeof operator can be used to get the size of the entire array). The disk file is read from disk and placed in another array by the fread() statement in line 32. These two statements move the entire array from main memory to the disk drive and back to another array in main memory. The printf() statement in line 33 is there just to prove that the direct I/O statements work.

The fread() statement requires four arguments. Its prototype declaration looks like this:

```
size_t fread( void *buffer, size_t size, size_t count, FILE *stream );
```

The first argument for the fread() function is *buffer*, which is a pointer to an array in the computer's memory. The array pointed to by *buffer* is where the data read from the disk will be stored. In Listing 6.5, *buffer* points to the double array y[].

Note that the I/O area specified in fread() is a user area separate from any file buffers used by the file. The direct I/O functions perform physical transfers of data to and from the buffers and then copy the data back and forth to the area pointed to by the fread() and fwrite() functions. A user I/O area does not have to be as large as a file buffer. It doesn't even have to be an integral multiple or divisor of the buffer size: The library routines take care of all coordination of data movement.

fread()'s second argument is *size*, which specifies the size of each member to be read or written. In Listing 6.5, the size is specified as the sizeof(y). This means that fread() will read an amount of data that is as large as the array y[]. You can use different *size* values from one fread() call to the next. For example, you can read the entire array in Listing 6.5 at one time, and then later read just single array elements (by specifying sizeof double). Thus, you can read entire records, parts of records, or just single bytes to suit the logic requirements of your program at any point during execution.

count, which is the third argument, tells fread() the number of members to read from the disk file. Because the *size* argument in Listing 6.5 is the size of the entire array in memory, the *count* argument is set to 1. In this sample program, you could just as easily have specified sizeof double and read three members to input the entire array.

The fourth and final argument is the *stream* pointer, which points to the stream associated with the disk file you are reading. Notice that the stream pointed to by `file_ptr` in Listing 6.5 is opened by the `if` statement found in lines 19 through 23. Notice also that the stream is opened in a binary-access mode.

`fread()` returns a `size_t` count of the number of items actually read. If the end-of-file character was reached or there was an error, the count returned will be less than you requested (it may be zero if nothing was read).

The `fwrite()` function is the inverse of the `fread()` function. `fwrite()` takes data that is stored in an area of memory and writes that data to a disk file. Like `fread()`, `fwrite()` has four arguments in its prototype declaration:

```
size_t fwrite( const void *buffer, size_t size, size_t count, FILE *stream );
```

In the `fwrite()` function, the `buffer` argument is a pointer to an area of memory from which data is to be written to the disk drive. In Listing 6.5, *buffer* contains the address of the `x[]` array. This array contains three double floating-point numbers that are copied to a disk file.

The *size* argument indicates the size of each member to be written to the disk file. The *size* argument in Listing 6.5 is the size of the entire `x[]` array. *size* indicates that `fwrite()` will copy the entire array to the disk with one write.

The `count` function specifies the number of members `fwrite()` will output. In Listing 6.5, *count* is equal to 1 because the entire array will be copied to the disk in one write statement.

Finally, the *stream* argument is a pointer that points to the stream to which data will be written.

The `fwrite()` function returns a `size_t` count of the number of items actually written. If there was an error, the count may be less than you requested, or it may be zero.

Many times, the `fread()` and `fwrite()` statements are used to process files that contain character data. Listing 6.6 shows how the `fread()` function can be used to extract information from an exported database file.

Listing 6.6. prtlab.c. The print-label program, using `fread()` to extract information from a database file.

```
1   /* PRTLAB.C  This program reads and prints the records in
2              an address label database file. The file can
3              contain a variable number of records.
4
5              Even though the number of records in the file
```

```
 6                 is variable, the size of each of the fields in
 7                 the records is fixed. The size of each of the
 8                 fields is determined by the typedef structure
 9                 address_t. */
10
11  #include <stdlib.h>
12  #include <stdio.h>
13  #include <string.h>
14  #include <stddef.h>
15
16  #define MAXLABS 180
17
18  typedef struct {
19    char name[36];
20    char street[36];
21    char apt[36];
22    char city[36];
23    char state[6];
24    char zip[5];
25    char fill[2];
26  } address_t;
27
28  void null_term( char* str, int length );
29  int compzip( const char*, const char* );
30
31  void main( int argc, char* argv[] )
32  {
33    int j = 0, k = 0;
34    FILE* adrfile;
35    FILE* labels;
36    char adrname[81];
37    char labname[81];
38    address_t* list;
39
40    if ( argc < 3 ) {
41      puts( "Command format is: prtlab addressfile labelfile" );
42      exit( 0 );
43    }
44
45    if ( NULL == ( list = malloc( MAXLABS*sizeof(address_t) ) ) ) {
46      puts( "Unable to acquire memory for address table." );
47      exit( 8 );
```

Listing 6.6. Continued.

```
48    }
49
50    strcpy( adrname, argv[1] );
51    strcpy( labname, argv[2] );
52
53    if ( NULL == ( adrfile = fopen( adrname, "rb" ) ) ) {
54      puts( "Can't open input address file." );
55      exit( 8 );
56    }
57    if ( NULL == ( labels = fopen( labname, "w" ) ) ) {
58      puts( "Can't open output label file." );
59      exit( 8 );
60    }
61
62    while ( j<MAXLABS-1 && fread( &list[j], sizeof(address_t), 1, adrfile ) ) {
63      list[j].fill[0] = ' ';
64      ++j;     /* go to next address record slot */
65    }
66    fclose( adrfile );
67
68    printf( "Read %d address records.\n", j );
69
70    qsort( list, j, sizeof(address_t), compzip );
71
72    for ( k=0; k<j; ++k ) {    /* null terminate line strings */
73      null_term( list[k].name,36 );
74      null_term( list[k].street,36 );
75      null_term( list[k].apt,36 );
76      null_term( list[k].city,36 );
77      null_term( list[k].state,6 );
78      null_term( list[k].zip,6 );
79    }
80    k = 0;
81    while ( k<j ) {
82      fprintf( labels, "%s\n", list[k].name );
83      fprintf( labels, "%s\n", list[k].street );
84      fprintf( labels, "%s\n", list[k].apt );
85      fprintf( labels, "%s  %s   %s\n", list[k].city,
86        list[k].state, list[k].zip );
87      fprintf( labels, "\n" );
```

```
88      ++k;
89    }
90    fclose( labels );
91  }
92
93  void null_term( char* str, int length )
94  {
95    static int i;
96
97    str += length - 1;    /* point to last byte */
98    for( i=length; i>0; --i ) {
99      if ( *str != ' ' ) {
100        ++str;
101        break;
102      }
103      --str;
104    }
105    if ( i == 0 ) ++str;
106    *str = '\0';
107  }
108
109  int compzip( const char* arg1, const char* arg2 )
110  {
111    return( strncmp( &arg1[offsetof(address_t,zip)],
112                     &arg2[offsetof(address_t,zip)], 5 ) );
113  }
```

Listing 6.6 is a utility program used to format a file of address labels. The input data for the program is a file that consists of a number of fixed-length records. Each of the fixed-length records is a complete address. If you look at the typedef in lines 18 through 26, you can see how each record is organized.

Lines 62 through 64 contain the fread() function that reads one record at a time from the address file. The records that are read are placed in the list[] that is set up in lines 45 through 48. Note the size argument for fread() in line 62. fread() reads enough data from the disk file to fill an address_t type record. Reading this much information enables fread() to retrieve an entire address record with one read.

After the list[] array is filled, the qsort() function is called to sort the entire list of addresses. qsort() is called in line 70.

qsort() is a library function that can be used to sort arbitrary arrays of data. qsort() is defined as:

```
void qsort( void *base, size_t num, size_t width,
    int (__cdecl *compare) (const void *elem1, const void *elem2));
```

In the function arguments list, base is the address of the array to be sorted, and width is the size of each element in the array.

The third parameter, however, is unique. compare is a pointer to a function that you write for use with qsort(). Elements are sorted by comparing each element to other elements in the array and determining whether an element is greater than, less than, or equal to the other elements. This information is then used to properly position the element into its sorted position in the array. By writing your own compare function, qsort() can be used to sort arrays that contain any type of data. Your compare function must have two arguments: elem1 and elem2 (short for *element1* and *element2*), which point to the array elements that are to be compared. The compare function must return a value less than zero if elem1 is less than elem2, zero if elem1 and elem2 are equivalent, or a value greater than zero if elem1 is greater than elem2.

Line 70 calls qsort(). Note that the third parameter, compzip, is the name of the compare function. compzip is defined in lines 109 to 113. Because this program bases its sort on the ZIP code field of the data record, each parameter is treated as a pointer to the address_t.zip field. compzip uses the strncmp() function to compare the ZIP code field as a string. strncmp() returns less than zero, zero, or greater than zero, depending on the collating order of its two string arguments.

After the records are sorted, each field in the record is stripped of excess trailing blanks. The for statement in lines 72 through 79 steps through each record in the list. As each record is accessed, the null_term() function is called to strip the blanks off each field in the record.

Finally, after the trailing blanks are removed, the fprintf() function is called to print a formatted address label. The formatted labels are written to a file on the disk so that the user can print them later.

Using the File-Positioning Functions

The direct I/O functions fread() and fwrite() are useful functions by themselves. These functions are even more useful, however, when you combine them with the file-positioning functions.

With the file-positioning functions, you can detect your current location in a file and change that location if you want. Being able to change your position in a file gives you greater flexibility in getting the data you want when you want it. This section shows you how to use the functions that indicate your current position in the file, as well as the functions that let you change your position.

Obtaining the Current File Position

Microsoft C/C++ has two functions that indicate your current file position: ftell() and fgetpos(). The value returned by ftell() is the current file position expressed as a byte offset from the beginning of the file. The value returned by fgetpos() is the value of the file pointer for a stream. The exact return value of the fgetpos() is irrelevant to you; only other functions like fsetpos() need the return value.

fgetpos() is called with two arguments. The fgetpos() prototype declaration shows the arguments and their types:

```
int fgetpos( FILE *stream, fpos_t *pos );
```

The *stream* argument is a pointer to the stream for which you want to determine the value of the current file pointer. *pos* points to an object that holds the current file position. Listing 6.7 shows how fgetpos() is called in a program.

Listing 6.7. getpos.c. A program that uses the fgetpos() function.

```
 1   /* GETPOS.C  This program uses the fgetpos() function
 2                 to determine the current file position. */
 3
 4
 5   #include <stdio.h>
 6   #include <stdlib.h>
 7
 8   main()
 9   {
10     FILE *file_ptr;
11     fpos_t position;
12     char text_out[] = "Extra string stuff.";
13
14     file_ptr = fopen( "junk.txt", "w+" );
15
16     fgetpos( file_ptr, &position );
17     printf( "Current position = %ld.\n", position );
18
19     fwrite( text_out, sizeof( text_out ), 1, file_ptr );
20
21     fgetpos( file_ptr, &position );
22     printf( "New position = %ld.\n", position );
23
24     fcloseall();
25     return 0;
26   }
```

You need to watch for two things when you use the fgetpos() function. First, make sure that you declare a variable of the type fpos_t (see line 11). The fpos_t type variable holds the current file position value. Second, make sure that you use the address-of operator when passing the position argument to the fgetpos() function (see lines 16 through 21).

The ftell() function is even easier to use than fgetpos(). ftell() needs to know only the name of the stream for which you want to determine the current file position. The following code fragment shows the use of ftell():

```
file_ptr = fopen( "junk.txt", "a+b" );
fprintf( file_ptr, "Additional information." );
printf( "The current offset is %ld.\n", ftell( file_ptr ) );
```

The ftell() function is called in the printf() statement on the last line. The value returned by ftell() is the current file position, which is printed by the printf() statement. Notice that ftell() is given an argument that points to the stream that was opened with the preceding fopen() function.

Setting a New File Position

Knowing the current file position is nice, but being able to change it easily is even better. You use three standard functions—rewind(), fsetpos(), and fseek()—to change the position of the file pointer.

The rewind() function sets the value of the file position indicator back to the beginning of the file. You invoke rewind() by calling it with a stream pointer argument. Note an example:

```
rewind( file_ptr );
```

This statement causes the file position indicator for the stream pointed to by file_ptr to be reset to the beginning of the file.

You use the fsetpos() function with the fgetpos() function. fsetpos() sets the file position indicator back to the value that was stored by fgetpos(). The declaration for fsetpos() looks like this:

```
int fsetpos( FILE *stream, const fpos_t *pos );
```

The first argument passed to fsetpos() is a pointer to the stream for which you want to change the file position indicator. The second argument is an fpos_t type variable, which should contain a file position indicator previously stored by the fgetpos() function.

The following code fragment shows how the fgetpos() and fsetpos() functions are used together:

```
FILE file_ptr;
```

```
fpos_t position;
...
fgetpos( file_ptr, &position );
...
fsetpos( file_ptr, &position );
```

In this code fragment, `fgetpos()` stores in the position variable the current value of the file position indicator. Later, when the `fsetpos()` function is called, the file position indicator is returned to the position indicated by the variable `position`.

Finally, the `fseek()` function is one of the most versatile file-positioning functions because it lets you move anywhere in the file. Note the format of the prototype declaration for `fseek()`:

```
int fseek( FILE *stream, long int offset, int origin );
```

The first argument points to the stream with which you will be working. The `offset` argument lets you specify the relative number of bytes you want to move the file position indicator. The value of the `offset` argument is combined with the value of the `origin` argument to determine exactly where you want to put the file position indicator. The `origin` argument can have any of the following values:

- `SEEK_CUR` is set to the same value as the file position indicator.
- `SEEK_SET` is set to the beginning of the file.
- `SEEK_END` is set to the end of the file.

Listing 6.8 uses the `fseek()` function to calculate the length of a file.

Listing 6.8. flength.c. A program that uses `fseek()` to calculate file size.

```
1   /* FLENGTH.C   This program uses the fseek() function to
2                  calculate the length of a file. */
3
4   #include <stdio.h>
5   #include <stdlib.h>
6
7   main()
8   {
9     FILE *file_ptr;
10    long file_size;
11
12    file_ptr = fopen( "junk.txt", "r+b" );
13
```

Listing 6.8. Continued.

```
14    fseek( file_ptr, 0, SEEK_END );
15    file_size = ftell( file_ptr );
16
17    fseek( file_ptr, 0, SEEK_SET );
18    file_size -= ftell( file_ptr );
19
20    fcloseall();
21    printf( "The file is %ld bytes long.\n", file_size );
22  }
```

In line 14, fseek() sets the file position indicator to the end of the file. In line 15, ftell() stores in the variable file_size the value of the file position indicator. In line 17, fseek() is called again. This time, fseek() sets the file position indicator to the beginning of the file. Then the difference between the end-of-file position and the beginning-of-file position is calculated. The result is stored in the file_size variable.

Handling File I/O Errors

The demonstration programs in this book do not check for many file errors because errors are not much of a problem in these sample programs. When you start writing production code, however, file errors can become critical. You need a way to detect a file error that occurs and correct the problem before much damage is done. This section shows you some of the Microsoft C/C++ functions that detect file I/O errors, report these errors, and deal with the error conditions.

Detecting File I/O Errors

One of the handiest error-detection functions is the feof() function. This function checks a stream to determine whether the end of the file has been encountered. If an EOF indicator is detected, feof() returns a nonzero value; otherwise, feof() returns 0. To use the feof() function, all you need to do is tell feof() which stream you want to check.

The following code fragment shows a common use of the feof() function:

```
while( !feof( file_ptr ) )
  char_in = getc( file_ptr );
```

Here the `getc()` function is executed as long as `feof()` does not detect the end of the file. This code fragment, then, reads the entire file pointed to by `file_ptr`.

The `ferror()` function tests a stream to see whether any error indicators have been set. If `ferror()` detects an error, `ferror()` returns a nonzero value. The stream's error indicator can be cleared with either the `rewind()` or the `clearerr()` function.

This next statement tests the stream to which `file_ptr` points:

```
if( ferror( file_ptr )
  printf( "An error has occurred.\n" );
```

If an I/O error has occurred on that stream, the `printf()` function is executed, alerting you that such an error has occurred.

Displaying and Clearing File I/O Errors

After you have determined that an error has occurred, you need to determine what the error is and clear it if possible. You use the `clearerr()`, `strerror()`, and `perror()` functions for these tasks.

The `clearerr()` function clears a stream's error and end-of-file indicators. To use `clearerr()`, you call `clearerr()` with a pointer to the stream for which you want to clear the error. The statement

```
clearerr( file_ptr );
```

clears the error and end-of-file indicators for the stream pointed to by `file_ptr`.

The `strerror()` function helps you diagnose what error has occurred. `strerror()` takes an integer argument that represents an error code and returns a pointer to an error-message string associated with that error. The following code fragment shows how you can use the `strerror()` function to display the error messages associated with error codes 1 through 10:

```
for( i = 1; i <= 10; i++ )
  printf( "%s", strerror( i ) );
```

In this code fragment, `strerror()` successively returns pointers to the message strings associated with error codes 1 through 10. A pointer to a message string returned by `strerror()` can be passed directly to the `printf()` function.

Finally, the `perror()` function causes the message associated with the current value of `errno` to be printed to the standard error device. `perror()` can take a string argument that will also be printed with the system error message.

Note how you can use the perror() function to display a file I/O error:

```
FILE *file_ptr;

if( ( file_ptr = fopen( "nonexist.txt", "r+b" ) ) == NULL )
  perror( "Sorry Charlie" );
```

In this code fragment, when the nonexist.txt file could not be opened, the perror() function was called. Because an error did exist, the perror() function caused an error message to be printed. The string "Sorry Charlie", which was passed to perror() as an argument, is therefore prefixed to the system error that perror() displays.

Exercises

These exercises give you practice using the following Microsoft C/C++ file I/O library functions: character and string I/O functions, formatted and unformatted I/O functions, and direct I/O and file-positioning functions.

1. Create a simple file program that uses the scanf() and printf() functions to enter and display data in the file. Take advantage of the formatted I/O capabilities so your program can handle integer, floating-point, and string data types.

2. Use a text editor to create a text file of moderate size. Then write a program that reads and displays the text file one character at a time.

3. To demonstrate the effects of buffer size, modify the program you created in the preceding exercise.

4. Use the fread() and fwrite() functions to copy a text file.

5. Use the fread() and fwrite() functions to copy a file composed of integer values.

6. Create a small text file and use the fseek() function to print every other character in the file.

7. Use the file I/O error-detection functions on two of the programs you created in this group of exercises.

Summary

In this chapter, you learned how to use the Microsoft C/C++ I/O library functions, which enable you to access the mass storage and other I/O devices on your computer. The following important points were covered in this chapter:

■ *A file is a collection of related data.* A file can be kept on a permanent storage device or transferred by an interactive device. A permanent storage device is an I/O device that can hold data for long periods of time, and an interactive device is an I/O device used to transfer data. An interactive device does not store data for long periods.

■ *Microsoft C/C++ uses streams to represent and transfer data from files.* Opening a file associates a stream with the file. When you open the file, a pointer to a FILE type data object is returned. The FILE type object contains information used to control the stream and manage the file's I/O buffer. Closing the file disassociates the stream from the file.

■ *Microsoft C/C++ has two types of streams: text streams and binary streams.* Certain characters from a file opened in text mode are converted to an internal format as the stream is processed—for example, carriage-return/line-feed characters are converted to the new-line character (\n). For a file opened in binary mode, no conversions are performed on the data in the file associated with the stream. A binary stream represents the original file bit-for-bit.

■ *You use the scanf() family of functions to input formatted data.* These functions enable you to specify the type and format of data to be input. The scanf() family of functions expect you to supply a format string argument specifying data types to input, as well as a list of addresses indicating where input data will be stored.

■ *You use the printf() family of functions to output formatted data.* These functions enable you to specify the type and format of data to be output. The print() family of functions expect you to supply a format string argument specifying data types to output, and a list of objects (not addresses) to be output.

■ *Microsoft C/C++ provides several functions that perform character and string I/O.* The ...get...() and ...put...() groups of functions provide for the input and output, respectively, of characters and strings. Some versions of these functions assume that the standard streams will be used, whereas other versions enable you to specify a stream.

■ *The setbuf() and setvbuf() functions provide complete control of file buffering.* These functions can increase the performance of your programs by providing a speed-matching service between the computer's slow devices and its fast memory and CPU.

■ *The fread() and fwrite() functions provide direct I/O service.* Using the fread() and fwrite() functions, you can control precisely the amount of data transferred at one time. Note that you cannot transfer more than 64K—16 bytes at a time. 64K is the 80x86 segment size, and DOS requires 16 bytes for a Memory Control Block (MCB).

■ *The file-positioning functions provide complete direct-access file service.* You can use `fgetpos()` and `ftell()` to determine the current file position, and you can use `fsetpos()` and `fseek()` to change the current file position.

■ *Several functions are available for detecting errors in your programs.* The `feof()` function detects the end of the file you are working with, and the `ferror()` function tests a stream for possible error conditions. If you have an error condition, `strerror()` and `perror()` functions can provide diagnostic messages to help you track down the error. The `clearerr()` function is useful when you want to clear any I/O or end-of-file errors posted for a stream.

Using Memory Models

I f you are new to C programming—especially if you are new to PC programming—you must learn how to use the computer's memory. The Intel family
of 80x86 processor chips uses a *segmented memory addressing scheme*. With a
segmented addressing scheme, you cannot use one type of pointer to access
every location in memory. Because the computer's memory is divided into
segments of 64K each, to access a particular location in memory, you must
know the correct segment address as well as the offset into the segment.
Simply put, this chapter shows you how your computer uses memory and how
you can control it.

The chapter also shows you how to take advantage of the Microsoft Overlaid
Virtual Environment (MOVE). MOVE technology enables you to create programs that are larger than those your computer can normally load. Using
MOVE, you can run a large program by keeping unused parts of it on disk, in
extended memory, or in expanded memory. When the extra parts of the
program are needed, they are loaded and executed. MOVE technology enables
you to create more powerful programs than ever before.

Microsoft C/C++ 7.0 also introduces a new virtual memory management system
that you can use to store extremely large amounts of data in extended memory
(EMS), expanded memory (XMS), on a disk, or a combination of all three.
Virtual memory is as easy to use as the standard `malloc()` function used in
nearly all C programs for dynamically allocating memory.

Introducing 80x86 Architecture

To get a grasp of how memory addressing works on Intel's line of processor chips, you need to know something about how the chips were made. When you understand the design of the processor chips, you can understand more easily how to use segmented addressing.

Understanding Segments, Paragraphs, and Offsets

The 8088 chip used in the original IBM PC is a 16-bit processor with a 20-bit address bus and an 8-bit data bus. The *data bus,* located on the system board, is the group of circuit traces that is used to transfer data from the CPU to the other devices. The *8-bit data bus* on the PC allows only eight bits (one byte) of data to be transferred at a time.

The *address bus* is the series of circuit traces that determines which memory location will be used. The number of memory addresses available is determined by the number of bus lines. You can calculate how many addresses are available by raising 2 (the number of values that can be represented on a single bus line) to a power equal to the number of bus lines available. For the PC, the number of memory locations available is equal to 2 raised to the 20th power, or 1M. (If you have an 8088-based computer, you know that you can use only 640K of memory; the remaining 384K of memory is available only for the system's use.)

The 8088 chip is a 16-bit microprocessor. Naturally, a 16-bit processor works with 16 bits of data at a time. Therefore, the largest integer value that the 8088 can use is 65,535, or 64K. The largest integer value that the processor can use determines the largest memory address that can be calculated.

You may be wondering how a CPU that can generate only a 16-bit value can control a 20-bit address bus. The secret is that the address is created with two *words* of memory (on the 8088, a word is two bytes). One word of memory contains an offset address, and the other word contains a segment address. The offset address is a 16-bit value that can address up to 64K of memory. The segment address is also a 16-bit value; however, because the segment address is considered to be *shifted four bits to the left,* the segment address represents a 20-bit value. The segment and offset addresses can be combined to access any memory location.

Take a look at the following example to see how shifting a 16-bit value four bits to the left can generate a 20-bit value:

	Binary Value	Hex Value
Before shifting	0001 0010 0011 0100	1234
After shifting	0001 0010 0011 0100 0000	12340

In this example, the value that would be stored in the segment address register is 1234, the 16-bit value on the first line. By itself, the 16-bit segment address value cannot address a memory location; the 16-bit value must be changed to a 20-bit value. Changing the value is accomplished by shifting the binary value four bits to the left. Shifting the value four bits is the same as multiplying the value by 16.

You can see on the second line of the preceding example that after the segment address value is shifted, the result is a 20-bit value. This 20-bit value is the actual address of a location in memory.

When you see a segment address written down, or when you check the value in a segment address register, the value that you see is a 16-bit value. To get the actual segment address, remember to add four zeros in binary notation (or one zero in hexadecimal notation) to the end of the 16-bit value. The result is the 20-bit segment address.

If you are mathematically inclined, you may have noticed that the segment address can address only every 16th byte of memory. This is true because the four-bit shift always leaves the last four bits equal to zero. Each of these 16-byte blocks is called a *paragraph*.

For addressing a particular location, the segment address must be combined with the offset address. The offset address holds a value that specifies the offset, in bytes, from the segment address. For example, if the segment address equals 2BC00 (hexadecimal notation) and the offset address equals 00FF, the actual memory address equals 2BCFF.

The standard notation for writing a memory address is `segment:offset`. The segment value that is written is the 16-bit value stored in the segment register. The memory location 2BCFF would then be written as 2BC0:00FF.

It is possible for offset values to overlap. With overlapping offset values, *different* addresses can refer to the same memory location. For example, the following addresses refer to the same location:

2BC0:00FF

2000:BCFF

2111:ABEF

2A00:1CFF

The idea that offset values can overlap becomes important when you are working with `far` and `huge` pointers. The next section of this chapter shows you what kinds of pointers are available and how they address your computer's memory.

Advanced Features of the 80286 and the 80386

Intel's 80286, 80386, and 80486 are newer microprocessors that are much more advanced than the 8088. Few programs, however, have been produced that take advantage of these chips' enhanced capabilities. Microsoft Windows 3.1 is changing all that. Windows 3.1 dramatically increases your productivity by taking advantage of the advanced hardware features of the 80286 and 80386 chips.

Because Part III of this book explores programming for the Windows 3.1 environment, you should be aware of some of the hardware features that Windows can use.

Like the 8088, the Intel 80286 is a 16-bit microprocessor. The 80286, however, has extra features that make it more powerful than the 8088. Some of these features are the following:

- A true 16-bit data bus capable of moving two bytes at a time.

- A 24-bit address bus that increases maximum RAM capacity to 16M.

- Multitasking capability that permits the processor to run more than one program at a time.

- Virtual memory that gives the computer access to more memory than is normally available on the computer. This "extra" memory is stored on disk and moved to RAM when needed. The 80286 virtual memory mode gives the processor access to one gigabyte of memory.

The 80386 has even more advanced features than the 80286. These features include the following:

- A true 32-bit processor that can process *and* transfer data four bytes at a time.

- A 32-bit address bus that gives you access to four gigabytes (four billion bytes) of memory.

- A virtual memory mode that can access 64 terabytes (64 trillion bytes) of memory by using a 46-bit memory address.

Understanding CPU Addressing Registers

To increase overall performance, the processor keeps often-used information stored inside the processor chip in several *registers*. The registers are special 16-bit memory locations that can be accessed quickly.

The 8088 chip has 14 registers that hold information and memory addresses. Figure 7.1 is a diagram of the registers used in the 8088. Not all the registers are used for addressing purposes. The functions of all the registers are explained here, however, in preparation for Chapter 10's discussion on using assembly language with C.

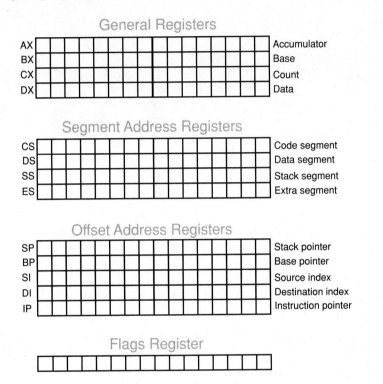

Figure 7.1.

The 8088 internal registers.

Although the general registers are used for a variety of tasks, each has some use usually associated with it. Here are some common uses of the general registers:

AX	Used for accumulating values and for mathematical operations
BX	Used in indexing operations
CX	Used in indexing and loop counting
DX	Used for general and mathematical operations

The registers AX, BX, CX, and DX are 16-bit registers, but they also can be accessed in 8-bit units. Each of these registers has these byte-sized counterparts:

AX = AH and AL

BX = BH and BL

CX = CH and CL

DX = DH and DL

For example, you may use AH to reference the upper byte of the AX register and AL to reference the lower byte.

The second group of registers is the segment address registers. Each of these registers stores a 16-bit segment address value. You can determine the actual segment address by shifting the segment address value four bits to the left. When combined with an offset value, the segment address value points to a 64K block of memory. The segment address registers and the blocks of memory that they point to are in the following list:

CS   The code segment address where the currently executing program is located.

DS   The data segment address where the data for the current program is stored.

SS   The stack segment address for the program's stack area. The stack acts as temporary storage that keeps track of what program functions are called and the values passed to the functions.

ES   The extra segment address used to store program data and to process data transfers between memory segments.

Each of the preceding segment addresses does not have to point to a different segment. In fact, all four pointers can contain the same address. The program's memory model determines whether the segment addresses are the same. Memory models are covered in the section "Using the Six Microsoft C/C++ Memory Models" later in this chapter.

The third group of registers consists of the offset address registers. You have already learned that an offset address is combined with a segment address to access a particular memory location. The next list shows what kind of data the offset addresses locate:

SP   The stack pointer is used with the SS (stack segment) register to find the exact location of the top of the stack.

BP   The base pointer is used to index into the stack to find arguments or automatic variables.

SI   The source index register can be used to index into the data segment. The SI register can also serve other general purposes.

DI   The destination index register is used the same way the source index register is used.

IP   The instruction pointer is used as a program counter for the program that is currently executing. The instruction pointer points to the next instruction to be executed. Microsoft C/C++ cannot directly access this register.

The flags register is a special register that stores information about the current status of the CPU and the instructions that have been executed. On the 8088 processor, the flags register occupies 16 bits. On the 80386 processor, the flags register occupies 32 bits. The extra 16 bits on the 80386 flags register store information specific to the 80386 chip and its processing modes.

Understanding *near, far,* and *huge* Pointers

You saw in Chapter 4 that a pointer is a data object containing the address of another data object. You saw also that you can have different types of pointers: pointers to integers, pointers to floating-point numbers, pointers to characters, and even pointers to functions. In this section, you learn that additional types of pointers are available. These pointers don't point to different types of objects, however, but to different locations in memory.

This section shows you that the type of pointer you use depends on whether the object pointed to is in the same memory segment as one of the segment registers. You also learn how to use the near, far, and huge pointers. Microsoft C/C++ also provides a fourth pointer type called a *based pointer*. Based pointers reference a memory address that is a 16-bit offset from a memory segment that you specify.

Choosing the Pointer Size You Want

Microsoft C/C++ has three different pointer sizes: near, far, and huge. The memory model that you use has one of these three types as the default pointer type. You can, however, explicitly declare a pointer to be any type you want. This section explains the distinctive features of each pointer type.

A near pointer is the easiest pointer to use; however, it is also the most limited because it can store only a 16-bit address. Because of its 16-bit address value, the near pointer can address just 64K. Remember that the maximum integer value that can be stored in 16 bits is 65,535. The near pointer's size, then, limits it to accessing one 64K block of memory.

In accessing an actual memory location, the near pointer must be combined with an address in one of the segment registers. That address points to the beginning of a block of memory, and the address in the pointer is an offset into that block. Which segment register is used depends on what type of object the pointer points to. The CS (code segment) register provides the segment address when a near pointer points to a function. The DS (data segment) register provides the segment address when a near pointer points to a data object.

near pointers are easy to use because you do not have to account for segment values when you are manipulating the functions. Because near pointers do not store segment values, the pointers can be directly compared. Arithmetic operations are also easier on near pointers because calculations do not have to handle segment values.

A far pointer is a 32-bit pointer that can access any memory location. A far pointer contains both a segment value and an offset value. The biggest advantage of far pointers is that they can access code and data segments that are larger than 64K. Thus, far pointers free your program and data from the 64K limit.

Using far pointers does create some problems. Earlier in the chapter, you saw that a single memory location can have several different segment:offset values. For example, the following three segment:offset addresses locate the same place in memory:

> 4000:000A
>
> 3FFF:001A
>
> 3ED2:12EA

Suppose that you have three far pointers, each of which contains one of the values in the preceding list. Each far pointer points to the same location in memory. If you tried to perform a logical comparison on the pointers, however, the comparison would indicate that the pointers are not equal. The *values* (addresses) stored in each of the three far pointers are not mathematically equal, although the pointers point to the same location. Thus, you have to be sure that the segment values are identical if you compare far pointers. If you need to perform logical comparisons, a near pointer or a huge pointer is easier to use than a far pointer.

Performing arithmetic operations on the address stored in a far pointer may not work the way you expect. When you add a value to, or subtract one from, a far pointer, only the offset value is affected. You cannot change the segment value in the far pointer with a mathematical operation. If the value 4000:FFFF that is stored in a far pointer is incremented by 1, the new value of the far pointer will equal 4000:0000 rather than 5000:0000.

Like a far pointer, a huge pointer contains a 32-bit address and can point to any location in memory. The distinguishing feature of a huge pointer is that the address stored in the huge pointer is normalized.

A *normalized pointer* is one that has had a conversion performed on the address stored in the pointer. That address has been changed so that as much of the address as is possible is stored in the segment value. The offset value, then, contains only the values 0 to F (hexadecimal).

The following example shows how the normalization process works (all values are in hexadecimal notation):

16-bit segment address:	3256
Left-shifted segment address:	32560
16-bit offset address:	00C4
20-bit memory address:	32624
Normalized segment address:	3262
Normalized offset address:	0004

Here the original 16-bit segment address is left-shifted to create a 20-bit segment address. The original offset address is then added. The actual memory location is indicated by the address 32624. After the actual address is calculated, the normalization process can start. The normalized segment address is equal to the first four high-order digits of the actual address. The remaining low-order digit from the actual address is the offset value for the new normalized address.

A normalized huge pointer has two advantages over a far pointer. First, logical operations can be performed on the huge pointer. Second, the huge pointer's segment value can be changed with a mathematical operation.

The normalization of a huge pointer lets you logically compare huge pointer values. With far pointers, two pointers could point to the same memory location and still have different segment and offset values. Because of normalization, however, any huge pointers that point to the same location compare as equal.

Unlike the far pointer, when the offset value of the huge pointer wraps around, the segment value is also changed. Because the segment value can be changed when you are working with huge pointers, a huge pointer can work with a single object larger than 64K.

The problem with huge pointers is that extra overhead is needed for huge pointer arithmetic. Special functions have to be called when you perform huge pointer arithmetic. Your processing speed is therefore reduced.

Using the *near, far,* and *huge* Specifiers

You can declare pointers in your programs either with or without the __near, __far, and __huge modifiers. Using a pointer modifier overrides the default type and creates a pointer of the type you specify. For example, the line

```
char __far *char_ptr;
```

declares a far character pointer regardless of the program's default pointer type. But the line

```
char *char_ptr;
```

declares a character pointer that will have the program's default pointer type. If the program is compiled with the tiny memory model, the default pointer type is near. If the program is compiled with the Large memory model, the default pointer type is far.

The short program in Listing 7.1 uses far pointers to keep track of a disk file that has been stored in the far heap.

 **NOTE**   Prior to version 6.0 of Microsoft C/C++, the compiler permitted the use of the near, far, and huge keywords to specify the pointer type. Beginning with version 6.0, Microsoft C/C++ expects these keywords to begin with two underscores: __near, __far, and __huge. To maintain compatibility with existing source code, the compiler continues to allow the use of near, far, and huge, and also _near, _far, and _huge, but you should switch to the new format for all newly written C code.

Listing 7.1. farmem.c. A demonstration of the use of far pointers.

```
 1   /*FARMEM.C  This program demonstrates the use of far
 2               pointers by allocating enough memory to
 3               hold an entire file. For this program to
 4               work correctly, it must be compiled under
 5               the Compact, Large or Huge Memory Model. */
 6
 7   #include <stdio.h>
 8   #include <stdlib.h>
 9   #include <malloc.h>
10   #include <fcntl.h>
11   #include <io.h>
12
13   main(){
```

```
14     unsigned long file_size;
15     unsigned long i;
16     int           file_handle;
17     char          *memory_ptr1;
18     char          *memory_ptr2;
19
20
21     if( (file_handle = open("printers.txt", O_RDONLY¦O_TEXT)
22         ) == -1 ) {
23       printf( "Could not open file.\n" );
24       printf( "Exiting program.\n" );
25       exit( 0 );
26     }
27
28
29     file_size = filelength( file_handle );
30     memory_ptr1 = _fmalloc( file_size );
31     if (memory_ptr1 == NULL ) {
32       printf( "Not enough memory to store file.\n" );
33       printf( "Exiting program.\n" );
34       exit( 0 );
35     }
36     else{
37       memory_ptr2 = memory_ptr1;
38       _read( file_handle, memory_ptr2, file_size );
39     }
40
41     for( i = 1; i <= file_size; i++ ) {
42       putchar( *memory_ptr2 );
43       memory_ptr2 ++;
44     }
45
46     close( file_handle );
47     _ffree( memory_ptr1 );
48     return 0;
49 }
```

Listing 7.1 shows how the memory model that is used to compile a program
affects the pointers declared in the program. Before you examine the Microsoft
C/C++ memory models, first review the purpose of the program in Listing 7.1.

The program farmem.c gets the size of a text file that is stored on disk, allocates enough memory to store the file in RAM, reads the file, and then prints the file.

Lines 21 through 26 use the open() function to open a text file stored on the disk drive. If the value returned by open() is equal to –1, the open() function failed and the program is aborted.

The function in line 29 gets the length of the file that is opened in lines 21 and 22. Then, in line 30, a buffer is allocated from the heap to hold the file. If _fmalloc() returns NULL, the allocation failed.

In line 38, a single function call to the _read() function reads the entire disk file and stores the file in the far heap. The _read() function is able to read the entire file with one function call because the value returned by filelength() tells _read() how many bytes to read from the disk file.

The for loop in lines 41 through 43 steps through the allocated memory block one byte at a time. This technique is not the most efficient way to display the data in the block, but it does provide an easy way to manipulate the block's data. Stepping through the block byte-by-byte makes it easy to come back and modify this program.

Listing 7.1 uses two pointers to index into the block of allocated memory. The two pointers are declared in lines 17 and 18. Although these pointers are declared without any modifiers, both pointers are far pointers because the Large memory model under which the program was compiled causes all pointers to have a default type of __far. It would be perfectly legal, but redundant, to code the declarations in this way:

```
char __far *memory_ptr1;
char __far *memory_ptr2;
```

Whenever you need to declare a pointer of a type that is different from the default type for the program, all you have to do is include the modifier in the declaration. Suppose, for example, that you needed to use a near pointer in Listing 7.1. The declaration for the pointer would look like this:

```
void near *extra_ptr;
```

Using the Six Microsoft C/C++ Memory Models

You have seen several references to memory models in this chapter. A *memory model* is just a compiler option that determines how much memory space to allocate for your program's code and data. This section gives you guidelines on choosing the memory model that is appropriate for your program.

Deciding Which Memory Model To Use

Microsoft C/C++ offers six different memory models from which you can choose. Each memory model has different features that affect how much space will be allocated for the code and data in your program. Table 7.1 lists the memory models and indicates their features.

Table 7.1. The Microsoft C/C++ memory models.

Model	Description
Tiny	This memory model is the smallest. A program compiled under the Tiny memory model can be converted to a .COM file. With this memory model, all four segment registers point to the same address. The program's code, data, and stack have to fit within 64K. You use the Tiny memory model when you don't have any space to spare.
Small	For the Small memory model, the code and data segments are different, but each segment is limited to 64K. The stack is included in the data segment. Many applications work well with the Small memory model. Because this memory model uses only near pointers, program performance is increased.
Medium	The Medium memory model uses the far pointer for the program's code and uses near pointers for the data. Therefore, the code for a Medium model program can occupy up to 1M, but the data is limited to 64K. This model is good for large, complicated programs that do not use data.
Compact	The Compact model is a mirror image of the Medium model, using near pointers for code but far pointers for data. The program's data can occupy up to 1M of memory, but the program itself is limited to 64K. The Compact model is good for shorter programs that handle large amounts of data.
Large	The Large model is used for big programs that work with large amounts of data. far pointers are used for both the program's code and data. Therefore, both code and data can occupy up to 1M of memory.
Huge	Like the Large memory model, the Huge memory model uses far pointers for the code and data. The difference between these two memory models is that the Huge memory model sets aside the 64K limit for static data. Static data can therefore use more than 64K. You use the Huge model for your largest programs.

You select which memory option you want before you compile your program. To select one of the memory options, choose the Language Options... command from the Options menu, and then choose either **C** Compiler Options or C++ Compiler Options, as appropriate.

On the appropriate Compiler Options dialog, use the Memory Model item to select the memory model that you want. Now, when you compile your program, the compiler will generate code that is appropriate for the selected memory model.

Because each memory model allocates code and data memory differently, each model has a unique set of default pointer modifiers. Table 7.2 summarizes the default pointer modifiers for each of the memory models. The default segment modifier is listed if the model's pointers are near pointers.

Table 7.2. Memory models and pointer modifiers.

Memory Model	Function Pointer	Segment Modifier	Data Pointer	Segment Modifier
Tiny	near	_cs	near	_ds
Small	near	_cs	near	_ds
Medium	far	N.A.	near	_ds
Compact	near	_cs	far	N.A.
Large	far	N.A.	far	N.A.
Huge	far	N.A.	far	N.A.

Programming with Mixed Models

A time probably will come when you link a program that has modules compiled under different memory models. Problems can occur if you are not careful when you link these mixed models.

Consider what happens when a module compiled with the Small memory model tries to call a function in a module compiled in the Large memory model. From Table 7.2, you can see that the Small module, by default, calls functions with near pointers, and that the Large module calls functions with far pointers. When a function in the Small module calls a function in the Large module, the function call is made with a near pointer. The function called in the Large module, however, requires a far pointer. This situation simply will not work.

There is a way to use mixed memory models and have functioning programs. The secret is to use a function prototype that explicitly declares the pointer type for the function. Listings 7.2 and 7.3 show two program modules, each compiled under a different memory model, that can be linked to form a functioning program.

Listing 7.2. module1.c. The first module of a mixed-model program.

```
1   /* MODULE1.C  This source code is the first program module
2                 used in the demonstration of mixed-model
3                 programming. This module was compiled under
4                 the LARGE memory model. */
5   int func1()
6   {
7     return 1;
8   }
9
10  int func2()
11  {
12    return 2;
13  }
```

Listing 7.3. module2.c. The second module of a mixed-model program.

```
1   /* MODULE2.C This source code is the second program module
2                used in the demonstration of mixed-model
3                programming. This module was compiled under
4                the SMALL memory model. */
5
6   #include <stdio.h>
7   #include <stdlib.h>
8
9   extern int __far func1();
10  extern int __far func2();
11
12  void main()
13  {
14    printf( "%d %d\n", func1(), func2() );
15  }
```

Listing 7.2 is a source file that contains functions called by another program module. Listing 7.2 was compiled to an object file under the Large memory model. The functions in Listing 7.2 are therefore called with far pointers.

Listing 7.3, which is the main source file for the mixed-model example, contains a main() function that calls the other functions located in Listing 7.2. Listing 7.3 was compiled to an object file under the Small memory model. The function calls made in Listing 7.3 are therefore made with near pointers.

Although the program in Listing 7.3 was compiled under the Small memory model, the program is able to call the far functions in Listing 7.2 because of the declarations in lines 9 and 10. Listing 7.3 contains declarations that explicitly declare the external functions as far functions. The explicit far function declaration causes far pointers to be used, although the default pointer type is near.

If the external declarations in Listing 7.3 were coded as

```
extern int func1();
extern int func2();
```

the linker would generate an error when the project file was compiled.

You also have to be careful about pointers passed as arguments. For example, if the function definition for func1() in Listing 7.2 were

```
int func1( int * i )
{
  ...
}
```

the function declaration for func1() in Listing 7.3 should be

```
extern int func1( int _far * i );
```

If you have a Small model program that needs to link in Microsoft C/C++ library routines, you may need to create a special header file. The library routines are Large model routines and use far pointers. To use the library routines with your Small model program, you need to make a special copy of the header file. In the new copy of the header file, you must declare explicitly all the functions and pointers as far type pointers.

Just remember that the success of mixed-model programming depends on using the right function and pointer declarations. If you throw in an extra measure of care, your mixed-model programs will work.

Creating .COM Executable Program Files

.COM files are executable files like .EXE files; however, .COM files have strict limits on the size of the code and data. This section explains the advantages of using .COM files and how you can create these executable files with Microsoft C/C++.

Using .COM Files

After you compile and link your source code, you have created an executable file, which has all the parts it needs to be run in DOS. Usually, the executable file you create has an extension of .EXE. However, you can create another type of executable file: the .COM file.

The size of a .COM file is its most distinguishing feature. Because a .COM file is compiled under the Tiny memory model, the .COM file's code, data, and stack must fit within one 64K block of memory. This 64K size is somewhat restrictive, but many programs can easily fit in this memory limit.

The biggest advantage of a .COM file is its speed. Because a .COM file always uses near pointers, you avoid all the overhead associated with far and huge pointers. The reduction in processing time needed for handling far and huge pointers increases the performance of your program. You can obtain an identical performance improvement using the Small memory model. From a performance perspective, the only difference between Tiny and Small is that the Small model produces a slightly larger .EXE file, which can imperceptibly increase the program load time. For all practical purposes, I recommend that you use the Small memory model in place of the Tiny model.

Listing 7.4 shows a simple filter program that was compiled under the Tiny memory model and linked as a .COM file.

Listing 7.4. little.c. A small program compiled and linked as a .COM file.

```
1   /* LITTLE.C  This program is compiled with the TINY
2              memory model in order to generate a .COM
3              file. The resulting .OBJ file must be linked
4              with TLINK to create the .COM file. */
5
6   #include <stdio.h>
7   #include <stdlib.h>
8   #include <ctype.h>
```

Listing 7.4. Continued.

```
9
10  main()
11  {
12    FILE *file_ptr;
13    char proc_char;
14
15    if( ( file_ptr = fopen( "printers.txt", "rt" ) ) == NULL )
16    {
17       printf( "Unable to open file.\n" );
18       printf( "Exiting program.\n" );
19       exit( 0 );
20    }
21    /* Read file characters, convert to uppercase, and print. */
22    while( proc_char != EOF ) {
23      proc_char = fgetc( file_ptr );
24      proc_char = toupper( proc_char );
25      putchar( proc_char );
26    }
27
28    fclose( file_ptr );
29    return 0;
30  }
```

The program in Listing 7.4 is well suited for linking as a .COM file. This short filter program reads a file and converts all lowercase letters to uppercase.

The heart of the program is contained in the while loop found in lines 22 through 26. The disk file is scanned one character at a time. If the character that is read is a lowercase letter, it is converted to an uppercase letter. The input character, converted if necessary, is then written to the screen.

The program is suitable for compiling and linking as a .COM file because it contains very little code and data. The only two variables in the program are a file pointer and a char type variable.

The program in Listing 7.4 was written and compiled to an object file in the Microsoft C/C++ PWB. Because the file was to become a .COM file, the Tiny memory model was selected.

 **NOTE** To compile and link this program, you must have the SLIBCE.LIB file, or its contents must be present in the combined library. This library file is constructed automatically during installation of Microsoft C/C++, but only if you have chosen to install the Tiny model libraries. If you chose not to install the Tiny model libraries, you will not be able to link this example program at this time.

Understanding the Microsoft Overlay Virtual Environment

For the first few years after the PC was introduced, programs were not overly complex. During this period, most programs worked with only 256K of memory. As the programs became more sophisticated, they required more memory. Adding memory was fine until the 640K barrier was reached. Making programs larger meant that entire programs would not fit in memory at one time. Programmers had to use overlays to store unused parts of the programs on disk.

With Microsoft C/C++ 7.0, Microsoft has introduced a new overlay technology with the Microsoft Overlay Virtual Environment (or MOVE). Using MOVE, you can create programs that are more powerful and useful than ever before. This section shows you how to start taking advantage of the new overlay utilities. First you learn how a typical overlay system works, and then you see how Microsoft's new system works.

Knowing What an Overlay Manager Does

To run a program that has become too large to fit in memory, you must first divide the program into pieces that can be called as needed. Each of these pieces is called an *overlay*. When a program needs to execute a function stored in an overlay, the appropriate overlay is loaded into memory and the function is executed.

The job of the overlay manager is to decide which overlay needs to be loaded in memory and which overlay can be stored on disk. The overlay manager is responsible for the initial loading of the overlay modules and for the swapping of modules as the program is executing.

Regular overlay systems, although not as sophisticated as MOVE, are still quite helpful. A regular overlay system is divided into two groups of functions: the root unit and the overlay units.

The root unit is the stable part of the program that stays loaded in memory as long as the program is executing. The functions in the root unit can be called by any overlay unit that is currently loaded in memory.

The overlay units do not always reside in memory; they are loaded only if they are needed. A function in an overlay unit can call functions located in the root unit or other parts of the same overlay unit. However, a function in one overlay unit cannot call a function in another overlay unit. The reason is that the typical overlay system allows only one overlay unit to be loaded in memory at a given time.

When a typical overlay program begins execution, it allocates only enough memory space to store the root unit and the largest overlay unit. Thus, when a new overlay needs to be loaded, the current overlay must be put away to disk to make sufficient room for the new overlay.

A typical overlay system is better than nothing, but it is still hard to work with. In such a system, each overlay unit must be self-sufficient. The way overlays are loaded into memory prevents one overlay from accessing any of the functions in another overlay. The only other unit that an overlay can access is the base unit.

The typical overlay system requires that you have complete knowledge of the interdependencies of your program's functions. To include a function in an overlay unit, you must be sure that the function does not call any function outside its overlay unit or the base unit. Keeping track of *all* the interdependencies of the functions in your program can be time-consuming.

Understanding MOVE

Microsoft has introduced a new overlay manager with Microsoft C/C++ 7.0. This new overlay manager is called *MOVE* for *Microsoft Overlay Virtual Environment.* MOVE is more sophisticated than many other overlay managers because it is more intelligent.

As noted before, with a conventional overlay manager, one overlay unit cannot call functions in another overlay unit. Using MOVE, a function in one overlay can call a function in another overlay, regardless of the segment in which the called function is stored. With a typical overlay manager, the basic division of a program is called a *unit.* With MOVE, each division of a program is called an *overlay* or *segment.*

Dynamic overlay swapping is what makes MOVE versatile. When a segment is needed, MOVE attempts to load that segment into the overlay cache buffer area in memory. If enough space is available in the overlay cache, the new segment is loaded and your program continues. If enough space is not available, MOVE looks for other segments that are not being used. Those segments are moved out to make room for the new segment. What if the entire cache area contains active segments when a new segment is called? In that case, MOVE selects a segment that is already loaded and removes it to make room for the new segment. Segments are removed until there is enough space to load the new segment. Dynamic segment swapping relieves you of the task of tracking every function's interdependency.

MOVE's initialization routine will automatically try to use extended or expanded memory, if it is available. The use of extended or expanded memory improves the performance of MOVE. If your computer has extended or expanded memory, segments that are swapped out will be stored there until they are needed again. Storing unused segments in extended or expanded memory is much faster that relying solely on the disk drive for storage.

 NOTE MOVE can be used only with programs compiled with either the Medium or Large memory models. The Tiny, Small, Compact, and Huge memory models cannot use overlays.

As you see in the next section, there is little for you to do to begin using overlays in your programs. The MOVE module that manages the overlaying process is automatically linked into your .EXE file by the linker when overlays are defined. The next section explains how to define your program's overlays.

Designing and Creating Overlay Programs

Although the concept of overlay programs is simple, it takes much code to manage an overlaid program. Until Microsoft C/C++'s MOVE became available, using overlay managers took a good deal of thought and planning. However, MOVE takes care of most of the details for you. Now you can spend more time developing your program and less time planning your overlay units.

Although MOVE is easy to use, some planning is required in setting up and compiling your program. This section shows you how to plan your program and, after you have written the program, how to build the executable file.

Deciding What Modules To Overlay

The nice thing about using MOVE is that you do not have to spend much time determining what you can and cannot overlay. Dynamic segment swapping makes all your overlays available when you need them. When you call a function, MOVE makes sure that the module containing that function is used, regardless of what other overlay is in memory.

You should give some thought, however, to how your functions call each
other. Suppose, for example, that you have the following overlays of code:

Overlay 1:

```
...
func1()
{
  func2();
}
...
```

Overlay 2:

```
...
func2()
{
  func3();
}
...
```

Overlay 3:

```
...
func3()
{
  printf( "Last call in chain.\n" );
}
```

Overlay 1 has to call overlay 2, and overlay 2 has to call overlay 3. If all three
overlays were small and could fit in memory, this would not be a problem. If
the overlays were large, however, overlays 1 and 2 would probably be moved
out of memory by the time overlay 3 was called.

If func1(), func2(), and func3() were all in the same overlay, the extra overlay
swapping would be avoided and the program would run faster. As you can see
from this example, grouping interdependent functions together enhances the
performance of your program. When you create a program, you might want to
put all the graphics functions in one overlay and all the help functions in
another overlay.

Some functions should not be overlaid. Functions that are designed to be
short, fast, or time-critical are better left resident. You should always leave a
time-critical function resident to ensure that the function is immediately
available when it is needed. Functions that handle system interrupts should
not be overlaid either. If an interrupt handler is not in memory when an
interrupt occurs, your program will probably blow up.

Each overlay can be up to 64K in size. For optimal overlay efficiency, however,
Microsoft suggests aiming for a 4K overlay size.

As you can see, dividing your program into overlay segments is simple. You should group logically related, interdependent functions in overlay segments and leave the time-critical functions and interrupt handlers resident. Dividing your program into logical segments usually results in good overall performance.

Compiling and Linking an Overlay Program

Creating an overlay program is easy. You design and write overlay projects just as you design and write other C projects. The only change you must make is the addition of a module definitions file, known as a .DEF file. The .DEF file contains special module definition statements that provide the Linker with information about your program. As you might expect, the .DEF file specifies which parts of your program go into which overlay sections. The .DEF file is easy to create; for overlays, you need to use only a single statement called SEGMENTS. The SEGMENTS function defines the overlays or segments used in your programs. The .DEF file is then included in the project file used to make your application. (You'll learn more about .DEF files in Part III, "Using Microsoft C/C++ with Windows," because all Windows programs must use .DEF files).

Before looking at what goes into the .DEF file, take a look at a group of source files that produce a program when they are compiled called ovrmain.exe. Listings 7.5 through 7.9 contain a very simple program made up of a main program—ovrmain.c—and four separate modules—ovrmod1, ovrmod2, ovrmod3, and ovrmod4—that will be placed into overlays using information provided in the DEF file.

Listing 7.5. The ovrmain.c program calls several functions that will be placed into overlays.

```
1   /* OVRMAIN.C  The main file in the overlay program
2                 project. This file will stay resident
3                 during the entire program execution. */
4
5   #include <stdio.h>
6   #include <stdlib.h>
7   #include <conio.h>
8   #include <graph.h>
9
10  /* From OVRMOD1.C */
11  extern void ovrfunc1( void );
12  extern void ovrfunc3( void );
```

Listing 7.5. Continued.

```
13
14   /* From OVRMOD2.C */
15   extern void ovrfunc2( void );
16
17   /* From OVRMOD3.C */
18   extern void ovrfunc4( void );
19
20   /* From OVRMOD4.C */
21   extern void ovrfunc5( void );
22   extern void ovrfunc6( void );
23
24
25   int global_i;
26   extern char *ovr1_msg;
27   extern char *ovr2_msg;
28
29   void rootfunc( void )
30   {
31     printf("Demonstrates calling a root function from an overlay.\n\n");
32   }
33
34   main( void )
35   {
36     _clearscreen( _GCLEARSCREEN );
37     printf( "In ovrmain.c. global_i and global_msg have "
38             "not been initialized.\n\n" );
39
40     ovrfunc1();
41     printf( "The first overlay module has been called.\n" );
42     printf( "global_i = %d.\n", global_i );
43     printf( "The overlay message = %s.\n\n", ovr1_msg );
44
45     ovrfunc2();
46     printf( "The second overlay module has been called.\n" );
47     printf( "global_i = %d.\n", global_i );
48     printf( "The overlay message = %s.\n\n", ovr2_msg );
49
50     /* Call routine back in overlay module 1 */
51     ovrfunc3();
52
```

```
53    /* Call routine in overlay module 4 */
54    ovrfunc4();
55
56    /* Both of the following functions are in the ovrmod4 module.
57       But only ovrfunc5() is overlaid, having been placed in overlay 2 */
58    ovrfunc5();
59    ovrfunc6();
60
61    printf( "Back in ovrmain.c module, ready to exit.\n" );
62    return 0;
63 }
```

Listing 7.6. ovrmod1.c. The first overlay manager.

```
1  /* OVRMOD1.C This is the first overlay module to
2                be called. The purpose of this module
3                is to set the values of the global
4                variables in ovrmain.c. */
5
6  extern int global_i;
7  char *ovr1_msg;
8
9  void ovrfunc1( void )
10 {
11   global_i = 10;
12   ovr1_msg = "Working in ovrmod1.c";
13 }
14
15 void ovrfunc3( void )
16 {
17   printf("This is coming to you from ovrfunc3 inside the first overlay.\n");
18 }
```

Listing 7.7. ovrmod2.c. The second overlay manager.

```
1   /* OVRMOD2.C  This is the second overlay module file. This
2                 file is called by the ovrmain.c module. */
3
4   extern global_i;
5   char *ovr2_msg;
6
7   void ovrfunc2()
8   {
9     global_i = 20;
10    ovr2_msg = "Working in ovrfunc2";
11  }
```

Listing 7.8. ovrmod3.c. The third overlay manager.

```
1   /* OVRMOD3.C  This is the third overlay module file. */
2
3   extern void rootfunc( void );
4
5   void ovrfunc4()
6   {
7     printf("Inside ovrfunc4(), we call the rootfunc().\n");
8     rootfunc();
9   }
```

Listing 7.9. ovrmod4.c. The fourth overlay manager.

```
1   /* OVRMOD4.C  This contains two functions, only one of which is overlaid */
2
3   void ovrfunc5()
4   {
5     printf("Inside ovrfunc5().\n");
6   }
7
8   void ovrfunc6()
9   {
10    printf("Inside ovrfunc6().\n");
11  }
```

The preceding three listings make a simple program. The main program module in Listing 7.5 makes calls to the overlay modules, which store values in global variables in the main module.

These three program modules were written and compiled like any normal project. You can compile and link all five files "as-is" and produce a normal, non-overlayed program.

Turning this program into an overlaid program requires the use of the definitions file to tell the linker which modules go into which overlay. Listing 7.10 shows a sample definitions file for use with these short program modules.

Listing 7.10. The ovrmain.def module definitions file.

```
1   SEGMENTS
2       OVRMOD1_TEXT  OVL:1
3       OVRMOD2_TEXT  OVL:2
4       OVRMOD3_TEXT  OVL:1
5       OVRMOD4_TEXT  OVL:3
```

The SEGMENTS keyword is the only statement that you need to place in your definitions file. You can place other statements, if needed; however, to describe overlays you need only the SEGMENTS keyword.

Each statement following SEGMENTS specifies a segment name, followed by the keyword OVL:, followed by an overlay number. The segment name corresponds to each .obj module name, in all capital letters, followed by _TEXT. Hence, OVRMOD1_TEXT corresponds to the module produced by compiling ovrmod1.c.

The number following the OVL: keyword tells the linker into which overlay the module should be placed. The statements in this DEF file cause ovrmod1 and ovrmod3 to be placed in overlay 1, ovrmod2 to be placed in overlay 2, and ovrmod4 to be placed in overlay 3. That's all there is to creating an overlaid program.

The Microsoft Linker automatically links in the MOVE library routines and structures your .EXE file appropriately for overlays. MOVE takes care of memory initialization and allocation and reads your overlay sections from disk when needed.

To compile and link your overlaid program, use the PWB to create a project file containing ovrmain.c, ovrmod1.c, ovrmod2.c, ovrmod3.c, ovrmod4.c, ovrmain.def, and graphics.lib. Remember to select either the Medium or Large memory model. Then build your project.

To compile and link using the command line compiler, enter the following command:

```
cl /AM ovrmain.c ovrmod1.c ovrmod2.c ovrmod3.c ovrmod4.c ovrmain.def graphics.lib
```

You must specify /AM to select the Medium memory model or /AL to select the Large memory model. The MOVE overlay manager routines are available only in the Medium or Large memory model libraries.

All the overlays are placed in a single .EXE file. This eliminates problems caused by other overlay systems that create one .EXE file and lots of .OVL (or similarly named) files containing each overlay.

This short project illustrates how the overlay manager works. A real program that benefits from using the overlay manager would be too large to include in this book. As you create more powerful programs, you will soon discover how useful the MOVE overlay manager can be.

Using Virtual Memory

All programs eventually run out of memory (or so it seems). There's a programming proverb that says "All programs will grow to fill the available memory size." No matter how much memory you have available today, your program will eventually need more. Microsoft's MOVE technology helps you manage the ever-expanding program code segments. When your program needs to access more data than can fit in DOS's limited memory space, you need to turn to virtual memory techniques.

At the simplest level, if the data required by your program does not fit into memory, you can always write the data to disk and read the data back piece-by-piece, as needed. This can be awkward, however, and will greatly slow your program's execution unless you use multiple file buffers and add a fair degree of complexity to your program.

Fortunately, you don't have to go to so much trouble. Microsoft C/C++ 7.0 offers virtual memory functions that enable you to manipulate data structures that require more memory than is available within the confines of DOS. Microsoft C/C++'s virtual memory manager automatically takes care of swapping your data to and from disk, extended memory, or expanded memory. In the latter case, your programs will run nearly as fast as if their data fit entirely into memory. Using virtual memory, your programs will now be able to conveniently access and use sizeable data structures that regular DOS programs can't touch unless they include lots of messy programming tricks.

Using the virtual memory manager is almost as easy as calling the malloc() function to allocate memory blocks. To begin using virtual memory, you must first call the _vheapinit() function to initialize the virtual memory management system. Then, call _vmalloc() to allocate blocks of virtual memory. _vmalloc()

is different than `malloc()`, however, in that `_vmalloc()` returns a handle, rather than a pointer, to memory. To access the virtual memory block, you must first call `_vload()` or `_vlock()` to ensure that your memory block is actually in DOS memory where your program can gain access to it.

Listing 7.11 illustrates an example usage of the virtual memory manager.

Listing 7.11. The vmem.c program shows how to allocate and use virtual memory.

```
1   /* VMEM.C Demonstrates use of virtual memory routines. */
2
3   #include <stdio.h>
4   #include <vmemory.h>
5
6   #define BLOCKSIZE 1024
7
8   main( void )
9   {
10    _vmhnd_t vmblock1, vmblock2;
11    char __far *bigblock;
12    int i;
13
14    /* Initialize the virtual memory manager */
15    if (_vheapinit( 8192/16, _VM_ALLDOS, _VM_XMS ) == 0) {
16        printf("Unable to initialize virtual memory manager.\n");
17        exit(1);
18    };
19
20    vmblock1 = _vmalloc( BLOCKSIZE );
21
22    bigblock = (char *) _vload( vmblock1, _VM_DIRTY );
23
24    /* Process the data in bigblock in the usual way */
25    for (i=1; i<=BLOCKSIZE; i++)
26      *bigblock++ = '!';
27
28    /* Allocate a second block */
29    vmblock2 = _vmalloc( BLOCKSIZE );
30    bigblock = (char *) _vload( vmblock2, _VM_DIRTY );
31
```

Listing 7.11. Continued.

```
32    for (i=1; i<=BLOCKSIZE; i++)
33      *bigblock++ = '*';
34
35    bigblock = (char *) _vload( vmblock1, _VM_CLEAN );
36    if (*bigblock == '!')
37      printf("First block contains ! characters.\n");
38    else
39      printf("Error: first block isn't correct.\n");
40
41    bigblock = (char *) _vload( vmblock2, _VM_CLEAN );
42    if (*bigblock == '*')
43      printf("Second block contains * characters.\n");
44    else
45      printf("Error: second block isn't correct.\n");
46
47    /* Terminate the virtual memory mgr; free up all resources */
48    _vheapterm();
49  }
```

Line 4 includes the vmemory.h header file. This is required when using the virtual memory features. Line 10 declares two handles to virtual memory blocks: vmblock1 and vmblock2. You must declare and use a handle for each virtual memory block that you allocate. The _vmhnd_t typedef is defined for you in vmemory.h.

The call to _vheapinit() (see line 15) initializes the virtual memory system and allocates a DOS memory area buffer for access to the virtual memory blocks. The first parameter to _vheapinit() is the minimum required memory for your application. Microsoft recommends that the minimum be at least several kilobytes in size. Note that the size specified in line 15 of this example program—8192 bytes—is divided by 16. This is because the memory size should be specified in paragraphs. Remember that the Intel family of microprocessors segments memory. The segment registers can address memory only in 16-byte increments. Hence, 8192 divided by 16 defines the number of 16-byte paragraphs to be allocated.

The next parameter defines the maximum number of paragraphs to allocate for the virtual memory buffers. If you use the constant _VM_ALLDOS, the virtual memory system will allocate up to the remaining free DOS memory.

The third parameter tells the virtual memory system where it should place the virtual memory blocks when they do not fit in DOS memory. You can place these blocks in extended memory, expanded memory, a disk file, or a combination of all three. As shown in line 15, the constant _VM_XMS requests that the virtual memory space be allocated in extended memory. The other constants you can use here are _VM_EMS, _VM_DISK, or _VM_ALLSWAP. _VM_ALLSWAP requests that all forms of additional memory be used; if some are not available, it will use only that which is present.

Line 20 calls _vmalloc() to allocate a block of virtual memory. It returns a handle rather than a pointer like malloc(). Before you can begin to use the allocated virtual memory block, you must use the _vload() (see line 30) or _vlock() functions (described a little later in this section) to load the block into the DOS memory area. Both functions return a far pointer to the virtual block. You can now use the virtual memory block as you would use any other dynamically allocated memory.

What happens when you allocate another block of memory and there isn't room in the virtual memory buffer? When this happens, the virtual memory system must throw out one of the blocks it currently has in memory. Blocks are selected using a Least-Recently-Used algorithm. In other words, a block that hasn't been used recently is discarded and its space is made available for a new block.

What happens to the data in a block that is about to be discarded? This depends on the second parameter used in the call to _vload(). In line 30, this parameter is set to _VM_DIRTY. This tells the virtual memory manager to automatically move the block from DOS memory out to the virtual memory area (XMS, EMS, or a disk file). If this parameter is set to _VM_CLEAN, the memory manager assumes that the data in the block has not been altered—in other words, it is *clean*. Clean blocks do not need to be written back to the virtual memory area because the virtual memory storage already has a copy of this block.

The first time you allocate and load a memory block, it is very important that you set this parameter to _VM_DIRTY. This ensures that any data you write to the block will be updated into the virtual memory storage area. Thereafter, if you wish only to read the data, you can set the parameter to _VM_CLEAN. If you wish to read and change the data, you must again set this value to _VM_DIRTY.

Using _vlock()

The data in a virtual memory block is only guaranteed between calls to the virtual memory functions. If you set a pointer to a block of data and then call another virtual memory function, your pointer may no longer be valid. Fortunately, you can force the virtual memory manager to lock your block in a safe memory location. _vlock()'s only parameter is a handle to a block and is called like this:

```
bigblock = (char *) _vlock( vmblock1 );
```

Now, the memory block is locked in memory and will not be discarded until you call _vunlock(). If the block is dirty and needs to be saved, write

```
_vunlock( vmblock1, _VM_DIRTY );
```

If the block is clean and can be safely discarded, write

```
_vunlock( vmblock1, _VM_CLEAN );
```

If you call _vlock() more than once using the same handle, the virtual memory manager increments a counter a maximum of 255 times. Subsequent calls to _vunlock() decrement the counter; when the counter reaches 0, the block is discarded.

Freeing up a Virtual Memory Block

To free up the virtual memory space occupied by a block, you can call _vfree (vmhandle). The block owned by vmhandle must not be locked when you want to free it.

Terminating Virtual Memory Usage

When you no longer need to use the virtual memory services, call _vheapterm(). This is extremely important! If you fail to call _vheapterm(), any extended or expanded memory blocks used by the virtual storage system may remain allocated until you reboot the computer.

Exercises

The following exercises give you practice in creating and compiling programs in different memory models, using pointers in different memory models, and using overlay programs:

1. Create a short program and compile it under the Small and Large memory models.

2. Make a Large model program that uses a pointer to a string. Use the FP_SEG() and FP_OFF() functions to examine the values of the far pointer.

3. Write a program that counts the number of Cs in a disk file. Compile the program to a .COM file using the Tiny memory model.

4. Create a mixed-model project that has a large module with at least three functions, and a small module with only a `main()` function. Have the `main()` function call each of the functions in the large module.

5. Write an overlay program that keeps the `main()` function resident and overlays two other functions. Have one overlay dump a text file in all lowercase letters, and have the other overlay dump a text file in all uppercase letters.

6. Write a program to read a file into a virtual array of line records. Allocate perhaps 500 blocks, each 80 bytes in size or of a size sufficient to hold text lines from a file. Read and copy an entire text file into the virtual memory blocks and print the contents of each block to the screen. By using the virtual memory manager in this fashion, you have the makings of a simple text editor program!

Summary

In this chapter, you saw how your Microsoft C/C++ programs use your computer's memory. The following important points were covered:

- *Because the Intel family of processor chips is based on a design that uses a 16-bit processor and a 20-bit address bus, the address of a memory location has to be divided into two parts: the segment address and the offset address.* By itself, the segment address cannot address a particular memory location. An offset address must be added to the segment address in order to access a particular memory location.

- *To increase CPU performance, the 8088 processor has a series of registers that store often-used data.* These registers store, among other things, segment and offset addresses for your program's code, data, and stack memory locations.

- *Microsoft C/C++ has three types of pointers: __near, __far, and __huge.* The __near pointer must be used with a segment value in one of the segment address registers. The __far pointer can access any memory location, but you cannot reliably compare or perform mathematical operations on __far pointers. The __huge pointer can access any memory location and can be successfully compared and manipulated. __huge pointers can work with objects larger than 64K. The normalization of the __huge pointer, however, requires extra function calls and consequently slows your program.

- *Microsoft C/C++ has six different memory models you can use when compiling your program.* They are the Tiny, Small, Medium, Compact, Large, and Huge models. The model you use determines how much memory will be available for the code and data in your program.

■ *Mixed-model programming requires that you explicitly declare the types of the functions and pointers in the external modules.*

■ *.COM files are executable files that have the program's code, data, and stack stored in the same 64K block of memory.* .COM files are useful for small programs that do not require much data. Such files are efficient because only near pointers are used.

■ *MOVE, the Microsoft Overlaid Virtual Environment overlay manager, controls the use of overlays in your program.* An overlay is a program segment that is stored on disk until it is needed. At that time, the segment is read from disk and executed.

■ *When designing an overlay program, try to keep interdependent functions in the same segment.* Keeping these functions together means fewer overlay swaps and better performance. Interrupt-handling and time-critical functions should not be overlaid. Overlaying an interrupt handler can cause odd program behavior.

■ *Microsoft C/C++ provides a easy-to-use virtual memory manager.* You can use the virtual memory functions to allocate and manipulate large data structures. This is especially helpful when your program's code has grown sufficiently large that there is very little DOS memory left over for your program's data.

The next chapter shows you how to use the Microsoft C/C++ video functions. These functions make it easy for you to control both your text and graphic video output.

Using the Microsoft C/C++ Video Functions

Microsoft C/C++ provides an extensive library of graphic and text video functions that enable you to create professional-looking screens, including presentation-quality graphics, quickly and easily.

The purpose of this chapter is to get you up and running with the Microsoft C/C++ video functions. The chapter is not designed to be an exhaustive reference on video programming; a complete reference requires more space than is available. The chapter does cover most of the video functions and shows you how to use some of the more popular ones.

Understanding the IBM/PC Text Modes

Video monitors work in two basic video modes: *graphics mode* and *text mode*. In graphics mode, because you have control of every pixel on the screen, you can display any type of image you want. In text mode, you are limited to displaying characters from the video adapter's character set. The advantages of text mode are the speed and ease with which character output can be formatted and displayed. This section provides an overview of how character data sent from your program is displayed on the screen.

Surveying PC Video Adapters and Screens

The video display system on your computer consists of two parts: the video adapter and the screen. Inside your computer, the *video adapter* is a group of circuits that translates the data output by your program to a video signal the monitor can use.

When your program outputs the letter *T*, the ASCII value that represents the letter *T* is sent to the video adapter. The video adapter uses the ASCII code to look up the shape of the letter in the adapter's ROM (read-only memory). The information from the ROM chip tells the adapter which pixels must be turned on to display the character on the screen. Finally, the character is displayed at either the current cursor position or a position you specify. Figure 8.1 shows the basic process of displaying a character on the screen.

Figure 8.1.

How a character is displayed.

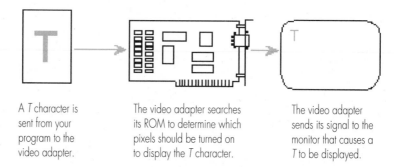

A *T* character is sent from your program to the video adapter.

The video adapter searches its ROM to determine which pixels should be turned on to display the *T* character.

The video adapter sends its signal to the monitor that causes a *T* to be displayed.

The process in Figure 8.1 shows how data is displayed on-screen in text mode—the display mode in which only character data can be displayed. See Appendix A for a list of the 256 ASCII characters that can be displayed in text mode.

Microsoft C/C++ supports five different text modes. These modes differ in the number of characters displayed on-screen and whether characters are displayed in black and white or in color. Table 8.1 lists the five text modes and their distinguishing features. The identifier listed beneath the *Mode* heading is used in conjunction with the _setvideomode() function.

Table 8.1. The Microsoft C/C++ text modes.

Mode	Features
_TEXTBW40	A black-and-white 40-column mode. This mode displays 25 lines, each of which can hold 40 characters. The characters are displayed in black and white.

Mode	Features
_TEXTC40	A color 40-column mode. The screen displays 40 columns and 25 rows of characters in color.
_TEXTBW80	A black-and-white 80-column mode. The screen displays 80 columns and 25 rows. The characters are displayed in black and white.
_TEXTC80	A color mode that displays 80 columns and 25 rows.
_TEXTMONO	A mode that displays monochrome text in 80 columns and 25 rows.

Understanding Memory-Mapped Screen I/O

So that the image on your monitor appears stable to the human eye, the video circuitry redraws the screen 60 times every second.

Fortunately, your program does not have to send data to the display adapter every time the screen is redrawn. When the program sends data to the display adapter, the data is stored in a special section of RAM reserved for *video memory*. Each time the video adapter redraws the screen, the adapter checks the video memory to see what should be put on-screen.

Each display location on the screen has a corresponding location in video memory. If there is a character in a video memory location, that character is drawn at the corresponding location on the video display.

Having a memory location for each location on the video display is the idea behind memory-mapped screen I/O. If you do not specify a memory location, display data that is output by your program is stored at the next available location in video memory. If you want, you can specify the memory address where your data is to be stored. Specifying the memory address lets you put display data at the exact screen location you want.

With the built-in Microsoft C/C++ video functions, you can create sophisticated images without having to worry about direct access to video memory. With these video functions, you can place data anywhere on the screen by using the correct row and column address. You do not have to use the actual video memory address. Microsoft C/C++ takes care of that for you.

When you are working in text mode, every location on the screen has two memory bytes associated with it. The first byte of memory stores the ASCII value of the character to be displayed. The second byte, called the *attribute byte*, stores information about the way the character is displayed. Figure 8.2 shows how a location in video memory is related to a location on the screen.

314

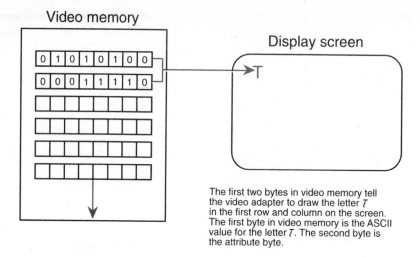

Video memory

Display screen

The first two bytes in video memory tell
the video adapter to draw the letter *T*
in the first row and column on the screen.
The first byte in video memory is the ASCII
value for the letter *T*. The second byte is
the attribute byte.

Controlling the Text Screen

The Microsoft C/C++ library of functions makes it easy for you to control the
appearance of the text-mode screen. Functions are available for selecting the
text mode to be used, the background color, and the attributes of the text.
This section shows you how to start using these text-mode control functions.

All screen control functions for both text and graphics modes are defined in
the graph.h header file. To use the text video functions, place the following
statement at the beginning of your source file:

```
#include <graph.h>
```

Selecting a Video Mode

The first text-mode control function that you need to call is the
_setvideomode() function. This function determines the number of characters
that can be displayed and whether color will be used. Note the format of the
_setvideomode() function:

```
_setvideomode( short mode );
```

mode is an integer value that determines which text mode will be used. You can
use either an integer value or a symbolic constant for the mode argument. The
symbolic constants and their integer values are listed in Table 8.2. The five
text modes shown in Table 8.2 were described in Table 8.1 in the preceding
section.

Table 8.2. The symbolic constants and integer values for _setvideomode().

Symbolic Constant	Integer Value	Usage
_TEXTBW40	0	Black-and-white 40-column
_TEXTC40	1	Color 40-column
_TEXTBW80	2	Black-and-white 80-column
_TEXTC80	3	Color 80-column
_TEXTMONO	7	80x25 monochrome
_DEFAULTMODE	−1	Restores to original mode

Selecting Text Colors

If you have a color monitor and you are using a color text mode, you can choose a background color and a foreground color independent of one another. For example, to select white text on a blue background, you would specify a white foreground color and a blue background color. You set the background color with the _setbkcolor() function, using the following format:

_setbkcolor(*long color*);

color is a long variable that determines which background color will be used where color has a value from 0 to 7, as shown in Table 8.3.

To set the foreground color of a displayed character, you use the _settextcolor() function call:

_settextcolor(*short pixel*);

pixel normally has a value from 0 to 15, as shown in Table 8.3. You can also make text blink by adding 16 to the pixel color value shown in Table 8.3. For example:

_settextcolor(7);

selects white text color, and

_settextcolor (7 + 16);

causes the white text to blink on the display.

Table 8.3 shows the values that you can use when selecting text colors. Only the first eight colors, numbered 0 to 7 are available as background colors. You can use all 16 values, 0 to 15, to select a foreground color.

Table 8.3. The text-mode foreground and background colors.

Color	Value	F = Foreground only B = Background only
Black	0	F/B
Blue	1	F/B
Green	2	F/B
Cyan	3	F/B
Red	4	F/B
Magenta	5	F/B
Brown	6	F/B
White	7	F/B
Dark gray	8	F
Light blue	9	F
Light green	10	F
Light cyan	11	F
Light red	12	F
Light magenta	13	F
Yellow	14	F
Bright white	15	F
Blinking	Add 16	F

If, for example, you make the following function call, the screen's background color is set to green:

```
_setbkcolor( 1 );
```

An actual call to _settextcolor() looks like this:

```
_settextcolor( 14 );
```

This call to _settextcolor() sets the text color, or foreground color, to yellow.

When _setbkcolor() and _settextcolor() are used, only the direct video functions that follow these functions are affected.

NOTE The graph.h header file defines several constants, such as _RED, _BLUE, _WHITE, and so on. Do not use these constants as parameters to _setcolor() or _setbkcolor(). These constants are intended for use with the EGA and VGA color palettes, described later in this chapter.

Displaying Text in Color

To display text using the selected color, you must use the special _outtext() function call. The standard output functions—such as printf(), puts(), cprintf(), or cputs()—are not affected by the settings of the _settextcolor() and _setbkcolor() functions.

To use _outtext(), you must place your desired output into an output buffer. A convenient method is to use the sprintf() function. Listing 8.1 shows how the _setbkcolor(), _settextcolor(), and _outtext() functions are used.

Listing 8.1. A demonstration using _setcolor() and _setbkcolor() to select color values for text output.

```
1   /* ATRDEMO.C  Text mode attribute demonstration program.
2                 This program uses _settextcolor() and _setbkcolor()
3                 to change the foreground and background text colors. */
4
5   #include <stdio.h>
6   #include <stdlib.h>
7   #include <conio.h>
8   #include <graph.h>
9
10  int main()
11  {
12    int i, j, k;
13    char buffer[255];
14    struct videoconfig config;
15
16    _setvideomode( _TEXTC80 );
17
18    for( i = 0; i <= 7; i++ ){
19      for( j = 0; j <= 15; j++ ){
20        _setbkcolor( i );
21        _settextcolor( j );
```

Listing 8.1. Continued.

```
22        _settextwindow( 10, 10, 20, 50);
23        _settextposition( 5, 20 );
24        sprintf( buffer, "Color: %d  Bkgrnd: %d", j, i );
25       _outtext(buffer);
26      }
27    }
28    return 0;
29  }
```

The program in Listing 8.1 uses the _setbkcolor() and _settextcolor() functions to change the text foreground and background colors. The program is composed of two loops. The two loops cycle through the background and foreground colors and to display a message in each of the possible color combinations.

The first loop, in lines 18 through 27, generates a value that is used to change the background color in line 20.

The second loop, in lines 19 through 26, generates a value that is used to change the foreground color in line 21.

Because the foreground color is determined by the second loop, the foreground color changes more rapidly than the background color.

Using the Window Functions

To give you more versatility in formatting your screen output, Microsoft C/C++ provides window functions with which you can define and use *text windows*. A text window is a rectangular area to which your output is limited. This section shows you how to set up and use the Microsoft C/C++ window functions.

The _settextwindow() function defines a rectangular area on the screen where the output is sent. Note the format for the call to the _settextwindow() function:

```
_settextwindow( short r1, short c1, short r2, short c2 );
```

The arguments passed to the _settextwindow() function are the *screen* coordinates of the upper-left and lower-right corners of the window. In text mode, the screen coordinates are specified in *1 origin format,* which means that the upper-left corner has coordinates (1,1) rather than (0,0). r1 and r2 are rows and c1 and c2 are text columns. In this way, r1 and r2 correspond to the y-axis—or vertical axis—on the screen, whereas c1 and c2 correspond to the x-axis—or horizontal axis—across the screen.

Every program that you write creates a window. If you do not explicitly call the _settextwindow() function in your program, a window is created by default. The size of the automatically created window is equal to the maximum size of the current text-mode screen. For a typical screen 80 columns wide by 25 rows high, this is equivalent to the following function call:

```
_settextwindow( 1, 1, 25, 80 );
```

Listing 8.2 demonstrates the use of the _settextwindow() function.

Listing 8.2. wnddemo.c. A demonstration of the _settextwindow() function.

```
1    /* WNDDEMO.C  This short program creates two different
2                  windows. The first window uses the entire
3                  screen. The second window only occupies
4                  the middle of the screen. The text sent
5                  to each window is a rolling ASCII pattern.
6                  The same test pattern is sent to each window.
7    */
8
9    #include <stdio.h>
10   #include <stdlib.h>
11   #include <conio.h>
12   #include <graph.h>
13
14   main()
15   {
16     int i,j;
17     char buffer[255];
18
19     _setvideomode( _TEXTC80 );
20     _setbkcolor( (long) 2 );
21     _clearscreen( _GCLEARSCREEN );
22
23     for( i=0; i<=100; i++)
24       for(j=48; j<=122; j++){
25         sprintf( buffer, "%c",j);
26         _outtext(buffer);
27         }
28
29     _settextwindow( 15, 5, 20, 75 );
30     _setbkcolor ( (long) 4 );
31     _clearscreen ( _GCLEARSCREEN );
32
```

Listing 8.2. Continued.

```
33    for( i=0; i<=100; i++)
34      for(j=48; j<=122; j++){
35        sprintf( buffer, "%c",j);
36        _outtext(buffer);
37        }
38
39    return 0;
40  }
```

Listing 8.2 is a small program that uses two different windows. The first window is created automatically when the program begins execution. By default, the first window occupies the entire screen. In line 20, the _setbkcolor() function is called to set the background color of the screen. The value of 2 passed to _setbkcolor() sets the background color to green.

The for loops in lines 23 through 27 print a rolling ASCII pattern. These for loops print the ASCII characters with values from 48 to 122. Notice that there are no new-line characters printed in the for loops. The output is allowed to scroll from one line to the next.

The second window that is used is defined by the _settextwindow() function call in line 29. _settextwindow() creates a window with the upper-left corner at position (5,15) and a lower-right corner at position (75,20). All the characters that are output using the _outtext() function in line 36 will be displayed inside the new window. Everything outside the new window will remain as it was. Note that when you use _settextwindow() or any of the graph.h defined functions, you must use _outtext(). The normal I/O functions, such as printf() or putch(), are not affected by the settings of _settextwindow().

Placing Text at a Specific Screen Location

The _outtext() function displays text at the current cursor location. You can set the cursor location to any point on the screen by calling _settextposition(), which is defined as

```
_settextposition( short row, short column );
```

To use _settextposition(), specify a new row and column position. For example, to move the cursor to row 5, column 20, write:

```
_settextposition( 5, 20 );
```

The next _outtext() function call begins writing text starting at column 20 on row 5.

The position specified by row and column is relative to the boundaries of the text window set with _settextwindow(). For example, if you set the text window boundaries to the lower-right corner of the screen, as with

```
_settextwindow( 13, 40, 25, 80 );
```

then subsequent _settextposition() calls set the cursor location relative to these boundaries. For instance,

```
_settextposition( 5, 10 );
```

positions the cursor at the physical screen location, row 13 + 5, column 40 + 10.

Determining the Current Text-Mode Settings

Microsoft C/C++ stores the text-mode settings in various internal data structures. Several functions return the current settings stored in these data structures. You use _gettextcolor() to obtain the current text color, _getbkcolor() to obtain the current text background color, _gettextposition() to obtain the current text-output location, and _gettextwindow() to obtain the current text window boundaries. The function _getvideoconfig() returns a structure containing a variety of graphics-related settings, including the maximum number of text columns and rows available on the current display screen.

Determining the Current Text Color Settings

To obtain the current foreground and background color settings, call the _gettextcolor() and _getbkcolor() functions, respectively.

_gettextcolor() has no parameters and returns the color value of the current foreground color. _gettextcolor() is defined as

```
short _far _gettextcolor(void);
```

_getbkcolor() returns the color value of the current background color. The declaration short _far means that _gettextcolor() is called as a far function, returning a short value. short is equivalent to an 8-bit integer. _getbkcolor() is defined as

```
long far _getbkcolor(void);
```

Determining the Current Text Window Boundaries

The boundaries of the current text window are obtained by calling
_gettextwindow(), which is defined as

_gettextwindow(*short__far *r1, short__far *c1, short__far *r2, short__far *c2*);

r1 and c1 describe the upper-left corner of the window, and r2 and c2 describe the lower-right corner of the window.

Determining the Current Text Output Position

You use _gettextposition() to obtain the current cursor location.
_gettextposition() returns a structure containing the row and column coordinate; hence _gettextposition() is defined as

```
struct rccoord {
  short row;
  short col;
  } __far _gettextposition( void );
```

where rccoord is a structure type defined in graph.h.

Determining Other Screen Attributes

You can obtain additional information about the video display by calling
_getvideoconfig(), which returns as a parameter a structure containing video
information. _getvideoconfig() is defined as

```
_getvideoconfig( struct videoconfig __far *config );
```

The videoconfig structure contains various video display information, as
follows:

```
struct videoconfig {
    short numxpixels;        /* number of pixels on X axis */
    short numypixels;        /* number of pixels on Y axis */
    short numtextcols;       /* number of text columns available */
    short numtextrows;       /* number of text rows available */
    short numcolors;         /* number of actual colors */
    short bitsperpixel;      /* number of bits per pixel */
```

```
    short numvideopages;      /* number of available video pages */
    short mode;               /* current video mode */
    short adapter;            /* active display adapter */
    short monitor;            /* active display monitor */
    short memory;             /* adapter video memory in K bytes */
};
```

Understanding the IBM/PC Graphics Mode

As noted earlier, you can use two groups of video modes: text mode and graphics mode. In the preceding sections, you learned how to use text mode to handle your character data. You use graphics mode to display your graphical data, such as charts, graphs, drawings, and other images. In this section, you learn what graphics mode is and how to start using it in your programs.

Understanding Pixels and Palettes

The *pixel* (short for *picture element*) is what graphics mode is all about. A pixel is a single dot on your screen. In graphics-mode processing, you control each pixel on your screen.

Each type of video adapter and screen supports a different number of pixels. For example, a CGA adapter and display can display a maximum of 640×200 pixels, whereas an IBM 8514 display can display up to 1024×768 pixels. *Screen resolution,* then, refers to the number of pixels your screen can display.

It is possible for an adapter and screen combination to support more than one resolution. The number of resolutions that can be displayed also depends on the software that controls the adapter and screen. Table 8.4 lists the video adapters and resolutions Microsoft C/C++ supports. The mode constant, shown at the right of the table, selects the video mode when used as a parameter to _setvideomode(). For example, to select 16-color, high-resolution EGA mode, you use the following:

```
_setvideomode( _HRES16COLOR );
```

The EGA, MCGA, and VGA adapters support all the CGA modes. VGA supports the EGA modes, except that not all monitors are capable of operating in EGA-compatible mode. The MCGA display also supports the VGA _VRES2COLOR and _VRES16COLOR modes.

Table 8.4. The video adapters and resolutions supported in Microsoft C/C++.

Type Description	Resolution(s)	# of Colors	Mode Constant
CGA Color Graphics Array	320 × 200	4	_MRES4COLOR
	320 × 200	4 gray	_MRESNOCOLOR
	640 × 200	2	_HRESBW
EGA Enhanced Graphics Adapter	320 × 200	16	_MRES16COLOR
	640 × 200	16	_HRES16COLOR
	640 × 350	2 gray	_ERESNOCOLOR
	640 × 350	4/16	_ERESCOLOR
VGA Video Graphics Array	320 × 200	256	_MRES256COLOR
	640 × 480	2	_VRES2COLOR
	640 × 480	16	_VRES16COLOR
Hercules Monochrome	720 × 348	2	_HERCMONO
Olivetti/AT&T 6300	see note	16	_ORESCOLOR
Selects default video mode			_DEFAULTMODE
Selects highest resolution graphics mode			_MAXRESMODE
Selects mode with the most color choices			_MAXCOLORMODE

Note: The Olivetti adapter supports the equivalent CGA, EGA, and VGA modes.

If you use _DEFAULTMODE, _setvideomode() automatically selects an appropriate default video mode. You should call _setvideomode(_DEFAULTMODE) just prior to termination of your program. Alternatively, you can select the mode with the highest resolution by using _MAXRESMODE or the mode with the greatest number of colors by using _MAXCOLORMODE.

Using Color Palettes

Each pixel on the screen has a corresponding memory location. The memory location holds a value that indirectly determines the color of the pixel. This determination is made because the value stored in memory is an offset into a table called a *palette*. The value in the palette determines the actual color to be displayed.

The palette is a list of all the colors that can be displayed on the screen at any given time. Many times, the number of colors listed in a palette is a fraction of the number of colors the screen can actually display. Except for the CGA display, the number of colors in a palette is normally limited by the amount of video memory available.

The color screens supported by Microsoft C/C++ can be divided into two groups by the way that colors are controlled. The first group is the CGA group for the CGA video modes. The second group is the EGA group, which includes the EGA and VGA adapters.

Using CGA Color Palettes

When you are using CGA-type screens, you can choose either the low- or high-resolution mode. The *low-resolution mode* displays 320×200 pixels in four colors. The *high-resolution mode* displays 640×200 pixels in two colors.

In CGA low-resolution mode, you can display only four colors at one time, determined by which of the four palettes you select. Each palette contains four colors, numbered 0 to 3. The first color in each palette, or color 0, corresponds to the current background color. The remaining three colors, numbered 1 to 3, contain predefined colors, depending on the palette.

Table 8.5 shows the fixed colors in each of the four palettes. The palette that you use is selected by calling the _selectpalette() function, like this:

```
_selectpalette( 0 );  /* Select palette # 0 */
```

Table 8.5. The CGA color palettes. Color #0, not shown here, corresponds to the current background color.

Palette #	Color 1	Color 2	Color 3
0	Green	Red	Yellow
1	Cyan	Magenta	Light gray
2	Light green	Light red	Yellow
3	Light cyan	Light magenta	White

The _MRESNOCOLOR CGA video mode is intended for use with black-and-white displays; however, if it is used with a color display, it will display the colors shown in Table 8.6.

Table 8.6. The _MRESNOCOLOR CGA video mode color palettes.

Palette #	Color 1	Color 2	Color 3
0	Blue	Red	Light gray
1	Light blue	Light red	White

Selecting a Background Color

The background color is chosen using the _setbkcolor() function, which I already introduced for use in selecting text colors. When _setbkcolor() is used in graphics mode, you can select the background color from one of the 16 colors shown in Table 8.7. For example:

```
_setbkcolor( 4 );      /* Select Red as the background color */
```

Table 8.7. Graphics mode background color choices.

Color	Parameter Value
Black	0
Blue	1
Green	2
Cyan	3
Red	4
Magenta	5
Brown	6
White	7
Dark gray	8
Light blue	9
Light green	10
Light cyan	11
Light red	12
Light magenta	13
Yellow	14
Bright white	15

Selecting Colors from the Current Palette

The foreground color is chosen from the current color palette by calling the _setcolor() function. _setcolor() is defined as

```
_setcolor( short color );
```

For the CGA video display modes, the `color` parameter has a value from 0 to 3 and selects a color entry from the current palette. For instance, if the current palette is #3, then

```
_setcolor( 1 );
```

sets the foreground color to light cyan.

Using CGA High-Resolution Mode

Using CGA high-resolution mode is less complicated than using CGA low-resolution mode. In high-resolution mode, each pixel can have a value of either 0 or 1. If the pixel value is 0, the pixel will be in the black background color. If the pixel value is 1, the pixel will be in the foreground color you select. You can use any of the 16 colors in Table 8.7 as a foreground color.

Setting the foreground color in CGA high-resolution mode is a little strange. To set the foreground color, you use the `setbkcolor()` function, which sets the hardware *background* color. You use this function because of a peculiarity in the CGA adapter. If, for example, you wanted to draw a CGA high-resolution figure in yellow, you would use the following:

```
setbkcolor( 14 );
```

This causes the circle-drawing function (in Microsoft C/C++, it is the `_ellipse()` function) to output the circle in yellow on a black background.

Selecting EGA/VGA Video Mode Colors

EGA and VGA graphics modes are similar to the CGA modes except that the default palette contains 16 colors, all of which can be displayed simultaneously on the screen. The VGA display also supports a 256-color mode. In the VGA `_MRES256COLOR` mode, the first 16 color entries in the 256-color palette correspond to the 16 colors in the EGA and VGA 16-color modes.

You can custom-design these 16 palette colors from a group of 64 possible colors (see Table 8.8). By default, the colors in the EGA palette correspond to the CGA text mode colors. Table 8.8 lists the EGA palette entries and their corresponding default color assignments.

Table 8.8. The 16 EGA palette colors.

Color #	Color	Constant
0	Black	_BLACK
1	Blue	_BLUE
2	Green	_GREEN
3	Cyan	_CYAN
4	Red	_RED
5	Magenta	_MAGENTA
7	White	_WHITE
8	Brown	_BROWN
9	Gray	_GRAY
10	Light blue	_LIGHTBLUE
11	Light green	_LIGHTGREEN
12	Light cyan	_LIGHTCYAN
13	Light red	_LIGHTRED
14	Light magenta	_LIGHTMAGENTA
15	Yellow	_YELLOW
16	Bright white	_BRIGHTWHITE

 NOTE The color number is used in conjunction with _setcolor() or _setbkcolor(). The color constant is used only with the _remappalette() function—or its cousin, _remapallpalette().

Custom Designing VGA Palette Colors

You can change individual palette entries with the _remappalette() function. For instance, you could change entry number 7 from white to light blue by writing

```
_remappalette( 7, _LIGHTBLUE );
```

This has the interesting effect of changing to light blue any existing white objects on the screen. After you call _remappalette(), all the existing white objects will have their color changed to light blue.

You can also create custom colors by taking advantage of the VGA hardware. The VGA hardware can display up to 262,144 different colors, although not all at the same time. Depending on the mode and the available video memory, the VGA can normally display 16 or 256 simultaneous colors. Each color is stored in a palette entry, and each entry can be set to any of the 262,144 possible color combinations.

Custom palette colors are mixed by combining various intensities of red, green, and blue. Each color intensity can have one of 64 possible intensity levels. Combined, the three color settings represent $64 \times 64 \times 64$—or 262,144—separate color selections.

In Microsoft C/C++, the color intensities are represented as byte values, with each byte storing a value from 0 to 63. The three byte values are combined into a long parameter value for passing to the `_remappalette()` function as follows, where the high order byte is byte 3, the low order byte is byte 1 and each *x* represents one bit position:

byte 3	byte 2	byte 1	byte 0
	Blue	Green	Red
unused	00xxxxxx	00xxxxxx	00xxxxxx

Each byte intensity value varies from 0 to 63. For example, if the blue intensity is set to 0, no blue color is mixed into the resulting color. If the blue intensity is set to 63, the maximum amount of blue is added. For example, the pre-defined graph.h constant _RED is defined as follows:

byte 3	byte 2	byte 1	byte 0
	Blue	Green	Red
unused	00000000	00000000	00101010

This bit pattern produces the following C macro definition statement:

```
#define _RED 0x00002AL
```

Other colors are defined by mixing the various color intensities. Magenta, for instance, is a combination of blue and red:

```
#define _MAGENTA 0x2A002AL
```

Using the `_remappalette()` function, any of the 262,144 possible colors can be assigned to a particular palette entry. For example, to set palette entry 1 to magenta, you might write:

```
_remappalette( 1, 0x2A002AL );
```

or

```
_remappalette( 1, _MAGENTA );
```

Custom Designing MCGA Color Palettes

The MCGA operates in all the CGA modes, plus the 2- and 16-color VGA modes _VRES2COLOR and _VRES16COLOR. In both of the VGA modes, you can custom program the MCGA's color palette just as you can the VGA's.

Custom Designing EGA Palette Colors

The EGA color palette, like the default VGA palette, contains 16 color entries, each of which is preset to the values shown in Table 8.7. You use the _remappalette() function to change the individual entries in the palette. To change entry number 1 to another color—such as green—you write:

```
_remappalette( 1, _GREEN );
```

Just as with the VGA palette, you can also program custom color combinations into the EGA palette. Each of the 16 palette entries can be set to any of the 64 possible color combinations. You select a color combination by mixing different intensities of red, green, and blue. Each color intensity varies from 0 to 3, providing for $4 \times 4 \times 4$—or 64—color combinations. The mechanism for mixing a custom color is identical to that used for the VGA, except that only two bits are used for each color intensity, as shown here:

byte 3	byte 2	byte 1	byte 0
	Blue	Green	Red
unused	00xx0000	00xx0000	00xx0000

Note that the EGA color intensity bits are located in the upper nibble (the first four bits) of each byte, and not, as you might expect, in the lower nibble (the last four bits) of each byte.

Introducing the Graphics Drawing Functions

Graphics programming is easy when you use Microsoft C/C++ and its library of drawing functions. Microsoft C/C++ provides standard drawing routines—such as _arc, _ellipse, _lineto, and _pie—and also a library of presentation graphics functions for drawing pie graphs, bar graphs, and line charts that include headings and data points. Before you can examine the drawing functions, however, you must first understand the graphics coordinate system.

Every point or pixel on the graphics screen is located relative to a horizontal x-axis and a vertical y-axis. The default coordinate system places (0,0) at the upper-left corner of the display. The x coordinate increases across the display to the right, and the y coordinate increases down the display toward the bottom. The maximum x and y values depend on the video adapter and video mode currently in use.

NOTE Graphics coordinates begin at (0,0), whereas text-mode coordinates begin at (1,1).

Traditionally, graphs have been drawn using different coordinate systems than those provided by the video hardware. Generally, the point (0,0) is positioned at the center of the display. The x values increase to the right of the screen center and decrease (become negative) to the left of the screen center. Similarly, the y values increase toward the top and decrease from the midpoint to the bottom of the display, as shown in Figure 8.3.

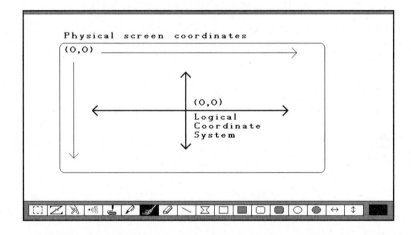

Figure 8.3.

A typical graphics coordinate system places (0,0) at the midpoint of the viewing screen.

To help you deal with the hardware coordinate system versus more traditional coordinate systems, Microsoft C/C++ provides two functions: _setvieworg() to position the origin to a new location and _setviewport() to position the graphics area to a subset region of the display.

Using _setvieworg()

The point (0,0) or the origin of a viewport is placed at the upper-left corner of the viewport, whether the viewport is the entire screen or a subset of the screen. By calling _setvieworg(), Microsoft C/C++ can automatically remap the origin to a new location within the viewport.

To understand the use of _setvieworg(), consider when the viewport covers the entire screen (this is the default viewport setting). To position the logical origin to the center of the screen, you call _setvieworg() with the hardware coordinates of the new logical origin. To determine the midpoint of the display (in the hardware coordinate system), you must first call _getvideoconfig() to obtain the current maximum x and y values. The maximum values are divided in half and passed to _setvieworg(). Here's an example:

```
struct videoconfig config;
...
_getvideoconfig( &config );
_setvieworg( config.numxpixels/2, config.numypixels/2 );
```

This creates the viewing region that has its logical origin at the center of the screen, as shown in Figure 8.4. Note that x values now run from a negative value at the left to a positive value on the right. Furthermore, y-axis values vary from negative values on top to positive values below the x-axis.

Figure 8.4.

Illustration of mapping logical viewing coordinates to physical screen coordinates.

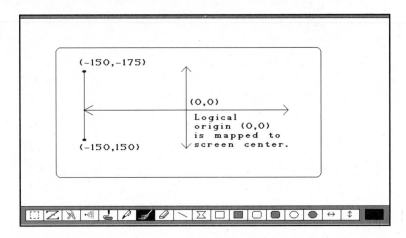

As you may have already guessed, you can reset the logical origin back to the hardware coordinates by using

```
_setvieworg( 0, 0 );
```

Using _setviewport()

You can set the viewing region to a subset of the display area by calling _setviewport(). For example, if you call _setviewport() as

```
_setviewport( 100, 50, 300, 150 );
```

you define the viewing region illustrated in Figure 8.5. Subsequent graphic output will be confined to this viewing region, with the origin (0,0) located at the upper-left corner of the viewport.

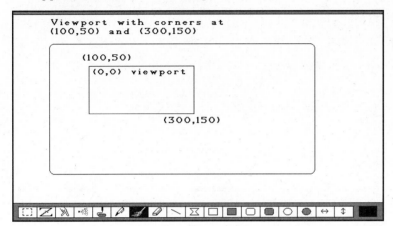

Figure 8.5.

Illustration of a viewport.

Like the physical screen coordinate system, the origin (0,0) is located at the upper-left corner of the viewport. You can move the origin to a new location inside the viewport by calling _setvieworg().

When a viewport is established, the Graphics Library establishes a *clipping boundary* at the edges of the viewport. All subsequent drawing functions will clip their output at the viewport boundary. This means that if you attempt to draw a line, an ellipse, or other graphic object, any portion of the object that would extend beyond the edges of the viewport is clipped and does not appear on the screen.

Using Window Coordinates

The viewport viewing region is fine if your drawing will use only integer-valued coordinates within the range of the screen or viewport resolution. If you want to use larger, smaller, or arbitrarily sized coordinates, however, you need another method to map those coordinates so that they fit within the viewport. Suppose, for instance, that your graphics application draws objects that are, from your application's perspective, 1200 × 800 units in size. You can manually scale your coordinate measurements to a smaller value so that they will fit within the screen resolution, or you can let Microsoft C/C++ handle the conversion automatically by using the _setwindow() function.

_setwindow() has five parameters, four of which define a real-world coordinate system:

```
_setwindow(short finvert, double wx1, double wy1, double wx2, double wy2);
```

You use _setwindow() to establish an arbitrary coordinate system based on the needs of your application. For instance, if you call _setwindow() with the following parameters:

```
_setwindow( TRUE, 1, 600, 1000, -600 );
```

you create the window shown in Figure 8.6. The finvert parameter specifies the location of the minimum and maximum y-axis values. When TRUE, the minimum y-axis coordinate defines the bottom of the window; when FALSE, the minimum y-axis coordinate defines the top of the window.

To use the window coordinate system, you must call the appropriate drawing functions that end in _w or _wxy suffixes. For instance, instead of calling _arc(), you should call _arc_w() or _arc_wxy().

Figure 8.6.

A window coordinate system mapped to a viewport coordinate system.

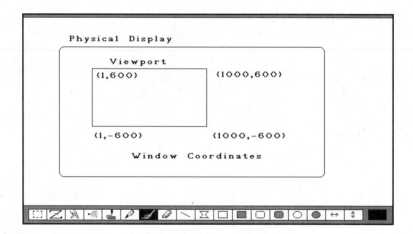

Using the Drawing and Filling Functions

The shapes you draw with the Graphics Library functions can be divided into two groups: unfilled objects and filled objects. The inside of an unfilled object is the same color as the background; you see only the outline or border of the object. The inside of a filled object is set to a color or pattern that you specify. In this section, you first learn how to use functions that draw unfilled objects. You then learn how to use functions that draw filled objects or fill areas on the screen.

In the Graphics Library, you can find the following drawing functions to draw unfilled objects:

_arc()	Draws an arc
_ellipse()	Draws an ellipse or circle
_lineto()	Draws a line from the current position to a position you specify
_pie()	Draws a section of pie (as in a pie chart)
_polygon()	Draws a polygon
_rectangle()	Draws a rectangle

Each of these functions includes a _w or _wxy companion function for use with window coordinates. These companion functions are described later in this section.

Listing 8.3 shows how easily you can use these drawing functions. Note that the next three listings were written for a VGA monitor. If you want the programs to work with a CGA monitor or another monitor, you need to change the values that control the size of the object being drawn.

Listing 8.3. graph1.c. A program that uses the basic drawing functions.

```
1   /* GRAPH1.C This program shows how easy it is to use the
2              graphics functions. */
3
4   #include <stdlib.h>
5   #include <stdio.h>
6   #include <conio.h>
7   #include <graph.h>
8
9   int main()
10  {
11
12      #define DIAMETER 75          /* Diameter of circle, in pixels */
13      #define PIXELWIDTH 640       /* Screen width, in pixels */
14      #define PIXELHEIGHT 480      /* Screen height, in pixels */
15
16      int i, x, y;
17
18      _setvideomode( _VRES16COLOR );
19
20      for( i = 1; i <= 100; i++) {
```

Listing 8.3. Continued.

```
21      /* Randomly select a coordinate on the screen */
22      x = rand() / 32767.0 * PIXELWIDTH/2 + DIAMETER;
23      y = rand() / 32767.0 * PIXELHEIGHT/2 + DIAMETER;
24      _ellipse( _GBORDER, x, y, x + DIAMETER, y + DIAMETER );
25      }
26
27      while( !kbhit() );
28      _setvideomode( _DEFAULTMODE );
29      return 0;
30  }
```

The short program in Listing 8.3 shows how to call the graphics functions. The program uses a for loop to draw a series of circles across the screen. Circles are drawn using the _ellipse() library function.

Before the graphics functions can be called, you must select and initialize graphics mode using _setvideomode() and an appropriate video mode constant.

When the graphics mode is initialized, you are ready to call a graphics function. The for loop in lines 20 through 25 draws a series of randomly positioned circles. The _ellipse() function draws both ellipses and circles, depending on its parameters. As shown here, the parameters describe a bounding box for the circle, with (x,y) defining the upper-left corner of the box and (x + DIAMETER, y + DIAMETER) defining the lower-right corner. _GBORDER specifies that only the boundary of the object should be drawn.

When you are through with graphics mode, switch back to regular text mode. The switch to text mode is made with the _setvideomode (_DEFAULTMODE) function in line 28.

Listing 8.4 shows how to call some of the other drawing functions in the library. These include the _pie(), _lineto(), _arc(), and _polygon() functions.

Listing 8.4. graph2.c. A program that uses more graphics functions.

```
1   /* GRAPH2.C This program shows how functions in the
2                library are called. */
3
4   #include <stdlib.h>
5   #include <stdio.h>
6   #include <conio.h>
7   #include <graph.h>
```

```
8
9   int main()
10  {
11      int i, x, y;
12      static struct xycoord polypoints[] = {
13                  10, 10,
14                  500, 10,
15                  500, 300,
16                  200, 300,
17                  10, 10 };
18
19      _setvideomode( _VRES16COLOR );
20
21      /* Draw an ellipse shape */
22      _setcolor ( 7 );
23      _ellipse( _GBORDER, 100, 100, 200, 75 );
24
25      /* Draw a pie wedge */
26      _setcolor( 4 );
27      _pie( _GBORDER, 100, 100, 300, 300, 300, 20, 0, 350 );
28
29      /* Draw an arbitrary shape using _lineto */
30      _setcolor( 3 );
31      _moveto( 300, 250 );
32      _lineto( 500, 200 );
33      _lineto( 500, 400 );
34      _lineto( 300, 425 );
35      _lineto( 300, 250 );
36
37      /* Draw an arc */
38      _setcolor( 6 );
39      _arc( 300, 100, 600, 200, 300, 30, 0, 300 );
40
41      _setcolor ( 2 );
42      _polygon ( _GBORDER, polypoints, 5 );
43
44      while( !kbhit() );
45
46      _setvideomode( _DEFAULTMODE );
47      return 0;
48  }
```

The _ellipse() function in line 23 draws an elliptical object on the screen. The first parameter, _GBORDER, specifies that the boundary of the ellipse object (as compared to its interior) should be drawn. The next four parameters are really two sets of paired arguments describing the upper-left and lower-right corners of a bounding rectangle. The ellipse is drawn in such a way that it fits inside the bounding rectangle. In line 23, the upper-left corner is positioned at (100,100) and the lower-right corner is at (200,75).

Line 27 uses the _pie() function to draw a wedge-shaped section of a circle or ellipse. The parameters to _pie() are a little more complicated than those for _ellipse(). Like _ellipse(), the first parameter, _GBORDER, specifies that the boundary of the pie slice is to be drawn. Also like _ellipse(), the next four parameters are paired coordinates describing a bounding rectangle which will contain the pie slice. The parameters in line 27 place the bounding rectangle at (100,100) and (300,300).

To draw just a slice of the pie, _pie() must be given a starting and ending position. These positions are given in the last four parameters, which are again two pairs of coordinates. The starting position is given as a vector from the center of the pie to the specified coordinate (300,20). The ending position is the vector from the pie's center to (0,350). Figure 8.7 shows how these parameters mark the starting and ending positions of the pie slice.

Figure 8.7.

A pie slice is drawn inside a bounding rectangle from a starting vector, shown here as (300,20), to an ending vector (0,350).

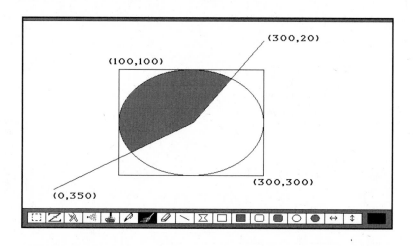

Lines 30 to 35 draw a sequence of lines across the display using _lineto(). The _moveto() function positions the graphics "cursor" or graphics-output position to the point (300,250) on the display. Each _lineto() draws a line beginning from the current graphics-output position to the point specified as _lineto()'s parameter. The current graphics-output position automatically moves to the new coordinate passed to _lineto().

Line 39 shows how an arc is drawn using the _arc() function. _arc()'s parameters are the same as the _pie() function—except that _arc() does not have an equivalent for the _GBORDER parameter. Instead, _arc()'s first four parameters identify the upper-left and lower-right coordinates of a bounding rectangle, and the next four parameters describe the starting and ending positions for the arc.

Arbitrary polygon shapes are drawn using _polygon(). _polygon()'s parameters include an array of points and the number of points in the array. Lines 12 through 17 initialize polypoints[] to five xycoord pairs, where xycoord is defined in graph.h. (Remember that an *n*-sided figure must have *n*+1 points; hence, five points define a four-sided figure). Line 42 calls _polygon(). The number of points in the array of points is passed as the third parameter.

Drawing Filled Objects

Many of the drawing functions can draw solid or filled objects. A special function _floodfill() fills an area on the screen. The functions that can fill an object are as follows:

_ellipse()	Fills the interior of an ellipse or circle
_pie()	Fills the interior of a pie section
_polygon()	Fills the interior of a polygon
_rectangle()	Fills a rectangle
_floodfill()	Fills a region on the screen

Using the filled-image functions is as quick and easy as using the unfilled-image functions. Listing 8.5 shows a program that draws several solid objects.

Listing 8.5. solid.c. A program that uses a filled-image function.

```
1   /* SOLID.C This program shows how to draw solid or filled
2           objects using the graphics functions */
3
4   #include <stdlib.h>
5   #include <stdio.h>
6   #include <conio.h>
7   #include <graph.h>
8
9   int main()
10  {
11      int i, x, y;
```

Listing 8.5. Continued.

```
12
13       _setvideomode( _VRES16COLOR );
14
15       /* Draw and fill an ellipse shape */
16       _setcolor ( 7 );
17       _ellipse( _GFILLINTERIOR, 100, 100, 200, 75 );
18
19       /* Draw and fill a pie wedge */
20       _setcolor( 4 );
21       _pie( _GFILLINTERIOR, 100, 100, 300, 300, 300, 20, 0, 350 );
22
23       /* Draw and fill an arbitrary shape using _lineto and _floodfill */
24       _setcolor( 3 );
25       _moveto( 300, 250 );
26       _lineto( 500, 200 );
27       _lineto( 500, 400 );
28       _lineto( 300, 425 );
29       _lineto( 300, 250 );
30       _floodfill( 301, 251, 3 );
31
32       /* Draw a filled rectangle */
33       _setcolor( 5 );
34       _rectangle ( _GFILLINTERIOR, 400, 50, 600, 200 );
35
36       while( !kbhit() );
37       _setvideomode( _DEFAULTMODE );
38       return 0;
39   }
```

Listing 8.5 is a simple program that draws a series of filled objects across the display. This program is nearly identical to Listing 8.4, but with a single parameter change in the drawing functions. By changing the first parameter from _GBORDER to _GFILLINTERIOR, the library routines draw each object with a special fill pattern. You can customize the actual pattern using _getfillmask() and _setfillmask(), which are described in the next section.

You can also fill a bounded region using _floodfill(). _floodfill() uses three parameters: The first two are the coordinate of any point location within the area to be bounded, and the third is the color of the boundary color. _floodfill() completely fills the bounded area out to the edges defined by the boundary color.

NOTE If the area is not actually bounded—because there is a hole in one or more sides of the object—`_floodfill()` will literally flood the entire screen. You can fill the area outside of an object by placing the initial y coordinate outside the object.

Controlling the Drawing Functions

Microsoft C/C++ provides several functions that let you take control of the drawing functions:

`_moveto()`	Moves the current position to (x,y)
`_getcurrentposition()`	Returns the current cursor location
`_getlinestyle()`	Gets the current line style
`_setlinestyle()`	Changes the current line style
`_getwritemode()`	Gets the mode used by line-drawing routines
`_setwritemode()`	Sets the mode used by line-drawing routines
`_getfillmask()`	Returns the user-defined fill pattern
`_setfillmask()`	Picks a user-defined fill pattern

Using _getcurrentposition()

`_getcurrentposition()` returns the location where the next graphics output will take place. `_getcurrentposition()` is defined as

```
struct _xycoord __far _getcurrentposition(void);
```

where `_xycoord` is defined as

```
struct _xycoord {
        short xcoord;
        short ycoord;};
```

By calling `_getcurrentposition()`, you can obtain the x and y coordinate positions where the next graphics drawing will appear.

Using _setlinestyle()

A call to the `setlinestyle()` function looks like this:

```
_setlinestyle( unsigned short mask );
```

The *mask* parameter specifies what line-drawing pattern will be used. *mask* is a 16-bit pattern, where each bit in the pattern corresponds to a pixel in the line. Each bit that is set to a 1 draws a pixel in the current drawing color, and each bit set to 0 leaves the screen unchanged. By varying the value of *mask*, you can create dotted or dashed lines. Figure 8.8 shows how to create a dashed line.

In Figure 8.8, _setlinestyle() uses a 16-bit wide mask to describe the line-drawing pattern. Each bit that is set is drawn in the current drawing color, whereas each cleared bit is left as the background color. The mask shown here, when repeated as part of a _lineto() function, displays a dashed line. The hex equivalent for this bit pattern is 0xF0F0.

Figure 8.8.

Using _setwritemode() and _getwritemode().

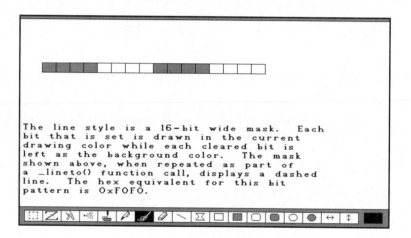

The _lineto(), _rectangle(), and _polygon() functions each draw their respective objects using the *write mode* established with _setwritemode(). The write modes enable you to choose how the line-oriented figures are drawn on the display. By default, when a line is drawn to the display, each pixel that appears in the line is set to the current color. However, there are other options. Instead of setting each pixel, you may wish to have each pixel in the line ANDed with the current screen pixel or to use some other binary operation. These operations and the constants that are passed to _setwritemode() are shown in Table 8.8.

To determine the currently active drawing mode, call _getwritemode(). _getwritemode() returns a short value containing one of the constant values shown in Table 8.9. The _GXOR option is often used for drawing line figures that are later moved or erased from the display. When a line is drawn using the exclusive-OR option, each pixel in the line is XORed with the pixel on the screen.

The result is that where a line crosses another line or object, the pixels under the intersection are cleared rather than set. This is because 1 XOR 1 is zero. You can use this feature to help you erase objects after they have been drawn. For example, if you draw a line using the _GXOR write mode, you can erase the line by merely redrawing the same line (be sure to use _GXOR both times).

Table 8.9. Mode constants used to select line-drawing options with `_setwritemode()`.

Constant	Result
_GPSET	Sets the screen pixel
_GXOR	Exclusive-ORs the existing display pixels with the new pixels
_GAND	ANDs the existing display pixels with the new pixels
_GOR	ORs the existing display pixels with the new pixels
_GPRESET	Clears the screen pixel

Using _setfillmask()

A call to the `setfillmask()` function looks like this:

```
_setfillmask( unsigned char _far * mask );
```

The `mask` parameter specifies the pattern used when you are drawing filled objects. The mask is an array of 8 × 8 bits—a structure that is conveniently organized as an array of eight character bytes. For each bit that is set to a 1, a pixel is drawn in the current foreground color. For each bit set to 0, the pixel is drawn in the background color. In this way, the 8 × 8 array of bits describes a pattern that is replicated over the entire region of the filled object. Figure 8.9 shows a *light fill* pattern, where only half the bits are drawn on the screen. This pattern corresponds to the hex string AA55AA55AA55AA55.

Listing 8.6 illustrates the use of `_setfillmask()`. Lines 12 through 21 provide several predefined fill patterns that you can use in your programs. Lines 14 and 15 define the light fill pattern shown in Figure 8.9.

Figure 8.9.

A pattern mask is an array of 8 x 8 bits, which describes the fill pattern used when drawing filled objects.

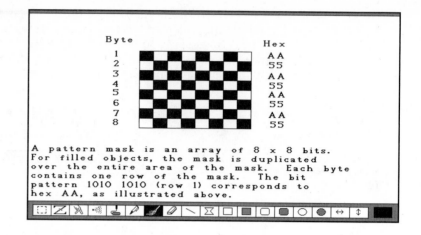

Listing 8.6. Example usage of the _setfillmask() function.

```
1   /* FILLMASK.C This program shows how to define a
2                 fill pattern for use with _setlinestyle() */
3
4   #include <stdlib.h>
5   #include <stdio.h>
6   #include <conio.h>
7   #include <graph.h>
8
9   int main()
10  {
11      int i, x, y;
12      static char solidfill[8] = {
13        0xFF, 0xFF, 0xFF, 0xFF, 0xFF, 0xFF, 0xFF, 0xFF };
14      static char lightfill[8] = {
15        0xAA, 0x55, 0xAA, 0x55, 0xAA, 0x55, 0xAA, 0x55 };
16      static char crosshatch[8] = {
17        0xFF, 0x88, 0x88, 0x88, 0xFF, 0x88, 0x88, 0x88 };
18      static char vert_line[8] = {
19        0x55, 0x55, 0x55, 0x55, 0x55, 0x55, 0x55, 0x55 };
20      static char horz_line[8] = {
21        0xFF, 0x00, 0x00, 0x00, 0xFF, 0x00, 0x00, 0x00 };
22
23      _setvideomode( _VRES16COLOR );
24
25      _setfillmask( lightfill );
```

```
26
27      /* Draw and fill an ellipse shape */
28      _setcolor ( 7 );
29      _ellipse( _GFILLINTERIOR, 100, 100, 200, 75 );
30
31      /* Draw and fill a pie wedge */
32      _setcolor( 4 );
33      _pie( _GFILLINTERIOR, 100, 100, 300, 300, 300, 20, 0, 350 );
34
35      /* Draw and fill an arbitrary shape using _lineto and _floodfill*/
36      _setcolor( 3 );
37      _moveto( 300, 250 );
38      _lineto( 500, 200 );
39      _lineto( 500, 400 );
40      _lineto( 300, 425 );
41      _lineto( 300, 250 );
42      _floodfill( 301, 251, 3 );
43
44      /* Draw a filled rectangle */
45      _setcolor( 5 );
46      _rectangle ( _GFILLINTERIOR, 400, 50, 600, 200 );
47
48      while( !kbhit() );
49      _setvideomode( _DEFAULTMODE );
50      return 0;
51  }
```

Clearing the Graphics Display Screen

When you start drawing on the screen, you will soon need to clear the screen and start over. Microsoft C/C++ has just the function for clearing the screen: the _clearscreen() function. When you call _clearscreen(_GCLEARSCREEN), the entire screen is erased and ready to use again. Optionally, you can use _GVIEWPORT and _GWINDOW as parameters to _clearscreen() to restrict the region you want to clear.

Controlling the Graphics Screen

Your graphics system has from one to four graphics pages you can use. A *page* is a block of memory that holds an entire graphics screen. The page where all the graphics functions send their output is called the *active page,* whereas the page that is being displayed is called the *visual page.*

Table 8.10 lists the adapters and modes that support more than one video page.

Table 8.10. The adapters and modes that support more than one video page.

Adapter	Number of Pages
EGA	Two or four pages
Hercules Mono	Two pages
VGA	Two pages

The `setactivepage( short page )` function sets the active page where graphics output is sent. `setvisualpage( short page )` selects the video page to be displayed. You can use this feature to create a complex drawing in an unused page. Then, by calling `_setvisualpage()`, you can instantly switch to the new drawing. For some applications, this provides a more pleasing effect for the user than watching each object appear one at a time.

Using Text in Graphics Mode

Displaying text in graphics mode is different from displaying text in text mode. Because you control every pixel on the screen in graphics mode, you have to control how the letters are drawn when you display text.

The easiest way to display text in graphics mode is to display characters that are already drawn. Using a pre-made set of characters can save you a great deal of time because you do not have to re-create the characters each time you need them.

A set of pre-made characters in the same style is called a *font.* Microsoft C/C++ 7.0 provides several fonts that you can use to display text information in your graphic images. This section shows how to use the fonts and graphics-mode text functions in Microsoft C/C++.

Understanding Fonts

Fonts are provided in two flavors: *bitmapped fonts* and *stroked fonts*. The difference between the two families of fonts becomes evident when you consider how the fonts are created.

A character in a bitmapped font is made by turning on or off each dot in a rectangular grid. The actual size of the grid (in pixels) can vary depending on the scaling factor used when the character is printed. The font can be scaled so that the displayed size of the font is larger than the defined size. When a bitmap font is displayed larger than its defining grid, the font can look coarse or chunky. The major advantage to bitmapped fonts is that they can be drawn on the screen very quickly.

The stroked fonts are fundamentally different from the bitmapped fonts. A character in a stroked font is made from a series of vectors that tells the program how to draw the font.

Because of the way stroked fonts are drawn, they can produce better results when they are enlarged. When you scale a bitmapped font, the basic grid pattern is simply enlarged. When a bitmapped font is made larger, the appearance of the font becomes more ragged. A stroked font can be enlarged, however, with good results. The vectors that define the stroked font create a good image whether the character is large or small.

Fonts are stored in font files that end with a .FON extension. .FON files that contain bitmaps often contain bitmaps for several different character sizes, such as 10×8, 12×9, and so on. In this way, the bitmaps can sometimes be mapped perfectly to your application.

Six fonts are standard with Microsoft C/C++ and are stored in the C700\LIB library directory. These fonts are shown in Table 8.11.

Table 8.11. Standard Microsoft C/C++ fonts.

Font	Font name	Type	Sizes	Spacing
Courier	`coure`	Bit	10×8, 12×9, 15×12	Fixed
Helvetica	`helv`	Bit	10×5, 12×7, 15×8, 18×9, 22×12, 28×16	Proportional
Times Roman	`tms rmn`	Bit	10×5, 12×6, 15×8, 16×9, 20×12, 26×16	Proportional
Modern	`modern`	Vector	Scaled	Proportional
Script	`script`	Vector	Scaled	Proportional
Roman	`roman`	Vector	Scaled	Proportional

Using the Graphics-Mode Text Functions

Microsoft C/C++ has several functions that enable you to control the size and appearance of the fonts. Listing 8.7 shows how some of these graphics-mode text-output functions can be used.

Listing 8.7. showtext.c. A program that uses fonts.

```c
/* SHOWTEXT.C   This program demonstrates the use of the
              fonts. */

#include <stdlib.h>
#include <stdio.h>
#include <conio.h>
#include <graph.h>

main()
{
  char test_str[] = "This is a test. This is only a test!";

  _setvideomode( _VRES2COLOR );
  _registerfonts( "\\windows\\system\\script.fon" );
  _setfont( "t'script'h32w20v" );        /* Select times roman font */

  _moveto( 100, 100 );
  _outgtext( test_str );

  _moveto( 100, 100 );
  _setgtextvector( 1, -1 );
  _outgtext( test_str );

  while( !kbhit() );

  _unregisterfonts();
  _setvideomode ( _DEFAULTMODE );

  return 0;
}
```

Before you can use any of the graphical text-output functions, you must be in graphics mode. You must register with the graphics system each font that you plan to use by calling _registerfonts(). The parameter to _registerfonts(), as shown in line 14, is a string containing a filename. This filename should be the name of a font file that you wish to register, or it may be a wildcard filename containing * or ? characters. In the case of a wildcard filename, _registerfonts() registers all fonts having filenames that match the wildcard file specification. _registerfonts() returns a number indicating the number of fonts that it successfully registered, or a negative value if an error occurred.

Next, you must specify information about the font that you want to use. _setfont() selects which of the potentially many registered fonts that your application will use for its current text output. You pass to _setfont() a string containing information about the font, including the desired pixel height and width. Table 8.12 shows the options that you can set in the _setfont() parameter string. Listing 8.7 uses _setfont() to select the script font and to select a character size of 32 pixels high by 20 pixels wide.

Table 8.12. _setfont() **codes passed in a character string to select specific features.**

Option character	Purpose
b	When you use a bitmapped font, _setfont() tries to select the best-matching font for the requested pixel height and width. If you do not specify the b option and your requested pixel height and width are not defined for the requested font, _setfont() will fail.
	When the b option is selected, you can specify height and width values that may not be defined for the requested font. In this situation, _setfont() tries four separate approaches to choosing the best match: (1) find a font size that matches the pixel height, (2) select a different typeface that matches, (3) match the width, or (4) select a typeface that is fixed or proportional, as requested.
	If the requested font size lies exactly midway between the sizes of two registered fonts, _setfont() chooses the smaller of the two fonts.
f	Select a fixed-space font.
h y	Specify desired height, in y pixels.
n m	Select font number m, where m ranges from 1 to the current number of registered fonts.
p	Select proportionally-spaced font.

continues

Table 8.12. Continued.

Option character	Purpose
r	Select raster (bitmapped) font.
t'*fontname*'	Select the font named in single quotes, where '*fontname*' may be 'courier', 'helv', 'modern', 'roman', 'script', or 'tms rmn' for the standard fonts provided with C/C++ 7.0.
v	Select the vector-mapped font.
w *x*	Specify desired width in *x* pixels.

_moveto() (line 17) positions the current graphic output position to (100,100). _outgtext() draws the content of its parameter string using the current type-face and font size. Note that _outgtext() has only a single letter different in its name from the similar _outtext().

You can draw text in different directions across the screen, beginning from the starting graphics output position. Line 20 positions the starting position to (100,100). Line 21 calls _setgtextvector() to specify a direction in which the text should be drawn. The parameters (1,–1) cause the text to be drawn at a 45-degree angle, descending to the right. Figure 8.10 shows the various positions at which text can be drawn. The parameters to _setgtextvector() describe a vector having its origin at the starting point of the string. Hence, (–1,1) is relative to the starting point (100,100).

Figure 8.10.

Use the coordinate values shown in the drawing to change the angle and position at which _outgtext() will draw the character string.

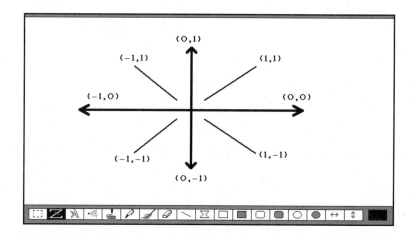

When your program no longer needs to use the fonts, you can free up the memory they require by calling _unregisterfonts(), as shown in Line 26 of Listing 8.7.

Using Microsoft Windows Fonts

The Microsoft C/C++ graphics functions are also compatible with the font files used in Microsoft Windows applications. If you have Microsoft Windows installed on your hard disk, the Windows font files are stored in the SYSTEM directory. For example, if Windows is installed in C:\WINDOWS, you can find these additional font files by typing the following DOS command:

```
DIR C:\WINDOWS\SYSTEM\*.FON
```

In addition to the standard fonts supplied by Windows, many application programs provide their own font files. If you choose to use the Microsoft Windows fonts with your C/C++ programs, you merely need to register the appropriate font file and then make the desired font the active font by calling _setfont().

The font name is embedded in the binary file and is often the same as the filename of the .FON file. For example, the Windows font file COURE.FON contains the font 'coure'. This is the name that should be used with the t'*fontname*' option of _setfont(). Font names are stored near the beginning of the file, and can often be located by loading the file into a text editor—but do keep in mind that the font file is a binary file and you may have to do some looking. Alternately, you can use _setfont()'s *n* option to select a registered font by number.

Using Other Font Functions

You can obtain information about the currently active font from _getfontinfo(). _getfontinfo() is defined as

_getfontinfo(*struct _fontinfo _far *fontbuffer*);

where _fontinfo is defined in graph.h. _fontinfo contains the following information about the current font:

```
struct _fontinfo {
    int type;          /* set = vector, clear = bit map */
    int ascent;         /* Pixel distance from top to baseline */
    int pixwidth;      /* Width in pixels, or 0 if proportional */
    int pixheight;      /* Height in pixels or 0 if proportional */
    int avgwidth;     /* Average character width in pixels */
    char filename[81];    /* File name including path */
    char facename[32];    /* Font name */
};
```

To learn the current setting of the graphics text vector (as set by
`_setgtextvector()`), call `_getgtextvector()`, which is defined as

```
short xycoord _far _getgtextvector( void );
```

The `xycoord` type contains two fields, `xcoord` and `ycoord`, containing the
current x and y values set by `_setgtextvector()`.

When you need to determine if a text string will fit within a region of the
display, call

```
_getgtextextent(unsigned char _far *text)
```

The `_getgtextextent()` function returns the width of the string in pixels.

Exercises

The following exercises give you practice in controlling your monitor's display
colors, using text windows, and using video graphics drawing functions:

1. Write a program that displays a message in as many different text modes
    as your monitor supports.

2. Change Listing 8.1 so that blinking text is turned on at least once every
    time the background color changes.

3. Write a program that displays the contents of a disk file in a window.

4. Write a program that sends the graphics output to a video page that is
    not being displayed. When several objects are drawn, display that video
    page.

5. Write a program that uses the `_lineto()` function and input from the
    cursor keys to create simple line drawings.

Summary

In this chapter, you learned how to use Microsoft C/C++'s text and graphics
video display functions. Specifically, you learned the following important
points:

■ *The PC uses a video adapter and a screen to display information.* The video
  adapter takes the output of your program and generates a signal that
  causes an appropriate image to be displayed on the screen.

■ *Microsoft C/C++ supports several different video adapters.* Some of the most
  popular are the CGA, EGA, VGA, and Hercules adapters.

■ *Two basic types of display modes are available: text mode and graphics mode.* Text mode displays only character data, whereas graphics mode displays any type of image you create. Each of these modes can be divided into several other modes, based on resolution and the number of colors used.

■ *You can set six different text modes with Microsoft C/C++.* The mode you select determines how many characters will be displayed and whether the display will be in color.

■ *In text mode, each character has its own attribute byte.* This byte determines the foreground and background color for each character displayed. Functions are available for changing the foreground and background colors.

■ *You use the* `_settextwindow()` *function to create a rectangular area on the screen where output from the* `_outtext()` *function will be sent.* The `_settextwindow()` function requires arguments that indicate the upper-left and lower-right corners of the new window.

■ *A pixel is a single dot on the screen.* Each pixel has a memory location associated with it. The memory location holds a value that is an offset into a palette table. The palette contains the actual color values of all the colors that can be displayed in the current video mode.

■ *When you want to enter graphics mode, you use the* `_setvideomode()` *function.* When you are through with graphics-mode processing, you call `_setvideomode( _DEFAULTMODE)` to shut down graphics mode.

■ *The drawing functions generally have two modes of operation: boundary drawing and solid or filled object drawing.* The mode is specified by passing `_GBORDER` or `_GFILLINTERIOR` as the first parameter to the appropriate drawing function.

■ *A viewport is a rectangular area on the screen to which the output of the graphics functions is limited.* You use the `_setviewport()` function to create a viewport. You can tell `_setviewport()` how large to make the viewport and where it will be located on the screen.

■ *Some video adapters support multiple video pages.* A video page is an area of memory large enough to hold an entire graphics screen. You can control which video page will receive the graphics function's output and which video page will be displayed.

■ *Fonts are collections of characters that can be displayed in graphics mode.* A character in a bitmapped font is stored as a rectangular grid of bits. The shape of a bitmapped character is determined by which bits are turned on and off in the grid. A character in a vector font is stored as a series of vectors that are used to draw the font. You get better results with an enlarged stroked font than with an enlarged bitmapped font.

■ *Although it is not described in this book, you should be aware that the Microsoft C/C++ Graphics Library contains a wealth of presentation graphics functions.* These functions are used to draw analytical charts such as pie, line, bar, column, and scatter diagram charts. The presentation graphics functions work with your raw numeric data and cleanly and easily convert the data into chart format, with data labels and chart titles. All the presentation graphics functions begin with the letters _pg...(). You can find more information about the _pg...() functions in the *Microsoft C/C++ 7.0 Run-Time Library Reference.*

Using CodeView and Profiler

When you want to produce fast, error-free code, you need to use *CodeView* and *Microsoft Profiler.* CodeView is a stand-alone debugging utility that comes with Microsoft C/C++ 7.0. Profiler is a new utility program. With Profiler, you can analyze the performance of your program. Profiler provides statistics on what was executed, how often it was called, and how long it took to execute. You have all the data necessary for deciding how to modify your program for increased performance.

CodeView has the same type of interface as the Programmer's WorkBench, so you can start productively using CodeView right away.

This chapter shows you how to set up and use CodeView and Microsoft Profiler. You learn how to set up your program so that it will be compiled with the information needed for debugging and profiling. You learn also how to start and use CodeView and Microsoft Profiler, as well as how to find errors and bottlenecks in your programs.

Keep in mind that this chapter is only an introduction to CodeView and Microsoft Profiler. The chapter is designed to give you a working knowledge of the most popular features of these utilities.

If you are developing Windows software, especially from within the PWB launched as a Windows application, you will want to use the CVW1 Windows-compatible CodeView debugger. CVW1 runs in a separate Microsoft Windows window, enabling you to debug and watch your application's output at the same time. If you elected to install the Windows development tools during the Microsoft C/C++ installation process, CVW1 was automatically installed in the Microsoft C/C++ file group in the Program Manager. You can access CVW1 by double-clicking its icon. You can also launch CodeView for Windows by running the CVW program at the DOS command line.

This chapter describes the use of CodeView only for MS-DOS.

Setting Up for Debugging

You can use CodeView as a stand-alone utility, or you can call it directly from within the PWB. In the past, debuggers were completely separated from the editor and compiler. Consequently, it was harder to start and use the debuggers.

 NOTE CodeView for MS-DOS requires at least two megabytes of memory managed by HIMEM.SYS (the Windows extended memory manager), 386MAX.SYS (which is part of the Microsoft C/C++ 7.0 package), or an EMM386.SYS expanded memory manager.

The first part of this section explains bugs and debugging programs. The second part of the section shows you how to set up your program with CodeView so that CodeView can be executed from within the PWB.

Understanding Bugs and Debuggers

Bugs are simply malfunctions in your program. These malfunctions can manifest themselves in a number of different ways. A bug that is a *data error* can result in your program producing the wrong answers. Data errors can occur when your program reads the wrong data, reads data incorrectly, or loses track of it's place in a large data structure. Note the following common data error:

```
scanf( "%d", i ); /* This statement does not work right */
```

This `scanf()` function call contains an error that is easy to make but hard to see. When you use the `scanf()` function, remember that you have to supply the address of where the input data will be stored. To tell `scanf()` the address of a variable with one of the basic data types, you have to precede the variable name with the & symbol. It can be hard to miss an address-of operator error because you know that the `scanf()` function needs the operator, and you tend to assume that the operator has been included.

Other bugs are *logic errors,* which are flaws in the program design. A logic error can occur when the program tries to handle something it was never programmed for or when you make a simple typographical error. Look at the following example:

```
int i;
int j = 0;
...
for( i = 0; j = 10; i++ )   /*This loop will never end*/
  printf( "i = %d\n", i );
```

In this code fragment, a logic error is in the `for()` loop. If you look closely, you will notice that the controlling expression for the loop is the expression `j = 10`, rather than the correct expression, which is `i = 10`. The logic error in the `for()` loop will cause the loop to run forever, or at least until you reboot your computer.

Here are some common errors that programmers make:

- *Incorrect use of C operators and punctuators.* Using the assignment operator (=) when you intend to use the equality operator (==) can dramatically change program execution. Depending on the compiler warning level that you have set, Microsoft C/C++ will warn you if it sees an assignment operator in a conditional statement. Another easy mistake is to put a semicolon in the wrong place.

- *Untidy errors.* The advice "When you are through with something, put it away!" also applies to programming. For example, if you start allocating memory and you don't free any of the allocated blocks, you can easily run out of memory space.

- *Side-effect errors.* It is possible for a function or macro to change the value of data or pointers in your program without your knowledge.

- *Unnoticed changes to global variables.* Before a function changes the value of a global variable, make sure that the changed value will not cause problems in the rest of the program.

- *Autovariable errors.* Automatic variables are created each time a function is called. An automatic variable ceases to exist when the function ends. Therefore, returning a pointer to an autovariable can cause bizarre results. Reusing a variable name can cause problems if the name is reused in the wrong location.

- *Use of integers of different sizes.* Be careful when you assign values to integers of different sizes. For example, you can assign the value of a long `int` to a short `int`. Because the value of the long `int` is truncated to fit in the short `int`, however, the two integer values will not be equal.

■ *Loop counter errors.* When you create a `for()` loop, use the correct controlling condition expression. For example, the loop

```
for( i = 0; i < 10; i++ )
```

counts from 0 to 9. But the loop

```
for( i = 0; i <= 10; i++ )
```

counts from 0 to 10. The first loop makes 10 passes, and the second loop makes 11.

■ *Operator precedence.* Remember that C operators are acted on in a definite order. Keep a chart of operator precedence handy when you are writing an expression that uses several operators.

Until recently, finding bugs in programs was difficult. It involved the tedious process of digging through listings and adding extra code to the program to dump the values of variables and to map the flow of program execution. Debugging was a long and involved process.

Now, with an animated debugger like CodeView, finding errors in programs is much easier. CodeView lets you watch your program as it runs. No longer do you have to add reams of `printf()` statements to see what is happening inside the program. Next, you learn the main features of CodeView and how to compile your program for debugging.

Preparing To Run CodeView from the PWB

CodeView is a stand-alone program, which means that it is a completely separate program from the Programmer's WorkBench; however, you can access and use the facilities of CodeView from within the PWB. CodeView can help you locate program defects through some of these powerful features:

■ *Tracing.* Tracing enables you to execute your program one line at a time and thus see the effect of every statement in your program. Animated tracing and stepping are special tracing modes.

■ *Stepping.* With this feature, you can trace your program one line at a time without having to trace into called functions.

■ *Animated tracing.* This feature enables you to run your program in slow motion. You can see what statements are executed and how the data changes.

■ *Viewing aspects of your program.* Viewing gives you a new perspective on your program. You use windows to view almost any part of your program, including the source code, data, stack, and CPU.

■ *Watching.* Watching lets you track the values stored in the variables during the execution of your program.

■ *Changing.* With CodeView, you can change the value of a variable while the program is running.

Although CodeView provides many features, it will not let you edit or recompile your program when you find a program bug. When you find a bug, you must switch back to the PWB to correct the problem and recompile your program.

Not every program can be debugged. Only programs compiled with the right options can be examined by CodeView. To work correctly, CodeView requires you to include extra information in your program's executable file. All you need to do is set an option to have the debugging information included in your program. You first select **O**ptions from the PWB and then select the Buil**d** Options command. When the Build Options dialog box appears, choose the Use **D**ebug Options radio button (see Figure 9.1). From now on, any program you compile will contain the information necessary for CodeView to work.

Figure 9.1.

The PWB debugging option.

If you are using the command-line compiler `cl`, you must use the `/Zi` compiler switch like this:

```
cl /Zi source.c
```

If you choose to link your program separately from the compile step, you must append the `/CO` (for CODEVIEW) switch to the LINK command line.

Using CodeView

This section gets you started using CodeView to examine your program. The first part of the section shows you how to load and execute a program under CodeView. The second part of the section explains how to change the data your program uses.

Running a Program with CodeView

CodeView is a stand-alone program, but you can start it from within the PWB or separately from the PWB. The easiest method to explain is starting CodeView from the DOS prompt. Just type the following:

`cv progname.exe`

This runs CodeView and loads the named program, here shown as `progname.exe`. CodeView is now ready for you to begin looking for bugs. Remember, when you find a bug, you will have to get out of CodeView, fix the problem, and recompile your programs.

CodeView can be run in 25-, 43-, or 50-line mode depending on your monitor. To select 43-line mode (for EGA displays), add the `/43` command-line switch just after `cv` on the DOS command line. To select 50-line mode (for VGA displays), add the `/50` command-line switch just after `cv`.

The second way to start CodeView is from inside the PWB. If your program is already compiled and linked using the Debug options, you can start CodeView by selecting **D**ebug from the **R**un menu. This loads and runs CodeView, automatically loading your program into CodeView, ready for debugging. Select Code**V**iew from PWB's **O**ptions menu to choose the number of lines that CodeView should display on your monitor.

Programs must be compiled with the debug options switched on. Select Buil**d** Options from the **O**ptions menu, and then select **D**ebug Options. If your program is not yet compiled or must be recompiled, select **B**uild or **R**ebuild All (as appropriate) from the **P**roject menu. When the compilation and link have finished, PWB displays a Build Operation Complete dialog box. At this box you can run the program, cancel program execution, or select the **D**ebug option. To enter CodeView, select the <**D**ebug> action button.

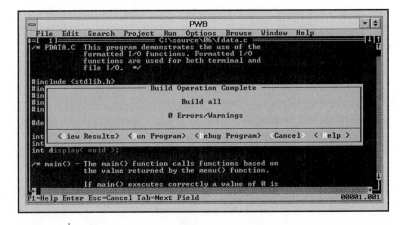

Figure 9.2.

Starting CodeView.

The primary advantage of starting CodeView from inside the PWB is the ease with which you can modify your program when you find a bug. When you are using CodeView and you find a bug in your program, you still have to get out of CodeView to fix the problem. Because CodeView was started from within the PWB, however, exiting CodeView puts you right back in the PWB. As soon as you get out of CodeView, you are ready to modify and recompile your program.

Within CodeView there are a number of ways you can run your program. Some of these methods are displayed on the prompt line at the bottom of the screen: `F8 to Trace`, `F10 to Step`, and `F5 to Go` or run your program. The **R**un menu displays some additional options, including **A**nimate.

In addition to the keystrokes and pull-down menu options, CodeView also has a command-driven mode of execution. In this form, you type commands in the CodeView Command window, where each command consists of one or two letters followed by options such as numbers or symbols. You will find that learning to use the Command window is easy and provides access to many more functions than those available through the pull-down menus.

The rest of this section examines the different ways you can run your programs under CodeView. The examples provided use the fdata.c program from Chapter 6.

The `F5=Go` keystroke command (on the **R**un menu) executes your program at full speed. You are put back in CodeView only when the program terminates, when a *breakpoint* is encountered, or when you press Ctrl-Break. A breakpoint is an indicator that you can put in the program with CodeView. The purpose of a breakpoint is to stop program execution so that you can see what is happening.

Several shortcut keys are shown at the bottom of the screen. For example, the shortcut key for the command that executes the program is F5, and the shortcut key for the Trace command is F8.

The Go command executes your program at full speed until the program terminates. If you want to have the program execute to a certain point and then stop, you can use a shortcut to set the breakpoint and execute the program. Using the mouse, move to the program line where you wish to have the program stop, and press the *right* mouse button. Or, using the keyboard keys, move the cursor to the line where you wish to have the program stop, and press F7. In either case, when you click the right mouse button or press F7, the program immediately executes down to the line you selected and then stops. This command is useful when you are checking a program and are interested only in what happens after a certain point in the program. Keep in mind that if the line you select is inside a section of code that is never executed, such as after an `if()` statement, it is possible that you will never encounter the breakpoint.

The F8=Trace command is perhaps the most important command in CodeView. Using Trace, you can execute one statement at a time. When this command encounters a function call, CodeView traces program flow into the called function.

The F5=Step command is similar to Trace, except that Step does not trace into called functions. Instead, Step follows your program's main flow of execution. A function call is treated like any other statement and does not result in tracing into the called function.

The best way to learn how to use CodeView is to use it. Use the PWB to open the program fdata.c from Chapter 6. Select Build Options from the Options menu. On the Build Options dialog box, select Use Debug Options.

Next, select Build from the Project menu to recompile fdata.c using the debug options. When the compilation and link have completed, select <Debug> from the Build Operation Complete dialog box. This will start CodeView and load the compiled fdata into CodeView, ready for debugging, as shown in Figure 9.3.

Figure 9.3.

The CodeView screen with fdata.exe ready for debugging.

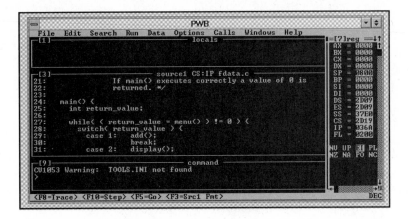

Notice that the cursor is automatically placed on the first *executable* line in the program. As you learned in an earlier chapter, the first executable statement in a C program is the call to the main() function. All the comments, macros, and variable declarations before main() are not executable statements because these instructions are handled during the compile and link process.

When you have fdata.exe loaded, press F8 to choose the Trace command. When you press F8, the Trace command executes the program up to the while() statement at the beginning of main(). The while() statement controls the execution of the menu() function for the fdata program. Therefore, when you press F8 again, the cursor moves to the menu() function. Continue pressing F8.

Notice that the screen flickers whenever a `printf()` call is encountered. The screen flickers because CodeView is actually switching screens and displaying the data in the `printf()` call. If you continue to press F8, you are eventually switched to the user screen when the program requests input. This screen is one of the nice features of CodeView: You can interact with your program while you are debugging it.

When the user screen is brought up and you are prompted for a response, enter the number 0. This response tells the program that you want to quit. Because there is no need to execute the rest of the program's instructions, select **R**estart from the **R**un menu. This causes CodeView to reset the program. The next time you execute any of CodeView's tracing commands, tracing will start at the beginning of the program.

The Step command works like the Trace command. The only difference is that Step does not trace into a called function. When Step encounters a function call, the function is executed at full speed; however, Step does not display the statements in the function.

After you reset the fdata program, use F10 to step through the program again. This time, you do not see the statements in the `menu()` function as they are executed. The only part of the `menu()` function that you see is the user screen prompting you for a menu selection. Enter 0 for the menu selection and continue using Step to trace through the program until it ends.

The Go command runs the program at full speed until the end of the program is reached or until a breakpoint is reached. The easiest way to set breakpoints (stopping points) is to use the mouse cursor to select each breakpoint. Double-click the left mouse button at each line where you wish to have the program stop. You can set more than one breakpoint if you wish (this is especially useful if your program branches and you are unsure which branch it will take). To illustrate, use the mouse to double-click the first line of the `menu()` function. Then choose Go to execute the program, running at full speed until the program enters the menu function.

You can set breakpoints with keystrokes also. To set a breakpoint using keystroke commands, use the keyboard keys to navigate to a desired line and then press F9. This sets a breakpoint at the line where the cursor is located.

The Animate command runs the program in slow motion. Selecting **A**nimate is like continually pressing F8 (Trace), except that selecting **A**nimate is easier. You can select the trace speed by choosing **T**race Speed from the **O**ptions menu, and then selecting **S**low, **M**edium, or **F**ast from the dialog box. You can stop the **A**nimate trace at any time by pressing any key on your keyboard or by clicking the mouse.

Mixing Source and Assembly Language

CodeView can optionally display your program in its original C (or C++) source text, in assembly language, or in a mixture of the two. In the latter situation, CodeView inserts the compiler-generated assembly statements between each of your C program statements. This is particularly useful during debugging of complex statements, such as if() statements, where debugging one C statement at a time does not provide enough detail to trace the execution of the program.

There are two ways to select the current viewing language:

On the Options menu, choose Source1 Window Options. Under the Display Mode heading, choose Source, Mixed Source and Assembly, or Assembly.

Press the F3 key repeatedly. Each time you press F3, CodeView cycles to the next source display option. If you begin with Source shown, pressing F3 will cause Mixed Source and Assembly to appear in the Source window. Pressing F3 again displays Assembly Language only. Pressing F3 once more reverts back to C source code.

Using the Command Window

If the command window is not already visible on your CodeView screen, you can select Command from the Windows pull-down menu (or press Alt-9). The command window displays a > (greater-than) symbol at the left side of the window, which acts as a prompt for your commands. Using command mode, you can control all aspects of your debugging session. This section, being only an introduction to CodeView, touches on only a few of the features that you can use at this prompt. Table 9.1 shows just a few of the more than 60 commands available in command mode. You can type multiple commands on one command line by separating each command with a semicolon. If you are a new user of CodeView, you will find it easier to stick with the pull-down menu interface than to use the command-line functions to make the command window active.

Table 9.1 A few of the commands available in command mode.

Command	Description
BP	Breakpoint Set: BP line number or symbol You can use BP to set a breakpoint at a specified line number or function name. CodeView offers a wide variety of breakpoint features; only some of those features are discussed in this book.

Command	Description
E	Animate The E command begins execution of the program, running it in "slow motion." Press any key to stop the program.
G	Go [*optional break address*] Begins execution of the program and continues running until the program terminates or reaches a breakpoint. You can optionally specify a breakpoint address on the command line. The breakpoint address can be the name of a function. For example, to execute the program down to the entry to a function named loop_count(), you type: G loop_count You may also specify labels, if your code uses labels. To specify a label, you must specify the function name and the name of the label inside the function, like this: G {loop_count}abort_*label*
H	Help: H command Displays a help message about the indicated command.
L	Restart Resets the program back to its beginning. This command is useful if you wish to begin a new debugging session using the current program.
Q	Quit Exits CodeView.
R	Registers: R *registername* [= *optional expression*] Displays the value of the indicated CPU register. If R is followed by an equals sign and an expression, the register is assigned the value of the expression.
T	Trace: T *count* Traces or single-steps through the program *count* number of times. For example, T 20 traces through the next 20 source lines or machine instructions, depending on the debugging mode.
T	Trace Speed: T S, T M, or T F When the T command is followed by S, M, or F, the Trace command sets the speed of tracing. The S option specifies a $\frac{1}{2}$-second delay between each instruction, M specifies a $\frac{1}{4}$-second delay, and F requests fast execution (no delay).
W	List Watch expressions Lists all current watch expressions.

continues

Table 9.1 Continued.

Command	Description
WC	Delete watch: WC *n* or WC * Use WC *n* to delete watch expression number *n* (from the List Watch listing). Use WC * to delete all watch expressions.
W?	Add watch: W? *expression* [, *optional format*] To add an expression to the watch window, type W? followed by the expression. For instance, to monitor the value of variable i, you type: W? i You may also enter an expression, such as: W? i * 25
@	Redraw the CodeView screen
\	View the program's output screen

Viewing Data

Tracing through your program is just one of the many features CodeView offers. Another major feature of CodeView is its capability to examine all the information associated with your program.

To view or *watch* the value of a variable or expression, use the **A**dd Watch... command on the **D**ata menu. You use the **D**ata menu to add or delete *watches* (and also to set or edit breakpoints using the menu system). **A**dd Watch... displays the dialog box shown in Figure 9.4. Enter a variable name or expression in the **E**xpression: input field. If you enter the name of a local variable, the variable must be in scope for you to see its value. You can enter a variable name while the variable is out of scope, but CodeView will indicate that it is unable to evaluate your expression at that point in the program.

To reference a variable declared within another function, such as a local static variable, prefix the variable name with {functioname}, like this:

```
{loop_count}i
```

This instruction tells CodeView to display the variable i defined inside the function named loop_count. The value of i, because it is a local variable, may only be valid when executing program statements inside loop_count. When executing other code, CodeView indicates that the expression cannot be evaluated.

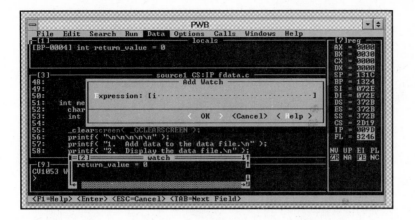

Figure 9.4.

Use the Add Watch dialog box to add a variable or expression to the Watch window. Use this feature to observe the values of variables during program execution.

All watch values are displayed in a watch window. If the window is not presently displayed on the CodeView screen, select the watch window from the **W**indows pull-down menu (or press Alt-2 as a short-cut key to display the watch window). To make the window disappear, select the window and then press Ctrl-F4 to close the window, or choose **C**lose from the **W**indows pull-down menu.

When a watch value is no longer needed, use the **D**elete Watch... function on the **D**ata menu to remove the watch. **D**elete Watch... displays a list box that contains all your current watch expressions. Move the cursor (or use the mouse) to select the watch you wish to delete. Then choose < OK > to delete your selected watch expression. You can erase all watches by choosing the < **C**lear All > button on the Delete Watch dialog box.

To see a list of the functions called so far, on the way down to the current location in the program, select the **C**alls menu. This displays a list of functions, with the most recently called function at the top. For instance, if a() calls b(), and b() calls c()—and you stop at a breakpoint in function c()—the **C**alls menu displays c() at the top of the list and a() at the bottom.

The *locals* window displays the name and value of each local variable in the current function, plus its stack location as an offset from the BP register. You can edit the values of variables shown in the locals window. Move the cursor to the item to be changed and type a new value. If the locals window is not already visible on the screen, choose Locals from the **W**indows pull-down menu (or press Alt-1).

If your program uses multiple modules (and most sizeable C programs do), you can open other modules using the Open **M**odule command from the **F**ile menu. With the Open **M**odule command, you get a window in which you can display other program modules.

You can also open multiple source windows using the **O**pen Source... command from the **F**ile menu.

The Registers window shows everything you ever wanted to know about the state of the CPU during program execution. Select Register (or press Alt-7) from the **W**indows menu to display the Registers window. The CPU window is especially useful for debugging in assembly language, working with programs without debugging information, or finding the elusive bugs. The Registers window shows the value of each CPU register, the CPU flags, the value of the stack registers, and the value currently at the top of stack.

To view an arbitrary location in memory, choose **M**emory1 from the **O**ptions menu. The Memory1 Window Options dialog has an input field for you to specify an address; a Display format options list box to choose Ascii, Byte, Integer, Hex, and so forth; and two check box items. If you check the Reevaluate expression always (live) box, CodeView will continuously update the contents of the memory display during program execution.

Setting Breakpoints

You learned earlier that the term *breakpoint* refers to the feature that stops the execution of your program during debugging. Although a breakpoint can simply stop the execution of your program, the breakpoint feature can actually be a great deal more versatile.

To understand the way a particular breakpoint works, note the following three pieces of information:

- *Where the breakpoint is located in your program.*

- *The triggering condition of the breakpoint.* A breakpoint can be triggered when the breakpoint location is encountered, when an expression evaluates as true, when the value of a data object changes, or when a pass count reaches a predetermined value.

- *The status of program execution after reaching a breakpoint.* When encountering a breakpoint, the program can either stop or continue. If program execution stops, you can examine any part of the program you want. If program execution is allowed to continue, you can specify that the value of an expression be logged or that an expression you supply be executed.

To set a breakpoint, select the **S**et Breakpoints command from the Data menu. Selecting the **S**et Breakpoints command pops up a dialog box that offers breakpoint options (see Figure 9.5).

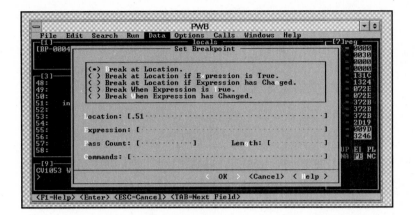

Figure 9.5.

The Breakpoint options dialog box.

The radio buttons shown at the top of the Set Breakpoint dialog box determine what happens when a breakpoint is encountered. **B**reak at location causes program execution to stop when a breakpoint is encountered. This always causes a breakpoint to be executed every time it is encountered during execution.

To set a nonconditional breakpoint at a specific program line number, select the **B**reak at Location radio button and move to the **L**ocation: input field. At the input field, type a period followed by the source code line number where the program should stop. There should be no space between the period and the line number, as in .12, which sets a breakpoint at line 12. If you omit the period, CodeView thinks you've typed a memory address and won't behave the way you'd like it to behave.

The Break at Location if E**x**pression is True option causes a breakpoint to be triggered only when the supplied expression is true. You can enter an expression similar to the type used for the watch expression, in the **E**xpression: input field. Break at Location if Expression has Cha**n**ged tells the debugger to break execution when a data value that you specify changes. You can also tell CodeView to break at any point in the program if the expression becomes true or if the value of the expression changes.

Pass Count: lets you specify a number of iterations to pass by the breakpoint without stopping. For instance, if you set a breakpoint in a loop and set **P**ass Count: to 5, CodeView will ignore the first five times that it encounters the breakpoint.

If you wish to change your breakpoint settings later, choose the **E**dit Breakpoints command from the **D**ata menu. This will display a list box of your currently active breakpoint settings. You can add new breakpoints, remove existing breakpoints, or modify the current breakpoint parameters.

Using Microsoft Profiler

Using Microsoft Profiler should become a new step in your program development cycle. After you write and debug your program, you can use Microsoft Profiler to analyze your program's efficiency. This utility can show you exactly where your program's time goes, such as the number of times a statement is executed and the amount of time spent executing the statement. By using this information, you can judge the statement's relative efficiency.

This section introduces you to profiling and shows you how to start analyzing your programs. The first part of the section explains the concept of profiling. The second and third parts show you how to set up and profile a program.

Knowing What Profiling Is

Profiling is the statistical analysis of the performance of code in your program. A profiler runs your program and records information indicating which statements are used, how often a statement is executed, and how long each statement takes to execute. You can use this information in deciding which statements need to be further refined or optimized. You can also use this information to help you decide which program sections are appropriate for compiling in p-code.

Another good use for Profiler is to compare different algorithms and different implementations to determine which is fastest. You can also use the Profiler to help with program testing. Because the Profiler can record each time that a particular program statement is executed, you can use the Profiler's analysis to determine if sufficient tests have been designed to ensure that every program statement gets executed at least once. If statements are not being executed, this is a clue that the tests are inadequate, the program logic is flawed, or unneeded code has been inserted into the program.

The Profiling Process

Optimizing and profiling are different processes. The Microsoft C/C++ compiler has options you can set that cause your program to be optimized when it is compiled. The optimizing process simply replaces time-consuming function calls with function calls that take less time. The profiling process analyzes your program so that you can change its basic structure and thus make the program more efficient.

Figure 9.6 shows the three steps in the profiling process.

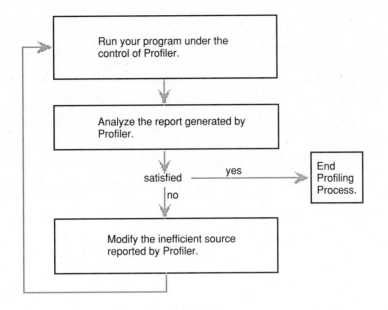

Figure 9.6.

The steps in the profiling
process.

You will probably go through the three profiling steps several times as you are fine-tuning your program. After you make one change in the program, you will likely find another area that you can make more efficient. You can repeat these three steps until you are satisfied with your program's performance.

The first step in the profiling process is to run your program under the profiler's control. Microsoft Profiler executes your program and collects information about how the program spends its time and what parts of the program are used. When Microsoft Profiler finishes running your program, the profiler generates data about the performance of the program. This report includes information about the number of times a statement was executed or the amount of time the statement took, and the overall percentage of processing time devoted to each statement.

The second step in the profiling process is to analyze Microsoft Profiler's report. The report can show you where time is being spent calling functions or calculating values, which parts of your program are executed, and how often they are used. With a little thought and research, you can learn a great deal about how your program really works.

When you determine where your program is spending too much time, the third step is to rewrite your source code so that the time-consuming routines are more efficient. Depending on how your program is spending its time, the task of rewriting your source code can be either simple or complex. At times, you may just need to replace one group of statements with another more efficient group to enhance performance. At other times, you may need to restructure your source code and possibly change the algorithms you use. The changes you make to your source code can easily be analyzed. All you have to do is recompile and reprofile the program to see whether performance was improved by your changes.

Starting Microsoft Profiler

Using Microsoft Profiler is a straightforward process; however, you need to compile your program with the debugging options turned on.

Before you begin profiling, it helps to separate sections of code that you already know need work. Separating code into logical sections makes it easier to see and analyze a particular inefficiency. Separating user-input routines also is helpful. Because user-input routines depend on the speed of the user and not the speed of the computer, profiling the user-input routines does little good. You may even want to replace these routines with a pre-made set of data from a disk file, with an array, or with random data generated by the computer.

It is important that you compile your program with full debugging information turned on. To turn on debugging information, select **O**ptions from the PWB main menu. Next pick the Buil**d** Options menu item and click the Use **D**ebug Options radio button. Microsoft Profiler has to have the debugging information so that the statistics for each line of your *source code* can be shown. When you begin profiling your program, make sure that Microsoft Profiler has access to both your .EXE file and the source code.

Knowing Basic Profiling Information

This section contains a profile of ptest1.c, a short program that displays the contents of a disk file on the screen. Listing 9.1 shows the source code for the ptest1.c program. Note that when you use the ptest1.c program, you need to provide a text.dat file for the program to read. You can easily create the text.dat file by using the DOS COPY command to copy the ptest1.c source code to text.dat.

Listing 9.1. ptest1.c. The first of two profile test programs.

```
1   /*  PTEST1.C  This program uses the character I/O functions
2              to demonstrate the use of Microsoft Profiler. */
3
4   #include <stdio.h>
5   #include <stdlib.h>
```

```
 6   #include <graph.h>
 7
 8   main()
 9   {
10     FILE *file_ptr;
11     char store;
12
13     if( ( file_ptr = fopen( "text.dat", "rt" ) ) == NULL ) {
14       _clearscreen( _GCLEARSCREEN );
15       printf( "Could not open data file.\n" );
16       printf( "Calling the exit() function.\n" );
17       exit( 0 );
18     }
19
20     _clearscreen( _GCLEARSCREEN );
21     while( ( store = fgetc( file_ptr ) ) != EOF ){
22       putchar( store );
23     }
24
25     fclose( file_ptr );
26     return 0;
27   }
```

The Microsoft Profiler is actually a set of programs: PREP, PROFILE, and PLIST. The PREP program scans a command file and readies your program for profiling. PROFILE executes your program and collects statistics. Finally, PLIST converts the collected statistics into an output file.

Each of these programs is controlled with special command files and numerous command-line switches, but you don't have to worry about all these details for simple profiling operations. Microsoft has conveniently provided a set of .BAT batch files that handle all the ugly details. All you need to do is invoke the appropriate batch file.

To determine which batch file to use, you must first understand the four different types of profiling:

Counting   The Profiler keeps a count of each time that a program line or function is executed.

Timing   The Profiler keeps track of how much time is spent executing each line or function. This mode of operation causes your program to run very slowly when it is being profiled.

Sampling   Using sampling, the Profiler periodically takes a look at what program lines or functions are in use. Over a lengthy period of time, this can produce a representative sample of your program's execution. Sampling will have the least effect on your program's execution speed.

Coverage   In this mode, the Profiler records which lines or functions have been executed. This is useful when you are testing your program to ensure that each line in the program is executed as a result of your testing.

To control execution of the profiling operation, Microsoft provides a total of eight batch files—four for selecting profiling by lines and four for selecting profiling by functions. The line-based profiling files are named

lcount.bat—for the counting profile

ltime.bat—for the timing profile

lsample.bat—for the sampling profile

lcover.bat—for the coverage-testing profile

The batch files for function analysis all begin with the letter *f*, so lcount.bat becomes fcount.bat, and so on. The Profiler also works with Windows programs. These files are named the same as the *l* and *f* batch files, except that they have a letter *w* added to the end of the batch file name, as in lcountw.bat. There is no fsamplew or lsamplew batch file as sampling cannot be used for Windows programs.

To profile the program ptest1.c (from Listing 9.1), compile and link ptest1 with the debug options enabled. Then type the following at the DOS command prompt:

```
lcount ptest1
```

The lcount.bat batch file automatically invokes PREP to build the necessary profiling information. Then the batch file turns over control to PROFILE, which executes the ptest1 application. When finished, the batch file runs PLIST to produce the output file ptest1.out. This output file is shown in Listing 9.2.

Listing 9.2. The output produced by the lcount profiling function.

```
Microsoft PLIST Version 1.20


Profile: Line counting, sorted by line.
Date:    Mon Feb 24 16:28:32 1992
```

```
Program Statistics
-----------------

    Total lines: 13
    Total hits: 1717
    Line coverage:  69.2%


Module Statistics for c:\profiler\bin\ptest1.exe
-------------------------------------------------

    Lines in module: 13
    Hits in module: 1717
    Module line coverage:  69.2%


Source file: c:\profiler\bin\ptest1.c


        Hit
Line  count   %   Source
------------------------
   1:                  /*  PTEST1.C  This program uses the character I/O functions
   2:                              to demonstrate the use of Microsoft Profiler. */
   3:
   4:                  #include <stdio.h>
   5:                  #include <stdlib.h>
   6:                  #include <graph.h>
   7:
   8:                  main()
   9:     1    0.1  {
  10:                      FILE *file_ptr;
  11:                      char store;
  12:
  13:     1    0.1      if( ( file_ptr = fopen( "text.dat", "rt" ) ) == NULL ) {
  14:     0    0.0         _clearscreen( _GCLEARSCREEN );
  15:     0    0.0         printf( "Could not open data file.\n" );
  16:     0    0.0         printf( "Calling the exit() function.\n" );
  17:     0    0.0         exit( 0 );
  18:                      }
  19:
  20:     1    0.1      _clearscreen( _GCLEARSCREEN );
  21:   571   33.3      while( ( store = fgetc( file_ptr ) ) != EOF ){
  22:   570   33.2         putchar( store );
  23:   570   33.2      }
  24:
  25:     1    0.1      fclose( file_ptr );
  26:     1    0.1      return 0;
  27:     1    0.1  }
```

The information presented in lines 21 through 23 indicates that more than 99 percent of the statements executed when this program runs are those confined within the while loop. Obviously, if you optimize this program, lines 21 through 23 are good candidates for improvement because any improvement here will dramatically improve the speed of the program.

The line count report, however, indicates only that these lines are executed many times. If you run the analysis by time, you get a different view of the program. Listing 9.3 shows the resulting time analysis.

Listing 9.3. Execution profile of ptest1.c, as measured by time spent in each line.

```
Microsoft PLIST Version 1.20


Profile: Line timing, sorted by line.
Date:    Mon Feb 24 19:19:30 1992



Program Statistics
- - - - - - - - - - - - - - - - -
     Total time: 2273.057 milliseconds
     Time before any line: 119.020 milliseconds
     Total lines: 13
     Total hits: 1717
     Line coverage:  69.2%


Module Statistics for c:\profiler\bin\ptest1.exe
- - - - - - - - - - - - - - - - - - - - - - - - - - - - - - - - - - - - - - -
     Time in module: 2154.037 milliseconds
     Percent of time in module: 100.0%
     Lines in module: 13
     Hits in module: 1717
     Module line coverage:  69.2%


Source file: c:\profiler\bin\ptest1.c


              Line        Hit
     Line     Time    %   count Source
- - - - - - - - - - - - - - - - - - - - - - - - - - - - - -
       1:          /*  PTEST1.C  This program uses the character I/O functions
       2:          to demonstrate the use of Microsoft Profiler. */
       3:
```

```
 4:                                #include <stdio.h>
 5:                                #include <stdlib.h>
 6:                                #include <graph.h>
 7:
 8:                                main()
 9:     0.000    0.0      1 {
10:                                    FILE *file_ptr;
11:                                    char store;
12:
13:     7.987    0.4      1   if( ( file_ptr = fopen( "text.dat", "rt" ) ) == NULL ){
14:     0.000    0.0      0       _clearscreen( _GCLEARSCREEN );
15:     0.000    0.0      0       printf( "Could not open data file.\n" );
16:     0.000    0.0      0       printf( "Calling the exit() function.\n" );
17:     0.000    0.0      0       exit( 0 );
18:                                    }
19:
20:     1.778    0.1      1   _clearscreen( _GCLEARSCREEN );
21:   445.446   20.7    571   while( ( store = fgetc( file_ptr ) ) != EOF ){
22:  1197.029   55.6    570       putchar( store );
23:   498.595   23.1    570   }
24:
25:     0.377    0.0      1   fclose( file_ptr );
26:     0.000    0.0      1   return 0;
27:     2.825    0.1      1 }
```

As expected, when you look at the program's profile by how much CPU time each line takes up, lines 21 through 23 are still at the top of the heap. Now note, however, that line 22 alone uses twice as much time as the lines on either side. For this reason, it is important that you profile your program carefully.

Consider what happens if you perform a line count profile analysis on a statement that calls a time-consuming function. The line count may show relatively few calls to the function. A time analysis, however, may reveal that the execution time spent inside the function is expensive and should be reduced. For this reason, you must always examine and interpret the results of a profile analysis carefully. If you fail to understand the data produced by the Profiler, you can waste time optimizing the wrong sections of your program.

Don't be surprised when you run this program and your execution statistics differ from the statistics listed in the book. The actual values of the statistics depend on the speed of your CPU, the speed of the disk, and the size and type of data files that you use.

Improving ptest1

If you look at line 22 in Listing 9.1, you see that it is a putchar() function. You now know that the ptest1 program is spending 98 percent or more of its time writing data to the screen. To improve the efficiency of this program significantly, you need to change the screen output. The easiest way to do that is to replace character output with string output. Listing 9.4, ptest2.c, shows how ptest1.c was modified.

Listing 9.4. ptest2.c. The second of two profile test programs.

```
1   /*  PTEST2.C  This program is a modification of the PTEST1.C
2               program. This program uses string I/O to
3               increase the performance of the program. The
4               result can be seen by using Microsoft Profiler. */
5
6   #include <stdio.h>
7   #include <stdlib.h>
8   #include <graph.h>
9
10  main()
11  {
12    FILE *file_ptr;
13    char *c_ptr;
14    char store[256];
15
16    if( ( file_ptr = fopen( "text.dat", "rt" ) ) == NULL ) {
17      _clearscreen( _GCLEARSCREEN );
18      printf( "Could not open data file.\n" );
19      printf( "Calling the exit() function.\n" );
20      exit( 0 );
21    }
22
23    _clearscreen( _GCLEARSCREEN );
24    while( c_ptr != NULL ){
25      c_ptr = fgets( store, 256, file_ptr );
26      puts( store );
27    }
28
29    fclose( file_ptr );
30    return 0;
31  }
```

In Listing 9.2, the data transfer from the disk file is done one string at a time instead of one character at a time (as with Listing 9.1). Running the executable version of Listing 9.4 through Microsoft Profiler shows how much speed you gain by using string I/O. Listing 9.5 shows the Profiler output for ptest2.

Listing 9.5. Line timing analysis of ptest2.

```
Microsoft PLIST Version 1.20


Profile: Line timing, sorted by line.
Date:    Mon Feb 24 19:17:04 1992



Program Statistics
- - - - - - - - - - - - - - - - -
    Total time: 590.240 milliseconds
    Time before any line: 14.392 milliseconds
    Total lines: 14
    Total hits: 92
    Line coverage:  71.4%

Module Statistics for c:\profiler\bin\ptest2.exe
- - - - - - - - - - - - - - - - - - - - - - - - - - - - - - - - - - - -
    Time in module: 575.849 milliseconds
    Percent of time in module: 100.0%
    Lines in module: 14
    Hits in module: 92
    Module line coverage:  71.4%


Source file: c:\profiler\bin\ptest2.c


          Line      Hit
  Line    Time   %  count Source
- - - - - - - - - - - - - - - - - - - - - - - - - -
    1:                    /*  PTEST2.C  This program is a modification of the PTEST1.C
    2:                                  program. This program uses string I/O to
    3:                                  increase the performance of the program. The
    4:                                  result can be seen by using Microsoft Profiler. */
    5:
    6:                    #include <stdio.h>
    7:                    #include <stdlib.h>
    8:                    #include <graph.h>
```

Listing 9.5. Continued.

```
 9:
10:                              main()
11:      0.000    0.0     1 {
12:                                 FILE *file_ptr;
13:                                 char *c_ptr;
14:                                 char store[256];
15:
16:      0.000    0.0     1     if(( file_ptr = fopen( "text.dat", "rt" ) ) == NULL ) {
17:      0.000    0.0     0         _clearscreen( _GCLEARSCREEN );
18:      0.000    0.0     0         printf( "Could not open data file.\n" );
19:      0.000    0.0     0         printf( "Calling the exit() function.\n" );
20:      0.000    0.0     0         exit( 0 );
21:                                 }
22:
23:     57.223    9.9     1     _clearscreen( _GCLEARSCREEN );
24:      0.000    0.0     1     while( c_ptr != NULL ){
25:     66.493   11.5    28         c_ptr = fgets( store, 256, file_ptr );
26:    448.400   77.9    28         puts( store );
27:      0.000    0.0    29     }
28:
29:      0.614    0.1     1     fclose( file_ptr );
30:      0.000    0.0     1     return 0;
31:      3.119    0.5     1 }
```

From the Profiler output, you can see that ptest2 required a total of just 575 milliseconds of execution time. Compare that time to the more than 2,000 milliseconds requirement of ptest1.

ptest2.exe still spent 85 percent of its time writing data to the screen. If you look at the overall time spent displaying information, however, ptest2.exe is significantly faster than ptest1.exe. Changing from character output to string output increased overall program performance by almost 400 percent. Notice that character input is almost as fast as string input. The time difference between the character-input statements and the string-input statements is about .02 of a second.

Selecting a Profiling Mode

The profiling mode you use determines what kind of information Microsoft Profiler collects and how quickly your program runs under Microsoft Profiler.

As explained previously, the Profiler has four separate profiling modes: counting, timing, sampling, and coverage.

In the timing mode, the Profiler maintains a count of how much time is spent executing each line or function. As you might expect, there is significant overhead in recording this data during your program's execution. Consequently, your program will run very slowly.

Counting also has a significant overhead (but less than timing) because it maintains a count that tracks the number of times each line or function is encountered.

Coverage requires less overhead than counting because coverage notes only that the line or function was executed at least once, not how many times it was executed.

Sampling is the least invasive profiling mode. In this mode, Microsoft Profiler regularly checks the status of your program. If your program is in a profiling area during a check, the execution counter or timer for that area is incremented. Using this mode results in less slow-down in program performance.

Although sampling results in less performance degradation, sampling doesn't come for free, either. Sampling cannot generate all the information of the other modes, and the timer results that you get can be somewhat inaccurate. The only type of information provided by sampling mode is timer counts. By its nature, sampling mode cannot generate instruction counts. Moreover, because sampling occurs only at periodic intervals, it is possible to miscalculate the time an area takes to execute. In fact, if the program section under analysis is fast, sampling may not even register that the area executed.

 NOTE Sampling is not available when you are profiling Windows applications.

Looking Toward Other Profiling Features

It is beyond the scope of this book to describe all the Microsoft Profiler features. You should know that as you progress, you can create your own command files for use with the Profiler. Using command files, you will be able to select from multiple files, specific line ranges (such as 100-400) within each source module, or individual functions or groups of functions.

Exercises

The following exercises give you practice in setting up and using CodeView and Microsoft Profiler:

1. Practice using CodeView by selecting Use **D**ebug Build Options from the Build Options dialog box, compiling a sample program, and then entering the CodeView debugger from within the PWB.

2. Write a simple loop program and trace through the program, using the F8=Trace command and the **A**nimate command under CodeView's **R**un menu selection.

3. Trace the loop program again. When you have made a few passes through the loop, use the locals window to change the value of the loop counter. Examine the effects of the change on the program.

4. Write a program that calls a function that adds the first 100 even numbers. Trace through the program by using both the Step and Trace functions.

5. Write a program that contains a structure and an array. Use the **A**dd Watch... command to view the contents of both.

6. Reload the program that sums the first 100 even numbers. Open a Watches window and watch the value of the accumulator variable as the program is traced with **A**nimate trace.

7. In the even-numbered program, set a breakpoint that will stop execution when the accumulator value reaches 110.

8. Profile the even-numbered program you wrote. Profile the program using the lcount and ltime batch files.

9. Write a program that calls three or four different looping functions. Profile the program in counting, timing, and sampling modes.

Summary

In this chapter, you learned how to use CodeView and Microsoft Profiler. These two programs help you create professional code more quickly and easily. The following important points were covered:

■ *A debugger is a utility that lets you examine your program while it is running.* A debugger can help you find logic bugs or data bugs. A logic bug is a problem with the basic design of your program. A data bug is a problem with the data your program uses.

■ *CodeView is a stand-alone debugger; however, it can be launched from within the Programmer's WorkBench.*

■ *When you trace your program, you run it one line at a time.* Tracing enables you to see the effect of each line in your program.

■ *CodeView has a number of tracing commands you can use.* Trace executes your program one line at a time, whereas **A**nimate cycles through several lines, one after the other. **R**un lets you run your program at full speed. You can also choose whether to trace into functions in your program.

■ *You can watch the data values in your program change while the debugger is executing the program.* You can even change the value of the data in your program to see what will happen.

■ *Breakpoints enable you to interrupt your program so that you can find out what the program is doing.* You can set breakpoints to stop the execution of your program so that you can check the program's status. You can set breakpoints also to log values automatically and continue processing. A breakpoint can be set so that it always stops program execution or stops execution only when a specific event has occurred.

■ *Microsoft Profiler is a stand-alone utility that analyzes the performance of your program.* With Microsoft Profiler, you can see exactly which statements are executed, how many times they are called, and how long they take to execute.

■ *To profile a program, you simply load the .EXE version of the program (compiled with the debug options enabled) and run it.* Microsoft Profiler collects all the statistics you want.

■ *The program you profile must be compiled with full debugging information turned on.* The debugging information lets Microsoft Profiler link the statement in the .EXE file with your source file.

■ *You can choose to profile your program by counting the number of times a line or function is executed, by keeping track of how much time is spent in a line or function, or by keeping track of which statements have been executed at all.*

Using Microsoft C/C++'s Advanced Features

T his chapter covers some of the advanced features of the Microsoft C/C++ compiler that are extensions to the ANSI C language.

Some other compiler vendors offer products with the features covered in this chapter. Some of these products have all the features presented here. Keep in mind, however, that some of these features are extensions to the ANSI standard C language, and their implementation is unique to Microsoft C/C++. They are not directly portable to any other brand of compiler. Don't let that stop you from using these features. When you design your programs, just remember that these features are not portable, in case you later want to port them to another compiler or operating system.

In this chapter, you learn about the following advanced programming topics:

- *Using assembly language with your C programs.* A good C compiler produces very efficient machine code. That, plus the fact that C is a marvelously powerful and flexible language, tends to make C programmers partial (if not prejudiced). Why use assembly language? By using it, you can get still more power and more use of all your computer's capabilities. A program that combines both languages can be an awesome performer. This chapter introduces you to writing assembly language routines and using inline assembly statements.

- *Using Microsoft C/C++ interrupt functions.* Microsoft C/C++ supports a full range of interrupt service routines and facilities. You can cause software interrupts, as well as trap and handle them. Using interrupt services can help you produce a production-quality program. You learn how to use software interrupts and how to trap and handle system-related interrupt events.

- *Using the Microsoft C/C++ program optimization features.* You can optimize your programs for size or speed. You learn when and how to optimize your programs, and you get a brief tour of compiler optimization strategies.

Using Inline Assembly Language

Inline assembly language is covered first because it is probably the most often-used method of mixing C and assembly language. Microsoft C/C++ (and other good compilers) produce reasonably efficient machine code, so in most cases you need to tune only isolated spots in your program to provide higher performance or additional functions.

Unfortunately, a C book is not the place to teach assembly language programming. I could cover part of the language, but how much coverage would be enough without leaving you dangling? For a full treatment of assembly language programming, you may want to consult Allen Wyatt's *Using Assembly Language* (Third Edition, Que, 1992). That book, which is packed with both tutorial and reference information, gives the subject the full-scale treatment it deserves.

This book, however, must concentrate on what you need to know so that you can interface assembly language routines with your C programs, with an emphasis on the C environment.

Understanding the Inline Assembly Environment

Inline assembly statements can appear directly in your Microsoft C/C++ programs, so the C language program is the surrounding environment for these statements. You should know two things before you can correctly and effectively use inline assembly statements. First, you must know how to compile a C program containing inline assembly (which is discussed in this section). Second, you must know what you can and cannot do in inline assembly statements (which is discussed in the next section).

Compiling a program that contains inline assembly statements is only a little more complex than compiling a simple C program. You can use the Microsoft Assembler to generate object modules that can be linked into your overall application. You can also place assembler statements directly into special __asm statements inside your C/C++ source. The Microsoft C/C++ compiler has a special built-in assembler that lets you write assembly language routines in the middle of your C code. The built-in assembler has a subset of the features found in the Microsoft Assembler, which is sold separately by Microsoft.

Using the __asm Keyword

To insert inline assembly statements directly in your C program, use the __asm keyword at the beginning of the statement. Here are several different ways you can code an __asm statement:

```
__asm assembly statement
__asm assembly statement
__asm assembly statement __asm assembly statement
__asm {
  assembly statement ; assembly statement
  ...
  assembly statement
  assembly statement
  assembly statement
  ...
}
```

Because each __asm statement counts as a single C statement, you can enclose a series of __asm statements in a block surrounded by braces, as shown in the preceding example. The __asm keyword acts as a statement separator, so no semicolons are used to separate assembly language statements. You can also write comments on an __asm statement: Just use the normal C comment syntax (/*-*/ for C, and // for C++). Note, however, that no inline assembly statement can be continued to another line.

When you write inline assembly statements in your program, you must become more conscious of memory models and pointer sizes. You must always be aware of segment arrangements and pointer sizes when you are mixing C and assembler. Listing 10.1 shows a program that contains inline assembly code and illustrates both memory model dependency and the use of the __asm keyword.

Listing 10.1. inline.c. A program that shows the use of inline assembly in a large-model C program.

```
1   #include <stdlib.h>
2   #include <stdio.h>
3
4   void increment( int* arg )
```

```
 5  {
 6      /* First parameter is at [bp+4], which is the address of arg */
 7      __asm {                  /* Get pointer to obj & deref */
 8        mov   si,[bp+4]        /* get offset adrs of arg */
 9        mov   ax,[si]          /* deref, pick up int */
10        inc   ax               /* increment */
11        mov   [si],ax          /* and save it */
12      }
13  }
14
15  void main()
16  {
17      int j = 3;
18
19      printf( "Initial value was %d\n", j );
20      increment( &j );
21      printf( "New value is %d\n", j );
22  }
```

Function increment adds 1 to the argument passed as a parameter. Because the parameter arg is a pointer value, the assembly code must load the address value into the si register, (line 8) and then load the value that [si] points to (line 9). When a function is called, the calling routine pushes the parameters to the function onto the stack. The assembly language call instruction then pushes the return address onto the stack.

On entering an assembly language routine, the BP register points to the area on the stack known as the *stack frame.* Assembly code must gain access to function parameters by accessing them as a byte offset from the BP register. Hence, the statement

```
mov   si, [bp+4]
```

copies the value at memory location [bp+4] to si. The address now in si, in turn, is used to access the value of the parameter. This value is incremented and then stored back to the argument's address. The reference [bp+4] only works for an assembly routine that is a near procedure. For a far procedure, use [bp+6].

Coding the correct assembly statements is probably the trickiest thing about mixing C and assembler. It is strictly up to you to write assembly language code that meshes properly with the memory model being used. You can use all the normal 8086 and 80286 instructions in your inline assembly statements, including the 80287 floating-point instructions. You can use also all the extended string instructions of the 8086 instruction set, including special byte and word forms.

The loop and jump instructions are supported, together with the lock and rep instruction prefixes. A jump target may be either a C label or a label defined in an __asm block. Unlike C labels, however, a label defined inside an __asm block is not case-sensitive whether it is used within an __asm block or referenced from C code.

You can use the EVEN and ALIGN assembler directives to force labels to be placed on specific memory address boundaries. On all the 80x86 processors except for the 8088 CPU, this causes instruction fetches to operate more efficiently.

You can write constants in either C or standard assembler notation. For instance, 0xFF in C is equivalent to 0FFh in assembler notation. Constants preceded by zero are normally treated as octal. You can also reference any constant declared in a C #define statement.

What registers can you use in general, and what are the restrictions on their use? The C function call environment expects you to preserve the BP, SP, CS, DS, and SS registers. If you use or modify them, you must be certain that they have been restored to their original values before exiting inline assembly statements. However, you can use the AX, BX, CX, and DX registers (and their 8-bit subregisters, such as AH and AL) as well as the ES and flags registers in any way you want: These are considered to be *scratch* registers, or registers that are available for any use. However, if you use the _fastcall calling convention (see later in this chapter), any function declared as _fastcall must preserve the CX and ES registers.

As just noted, certain registers must be restored before returning to C code. Is there ever a time when you should modify those registers? First, there are two registers that you should consider inviolable: the CS and SS registers. Just don't modify these registers (other than indirectly—such as modifying CS through a CALL instruction). You will certainly regret it if you modify them, unless you are an expert assembly programmer.

Frequently, you will find it necessary to use the DS and ES registers to support certain instruction sequences. Using the ES register is no problem; it is a scratch register anyway. But the DS register is critical to the continued functioning of your C program: Always save the value of DS on entry to any routine that must change the value in DS, and then restore the DS register before returning from the assembly function. Your best bet is to save DS on the stack using push ds and, at the end of your assembly procedure, pop ds.

Assembly code that does much of anything often uses indirection to access memory locations (just like C programs). This means that you will have to manipulate segment registers fairly often. Furthermore, you should know which segment registers to manipulate. For your convenience, Table 10.1 shows which segment registers are assumed by the various operand formats and their corresponding addressing modes.

Table 10.1. Assumed segment registers for operand formats and addressing modes (8088 registers).

Segment Register	Operand Format	Addressing Mode
(None)	reg	Register operand
(None)	data	Immediate operand (in instruction)
DS	displacement	Direct-memory operand
DS	label	Direct-memory operand
DS	[bx]	Indirect operand
SS	[bp]	Indirect operand
DS	[si]	Indirect operand
DS	[di]	Indirect operand
DS	[bx+disp]	Base-relative operand
SS	[bp+disp]	Base-relative operand
DS	[di+disp]	Direct-indexed operand
DS	[si+disp]	Direct-indexed operand
DS	[bx][si]+disp	Base-indexed operand
DS	[bx][di]+disp	Base-indexed operand
SS	[bp][si]+disp	Base-indexed operand
SS	[bp][di]+disp	Base-indexed operand

The program in Listing 10.1 does not make clear that you can generally use the label of any C identifier that is currently in scope when inline assembly statements appear in the code. Such use can make life much simpler in many cases.

In this program, for example, you could have written the statements that load the pointer into SI by using the arg label, because that name is in scope for the duration of the increment() function. Those lines would have the following appearance:

```
mov  si,word ptr arg    /* Get offset adrs of arg */
```

An exception to this rule crops up when you attempt to refer to the label of a C++ class member variable in inline assembly language. In Part II of this book, you discover that a C++ class has its own unique scope. The labels of member variables are therefore not available to inline assembly statements.

Using Interrupt Functions

This section leads you through the Microsoft C/C++ facilities for using 80x86 interrupt architecture. You learn first how to cause 80x86 and DOS interrupts and then how to handle interrupts caused by other parts of the system.

Understanding 80x86 Interrupt Architecture

80x86 interrupts can be caused by hardware (such as I/O devices) or by software (such as the int assembly instruction). When an interrupt occurs, the CPU saves its current status—including the address of the next instruction to be executed—the system flags, and the system registers.

What happens next depends on what interrupt number is associated with the interrupt. For hardware interrupts, a support chip generates and supplies the interrupt number. For software interrupts, the interrupt number is supplied by the int instruction's operand.

Now the 80x86 CPU uses the interrupt number as an index into a table of interrupt vectors; an *interrupt vector* is nothing more than a far (four-byte) pointer. The pointer for an interrupt contains the address of the interrupt service routine (ISR) that will handle the new conditions.

As you might imagine, the interrupt vector table is not placed just anywhere in memory. It has a fixed location at the beginning of RAM, at address 0000:0000. Figure 10.1 shows the relative location of the interrupt vector table, together with the rest of the RAM organization in an IBM PC or a compatible computer.

Figure 10.1.

Memory organization,
including interrupt vector
locations, for the IBM PC
and compatibles.

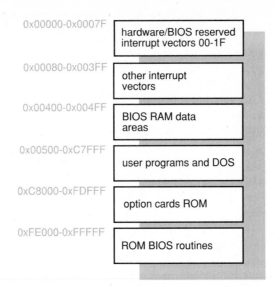

Because the interrupt vector table occupies the first 1,024 bytes of RAM, there can be a maximum of 256 interrupt vectors. The interrupt vectors are organized in groups, as shown in Table 10.2, according to purpose and what kind of ISR will handle the interrupt condition. For complete coverage of specific interrupts and their uses, you may want to consult *DOS Programmer's Reference* (Second Edition, Que Corporation, 1989).

Table 10.2. Summary of 80x86 interrupt vector usage on IBM and compatible ISA/EISA and MicroChannel computers.

Interrupt Invoked By	Interrupt Handled By	Interrupt Vector Numbers (Hex)
Hardware	User, system handler	00-0F
User, DOS	ROM BIOS	10-1F
User	DOS	20-3F
DOS, dvc drvrs	BIOS, device drivers	40-5F
User	(Reserved for users)	60-66
User	LIM EMS driver	67
Hardware	Device drivers	70-77
BASIC	BASIC	80-F0
(Not used)	(Not used)	F1-FF

As you can see in Table 10.2, most interrupts are handled by the system: Either the BIOS or DOS will do the work. In a few circumstances, your program can "hook" itself into the interrupt vector table and provide the ISR for an interrupt vector. You see how to do that in the section "Using Interrupt Handlers" later in this chapter. Before you move to that more complicated task, however, you need to consider how to cause system interrupts in a controlled and useful manner.

Using the Microsoft Interrupt Interfaces

Microsoft C/C++ provides two library functions for causing generic 80x86 interrupts and two functions for causing DOS interrupts. These functions are int86(), int86x(), intdos(), and intdosx().

All four of these interrupt-causing functions must use the union name REGS (declared in dos.h) to store and read back copies of the system registers. This is important because the system registers must be used to communicate parameters to the interrupt handlers (ISRs) within the BIOS and DOS. The int86x() and intdosx() functionsadditionally affect the DS and ES registers through the SREGS structure (also declared in dos.h), but these functions are not discussed here. This discussion instead focuses on the int86() and intdos() functions. (Logic involving the modification of DS and ES is best left to assembly language, and you already know how to use assembly language).

The REGS union has two member structures. The h structure contains unsigned char declarations for all the byte registers (ah, al, bh, bl, and so on). The x structure member contains unsigned int declarations for all the word registers (ax, bx, cx, and the rest). Note that the register variable names are written in lowercase letters. Thus, a REGS union object named reg contains a member named reg.h.al that holds a copy of the system AL register and a member named reg.x.ax that holds a copy of the system AX register. Finally, note that assigning a value to reg.x.ax implicitly places a value in reg.h.ah and in reg.h.al (remember the overlay nature of unions).

The general sequence for invoking a BIOS interrupt involves first loading the AH system register with a function code (a number indicating the specific action to be taken) and then executing the int instruction that specifies the interrupt number as its operand. In the next program, for example, the 0x13 interrupt—function code 0x19—is used to park the heads of a fixed disk drive. The assembly language sequence for accomplishing this action is the following:

```
...
mov     ah,19h    ; function code for park heads
mov     dl,80     ; do it for drive C:
int     13h       ; get BIOS to do it
...
```

When using the int86() function, of course, you do not load system registers directly; their values are extracted by the int86() function from the REGS union you set up before calling the function. You do not invoke the interrupt directly, either; the int86() function does that after setting the real system registers properly. Listing 10.2 shows how to use the int86() function to park the heads on all the fixed disk drives on your system.

Listing 10.2. fdpark.c. A program that uses the int86() function to park heads for all system fixed disk drives.

```
1   /* FDPARK.C ----- Use INT86() function to park all fixed
2                     disk drives in the system
3   */
4
5   #include <stdio.h>
6   #include <stdlib.h>
7   #include <dos.h>
8
9   void main()
10  {
11    union REGS reg;   /* Register structs declared in dos.h */
12    unsigned char driveid = 0;            /* Begin with C: */
13
14    while ( 1 ) {
15      reg.x.ax = 0x1900;
16      reg.h.dl = 0x80 ¦ driveid;
17      int86( 0x13, &reg, &reg );
18      if ( reg.h.ah ) break;   /* Error code means no more */
19      printf( "Parked heads for drive %c:...\n",
20              driveid++ + 67 );
21    }
22  }
```

Notice how the reg object is used in the int86() interrupt call in line 17. Always be sure to pass the address of the union to int86(). The first argument is the address of the register variables union used as input to int86(): The function will extract the setup values from the first argument. The second argument is the address of the register variables union that will be output from int86(): The values of the resulting registers are placed there.

The program in Listing 10.2 also illustrates the fact that BIOS interrupt functions often return a status code reflecting the outcome of the operation. In this case, register AH is zero if the head-parking operation was successful;

however, the register contains an error code if the operation was not successful. (The logic uses the error code to detect an absence of any more fixed disk drives.) Again, you do not access the system register AH directly. You get the value of that register as reported by int86() from the REGS union.

The head-parking program has some limitations you should know about. Although the program will work with almost all recent computers, some users may have an older computer with a fixed disk drive tacked on it. BIOS interrupt 0x13, function 0x19 works only for the following personal computers:

- The PC/AT with BIOS dated after 11/15/86, or completely compatible computers.

- The PC/XT with BIOS dated after 1/10/86, or completely compatible computers.

- The entire PS/2 line of computers and compatibles.

If your computer does not fall into one of these groups, fdpark.c won't hurt anything, but it won't do anything, either.

Because Microsoft C/C++ is such a complete package, there are only a few times when you need to use the int86() function. Parking fixed disk heads is clearly one of those times. Using the intdos() function is even more rare, but I discuss it here for the sake of completeness.

DOS functions are available to users (meaning programmers) through the 80x86 interrupt number 0x21, with many associated function codes. Because DOS calls fall into a class by themselves, Microsoft C/C++ provides the intdos() function, which assumes that the interrupt number is 0x21. Frankly, there is little reason to use this function in ordinary code because the ANSI standard library functions, plus the Microsoft-supplied additional functions, cover just about every contingency. This is true of the program in Listing 10.3, which uses the DOS function code 0x2A to get the system date and the weekday from DOS.

Listing 10.3. calldos.c. A program that uses the intdos() function to get the system date and weekday.

```
1   /* CALLDOS.C ----- Use INTDOS() function to get the system
2                      date and weekday
3   */
4
5   #include <stdio.h>
6   #include <stdlib.h>
7   #include <dos.h>
8
9   char *months[] = {
```

```
10    "",
11    "January",  "February","March",    "April",
12    "May",      "June",    "July",     "August",
13    "September","October", "November","December",
14  };
15
16  char *days[] = {
17    "Sunday",   "Monday", "Tuesday", "Wednesday",
18    "Thursday", "Friday", "Saturday",
19  };
20
21  void main()
22  {
23    union REGS reg;   /* Register structs declared in dos.h */
24
25    reg.x.ax = 0x2A00;    /* Set up call code for int. 0x21 */
26    intdos( &reg, &reg );        /* Get the date & weekday */
27    printf( "The current date is %s, %s %d, %d.\n",
28            days[reg.h.al], months[reg.h.dh],
29            reg.h.dl, reg.x.cx );
30  }
```

The intdos() function is almost exactly the same as the int86() function in its use and arguments, except for the name and the absence of the interrupt number. Again, if you want details about all the DOS interrupts, you can consult the *DOS Programmer's Reference*.

Using Interrupt Handlers

An interrupt handler is an ISR. That's simple enough. But what if you want to take over the handling of an interrupt, instead of allowing the BIOS code or DOS to do it? Microsoft C/C++ provides for this contingency as well, by offering the __interrupt specifier. You can use the __interrupt specifier to identify one of your own C functions as an ISR. In this section, you learn what that means and how to do it. You also have a little fun writing an ISR that displays a real-time clock on the screen while your program goes about its other business.

Declaring Interrupt Handler Functions

The general form of an interrupt handler function is the following:

```
void __interrupt __far newint60(   unsigned _es, unsigned _ds,
                                    unsigned _di, unsigned _si,
                                    unsigned _bp, unsigned _sp,
                                    unsigned _bx, unsigned _dx,
                                    unsigned _cx, unsigned _ax,
                                    unsigned _ip, unsigned _cx,
                                    unsigned flags );
{
    /* Do something in here */
}
```

When an interrupt has caused your ISR to be executed, the system has already pushed the flags, the CS register, and the IP (instruction pointer) register onto the system stack. Code that Microsoft C/C++ generated and prefixed to your ISR function has also pushed the remaining registers onto the stack, in the order shown in the preceding code fragment (remember that Microsoft C/C++ scans argument lists from right to left). You do not have to declare all the system registers for every ISR function. In fact, many ISR functions that you write may have no arguments. If you use some of the registers, however, you cannot skip any or alter the order shown here: If you need register ax, you must declare in the parameter list all the registers before that one.

The body of your ISR function can modify any or all of those registers by assigning new values to the register arguments passed to the function; this has the effect of altering a register's contents as it sits on the stack. When that register is popped off the stack (when the ISR returns), it contains the new value. Common sense—as well as the restrictions on preserving registers, which were detailed earlier in this chapter—indicates which registers you can alter safely.

Aside from altering system registers in an ISR, you can do a number of useful things in the ISR's function body. You can update variables that are in scope for the ISR function (its own local variables and global static data), read and write data from a communications port, display information on the screen, and even cause further interrupts (nested interrupts). There is one thing that you should not do, however, if you want your program to continue running and your disks to remain uncorrupted (unless you are a DOS and an assembly expert): *Do not attempt to perform disk file I/O.*

Microsoft recommends that you avoid calling any standard library functions unless you are certain that the library function does not call the DOS INT 21H interface or the BIOS calls. Functions that use DOS INT 21H include all of the library I/O functions and all of the _dos...() functions. There are instances where you can get away with violating these rules, as in the example program that comes later in this section, but generally you should follow these guidelines to keep your program safe.

The reason for these severe restrictions is that interrupts occur at unpredictable times—for instance, when DOS is already in the middle of doing other file functions. Furthermore, DOS is a single-tasking (single-threaded) operating system, and you may cause that wonderful simpleton to lose track of its internal stack (it actually has two stacks, which is even worse) and completely wreck whatever it was in the process of doing.

There are still many useful things you can do with ISRs, however, as you are about to find out. First, you need to know the basics of setting up the ISR and hooking into the interrupt vector that the ISR will be servicing. In broad strokes, you should perform the following tasks when installing your own ISR:

- *Preserve the old interrupt vector.* Microsoft C/C++ provides the _dos_getvect() function for this purpose. You can save this far pointer in a pointer to a function.

- *Hook the address of your ISR function into the interrupt vector.* The _dos_setvect() library function performs this task

- *Before your program exits to the system, restore the old interrupt vector.* Use the _dos_setvect() function again, with the old ISR address you saved before.

Implementing a Timer Tick Interrupt Handler

This section presents an actual ISR application. It intercepts the system clock tick interrupt and uses the opportunity to display a real-time clock in the upper-left corner of the screen. After you set up the ISR, the rest of the program goes about its business—at the same time that the clock is being continuously updated.

The timer tick interrupt (number 0x08) is one of those interrupts that is hardware generated. When the system interval timer goes off, it activates an interrupt request circuit (a physical electronic circuit) that is gated to the interrupt 0x08 vector. Even more interestingly, the BIOS ISR for interrupt 0x08 invokes another software interrupt: vector 0x1C.

The purpose of interrupt 0x1C is to allow user programs to intercept it and do something useful with it. You should generally leave the BIOS ISR alone, because it does such things as turning off disk drive motors that have been left running. (It is possible to intercept interrupt 0x08, but that won't be shown here.)

Figure 10.2 shows the flow of instruction execution when a timer tick occurs. The user program is temporarily suspended, and the interrupt 0x08 ISR is executed; it in turn invokes interrupt 0x1C.

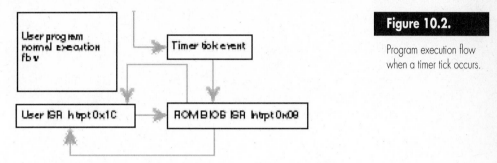

Figure 10.2.

Program execution flow when a timer tick occurs.

When the real-time clock ISR is finished, execution flow trickles back up through the 0x08 ISR, and finally back to the user program, exactly where it was suspended. The user program then continues running, none the wiser. The net effect, of course, is the appearance of having two programs running at the same time: one for the clock and one for the more mundane code. The program that handles all this, ticker.c, is shown in Listing 10.4.

Listing 10.4. ticker.c. An ISR routine that intercepts timer ticks and displays a real-time clock on-screen.

```
1   /* -------------------------------------------------
2        TICKER.C contains an interrupt service
3        routine (ISR).
4        ------------------------------------------- */
5   #include <stdlib.h>
6   #include <stdio.h>
7   #include <dos.h>
8   #include <conio.h>
9   #include <graph.h>
10
11  void( __interrupt __far *oldint1c)();
12
13  unsigned char hour, min, sec;
14  unsigned sc0_base = 0xb800; /* base adrs for cga/ega/vga */
15  int todx = 1, tody = 1;
```

Listing 10.4. Continued.

```
16  char tstring[9];
17
18  void __interrupt __far newint1c()
19  {
20    static unsigned int count = 18;
21
22    if ( --count == 0 ) {
23      count = 18;
24      __asm {                 /* Get time function */
25        sti
26        mov  ah,02h
27        int  1ah              /* Invoke BIOS BCD time    */
28        mov  hour,ch
29        mov  min,cl
30        mov  sec,dh
31      }
32      tstring[0] = ( hour >> 4 ) + '0';   /* Unpack BCD time */
33      tstring[1] = ( hour & 0x0F ) + '0';
34      tstring[2] = ':';
35      tstring[3] = ( min >> 4 ) + '0';
36      tstring[4] = ( min & 0x0F ) + '0';
37      tstring[5] = ':';
38      tstring[6] = ( sec >> 4 ) + '0';
39      tstring[7] = ( sec & 0x0F ) + '0';
40      __asm {                 /* Get it on the screen - quickly */
41        xor  dx,dx
42        mov  ax,tody
43        dec  ax               /* adjust to 0-origin adrs */
44        mov  si,160
45        mul  si               /* line offset in AX        */
46        mov  cx,ax            /* save line offset         */
47        mov  ax,todx
48        dec  ax
49        shl  ax,1             /* byte offset              */
50        add  cx,ax            /* total offset CX          */
51        mov  di,cx
52        cli
53        push es
54        mov  es,sc0_base      /* ES points to output RAM */
55        mov  cx,8             /* 8 bytes out              */
56        mov  si,0
```

```
57        }
58   show_tick:
59      __asm {
60         mov  bl,tstring[si] /* pick up display byte    */
61         mov  bh,70h         /* normal video attribute  */
62         mov  ax,bx          /* recover bytes           */
63         stosw               /* output, di auto incr    */
64         inc  si
65         loop show_tick
66         pop  ax
67         mov  es,ax
68         sti
69      }
70   }
71   }
72
73   void start_ticker( void )
74   {
75     oldint1c = _dos_getvect( 0x1c );
76     _dos_setvect( 0x1c, newint1c );
77   }
78
79   void stop_ticker( void )
80   {
81     _dos_setvect( 0x1c, oldint1c );
82   }
83
84   void main()
85   {
86     char ch;
87     int quit = 0, i = 1, incr = 1;
88
89     _clearscreen( _GCLEARSCREEN );
90     _settextposition( 12, 24 );
91     _outtext( "Strike Esc to stop the demo." );
92     start_ticker();
93     _settextwindow( 14, 12, 24, 68 );
94     while ( !quit ) {
95       if ( kbhit() ) {
96         if ( 0 == ( ch = getch() ) ) ch = getch();
97         if ( ch == 27 ) ++quit;
98       }
99       _settextposition( i, i*5 );
```

Listing 10.4. Continued.

```
100     _outtext( "Hello" );
101     i += incr;
102     if ( i == 10 ) { incr = -1; }
103     if ( i == 1 )  { incr = 1; }
104     }
105     stop_ticker();
106     _settextwindow( 1, 1, 25, 80 );
107     _clearscreen( _GCLEARSCREEN );
108 }
```

Line 11 declares oldint1c to be a pointer to an interrupt routine. This pointer is used in line 75 as a place to hold the current 0x1C interrupt address. After the program has completed execution, the original interrupt address is restored from the value saved in oldint1c (see line 81).

The main body of the program executes within the main() procedure. At line 92, start_ticker is called to install the new int 0x1C interrupt handler. start_ticker saves the current interrupt address in oldint1c and then resets the interrupt table entry to the address of newint1c. Then, main() enters a loop, displaying the message Hello at various places on the screen. This loop continues to execute until the user presses the Escape key to terminate the program.

Meanwhile, now that newint1c has hooked into the 0x1C timer interrupt, each time the system clock generates a timer interrupt, newint1c executes. Timer interrupts are generated 18.2 times per second. To display the time on the screen once per second, newint1c maintains a count variable. count is initially set to 18 and decremented at each timer interrupt. When count reaches 0, a new time string is placed on the screen, count is reset to 18, and the process repeats, waiting for the next one-second interval.

The newint1c() routine calls the BIOS function 0x1A to obtain a BCD string holding the current time. This BCD value is converted to an ASCII string (lines 32 through 39) and is then written to the upper-left corner of the screen.

One of the most important things to remember about writing an ISR for the timer tick is that no timer ticks can occur while your ISR is running. When an interrupt occurs, the system disables additional interrupts until the current interrupt is processed. Therefore, your ISR had better finish its work before the next timer tick occurs, or the system clock will get further behind. Moreover, if you cut it too close, there may be little or no time left for the main program to do any of its work. All things considered, the faster the ISR runs, the better it will be. For that reason, most of the 0x1C ISR function has been coded with inline assembly.

Whenever you intercept an interrupt, particularly one such as the timer interrupt that may be "hooked" by several programs or TSRs, you should always call the original interrupt when you are finished with your processing. This gives all other tasks a chance to process the interrupt, too. For the sake of simplicity, however, the old interrupt was not called in this sample ISR.

Using Program Optimization Features

The Microsoft C/C++ package has many program optimization features that are geared to producing faster or smaller programs. This section takes a look at how you can employ some of these features in your program applications.

When functions are called, Microsoft C/C++ generates code to push the value or address of a function argument onto the stack. If you place the keyword __fastcall in front of a function declaration, Microsoft C/C++ uses a special calling convention that places parameters into registers, if possible, before calling the function. This can eliminate the extra overhead of stacking parameters and accessing their values through indirect addressing. If there are more parameters than available registers, Microsoft C/C++ goes ahead and pushes the extra arguments onto the stack.

If __fastcall is in effect, the compiler will try to match function arguments to registers as follows:

Argument data type	Target registers
char/unsigned char	AL, DL, or BL
int/unsigned int	AX, DX, or BX
long/unsigned long	DX:AX
near pointer	BX, AX, or DX
far/huge pointers	passed on stack

Structures, unions, and all floating-point values are always placed on the stack and are never represented in registers.

When compiling your programs, you can set certain global options that affect the entire compilation. Depending on your goal, you can choose to produce the fastest-executing code or the smallest code size. In most instances, you must trade execution speed for code size. If you are using the command-line compiler cl, specify the switches shown in Table 10.3.

Table 10.3. cl switches for selecting optimizations.

Desired Compiler Output	Use These Compiler "switches"
Fastest code	/Oxaz /Ob2 /Gr
Small code	/Osae /Gs
p-code*	/Oqc

* The p-code option requires an additional 9K interpreter, so its code reduction is advantageous for larger programs only.

If you are using the PWB, select the **O**ptions menu and then the Lang**u**age Options item. This displays a submenu: Select either **C** compiler options or C++ compiler options, as appropriate. On the Compiler Options dialog, select the <**O**ptimizations> button. This displays yet another dialog: the Optimizations dialog (hopefully you haven't gotten lost in a twisty maze of dialogs). On this screen, select Optimize for **t**ime or Optimize for **s**pace as required. Under the *Specific* heading, check the items for which you wish to have optimization performed, such as **L**oop code optimization.

There are many ways that a compiler can optimize your program. For example, in the case of a loop, such as the following for loop:

```
for (i=0; i<999; i++ ) { ... }
```

it may be advantageous to keep the value of i in a CPU register. Depending on the content of the loop, this can greatly improve execution speed.

A compiler can also spot redundant code. For instance, the following two statements contain a repeated expression:

```
A = B + B * ( D - X + Y );
C = F + F * ( D - X + Y );
```

A good optimizing compiler recognizes the duplicate code and automatically assigns the value of the expression (D - X + Y) to a temporary variable or register. Internally, the code generated looks more like the following:

```
Temp = ( D - X + Y );
A = B + B * Temp;
C = F + F * Temp;
```

If your program makes much use of floating-point operations, be sure to select the appropriate floating-point library routines. To do this, go back to the Compiler Options dialog and select <**A**dditional Release Options>. This displays yet another dialog, from which you can select the floating-point operations. Microsoft C provides five separate floating-point operation modes, described in Table 10.4. Each has benefits and each has disadvantages, depending on your application and the target machine in use.

Table 10.4. Microsoft C/C++ Floating-Point Library Options.

PWB Option	cl Option	Advantages and Disadvantages
Inline Emulation	/FPi	Fastest emulation package. It works with or without an 80x87 math coprocessor. If the coprocessor is available, it is used, otherwise the library routines simulate the 80x87 coprocessor. The major disadvantage is that this option generates more code. Also, the emulation routines run slightly slower than the Alternate math library in exchange for providing higher accuracy and 80x87 compatibility.
Inline 80x87	/FPi87	Fastest method when 80x87 is guaranteed to be present. The only disadvantage is that programs compiled using this option will not run unless the 80x87 math coprocessor is available.
Fast Alternate Math	/FPa	If a coprocessor is not available, this results in the fastest execution and the least amount of memory. The disadvantage is slightly less accuracy than available with the emulation package.
Emulation Calls	/FPc	Similar to inline emulation but runs slightly slower. It works with or without an 80x87 coprocessor.
80x87 Calls	/FPc87	Slightly less efficient than the inline 80x87 calls, but it enables you to link with the emulator library if no 80x87 is available. You do this by explicitly including *m*LIBCE.LIB in the link, where *m* denotes the appropriate memory model in use (such as S or L, for example).

If the PC that will run this application does not have an 80x87 math coprocessor and 80x87 compatibility is not important, select the **F**ast Alternate Math library. If the target machine definitely contains an 80x87 math coprocessor, select the **I**nline 80x87 instructions option. If you don't know whether or not the target machine has a math coprocessor but you'd like to be able to support it if it is available, choose either emulation calls or inline emulation.

Using p-code

Normally, the Microsoft C/C++ compiler outputs 80x86 native machine code. Through the use of the p-code options, however, the compiler can produce special *packed code* that reduces the overall program size at the expense of slower execution. For this reason, most applications that use p-code will want to ensure that they do so only for areas that are not time-sensitive. User interface routines that handle line editing, for instance, are a good candidate for conversion to p-code.

To select p-code generation for an entire module, use the **O**ptions menu's Project **T**emplate option. Then choose **S**et Project Template, and choose the DOS p-code .EXE template.

Rather than compile entire modules into p-code, the compiler provides a special *pragma* for turning p-code compilation on and off selectively. Through the use of the pragma, you can hand-tailor p-code usage to provide the greatest size reduction without compromising overall program performance. To turn on p-code generation, place the following statement at the beginning of a module or before the definition of a function:

```
#pragma optimize("q", on)
```

To turn off p-code generation, use

```
#pragma optimize ("q", off)
```

Note that p-code generation can be enabled or disabled only for an entire module or an entire function.

For all programs that use p-code, the Microsoft Linker attaches in a 9K-sized p-code interpreter. Obviously, for small programs, the extra p-code interpreter negates the savings of using p-code.

Microsoft recommends using native code for all speed-critical functions or functions that are called within loops. You can use p-code for user interface code, especially code that does much waiting for keystrokes. It is also recommended that you use p-code for functions that are seldom used, such as error handlers or other features that are seldom used.

Exercises

The following exercises reinforce what you have learned about inline assembly, the writing of separately assembled C-callable modules, and interrupt handlers:

1. Using inline assembly language, write a function that raises one integer to an integral power. The function prototype might look something like this:

   ```
   int ipower( int arg1, int arg2);
   ```

   Use the Small memory model so that *arg1* can be located by [bp+4], and *arg2* can be located by [bp+6]. Tip: leave the result in the ax register and return from the function with this statement:

   ```
   return _AX;   /* Use the _AX pseudo-variable */
   ```

2. Write an assembly language routine that mimics strcat(). Experiment with the use of different memory models. Write one version to work with the small memory model and one to work with the Large memory model. Note that when you are using far memory addressing, argument addresses placed on the stack contain both a segment and an offset value. Your assembly language needs to take this into consideration.

3. Modify the ticker.c program to enable a user to use the arrow keys to move the real-time clock around the screen. Tip: you will have to unhook your ISR temporarily and reinstate it after adjusting the todx and tody variables.

4. Write a sample program (or use one of the programs presented in this book) and use #pragma optimize to turn on and off p-code generation for the module and also for individual functions. Compare the resulting .EXE file sizes and execution times.

Summary

The Microsoft C/C++ package provides tools to meet all your programming needs. This chapter showed you how to use these tools. Specifically, you learned how to do the following:

- ■ *Write inline assembly statements in your programs.* You can insert assembly statements directly into your programs using the __asm keyword.

- ■ *Use 80x86 and DOS interrupts to provide sophisticated services for your program.* Using interrupts makes available the full power of the system BIOS and the DOS operating system.

■ *Write an ISR to handle asynchronous (unpredictable) system events.* An interrupt service routine (ISR) lets your program perform sophisticated tasks. You can even implement a small degree of multitasking simulation using ISRs.

■ *Select compiler optimization options and use the floating-point libraries.*

This is all pretty heady stuff, but there is more to come. In Part II, you learn about object-oriented programming, using Microsoft C/C++ at an intermediate to advanced level. Part III introduces you to the world of Windows 3.1 applications programming. We hope you have the entire weekend free!

PART

II

OUTLINE

11 Using C++ Classes

12 Creating C++ Objects

13 Accessing C++ Objects

14 Using Overloaded Functions and
    Operators in C++

15 Using C++ Constructors and
    Destructors

16 Using C++ Streams

17 Using C++ Derived Classes

18 Object Control and Performance
    Issues

Using Microsoft C/C++'s Object-Oriented Features

Using C++ Classes

C ++ was originally called "C with classes." The class concept, which is central to C++, gives the language its unique capabilities. Microsoft C/C++ supports all the most recent class-definition features. This chapter presents a thorough introduction to C++ class fundamentals.

You should be aware, however, that C++ is not a programming language for beginners. A beginner can learn C++, but even fundamental C++ features embody some rather sophisticated C concepts. From this chapter on, therefore, the text is directed to those users who are at least moderately proficient with standard C and its terminology.

To understand Microsoft C/C++, you must understand C++ classes. A *class* is a user-defined *type*. The idea of a class as a type goes considerably further than the typedef you have already seen. typedef is merely a way to create new names as synonyms for existing C types. A C++ class declaration enables you to define a completely new kind of object—a class object—with properties you specify. The difference between C data types and C++ classes is so significant that the terms *data object* and *class object* are used to distinguish the two concepts.

As the discussion of classes develops, you will sometimes see references to the C++ base document. The base document for C++ is the book entitled *The Annotated C++ Reference Manual*, by Margaret A. Ellis and Bjarne Stroustrup (Addison-Wesley, 1990). This book embodies the current standard of C++ practice. Microsoft C/C++ is almost entirely in conformity to this standard.

Important Features of C++

C++ adds several significant and powerful features to the C programming language. *Object-oriented programming* (OOP), one of the most important features of C++, is an approach to software engineering that has demonstrated significant improvements in the productivity and reliability of software projects. In C++, the class is the key to unlocking the capabilities of OOP.

Through a built-in *inheritance* mechanism, you can create new classes of objects from prebuilt classes. The ability to inherit functionality means that new class objects are defined as being like another class, but perhaps with changes or extensions. Inheritance has become the key to a generalized and adaptable approach to sharing and reusing code. This results in greater productivity and higher reliability because previously tested and completed code can be incorporated quickly into new applications. The concepts of the C++ class and the capabilities of inheritance are the two most important features of C++.

C++ also introduces the concept of *overloaded* functions and operators. This enables you to create multiple functions that have the same name, such as a square root function for a variety of data types:

```
float sqrt( long x );
float sqrt( int x );
float sqrt( real x );
```

The C++ compiler automatically selects the appropriate function, based on the type of the function's parameter(s).

By overloading operators, such as the arithmetic + or –, you can extend the capability of the language to provide arithmetic operations on any type of data or objects, such as complex numbers or other units of data. Overloaded operators are discussed in Chapter 14, "Using Overloaded Functions and Operators in C++."

C++ contains a new I/O mechanism based on C++ streams (which are significantly different than C streams). For a complete description, see Chapter 16, "Using C++ Streams."

How to Access C++ Features

The Microsoft C/C++ compiler distinguishes between standard C and C++ programs by checking the filename extension of your source files. If your source filename ends in *.c* then the compiler treats the source as a C program. If the source filename ends in *.cpp* then the compiler enables you to use the C++ features. For example, source.c is a standard C program, and source.cpp is a C++ program. By convention, header files for C++ are written with the *.hpp* extension, but you can use *.h* if you wish.

You cannot access the features of the C++ language unless you make the compiler aware of your use of C++ features. Therefore, be sure to use the *.cpp* extension on all your C++ programs. Because C is a proper subset of C++, you can use the *.cpp* extension for all your applications.

Derived Types in C and C++

In standard C, *derived types* (arrays, structures and unions, function types, and pointer types) are all derived from the basic data types. You can derive a more complex type from a simpler one by grouping basic type objects together (as in a structure), or by using a basic object type in a new way (as in forming a pointer to an integer). You can also use the typedef keyword to associate a new type name with the derived object.

The *structure* is a particularly useful and interesting derived data type for two reasons. First, the structure permits you to group together data objects having many different basic types (even other structures) and to treat the result as a single entity. The standard C structure is a very useful type, even if no further capabilities are added to it. Second, the structure is the underlying basis for the C++ class. What this means becomes apparent as you read through this chapter.

There are some things you cannot do with a standard C structure, however. You cannot use a structure directly as part of an expression (although you can write a function that "adds" two structures), and you cannot define a function within a structure (although you can declare a pointer to a function within a structure). You can define a C++ class that allows objects of that class to do both of these things, and more.

Redefining "Derived" in C++

With standard C, you can derive new groupings and new uses of predefined data types, but you cannot alter the nature—the fundamental behavior—of any predefined type. Therefore, the type-definition facility of C can never be more than a means of applying new names (synonyms) to something that already exists.

C++ not only allows you to define the existence and contents of a class type, but also requires you to define the type's behavior. Thus, a class can be considered a data type, but a class is not truly a derived type. A class is a *new* type. It is more appropriate to speak of C++ classes as *user-defined* types rather than as derived types.

You can use the features of standard C to approach the functionality of C++ class objects, but C can never match either the power or the elegance of the class object. You can write a function that sums two arrays of integers, for example, but standard C cannot permit the following use of array names:

```
int a[10];
int b[10];
int c[10];
...
c = a + b;   /* ILLEGAL IN STANDARD C */
```

You *can* design a C++ class, however, that supports the use of the addition operator with objects of that class. The following code fragment briefly shows how to define the addition operation for array *class* objects:

```
class arrayplus { // skeleton class declaration
  int data[10];
public:
  arrayplus operator+( arrayplus& );
  ...
};
...
arrayplus arrayplus::operator+( arrayplus& op2 )
{
  int i;
  arrayplus hold; // define a temporary object

  for ( i=0; i<10; ++i )
    hold.data[i] = data[i] + op2.data[i];
  return hold;                // return by value
}
...
arrayplus a, b, c;   // Define some class objects
c = a + b;           // this is legal, now
```

This code fragment contains a number of new features that are explained throughout this chapter and the following chapters. You should be able to detect three things in the code fragment, however, without a detailed knowledge of C++ syntax:

■ *C++ classes define both the content and the behavior of new (user-defined) types.* In the preceding code fragment, the arrayplus class defines both the structure of an array's data elements and the method used to add two arrayplus objects. The *method* (a technical word borrowed from OOP) is given in the form of a *member function* (a function that actually belongs to the class). The member function in this case is operator+().

- *Class declarations can and do have intimately associated functions that control the behavior of the class.* Standard C structures can contain a pointer to a function, but not embedded function definitions. A C structure cannot own a function as a class can. Note the similarity of the class definition for the class arrayplus to the format used for a struct definition. A class is similar to the basic C structure, but it contains both data and function declarations within the class. You learn how functions are associated with classes in the next section.

- *C++ comments differ greatly from C comments.* C++ comments are introduced by two consecutive slashes and are terminated only by the end of the source line. Thus, C++ comments must be either the last thing on a source line or the only thing on a source line.

As you can see, you can arrange a C++ class declaration so that an object having that class (that is, having that user-defined type) can be used directly in an expression. Although controlling a class object's behavior is not nearly all that you can do with class definitions, it is one of the most important things you can do with them.

Understanding C++ Encapsulation

It should be clear by now that classes are used to bundle together an object's data structure and the methods for controlling the object's data. (Think of a method as being similar to a function.) This approach to defining objects arises naturally out of the more general theory of OOPS (object-oriented programming systems). Bundling data and methods together is called *encapsulation*.

Encapsulation is an important part of the design of C++. Encapsulation accomplishes three things: (1) it hides complexity, (2) it discourages the programmer from tampering with code that already works, and (3) it promotes the reuse of previously developed code.

C++ encapsulates class objects by using structures (with either the struct or class keyword). Ordinary C structures contain data members that belong to the structure and which cannot be accessed apart from the structure. Class declarations go a step further and permit data members *and* member functions, both of which *belong to the class*.

Thus, C++ uses the struct type as a foundation for class objects, but C++ structures and classes can do many things that C structures cannot do. Ownership of functions as well as data gives C++ classes an added dimension, of sorts, as shown in figure 11.1.

Figure 11.1.

C structures own data members, but C++ classes own both data members and member functions.

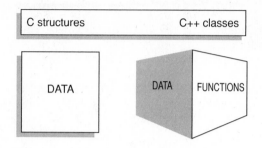

C++ classes use encapsulation to hide complexity in two ways: by concealing internal data structures and functions, and by providing a user (that is, programmer) interface that does not require knowledge of a class object's internal workings. Just as you do not have to know the bit structure of a floating-point number, or what goes on behind the scenes when floating-point numbers are multiplied together, you also do not need to focus on a class object's internal structure or internal functions in order to use the class object. You only need to call the object's public member functions to interface with the object. The concept of encapsulation is illustrated in figure 11.2.

Figure 11.2.

C++ encapsulation of class objects hides the object's internal workings from a user of the object.

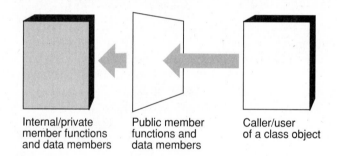

Encapsulation also discourages programmers from unnecessarily tampering with data structures and functions that are already functional. The urge to take shortcuts is sooner or later irresistible to the ordinary programmer. The danger of modifying data with a shortcut method is that you are likely to forget some necessary part of the process, and therefore likely to corrupt the data.

When data structures and the functions authorized to modify them are placed out of sight through encapsulation, the temptation to tamper with complex structures is reduced. Although encapsulation may seem, at first, like an irritating restriction, you will find with experience that there are definite benefits involved. Encapsulation really does reduce the incidence of accidental damage to data structures. In the end, the need for debugging large projects can be drastically reduced.

Encapsulation also provides, in a roundabout way, shortcuts to manipulating data structures. Such shortcuts are possible because class objects are self-contained; you do not have to remember constantly all the complexities of manipulating class objects. The objects themselves take care of handling the data structures.

Finally, the self-contained nature of encapsulated objects encourages the use and reuse of already developed code. C++ classes are easily reusable because class objects tend to be both robust and capable. They are generally robust because it is easier to write sophisticated code in a C++ class than in a plain C program (another benefit of encapsulation). You are therefore more apt to write class declarations that anticipate all uses of the class.

Declaring Classes with *struct*

In the preceding section, you learned that a class object's public member functions provide an "interface" with users of the object (that is, public member functions of a class object can be called by other functions that want to use the object). Thinking of public member functions as an interface to a class object is a helpful notion, but C++ has no formal "implementation definition" or "interface module" as some other object-oriented languages do.

Languages such as Simula do have an interface definition that places user-defined objects in memory outside the main program. The advantage of handling object interfaces this way is that a change made to the class object does not affect the main program. It does not need to be recompiled when changes are made to a class definition.

A formal interface module that must be used to access every class object has a great disadvantage, however: it's *slow*. A lack of execution speed is, in fact, one of the primary reasons OOPS languages did not become popular sooner.

C++ overcomes the speed barrier by treating user-defined objects in almost exactly the same way that it treats built-in object types. The compiler always knows the size and internal structure of a class object, even if the programmer does not. But treating classes this way means that everything about the class *must be known at compile time*. Interpretation of class code is not done at runtime.

Therefore, if any changes are made to a class (even the private, "invisible" parts), any program that uses the class must be recompiled and relinked, or the program will still use the old version of the class. The great advantage of this approach is that it allows a main program to access objects directly, which is in keeping with the original C philosophy of generating trim, fast runtime code. You do not have to use pointers (or any other additional interface) to an object unless you want to use them.

Although C++ does not place artificial barriers in the way of using class objects, it does observe certain conventions in determining which data members and member functions of a class can be accessed by functions not belonging to the class. A class object has both private and public members:

- *Private data members and member functions can be used only by member functions of the class and by functions that are friends of the class.* Members of a class are private by default when the class is declared with the class keyword. You can allow class members to default to private access or you can specify them to be private members to hide a class object's complexity. Declaring classes with the class keyword is covered in the next section, and friend functions are discussed at the end of this chapter.

- *Public data members and member functions can be used by any function.* Members of a class are public by default when the class is declared with the struct or union keyword. The rest of this section covers the use of struct and union to declare a class.

Declaring a class with a struct or union keyword is the most straightforward way to give immediate, direct access to a class and its members. All the members (data and functions) of a C++ struct enable public access from anywhere in the program. A class declared with union also enables public access by default and has the additional characteristic of having only one member active at a time (in keeping with the notion of unions as overlays of the same area of memory). The following discussion refers only to structures, but the same rules also apply to unions.

In C++, a structure *is* a class and, at the same time, a true structure (avoiding many compatibility problems with C). Comparing C++ structures to C structures is helpful in understanding the additional capabilities of the C++ variety. Recall the general syntax for declaring a structure object:

struct *tag*$_{opt}$ { *member-list*$_{opt}$ } *identifier-list*$_{opt}$;

The struct syntax should be familiar to you. You can use it as you ordinarily would in C, or you can use it in C++ to define a true class type. When you use struct to declare a class, a number of new things begin to happen. Listing 11.1 shows you some of them. Look at the code carefully and notice the use of the .cpp filename extension for the source file.

Listing 11.1. structob.cpp. Using struct to declare a class.

```
1   #include <stdlib.h>
2   #include <stdio.h>
3
4   struct myclass {
5       int a;
```

```
 6    myclass();
 7    void showclass();
 8  } my_obj;
 9
10  myclass::myclass()
11  {
12    a = 37; // initialize the object
13  }
14
15  void myclass::showclass()
16  {
17    printf( "The value of my object is %d\n", a );
18  }
19
20  void main()
21  {
22    // ----- Prove that everything in a class
23    // ----- declared with struct is accessible
24
25    my_obj.a = 64;  // ref. just like a C struct
26    my_obj.showclass();
27  }
```

Some parts of the program in Listing 11.1 should present no problem to you at all. The #include statements in lines 1 and 2 are old friends, and so is the general layout of the main() function.

The main() function has been declared as void. Many experienced C programmers are accustomed to declaring main() with no return type at all. Failure to specify a return type for main(), however, causes Microsoft C/C++ to generate a compile-time warning message. If you don't mind the warning message, you can code main() without a return type.

References to structure members, in lines 25 and 26, also should be familiar. The syntax of a reference to a structure data member is still the same as in ordinary C. If you look closely at line 26, however, you see that the reference made there is to a member *function*—something you cannot include within a C structure.

There are further aspects of the structure declaration in Listing 11.1 that are not yet familiar to you. Look first at lines 4 through 8. The structure is declared in those lines, but remember that this is C++, and the struct declaration actually defines a *class*.

Notice particularly that lines 6 and 7 contain function prototypes for the class's member functions. Function prototypes are definitely not allowed in C structures! Several points about member function declarations are not obvious from the sample code:

- *C++ classes can declare special functions—constructor and destructor functions—that are not allowed elsewhere in the program.* Constructor functions are used to set up and initialize class objects, and destructor functions are used to destroy class objects (that is, to release their memory if necessary). These functions are covered in a section later in this chapter, as well as in Chapter 15, "Using C++ Constructors and Destructors."

- *Special methods are required for associating class member functions with the class.* The syntax for associating a member function with its class is like nothing you have seen in C. The details for setting up member functions are given in the section "Writing Member Functions for a Class" later in this chapter.

- *C++ function prototypes of the form* function() *do not imply the old-style (Kernighan and Ritchie) practice of allowing the function definition to assume any function parameters it likes.* In old-style (K&R) C, an empty formal parameter list meant the corresponding function definition could declare any parameters it was suitable to declare. You just had to make sure that a function call to that function actually passed the expected number and type of arguments.

- In C++, an empty formal parameter list has the same meaning as the ANSI standard syntax function(void). In other words, *no* arguments are permitted. This rule also applies to *any* function declared in a C++ program.

- *C++ considers old-style function definitions to be anachronistic.* Function definitions of the following form used to be quite common:

```
sum( a, b )
  int a;
  int b:
{
  return a + b;
}
```

Both ANSI C and C++ still permit this form of function definition, but both types of compilers consider the practice to be dangerous and out-of-date. Furthermore, C++ does *not* allow class member functions to be defined with this syntax; you must use the full function prototype for class member functions.

Lines 10 through 18 in Listing 11.1 contain the code defining the class member functions. The class's constructor function (one of those special functions) appears in lines 10 through 13. This particular constructor function is a simple one: It initializes the integer member variable a. The syntax of the constructor function for a class is distinctive in that no return type is permitted, and the constructor function name is exactly the same as the class name. The most interesting thing about this member function is the way that it accesses the member variable a. Because the function is a member of the class, the function is not required to use the structure member operator (.) that was required in main().

The other member function, showclass(), is shown in lines 15 through 18. Its sole purpose is to display the value of the member variable a. Like the constructor function, the most distinctive feature of showclass() is that it doesn't need to use the structure member operator to access a member variable.

The last thing you should notice in Listing 11.1 is the direct definition in line 8 of a struct object, my_obj, together with the struct declaration. Although such a definition is perfectly legal, class objects are almost never defined in this manner in C++ (regardless of whether the class or struct keyword is used). Normal usage looks like this:

```
struct myclass {    // Declare the class here
  int a;
  myclass();
  void showclass();
};


    ...


void main()
{
  myclass my_obj;    // Declare the class OBJECT here

  my_obj.a = 64;
  my_obj.showclass();
}
```

The main reason for using local object definitions (which, like other local variables, have auto duration) is to avoid the use of global variables. Because C++ class objects are typically much larger than standard C data objects, globally defined class objects take up a lot of memory space in your programs. The goal is to allow class objects to disappear whenever possible, and as soon as possible. Other reasons for using local objects involve issues of performance and garbage collection. Class object behavior and performance are discussed in Chapter 18, "Object Control and Performance Issues."

Other parts of Listing 11.1 are obviously worth examining. Elements common to all classes are discussed in the next section. From this point on, classes are declared with the class keyword. This does not mean that classes declared with struct are undesirable—only that they are not as common.

Declaring C++ Classes

The members of a class (both data and functions) declared with the `class` keyword are private by default; that is, they can be accessed only by member functions (and *friend* functions) of the class. The fact that class members have by default a private attribute can cause unexpected problems in designing classes. This issue deserves more explanation.

The key concept in understanding the public or private nature of member objects is that the private attribute controls *access* to member objects, *not visibility* of member objects. To help you understand the difference between access control and visibility (that is, classical C scope), two C++ programs are presented here. One of them works, but not as expected; the other doesn't even compile correctly.

The first program, named access.cpp, has two classes: cp1 and cp2. The member function show() in class cp2 attempts to access the member variable A in class cp1. The program is shown in Listing 11.2.

Listing 11.2. access.cpp. Access control does not affect this program, but visibility does.

```
1   #include <stdlib.h>
2   #include <stdio.h>
3
4   int A; // this is a global data object
5
6   class cp1 {
7     int A; // this is a private member data object
8   public:
9     cp1() { A = 37; }
10  };
11
12  class cp2 {
13  public:
14    void show() { printf( "%d\n", A ); }
15  };
16
17  void main()
18  {
19    cp1 X;
20    cp2 Y;
21
22    Y.show(); // this gets to global A
23  }
```

In Listing 11.2, the classes cp1 and cp2 are unrelated; they are separate classes. Therefore, when the member function show() of cp2 (written as cp2::show()) attempts to access a variable named A (line 14), it is the global variable A (line 4) that is both visible and accessible to the function, not the intended variable in cp1.

Accessibility is not even possible for the cp1 member variable A in Listing 11.2. That variable is completely invisible to the function cp2::show(). You might try to force access to the variable cp1::A by rewriting line 14 and using the scope resolution operator:

```
void show() { printf( "%d\n", cp1::A ); }
```

If you do this, however, the compiler mistakenly assumes that you are referring to a bit-field object and produces an error message. (Scope resolution is discussed later in several places, including Chapter 13, "Accessing C++ Objects.") Access to the member variable A is controlled by the following considerations:

- *A C++ struct or class has its own scope.* Therefore, when the compiler finds a reference to a variable identifier A in a member function of cp2, the compiler first searches the scope of cp2 for the identifier. It is not found there.

- *The ordinary scoping rules of C require that the scope surrounding the reference be searched for the identifier referred to.* The surrounding scope, however, does not include the members of cp1 because that class has its own scope (which is why cp1::A is completely invisible to cp2). The result is that the global copy of A is found and used.

If the program in Listing 11.2 is rewritten so that class cp2 is derived from class cp1, access control becomes the dominant issue. Deriving classes (class inheritance) is explained in Chapter 17, "Using C++ Derived Classes." For now, the important thing to know about deriving classes is the derived class inherits (carries along) many of the characteristics of its base class (the one from which it is derived). If properly declared, the derived class can also have access to the public members of the parent class. The rewritten program is shown in Listing 11.3.

NOTE Compiling access2.cpp results in a compiler error message for reasons described in the text.

Listing 11.3. access2.cpp. Access control is the important issue here because C++ structs (including classes) have their own scope.

```
1   #include <stdlib.h>
2   #include <stdio.h>
3
4   int A; // this is a global data object
5
6   class cp1 {
7     int A; // this is a member data object
8   public:
9     cp1() { A = 37; }
10  };
11
12  class cp2 : public cp1 { // inherit from cp1
13  public:
14    void show() { printf( "%d\n", A ); }
15  };
16
17  void main()
18  {
19    cp1 X;
20    cp2 Y;
21
22    Y.show(); // this gets to global A
23  }
```

In Listing 11.3, when the member function cp2::show() attempts to access the variable A, the global integer A is not what is accessed. Global A is in fact still visible, but the following new considerations apply in determining which instance of A is meant:

1. A C++ struct or class has its own scope. Therefore, no attempt is made to access the global copy of A; the local scope is searched for the referenced identifier first.

2. Because the function show() is a member function of cp2, the compiler attempts to locate a matching variable identifier within its scope (that is, within the class's *name space*). No such identifier is present in the scope of cp2.

3. Because cp2 is *derived from* cp1, and the base class was declared public (line 12), the compiler attempts to locate a matching identifier in the cp1 name space. Such a variable identifier does exist, but it has the private

attribute and is not accessible from within a `cp2` member function. Only the `public` members of the base class (parent class) are available. A compile-time error results.

The critical point in this discussion is that a C++ `struct` or `class` has its own scope. It is easy to code yourself into a corner so that you cannot legitimately make reference to a member variable. Object-oriented encapsulation is fully enforced within C++ classes, requiring you to design your classes carefully with regard to visibility and accessibility.

You must be especially careful to choose which class members (data or functions) you want to specify as being public members. You learn how to make those choices in the next section. Scope resolution methods and issues are discussed in greater detail in the section "Using the `public`, `private`, and `protected` Keywords" later in this chapter, as well as in Chapters 13 and 17.

Understanding the *class* Declaration

A *class* is a new type, not merely a synonym for an existing type. Because a class is a new type, you must consider the following points when declaring a class:

■ *You must decide how to package the class.* That is, you must determine whether to use the `class`, `struct`, or `union` keyword to declare the class. This decision is influenced by the kind of class-member access control you want to establish for objects of that class, as discussed in the preceding section. As noted earlier, you generally will use the `class` keyword.

■ *You must design the internal structure of the new object type.* Deciding which member data objects must be included, as well as how they are to be used, is an important part of class design. You must include everything necessary for the efficient use of objects of the class, but you certainly don't want to include unnecessary members (which would uselessly increase the size of class objects).

■ *You must decide how objects of the new class behave.* Do you want to be able to use class objects in arithmetic expression? Then you must provide member functions that describe how addition, subtraction, and other operations will work. Do you want class objects to be able to write themselves to the system printer or a disk file? Then you must write member functions that handle such an action.

Clearly, there are many more decisions involved in writing a class declaration than there are in declaring an ordinary structure. Time and practice will assist you in making those decisions, as will the analysis of class declarations that others have written. (You have ample opportunity to analyze many classes as you read this book.)

Using Class Declaration Syntax

Before you can approach high-level design decisions, however, the mechanics of class declarations must be firmly within your grasp. The best place to begin is with the simplest form of the class declaration. Its general syntax is this:

```
class-key class-name_opt { member-list_opt } obj-name_opt ;
```

Notice that the only required parts of the declaration are the class-key, the curly braces, and the terminating semicolon. The remaining items are optional. If class is the keyword being used, a class declaration is usually written in the following physical format (indentation and whitespace may vary, as in ordinary C):

```
class class-name {
  data-members
public:
  member-function-prototypes
  inline-member-functions
};
```

```
member-function-definitions
```

You now have before you a syntax guideline and a formatting guideline for declaring classes. With these guidelines in mind, note that the syntax controls a class declaration in the following ways:

■ *The class-key may be one of the following keywords:* class, struct, *or* union. The differences between these keywords have already been discussed. Remember that the most important difference between them is access control, not visibility. In the rest of this book, the class keyword is used exclusively.

■ *The class-name becomes a type name and is a reserved word (a user-defined keyword) within the scope in which it is defined.* Just as a struct can have block scope or file scope, so can a class declaration. However, for the compiler, class names have a syntactical significance like that of the keyword int—a significance that goes far beyond that of an ordinary structure tag, because your class name is considered a reserved word for the duration of the program.

Furthermore, it is possible to write an unnamed class declaration, one that does not have a class name (like leaving out a structure tag). Class objects defined with unnamed classes are called *singleton objects*. Here are some restrictions on what you can do with unnamed classes and singleton objects:

1. To define a singleton object of the unnamed class, you must use the *obj-name* (which is otherwise optional) just before writing the final semicolon. Because there is no class name, there is no type name

that can be used later to define a normal class object. Note this example:

```
class{  // declare an unnamed class
...
} anyobject ;  // define a singleton object
```

2. An unnamed class may not have constructor or destructor member functions. Because there is no class name, the compiler has no way to associate the correct constructor and destructor functions with the class.

3. A singleton object of an unnamed class cannot be passed as an argument to a function. The compiler is unable to perform proper type checking on a parameter that has no class name. You can get around this restriction by using the variable parameter list ellipsis (...) in the called function's prototype. However, the called function can know the object's size only if the object has file or enclosing block scope—in which case there is no need to pass the object as an argument anyway.

4. You cannot return an object of an unnamed class from a called function at all. Again, the reason is that there is not enough information present to permit type checking, and there is no variable list support for returning values.

■ *The* `member-list` *specifies the class member data objects and functions.* A class member list is similar to the member list for an ordinary structure, except for the following differences:

1. A member list may contain member function prototypes (or perhaps inline functions—see the section "Writing Member Functions for a Class" later in this chapter).

2. A class member list may be completely empty. Such a class is called an *empty class*. For example, you could declare a class in this way:

```
class some_class {}; // no member data or functions
```

Empty classes are used mostly during program development as placeholders, when you don't yet know what should go into the class declaration. Even though a class is empty, it does not have zero size. An empty class has a small but definite size because of the invisible overhead information necessary for controlling the class.

3. The formatting guideline given earlier in this section does not specify an absolutely required style for writing a member list. It is a common practice to place the data members in the private part of the declaration and to place member functions in the public part. The sample arrangement is not cast in concrete, however. At times, you

may need to place some data members in the public part, and some member functions (those that should be used only by other member functions) in the private part.

4. The class member list may also include enumerations, bit-fields, structures, unions, other classes, friend functions, and type names (nicknames). That is, you can include within the member list all the object types you usually include in a struct declaration, plus some more object types that are peculiar to C++ classes. Note that nested classes are supported in Microsoft C/C++.

Another class can be declared within an enclosing class declaration. When you write such a *nested class*, remember that a C++ class is a scope, and (in this case) visibility (scope) can become a definite issue. *The nested class is visible only within the scope of its enclosing class.* A nested class can use only type names, static members, and enumerators from its enclosing class (but a nested class can refer to other types indirectly by using pointers, references, and explicit resolved object names). Consider, for example, the following short program:

```
double A;
double Z;

class outer {
public:
  double A;
  static double B;

  class inner {
    outer X;            // WRONG. 'outer' not complete yet.

    void f( double C )  // Declare inline function.
    {
      A = C;            // WRONG. Enclosing A not static.
      X.outer::A = C;   // WRONG. Must have a specific
                        //        object, and none can
                        //        exist yet.
      ::A = C;          // OK. Global A accessed.
      B = C;            // OK.
      Z = C;            // OK. Global Z is visible.
    }
  };
};

main()
{
```

```
    inner obj = 3.1415926; // ERROR: 'inner' not in scope.
}
```

The comments in this code fragment tell the tale: A nested class is sharply restricted as to what object references it can make.

As mentioned earlier, a *nickname* can be used in a class member declaration. A nickname is a *typedef-name* that names a class.

■ *An object name is only used following a class declaration to define an object of an unnamed class.* Defining objects of unnamed classes, however, is not a recommended or common practice.

Declaring Class Members

Several other rules govern the declaration and use of member objects and functions. Some of the following rules have a basis in standard C, whereas others relate only to C++:

■ *Member names must be unique within the scope of the class.* This means that you cannot declare data members more than once within the same class. You cannot add a class member to the class by using a declaration outside the class (the member list in the class declaration completes the class entirely). Notice that you can use the same identifier more than once in a program if the identifier is used in different classes. Member functions are grouped separately in the next rule.

■ *You can use member function names more than once in the same class only if the combinations of function parameters and return types are sufficiently different.* This strategy is called *function overloading.* Overloading is discussed in Chapter 14.

■ *A member declaration cannot include an initializer.* This rule may seem too restrictive until you remember that a class is a type specification and not an object definition.

Other rules control what you may do with member object declarations contained in more advanced class declarations. Those rules appear when the advanced uses are covered in succeeding chapters.

Building a LIFO Stack Class

For now, you need to use C++ classes, even if you don't understand everything you see. You have enough rules to begin using C++ classes. It's time to apply those rules in a concrete way.

Designing and coding a useful class will help you to understand how to build class declarations. The example in the following discussion is a class for generalized LIFO (last-in-first-out) stack objects.

What is a generalized LIFO stack? The answer has three parts. First of all, a *stack* is an area of memory (RAM) in which temporary variables are stored. (Microsoft C/C++ auto variables are created on the system stack, and parameter values are placed there as well.)

Second, data on the stack can be stored and retrieved only in a certain sequence. The last object *pushed onto* the stack (placed in the stack's memory) is the first *popped off* the stack (removed from the stack's memory). Older data objects on the stack can be used but not removed before younger data objects are popped off the stack. Thus, the *last-in-first-out* sequencing of objects on the stack yields the acronym LIFO for this kind of memory use.

Third, the stack used by your PC's hardware can (and does) hold all sorts of different data objects. The class used in this discussion should therefore be designed to control a *generalized stack* of objects—a stack that can handle just about anything.

How do you control the memory that a LIFO stack uses? To understand how this is done, think of a stack as being similar to a can of three tennis balls. The first ball put in the can is at the bottom, and the last ball put in the can is at the top. Furthermore, the last item pushed onto a stack is said to be on the top of the stack. Figure 11.3 illustrates the memory layout of a LIFO stack.

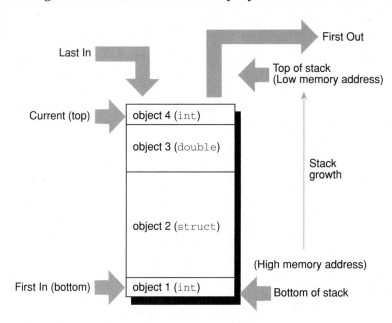

Figure 11.3.

A LIFO stack grows from the bottom (high memory address) to the top (low memory address).

Figure 11.3 shows that stacks are positioned with the "bottom" at the highest memory address, and the "top" at the lowest memory address. The only reason for this is that diagrams of system memory are traditionally drawn this way. There is no physical reason why you could not arrange stack growth to proceed from low to high memory.

As Figure 11.3 illustrates, you need to keep track of several addresses related to the stack and its contents. You need to know how big the stack is; therefore, the addresses of the top and bottom limits are required. Because the top object on the stack is the only object that can be popped off, you need just one more address to control the stack: the address of the top, or current, object. You can store all these addresses in C pointers.

In addition to keeping track of the addresses, you need to know the rules for stack control before you can begin coding the stack class declaration:

- *Memory for the body of the stack is acquired outside the boundaries of any particular class object.* The purpose of this rule is to keep the size of a stack object small, even though keeping stack contents outside the class object is technically a violation of OOPS encapsulation.

- *The pointers used for stack control are named* top, bottom, *and* current *so that their uses are obvious at a glance.* The top pointer is initially set to the address of the top byte in the stack (the lowest memory address actually in the stack). Both the bottom and the current pointer are set to the address of the first byte *beyond* the bottom byte of the stack (the address of the byte that is one byte higher than the highest address actually in the stack).

- *Stack class member functions use only void pointers so that any object, of any size, can be placed on the stack.* (The term *generalized* LIFO stack is derived from this rule.)

- *An object is pushed onto the stack in the following manner:*

  1. The current pointer is compared to the top pointer to determine whether there is room on the stack for the object being pushed (the object's size is used to perform this calculation). If no room is available, a zero value (*false*) is returned immediately and no pointer is modified.

  2. If there is room for the object, the current pointer is decremented by an amount equal to the size of the object, and the object is copied to the memory pointed to by current. Then a nonzero (*true*) value is returned, and the current pointer is left pointing to the last object pushed onto the stack.

- *An object is popped off the stack in the following manner:*

  1. The current pointer is compared to the bottom pointer to determine whether there are enough bytes still on the stack (a number of bytes equal to or greater than the size of the requested object). If enough bytes aren't available, a *null pointer* value is returned immediately.

2. If a sufficient number of bytes is on the stack to satisfy the request, the current pointer is *incremented* by an amount equal to the size of the requested object, and a pointer to the top object on the stack is returned. Thus, the object just popped off the stack is positioned *above* the current address of the new top object on the stack. That is, the object just popped off is no longer "on the stack."

The LIFO class has two more features that need mentioning before the code is presented. First, a temporary-object allocation member function is also provided so that you can create local class objects on the stack, similar to the way that Microsoft C/C++ allocates auto variables on the system stack. The allocation algorithm is a minor variant of the push() member function. You delete temporary objects from the stack with the pop() member function. You can create true class objects on a LIFO stack; you see how to do this in the discussion of Listing 11.6 later in the chapter.

Second, three function-like macros—PUSH, POP, and ALLOC—are provided so that you can call stack class member functions by using a type name to set the object size, instead of having to state explicitly the number of bytes to be pushed or popped.

Because the stack class is useful enough to include in many other programs, compiling the class code separately is worthwhile. To compile the class code separately, you need to arrange the class declaration into two source files: a header file (lifo.hpp), which contains the class declaration and member function prototypes; and a source code file (lifo.cpp), which contains the member function definitions. Listing 11.4 shows the lifo.hpp header file.

Listing 11.4. lifo.hpp. Class declaration for a LIFO (last-in-first-out) generalized stack object.

```
1   #include <stdlib.h>
2   #include <string.h>
3
4   class lifo {
5     char *top;
6     char *bottom;
7     char *current;
8     char *work;
9   public:
10    lifo();                  // default constructor
11    lifo( unsigned size );   // constructor with parameter
12    ~lifo();                 // destructor
13    int push( unsigned bytes, void *obj );
14    void *pop( unsigned bytes);
```

```
15    void *get_block( unsigned bytes );
16  };
17
18  #define PUSH(type,obj)  push( sizeof(type), obj )
19  #define POP(type)       pop( sizeof(type) )
20  #define ALLOC(type)     get_block( sizeof(type) )
```

In Listing 11.4, lines 1 and 2 contain `include` directives for stdlib.h and string.h, respectively. These directives are placed here so that you don't forget, when including lifo.hpp itself at a later time, that the `includes` are required for the correct compilation of the `lifo` class member functions. It won't hurt anything if you also `include` them elsewhere because Microsoft has written its standard headers using conditional preprocessing logic to determine whether `included` code is already present.

The `lifo` class declaration is found in lines 4 through 16 of Listing 11.4. Notice that the `top`, `bottom`, `current`, and `work` pointers are declared above the `public` keyword. Because the `class` keyword (rather than `struct`) is used, all those pointers have private access by default. The `work` pointer might have been declared as a local variable in each member function that needs it. Instead, the `work` pointer was declared as a private member variable; therefore, the pointer is created only once (when a `lifo` object is created) and is shared by all member functions. No further setup overhead is involved in using the `work` pointer when a member function needs it.

The `public` keyword in line 9 introduces the part of the class member declarations that can be accessed by functions outside the class. For the `lifo` class, that part includes all the member functions, but none of the member data objects.

The member functions declared in lines 10 through 12 deserve special mention. The two member functions in lines 10 and 11 have the same name as the class itself. These functions are the *constructor* functions for the class. You use constructor functions to set up and initialize class objects. A common use for constructor functions is to acquire extra memory residing outside the class object (as with the `lifo` class).

Chapter 15 discusses constructor functions (as well as destructor functions), but you should know some things right away. Be aware of the following requirements for constructor functions:

■ *A constructor function for a class must have the same name as the class.* This requirement is not optional. You can write a class declaration without specifying a constructor (thus allowing the compiler to supply a default constructor), but if you supply one or more constructors, each constructor must have the same name as the class.

- *A constructor function declaration cannot specify a return type.* The compiler has its own internal return type for constructors. You cannot code one.

- *When you code more than one constructor function declaration, the parameter list for each one must be different from all the others.* In C++, writing more than one function with a single name is called *overloading*. The only way the compiler can distinguish between different "versions" of an overloaded function is to compare parameter lists (and return types too, but they are not permitted in constructors or destructors).

The `lifo` class declaration features two constructor function declarations. The first, in line 10, is the *default constructor*; it has no formal parameter list and accepts no arguments. For the `lifo` class, the default constructor is designed to acquire a 2K block of memory to hold stack data. The second constructor function declaration, in line 11, accepts an unsigned integer as an argument, and the corresponding constructor function attempts to acquire a block of memory equal in size to that argument to hold stack data.

You use a destructor function to clean up after a class object has been destroyed—for example, when a local class object goes out of scope. You need to code a destructor function when you use the constructor function—for instance, to acquire outside memory (as with `lifo` class objects). Follow these rules for destructor functions:

- *A destructor function for a class must have the same name as the class, except the first character of the destructor function name must be a tilde (~).* In Listing 11.4, the destructor function name is `~lifo()`. You can write a class declaration that has no explicit destructor and allow the compiler to supply a default function, just as you can omit the constructor.

- *A destructor function cannot specify a return type.* The compiler also has its own special return type for destructor functions.

- *A destructor function cannot accept arguments.* Without a parameter list, overloading is not possible. Only one destructor function, therefore, is permitted in a single class declaration.

The remaining member function declarations are found in lines 13 through 15 of Listing 11.4. These functions include methods for pushing an object on the stack, popping an object off the stack, and allocating space on the stack for an arbitrary object. All these functions are covered in the discussion of Listing 11.5.

The function-like support macros, lines 18 through 20, appear only in the lifo.hpp header file in Listing 11.4. The three support macros are PUSH(), POP(), and ALLOC(). They correspond to the member functions push(), pop(), and get_block(), respectively. You can see from these names that C (including C++) is usually a case-sensitive language: PUSH is not the same as push to the compiler.

The sole purpose of the support macros is to enable you to call the `lifo` member functions by using a type name, instead of having to specify the number of bytes to push, pop, or allocate on the stack. Suppose, for example, that you have declared the following `lifo` class object named `stack`:

```
lifo stack;
```

To push a long integer onto `stack` without the assist macro, you would have to use code like this:

```
long x;
...
stack.push( 4, &x );
```

With the `PUSH()` support macro, however, you could write

```
stack.PUSH( long, &x );
```

which would be expanded by the preprocessor into the following compile-time code:

```
stack.push( sizeof(long), &x );
```

The advantage of the support macros is obvious. You can use type names to specify implicitly the size of the object being pushed or popped, and thus avoid inadvertent size errors. In writing these fragmentary code lines, for instance, a size of 2 was mistakenly specified at first (because of focusing on integers) rather than the 4 bytes required for a long integer.

The preceding discussion of constructor, destructor, and member functions helps you to understand the class member function definitions. The `lifo` class member function definitions are shown in Listing 11.5.

Listing 11.5. lifo.cpp. Class member function definitions for `lifo` objects.

```
1   #include "lifo.hpp"
2
3   // ------------------------------------------------------------
4   // Both constructors get space on the free store for a stack
5   // ------------------------------------------------------------
6
7   lifo::lifo()
8   {
9     if ( NULL == ( top = new char[2048] ) ) abort();
10    bottom = current = top + 2048;
11    work = NULL;
12  }
13
```

Listing 11.5. Continued.

```cpp
14  lifo::lifo( unsigned size)
15  {
16    if ( NULL == ( top = new char[size] ) ) abort();
17    bottom = current = top + size;
18    work = NULL;
19  }
20
21  lifo::~lifo()
22  {
23    delete top;
24  }
25
26  // ------------------------------------------------------------
27  // lifo::push() places a nonspecific object on the stack,
28  //              if there is room for it. Returns 1 if
29  //              successful, 0 if failure.
30  // ------------------------------------------------------------
31
32  int lifo::push( unsigned bytes, void *obj )
33  {
34    if ( top > ( current - bytes ) ) return 0;
35    current -= bytes;
36    memmove( current, obj, bytes ); // push object
37    return 1;
38  }
39
40  // ------------------------------------------------------------
41  // lifo::pop() retrieves the next object on the stack.
42  //              Returns (void *) on success, NULL on failure.
43  // ------------------------------------------------------------
44
45  void *lifo::pop( unsigned bytes)
46  {
47    if ( bottom < ( current + bytes ) ) return NULL;
48    work = current;
49    current += bytes;
50    return work;
51  }
52
53  // ------------------------------------------------------------
```

```
54   // lifo::get_block() allocates n bytes on the stack, but
55   //                    does not push any data. Used to
56   //                    allocate "local object" space.
57   //                    Returns (void *) on success, NULL on
58   //                    failure.
59   // ------------------------------------------------------------
60
61   void *lifo::get_block( unsigned bytes )
62   {
63     if ( top > ( current - bytes ) ) return NULL;
64     current -= bytes;
65     return current;
66   }
```

Implementing the lifo class member functions according to the specifications given earlier is fairly straightforward. A lifo stack is a simple object, and you just need to know how to package the functions. Given the specifications for the class's behavior, the logic of the member functions is self-explanatory.

The member function definitions (declaration parts plus function bodies) are written outside the class declaration for the lifo class. This method is the usual way of writing member functions. The only problem associated with member functions positioned outside the class declaration is this: how to let the compiler know to which class a particular function definition belongs. You can resolve this problem in C++ by prefixing the class name to the function name, using the following syntax:

```
return-type class-name::function-name( parm-list )
{
   ... // function body
}
```

The double colon between the class-name and the function-name is called the *scope resolution operator*. It is used to determine scope in C++ when a reference to a function or data member would otherwise be ambiguous. You learn more about the scope resolution operator (as well as other methods of packaging member functions) in the section "Associating Member Functions with a Class" later in this chapter. For now, be aware that the scope resolution operator is used in lines 7, 14, 21, 32, 45, and 61 of Listing 11.5 so that those functions are associated with the lifo class declaration.

You should notice two other features in Listing 11.5. First, recall that lifo.cpp is intended to be compiled to object code (pardon the pun) separately from any other programs that may use lifo objects. Thus, an include for lifo.hpp appears at the beginning of this source file (in line 1).

Second, lifo.cpp contains two operators you have not seen before. Lines 9 and 16 use the operator new to allocate memory on the free store. The new operator acquires memory as if new were a cross between malloc() and calloc(). The C++ *free store* is an area of dynamic memory similar to the familiar C heap. (In Microsoft C/C++, it is the heap, but C++ rules do not require this equivalence.) Both the operator new and the free store are covered in detail in Chapter 15. Their general purposes and uses are clear enough at this time.

The other operator new to you is delete (see line 23). It performs the companion function to new, releasing memory acquired on the free store. The delete operator also is covered more thoroughly in Chapter 15.

Using the *this* Pointer

By now, you should understand how the compiler associates member functions with class declarations. You may be wondering, though, how a *member function* knows which instance of a class object it is dealing with. Detecting the current instance of a class object is a little tricky. Suppose, for example, that you have declared three different lifo objects:

```
lifo stack1, stack2, stack3;    // Just like C, right?
int a;                  // Set up something to work with
...
stack2.PUSH( int, &a ); // Now call the member function
```

From the point of view of the *caller* of a member function, it's clear which instance object is meant. You just qualify the reference to the member function with the class (or structure) name, using the structure member operator (.). It is not obvious, however, to the member function lifo::push() that stack2, in the preceding code fragment, is the object with which lifo::push() is dealing. You need some method of steering the member function to the correct object.

The method you use to connect member functions and the current object involves a pointer. The compiler provides, behind the scenes, a special pointer for each class and its member functions. This pointer is made to point to the correct object when a member function is called. The pointer has a special name: this. How it selects instance objects is illustrated in figure 11.4.

Note the following points about the this pointer:

- *The this pointer is handled entirely behind the scenes.* You don't declare this yourself, you don't have to initialize it, and you should (normally) not place any address values in it. The compiler secretly generates code that does all the necessary work with this before a member function executes.

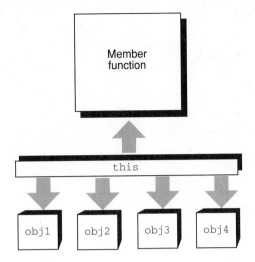

Figure 11.4.

this is made to point to
the correct instance object
during a member function
call.

■ *C++ makes the use of the* this *pointer entirely transparent to the member function using it.* In plain C, whenever you use a pointer to access structure members, you must use the structure pointer operator (->) to access the data object. In C++, it is understood that something different—something special—is going on, and the syntax is adjusted accordingly. Note carefully that *within a class member function, access to class data members and other member functions of the same class appears direct and uncomplicated.* Inside a member function, you don't need to use the class or structure name as a prefix to the member name, nor do you need to use structure member operators.

The completely transparent access to member data and functions within the boundaries of the active member function makes writing the member functions simple (as far as member access is concerned, at least). For example, look again at the code for the function body of lifo::push() in lines 34 through 37 of Listing 11.5. Both the current and top members are used, as if they are directly available—and they are. No pointer dereferencing or structure pointer operators are needed. Yet this single member function can service many different instance objects; therefore, copies of current and top can be unique to each instance object. All copies of instance objects and their member data are distinguished from each other and controlled by the behind-the-scenes action of this.

As soon as you are comfortable with the appearance and methods of Listing 11.5, move to Listing 11.6. This program listing contains the source code for uselifo.cpp, which uses the lifo class in various ways. Unless you are already experienced with C++, don't expect to understand everything you see yet.

Listing 11.6. uselifo.cpp. A demonstration program that uses a `lifo` class object.

```
1  // ------------------------------------------------------------
2  // USELIFO.CPP
3  //    To build the executable file for this program, you
4  //    need to set up a project file with these entries:
5  //       USELIFO.CPP
6  //       LIFO.CPP
7  //    You can create lifo stack objects in programs using
8  //    any memory model, but you may run out of heap space
9  //    if you use the small or tiny models.
10 // ------------------------------------------------------------
11 #include <stdio.h>
12 #include <stdlib.h>
13 #include <string.h>
14
15 #include "lifo.hpp"
16
17 //
18 // declare a simple class for use in testing lifo class
19 //
20 class simple {
21   int stuff;
22 public:
23   simple() { stuff = 2; }
24   ~simple() {}  // default destructor
25   void showit() { printf ( "%d\n", stuff ); }
26 };
27
28 //
29 // Overload global operator new()
30 //
31 void* operator new( size_t size, void *ptr )
32 {
33   size = size; // Dummy statement
34   return ptr;  // Here is what we are after
35 }
36
37 void main( void )
38 {
39   unsigned char byte = ' ';
```

```
40    char test_str[] = "Well, hello, there!";
41    char *fetch;
42    lifo stack;
43
44    //
45    // Fill up and empty the stack
46    //
47    while ( stack.push( 1, &byte ) ) ;
48    printf( "The stack is full.\n" );
49    while ( NULL != stack.pop( 1 ) );
50    printf( "The stack is empty again.\n" );
51    //
52    // Push and pop something significant
53    //
54    stack.push( strlen(test_str)+1, test_str );
55    fetch = (char *)stack.pop( strlen(test_str)+1 );
56    printf( "%s\n", fetch );
57    //
58    // Use lifo::getblock() to allocate space on the
59    // stack and create a class object directly in that
60    // spot.
61    //
62    fetch = (char *)stack.get_block( sizeof( simple ) );
63    simple* X;
64    X = new(fetch) simple;
65    X->showit();
66    X->simple::~simple();      // explicitly delete object
67    stack.pop( sizeof( simple ) );      // throw it away
68    //
69    // Now demonstrate the support macros
70    //
71    int one = 1, two = 2, three = 3;
72    int a, b, c;
73    stack.PUSH( int, &three );
74    stack.PUSH( int, &two );
75    stack.PUSH( int, &one );
76    a = *(int *)stack.POP( int );
77    b = *(int *)stack.POP( int );
78    c = *(int *)stack.POP( int );
79    printf( "%d %d %d\n", a, b, c );
80    fetch = (char *)stack.ALLOC( simple );
81    X = new(fetch) simple; // reuse simple object pointer
```

Listing 11.6. Continued.

```
82    X->showit();
83    X->simple::~simple();      // explicitly delete object
84    stack.POP( simple );                // throw it away
85  }
```

The program in Listing 11.6 contains a mixture of simple and sophisticated code. In the following discussion, every technique in uselifo.cpp is identified, but the main purpose of this program's discussion is to showcase the use of lifo class objects. The more advanced techniques are discussed in later chapters. Overriding operator new() and operator delete(), for example, is covered in Chapter 15.

The comments in lines 1 through 10 of Listing 11.6 are important for this program. The comment lines indicate that lifo.cpp resides in a separate source file; you therefore need to construct a project file to compile and link uselifo.cpp. A simple project file, consisting of the names uselifo.cpp and lifo.cpp, is sufficient.

The comments indicate also that you can compile uselifo.cpp with the small model. If, however, you are going to write a more ambitious program (one in which many lifo class objects as well as other class objects are declared and used), you should consider using the large model for the program. The large model provides a full 64K free store (heap), but the smaller models do not.

Preliminary matters are taken care of in lines 11 through 35 of Listing 11.6. These lines contain the include statements for library functions (plus an include directive for the lifo header); a declaration for a different class (a class named simple), which is used to demonstrate lifo stacks; and a function definition for operator new().

The function definition for operator new() is potentially the most confusing item. If operator new() is supplied by the compiler, why does it need to be redefined? The answer is that operator new(), as used here, is different from the standard global operator new(). Specifically, operator new() *controls the address* at which memory is acquired—in this program, memory is not acquired from the free store but is located on the lifo stack object. Once again, such control of the operators new() and delete() is explained more fully in Chapter 15.

Lines 39 through 42 contain a selection of object definitions. Included are character and string objects, which will be pushed on and popped off the stack, and the lifo class object itself, appropriately named stack. Did you notice in line 42 how simple it is to declare a class object? It's as easy as declaring an int variable; all the real work was done in designing the class header and member function source files.

The first demonstration of `lifo` class objects appears in lines 45 through 50. These lines show how to invoke the `lifo::push()` member function, by pushing characters onto the stack until it is full. Then the `lifo::pop()` member function is used to pop them all back off again (and to discard them).

Lines 52 through 60 show how to push a whole string onto the stack, and how to address that string once more when it has been popped. Popping the string off the stack also illustrates why the `lifo::pop()` routine preserves the address of the `current` pointer to use as the return value, before adjusting `current` to its new value. If this were not done, the object would be popped and then completely lost.

Lines 57 through 67 represent fairly sophisticated C++ code. They show how to allocate space on a `lifo` stack and how to create, use, and delete another class object in the allocated space. Some of the code from that section of the program is reproduced here:

```
62    fetch = (char *)stack.get_block( sizeof( simple ) );
63    simple* X;
64    X = new(fetch) simple;
65    X->showit();
66    X->simple::~simple();     // explicitly delete object
67    stack.pop( sizeof( simple ) );      // throw it away
```

Line 62 allocates the space on `stack` in an amount equal to the size of a `simple` class object. Because `fetch` is a pointer to `char`, the resulting void pointer must first be cast to `(char *)` before it can be assigned to `fetch`.

Because space allocation for the `simple` object is handled explicitly, instead of allowing the global operator `new` to handle it, line 63 declares only a *pointer* to `simple` rather than a `simple` *object*.

The code in line 64 creates the `simple` object, using the redefined (that is, *overloaded*) global operator `new()`. Notice that this statement causes the `simple` class constructor to be called (the compiler secretly generates the code to do that) so that initialization can be performed. Remember, too, that the overloaded operator `new()` is set up to point wherever you like—in this case, to the space on the stack pointed to by `fetch`.

Line 65 calls a member function of the `simple` class object. Because this object was created with `new()`, and because only a pointer to the object was retained, the call must use the structure pointer operator to get to the member function. Don't be confused by this requirement. Logic *inside* the member function still requires *no* dereferencing syntax to access other member functions and variables. The *caller* here must deal with the fact that a pointer is used to locate the object.

Line 66 contains a special function call. The destructor for the `simple` object is called directly—something you rarely need to do. More about this technique is provided later in the section "Providing Constructor and Destructor Functions," but a question needs to be answered right now. Why call the destructor for a class object when destructor calls are usually automatic (invoked when the object goes out of scope)? You need to call the destructor for the `simple` object precisely because it was created at a specific address (not on the free store) with an overloaded `new()` call. A class object created at a specific address never goes out of scope, and cleanup is left entirely to you: the destructor is not automatically called for such an object.

Line 67 completes the program portion in Listing 11.6. This line's action is simply to pop off the stack the space used by the `simple` object, freeing the stack for other use.

The remaining code in Listing 11.6 demonstrates the use of the support macros. One of the most interesting aspects of this section of code is the declaration of local variables in lines 71 and 72. Standard C permits the declaration of objects local to a block only at the top of the block. C++ is more flexible: You can declare local objects anywhere within a block.

Using the support macros is straightforward. Remember that the `lifo` member functions return a void pointer, which must be cast before assigning its value to another pointer (as in lines 76 through 78, for example). A void pointer can receive any pointer type in an assignment without a cast; to *send* a void pointer across the assignment operator requires a cast to the receiving pointer type.

Using the *public, private,* and *protected* Keywords

You already know members of a class declared with `class` are private by default, and members of a class declared with `struct` (or `union`) are public by default. Access to member objects can be overridden. You can override access to a class member by using two keywords you already know (`public` and `private`) and one you don't yet know (`protected`). These keywords control access to class members in the following ways:

■ `public`

Class members that are declared to be `public` (or are public by default) can be used (when they are data members) or called (when they are member functions) by any function. The calling function does not need to belong to the class (or any class).

■ `private`

Class members that are declared to be `private` (or are private by default) can be used or called only by member functions of the same class, or by *friends* of that class (see the section "Using Friend Functions" later in this chapter).

■ `protected`

Class members that are declared to be `protected` can be used only by member functions and friends of the same class, or by member functions and friends of another class *derived* from the original class. In other words, the `protected` keyword provides access protection for members *inherited* from a higher class. Class derivation and inheritance are explained in Chapter 17.

The `public`, `private`, and `protected` keywords are called *access specifiers*. You use the following syntax for writing access specifiers:

```
access-specifier : member-list_opt
```

The `member-list` is optional. Even though you can have an empty member list following an access specifier, the colon (:) is required. All the member identifiers following an access specifier have the indicated access. You can use any combination of access specifiers in a class declaration; no particular order of appearance is required.

The base document makes a point about access control that is worth summarizing here. The C++ access control mechanism is intended to guard class members against accidental misuse, *not* against deliberate abuse.

Nothing can stop you from taking the address of a class object and casting that pointer to another class. Accessing the object through the second pointer prevents the compiler from providing type protection according to the original class declaration. Furthermore, nothing can protect a program against the meddling of another (perhaps unscrupulous) programmer who has access to the source code. Such a programmer can change the class declaration, leaving a "back door" entry to presumably protected member objects.

If you usually think of access control as a security measure, think again. You need some other means of protecting your code.

Writing Member Functions for a Class

In this chapter, you have seen a number of class declarations and their member objects and functions. As the chapter progressed, the explanation of C++ syntax and source code arrangement became more specific. In this section, you learn the explicit rules for declaring and defining class member functions. The rules for declaring and defining friend functions of classes are presented in the last section of the chapter.

Associating Member Functions with a Class

The advances in programming language that are incorporated in C++ have only one purpose: to help the programmer control complexity. For that reason, you often find that C++ code is used to implement large, complex programs. In such programs, you most often find separate compilation used to build the final module.

Compiling Member Functions Separately

Because separate compilation is the technique you will probably use the most, the first packaging method presented here is for placing class member function definitions *outside* the class declaration. To simplify the presentation, both the class declaration and the member function definitions appear together in the next code fragment. The comments in the code fragment indicate which parts of the fragment belong in a separate source file. Here is the code fragment, showing how to package member function definitions outside the class declaration:

```
// ----------------------------------------------------------
// Declare a class with member function definitions outside
// the class declaration
// ----------------------------------------------------------

// THIS IS THE PART THAT GOES IN THE HEADER (.HPP) FILE
class A {
  int i;
public:
  void f1( int );        // function declarations only here
  void f2( int );
};
// **********************************************************

// THIS IS THE PART THAT GOES IN THE MEMBER FUNCTION
// DEFINITION SOURCE (.CPP) FILE
                         // function definitions begin here
void A::f1( int arg )    // scope resolution operator defines
{                        // which class function belongs to
  i = arg * 2;
}

void A::f2( int arg )
{
  i = arg / 2;
}
```

When class member functions are defined outside the class declaration, you must use the fully qualified function name to identify the function:

```
return-type class::function( parms ) { ... }
```

The class name is specified first, then the scope resolution operator (::), and then the function name. The class name and scope resolution operator indicate to the compiler that the function definition belongs to, and is in the scope of, the associated class.

To call a class member function (sometimes loosely called a *method*), you must use the *class member syntax*. This just means that you use the name of a specific class object, followed by the structure member or structure pointer (as needed), and then the function call syntax. The following is an example:

```
A stuff; // define stuff with class A
...
stuff.f1( 4 ); // call stuff's f1() member function
```

Keep in mind that member functions must already have been declared in the class declaration, but not yet defined. You can neither redeclare nor redefine a class member function. Furthermore, you cannot add a class member function that was not declared in the class (this would violate all protection and access control).

Finally, you should know that each class member function defined outside the class declaration must have exactly one definition, regardless of the number of source files used to build the complete program. You can still overload a member function (provide several functions of the same name, but with different arguments and perhaps a different return type).

Declaring Inline Member Functions

You can also package class member functions *inline*. To write an inline member function, you *define* it within the class declaration, instead of simply declaring the function. The following code fragment shows how this is done:

```
// ----------------------------------------------------------
// Declare a class with inline member function definitions
// ----------------------------------------------------------

// THIS ALL GOES IN THE SAME SOURCE FILE AS THE PROGRAM
// USING THE CLASS
class B {
  int i;
public:
                // very short functions are suitable for
```

```
                      // inline definition, but note restrictions
                      // in the text
        void f1( int arg ) { i = arg * 2; }
        void f2( int arg ) { i = arg / 2; }
    };
```

Inline definitions such as the one in this code fragment have exactly the same effect as using the `inline` keyword on a member function defined outside the class declaration. For example, the `B1::f1()` member function could be written this way:

```
class B {
    ...
    void f1( int );
};


inline void B::f1() { i = arg * 2 }
```

Requesting the compiler to regard a member function as `inline` (by either method) means that, whenever a call to the function is encountered, you want the function body to be directly inserted into the code. The resulting straight-line code eliminates the overhead of a function call. Function syntax and type checking still apply, however. Notice also that you can use `inline` on an ordinary (nonmember) function.

Inline functions are suitable when a function is very short. How short is that? As a rule of thumb, if the function is short enough to strike you as trivial (not unimportant, just very concise), it is short enough to be an `inline` candidate. The presence of too many inline functions can increase the size of a program dramatically, so be conservative in your choices.

The rules for inline functions are slightly different from those for member functions defined outside a class. The most significant difference is that inline member functions may be defined more than once, in several source files. Multiple definitions are possible because the class declaration is most often found in a header file that is included, perhaps several times, in multiple source files.

There is an important restriction on multiple definitions of inline member functions. In every case, the `inline` member function must be defined in *exactly* the same way. Otherwise, the confusion that would result is obvious. Furthermore, you should understand that coding an `inline` function is only a *request* that the compiler use inline construction. You have no guarantee that the compiler will do so (just as you have no guarantee that a `register` variable will actually reside in a system register).

Specifying Default Arguments for Member Functions

C++ provides another feature for declaring functions that goes beyond standard C: *In a member function's declaration, you can specify default arguments for the member function.* Listing 11.7 contains a simple example of how this is done.

Listing 11.7. defarg.cpp. A program that uses default argument values in a member function declaration.

```
1   #include <stdio.h>
2
3   class A {
4     int m;
5   public:
6     void incr_m( int = 1 );
7     void show() { printf( "%d\n", m ); }
8   };
9
10  void A::incr_m( int amt )
11  {
12    m += amt;
13  }
14
15  void main()
16  {
17    A obj; // declare an A object
18
19    obj.incr_m( 2 ); // increment by two
20    obj.show();
21    obj.incr_m();    // increment by default amt
22    obj.show();
23  }
```

Line 6 of Listing 11.7 shows the member function prototype for `A::incr_m()` with a default argument supplied. Lines 19 and 21 show how you can call the same member function in two different ways—once by supplying an argument, and once by assuming the default argument value.

You can also write default arguments into inline function definitions. You might write line 6, for example, as

```
void incr_m( int amt = 1 ) { m += amt }
```

and then delete lines 10 through 13 (the *out-of-line* member function definition).

The following rules govern the use of default arguments (aren't there always rules?):

■ *You don't have to supply defaults for all arguments.* Once a default is supplied, though, all subsequent arguments in that same list must have default values. The following examples are not meant to be redeclarations of each other:

```
func( int, int );          // OK, no defaults
func( int, int=1, int=2 ); // OK, trailing args have values
func( int, int=1, int );   // ERROR, 3rd arg has no default
```

Trailing arguments not supplied in a member function call are supplied with values from the defaults (an error occurs if you don't supply defaults).

■ *If a default was supplied in a previous declaration of a member function, you don't have to specify the default again when redeclaring the function.* For example:

```
func( int, int=2 );
func( int=1, int ); // OK 2nd arg already given
```

■ *You* can *redeclare a member function prototype, supplying defaults that were not previously supplied.* For example:

```
func( int, int );
func( int=1, int=2 ); // OK, supplies missing defaults
```

■ *You* cannot *redefine a default argument that has already been declared.* For example:

```
func( int=1, int=2 );
func( int=1, int=2 ); // ERROR, both args already declared
```

Notice that you cannot redefine a default argument, even to the same value.

Providing Constructor and Destructor Functions

Although you learn about constructor and destructor functions (plus some related topics) in Chapter 15, you need to prepare to write C++ classes as quickly as possible. The general rules that apply to these special functions are therefore presented here.

Constructor and destructor functions have been used in this chapter, but without much explanation about them. You have learned only that these functions cannot have a return type, and that they must have the same name as the class (plus a prefixed tilde (~) for the destructor function name). Listing 11.8 shows several styles of constructor functions, giving a more rounded picture of what you can do with them.

Listing 11.8. constr.cpp. A program that contains several different (overloaded) constructors, including a default constructor with default arguments.

```
1   #include <stdio.h>
2
3   class A {
4      int a, b, c;
5   public:
6      A( int=1, int=2, int=3 );    // constr. 1. (default)
7      A( double, double, double);  // constr. 2.
8      A( long );                   // constr. 3.
9      A( A& );                     // constr. 4. (copy constr)
10     void show() { printf( "%d %d %d\n", a, b, c ); }
11  };
12
13  A::A( int i1, int i2, int i3 )
14  {
15     a = i1; b = i2; c = i3;
16  }
17
18  A::A( double f1, double f2, double f3 )
19  {
20     a = (int)f1; b = (int)f2; c = (int)f3;
21  }
22
23  A::A( long n )
24  {
25     a = b = c = (int)n;
26  }
27
28  A::A( A& other ) {
29     a = other.a;
30     b = other.b;
31     c = other.c;
32  }
33
34
```

Listing 11.8. Continued.

```
35  void main()
36  {
37    A x1;        // use default with def. args (constr 1)
38    x1.show();
39
40    A x2( 3 );  // use only 1 default arg      (constr 1)
41    x2.show();
42
43    A x3( 3, 1 );  // use 2 default args       (constr 1)
44    x3.show();
45
46    A x4( 3.14, 2.414, 6.28 );  // double args(constr 2)
47    x4.show();
48
49    A x5( 53L );                // long arg (constr 3)
50    x5.show();
51
52    A x6 = x5;       // use copy constructor (constr 4)
53    x6.show();
54  }
```

In Listing 11.8, notice that the first constructor function (line 6) is called the
default constructor. You can specify a default constructor in three ways:

■ *You can let the compiler generate a default constructor.* The compiler generates a default constructor function, but only if you have provided no
other constructor function at all. If you provide any constructors, you
need one that can serve as the default (as defined in the next two items
of this list). When generating a default constructor for you, the compiler
initializes any member data objects to a value of zero (consistent with
standard C rules for initialization of basic, derived, and aggregate
objects).

■ *You can provide a constructor function with no arguments.* The oldest, and
still most consistent, definition of a default constructor is a constructor
function that accepts no arguments. Such a default constructor for the
program in Listing 11.8, for example, might look like this:

```
class A{
...
A();
...
```

```
    }

    A::A()
    {
        a = 0; b = 0; c = 0;
    }
```

You can think of this form of default constructor functions as the classical form.

■ *You can provide a constructor function with all default arguments.* Recent versions of C++ allow a constructor function that has default values for every argument, *and can therefore be called with no arguments at all,* to play the role of default constructor function. This form of default constructor is used in line 6 of Listing 11.8.

The classical form of the default constructor (as explained in the second item in this list) and the form with default arguments cannot be used together. The meaning of the two forms used together is ambiguous—the compiler will not be able to determine which one to call. Consider the default constructor call implied by the declaration of obj in the following code fragment:

```
class A{
...
A();
A( int=1, int=2, int=3 );
...
}
...
void main()
{
    A obj; // Which constructor now?
}
```

The declaration A obj; is the correct format for invoking either form of the A class constructor. Because enough information is not present for the compiler to determine which of the two functions is meant, a compile-time error results. This is not much of a problem, though. Either form of the default constructor works; the only practical difference is that the form with all the default values is probably more flexible.

Lines 7 and 8 in Listing 11.8 illustrate that you can code (nondefault) constructor functions of several varieties. In other words, you can supply several overloaded constructors. None of the constructor functions can have a return value—that is illegal for *all* constructors—and each version of the function must have clearly different arguments. In this program, the purpose of the overloaded constructors is to allow the declaration of class objects that can be initialized several different ways. Lines 46 and 49 show how to declare objects by using nondefault constructors. Notice that the call arguments are used just as for a normal function call, even though these lines are object declarations that are semantically equivalent to int i.

The last kind of constructor is the *copy constructor*. This form permits a class object to be declared and initialized by copying the contents of another class object. Notice the general syntax of a copy constructor:

classname(otherclassname &);

As used here, the ampersand (&) is called the *reference operator*. A reference has a close family connection to a pointer to an object, but does not require dereferencing as pointers do. (A detailed description of references is provided in Chapter 13.) The copy constructor in Listing 11.8 is declared in line 9, and the copy constructor function definition appears in lines 28 through 32. Line 52 shows a sample of using a copy constructor in declaring a class object. For now, just write your copy constructors by mimicking this sample code.

The compiler generates a default destructor function for a class if you don't declare one, just as the compiler generates a constructor function. Like constructors, destructor functions cannot specify a return type. They are different from constructors, however, in several important ways:

■ *A destructor function has the same name as the class, but the tilde (~) character appears before the function name.* A destructor function declaration looks like this:

```
class A {
...
public:
...
~A();
};


A::~A() { ... } // destructor function definition
```

The tilde is the same character used for the standard C *one's complement* operator; the context of the character's use tells the compiler which use is meant. A destructor function can be an inline function.

■ *The destructor function for a class cannot accept arguments.* Whether you write the destructor yourself or allow the compiler to generate a default destructor, a destructor function cannot accept function arguments.

■ *A class can have only one destructor function.* This point is really a consequence of the preceding point. If a destructor cannot specify a return type or an argument list, you cannot produce different versions of the destructor function.

Simple class objects (particularly ones that do not acquire memory outside the object's boundaries) can usually do quite well with a compiler-generated destructor. If the memory for the whole object is going to be released, whether or not a member integer is first set to zero doesn't matter much.

Other class objects (such as the lifo class objects shown earlier in this chapter) require you to write an explicit destructor function that frees acquired memory or performs other cleanup tasks.

Using Friend Functions

Friend functions are *not* class member functions, but are granted access even to private member objects of a class. You use friend functions to keep class object size to a minimum, and to enhance class object performance. These uses of friend functions are covered in detail in Chapter 18, "Object Control and Performance Issues," but you need to know now how to declare such functions in order to complete your overview of basic class declarations.

Including Friend Functions in a Class

Declaring a function to be a friend of a class is easy. You just supply a function prototype for the friend function in the class declaration, and you prefix the prototype declaration with the keyword friend. Note the following example:

```
class A {
  int value;
public:
...
  friend int peekA( A ); //Here is the friend prototype
};
```

If you write the friend function definition out-of-line, no further special keywords are needed. The function definition for the peekA() function in the preceding code fragment would then look like this:

```
int peekA( A obj )
{
  printf( "%d\n", obj.value );
}
```

This second code fragment illustrates two important points about friend functions. First, friend functions *can* access private member variables in the class for which such functions are defined as a friend. Second, you *do* have to use structure member syntax, as shown here, to gain access to class members, and you *do* have to tell the friend function which object is meant (with an argument). There is no automatic assignment of the correct object address to the `this` pointer, as there is on behalf of member functions. You should also realize that friend functions defined out-of-line are *not* within the scope of the class (as member objects are).

Friend functions may also be defined inline. For example, you can combine the preceding two code fragments by using an inline definition in this way:

```
class A {
  int value;
public:
...
  friend int peekA( A ) //Here is the inline friend
  {
    printf( "%d\n", obj.value );
  }
};
```

The main difference between friend functions defined out-of-line and those defined inline is that inline friend functions are within the scope of the class where they are defined.

There are also some important restrictions on which functions can be declared to be friends of a class. You *cannot* declare the following kinds of functions as friends: constructors, destructors, virtual functions, assignment operator functions, and class type cast operator functions. (Assignment and cast operator functions are covered in Chapter 14.)

Whether a friend function is defined inline or out-of-line, you do not have to use the member access syntax (structure member operator or pointer) to call it; a friend function is not a member of the class that declared the function as friend. The `peekA()` friend function defined in the last code fragment, for instance, should be called in this way:

```
main()
{
  A obj1; // declare an A class object
  ...
  peekA( obj1 ); // pass object as arg
}
```

Deciding When To Use a Friend Function

In Bjarne Stroustrup's original book that introduced the new C++ language (*The C++ Programming Language*, Addison-Wesley, 1987), readers were urged to avoid friend functions, with three exceptions. Friends were considered suitable whenever it was necessary to avoid the use of global data, global nonmember functions, or public data members.

Subsequent experience has apparently changed the prevailing attitude toward friend functions. Friend functions are now in common use. The base document recommends the use of friend functions for a variety of reasons, including these:

- *Friend functions can improve the efficiency and performance of class objects and provide (in some circumstances) a cleaner programming interface to class members.* In many cases, using a member function would require passing whole class objects as arguments to and from class member functions. Using friend functions to implement specific kinds of class behavior can avoid much of this inefficiency (as explained in Chapter 18). A function can also be a friend to more than one class, helping to eliminate instances in which a global function would otherwise be necessary to provide a function common to more than one class.

- *Friend functions can make more flexible the implementation of overloaded operator functions for classes.* If you define a class on which you want to be able to perform addition, you must also write a function (member or friend) that defines how addition is to be performed on objects of that class. The significance of using friend functions to make such functions more flexible is clearly explained in Chapter 14.

- *You can use friend function declarations to provide access to class members for a routine written in another language.* Member functions obviously have to be written in C++ because of the special syntax and scope requirements. You may want to write a high-performance service routine in assembler. In that case, you can declare the routine a friend and link it in the finished program later.

In short, use friend functions conservatively, but don't be afraid to use them.

Exercises

The following exercises give you practice in declaring classes, defining member functions, and using class objects:

1. Review the class syntax and formatting guidelines and then answer the following questions: What is the general syntax of a class declaration? How are class declarations commonly formatted in source code? How are class declarations packaged for separate compilation?

2. Review the differences between class objects created with the `struct` keyword and the `class` keyword. When would you choose one keyword over the other, and why?

3. Modify the `PUSH()` macro shown in Listing 11.4 so that the second argument in the macro call does not require the address-of operator (&) Remember that the `lifo::push()` member function requires as its second argument a void pointer to the object being pushed. Examine the macro closely to see what will actually result from the macro expansion.

4. You might be tempted to modify the `POP()` macro in Listing 11.4 so that you don't have to cast the type of object just popped off the stack. The most obvious modification looks like this:

```
#define POP(type)      *(type *)pop( sizeof(type) )
```

This modification won't work, however. No errors are flagged in the header file during compilation, but the source file containing `POP()` macro calls (see Listing 11.6, for example) gets a lot of errors during compilation. Why doesn't this modification work? (Hint: Expand a macro call like `stack.POP( int )` by hand and see what you get.)

5. Review the header file lifo.hpp in Listing 11.4, observing what members are `private` (by default) and what has been made `public`. Why do you think the class declaration was arranged this way?

6. Write a class declaration with several overloaded constructor functions. Write the default constructor, using all default arguments. Use this class in a C++ program. Repeat the exercise but use a copy constructor rather than a default constructor.

7. Write a class declaration with at least one friend function. Declare a class object and access it through the friend function.

Summary

This chapter covered some of the most important concepts associated with C++. Before continuing with the next chapter, be sure you understand the following points:

■ *C++ classes define truly new types, whereas the standard C* `typedef` *provides only a synonym facility.* When you declare a C++ class, you declare not merely the contents of a data structure, but the behavior of that new type as well.

■ *C++ classes can be declared with the* `class`, `struct`, *or* `union` *keyword.* Classes declared with the `class` keyword permit `private` access to member data and functions by default; the other classes permit `public` access by default.

■ *Class member functions are always declared within a class and may optionally be defined inline.* Member functions define the behavior of class objects. If a member function is defined out-of-line, you use the scope resolution syntax (the function's *fully qualified name*) to associate the definition with the class to which it belongs:

```
class A {
...
public:
... int show();
};
...
int A::show() { ... }
```

If you define a member function inline, the fully qualified name is not necessary.

■ *You declare class objects as you would any other typed object.* For example, you can declare a local class A object in this way:

```
main()
{
  A my_obj; // declare a class A object
}
```

Other ways to create instance objects are discussed later, particularly in Chapter 15.

■ *Class member functions can access both private and public member data and functions directly.* Remember that the compiler generates a pointer named `this` for each instance object. When a member function is called, hidden code sets the `this` pointer to the correct address for the object. If, however, a member function accesses members of a *different* instance of the same class, the member function must use the member access syntax.

■ *Nonmember functions can access only public member data and functions, and must use the member access syntax for that purpose.* Some of the member data and functions of a class need to be visible only internally; they should not be accessed by nonmember functions. *Encapsulation* provides protection against accidental (though not fraudulent) access of private members. Furthermore, nonmember functions (other than friend functions) can access private members only through the member access syntax, as shown in this example:

```
class A {
public:
  int i;
  ...
};
```

```
...
main()
{
  A someobj;
  ...
  someobj.i = 0;
}
```

In other words, you use the structure member operator (.) or structure pointer operator (->) to access the member. This requirement should not be surprising because classes are based on advanced implementations of structures.

■ *Friend functions can access both private and public class members, but must still use the member access syntax.* Note the following short program:

```
#include <stdlib.h>
#include <stdio.h>

class A {
  int i;
public:
  friend int report( A obj ) { return obj.i; }
};

main()
{
  A myobj;

  printf( "%d\n", report( myobj ) );
}
```

Friend functions defined out-of-line are not in the class scope; those defined inline are in the class scope. Friend functions can be quite useful, particularly in boosting program performance (see Chapter 19).

If you have mastered these basic concepts, you are ready to begin reading the next chapter, "Creating C++ Objects."

Creating C++ Objects

K nowing the rules for declaring classes is something like having a theoretical knowledge of aerodynamics: It doesn't necessarily mean you can get in an airplane and fly away. A more practical kind of instruction is necessary first. That is what this chapter is about—the practical aspects of using class objects.

The contents of this chapter can be divided into two main categories: creating and initializing class objects. In creating and initializing class objects, you define objects and supply initial values for member data objects. Chapter 13, "Accessing C++ Objects," continues the discussion of the practical aspects of using class objects and deals with gaining access to objects.

Defining C++ Objects

The first order of business is the creation of class objects. Because a class defines a new type (not just a synonym), you can at times declare just a class object, much as you declare any other C variable. At other times, you might want an object to persist indefinitely. In that case, you need to create the object on the free store, which is analogous to acquiring storage with `malloc()` and `calloc()`.

Simple class object declarations are close to standard C syntax, but more advanced declarations, not surprisingly, exhibit some differences from familiar methods of declaration. Initialization of class objects also has its differences from the familiar initialization methods.

Assigning Storage Classes to Class Objects

Think back for a moment about the rules for C scope, linkage, and duration. Fortunately, almost all you learned about these rules in mastering standard C still applies to C++. The great exception is that a C++ class has a scope—which by definition could not arise in standard C.

When local, global, and arbitrary objects are referred to in this chapter, the primary concern is the *duration* of class objects (understanding duration in the standard sense). Class object duration is still related to the object's scope, as you have already learned. That is, local objects (objects declared with block scope) by default have auto duration; global objects (objects declared with file scope) by default have static duration.

Furthermore, you can use the *storage class specifiers* (auto, register, static, and extern) with class object declarations in the same way you use them with, for example, the declaration of an int. Because you are now writing C++, however, the significance of using one of the storage class specifiers may be slightly different from that in standard C. Notice the following guidelines for using storage class specifiers in C++:

■ *You can apply the auto and register specifiers only to objects declared with block scope.* In Microsoft C/C++, an auto object is created on the system stack. The object goes away when the function owning the object returns to its caller. It is therefore a contradiction in terms to apply auto to a global object (which is stored in the data segment rather than the stack).

Because register objects are also auto objects, the same restrictions apply to both kinds of objects. In C++, the register keyword serves as a suggestion that the object is frequently used, and has little to do with placing the variable in a hardware register. Moreover, C++ allows the address of a register object to be taken (that is, the address-of operator, &, can be used on it), which is illegal in standard C. Because of this new capability, most implementations ignore the suggestion.

Microsoft C/C++ limits the use of the register keyword to integral object types, and even then it is still only a hint. Microsoft C/C++ uses hardware registers whenever possible, anyway. Forcing a variable into a register could actually hurt performance by disturbing normal register usage and compiler optimization.

Neither the auto nor the register keyword is allowed for class member objects. A whole class object may be auto, however.

■ *You can apply the static specifier to objects anywhere.* You can apply the static keyword only to objects and functions—not, for example, to a class declaration. The static keyword can be used at file scope (limiting an object or function to internal linkage only), at block scope (giving a local object static duration), and with a member data object within a *global class declaration.* (See the section "Using Scope Resolution for Syntax Control" in Chapter 13, "Accessing C++ Objects," for details on how to create a `static` member object in a global class.) Because a local class declaration (naturally) goes out of scope often, `static` members are meaningless within such a declaration. (Locally declared classes are severely restricted in what they can do and in what objects they can refer to. The best rule of thumb for handling locally declared classes is not to use them, even though they are legal.)

■ *You cannot use the `extern` keyword with class members.* Otherwise, you can use the `extern` keyword as you always have, with the additional capability of declaring whole class objects `extern`.

Static data members of a class deserve a little more discussion because they have an interesting characteristic: Static data members are not part of any object of that class. This means a static data member can be referenced through a class object (the member was declared, after all, as a class member) and the static data member can be referenced independently of any particular class object. The following code fragment, for example, is perfectly legal (and usable):

```
class task {
  ...
public:
  static int numberoftasks; // Not a definition!
};
...
int task::numberoftasks = 1; // Here's the definition!
...
void main()
{
  int maxtasks = 16;
  task user1; // declare a class object
  printf( "%d\n", user1.numberoftasks );

  printf( "Inactive tasks: %d\n",
          maxtasks - task::numberoftasks );
}
```

In this code fragment, the only thing necessary for referring to the static member integer `numberoftasks` apart from any particular object is to fully qualify the identifier with the class name *classname::identifier*.

You should also notice the comments in the preceding code fragment. Observe particularly the comment that the declaration of the static object within the class is *not a definition*. A static data member must be defined elsewhere in the program. The definition of the static member object directs the compiler to allocate space for the object and to initialize it.

The numberoftasks static data member is explicitly initialized to 1 in the code fragment. This action illustrates another interesting characteristic: Static data members (of a global class declaration) are *initialized just like all other global objects,* but they otherwise obey normal class member access rules. A global object has a default value of zero, and so has a static data member. A global object definition can have an initializer, and so can a static data member. (An ordinary class data member cannot have an initializer.)

A final characteristic of static data members is important: Only one copy of a static data member is available, and it is shared by all objects of its class. When all objects of a class must communicate with each other, you can use a static data member instead of an ordinary global variable (which is more susceptible to corruption by uncontrolled access). Additionally, declaring a data member to be static helps decrease the size of class objects. Reducing the size of a class object is not a sufficient reason to use static data members, however. Let your program's logistical requirements guide that decision.

You can also declare class member functions to be static. The significance of static member functions is discussed in the section "Understanding *this" in Chapter 13.

Defining Arbitrary-Duration Class Objects

Most C++ authorities (including Stroustrup) recommend that programmers avoid global objects whenever possible. The reason is that C++ objects tend to be memory-intensive; using many global class objects can inflate the size of a program. At times, however, the logic of your program simply demands a global object. The alternatives to global objects are, of course, local objects and arbitrary objects. Local objects, which are declared in a block, go away when the block is exited. Arbitrary objects, which you explicitly create, do not go away until you explicitly delete them.

C++ arbitrary objects are created with the new operator and deleted with the delete operator, both of which are unique to C++. Arbitrary objects have the same advantage global static objects have: They persist for as long as you want them to remain. Furthermore, when you use arbitrary objects, you avoid the disadvantage of inflated program size because they do not exist until they are created during program execution.

You can see how arbitrary objects are used in the following illustration of a class and support program for controlling a Microsoft mouse. The mouse, if used at all during a program, is something you usually want available throughout program execution. A mouse class object can thus be considered for use as a global static object, but can work equally well as an arbitrary object.

Implementing a mouse class object as an arbitrary object is particularly attractive because the private data for the class contains several large structures, and a number of support functions are involved in the class. Furthermore, because there is no need to define more than one mouse object for a given program, there is no corresponding need to declare such objects with the frequency and ease of, say, integer objects.

The mouse class is named msmouse. Notice that the following characteristics should be included in this class:

■ *The class should include a member function that reports the success or failure of mouse initialization.* If the hardware system on which your program is running does not have a mouse, or if the mouse driver software was not installed (or was improperly installed) when the system was booted, the program needs to be able to discover that fact.

■ *The class should include mouse support for both text and graphics modes.* Using a text mouse is quite common, but mouse support in graphics mode programs has become increasingly necessary in the last couple of years. The program should be able to support a mouse in either mode. Additionally, the program should be able to respond to changes "on the fly" in video modes during program execution; a "reset" member function that can adjust to changing video modes is therefore helpful.

■ *Mouse coordinates and virtual screens should be completely hidden from the programmer.* The Microsoft mouse software addresses screen RAM in terms of virtual-screen coordinates. A virtual screen is an imaginary screen that, as far as the mouse driver is concerned, is never less than 640-by-200 pixels in size. The physical-screen dimensions for a given video mode and screen type vary considerably, requiring the program to convert physical to virtual coordinates, and virtual to physical coordinates. The msmouse class should include member functions that allow the program both to set and to report mouse coordinates *as if they were physical-screen coordinates*—no matter what video mode is active. Thus, the programmer is required to deal with only one set of coordinates while using the mouse.

Although many of the requirements for mouse programming are touched on in the explanation of the msmouse class, you should be aware that mouse-programming technology is fairly complex (especially for some of the advanced features the Microsoft mouse supports). If you want to know more about mouse-programming theory, you should get a copy of *Microsoft Mouse Programmer's Reference* (Microsoft Press, 1989). For other practical examples of mouse programming, you can consult Jack Purdum's *C Programmer's Toolkit,* 2nd Edition (Que, 1992), which also has a companion software disk.

Separate compilation was used to develop and test the msmouse class. The three source files involved in demonstrating a mouse object as an arbitrary-duration class object are these: (1) msmouse.hpp, a header file containing the class declaration; (2) msmouse.cpp, a file containing the member function definitions for the class; and (3) usemouse.cpp, a demonstration program that creates and uses a mouse class object. You at least need the following entries in a project make file if you use the PWB to compile and link the mouse sample programs:

```
usemouse.cpp
msmouse.cpp
graphics.lib
```

Alternatively, you can compile and link using the command line compiler, by typing:

```
cl usemouse.cpp msmouse.cpp graphics.lib
```

The header file msmouse.hpp is shown in Listing 12.1.

Listing 12.1. msmouse.hpp. A header file that contains the class declaration and support declarations for the Microsoft mouse class.

```
1   #if !defined( MSMOUSE )
2   #define MSMOUSE
3
4   #include <dos.h>
5   #include <graph.h>
6   #include <conio.h>
7
8   #define callmouse int86( 0x33, &reg, &reg )
9   #define NOBUTTON    0
10  #define LEFTBUTTON  1
11  #define RIGHTBUTTON 2
12  #define BOTHBUTTON  3
13  #define vmaxx 0
14  #define vmaxy 1
15  #define xsize 2
16  #define ysize 3
17
18  // Screen table can be used to convert mouse to
19  // real coordinates:
20  //     mousex = ( x - 1 ) * screentab[crtmode][xsize]
21  //     mousey = ( y - 1 ) * screentab[crtmode][ysize]
22  //     x = ( mousex / screentab[crtmode][xsize] ) + 1
23  //     y = ( mousey / screentab[crtmode][ysize] ) + 1
24  // This will take into account the difference between
25  // PC 1-origin and mouse 0-origin coordinate systems
26  // in text modes. Graphics modes already use 0-origin
```

```
27  // coordinates.
28
29  extern int screentab[20][4];
30
31  typedef struct {
32    int verify;
33    int crtmode;
34    int cursoron;
35    int buttons;
36    int numpress;
37    int x;          // x and y are in screen coordinates
38    int y;
39    int minx;       // min-max values are in mouse coordinates
40    int maxx;
41    int miny;
42    int maxy;
43    int crtpage;
44  } mstat_t;
45
46  class msmouse {
47    union REGS reg;
48    struct SREGS seg;
49    mstat_t mstat;
50  public:
51    void reset();
52    msmouse();
53    ~msmouse();
54    int initok() { return mstat.verify; }
55    void showcursor();
56    void hidecursor();
57    mstat_t *getposition();
58    void setposition( int = 0, int = 0);
59    mstat_t *getbutton( int );
60    mstat_t *releasebutton( int );
61    mstat_t *zonex( int, int );
62    mstat_t *zoney( int, int );
63  };
64
65  #endif
```

The first feature you should notice in Listing 12.1 is that the entire header file is controlled by an #if defined compiler directive. Using this directive is important when you begin to develop serious multiple source-file programs—and most C++ programs turn out to be serious programs because the OOPS approach encourages you to pack features into an object.

Various support macros appear next in Listing 12.1. Lines 8 through 12 define macros useful for identifying button presses that result from calling the `msmouse::getposition()` member function. (These macros are not used in the demonstration program, Listing 12.3, but are provided so you won't have to code them later.) Lines 13 through 16 provide macro names for subscripts into the screen conversion table named `screentab` (used to convert to and from mouse virtual-screen coordinates).

Lines 31 through 44 provide a `typedef` name, `mstat_t`, for a structure that is frequently used by member functions to report mouse status. That structure, `mstat`, is declared as a private data member in line 49 even though several of the member functions return a pointer to it. Returning a pointer to a private member is, strictly speaking, a violation of encapsulation for the class, but there are two good reasons for doing so for this class. First, the structure is used only to report status, not to control or modify the object. Second, the pure convenience of the technique makes using such a pointer desirable.

Member function prototype declarations for the `msmouse` class are shown in lines 51 through 62 of Listing 12.1. These member function declarations aren't notable, except that `msmouse::initok()` is an inline function. `initok()` returns the verify flag, which is set to 1 (a true condition) by the constructor *only* if mouse initialization was acceptable.

The next step, of course, is to write the member function definitions for the `msmouse` class. These definitions are shown in Listing 12.2.

Listing 12.2. msmouse.cpp. Member function definitions for the `msmouse` class.

```
1   #include <stdlib.h>
2   #include <dos.h>
3   #include "msmouse.hpp"
4
5   int screentab[20][4] = {
6
7   // -------------------------------------
8   //   vmaxx vmaxy xsiz ysiz      crtmode
9   // -------------------------------------
10       640,  200,  16,  8,       // mode 0
11       640,  200,  16,  8,       // mode 1
12       640,  200,   8,  8,       // mode 2
13       640,  200,   8,  8,       // mode 3
14       640,  200,   2,  1,       // mode 4
```

```
15      640,  200,   2,  1,      // mode 5
16      640,  200,   1,  1,      // mode 6
17      640,  200,   8,  8,      // mode 7
18        0,    0,   0,  0,      // mode 8
19        0,    0,   0,  0,      // mode 9
20        0,    0,   0,  0,      // mode A
21        0,    0,   0,  0,      // mode B
22        0,    0,   0,  0,      // mode C
23      640,  200,   2,  1,      // mode D
24      640,  200,   1,  1,      // mode E
25      640,  350,   1,  1,      // mode F
26      640,  350,   1,  1,      // mode 10
27      640,  480,   1,  1,      // mode 11
28      640,  480,   1,  1,      // mode 12
29      640,  200,   1,  1,      // mode 13
30  };
31
32  void msmouse::reset()
33  {
34    reg.x.ax = 0x0F00;
35    int86( 0x10, &reg, &reg );
36    mstat.crtmode = reg.h.al;
37    mstat.crtpage = reg.h.bh;
38    mstat.verify = 0;
39    reg.x.ax = 0;      // reset mouse driver
40    callmouse;
41    if ( reg.x.ax == -1 ) {
42      mstat.verify = -1;
43      mstat.cursoron = -1;
44      mstat.buttons = NOBUTTON;
45      mstat.numpress = 0;
46      mstat.x = mstat.y = 0;
47      mstat.minx = mstat.miny = 0;
48      mstat.maxx = screentab[mstat.crtmode][vmaxx] - 1;
49      mstat.maxy = screentab[mstat.crtmode][vmaxy] - 1;
50    }
51  }
52
53  msmouse::msmouse()  // reset mouse, status in AX
54  {
55    unsigned char first_byte;
56    void (_interrupt _far * oldx33)();
```

Listing 12.2. Continued.

```
57
58    oldx33 = _dos_getvect( 0x33 );
59    first_byte = *(unsigned char far *)oldx33;
60    if ( NULL == oldx33 || first_byte == 0xcf ) return;
61    reset();
62  }
63
64  msmouse::~msmouse()
65  {
66    reg.x.ax = 0;      // reset mouse driver
67    callmouse;
68  }
69
70  void msmouse::showcursor()  // display mouse cursor
71  {
72    reg.x.ax = 1;
73    callmouse;
74  }
75
76  void msmouse::hidecursor()
77  {
78    reg.x.ax = 2;
79    callmouse;
80  }
81
82  mstat_t *msmouse::getposition()
83  {
84    // Button status data is trapped only if a button
85    // is being HELD DOWN.
86
87    int ofs;
88
89    if ( mstat.crtmode > 3 ) ofs = 0;
90      else ofs = 1;
91    reg.x.ax = 3;
92    callmouse;
93    mstat.buttons = reg.x.bx;
94    mstat.x =
95      ( reg.x.cx / screentab[mstat.crtmode][xsize] ) + ofs;
96    mstat.y =
97      ( reg.x.dx / screentab[mstat.crtmode][ysize] ) + ofs;
```

```
 98    return &mstat;
 99  }
100
101  void msmouse::setposition( int x, int y )
102  {
103    int ofs;
104
105    if ( mstat.crtmode > 3 ) ofs = 0;
106      else ofs = 1;
107    mstat.x = x;
108    mstat.y = y;
109    reg.x.cx =
110      ( mstat.x - ofs ) * screentab[mstat.crtmode][xsize];
111    reg.x.dx =
112      ( mstat.y - ofs ) * screentab[mstat.crtmode][ysize];
113    if ( reg.x.cx < mstat.minx ¦¦ reg.x.dx < mstat.miny ) {
114      mstat.x = mstat.y = 0;
115      reg.x.cx = reg.x.dx = 0;
116    }
117    if ( reg.x.cx > mstat.maxx ¦¦ reg.x.dx > mstat.maxy ) {
118      mstat.x = mstat.y = 0;
119      reg.x.cx = reg.x.dx = 0;
120    }
121    reg.x.ax = 4;
122    callmouse;
123  }
124
125  mstat_t *msmouse::getbutton( int button )
126  {
127    int ofs;
128
129    if ( mstat.crtmode > 3 ) ofs = 0;
130      else ofs = 1;
131    reg.x.ax = 5;
132    reg.x.bx = button;
133    callmouse;
134    mstat.buttons = reg.x.ax;
135    mstat.numpress = reg.x.bx;
136    mstat.x =
137      ( reg.x.cx / screentab[mstat.crtmode][xsize] ) + ofs;
138    mstat.y =
139      ( reg.x.dx / screentab[mstat.crtmode][ysize] ) + ofs;
```

Listing 12.2. Continued.

```
140    return &mstat;
141  }
142
143  mstat_t *msmouse::releasebutton( int button )
144  {
145    int ofs;
146
147    if ( mstat.crtmode > 3 ) ofs = 0;
148      else ofs = 1;
149    reg.x.ax = 6;
150    reg.x.bx = button;
151    callmouse;
152    mstat.buttons = reg.x.ax;
153    mstat.numpress = reg.x.bx;
154    mstat.x =
155      ( reg.x.cx / screentab[mstat.crtmode][xsize] ) + ofs;
156    mstat.y =
157      ( reg.x.dx / screentab[mstat.crtmode][ysize] ) + ofs;
158    return &mstat;
159  }
160
161
162  mstat_t *msmouse::zonex( int minx, int maxx )
163  {
164    int ofs;
165
166    if ( mstat.crtmode > 3 ) ofs = 0;
167      else ofs = 1;
168    reg.x.ax = 7;
169    reg.x.cx =
170      ( minx - ofs ) * screentab[mstat.crtmode][xsize];
171    reg.x.dx =
172      ( maxx - ofs ) * screentab[mstat.crtmode][xsize];
173    callmouse;
174    mstat.minx = minx - ofs;
175    mstat.maxx = maxx - ofs;
176    return &mstat;
177  }
178
179  mstat_t *msmouse::zoney( int miny, int maxy )
180  {
181    int ofs;
```

```
182
183     if ( mstat.crtmode > 3 ) ofs = 0;
184       else ofs = 1;
185     reg.x.ax = 8;
186     reg.x.cx =
187       ( miny - ofs ) * screentab[mstat.crtmode][ysize];
188     reg.x.dx =
189       ( maxy - ofs ) * screentab[mstat.crtmode][ysize];
190     callmouse;
191     mstat.miny = miny - ofs;
192     mstat.maxy = maxy - ofs;
193     return &mstat;
194   }
195
```

Lines 5 through 30 of Listing 12.2 contain the screentab coordinate-conversion array. The array contains 20 rows of 4 entries, with each row corresponding to a PC video mode, for modes 0x00 through 0x13 (notice that modes 0x08 through 0x0C are no longer used). Within a row i, the elements screentab[i][vmaxx] and screentab[i][vmaxy] give the resolution of the mouse virtual screen, which is always in pixels, even in text modes. Next, the elements screentab[i][xsize] and screentab[i][ysize] give the number of virtual-screen pixels per physical display location on the screen.

You must also take into account the fact that mouse virtual coordinates and Microsoft C/C++ graphics-mode physical coordinates identify screen positions (both x and y positions) beginning from position 0, whereas Microsoft C/C++ text modes identify positions beginning from position 1. Member functions performing coordinate conversion must calculate an adjustment value of 0 or 1, depending on the active video mode. Whether the offset value is added or subtracted from the coordinate depends on the direction of conversion. You can examine the member functions to see how the adjustment value is computed and used.

Suppose, for example, the screen is running video mode 0x03 (color text, 80x25) and the member function msmouse::getposition() internally determines that the mouse position is on the 0th row and 11th column of the mouse virtual screen. How is the function going to convert these mouse coordinates to text coordinates for reporting to the caller?

First, the x-position, 11, is divided by the xsize value for this video mode, and the remainder is thrown away. The result so far is 1, but an adjustment of 1 must be added to the result to convert to a text-origin coordinate. Thus, the text x-position is column 2. A similar operation on the row, or y-position, gives the result of 1. Therefore, the mouse position in physical-screen coordinates (x,y) is (2,1).

You can find further details on how the member functions do their jobs by consulting the mouse technical documentation previously mentioned. All you need to remember is that you always communicate mouse coordinates to msmouse class objects in terms of the correct physical-screen coordinates for the active video mode.

The sequence of calls to msmouse member functions is also important. The best way to indicate what sequences are required is to show you. Look now at usemouse.cpp in Listing 12.3.

Listing 12.3. usemouse.cpp. A program that demonstrates the msmouse class in both text and graphics modes, using arbitrary-duration objects.

```
1   // ----------------------------------------------------------
2   // USEMOUSE.CPP
3   //   Demonstrates the Microsoft Mouse class in both text
4   //   and graphics modes.
5   // ----------------------------------------------------------
6
7
8
9   #include "msmouse.hpp"
10
11  #include <stdlib.h>
12  #include <stdio.h>
13  #include <dos.h>
14  #include <conio.h>
15  #include <graph.h>
16
17  int numitem = 10;
18  char *item[] = {
19    " initok()",
20    " showcursor()",
21    " hidecursor()",
22    " getposition()",
23    " setposition()",
24    " getbutton()",
25    " releasebutton()",
26    " zonex()",
27    " zoney()",
28    " reset()",
29  };
30  char *blurb[] = {
```

```
31    "initok() returns -1 if mouse driver initialized OK.",
32    "showcursor() turns on the mouse cursor.",
33    "hidecursor() turns off the mouse cursor.",
34    "getposition() returns x,y in mouse status block.",
35    "setposition() uses x,y to set mouse x,y.",
36    "getbutton() gets last x,y & clicks for button.",
37    "releasebutton() gets x,y & releases for button.",
38    "zonex() sets x1-x2 range for mouse cursor.",
39    "zoney() sets y1-y2 range for mouse cursor.",
40    "reset() re-initializes mouse after mode change.",
41  };
42
43
44  void eraseol( void );
45
46  void main()
47  {
48    int i;
49    char buffer[80];
50    mstat_t *mstat; // pointer to status block
51
52    msmouse *mouse;   // pointer to mouse object
53
54    mouse = new msmouse; // create mouse object
55    if ( mouse->initok() != -1 ) {
56      puts( "This system does not have a mouse attached." );
57      exit( 0 );
58    }
59
60    _settextcolor( 7 );
61    _setbkcolor( 1 );
62    _clearscreen( _GCLEARSCREEN );;
63    _settextcolor( 0 );
64    _setbkcolor( 7 );
65    _settextwindow( 5, 10, 15, 70 );
66    _settextposition( 1, 1 );
67    for ( i=0; i<numitem; ++i ) {
68      sprintf( buffer, "%s\r\n", item[i] );
69      _outtext( buffer );
70    }
71
72    _settextwindow( 17, 10, 25, 70 );
```

Listing 12.3. Continued.

```
73     _settextcolor( 7 );
74     _setbkcolor( 1 );
75     _settextposition( 1, 1 );
76     _outtext( "Click the RIGHT BUTTON for GRAPHICS demo." );
77     _settextposition( 2, 1 );
78     _outtext( "Click the LEFT BUTTON on item to SELECT." );
79     _settextwindow( 20, 10, 25, 70 );
80     _displaycursor( _GCURSOROFF );
81     mouse->zonex( 10, 70 );
82     mouse->zoney( 5, 15 );
83     mouse->setposition( 10, 5 );
84     mouse->showcursor();
85     while ( 1 ) {
86       mstat = mouse->getbutton( 1 );
87       if ( mstat->numpress ) break;
88       mstat = mouse->getbutton( 0 );
89       if ( !mstat->numpress ) continue;
90       i = mstat->y - 5; // scale to index value
91       if ( i >= 0 && i < numitem ) {
92         _settextposition( 4, 1 );
93         eraseol();
94         sprintf( buffer, "Last item clicked was: %s", item[i] );
95         _outtext( buffer );
96         _settextposition( 5, 1 );
97         sprintf( buffer, "%s", blurb[i] );
98         _outtext( buffer );
99       }
100    }
101
102    _settextwindow( 1, 1, 25, 80 );
103    mouse->hidecursor();
104    _setbkcolor( 0 );
105    _settextcolor( 7 );
106    _clearscreen( _GCLEARSCREEN );;
107    _displaycursor( _GCURSORON );
108
109    // msmouse.hpp already has graph.h included
110    // so go ahead with graphics mode demo
111
112
113    // Set up graphics video mode
```

```
114    //
115
116    _setvideomode ( _VRES16COLOR );
117
118    if (_grstatus < _GROK )
119    {
120        printf("Graphics error: %d\n", _grstatus);
121        printf("Press any key to halt:");
122        getch();
123        exit(1);
124    }
125
126    // -----------------------------------
127    // Important to reset after mode change
128    // -----------------------------------
129    mouse->reset();
130    // -----------------------------------
131
132    // draw a stopsign
133
134    char prompt[] = "Click the STOP SIGN to end demo";
135    char stop[] = "Stop";
136
137    struct videoconfig cf;
138    _getvideoconfig( &cf );
139    struct xycoord wholescreen[] = {
140        0, 0,
141        cf.numxpixels, 0,
142        cf.numxpixels, cf.numypixels,
143        0, cf.numypixels,
144        0, 0
145    };
146
147    int gx = cf.numxpixels / 2;
148    int gy = cf.numypixels / 2;
149    struct xycoord stopsign[] = {
150        gx-40,gy-40,
151        gx+40,gy-40,
152        gx+40,gy+40,
153        gx-40,gy+40,
154        gx-40,gy-40
155    };
```

Listing 12.3. Continued.

```
156
157    _setcolor( 1 );   // color BLUE
158    _polygon( _GFILLINTERIOR, wholescreen, 5 );
159
160    _setcolor( 4 ); // color RED
161    _polygon( _GFILLINTERIOR, stopsign, 5 );
162
163    _registerfonts("\\C700\\LIB\\ROMAN.FONT");
164    _setfont( "t'roman'h32w20v" );
165
166    _setcolor( 7 );
167    _moveto( gx - _getgtextextent( stop )/2, gy );
168    _outgtext( stop );
169    _moveto( gx - _getgtextextent( prompt )/2, gy+80 );
170    _outgtext( prompt );
171
172    mouse->showcursor();
173    while ( 1 ) {
174      mstat = mouse->getbutton( 1 );
175      if ( mstat->numpress ) break;
176      mstat = mouse->getbutton( 0 );
177      if ( mstat->numpress ) {
178        if ( mstat->x > stopsign[0].xcoord &&
179          mstat->x < stopsign[1].xcoord &&
180          mstat->y > stopsign[0].ycoord &&
181          mstat->y < stopsign[2].ycoord ) break;
182      }
183    }
184
185    _setvideomode( _DEFAULTMODE );
186
187    delete mouse;   // don't forget to shut mouse down
188
189  }
190
191
192  void eraseol(void)
193  /* Erases from the current cursor location to the right
194     edge of the line */
195  {
```

```
196     char empty[80];
197     struct rccoord coord;
198
199     coord = _gettextposition();
200     sprintf( empty,"%*c",80-coord.col,' ' );
201     _outtext( empty );
202     _settextposition ( coord.row, coord.col );
203 }
```

The first thing to notice about controlling the mouse is that the constructor function for the class contains all the mouse initialization code. Therefore, a user of the msmouse class needs only to define a mouse object in order to initialize the mouse software. In Listing 12.3, line 54 contains this definition, using the new operator to create an msmouse object of arbitrary duration. Because the new operator always returns a pointer of the correct type of object, a pointer for the mouse object is set up in line 48. Even though this code appears within the main() function, the use of the new operator dictates that this object has arbitrary duration, not auto duration.

Lines 55 through 58 check for the correct initialization of the mouse by calling the msmouse::initok() member function. Because the mouse driver returns a value of –1 when the mouse cursor is hidden (invisible), this function returns a –1 if initialization was correct. The mouse cursor is always hidden when you first initialize the mouse; you must unhide the mouse cursor later, after you have set the screen the way you want it.

Lines 60 through 80 set up the display by painting a list of the mouse functions and finally by hiding the normal cursor, using the Microsoft C/C++ _displaycursor(_GCURSOFF) function call. The only cursor you want on the screen is the mouse cursor. Here, at the beginning of the demonstration program, the screen is still in text mode, so text coordinates must be used to communicate with the member functions.

Next, lines 81 through 82 define the region of the display screen in which the mouse cursor is allowed to appear. This is accomplished with the msmouse::zonex() and msmouse::zoney() member functions. Once more, remember that the coordinate values you specify in these function calls are physical-screen coordinates, not mouse coordinates. The member functions convert them internally to the correct values before passing on the request to the mouse driver software. After all that has been accomplished, the mouse cursor is finally turned on in line 78.

The code for decoding and interpreting mouse actions is shown in lines 85 through 100 of Listing 12.3. Because the lines are an important logic sequence, they are reproduced here for closer scrutiny:

```
while ( 1 ) {
  mstat = mouse->getbutton( 1 );
  if ( mstat->numpress ) break;
  mstat = mouse->getbutton( 0 );
  if ( !mstat->numpress ) continue;
  i = mstat->y - 5; // scale to index value
  if ( i >= 0 && i < numitem ) {
    _settextposition( 4, 1 );
    eraseol();
    sprintf( buffer, "Last item clicked was: %s", item[i] );
    _outtext( buffer );
    _settextposition( 5, 1 );
    sprintf( buffer, "%s", blurb[i] );
    _outtext( buffer );
  }
}
```

The mouse control and decoding are accomplished with a while loop. Notice that the conditional expression for the while loop is just 1 (an expression that is always true); logic within the loop must be used to break out at the correct time. That logic depends on which mouse button the user presses.

Right-button presses are checked for in lines 86 and 87. The msmouse::getbutton() function (following the Microsoft internal requirements) requests the status of button "1"—the *right button.* Be careful here: This value does not correspond to the LEFTBUTTON macro shown in line 10 of Listing 12.1. The macros defined in Listing 12.1 are intended to support the msmouse::getposition() function, not button status reporting functions.

The getbutton() function reports several things to the caller. Most important, the function reports the number of times the requested button has been pressed since the last call to that function. getbutton() returns the address of the status block mstat in which the number of button presses was reported. Line 87 then tests that value; if the value is nonzero, the break command exits the while loop.

The real fun begins in line 88, which requests the left-button status. The left button is the one used to determine which line of the display the user clicks with the mouse. To compute which line was clicked, the minimum and maximum mouse cursor positions allowed must be taken into account. If you look back at line 82, you can see the mouse cursor is constrained to y coordinates from line 5 to line 15, inclusive.

Because the mouse cursor can be positioned no higher than line 5, line 90 subtracts 5 from the detected vertical mouse position. Mouse coordinates are set and reported independently of any windowing Microsoft C/C++ might be doing. If, for example, the mouse is positioned on the top line of that box when the user presses the left button, the position reported is 5. Then subtracting 5 yields 0, which is a handy number for indexing into the `blurb` array. As you may guess, the `blurb` array contains a list of short explanations of the various mouse functions.

The remaining lines of logic within the `while` loop, lines 91 through 99, verify the mouse indeed was clicked at one of the function name lines, and then select and display the corresponding `blurb` entry.

The second half of the demonstration begins only when the user clicks the right button (anywhere on the screen). This second phase involves switching to graphics mode and detecting a mouse click within a small area on the screen (a stop sign in a red square).

The most important line of code in this part of the program is line 129, where the `msmouse::reset()` member function is called. It is true that the Microsoft RAM-resident mouse driver already knows about the mode change (the driver is hooked into the BIOS interrupt), but the software is not yet aware of it. Hence, a specific function is called that can test the video mode and adjust `msmouse` parameters accordingly.

The detection and decoding loop for the graphics mode demonstration is shown in lines 173 through 183 of Listing 12.3. This loop is constructed almost exactly like the text mode loop, particularly in that physical-screen coordinates are used to detect the mouse cursor location.

Line 187 contains another important line of code. The `delete` operator is used to destroy the `msmouse` object, which was created with `new`. There are two important reasons to remember to delete objects that are no longer needed. The first reason is to maintain efficient garbage collection. This program has only one object, which lasts for the entire run of the program. In other cases, however, you may need many different objects—so many that memory utilization can become a problem. Additionally, it is bad practice to assume the operating system cleans up your messes after program termination. The system usually does just that, but in some instances, memory cleanup can be overlooked. Be safe and be sure. If you create it, you clean it up.

The second reason for deleting objects created with `new` is that they remain effective until you delete them. In this case, the mouse stays active for the life of the object. During the development of the `msmouse` class, it became evident that leaving the mouse active after a program terminates can lead to some strange errors. Other objects may be hooked into the operating system, or they may be performing some other sensitive function that requires cleanup. The best medicine, once again, is to be sure—delete the object when you are done with it.

Defining Local (*auto*) Class Objects

In this section, you learn how to define local (auto) class objects. A useful class, dbllist, is presented to illustrate local objects. The dbllist class is one that supports the construction and manipulation of doubly linked lists. Notice the following features of the dbllist class:

■ *All dbllist objects maintain only control information within the class object.* That is, only pointers to the list and the member function prototypes are declared within the class. Thus, you can build practical doubly linked lists that can be as large as the available storage permits, without inflating the size of the object or your program.

■ *An element in a dbllist linked list can be any size.* As for the lifo class discussed in Chapter 11, "Using C++ Classes," an element body of any size can be handled—even different sizes in the same list. A typedef named dblentry is provided that contains a de_size variable so that individual sizes can be tracked. An element body is assumed to be arbitrarily large; it can be up to 65536 bytes long.

■ *Elements in a dbllist linked list can be either inserted in order or appended to the list as the elements appear.* For a list in which order is not important, you can just append the elements to the end of the list as you build it. You also can build an ordered list by inserting the new elements as you build the list. The insertion logic compares the entire element body (not counting control information) to surrounding element bodies to determine the element's position in the list. The list is built in ascending order.

■ *Complete navigation facilities are included in the dbllist class.* Member functions are available for positioning to the head or tail of the list, and for traversing the list either forward or backward.

The header file for the dbllist class, containing support declarations and the class declaration itself, is found in Listing 12.4. As you read over the listing, notice again that #if defined() logic is used to prevent redeclaring the class or the companion typedef in multiple source-file programs.

Listing 12.4. dbllist.hpp. A header file that contains the class declaration for doubly linked list objects.

```
1   #if !defined( DBLLIST )
2   #define DBLLIST
3
4   #include <stdlib.h>
5   #include <stdio.h>
6   #include <string.h>
```

```
 7  #include <conio.h>
 8
 9  typedef struct de_type {
10    struct de_type *prev;
11    struct de_type *next;
12    void *de_body;
13    unsigned de_size;
14  } dblentry;
15
16  class dbllist {
17    dblentry *anchor;
18    dblentry *base;
19    dblentry *hold;v
20    dblentry *create( void *, unsigned );
21  public:
22    dbllist();
23    ~dbllist();
24    void kill();
25    void *gohead();
26    void *gotail();
27    void *gonext();
28    void *goprev();
29    void *append( void *, unsigned );
30    void *insert( void *, unsigned );
31  };
32
33  #endif
```

From the dbllist class declaration in Listing 12.4, you can see the class itself is straightforward. The declaration contains some pointers to list elements, as well as a member function in the private portion of the declaration. The other member functions, including a constructor and a destructor, are also fairly simple.

A careful look at the typedef for a list element (dblentry) shows that the physical construction of the list is not so simple, however. Figure 12.1 shows how the parts of the list are brought together by the class.

As you can see from Figure 12.1, a dbllist doubly linked list has three components: (1) the dbllist class object, which contains all the control information and member function names; (2) a doubly linked list of dblentry structures, each of which contains linkage pointers, size information, and a pointer to the last component; and (3) the element body, which contains any amount of user data you want to store.

Figure 12.1.

Physical construction of the doubly linked list for the dbllist class.

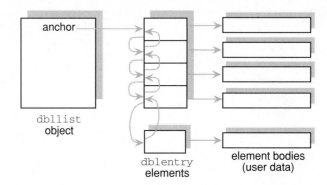

dbllist
object

dblentry
elements

element bodies
(user data)

Although much of the information is physically outside the class object, the linked-list data is nevertheless well protected because the only access to it is through the class object. Even the means of physically creating a new entry in the list is kept in the private portion of the object (that is, the dbllist::create() member function is private). A user of the class can create new objects only indirectly, by means of the append() and insert() member functions.

Why has the dbllist class been arranged this way? Any useful linked-list data would be impossibly huge for a class object declared locally or globally. If the linked list itself were included within the boundaries of a linked-list class object, you would be able to create such objects only with arbitrary duration—that is, you could use only new and delete to create and destroy them.

Furthermore, the logistics of handling a completely unpredictable amount of data within the boundaries of a class object would be truly formidable. As the dbllist class is designed, however, you can declare such objects anywhere and in any way, without inflating the size of your class objects or your EXE program file. This claim is proved in a moment, but first look at the member function definitions, shown in Listing 12.5.

Listing 12.5. dbllist.cpp. Class member function definitions for the dbllist class.

```
1   #include "dbllist.hpp"
2
3   dblentry *dbllist::create( void * data, unsigned bytes )
4   {
5     if ( NULL == ( hold = (dblentry *)malloc( sizeof( dblentry ) ) ) )
6       return NULL;
7     if ( NULL == ( hold->de_body = malloc( bytes ) ) ) {
8       free( hold );
9       return NULL;
```

```
10    }
11    memmove( hold->de_body, data, bytes );
12    hold->prev = hold->next = NULL;
13    hold->de_size = bytes;
14    return hold;
15  }
16
17  dbllist::dbllist()
18  {
19    anchor = base = hold = NULL;
20  }
21
22  dbllist::~dbllist()
23  {
24    kill();
25  }
26
27  void dbllist::kill()
28  {
29    base = anchor;
30    while( base ) {
31      hold = base->next;
32      free( base->de_body );
33      free( base );
34      base = hold;
35    }
36    anchor = base = hold = NULL;
37  }
38
39  void *dbllist::gohead()
40  {
41    base = anchor;
42    if ( base ) return base->de_body;
43    else return NULL;
44  }
45
46  void *dbllist::gotail()
47  {
48    if ( base ) {
49      while( base->next ) base = base->next;
50      return base->de_body;
51    }
```

Listing 12.5. Continued.

```
52    else return NULL;
53  }
54
55  void *dbllist::gonext()
56  {
57    if ( base ) {
58      if ( base->next ) {
59        base = base->next;
60        return base->de_body;
61      }
62      else return NULL;
63    }
64    else return NULL;
65  }
66
67  void *dbllist::goprev()
68  {
69    if ( base ) {
70      if ( base->prev ) {
71        base = base->prev;
72        return base->de_body;
73      }
74      else return NULL;
75    }
76    else return NULL;
77  }
78
79  void *dbllist::append( void *data, unsigned bytes )
80  {
81    dblentry *temp;
82
83    if ( NULL == ( temp = create( data, bytes ) ) )
84      return NULL;
85    gotail();
86    if ( !base ) {
87      anchor = base = temp;
88    }
89    else {
90      base->next = temp;
91      temp->prev = base;
92      base = temp;
```

```
93     }
94     return base->de_body;
95  }
96
97  void *dbllist:: insert( void * data, unsigned bytes )
98  {
99     dblentry *temp;
100
101                               // if empty list, just add it on
102
103    gohead();
104    if ( !base ) return( append( data, bytes ) );
105
106                               // create the new entry
107
108    if ( NULL == ( temp = create( data, bytes ) ) )
109      return NULL;
110
111        // position to entry before which this one belongs
112
113    while ( base->next
114     && memcmp( data, base->de_body, bytes ) > 0 )
115       base = base->next;
116               // if data still greater than last, append it
117    if ( !base->next
118     && memcmp( data, base->de_body, bytes ) > 0 ) {
119      base->next = temp;
120      temp->prev = base;
121      base = temp;
122    }                         // otherwise insert the entry
123    else {
124      hold = base->prev;
125      temp->prev = hold;
126      temp->next = base;
127      base->prev = temp;
128                              // Fix anchor when prepending
129      if ( !hold ) anchor = temp;
130      else hold->next = temp;
131      base = temp;
132    }
133    return base->de_body;
134  }
```

The only private member function in the dbllist class is dbllist::create(). It appears in lines 3 through 15 of Listing 12.5. create() can therefore be called only by other member functions of the class or by friends of the class (in this case, there are no friends). The insert() member function (which creates an ordered doubly linked list) and the append() member function (which creates an order-of-appearance doubly linked list) call create() to set up a new list entry and enter it in the list.

create() accepts as arguments a void pointer to the user data to be placed in the list, and an unsigned byte size of the object. create() first acquires memory for the dblentry structure for the element and then acquires memory for the user data. A pointer to the user data and its size are recorded in the dblentry structure, and a pointer to the dblentry structure is returned to the caller. Notice that no attempt is made at this point to link the entry into the list; responsibility falls to either insert() or append(). Notice also that the logic of create() allows you to create entries of any size and to mix entry sizes in a single list. Each entry records its own size.

In Listing 12.5, look also at the use of the structure pointer operator (->) in the create() member function. There are various references to hold->de_body, hold->next, and others. The hold variable is a data member of the dbllist class. Recall that because member functions of a class have the this pointer available to them, structure member and structure pointer operators are unnecessary for accessing member data variables (or functions, for that matter). So why do so many structure pointer operators appear here?

If you examine the create() member function code, you can see the structure pointer operator is not used to access the hold variable. The hold variable is itself a pointer to a dblentry structure; therefore, access to a dblentry member does require the pointer notation. If dbllist were an ordinary C structure, for example, you would have to write something like this in order to access hold and any structure members it refers to:

```
dbllist obj; // pretend dbllist is an ordinary structure
...
obj->hold->next = NULL; //WAIT! This isn't plain C!
```

Fortunately, this is not plain C, as the comment in the preceding code fragment proclaims. The first structure pointer operator is therefore unnecessary; this provides direct access to the class members. (Because hold is a private variable, this code fragment would not compile anyway.) In short, you will see many structure pointer operators in the member functions just because this particular class contains many data members that also happen to be pointers to structures.

Because most of the remaining dbllist member functions deal with the ordinary manipulation of doubly linked lists, only three more member functions of dbllist need to be mentioned: the dbllist() constructor function, the ~dbllist() destructor function, and the kill() member function.

The dbllist() constructor function is shown in lines 17 through 20 of Listing 12.5. Because no list element is yet present in the list, this function's sole purpose is to initialize the anchor, base, and hold pointers to a null value. The anchor pointer either will be NULL or will always point to the first dblentry structure in the linked list. That is why this pointer is named anchor: It anchors the entire list. You can always find the beginning of the list by running it backward until there is no further previous-entry pointer, but it's much faster to assign the value of anchor to the pointer locating the current entry.

Locating the current list element is the job of the base pointer. Its value *floats* up and down the list, depending on which direction the list is being run. You can see how base is used by examining the gohead(), gotail(), gonext(), and goprev() member functions in Listing 12.5.

The ~dbllist() destructor function is equally simple. All it does is call the dbllist::kill() function to free the storage tied up in each dblentry element and the associated user data. Hidden code generated by the compiler takes care of destroying the dbllist class object itself.

The kill() member function in lines 27 through 37 is interesting in its own right. Its purpose is to remove all the entries in the list, thus reestablishing an empty list. Why would you want to do this? You might want to repopulate the list with different data when you navigate from a disk directory to a sub-directory. In fact, you will learn how to navigate and repopulate a directory list later (in Listings 12.7, 12.8, and 12.9). First you need to see how a dbllist object is declared and used with block scope (a local object with auto duration).

The program usedbl.cpp shown in Listing 12.6 declares a dbllist class object that is local to the main() function. The amount of data stored in the list in this sample program is small, but none of the data goes on the system stack (where all auto objects go, whether C or C++) except the dbllist object itself. (There is little danger of overflowing the stack with a large list.)

Listing 12.6. usedbl.cpp. A program that demonstrates the dbllist class, using a local class object.

```
1   #include <graph.h>
2   #include "dbllist.hpp"
3
4   void main()
5   {
6     char *word = NULL;
7     dbllist lex;
8
9     _clearscreen( _GCLEARSCREEN );
```

Listing 12.6. Continued.

```
10      lex.append( "roger", 6 );
11      lex.append( "dodger", 7 );
12      lex.append( "codger", 7 );
13
14      word = (char *)lex.gohead();
15      while ( word ) {
16        printf( "%s\n", word );
17        word = (char *)lex.gonext();
18      }
19
20      lex.kill();
21
22      lex.insert( "roger", 6 );
23      lex.insert( "dodger", 7 );
24      lex.insert( "codger", 7 );
25
26      word = (char *)lex.gohead();
27      while ( word ) {
28        printf( "%s\n", word );
29        word = (char *)lex.gonext();
30      }
31
32      word = (char *)lex.gotail();
33      while ( word ) {
34        printf( "%s\n", word );
35        word = (char *)lex.goprev();
36      }
37  }
```

To compile and link the usedbl.cpp program inside the PWB, you need to create a project make file with at least the following entries:

```
usedbl.cpp
dbllist.cpp
```

Notice how easily you can create a doubly linked list as a local "variable." All you need is a line of code such as the one in line 6 of Listing 12.6:

```
dbllist lex; // This is all there is to it!
```

When this statement is executed, the doubly linked list is created (on the system stack), and everything is set up for you, ready to begin populating the list, using the append() or insert() member function.

Lines 10 through 12 populate the list with three words (hence, the object name lex) in an order-of-appearance list, using the append() member function. Lines 14 through 18 then show you how to use the gohead() member function to get to the beginning of the list, and how to use the gonext() member function to run the list forward. After that, the kill() member function in line 20 empties the list for the next part of the demonstration.

Creating an ordered doubly linked list (that is, creating the list in ascending sequence) is just as easy. You use the insert() member function as shown in lines 22 through 24. Notice that the words are not in alphabetical order as they are presented to the insert() function, but they will be in order when lines 26 through 30 print the list in the forward direction.

The kill() member function does not appear at this point in the program. Rather, the gotail() function is used to position the list for scanning backward. This procedure is demonstrated in lines 32 through 37 of Listing 12.6.

Doubly linked lists are tremendously powerful and flexible. They are frequently used in sophisticated programs, and you will find many opportunities to use doubly linked lists as you get used to them.

Defining Global (*static*) Class Objects

To complete the demonstration of local, global, and arbitrary object declarations, this section shows you how to declare and use global class objects. In the examples provided, you can see how to build a directory object. The dir class is a snap to create because the dbllist class is already available, and the C libraries provide built-in functions for accessing disk directories (see the Microsoft C dos.h header file).

As always, the first thing to do is to write the class declaration and place it in the header file (assuming you intend to use separate compilation). The header file dir.hpp is shown in Listing 12.7.

Listing 12.7. dir.hpp. A header file that contains the class declaration for the DOS directory class.

```
1   #if !defined( DOSDIR )
2   #define DOSDIR
3
4   #include <direct.h>
5   #include <dos.h>
6
7   #include "dbllist.hpp"
8
```

Listing 12.7. Continued.

```
 9  class dir {
10    struct _find_t dirblock;
11    dbllist *dirlist;
12    int complete;
13    int scanning;
14    char path[41];
15    char mask[13];
16    char search[53];
17    struct _find_t *current;
18  public:
19    dir();
20    dir( char *, char * );
21    ~dir();
22    void reset( char *, char * );
23    struct _find_t *getcurrent();
24    struct _find_t *getnext();
25    struct _find_t *getprev();
26    void navigate();
27  };
28
29  #endif
```

Did you notice dir.hpp contains an include for dbllist.hpp? If you look a little further (in line 11), you see a pointer to a dbllist object. The intention here clearly is to use the doubly linked list class as a base from which to develop the directory class.

Full use is also made of the built-in Microsoft C/C++ directory-access functions, _dos_findfirst() and _dos_findnext(). You might want to review the operation of these functions in your *Microsoft C Run-Time Library Reference*.

The dir class takes advantage of overloaded constructor functions, as discussed in Chapter 11. There are two constructors for the dir class. One is the default constructor, which initializes the object by reading the entire *current* directory, using the file mask *.*. The other constructor accepts two string pointers (char *) as arguments. The first string specifies the search *path*, which can include drive and directory path information, and can either have or omit a trailing backslash (\) character. (If absent, this character is supplied when the complete search string is built.) The second string can be the file mask and can include up to 12 characters in the format *filename.ext*, with or without DOS wildcard characters (* and ?).

Lines 23 through 25 show the declarations for the `getcurrent()`, `getnext()`, and `getprev()` member functions. These names are much like the corresponding `dbllist` member functions `gonext()` and `goprev()`. Indeed, the `dir` functions use the `dbllist` functions to get their work done. There is an important distinction between the two classes, however. A `dbllist` linked list is populated with entries by repeated user calls to the `insert()` or `append()` function, after the object has been created (by either defining it or creating it with `new`). A `dir` class object, though, is completely built by the class constructor. That is, you can create a doubly linked list of directory entries for the directory currently being listed with just the following two lines of code:

```
#include dir.hpp
...
dir workdir();

    // workdir already contains the directory list
    // when you get here!
```

Therefore, the `dir` class member functions `getnext()` and `getprev()` are purely navigation functions for traversing the directory list. There is no `dir` class counterpart to the `dbllist` class `insert()` or `append()` function.

With the difference between the directory class and the doubly linked list class firmly in mind, now look at the code for the `dir` class member function definitions in Listing 12.8.

Listing 12.8. dir.cpp. Class member functions for the `dir` class.

```
1
2   #include "dir.hpp"
3
4   dir::dir()
5   {
6     complete = 0;
7     scanning = 0;
8     strcpy( path, "" );
9     strcpy( mask, "*.*" );
10    strcpy( search, path );
11    if ( '\\' != search[ strlen( search ) - 1 ] )
12      strcat( search, "\\" );
13    strcat( search, mask );
14    dirlist = new dbllist;
15    complete = _dos_findfirst( search, 0xFF, &dirblock );
16    while ( !complete ) {
```

Listing 12.8. Continued.

```
17        dirlist->append( &dirblock, sizeof( struct _find_t ) );
18        complete = _dos_findnext( &dirblock );
19     }
20     current = (struct _find_t *)dirlist->gohead();
21     if ( current ) scanning = 1;
22  }
23
24  dir::dir( char *where, char *how )
25  {
26     complete = 0;
27     scanning = 0;
28     strupr( where );
29     strupr( how );
30     strcpy( path, where );
31     strcpy( mask, how );
32     strcpy( search, path );
33     if ( '\\' != search[ strlen( search ) - 1 ] )
34        strcat( search, "\\" );
35     strcat( search, mask );
36     dirlist = new dbllist;
37     complete = _dos_findfirst( search, 0xFF, &dirblock );
38     while ( !complete ) {
39        dirlist->append( &dirblock, sizeof( struct _find_t ) );
40        complete = _dos_findnext( &dirblock );
41     }
42     current = (struct _find_t *)dirlist->gohead();
43     if ( current ) {
44        scanning = 1;
45        dirblock = *current;
46     }
47  }
48
49  dir::~dir()
50  {
51     delete dirlist;
52  }
53
54  void dir::reset( char *where, char *how )
55  {
56     dirlist->kill();
```

```
57    complete = 0;
58    scanning = 0;
59    strcpy( path, where );
60    strcpy( mask, how );
61    strcpy( search, path );
62    if ( '\\' != search[ strlen( search ) - 1 ] )
63      strcat( search, "\\" );
64    strcat( search, mask );
65    dirlist = new dbllist;
66    complete = _dos_findfirst( search, 0xFF, &dirblock );
67    while ( !complete ) {
68      dirlist->append( &dirblock, sizeof( struct _find_t ) );
69      complete = _dos_findnext( &dirblock );
70    }
71    current = (struct _find_t *)dirlist->gohead();
72    if ( current ) {
73      scanning = 1;
74      dirblock = *current;
75    }
76  }
77
78  struct _find_t *dir::getcurrent()
79  {
80    if ( current ) return &dirblock;
81    else return NULL;
82  }
83
84  struct _find_t *dir::getnext()
85  {
86    struct _find_t *temp;
87
88    if ( !current ) return NULL;
89    temp = current;
90    if ( NULL == ( current =
91      (struct _find_t *)dirlist->gonext() ) ) {
92      current = temp;
93      return NULL;
94    }
95    else {
96      dirblock = *current;
97      return &dirblock;
98    }
```

Listing 12.8. Continued.

```
 99  }
100
101  struct _find_t *dir::getprev()
102  {
103    struct _find_t *temp;
104
105    if ( !current ) return NULL;
106    temp = current;
107    if ( NULL == ( current =
108      (struct _find_t *)dirlist->goprev() ) ) {
109      current = temp;
110      return NULL;
111    }
112    else {
113      dirblock = *current;
114      return &dirblock;
115    }
116  }
117
118  void dir::navigate()
119  {
120    char *temp;
121    char tpath[41];
122    char tmask[13];
123
124    if ( !current ) return;
125    if ( dirblock.attrib != _A_SUBDIR ) return;
126    if ( !strcmp( dirblock.name, "." ) ) return;
127
128    strcpy( tpath, path );
129    strcpy( tmask, mask );
130    if ( '\\' == tpath[ strlen( tpath ) - 1 ] )
131      tpath[ strlen( tpath ) - 1 ] = '\0';
132    if ( !strcmp( dirblock.name, ".." ) ) {
133      temp =tpath + strlen( tpath ) - 1;
134      while( *temp && *temp != '\\' ) temp--;
135      *temp = '\0';
136      strcat( tpath, "\\" );
137    }
138    else {
139      strcat( tpath, "\\" );
```

```
140        strcat( tpath, dirblock.name );
141        strcat( tpath, "\\" );
142    }
143    reset( tpath, tmask );
144  }
```

The default and overloaded constructor functions are found in lines 4 through 22 and lines 24 through 47, respectively, of Listing 12.8. The main difference between the two constructor functions is the default version uses hard-coded string constants to initialize the search path and search mask, whereas the overloaded version of the constructor function uses the received function arguments to initialize the search path and mask. Both constructor functions initialize the pointer to the directory linked list by simply using the new operator to create a dbllist object and to get its address:

```
dirlist = new dbllist; // Boy, this is easy!
```

The destructor function for the dir class, in lines 49 through 52, deletes the linked list.

The dir::reset() function in lines 54 through 76 is important, but not because of its internal logic or features. This function is similar to the overloaded version of the constructor because this function accepts new values for the search path and mask. The function is different because it begins by calling the dirlist->kill() to empty the linked list without destroying the linked list object. reset() then rebuilds the list by using the new search values. That is, reset() rebuilds the list for what will presumably be a completely different directory.

You have probably already guessed the real significance of the reset() member function: It is used to repopulate the directory linked list when you want to "navigate" subdirectories without having to start over. In fact, that is the purpose of the dir::navigate() member function shown in lines 117 through 143 of Listing 12.8. The navigate() member function assumes you want to move to either the next lower or the next higher subdirectory in the directory tree. The function also assumes the directory entry currently being pointed to is the entry for the new target subdirectory.

The navigate() member function first checks to see whether its function can be performed (see lines 123 through 125). navigate() performs the following checks:

1. If there is no current directory entry being pointed to, the directory is empty, so get out.

2. If the current directory entry being pointed to does not have the directory attribute, subdirectory navigation is impossible, so get out.

3. If the name field of the current directory entry being pointed to is a single period (.), you are positioned on the placeholder for the directory *two* levels above the one in the linked list. Navigation to this directory is not allowed, so get out.

The rest of the logic in dir::navigate() involves only the string manipulation required to rebuild the search path. If the name field of the current entry is two periods (..), the last level of the directory path must be stripped off to get to the next higher level. If the name field of the current entry is anything else (but still a directory-type entry), that name must be suffixed to the search path in order to descend to the next lower level of the directory tree. Finally, navigate() merely calls reset() with the resulting new search arguments, and away you go!

The list-traversing member functions—getcurrent(), getnext(), and getprev()—need only a little discussion. The getcurrent() function returns the address of the dirblock structure if the current entry pointer current is not NULL. In other words, getcurrent() assumes nothing has happened, but you want to get a new copy of the current entry pointer for some reason (there is one good reason, as shown in Listing 12.9).

getnext() and getprev() move to the next or previous directory list entry, respectively, assuming there is another entry in the indicated direction. If repositioning does occur, the directory block structure (which is an exact copy of the Microsoft C/C++ struct _find_t) is copied into the dirblock structure, which is part of the dir class object itself, and the address of dirblock is returned to the caller. Notice also that both these functions take precautions to prevent the current pointer from "falling off the ends" of the list; current is never NULL unless the list is empty.

Once again, all the hard work is finished when you have designed and coded the class declaration and member functions. Using the dir class is simple enough, as illustrated by the program usedir.cpp in Listing 12.9.

Listing 12.9. usedir.cpp. A program that demonstrates the dir class, using a global class object.

```
1   #include "dir.hpp"
2
3   dir workdir( "c:\\source\\12", "*.*" );
4
5   void main()
6   {
7     struct _find_t *entry;
8
9   // ------------------------------------------------------------
10  // Display the directory as requested
```

```
11    // ----------------------------------------------------------
12
13      entry = workdir.getcurrent();
14      while ( entry ) {
15        printf( " %-15s %6ld\n", entry->name, entry->size );
16        entry = workdir.getnext();
17      }
18
19    // ----------------------------------------------------------
20    // Find and navigate to the next higher directory
21    // ----------------------------------------------------------
22
23      getch();
24      while( NULL !=
25        ( entry = workdir.getprev() ) ) ;
26
27      entry = workdir.getcurrent();
28      while ( entry ) {
29        if ( !strcmp( entry->name, ".." ) ) break;
30        entry = workdir.getnext();
31      }
32      workdir.nagate();
33
34      entry = workdir.getcurrent();
35      while ( entry ) {
36        printf( " %-15s %6ld\n", entry->name, entry->size );
37        entry = workdir.getnext();
38      }
39
40    // ----------------------------------------------------------
41    // Display an altogether different directory
42    // ----------------------------------------------------------
43
44      getch();
45      workdir.reset( "\\", "*.bat" );
46
47      entry = workdir.getcurrent();
48      while ( entry ) {
49        printf( " %-15s %6ld\n", entry->name, entry->size );
50        entry = workdir.getnext();
51      }
52
53    }
```

Using dir class objects is so simple, in fact, that only one thing in Listing 12.9 needs to be explained. You should supply a pointer to a struct _find_t and initialize it with the getcurrent() member function in the following circumstances:

■ *When you first create the dir object (by declaring it or creating it new).* You need to pick up the address of the first entry in the list at this time.

■ *When you use the reset() member function to switch to a different directory.* Because the list is reinstated at this time, the old pointers no longer apply.

■ *When you use the navigate() member function to move up or down the directory tree.* Because navigation is just another method of selecting a new subdirectory and resetting, the list is reinstated in this case also.

■ *When you use the getnext() or getprev() function until your working pointer is NULL.* The dir class member functions never allow the *internal* entry pointers to become NULL (unless the list is empty), but such functions may *return* a null pointer if you attempt to run off either end of the list.

The fourth item in the preceding list requires a little amplification. Suppose, for example, you are traversing the list forward, using getnext(). When the internal current pointer is already positioned on the last entry in the list, getnext() returns NULL, but current is not changed. Therefore, calling getcurrent() initializes your local pointer with a valid address—the address of the last element in the list. The same principle also applies to traversing the directory list backward.

Initializing Class Objects

When you declare an integer data object with an initializer, you can easily see what happens when the integer is initialized. Notice, for example, the following line of code:

```
int a = 37;
```

There is no doubt that an integer a is being defined and that the value 37 must be assigned to it.

What must happen when a class object is created and initialized is perhaps not so obvious. Class objects can have constructors, copy constructors, and overloaded constructors. You can use constructors to implicitly convert other types to initialize a class object, and some class objects can take plain initializer lists. These options are discussed in this section.

Using Constructors To Initialize Class Objects

The `dir` class presented in Listings 12.7 and 12.8 illustrates two ways you can use constructors to initialize a class object. The `dir` class has both a default constructor (which can be called with no arguments) and an overloaded constructor (which can be called with arguments). Remember, you can have more than one overloaded version of the constructor.

The constructor's main job is to initialize the object—to take a block of memory and shape it into a valid class object. A constructor can do three things toward this end:

■ *A constructor function can call other member functions of the same class.* You may have designed some member functions whose purpose is to control or modify the object. You can call those member functions freely from the constructor function.

■ *A constructor function can access all data members, both private and public.* Class member data objects have many of the same characteristics of plain C data objects. Because one of those characteristics is the need for initialization, the constructor should ensure that all member data variables have a legal initial value. Referring to an uninitialized class member *pointer*, for example, can have the same result as referring to any other uninitialized pointer—disaster!

■ *A constructor function can call any of the compiler's library functions.* You need to be sure the correct header file has been included in the source module where the call to the library function occurs.

The ability to call any of the standard (or Microsoft C/C++ extended) library functions from a constructor is important, even critical. It would not have been possible, for example, to write the `msmouse` class if the `int86()` library function were not available to initialize and control the mouse. Yet C is a "foreign" language to C++. A linkage specification is required to allow calls to both C and C++ functions within the same program. A linkage specification informs the compiler of which language the called function uses.

The default linkage specification in C++ is to C++ functions, but the Microsoft C/C++ standard headers are already set up to prevent confusion and allow free access to all library functions from a C++ program. How Microsoft C/C++ does this, along with how you can set up your own header files to do the same thing, is covered in Chapter 14, in the section "Controlling Linkage Problems with Standard C Include Files."

The job of the constructor function is to make sure every data object and pointer member is given a legal starting value. If the class has multiple overloaded constructors, you must make sure each version does the job completely.

Furthermore, a constructor can be invoked in several different ways (which is the same as saying that a class object can be declared in several different ways). The default constructor can be invoked in two ways. You can use the constructor to convert another (basic) object type, and you can invoke the constructor directly. Listing 12.10 shows all these methods.

Listing 12.10. colorobj.cpp. A program that demonstrates the use of constructors in initializing class objects.

```
1   #include <stdlib.h>
2   #include <stdio.h>
3
4   #define RED    0
5   #define BLUE   1
6   #define GREEN 2
7
8   char *colornames[] = {
9     "Red", "Blue", "Green"
10  };
11
12  class colorobj {
13    int color;
14  public:
15    colorobj() { color = RED; }
16    colorobj( int icolor ) { color = icolor; }
17    colorobj( colorobj &other ) {
18      color = other.color;
19      printf( "My new color is %s!\n",
20             colornames[color] );
21    }
22  };
23
24  void main()
25  {
26    colorobj c1;                      // create a RED object
27    colorobj c2();               // create another RED object
28    colorobj c3 = BLUE; // create BLUE object by conversion
29    colorobj c4 = colorobj( GREEN ); //now call constructor
30    colorobj c5 = c4;            // use the copy constructor
31  }
```

Lines 26 and 27 of Listing 12.10 are equivalent. Both these class object definitions cause the default constructor to be invoked. As you can see by comparing these two lines, using the default constructor means you can either specify an empty argument list or just leave it off altogether.

Line 16 declares a constructor that accepts one argument (an integer specifying the desired color). You can, of course, define a class object by using this constructor in the usual manner:

```
colorobj cobj( RED ); // Use a macro name for argument
```

What is not so apparent in line 16 is that a constructor which accepts a single argument means a conversion from the argument type to the class type is to be performed. This in turn means the preceding line of code is equivalent to line 28 of Listing 12.10. You could code line 28 in this way:

```
colorobj c3( BLUE );
```

This line achieves exactly the same result.

Finally, you can invoke the constructor explicitly, as shown in line 29 of Listing 12.10. Notice that the constructor/class name on the right side of the assignment in line 29 specifies no object name: The constructor is being called directly. Notice, too, that this is not the same thing as invoking the copy constructor. Even though the right side of the assignment must obviously be copied to the object on the left, the user's copy constructor is not used to do so.

Line 29, when executed, does not cause the copy constructor (lines 17 through 21) to be executed. You can tell this because the copy constructor displays a message on the system console when the copy constructor is executed. Line 30, however, is a classic instance of using the copy constructor to initialize one object from another. In fact, line 30 is included in this sample program simply to demonstrate that the other methods do not involve a user-defined copy constructor.

Using Initializer Lists

Just as you can initialize a plain C aggregate object (structure, union, or array) with an initializer list, you can initialize a class object with an initializer list—if certain stringent requirements are met. To have an initializer list, a class object cannot have a constructor function (not even a default one), private or protected members, virtual functions, or base classes (that is, the class object cannot be an object of a derived class). In other words, initializer lists are useful mainly with objects of a class declared with the struct keyword. For example, look at the following class declaration:

```
struct IL {
  int a, b, c;
};
```

The class object shown here meets all the requirements for an initializer list. You can then initialize an IL class object like this:

```
IL threeints = { 1, 2, 3 };
```

An interesting and useful variation on the theme of initializer lists is the array of class objects. When you define an array of class objects, you can write an initializer list for the array, and each array element—which is a class object—can have a constructor. Suppose, for example, you are writing a large and complicated modeling program that requires six lifo arrays (refer to Chapter 11) for various purposes. You can write the array definition like this:

```
lifo request_que[6] = {
  lifo( 4096 );
  lifo( 8192 );
};
```

But wait! The array of lifo objects has six elements, yet only two entries are specified in the initializer list. What happened to the other four initializers? The compiler will generate the other four initializers with explicit calls to the default lifo constructor. The preceding code fragment, then, is equivalent to the following fragment:

```
lifo request_que[6] = {
  lifo( 4096 );
  lifo( 8192 );
  lifo();
  lifo();
  lifo();
  lifo();
};
```

Even though the lifo class has constructor functions, it is not the class for which the initializer list is provided; the initializer list is supplied for the array. There is one catch: If you omit any of the initializers, the class being used must have a default constructor. Conversely, if the class being used in an array has no default constructor, you cannot omit any of the initializers.

Exercises

The following exercises give you practice in defining and using Microsoft C/C++ class objects:

1. Get a copy of the *Microsoft Mouse Programmer's Guide* and review the mouse functions available. Extend the capability of the msmouse class to include more of these functions. Don't forget to declare new member functions in msmouse.hpp and to define the functions in msmouse.cpp.

2. To determine the size of a class object, first realize that the class declaration's function prototypes serve two purposes: to provide a prototype declaration and to establish the relationship of the class with an associated member function. Neither inline nor out-of-line member functions physically reside in the class object. A Microsoft C/C++ class object's size is thus the sum of the sizes of the data members, and nothing more. Recall also that static data members reside outside an object.

   Armed with that knowledge, make an estimate of the size of a `dbllist` linked list object and then investigate what circumstances would require you to use global, local, and arbitrary-duration objects. What kind of design consideration is most important in reaching your decision? Here's a tip: Storage for the list elements themselves resides *outside* the class object.

3. Add support macros to the `dbllist` class to allow calls to member functions, using a type name rather than a specific byte count. You may want to refer to Chapter 11 to review how such macros were constructed for the `lifo` class.

4. Write another version of the usedir.cpp program. Include such features as mouse support and a scrollable window for the directory list, using the Microsoft C/C++ `_settextwindow()` function. Mouse support can consist of scrolling a text file when the user clicks the left button on the file's directory entry, and navigating to a new subdirectory when the user clicks the right button on the file's list entry. This exercise is fairly advanced, so don't get discouraged if it takes a while to write the program.

5. Design and code a class that has several constructors. Write a sequence of code defining objects of that class and invoking the constructors in several different ways.

6. Design and code a class declaration that uses the `class` keyword to declare the class but can still permit an object definition with an initializer list. What did you have to do to get the code to compile correctly?

Summary

This chapter covered the basics of defining local, global, and arbitrary class objects, as well as how to initialize class objects. You learned the following important points:

- *You can define local, global, and arbitrary class objects.* Class objects generally follow the scope and duration rules of other C objects. Access to class object members, however, is complicated by the fact that a class is a scope in C++.

■ *You can write a variety of constructor functions for initializing class objects.* These functions include default constructors, overloaded constructors, and copy constructors. Furthermore, you can invoke a constructor (that is, define a class object) in various ways: using the default constructor, using a constructor to convert types across the assignment operator, and explicitly invoking a constructor.

■ *In certain cases—most notably when the class has no constructor—you can initialize a class object by using an initializer list, just as you can for aggregate C objects.*

Accessing C++ Objects

You saw in Chapter 12, "Creating C++ Objects," that declaring class objects involves more technique than declaring plain C objects. Accessing class objects is also more complicated than accessing plain C objects. This chapter examines in detail some of the complex methods of accessing class objects and their member components.

Specifically, you learn about the scope resolution operator; look more closely at the C++ scoping rules; learn how to use the this pointer to communicate with class objects (as well as how to control this); become familiar with the reference operator, its evolution, and its use; and take a look at using class objects as arguments to functions (both member and nonmember).

Using the Scope Resolution Operator

You have already seen in the preceding chapters what the scope resolution operator is and how it works. This section provides more detail on the subject of scope resolution, expanding on familiar topics and introducing advanced topics. You learn about the general uses of the scope resolution operator, the use of scope resolution for syntax control, and the control of ambiguities with the scope resolution operator.

508

Using Scope Resolution In General

The scope resolution operator (::) was first introduced in Chapter 11, "Using C++ Classes," in a discussion of the difference between visibility and access control. This section clarifies some of the concepts presented there.

Recall that the general syntax for using the scope resolution operator looks like this:

```
classname::membername
```

This form of *membername* is called the *fully qualified member name,* or just the *qualified name.* The method of writing it is like that of writing a fully qualified filename for DOS—by using the drive, path, filename, and filename extension. In either case, the notation fully specifies which object (or file) is to be referenced. One significant difference, of course, is that a class member can be either a data object or a member function. The scope resolution operator tells C++ which member function to execute also. More than one class can have member functions with the same name.

You can also use the scope resolution operator to inform the compiler that you want to refer to the *global copy* of a variable or function name, not to a class member version. In this case, you write the scope resolution operator *without* the preceding class name:

```
::objectname
```

An important use for this form of the scope resolution operator is to *unhide* a global function or variable. A function or variable can become hidden (from the perspective of class members) when both a global copy and a member copy of an object exist with the same name. Look, for example, at the following code fragment:

```
int A;
...
class sumpin {
  int A;
public:
  void showit() {
    printf( "%d\n", A );    // display member A
    printf( "%d\n", ::A );  // display global A
  }
};
```

By the same token, you can contrive a case in which the class name is hidden. You can hide a class name by declaring an object (a nontype, nonclass name, such as an int object), function, or enumeration in the *same scope* with the class declaration. Now you have both an *object* and a *type* with the same name.

In this case, the scope resolution operator won't help you much. Scope resolution helps you choose which of several possible objects to use, but it can't unravel the difference between an object name and a type name. In the following short program, the class is hidden (and the program won't compile either):

```
#include <stdio.h>

class A {
public:
  static int qq() { return 37; }
};

int A = 64; // This is the culprit -- it hides class A

void main()
{
  A doodad; // We want a class object, but no dice

  printf( "%d\n", doodad.qq() );
}
```

When you try to compile this program, Microsoft C/C++ does fine until it reaches the definition A doodad. The intention is to define a doodad class object, but it is masked by the int A object. The compiler devoutly declares that doodad is undefined.

If you can't use the scope resolution operator to get out of this scrape, what can you do? Is it still possible to have a class A and an integer A? It is possible if you use the class keyword (or the struct or union keyword) to inform the compiler just what kind of object you mean to define. Here is the doodad program rewritten so that it compiles and runs correctly:

```
#include <stdio.h>

class A {
public:
  static int qq() { return 37; }
};

int A = 64;  // Still hides the class, but there's a cure ...

void main()
{
  class A doodad; // This is how you get out of the bind

  printf( "%d\n", doodad.qq() );
}
```

To unhide the class name, you just add the `class` keyword to the declaration: `class A doodad`. Thus, even though the scope resolution operator is not a cure for all ills, it is still nice to have a `class A doodad` handy, don't you think?

The ANSI base document also allows the use of multiple scope qualifiers to access members of nested classes. The following code fragment provides an example:

```
#include <stdio.h>

struct A {
  struct B {
    static double pi;
  };
};

double A::B::pi = 3.1415926;


void main()
{
  printf( "%lf\n", A::B::pi );
}
```

True nested classes are new to the C++ language and are fully supported in Microsoft C/C++.

Using Scope Resolution for Syntax Control

Two uses of the scope resolution operator are related specifically to syntax requirements. You have already seen one of these uses repeatedly in sample code here, and the other use has been presented briefly. Follow these rules for the two uses relating to syntax control:

■ *You must use the scope resolution operator when defining an out-of-line class member function.* The sole purpose of this rule is to provide a vehicle for informing the compiler of the class to which a member function belongs (other classes may have identical member function names). It is quite common to define functions out-of-line, as illustrated by the syntax of the following code fragment:

```
class book{
...
    int page;
public:
...
```

```
int turnpage();    // Member function declaration
};
...
int book::turnpage() // Out-of-line member function definition
{
  return ++page;
}
```

■ *You must use the scope resolution operator when referring to a static class data member without using a specific class object.* Static data members exist independently of any particular class object, and one copy of a static member is common to all objects of that class. These facts explain the behavior of the following short program:

```
#include <stdlib.h>
#include <string.h>

class star {
public:
  static char name[21];
  star() { strcpy( name, "NONAME" ); }
  star( char *sname ) { strcpy( name, sname ); }
  void tellname() { printf( "%s\n", name ); }
};

char star::name[21]; // Define storage for static star::name

void main()
{
  star s1 = "Betelgeuse";
  star s2 = "Rigel";

  s1.tellname();    // Both objects report name as RIGEL
  s2.tellname();

  strcpy( star::name, "Aldebaran" ); //No particular object!
  printf( "%s\n", star::name );

  s1.tellname();   // Now both objects report name as ALDEBARAN
  s2.tellname();
}
```

Because there is only one copy of the member variable `star::name`, any change to that variable (regardless of which object is referenced) changes the name for all objects. Additionally, the variable can be referenced independently of any particular class object because of the fully qualified name `star::name`. Notice that while `name` is defined within the class definition, storage for `name` must be allocated independently of any class, hence, the declaration

```
char star::name[21];
```

that follows the class definition for `star`.

Controlling Ambiguities with Scope Resolution

In the last section, you saw how the presence of a class declaration and type definition with the same name in the same scope hides one of the names from the compiler. When a name is hidden, the compiler knows only about one of the declarations. It is also possible to use the same name for a class member that *appears in more than one class* in such a way that the compiler can't determine which member you mean when referring to the member. The compiler considers a reference to that member name *ambiguous*. Most ambiguities of reference occur when you are deriving one class from another.

In fact, all the uses of the scope resolution operator covered in this section look ahead to the subject on derived classes. Even though class derivation is not fully covered until Chapter 17, "Using C++ Derived Classes," all the major uses of the scope resolution operator are documented in this chapter.

For now, class derivation can be defined as instructing the compiler to create a new class just like an old one—except for a few differences. The old class is called the *base class*, and the new class is called the *derived class*.

All the members of the base class can be accessed as if they were members of the derived class *unless* you redefine the base class members in the derived class (this is how you tell the compiler what is different). The basic methods of class derivation are illustrated in the sample program in Listing 13.1.

Listing 13.1. docu.cpp. A program that derives classes from other classes.

```
1   #include <iostream.h>
2
3   class document {
4   public:
5     int pages;
6     void blurb() {
7       cout << "I have " << pages << " pages.\n";
8     }
9   };
```

```
10
11   class pamphlet : public document {
12   public:
13     pamphlet() { pages = 10; }
14   };
15
16   class book : public document {
17   public:
18     int chapters;
19     book( int np, int nc ) {
20       pages = np;
21       chapters = nc;
22     }
23     void blurb() {
24       cout << "I have " << pages << " pages and "
25             << chapters << " chapters.\n";
26     }
27   };
28
29   void main()
30   {
31     pamphlet flyer;
32     book uc( 900, 21 );
33
34     flyer.blurb();
35     uc.blurb();
36     uc.document::blurb();
37   }
```

The program in Listing 13.1 declares a base class, document, from which the classes pamphlet and book are then derived. This listing contains a new keyword count and the inserter operator <<. count is used to create program output. The use of count is fully explained in Chapter 16, "Using C++ Streams."

A pamphlet needs to record only page count (which is fixed at 10 pages), whereas a book must record both page count and chapter count. Because of this difference between the two derived classes, the blurb() member function must be different for the two classes.

Notice the basic, uncomplicated blurb() function is defined inline in the base class document (lines 6 through 8). The base class version of blurb() reports only page count for the document. Because a pamphlet is a document that needs only a page count, no data members are declared within the pamphlet class. A pamphlet, you may notice, can still get to the pages data member, which is declared only in the document base class (line 5).

A book is a more complicated form of document, however. A book must keep track of chapters as well as pages. The book class therefore declares the chapters data member (line 18) and relies on the base class declaration of pages. Furthermore, because the reporting process for a book is usually more complicated, the book class redefines the base class's blurb() member function.

Now consider the use of the scope resolution operator with base and derived classes. Line 35 of Listing 13.1 shows a normal call to a book's blurb() function. Both the page count and the chapter count are reported as a result of a call to blurb().

It is possible, however, to report only the page count for a book object if the *base class version* of blurb() can be reached. As illustrated in the function call in line 36, you can indeed reach the base class version by fully qualifying the function name with the base class name.

The blurb() member function shown in Listing 13.1 is not really ambiguous. The *derived class's* member function (or data object) is always meant, unless you override the reference by using the scope resolution operator.

Ambiguities can arise quickly, though, when a derived class inherits from two base classes instead of one. Suppose you have a chapter class and a page class, both of which have a size() member function. Partial declarations for these classes might look like this:

```
class chapter {
  unsigned numpages;
public:

  ...
  unsigned size() { return numpages; }
};

class page {
  unsigned numchars;
public:

  ...
  unsigned size() { return numchars; }
};
```

The purpose of the size() function is clearly different in the chapter and page classes. Now suppose a book class is to be derived from both of the preceding classes, and the book class is to have its own size() member function. The member function book::size() is to compute the total book size, using the size() functions of its base classes.

Whew! How in the world can you keep track of which `size()` function is meant at a given point in the code? Again, using the scope resolution operator is the answer. The `book` class, together with its `size()` function, can be written in this way:

```
class book : public chapter, public page {
  unsigned numchaps;
public:
  unsigned size() {
    return numchaps * chapter::size() * page::size();
  }
};
```

Here, class `book` is derived from both the `chapter` and `page` classes. This is known as *multiple inheritance*—where a derived class inherits characteristics from more than one class. In this example, it is assumed every chapter has the same page count and every page has the same character count. Nevertheless, you can see the scope resolution operator at work, resolving otherwise ambiguous references.

Deriving classes from other classes can cause other kinds of ambiguity—for example, when the base class contains *virtual* member functions. Virtual functions provide a *pass through* feature for derived classes that simplifies the process of selecting the correct copy of otherwise identical member functions. The classic example of this feature is a `shape` class, which is the base class for a number of specific classes, such as `circle`, `square`, `arc`—each of which has its own `draw()` member function. You can code the shape class like this:

```
class shape {
  ...
public:
  virtual void draw() {
    setgraphmode( getgraphmode() );
  }
  ...
};
```

This declaration sets up a member function so that a derived class can declare a member function with the *same type* (that is, having *both* the same return type and the same function parameters). The derived class's copy of the member function is the one that is now called, even if you should call it through a pointer to the base function's type. Using the `class shape` declaration just given, you might derive the following `class circle`:

```
class circle : public shape {
  int xcenter, ycenter, radius;
  ...
```

```
public:
  void draw() {
    circle( xcenter, ycenter, radius );
  }
};
```

The virtual function facility guarantees that the correct version of the draw routine is called for a specific class object. For example, if you now define a circle object and draw() it, the circle::draw() function is invoked:

```
void main()
{
  circle c1;

  c1.draw(); // Use the circle virtual draw() function
}
```

The virtual function facility, however, guarantees the circle::draw() member function is used even if the object is accessed through a pointer that has type *pointer to* shape. That is, the following code fragment still uses the circle::draw() member function, even though a pointer that has been forced to type pointer to shape is used:

```
void main()
{
  shape *x1;   // Here is a pointer to base class
  circle c1;   // Here is the derived class object

  x1 = &c1     // Convert *circle to *base
  x1->draw(); // Use the circle virtual draw() function
}
```

What does all this have to do with the scope resolution operator? For an answer to this question, consider the possibility that you may want to use a virtual function (guaranteeing that the derived class's version is normally used) and still be able to access the base class's copy of the function. The scope resolution operator does the trick, *suppressing the virtual call mechanism.*

In the case of the shape and circle functions just shown, you might want to access the shape::draw() function from within the circle::draw() function (perhaps to initialize the screen before drawing the circle). To accomplish this, you can modify the circle::draw() function:

```
class circle : public shape {
  int xcenter, ycenter, radius;
  ...
public:
```

```
void draw() {    // this is circle::draw()
  shape::draw(); // call base class version
  circle( xcenter, ycenter, radius );
}
};
```

You may rarely need to use both versions of a virtual function (or to override the version that is used), but the scope resolution operator enables you to do so.

Understanding the C++ Scope Rules

The concept of the scope of a name in C++ is identical to the concept of scope in plain C. The *scope* of a name is just the part of the program's source code that can refer to the name. In C++, as in plain C, the scope of a name implies something about both its *visibility* and its *duration*.

Specific scope rules in C++ differ somewhat from plain C scope rules, however, because of the added requirement that in C++ a class object has its own scope. This section first examines the differences between C++ and C scope rules and then summarizes C++ scope rules.

Understanding the Differences Between C and C++ Scope

C and C++ have several scope and scope-related differences. These differences become important if you must "switch gears" mentally between the two languages. The greatest problem caused by these differences is, of course, you can forget momentarily whether you are using C or C++ because the languages are so similar. The following list shows the main differences between the two languages:

- *C++ scope rules generally follow the ANSI C standard scope rules.* When you are not dealing with classes and class objects directly, or with one of the exceptions noted in this list, you should handle C++ scoping issues just as you handle C scoping issues.

- *C++ allows the declaration of local (auto) variables anywhere a C statement can appear.* Remember that plain C requires the declaration of auto variables at *the top of the block* in which they appear. The following code fragment, for example, is legal in C++ but not in standard C:

```
void some_function( int number )
{
```

```
    int i = 0; // here's a local variable

while ( number ) {
  --number;
  ++i;
}

    int j = 0; // here's another local variable

while ( i ) {
  --i;
  ++j;
}
}
```

■ *A C++ function cannot be called before it is declared.* In plain C, you can
call a function that has not yet been declared. The C compiler assumes
that it is to do no type checking of arguments, and also that the function
returns an `int`. In fact, declaring a plain C function *later* (with different
parameters or return type) causes a redefinition compiler error. A C++
compiler makes no such dangerous assumptions. You *must* declare a
function in C++ before you call it.

■ *A class name can be hidden accidentally by an explicit declaration of an
object within the class.* Because a `struct` or a `class` is a scope in C++, you
can unintentionally hide a type name (a class name) by declaring an interior object that has the same name as the `class` or `struct`, or by declaring
a nonmember variable in the same scope as the class having the same
name.

Accidentally hiding a class name is not as much of a problem in plain C (although you can rather easily block visibility to an object of the same type in an
outer scope). For example, the following code fragment (in plain C) shows that
a `struct` containing a member with the same name as the `struct` tag does not
hide the structure name:

```
#include <stdio.h>
#include <stdlib.h>

struct xxx {
  int xxx;
};

struct xxx obj;

void main()
```

```
{
  obj.xxx = 37;
}
```

This code fragment compiles with no errors and runs properly. No conflict occurs between the member integer xxx and the structure name xxx. A problem can arise, however, because C++ permits you to define your own types, and those type declarations (that is, the class declarations) comprise their own scope. A member variable with the same name as the class can hide the class name, requiring the use of the scope resolution operator in member functions to sort out the intended reference. Alternatively, a nonmember variable in the same scope as the class can also hide the class name, requiring the use of the class or struct keyword to clarify the reference. Samples of both these cases are shown earlier in this chapter.

Examining the C++ Scope Rules

C++ has four kinds of scope: local, function, file, and class. Notice the significance of each kind:

■ *Local scope*

C++ local scope is the same as for plain C. A name declared within a block (that is, an auto variable) is local to that block. A local variable can be used, after the point of declaration, only within that block and within inner blocks enclosed by it. Notice the *point of declaration* is defined to be directly after the complete declaration but before any initializer for the object. Notice, too, that class *objects* can be local variables just like anything else. Finally, remember that a C++ local declaration does not have to be at the top of the block—such a declaration can be anywhere within the block.

■ *Function scope*

Only labels have function scope, and they are in scope only within the function in which they appear. Therefore, the same label name can be used in different functions without confusion.

■ *File scope*

File scope is the same as global scope. A name declared outside any block or class declaration has global scope. A global name can be used anywhere within the source file, after the point of declaration.

■ *Class scope*

Class scope is new with C++ and does not exist in plain C. The name of a class *member* (object or function) is local to the class. A class member name can be used in the following ways:

1. A class member name can be used directly, without qualification, only by a member function of the same class.

2. A class member name can be referred to by a function outside the class, through the class member operator (.). This, of course, is true only if you are not using a pointer to the class object and only if the member has `public` accessibility.

3. A class member name can be referred to by a function outside the class, when the class object is being accessed by a pointer, through the class member pointer operator (`->`). Accessibility rules apply here, also.

4. A class member name can be referred to in some circumstances if you use the fully qualified name with the scope resolution operator. Using the `class::member` notation is sometimes needed to resolve ambiguities, as noted earlier in this chapter.

These C++ scoping rules deal with both ordinary and class objects:

■ *C++ names are tested for ambiguity first.* You have already seen that more than one class can use the same member names (because they are different scopes), that function definitions can be overloaded (resulting in multiple functions with the same names but different types), and that class inheritance can cause some ambiguity in the use of names. All these sources of confusion must be resolved first. Only when a name is completely unambiguous does the C++ compiler begin to apply access rules. Finally, when it has been determined there are no access errors, object type checking is performed.

■ *Global objects, functions, and enumerations are tested next.* These entities must have the following characteristics:

1. They are declared *outside* any block or class declaration.

2. They *can* be prefixed with the unary scope operator (`::`). When the scope operator is used without a class name in front of it, the global copy of the object, function, or enumerator is meant. You see this use later, particularly in Chapter 15, "Using C++ Constructors and Destructors."

3. They *cannot* be qualified with the binary scope resolution operator (`class::name`), and they *cannot* be qualified with either form of the class member operator. (That is, `obj.name` and `ptr->name` are by definition not global names.)

■ *Class membership is tested next.* If a qualified name (`class::name`, `obj.name`, or `ptr->name`) is used, `name` must be either a member of class or a member of another class derived from class. Furthermore, if a name such as `B->name` is used, where `B` is a class that has overloaded the `->` operator, `B->` must eventually resolve to `A->` (that is, `B->` must resolve to a simple pointer to a class object somewhere in the chain). Notice, for example, the following code fragment:

```
#include <iostream.h>

class A {
public:
  void blurb() { cout << "Hello!\r\n" ; }
};

class B : public A {
public:
  A* operator->() { return (A *)this; }
};

void main()
{
  B obj;  // Note that this is not a pointer!!

  obj->blurb(); // Route through operator->() logic
  obj.blurb();  // Do not route through operator->() logic
}
```

The class object `obj` is not a pointer, but the overloaded `operator->()` creates a simple pointer, as if `obj->A::blurb()` had been originally coded. The fact that class B here is derived from class A is only incidental.

■ *Ordinary local variables are checked next.* These names are not qualified in any of the ways described so far but are used in nonmember functions. If a name is used within a block but not declared within that same block, the compiler first checks to see whether the name is declared in an enclosing block, and only then checks to see whether the name is a global name. As mentioned earlier, local names hide names that are the same (regardless of type) and that reside in enclosing blocks or in file scope. An interesting side effect of this rule is that names in different scopes can never be overloaded versions of one another.

■ *Local variables in nonstatic member functions are checked next.* This phase of scope resolution proceeds exactly as for ordinary local variables, with one additional restriction. The declaration of a member name can hide member names in base classes, as well as those in enclosing blocks and global names.

■ *Local variables in static member functions are checked next.* If none of the preceding restrictions apply, a local variable in a static member function must be declared within that static function, must be declared within an enclosing block, must be a static member of the class or a base class, or must be a global name.

■ *The scope of function arguments is checked next.* The scope of function argument names depends on whether a function *declaration* or a function *definition* is being checked. If a function declaration is being checked, the argument name goes out of scope as soon as the declaration is complete. (That is why formal parameter names do not have to be the same as argument names in the function definition.) If a function definition is being checked, the argument names have scope local to the function. (That is why argument names can be used anywhere in the function body, and also why actual argument names do not have to match formal argument names.)

■ *The scope of constructor initializers is checked last.* A constructor initializer is a sophisticated feature that allows constructor function arguments to be manipulated. Constructor initializers are covered in Chapter 15. For now, the essential point is that a constructor initializer can refer to the constructor's argument names.

Special circumstances in scoping arise when functions are declared to be friends of a class. Friend functions have the following characteristics:

■ *Friend functions are not within the scope of the class.* When a function is declared to be a friend of a class (this is done by the class declaration, as explained in Chapter 11), the function is still not within the scope of the class. That is why friend functions must be passed an argument indicating which specific class object the friend function is to manipulate. Notice, for example, the following code fragment:

```
class A {
  int priv_data;
  ...
public:
  friend int get_data( A& );
...
};
...
int get_data( A& argobj )
{
  return argobj.priv_data; //must qualify member name
}
```

■ *Friend functions have access to private and protected members of a class.* The preceding code fragment also illustrates this point. Clearly, friend functions are an important part of the interface to a class object, even though they are not part of the class's scope. Because a class declaration must grant class friendship (it cannot be usurped), there is no violation of the class protection mechanism.

Communicating with C++ Objects

In plain C programs, you have data (which is manipulated), and you have functions (which perform the manipulations). Data and functions are two clearly different things with different purposes.

Even in plain C, however, there is a slight blurring of the distinction between data and functions. A function has a return type that must be a *data* type, and a function *call* can be placed directly in expressions and statements. Function calls are used the same way variables are. Notice the following example:

```
x = sqrt( 3.0 ); /* Take the square root of three */
```

There is an even greater blurring of the distinction between functions and data in C++ because class objects contain both data and functions. The structure of C++ encourages you to think of class objects as having some intelligence (only in the computer meaning of the word) and as being able to perform their own data manipulations. In OOP systems generally, the concept is one of *sending messages* to objects instead of calling functions and pointing them at some data.

Even so, you would not expect C++ to be unrecognizable to the C programmer, and it is not. Naturally, the method of sending messages to C++ class objects is simply to call a member function.

Sending Messages to Objects

You are already familiar with the plain C structure member operator (.) and the structure pointer operator (->). Now you need to become familiar with the C++ syntax that allows you to declare functions within a structure or class without having to resort to pointers to functions to do so.

If you have kept up with the developments in ANSI C, you may be somewhat familiar with the C++ syntax for calling a member function. Consider, for example, the following short program, which is 100-percent plain (ANSI) C:

```
#include <stdlib.h>
#include <stdio.h>

void message( void );  /* Prototype the message function */

struct holder {
  void (*router)( void ); /* Pointer to message function */
};

void main()
```

```
{
  struct holder mobj;                /* Declare the struct */

  mobj.router = message;    /* Initialize ptr to function */
  (*mobj.router)();          /* Call it the classic C way */
  mobj.router();             /* Call it the ANSI C way */
}

void message( void )
{
  puts( "What a funny way to invoke a function!" );
}
```

Notice in this short program that the structure declaration (this is not a class, remember) contains a pointer to a function, coded in the usual manner for C function pointers. Later, in the main() function, that pointer is first initialized and then the function is actually called in a way instantly recognizable to pre-ANSI C programmers. The last statement in main(), however, introduces something new with ANSI C. Once the pointer to a function is properly set up, the function can be called *without* the older syntax of an indirection operator surrounded by parentheses.

That isn't very difficult, is it? Well, if you followed that development, you just mastered the basic C++ syntax for calling a member function! You shouldn't be too surprised. Remember that C++ classes are C structures with extended capabilities, and there is no surprise at all.

Generally, then, you can call a class object's member function by using the structure member operator (now called the *class member operator*) or the structure pointer operator (now called the *class pointer operator*). Notice the syntax for these methods of calling member functions:

```
objectname.memberfunction( mbrfunction args );
objectname->memberfunction( mbrfunction args );
```

It seems that the more things change, the more they stay the same, doesn't it? Now that you know the basic rationale for calling member functions (sending messages to class objects), you can examine a real class—one that does something useful—and see how to communicate with it by calling member functions.

Consider, for example, the lib class, which is a library object class. What is a library? A library is a file that contains multiple subfiles (a subfile is called a library member). Each member of a library is a file in its own right—it just happens to be contained within the library file. A member of a lib file can be anything you want it to be, such as a text file, a binary file, or an EXE file.

You may be asking yourself, isn't this the same thing as the library files that come with my C++ compiler? The lib class libraries do have some similarities, but the differences are quite important. The lib class in this illustration, then, has been designed to force a file extension of LBR for lib files to keep them separate from other LIB files.

There are two ways to distinguish lib library files. They are distinguished first by the way they organize member files internally, and second by the way they handle waste space after a member is deleted.

So that the physical organization of a lib file is maintained, a variation on a familiar technology is used here: doubly linked lists. The variation is that the link addresses are disk addresses, not memory addresses. In fact, to organize a library's contents and to manage free (waste) space at the same time, a lib file contains *two* linked lists, as shown in Figure 13.1.

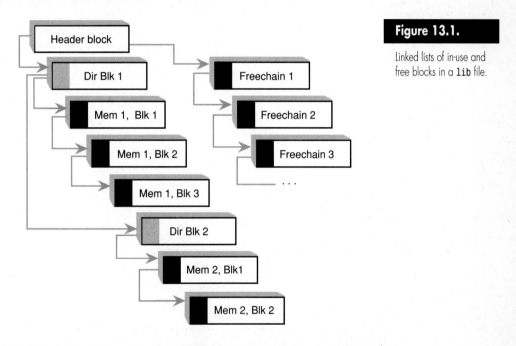

Figure 13.1.

Linked lists of in-use and free blocks in a lib file.

Figure 13.1 shows that the whole library file is anchored by a *header block*. Always the first block in the file, the header block is 19 bytes long. This block contains a disk address pointing to the first *data block*, and another disk address pointing to the first *free block*. All the data blocks are linked together, forming the *in-use* chain; and all the free blocks are linked together, forming the *free chain*. Figure 13.1 does not show all the detail, but the in-use and free chains are in fact doubly linked, much like a linked list kept in RAM.

The free chain is a simple doubly linked list, with no complications. All the empty data blocks (which are created when a member is deleted from the library) are kept in a single list so that one can be recovered and used when a new member is created or when an existing member needs more space. Recovering data blocks in this manner enables you to maintain a *self-reorganizing* library and thus avoid having to copy all the remaining members into another library file to eliminate dead space.

The in-use chain is a little more complicated. It is actually an indeterminate number of sublists woven together. The first of these sublists is the library's *directory*. The address in the header block pointing to the first in-use block actually points to the first directory block. Although there is only one anchor in the header for the in-use chain, there are any number of anchors in the directory entries for the member files. Each member file occupies a discrete linked list of data blocks, anchored by a directory entry but separate from the directory's list. Figure 13.2 illustrates the directory arrangement more clearly.

Figure 13.2.

Expanded view of a `lib` directory data block.

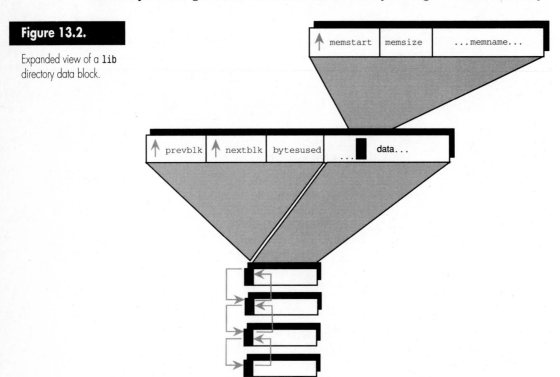

Like the data in a member file, the contents of a directory block reside in a data block. The data portion of the directory's linked list, as shown in Figure 13.2, contains a number of directory *entries* (each of which is 21 bytes long). A directory entry contains the following three fields:

- *The member's starting disk address.* The starting address of each member is kept in an `unsigned long` variable, as obtained by the ordinary `ftell()` function.

- *The member's length.* The length of each member is recorded as an unsigned long integer. This means that the size of each member conceivably could be as large as DOS allows a file to be.

- *The member's name.* A member name is the same as a DOS file (without drive or path information). This makes good sense because members are loaded from, and extracted to, ordinary DOS disk files.

Little more can be said about lib objects until you examine how the class is put together. Take a look at Listing 13.2, which contains the lib.hpp header file for the class.

Listing 13.2. lib.hpp. A header file for the library object.

```
1   #include <stdlib.h>
2   #include <stdio.h>
3   #include <string.h>
4   #include <direct.h>
5   #include <dos.h>
6
7   #define FALSE 0
8   #define TRUE 1
9
10  typedef struct {        // 19 byte header
11    char signature[7];        // signature string "LIBV10"
12    unsigned long dir;        // offset of first directory block
13    unsigned long freechain;  // offset of first free block
14    unsigned long eof;        // offset of end of freechain
15  } header;
16
17  typedef struct {        // 128 byte data blocks
18    unsigned long prevblk;    // offset of prevs blk in chain
19    unsigned long nextblk;    // offset of next blk in chain
20    int bytesused;            // bytes used in this block
21    unsigned char data[118];  // data storage for block
22  }datablock;
23
24  typedef struct {        // 21 byte directory entry
25    unsigned long memstart;   // first block of member
26    unsigned long memsize;    // size of member in bytes
27    char memname[13];         // mem name, with null byte
28  } entry;
29
30  typedef struct {        // struct for libseek and libtell
```

Listing 13.2. Continued.

```
31    unsigned long blockadr;    // byte address of disk block
32    int blockindex;            // byte index value at location
33  } lib_pos_t;
34
35  // ---------------------------------------------------------
36  // CLASS DECLARATION for lib object
37  // ---------------------------------------------------------
38  class lib {
39    header *hdr;
40    datablock *blk;
41    entry *ent;
42    int incore;              // flag on when unwritten block
43    lib_pos_t diradr;
44    lib_pos_t memadr;
45    FILE *libfile;
46    char *library;
47    int byteindex;
48    unsigned long bytecount; // for comparison to memsize
49    unsigned long curblock;  // disk address of cur datablock
50  public:
51    lib( char *libname );
52    ~lib();
53    void purgeblk();
54    void purgedir();
55    int readblk();
56    int writeblk();
57    int libseek( lib_pos_t *adr );
58    int libtell( lib_pos_t *adr );
59    int readhdr();
60    int writehdr();
61    int readn( unsigned char *buf, unsigned numbyte );
62    int writen( unsigned char *buf, unsigned numbyte );
63    int acquireblk();
64    int releaseblk();
65    int getnextblk();
66    int getprevblk();
67    int locate( char *member );
68    void listdir();
69    int addmem( char *member );
70    int delmem( char *member );
71    int listmem( char *member );
```

```
72    int extractmem( char *member, char *oname );
73    int unload( char *path );
74  };
```

The first thing you encounter in the lib.hpp header file, after the usual #include and #define directives, is a series of typedefs for the various structures used in the lib class. The typedef declarations provide storage layouts for a header type (the overall library header block), a datablock type (the linked record used for both data and free blocks), an entry type (a directory entry), and a lib_pos_t type (for reporting and setting the read/write position within a library member). All these typedefs appear in lines 10 through 33 of Listing 13.2.

The lib class declaration itself begins in line 38. Structured objects of the types just defined are declared, and several other important variables are declared in the private portion of the class. The integer incore is used internally to signal that a datablock buffer has received new data and needs to be written physically to disk. The libfile and library variables are the FILE and string objects, respectively, for manipulating and naming the library file.

The byteindex variable (line 47) is used internally to note the position of the next read or write, which uses the datablock currently in memory. The bytecount field appearing next keeps a running count of a member's size as it is being created or read back in. Finally, curblock keeps the physical disk address of the current datablock being read or written. If any of the member variables named in this paragraph should ever get out of kilter while a library file is being written, the file will be destroyed (so be careful not to misinterpret the use of member variables when modifying this program).

Most of the member function names declared in Listing 13.2 at least give a hint about what they do. Glance at the function declarations and then look over the lib.cpp source file shown in Listing 13.3. Following the listing is an explanation of how the member functions work.

Listing 13.3. lib.cpp. The member functions for the library object.

```
1  #include "lib.hpp"
2
3  // ------------------------------------------------------------
4  // lib() -- Constructor for lib object
5  // ------------------------------------------------------------
6  lib::lib( char *libname )
7  {
8     hdr = new header;
9     blk = new datablock;
```

Listing 13.3. Continued.

```
10    ent = new entry;
11    library = new char[81];
12
13    strcpy( library, libname );
14    if ( NULL == ( libfile = fopen( library, "rb+" ) ) ) {
15      if ( NULL == ( libfile = fopen( library, "wb" ) ) ) {
16        this->lib::~lib();    // if nothing works, kill it all
17      }
18      else {
19        strcpy( hdr->signature, "LIBV10" );
20        hdr->dir = 0UL;          // initialize the header block
21        hdr->freechain = 0UL;
22        hdr->eof = 0UL;
23        writehdr();
24        fclose( libfile );   // close-reopen the file normally
25        libfile = fopen( library, "rb+" );
26        byteindex = 0;                  // init internal variables
27        bytecount = 0;
28        curblock = 0UL;
29        diradr.blockadr = 0UL;
30        diradr.blockindex = 0;
31        memadr.blockadr = 0UL;
32        memadr.blockindex = 0;
33        incore = FALSE;
34      }
35    }
36    if ( !readhdr() )
37      this->lib::~lib();      // if you can't read header block
38    if ( strcmp( hdr->signature, "LIBV10" ) )
39      this->lib::~lib();          // or signature doesn't match
40  }
41
42  // ----------------------------------------------------------
43  // ~lib() -- Destructor for lib object
44  // ----------------------------------------------------------
45  lib::~lib()
46  {
47    delete hdr; // free all acquired areas
48    delete blk;
49    delete ent;
50    delete library;
```

```
51    fclose( libfile );
52  }
53
54  // ----------------------------------------------------------
55  // purgeblk() -- Clear all data from block buffer
56  // ----------------------------------------------------------
57  void lib::purgeblk()
58  {
59    blk->prevblk = 0UL;              // clear out the block buffer
60    blk->nextblk = 0UL;
61    blk->bytesused = 0;
62    memset( blk->data, '\0', 118 );
63
64  }
65
66  // ----------------------------------------------------------
67  // purgedir -- Clear directory entry buffer
68  // ----------------------------------------------------------
69  void lib::purgedir()
70  {
71    ent->memstart = 0UL;
72    ent->memsize = 0UL;
73    memset( ent->memname, '\xFF', 13 );
74  }
75
76  // ----------------------------------------------------------
77  // readblk() -- Physical read of block at curblock,
78  //              do not update curblock
79  // ----------------------------------------------------------
80  int lib::readblk()
81  {
82    byteindex = 0;
83    if ( 0 != fseek( libfile, curblock, SEEK_SET ) )
84      return FALSE;
85    if ( 1 > fread( blk, sizeof( datablock ), 1, libfile ) )
86      return FALSE;
87    incore = TRUE;
88    return TRUE;
89  }
90
91  // ----------------------------------------------------------
92  // writeblk() -- Physical write of block at curblock,
```

Listing 13.3. Continued.

```
93   //                    do not update curblock
94   // ----------------------------------------------------------
95   int lib::writeblk()
96   {
97     byteindex = 0;
98     if ( 0 != fseek( libfile, curblock, SEEK_SET ) )
99       return FALSE;
100    if ( 1 > fwrite( blk, sizeof( datablock ), 1, libfile ) )
101      return FALSE;
102    incore = FALSE;
103    return TRUE;
104  }
105
106  // ----------------------------------------------------------
107  // libseek() -- Seek to offset within a particular block
108  // ----------------------------------------------------------
109  int lib::libseek( lib_pos_t *adr )
110  {
111    curblock = adr->blockadr;
112    if ( !readblk() ) return FALSE;
113    byteindex = adr->blockindex;
114    return TRUE;
115  }
116
117  // ----------------------------------------------------------
118  // libtell() -- Report current block and offset position
119  // ----------------------------------------------------------
120  int lib::libtell( lib_pos_t *adr )
121  {
122    adr->blockadr = curblock;
123    adr->blockindex = byteindex;
124    return TRUE;
125  }
126
127  // ----------------------------------------------------------
128  // readhdr() -- Physical read of header
129  // ----------------------------------------------------------
130  int lib::readhdr()
131  {
132    if ( 0 != fseek( libfile, 0, SEEK_SET ) )
133      return FALSE;
```

```
134     if ( 1 > fread( hdr, sizeof( header ), 1, libfile ) )
135       return FALSE;
136     else
137       return TRUE;
138   }
139
140   // -----------------------------------------------------------
141   // writehdr() -- Physical write of header
142   // -----------------------------------------------------------
143   int lib::writehdr()
144   {
145     if ( 0 != fseek( libfile, 0, SEEK_SET ) )
146       return FALSE;
147     if ( 1 > fwrite( hdr, sizeof( header ), 1, libfile ) )
148       return FALSE;
149     else
150       return TRUE;
151   }
152
153   // -----------------------------------------------------------
154   // readn() -- read n bytes from member / directory
155   // -----------------------------------------------------------
156   int lib::readn( unsigned char *buf, unsigned numbyte )
157   {
158     unsigned i = 0;
159
160     for ( ; numbyte>0; --numbyte ) {
161       if ( byteindex >= 118 )
162         if ( !getnextblk() ) return FALSE;
163       if ( byteindex >= blk->bytesused )
164         return FALSE;         // leave byteindex where it is
165       buf[i++] = blk->data[byteindex++];        // get a byte
166     }
167     return TRUE;
168   }
169
170   // -----------------------------------------------------------
171   // writen() -- write n bytes to member / directory
172   // -----------------------------------------------------------
173   int lib::writen( unsigned char *buf, unsigned numbyte )
174   {
175     unsigned long oldblock, newblock;
```

Listing 13.3. Continued.

```
176    unsigned i = 0;
177
178    for ( ; numbyte>0; --numbyte ) {
179      if ( byteindex >= 118 ) {   // chain to next block
180
181        if ( !writeblk() ) return FALSE;  // write full block
182
183        if ( !getnextblk() ) { // no next block, make new one
184
185          oldblock = curblock;           // save old block adr
186
187          if ( !acquireblk() ) return FALSE;
188          newblock = curblock;
189          blk->prevblk = oldblock; // point back from new blk
190          if ( !writeblk() ) return FALSE;
191
192          curblock = oldblock;
193          if ( !readblk() ) return FALSE;
194          blk->nextblk = newblock;  // point fwd from old blk
195          if ( !writeblk() ) return FALSE;
196
197          curblock = newblock;
198          if ( !readblk() ) return FALSE;     // now continue
199        }
200      }
201
202      blk->data[byteindex++] = buf[i++];       // write a byte
203      if ( byteindex > blk->bytesused-1 )
204        blk->bytesused++;                    // update control info
205    }
206    return TRUE;
207  }
208
209  // ----------------------------------------------------------
210  // acquireblk() -- Get a free block from Q or create one.
211  //                 curblock will point to acquired block.
212  // ----------------------------------------------------------
213  int lib::acquireblk()
214  {
215    unsigned long newblock;
```

```
216
217    byteindex = 0;
218                                   // If there is no free chain,
219                                   // go to EOF and create blk
220    if ( hdr->freechain == NULL ) {
221      if ( 0 != fseek( libfile, 0, SEEK_END ) )
222        return FALSE;
223      curblock = ftell( libfile );
224      purgeblk();            // clear blk buf
225      if ( !writeblk() ) return FALSE;
226      return TRUE;
227    }
228                                   // Take last freechain block
229    curblock = hdr->eof;
230    if ( !readblk() ) return FALSE;
231
232    newblock = curblock;                  // hold it a minute
233
234    if ( blk->prevblk ) {           // try to back up 1 block
235      if ( !getprevblk() ) return FALSE;
236      hdr->eof = curblock;          // note new end of freechain
237      if ( !writehdr() ) return FALSE;
238      blk->nextblk = 0UL;
239      if ( !writeblk() ) return FALSE;
240      curblock = newblock;
241      purgeblk();
242      return TRUE;
243    }
244    else {                          // was only 1 blk in freechain
245      hdr->freechain = 0UL;
246      hdr->eof = 0UL;
247      if ( !writehdr() ) return FALSE;
248      purgeblk();
249      return TRUE;
250    }
251  }
252
253  // ----------------------------------------------------------
254  // releaseblk() -- Put an exisiting datablock into the
255  //                 freechain. curblock must point to the
256  //                 block to release.
257  // ----------------------------------------------------------
```

Listing 13.3. Continued.

```
258  int lib::releaseblk()
259  {
260    unsigned long holdblock;
261    unsigned long oldend;
262
263    holdblock = curblock;
264    byteindex = 0;
265    if ( !hdr->freechain ) {        // if there is no freechain
266      hdr->freechain = curblock;
267      hdr->eof = curblock;
268      if ( !writehdr() ) return FALSE;
269      purgeblk();
270      if ( !writeblk() ) return FALSE;
271      return TRUE;
272    }
273                                    // Add after last block of freechain
274    curblock = hdr->eof;
275    if ( !readblk() ) return FALSE;
276
277    oldend = curblock;
278
279    blk->nextblk = holdblock;                   // chain it on
280    if ( !writeblk() ) return FALSE;   // update old endchain
281
282    curblock = holdblock;              // relocate freed block
283    hdr->eof = curblock;
284    if ( !writehdr() ) return FALSE;
285    if ( !readblk() ) return FALSE;    // and update its link
286    purgeblk();
287    blk->prevblk = oldend;
288    if ( !writeblk() ) return FALSE;
289
290    return TRUE;
291  }
292
293  // ----------------------------------------------------------
294  // getnextblk() -- Read the next chained datablock
295  // ----------------------------------------------------------
296  int lib::getnextblk()
297  {
298    if ( !blk->nextblk ) return FALSE;
```

```
299    curblock = blk->nextblk;
300    if ( !readblk() ) return FALSE;
301    return TRUE;
302  }
303
304  // ----------------------------------------------------------
305  // getprevblk() -- Read the previous chained datablock
306  // ----------------------------------------------------------
307  int lib::getprevblk()
308  {
309    if ( !blk->prevblk ) return FALSE;
310    curblock = blk->prevblk;
311    if ( readblk() ) return TRUE;
312    else return FALSE;
313  }
314
315  // ----------------------------------------------------------
316  // locate() -- Find a member in the directory
317  // ----------------------------------------------------------
318  int lib::locate( char *member )
319  {
320    if ( !hdr->dir ) return FALSE;
321    curblock = hdr->dir;
322    if ( !readblk() ) return FALSE;
323    libtell( &diradr );
324    while ( readn( (unsigned char *)ent,sizeof( entry ) ) ) {
325      if ( ent->memname[0] == '\xFF' ) {
326        libtell( &diradr );
327        continue;
328      }
329      if ( 0 == strcmp( ent->memname, member ) )
330        return TRUE;
331      libtell( &diradr );
332    }
333    return FALSE;
334  }
335
336  // ----------------------------------------------------------
337  // listdir() -- Display a directory list
338  // ----------------------------------------------------------
339  void lib::listdir()
340  {
```

Listing 13.3. Continued.

```
341    printf( "Directory List for %s\n", library );
342    printf( "=============\n" );
343
344    if ( !hdr->dir ) return;
345    curblock = hdr->dir;
346    if ( !readblk() ) return;
347    while ( readn( (unsigned char *)ent,sizeof( entry ) ) ) {
348      if ( ent->memname[0] == '\0' ) break;
349      if ( ent->memname[0] == '\xFF' ) continue;
350      printf( "%-15s%12ld\n", ent->memname, ent->memsize );
351    }
352    return;
353  }
354
355  // ------------------------------------------------------------
356  // addmem() -- Add a new member to library
357  // ------------------------------------------------------------
358  int lib::addmem( char *member )
359  {
360    int i;
361    char *ptr;
362    unsigned char ch;
363    FILE *infile;
364
365
366    printf( "LIB: Adding member - %s\n", member );
367
368    // -- open file successfully
369
370    if ( NULL == ( infile = fopen( member, "rb" ) ) ) {
371      fclose( infile );
372      return FALSE;
373    }
374
375
376    // -- bypass any path info if present
377
378    i = strlen( member ) - 1;
379    while ( i>0 && member[i] != '\\' && member[i] != ':' )
380      --i;
381    if ( i > 0 ) ++i;
```

```
382    ptr = &member[i];
383
384    // -- check to see if it already exists
385
386    if ( locate( ptr ) ) return FALSE;
387
388    // -- find directory entry - note position
389
390    if ( !hdr->dir ) {
391      if ( !acquireblk() ) return FALSE;
392      libtell ( &diradr );
393      hdr->dir = curblock;
394      if ( !writehdr() ) return FALSE;
395    }
396    else {
397      curblock = hdr->dir;
398      if ( !readblk() ) return FALSE;
399      libtell( &diradr );
400      while ( readn( (unsigned char *)ent,sizeof( entry ) ) ) {
401        if ( ent->memname[0] == '\xFF' ) break;
402        libtell( &diradr );
403      }
404    }
405    strcpy( ent->memname, ptr );
406
407    // -- acquire first data block - note position
408
409    if ( !acquireblk() ) return FALSE;
410    ent->memstart = curblock;
411    ent->memsize = 0UL;
412
413    // -- read file - write member - count bytes
414
415    while ( 0 < fread( &ch, 1, 1, infile ) ) {
416      if ( !writen( (unsigned char *)&ch, 1 ) )
417        return FALSE;
418      ent->memsize++;
419    }
420
421    // -- if incore flag on, write last block
422
423    if ( incore )
```

Listing 13.3. Continued.

```
424        if ( !writeblk() ) return FALSE;
425
426     // -- close file
427
428     fclose( infile );
429
430     // -- update directory
431
432     if ( !libseek( &diradr ) ) return FALSE;
433     if ( !writen( (unsigned char *)ent,sizeof( entry ) ) )
434        return FALSE;
435     if ( incore )
436        if ( !writeblk() ) return FALSE;
437
438     return TRUE;
439  }
440
441  // ----------------------------------------------------------
442  // delmem() -- Delete a member from library
443  // ----------------------------------------------------------
444  int lib::delmem( char *member )
445  {
446     unsigned long datablk;
447
448     printf( "LIB: Deleting member - %s\n", member );
449
450     if ( !locate( member ) ) return FALSE;
451
452     datablk = ent->memstart;
453
454     purgedir();
455     if ( !libseek( &diradr ) ) return FALSE;
456     if ( !writen( (unsigned char *)ent, sizeof( entry ) ) )
457        return FALSE;
458     if ( incore )
459        if ( !writeblk() ) return FALSE;
460
461     curblock = datablk;
462     while ( curblock ) {
463        if ( !readblk() ) return FALSE;
464        datablk = blk->nextblk;
```

```
465     if ( !releaseblk() ) return FALSE;
466     curblock = datablk;
467   }
468   return TRUE;
469 }
470
471 // ---------------------------------------------------------
472 // listmem() -- Display a single member
473 // ---------------------------------------------------------
474 int lib::listmem( char *member )
475 {
476   int i;
477
478   printf( "LIB: Showing member - %s\n", member );
479
480   if ( !locate( member ) ) return FALSE;
481   curblock = ent->memstart;
482   if ( !readblk() ) return FALSE;
483   while ( curblock ) {
484     curblock = blk->nextblk;
485     for ( i=0; i<blk->bytesused; i++ )
486       putchar( blk->data[i] );
487     if ( !readblk() ) break;
488   }
489   return TRUE;
490 }
491
492 // ---------------------------------------------------------
493 // extractmem() -- Read a member from the lib and write
494 //                 to a file
495 // ---------------------------------------------------------
496 int lib::extractmem( char *member, char *oname )
497 {
498   int i;
499   FILE *ofile;
500
501   printf( "LIB: Unloading member - %s\n", member );
502
503   if ( oname[0] == '\0' ) strcpy( oname, member );
504
505   if ( NULL == ( ofile = fopen( oname, "wb" ) ) )
506     return FALSE;
```

Listing 13.3. Continued.

```
507
508    if ( !locate( member ) ) return FALSE;
509    curblock = ent->memstart;
510    if ( !readblk() ) return FALSE;
511    while ( curblock ) {
512      curblock = blk->nextblk;
513      for ( i=0; i<blk->bytesused; i++ )
514        if ( 1 > fwrite( &blk->data[i], 1, 1, ofile ) ) {
515          fclose( ofile );
516          return FALSE;
517        }
518      if ( !readblk() ) break;
519    }
520    fclose( ofile );
521    return TRUE;
522 }
523
524 // ---------------------------------------------------------
525 // unload() -- Unload entire library
526 // ---------------------------------------------------------
527 int lib::unload( char *path )
528 {
529    char out[81];
530    char holdname[13];
531    lib_pos_t here;
532
533    if ( !hdr->dir ) return FALSE;
534    curblock = hdr->dir;
535    if ( !readblk() ) return FALSE;
536
537    while ( readn( (unsigned char *)ent,sizeof( entry ) ) ) {
538
539      if ( !libtell( &here ) ) return FALSE;
540      if ( ent->memname[0] == '\0' ) break;
541      if ( ent->memname[0] == '\xFF' ) continue;
542
543      strcpy( out, path );
544      strcat( out, ent->memname );
545      strcpy( holdname, ent->memname );
546
```

```
547       if ( !extractmem( holdname, out ) ) return FALSE;
548       if ( !libseek( &here ) ) return FALSE;
549     }
550     return TRUE;
551 }
552
```

The lib.cpp source file in Listing 13.3 contains some tricky code. If you ever want to modify the program, be sure you completely understand what the existing code does before starting in. Now take a look at the member function definitions to see how they work.

The lib class has only one constructor function, shown in lines 6 through 40 of Listing 13.3. The constructor function accepts as an argument a string pointer to the library's filename. There is no default constructor—that would be pointless.

The constructor's job is to open the library file—creating one if necessary—in update mode and to initialize the internal control variables. Notice that the memory for the header, data block, directory entry, and filename string are acquired and maintained outside the boundaries of the lib object. If the library can be successfully opened (or created), the header block is read in, and the *signature* is verified. The signature is just the string "LIBV10", which occupies the first six bytes in the library file.

The lib destructor (lines 45 through 52) is especially simple. It releases the memory for control structures and closes the library file.

Both the purgeblk() function (lines 57 through 64) and the purgedir() function (lines 69 through 74) set something to nulls. The purgeblk() function reinitializes an in-memory data block when a data block is either newly acquired or released. The purgedir() function reinitializes the in-memory directory entry when a member file is being deleted, and also sets the member name to all '\xFF' values. That way, the block can be reused later.

The readblk() function (lines 80 through 89) performs a physical read of a 128-byte data block (which can contain either member or directory data) from the library. readblk() assumes that some other member function has correctly set the value of the member variable curblock to the physical disk address of the block. Because the block may need to be rewritten after receiving file data, readblk() does not change the value of curblock. Notice that the standard C fseek() and fread() functions are used to read blocks. Notice especially that the incore flag is set *on* (set to TRUE) when a block is read.

writeblk() performs the complementary task of writing a data block to physical disk storage, also using standard C library functions. Notice that whenever a block is physically written, the incore flag is turned *off* (set to FALSE).

The next two member functions, `libseek()` and `libtell()`, perform tasks for a `lib` file that are similar to those performed by `fseek()` and `ftell()` in plain C. The `libtell()` function (lines 120–125) reports the current read-write position within a member (or directory) by simply capturing `curblock` and `byteindex`. Remember that curblock always contains the disk address of the data block currently in memory, and `byteindex` has the offset (subscript) of the current byte in that block. The `libseek()` function (lines 109 through 115) performs the complementary task by reading in the indicated data block and setting `byteindex` to the correct value.

Another pair of member functions of critical importance to the `lib` class is `readn()`, in lines 156 through 168, and `writen()`, in lines 173 through 207. These functions read and write, respectively, n characters from the `lib` file. These functions are especially important because they provide the main I/O interface to the class.

The self-reorganizing characteristic of `lib` files is provided by the `acquireblk()` member function (lines 213 through 251) and the `releaseblk()` member function (lines 258 through 291). `acquireblk()` gets a data block from the free chain, if one is available, and makes the data block available for use. `releaseblk()` performs the opposite function of returning a discarded data block to the free chain (blocks are discarded when a member is deleted).

Processing a `lib` file member in a sequential manner naturally involves reading or writing blocks from the doubly linked chain of data blocks. *Running the chain* can be performed in the forward direction by the `getnextblk()` function (lines 296 through 302) and in the backward direction by the `getprevblk()` function (lines 307 through 313). These functions are relatively simple compared to the others discussed so far and require only picking up and using address pointers (*disk* addresses) with the same techniques you use for doubly linked lists in memory. To start processing a member file, you need to use the `locate()` member function found in lines 318 through 334. This member function finds and reads in the directory entry for a member (if, in fact, such an entry exists).

The remaining member functions (from line 336 to line 552) provide higher-level functionality for library objects. They all use the previously described member functions to carry out their tasks. The higher-level service member functions include the following:

■ `listdir()`

`listdir()` reads the entire library directory and reports each member name and member size on `stdout`.

■ `addmem()`

`addmem()` adds a new member file to the library. This function fails if the member filename is already present. `admem()` also assumes that there may be drive and path information present in the member name string (so that `lib` users can use wildcard characters to input member names). If such information is present, it is stripped off before the member name is recorded. This member function provides some good sample code for manipulating a library file, including the method for updating the directory when a member is added.

■ `delmem()`

`delmem()` deletes a member file from the library file. This function's manner of processing the directory is analogous to that used by `addmem()`, except that the directory entry is purged before writing back to disk instead of being filled in with information.

■ `listmem()`

`listmem()` locates a member file (if it is present in the library) and sends it to `stdout`. Because `stdout` is used, you can redirect output to the printer (using the DOS command-line redirection command `>PRN`).

■ `extractmem()`

`extractmem()` is the mirror image of `addmem()`. The `extractmem()` function reads a member file from the library and writes that file to an outside file. As with `addmem()`, it doesn't matter whether the member file read and written by `extractmem()` is text, binary, or something else. All member files are processed in binary mode so that every bit is reproduced faithfully.

■ `unload()`

`unload()`, the last member function in the `lib` class, is a powerful function that calls `extractmem()` for *every* member in the library. You might use `unload()`, for example, if a set of files has been transported (or distributed) in a `lib` file and you want to recover all the original files.

Many functions are available in the `lib` class, but it will not be useful without some code that can drive it. A driver program, pds.cpp, is provided in Listing 13.4. The program name is borrowed from the mainframe computing environment. The acronym *pds* means *p*artitioned *d*ata *s*et—partitioned, that is, into multiple subfiles, or members.

Listing 13.4. pds.cpp. A self-reorganizing library program that uses `lib` class objects.

```
1   #include <conio.h>
2   #include <dos.h>
3   #include "lib.hpp"
4
5   // --------------------------------------------------------------
```

Listing 13.4. Continued.

```
6   // main() -- Driver for testing lib object
7   // ------------------------------------------------------
8   void main(int argc, char *argv[] )
9   {
10     char lname[81];
11     char mname[81];
12     char oname[81];
13     char action;
14     struct _find_t dosdir;
15     int retn, i;
16     char dirpath[81];
17     char searcharg[81];
18
19     puts( "+--------------------------------+" );
20     puts( "+                                +" );
21     puts( "+ PDS Library Utility Version 1.1 +" );
22     puts( "+                                +" );
23     puts( "+--------------------------------+" );
24
25     if ( argc < 3 ) {
26       puts( "The correct format for the lib command is:" );
27       puts( "" );
28       puts( "    pds a lname mname [oname]" );
29       puts( "" );
30       puts( "where a is the action character:" );
31       puts( "    a - add member" );
32       puts( "    d - delete member" );
33       puts( "    x - extract member" );
34       puts( "    u - unload library" );
35       puts( "    l - list directory" );
36       puts( "    s - list member" );
37       puts( "and:" );
38       puts( "    lname - library file name (required)" );
39       puts( "    mname - member name" );
40       puts( "            required unless action=l" );
41       puts( "            (path spec if unloading)" );
42       puts( "    oname - opt. output file for extract" );
43       exit( 0 );
44     }
45
46     action = argv[1][0];
```

```
47    strcpy( lname, argv[2] );
48    mname[0] = '\0';
49    if ( argc > 3 ) strcpy( mname, argv[3] );
50    oname[0] = '\0';
51    if ( argc > 4 ) strcpy( oname, argv[4] );
52
53    if ( strchr( lname, '.' ) ) {      // force extension to .LBR
54      i = strlen( lname ) - 1;
55      while ( i>0 && lname[i] != '.' ) --i;
56      lname[i] = '\0';
57    }
58    strupr( lname );
59    strcat( lname, ".LBR" );
60
61    lib pds( lname );                  // create a library object
62
63    strupr( mname );
64
65    switch ( action ) {
66      case 'a':
67      case 'A': if ( strpbrk( mname, "?*" ) ) {
68                  strcpy( searcharg, mname );
69                  strcpy ( dirpath, mname );
70                  i = strlen( dirpath ) - 1;
71                  while ( i>0 && dirpath[i] != '\\'
72                          && dirpath[i] != ':' ) --i;
73                  if ( i > 0 ) ++i;
74                  dirpath[i] = '\0';
75             retn = _dos_findfirst( searcharg, 0xFF, &dosdir );
76                  strcpy( mname, dirpath );
77              strcat( mname, dosdir.name );
78                  while ( !retn ) {
79                if ( !( dosdir.attrib & _A_SYSTEM )
80                   && !( dosdir.attrib & _A_VOLID )
81                   && !( dosdir.attrib & _A_SUBDIR ) )
82                          pds.addmem( mname );
83                retn = _dos_findnext( &dosdir );
84                      strcpy( mname, dirpath );
85                strcat( mname, dosdir.name );
86                    }
87                    break;
88                  }
```

Listing 13.4. Continued.

```
89                 pds.addmem( mname ); break;
90      case 'd':
91      case 'D': pds.delmem( mname ); break;
92      case 'x':
93      case 'X': pds.extractmem( mname, oname ); break;
94      case 'u':
95      case 'U': if ( mname[strlen(mname)-1] != '\\'
96                  && mname[0] != '\0' )
97               strcat( mname, "\\" );
98               pds.unload( mname ); break;
99      case 'l':
100     case 'L': pds.listdir(); break;
101     case 's':
102     case 'S': pds.listmem( mname ); break;
103   }
104 }
```

A great deal of code has been presented here (hope you can use it!) to illustrate the methods of communicating with member functions. All the calls to member functions in Listing 13.4 are of the form *object.function()*. The amazing thing, again, is how much you can do with a fairly simple program once the complex code has been developed and encapsulated in a C++ class.

Understanding *this*

The this pointer, which was mentioned briefly in the discussion of the lifo class in Chapter 11, is available to member functions for accessing a particular instance object. Suppose, for example, you wrote a program that used the following two lib class objects:

```
lib libfile1( "DOCS.LBR" );
lib libfile2( "KEYWORDS.LBR" );
```

Having declared two distinct library objects, now suppose you want to display the directory for each. You could write these statements to accomplish that:

```
libfile1.listmem();
libfile2.listmem();
```

In both cases, the lib::listmem() function is called. As you may recall from Chapter 11, each access implies that a *behind-the-scenes* pointer (this) is in place (although you do not, in this circumstance, have to do any dereferencing). How does the presence of `this` affect the operation of `listmem()`? Look, for example, at line 481, reproduced from Listing 13.3:

```
curblock = ent->memstart;
```

How does the member function know which `curblock` to refer to? There is, after all, a separate copy of the variable for each `libfile1` and `libfile2`. The trick is to understand that the preceding statement is equivalent to the following statement:

```
this->curblock = ent->memstart;
```

The nice thing about the way `this` works is that you do not have to write the pointer reference yourself within a member function when referring to member data (not even if the object was created with `new` and is being controlled through a pointer).

You rarely use the `this` pointer with the most current C++ compilers. There are instances, however, in which you need to know that `this` exists and what it signifies. These instances are covered in the next few sections, which deal with C++ references and the passing and returning of class objects to and from member functions.

Using the Reference Operator

The *reference operator*, as its name implies, enables you to treat a *pointer* to an object as if it were simply an *object*. This concept is extremely important in C++. It vastly simplifies much syntax and makes possible some operations on class objects that would otherwise be difficult or impossible. References can be used on ordinary C objects and on class objects.

Evolving the Reference Operator from the Address-Of Operator

Once you understand that a reference uses a pointer behind the scenes, you should not be surprised that the reference operator uses the same character as the address-of operator (`&`). Then it is only a short step to understanding that the reference generated by the reference operator is merely an alternative name for an object. Consider, for example, the following code fragment:

```
int a = 37;            // declare and init an integer
int& b = a;            // declare a reference to a
```

The first line of this code fragment is just as straightforward as it looks. The second line is straightforward also, if you know that a reference is being declared. You could read the second line as "b is a reference to the integer a." Because b references a, b is said to be an *alias* to a.

Notice also where the reference operator appears in the second line of code: The operator is on the left side of the assignment, not in the position of the address-of operator. Furthermore, this code fragment makes it appear as if a is being assigned to b. *That is not the case.* Remember that references deal with pointers, but behind the scenes. Thus, the preceding code fragment is the *working equivalent* of the following code fragment:

```
int a = 37;          // define the integer again
int *b;              // define a pointer
b = &a;              // b contains address of a
```

When you compare these two equivalent code fragments, you can see that a reference is just a pointer in disguise. Moreover, the first code fragment makes another rule clear: *References always bind to objects, not to addresses.* This doesn't mean that addresses aren't being generated and used internally. It only means that *you* don't have to do it, nor do you have to write address notation in the code when using references.

Understanding the Reference Operator

References have two main purposes in C++. Stating these purposes is easy; appreciating their significance may be more difficult. Here are the main purposes for using references:

- *You can use references to specify operations for user-defined types.* As an alternative name for an object, a reference can serve as an *object locator* for the object. If you recall your ANSI C theory, this means that using a reference can enable you to use class objects in expressions with operators, and perhaps to stand as lvalues. Using references for this purpose is covered in Chapter 14, "Using Overloaded Functions and Operators in C++," and in Chapter 18, "Object Control and Performance Issues."

- *You can use references to reduce overhead in passing and returning class objects as arguments.* Passing large objects on the stack takes not only stack space but also *time.* If you can avoid placing large amounts of data on the stack, you should do so. References physically place on the stack only addresses of objects. That can mean better performance.

Sometimes these two purposes are at work at the same time: Returning a reference to an object from a member function is always efficient, but in some cases it may also be required to implement class operator functions. Before you go blazing off to write some code that uses the reference operator, however, you need to know a couple of rules about references:

- *You cannot manipulate a reference directly.* This may not make sense immediately because you can manipulate pointer values, and references are disguised pointers. Why, then, can't you tinker with a reference directly? The following code fragment illustrates the reason:

```
double count = 0;          // here is a count field
double& number = count;    // here is a reference to it
...
++number;          // count is now 1 !
```

  Remember that a reference is an alternative name, and references always bind to objects. Any reference to number, as shown in this code fragment, is an implicit reference directly to count.

- *You can use a reference to take the address of an object.* This rule also works because references bind to objects. Consider, for instance, this code fragment:

```
int a;      // declare an integer
int& b = a; // b is reference to a
int *c;     // declare a true pointer to integer
...
c = &b;     // taking address of b same as taking address of a;
            // *c == a
```

Even though the examples here have been trivial, you can do some pretty amazing things with references. In the next section, you get an idea of what those things are. Later on, references will become old friends.

Using Objects as Function Parameters

Class objects, like ordinary C objects, can be passed as arguments to functions and returned from them. This section discusses the use of class objects as function parameters and return values.

Passing Objects by Value and by Reference

You can pass class objects to a function both by value and by reference, just as you can with ordinary arguments in ordinary functions. Passing class objects by value has the same consequences as for ordinary C objects: You get only a copy of the object to work with. For example, look closely at the following short program:

```
#include <stdlib.h>
#include <stdio.h>

class OP {
  int value;
public:
  OP() { value = 37; }
  friend void changeit( OP );
  void show() { printf( "%d\n", value ); }
};

void changeit( OP someop )
{
  someop.value = 64;
}

void main()
{
  OP x;

  changeit( x );
  x.show();        // displays a value of 37
}
```

In this program, a friend function is used so that the private member variable value can be accessed. Do you think that the final call to OP::show() will display a value of 37 or 64? It will, in fact, display the value 37 because only a copy of the object is placed on the stack and passed to the friend function changeit(). Only that copy is modified, and the temporary object on the stack is thrown away when changeit() returns to its caller. The state of the original object is completely untouched by this operation.

Passing class objects to functions by reference has the same consequences as passing ordinary objects by reference (although the phrase *by reference* now takes on an added dimension). Suppose the preceding program was coded a bit differently, to allow changeit() to accept a reference to an OP object:

```
#include <stdlib.h>
#include <stdio.h>

class OP {
  int value;
public:
  OP() { value = 37; }
```

```
  friend void changeit( OP& ); // ACCEPT REFERENCE
  void show() { printf( "%d\n", value ); }
};

void changeit( OP& someop ) // REFERENCE HERE TOO
{
  someop.value = 64;
}

void main()
{
  OP x;

  changeit( x ); // NO CHANGE, REF'S BIND TO OBJECTS
  x.show();       // DISPLAYS A VALUE OF 64 NOW
}
```

In the second version of this program, no longer is a copy of the whole object placed on the stack and passed to the `friend` function; only a disguised pointer is placed there and passed to `friend`. Thus, the original object is available to the function, resulting in an altered value of `value`.

Accessing Other Objects from a Member Function

If a member function has a parameter that is also a class object, that member function can refer to the other class object. With class objects, however, you must still take into account the point of declaration of a class, as well as some more C++ scoping rules when you write references to other objects. Besides covering how to set up class objects as parameters, these rules deal with accessing other objects from within class objects. The additional scoping rules include the following:

■ *You cannot refer to objects of a class that has not yet been declared.* You can use an incomplete declaration of a class, however, to forward-declare the class to which you want to refer. Consider, for example, the following short program:

```
#include <iostream.h>

class A; // FORWARD-DECLARE THIS CLASS

class B {
  int bval;
```

```
public:
  B() { bval = 16; }
  int dosum( A& );
};

class A { // COMPLETE THE DECLARATION FOR CLASS A
  int aval;
public:
  A() { aval = 16; }
  int getval() { return aval; }
};

int B::dosum( A& aobj ) {
  return bval + aobj.getval ();
}

void main()
{
  A aobj;
  B bobj;

  cout << bobj.dosum( aobj );
}
```

This sample program uses an incomplete declaration of class A so that the argument type in B::dosum() can compile correctly. Notice, however, that the member function definition for B::dosum() is not coded until the declaration for class A has been completed. If dosum() had been coded inline, the function would have referred to members of class A— A::getval() specifically—before their point of declaration. In that case, the program would not compile correctly.

■ *Class member functions can declare and use local objects that have their own class type.* For example, the class A shown in the preceding program could have contained a member function that declared a local class A object! A class member function can locally define an object of its own class because member functions are invoked on behalf of specific class *objects*, not classes in general. Thus, the local object is a different object, even though the local object has the same class as the member function declaring it. All local objects go out of scope and are destroyed when the member functions return.

■ *Class member functions can be passed references to objects of other classes, and can define local objects of other classes.* You can use objects of another class as arguments or local variables provided, of course, that the other class has been completely declared by the time you get around to writing the current class's member function *definition*.

■ *Member functions or entire classes can serve as friends of a class.* This is a sneaky (but legitimate) way to gain access to an object of another class. You have already seen how `friend` functions are declared. Whole classes can be declared as friends in the following manner:

```
class A { ... };
class B {
  ...
friend A; // all class A member functions now friends
};
```

Once again, the function body of a member function cannot refer to any part of another class that has not yet been declared.

There are, in fact, even more rules of this kind that deal with class inheritance. For more information on such rules, refer to Chapter 17.

Using Pointers to Objects

Until now, most of the examples in this book have used either global or local class objects to illustrate class object access. Such objects use the structure member operator (.) to access class members. As you may guess, nothing prevents you from declaring a pointer to a class object. Class objects accessed through a pointer must use the structure pointer operator (->) to access members.

Understanding When Pointers Are Required

In only one instance *must* you use a pointer to access a class object: when the object is created on the free store. As you may recall, objects are created on the free store with the `new` operator. For example, the following short program uses `new` to create a class object, and must therefore access the object's member functions by means of a pointer:

```
#include <iostream.h>

class car {
  int drive;
  int cyls;
  int seats;
  int doors;
public:
  car ( int odrive = 2, int ocyls = 8,
```

```
          int oseats = 5, int odoors = 4 );
    void ctell();
};

car::car ( int odrive, int ocyls,
          int oseats, int odoors )
{
    drive = odrive;
    cyls = ocyls;
    seats = oseats;
    doors = odoors;
}

void car::ctell()
{
    cout << "This car has " << drive << " wheel drive, "
         << cyls << " cylinders, " << seats << " seats, and "
         << doors << " doors.\r\n";
}

void main()
{
    car *jaguar = new car;

    jaguar->ctell(); // MUST use a pointer for this access!
}
```

The last line of code in the `main()` function of this short program shows how to use the structure pointer operator to access a class object through a pointer. The technique is quite simple. The syntax is like the new, simplified ANSI syntax for calling functions through pointers, shown in the section "Sending Messages to Objects" earlier in this chapter.

A question may occur to you at this point. Why can't you use the more familiar `calloc()` or `malloc()` function to create class objects? You may, for instance, want to write something like this:

```
car *jaguar = (car *)malloc( sizeof( car ) );
```

There are two problems with this line of code: You must manually cast the pointer returned by `malloc()` to the car type; and it does not invoke the car class constructor in any way. In other words, you can certainly get sufficient space on the stack for a class object with `malloc()` or `calloc()`, but you cannot create a class object with either of them. The `new` operator, however, returns the correct type of pointer, and invokes the class constructor as well.

Declaring Pointers and Arrays of Objects

You can do with class objects just about anything you can do with data objects. You can, for instance, declare an array of objects (which does not require new), an array of pointers to objects (which requires new), or a pointer to an array of objects (which requires new).

Consider the most difficult case first: declaring an array of pointers to objects. This grouping is the most difficult to declare and does require the structure pointer operator in order to access a class member. Assume for a moment that you are still dealing with the car class. Look at the following new version of the main() function, using that class:

```
void main()
{
  int i;
  car *jaguar[4];  // array of 4 pointers to objects

  for ( i=0; i<4; ++i ) jaguar[i] = new car;
  for ( i=0; i<4; ++i ) jaguar[i]->ctell();
  for ( i=0; i<4; ++i ) delete jaguar[i];
}
```

The declaration car *jaguar[4] declares an array of pointers to class objects. Because of that, the new operator must be used for each array element. That is, new always returns a single pointer. The use and destruction of each of the class objects follows directly from that fact—you must use the structure pointer operator to access an array element's member function (a class object's member function), and you must use delete explicitly for each object pointed to by the array.

Now suppose you create another fleet of four expensive cars, but the easy way—a whole fleet at a time. In this instance, you need a true default constructor such as this one:

```
class car {
  ...
public:
  car();
  ...
};

car::car()
{
  drive = 2;
```

```
    cyls = 8;
    seats = 5;
    doors = 4;
}
```

In some circumstances (that is, when deriving classes), a default constructor may be a constructor with no arguments (as shown here), or it may be one with *all default* arguments (as shown in the original car class). In *this* circumstance—creating an array of objects with new—*only* a default constructor function with no arguments will do. Microsoft C/C++ refuses to compile the following main() function unless a true default constructor function is provided:

```
void main()
{
    int i;
    car *jaguar;   // ONE pointer to array of objects

    jaguar = new car[4]; // create them all!

    for ( i=0; i<4; ++i ) jaguar[i].ctell(); // no ptr deref!

    delete [4] jaguar; // destroy them all !
}
```

Here the pointer declaration car *jaguar has been left alone just to show that jaguar is *one* pointer. You instead could replace the fourth and fifth lines with the following single line:

```
car *jaguar = new car[4];
```

Whether you use one or two lines of code, the result is the same. The new operator does the following:

1. new creates a contiguous array of class objects on the free store.

2. As each class object is created on the free store, new invokes the default constructor for the class to initialize the object.

3. new finally returns a single pointer, which contains the address of the first class object in the array.

The use of subscripts with the jaguar array in the for loop in the preceding code fragment illustrates another interesting point: Even when dealing with arrays of class objects, you can still count on the equivalence of pointers and subscripts. If you recall your basic C theory, *jaguar, then, is the same as jaguar[0]. Therefore, you can refer to the array elements (which are class objects) as shown in the for loop in this code fragment.

Finally, you can get rid of the entire array of class objects with a single use of the delete operator. Look at the preceding code fragment carefully to see how this is done. The syntax delete [4] jaguar should be read as "delete four instances of the jaguar object, all found in a contiguous array."

Exercises

The following exercises give you practice in accessing class member functions, controlling the scope of class members, using C++ references, and using arrays of class objects:

1. Review the rules for using the scope resolution operator, as well as the general rules governing C++ scope. Trying to imagine what kind of code requires these rules may seem like a useless exercise, but the rules are quite necessary when such code crops up naturally (you will reach that point sooner than you think).

2. Write several class declarations for various kinds of objects that interest you, and practice sending messages to them (calling member functions). Create some of the class objects locally and create some on the free store with new.

3. Experiment with the reference operator. Use it to access ordinary objects and class objects. Try using it to pass class objects as arguments to functions.

4. Imagine a class of objects that seems to belong naturally in a group or an array. Write the class, making it as full-featured as you can. Create an array of these objects.

Summary

Accessing a C++ object requires some sound knowledge of how class objects are used in C++. In this chapter, you learned the following points:

■ *The scope resolution operator is used for general purposes, for controlling syntax, and for resolving ambiguities of reference.* You should have a good understanding of how to use the scope resolution operator before you approach Chapter 17 because derived classes frequently require its use.

■ *C++ scope rules for class objects go considerably beyond plain C scope rules.* Remember that a class is a scope! C++ scope rules are accordingly more complicated. It is possible to use the same name in different scopes, or to use the same name for a class and a type definition, and thus inadvertently hide one of the names.

■ *You send messages to objects by calling member functions.* The `this` pointer contains the address of the correct instance object when a member function is entered.

■ *References are disguised pointers to objects.* A reference provides an alternative name for an object, and references *always bind to objects.* A reference can therefore be an *lvalue* (be used on the left side of an assignment statement). References prove to be quite important when you begin to write overloaded operator functions for your classes.

■ *You can pass a class object to a function, both by value and by reference, and return a class object or reference to a class object from a function.*

■ *The `new` operator can create an array of class objects at one time, calling the default constructor for each element (class object) in the array.* The `delete` operator can destroy a whole array of class objects at once.

With this material as background, you are now ready to learn about overloading functions and operators in C++.

Using Overloaded Functions and Operators in C++

When you overload a function or operator, you define multiple versions of it. Overloading is one of the distinctive and powerful features of C++.

If you consider C++ from the designer's point of view, it is not surprising that C++ enables you to overload functions and operators. Overloading is required for the C++ user-defined types that are the main feature of C-based OOP systems—you must define not only the object type but also the new type's behavior. Defining member functions that belong to a user-defined type (a class) is a straightforward way to define a class's behavior, and defining how the C operator set is to behave with the class is a natural extension of the concept.

Overloading Member Functions

Overloading member functions is easier to understand than overloading operators on a class basis simply because overloaded functions are declared with a familiar syntax. Overloaded operators are also declared, but not quite in the same way that you declare overloaded member or nonmember functions. This discussion therefore begins with the techniques for overloading member functions.

You have already seen one function for which you might want to provide several versions for a class: the constructor function. It is often convenient to have available several different constructor functions so that objects of the class can be created in different ways.

The idea applies to ordinary member functions as well. It may be convenient or necessary to provide several ways to manipulate class objects. A `temperature` class object, for example, may need two methods of setting a thermostat, depending on whether the Fahrenheit or Celsius scale is used. This particular example, as well as a need for multiple constructor functions, suggests the more general idea that overloaded functions are appropriate when you want to avoid the overhead involved in function argument conversions, or when you want to perform the same basic member function with different sets of arguments.

Keeping in mind the notions of conversion avoidance and multiple methods of performing a task, you can begin to discover all kinds of classes that might need or use overloaded member functions. In deciding what functions to overload and how to overload them, you should consider both *calling efficiency* and *calling convenience*.

Understanding C++ Overloading

You have just learned that overloading a function means providing multiple versions of that function. Although the feature is handy, it creates a problem immediately. If you have several versions of a function—`function_a()`, for instance—how does the compiler know at any given place in the source code *which* version of the function you mean to call? This problem is illustrated in Figure 14.1.

A number of necessary features were deliberately left out of the functions shown in Figure 14.1 to drive home a point. The C++ compiler can distinguish among multiple functions with the same name *only if they have different types, or the functions have different arguments*.

You have already learned about function type in plain C. A plain C function is a derived type: specifically, a function has type *function returning type*. That is, a plain C function is typed according to the fact that it *is* a function and also that it returns a given data type.

If C++ were to type functions according to the plain C rule, the compiler designer would have difficulty implementing function overloading. The reason is that changing only the return type is considered a signal that the function has been improperly redeclared. C++ needs something besides the return type in order to distinguish between two functions with the same name. That extra something is the *number and type of arguments*.

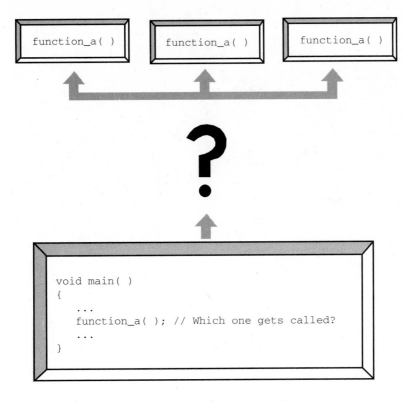

Figure 14.1.

Distinguishing among multiple functions with the same name creates a problem for the compiler designer.

C++ goes beyond plain C in that it can match both the return type and the argument list of a function call to the *best matching* declaration. (This is one of the reasons that C++ requires full function prototyping of functions.) Because of this capability, the compiler can determine rather easily which function is intended in a particular function call (see Figure 14.2).

Thus, you can overload functions by declaring multiple functions with the same name and varying the number and type of arguments, or by varying both the return type and the arguments. You *cannot* overload functions by varying only the return type.

Now you have seen how to overload a member function and how to write a function call for an overloaded function. How do you suppose the compiler determines which particular function you meant to call? The search for the corresponding function proceeds in this order:

1. *All the functions with the same name and in the same scope as the function call are considered.* Restricting the search for a matching name is more important than you might expect. If overloading of functions in different scopes were allowed, you could easily overload a function by accident. For member functions, this rule means that only other member functions in the same class are considered (remember that a class is a scope). If there is only one such function, it is selected immediately.

Figure 14.2.

The combination of arguments and return type identifies an overloaded function precisely.

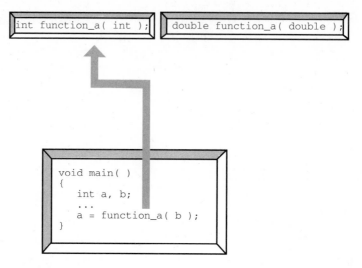

2. *A function with matching return type and arguments is searched for.* If a function call's arguments require no conversion or promotion to match one of the candidates, that function is called immediately.

3. *Possible conversions of the function call's arguments are examined.* If the function call's arguments can be converted in some way to match one of the overloaded function candidates, the matched function is called, using the converted or promoted arguments.

4. *If none of the preceding actions are successful, the call is illegal.* Only after every attempt has been made to match return type and arguments as closely as possible is the function call flagged as a compile-time error.

The C++ compiler uses a best-match algorithm in searching for a set of conversions or promotions for the function arguments. (Type conversions and promotions are covered in Chapter 2, "Understanding the Foundations of C.") The controlling principle used in the best-match search is that the overloaded function requiring the least argument conversion is the best match. The compiler follows these rules for performing the best-match search:

1. *Exact matches are best of all.* Obviously, if no conversion or promotion of arguments is required, the cleanest, fastest code is the result. There can also be no doubt which is the correct function.

2. *Matches requiring only argument promotions are the next best fit.* If promoting integers to more capable integers, or `floats` to `doubles`, is all that is needed for matching a function's argument types, that function is selected (failing an exact match). If several functions can be matched with promotions only, the function with the least number of promotions is best. (The base document says that the selected function must have at least one argument that is a better match than all other possible matches.)

3. *Matches requiring trivial or standard conversions are the next best fit.* Standard conversions (see Chapter 2) and trivial conversions are checked next. Again, the match requiring the least number of conversions is better. Trivial conversions are summarized in Table 14.1.

4. *Matches requiring user-defined conversions are the next best fit.* You can write your own cast operator definitions (overload the cast operator) for your classes. User-defined casts can be used in matching arguments for an overloaded function call.

5. *Matches involving functions that use the ellipsis (. . .) are the worst match of all.* The ellipsis indicates a variable number of unknown arguments. How can the compiler guarantee that variable arguments will match? Nevertheless, this criterion is used if all else fails.

Table 14.1. C++ trivial conversions.

Original Type		New Type	
object	`(T)`	reference	`(T&)`
reference	`(T&)`	object	`(T)`
subscript	`(T[])`	pointer	`(T*)`
call	`(T(args))`	call	`((T)(args))`
object	`(T)`	constant	`(const T)`
object	`(T)`	volatile	`(volatile T)`
pointer	`(T*)`	const pointer	`(const T*)`
pointer	`(T*)`	volatile pointer	`(volatile T*)`

These rules cover just about all the theory of matching function arguments you will ever need. The next section shows you how to write overloaded functions.

Declaring Overloaded Member Functions

When C++ was first introduced in 1986, people tended to think of function overloading as an exotic technique to be avoided. Even though *member* functions and class object operators could be overloaded with no extra syntactical requirements, overloading a *nonmember* function required the use of the `overload` keyword in a declaration. Overloaded declarations for a `cube_root()` function, for example, had to be written like this:

```
overload cube_root;        // THIS IS OBSOLETE !!
double cube_root( double );
double cube_root( float );
double cube_root( int );
double cube_root( long );
```

Now, though, overloading is regarded as an integral part of the user-defined type (class) definition process. The overload keyword is now obsolete and is not supported at all. Microsoft C/C++ allows (and prefers) you to declare overloaded functions without any extra keywords.

Overloading functions is particularly easy within a class declaration; overloading seems to flow naturally from the programming environment. To overload a class member function, you just write more than one prototype declaration for the function name. Listing 14.1 illustrates how to overload class member functions in a simple, uncluttered program.

Listing 14.1. strings.cpp. A program that shows overloading of class member functions.

```
1   #include <string.h>
2   #include <stdlib.h>
3   #include <iostream.h>
4
5   class string {
6     int length;
7     char data[256];
8   public:
9     string() { length = 0; strcpy( data, "" ); } // Here
10    string( char * );                            // are four
11    char *search( char );                        // overloaded
12    char *search( char * );                      // functions
13  };
14
15  string::string( char *text )
16  {
17    if ( strlen( text ) < 256 )
18      strcpy( data, text );
19    else
20      strncpy( data, text, 255 );
21    length = strlen( data );
22  }
23
```

```
24   char *string::search( char arg )
25   {
26     return strchr( data, arg );
27   }
28
29   char *string::search( char *arg )
30   {
31     return strstr( data, arg );
32   }
33
34   void main()
35   {
36     string hellomsg = "Hello, there, I'm a string!";
37     char *found;
38
39     cout << hellomsg.search( 't' ) << "\r\n" ;
40     cout << hellomsg.search( "string" ) << "\r\n" ;
41   }
```

Notice in Listing 14.1 that both the `string::string()` constructor and the `string::search()` member functions are overloaded (lines 9 through 12). The syntax for overloading these functions is simple, consisting of otherwise ordinary prototype declarations.

The class member function definitions (lines 15 through 32) are coded just like any class member functions—with the fully qualified names (except for the inline constructor, of course) followed by the formal parameter lists. Lines 39 and 40, within the `main()` function, show how the member functions are called. You just supply the desired argument types, and the compiler generates the call code for the correct version of the function.

Overloading Friend and Nonmember Functions

After member functions, functions that are friends of classes and functions that are not members of classes complete the inventory of the possible kinds of functions you can write in your C++ programs. All these kinds of functions can be overloaded. This section presents examples of overloading both friend and nonmember functions.

Overloading Friends of a Class

Overloading friend functions is nearly as easy as overloading ordinary member functions. The only difference between overloading friend and member functions is that the `friend` keyword is necessary, as it is for any friend function. You just write the friend function declarations, varying the arguments and possibly also the return types, just as for member functions. Friend function declarations are illustrated in the header file keynew.hpp (a keyboard handler class) in Listing 14.2.

Listing 14.2. keynew.hpp. A header file for the keyboard class, including overloaded friend functions.

```
 1   #define NORM 0
 2   #define EXT  1
 3
 4   #define F1 59
 5   #define F2 60
 6   #define F3 61
 7   #define F4 62
 8   #define F5 63
 9   #define F6 64
10   #define F7 65
11   #define F8 66
12   #define F9 67
13   #define F10 68
14   #define F11 87    // May not work on some machines
15   #define F12 88    // May not work on some machines
16   #define INS 82
17   #define DEL 83
18   #define HOME 71
19   #define END 79
20   #define UPA 72
21   #define DNA 80
22   #define LFA 75
23   #define RTA 77
24   #define PGU 73
25   #define PGD 81
26
27   #define MAXPUSH 4096
28
29   class keynew {
```

```
30    int state;
31    int ch;
32    int lastpush;
33    int pushbuf[MAXPUSH][2];   //LIFO push buffer
34  public:
35    keynew( void );
36    void *operator new( size_t );   // Class operator new
37    void operator delete( void * ); // Class op. delete
38    void next( void );      // Get next state and character
39    void nexte( void );     // Get next state, character, echo
40    void push( int, int ); // Push state and character
41    void loadmac( char * );
42    friend int keystate( keynew & );   // Overloaded
43    friend int keystate( keynew * );   //    friend
44    friend int keyval( keynew & );     //      function
45    friend int keyval( keynew * );     //       prototypes
46  };
47
```

The overloaded friend functions in Listing 14.2 are in lines 42 through 45. There are two versions of the `keynew::keystate()` function and two versions of the `keynew::keyval()` function. One version of each function accepts a reference to a `keynew` class object. The other version accepts a pointer to a `keynew` class object.

Before turning to the `keynew` class, you might want to notice the MAXPUSH object-like macro in line 27. MAXPUSH defines the size of the push buffer array—an array for recording both the key state (normal or extended ASCII) and the key value. Furthermore, the array is an array of `int`, not `char`. Because MAXPUSH is set to 4096, 16K of RAM are set aside for the push buffer. The point here is that you probably will want to create `keynew` objects only on the free store (with `new`), rather than globally (directly in the program) or locally (on the stack). An alternative, of course, is to reduce the size of the push buffer.

The friend function definitions for the `keynew` class are equally simple. You do not have to fully qualify the function names because friend functions do not belong to (are not in the scope of) their associated classes. You write the function definitions directly, as always, providing the required number of overloaded definitions. Both the member and friend function definitions for the `keynew` class are shown in Listing 14.3.

Listing 14.3. keynew.cpp. Class member functions for the keyboard class.

```
1   #include <stdlib.h>
2   #include <stdio.h>
3   #include <string.h>
4   #include <conio.h>
5
6   #include "keynew.hpp"
7
8   keynew::keynew( void )
9   {
10     state = NORM;
11     ch = '\0';
12     lastpush = MAXPUSH;
13  }
14
15  void *keynew::operator new( size_t size )
16  {
17     return::new unsigned char[size]; // Call global new
18  }
19
20  void keynew::operator delete( void *objptr )
21  {
22     ::delete objptr;                 // Call global delete
23  }
24
25  void keynew::next( void )
26  {
27     if ( lastpush < MAXPUSH ) {    // Get it from push buffer
28       state = pushbuf[lastpush][0];
29       ch = pushbuf[lastpush][1];
30       ++lastpush;
31     }
32     else {
33       state = NORM;
34       ch = getch();
35       if ( !ch ) {
36         state = EXT;
37         ch = getch();
38       }
39     }
40  }
```

```
41
42   void keynew::nexte( void )
43   {
44     if ( lastpush < MAXPUSH ) {    // Get it from push buffer
45       state = pushbuf[lastpush][0];
46       ch = pushbuf[lastpush][1];
47       ++lastpush;
48     }
49     else {
50       state = NORM;
51       ch = getch();
52       if ( !ch ) {
53         state = EXT;
54         ch = getch();
55       }
56     }
57     if ( !state ) putchar( ch ); // if not ext ASCII
58   }
59
60   void keynew::push( int kstate, int kval )
61   {
62     if ( lastpush > 0 ) {
63       --lastpush;
64       pushbuf[lastpush][0] = kstate;
65       pushbuf[lastpush][1] = kval;
66     }
67   }
68
69   void keynew::loadmac( char *msg )
70   {
71     char *p;
72     int i;
73
74     p = msg + strlen( msg ) - 1; // Push down kybd macro
75     for( i=strlen(msg); i>0; --i ) push( 0, *p-- );
76   }
77
78   int keystate( keynew &kybd )   // Overloaded friend
79   {                              //  functions start
80     return kybd.state;           //    *** HERE ***
81   }
82
```

572

Listing 14.3. Continued.

```
83  int keystate( keynew *kybd )
84  {
85    return kybd->state;
86  }
87
88  int keyval( keynew &kybd )
89  {
90    return kybd.ch;
91  }
92
93  int keyval( keynew *kybd )
94  {
95    return kybd->ch;
96  }
```

The function definitions for the overloaded keynew friend functions are found in lines 78 through 96 of Listing 14.3. The function bodies, like the function declarations, merely reflect the different kinds of arguments accepted by the different functions.

To complete the demonstration, Listing 14.4 shows a main program that uses the keynew class. The program's sole purpose is to load text data into the push buffer, using the keynew::loadmac() member function, and then to extract the data again.

Listing 14.4. testnew.cpp. A program that tests and exercises the keyboard class.

```
1   #include <stdlib.h>
2   #include <stdio.h>
3   #include <string.h>
4
5   #include "keynew.hpp"
6
7   main()
8   {
9     int i;                    // Declare an ordinary object ...
10    keynew *kybd = new keynew;  // Create keyboard object
11
12    char *msgs[] = {
```

```
13    "This is a keyboard object message block."
        " It was created\n",
14    "just to test the keyboard macro facility."
        " You don't have\n",
15    "to do anything, just watch the message roll"
        " up on the screen.\n",
16    "To exit the program, strike Enter.\n",
17    };
18                        // Load the macro lines backwards, so
19                        // they will read forward
20
21    for ( i=3; i>=0; --i ) kybd->loadmac( msgs[i] );
22
23                    // Call to keyval() uses overloaded friend
24
25    do { kybd->nexte(); } while ( keyval( kybd ) != 13 );
26    }
```

In Listing 14.4, look at line 25—the point of interest here. The keyval() function is called, using the object name kybd as an argument. Because kybd is a pointer to a keynew object, the corresponding overloaded friend function is invoked (the function defined in lines 93 through 96 of Listing 14.3).

Overloading Nonmember Functions

Declaring overloaded nonmember, nonfriend functions is the simplest form of function overloading. Because C++ functions *must* at least be declared before they can be called, you need merely to write the multiple declarations for the different versions of the function. The cube_root() function mentioned earlier in this chapter is a good example of this kind of overloaded function declaration. You write the declarations like this:

```
double cube_root( double );
double cube_root( float );
double cube_root( int );
double cube_root( long );
```

This time, notice that the overload keyword is nowhere in sight. Because Microsoft C/C++ is compatible with the ANSI C++ 2.1 standards, the overload keyword is obsolete.

You should consider two additional issues when overloading functions, whether they are member, friend, or nonmember functions. These issues are the handling of *functions with default arguments* and the handling of *functions with unused formal arguments*.

Because functions with default arguments and functions with unused formal arguments are unique to C++, questions about handling them do not arise when you write plain C programs. The following short program (which compiles and runs under Microsoft C/C++) incorporates examples of default arguments and unused formal arguments in one function:

```
#include <iostream.h>
#include <stdlib.h>

int f1( int = 0, int = 0 );

void main()
{
   cout << f1() << "\r\n" ;
}

int f1( int value, int )
{
   return value;
}
```

This program shows only one nonmember function, but the following discussion applies to member and friend functions as well.

Notice that the function f1() has two default arguments. Therefore, for purposes of argument matching for overloaded functions, C++ assumes that there are *three* overloaded functions with different numbers of arguments. This makes sense when you realize that f1() can legally be called in the following three ways:

```
f1();
f1( 0 );
f1( 0, 0 );
```

Generally, then, a function with n default arguments is considered (for argument-matching purposes) as $n + 1$ functions having the same name and different numbers of arguments. The point, naturally, is that if you write a call to a function with default arguments so that argument conversions are necessary, a complicated matching sequence (and a needlessly inefficient call) might result.

Now notice that the function *definition* for f1() does not name the second (unused) formal argument. A couple of things are going on here. First, even if an unused formal argument is unnamed, a call to that function must still specify an argument to be passed to the function. Next, the short program just shown has default arguments, which masks the first fact. The important point to understand is this: Although unused formal arguments do not appear in the function body, they *do* participate in argument matching for overloaded functions.

Understanding Type-Safe Linkage

Because the `overload` keyword is now obsolete, the C++ compiler has more responsibility in detecting overloaded functions and sorting out the calls to such functions. That is, the compiler must provide *type-safe linkage* to functions. The solution to any design problems that may result is *function mangling* (the C++ method of typing functions). Making some changes in the way linkage is handled in C++ programs may be required also. Both these subjects are discussed in this section.

Understanding Function Mangling

What's in a name? Everyday wisdom holds that a name is only a surface label and does not change the internal substance of a person or thing. This is only partly true for the compiler designer and, indirectly, for the compiler user.

What's in a C++ name? Function overloading makes it appear—at the source-code level—that you can have the same name for several different functions. This is true only at the source-code level, and then only *apparently* true. In the more technical language of the base document and of compiler design theory, overloading function names is just a *syntactical convenience* for the programmer. When processing source code, the compiler must generate a *unique name* for every distinct object and function. Otherwise, the compiler could never locate the precise object or function again.

A unique internal name is provided during compilation through the process of *function mangling*. The internal name (which exists on the symbol table during compilation) consists of the function name, return type, and signature. A function's signature is nothing more than its argument list. The signature is what primarily distinguishes a particular overloaded function. The signature is unique because of the exact number and type of arguments for the function. Forming unique internal identifiers for an overloaded function name is illustrated in Figure 14.3.

A problem now arises. How can the compiler know beforehand which functions are overloaded (and therefore need mangling) and which functions are not? The compiler cannot know, but there is a solution to the problem: Microsoft C/C++ and comparable C++ compilers mangle *all* functions.

You might think that mangling all functions would solve every possible problem related to redefining and overloading functions. Unfortunately, that is not the case.

Figure 14.3.

Each mangled name for an overloaded function constitutes a unique identifier and type for the function during compilation.

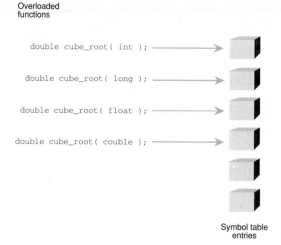

Overloaded functions

```
double cube_root( int );
double cube_root( long );
double cube_root( float );
double cube_root( couble );
```

Symbol table entries

Controlling Linkage Problems with Standard C Include Files

A problem with function mangling and type-safe linkage occurs when you mix modules from other languages with C++ modules. Surprisingly, plain C must be considered a different language for this purpose. It may seem reasonable to expect to directly call plain C standard library functions, but that just won't work—unless something is done to make it work.

You cannot call these library functions directly because of function mangling. A mangled function name is not the same as an unmangled name (which does not contain return type and signature data). Therefore, if C++ mangles *all* function names, how can it ever find, say, the standard printf() function during linkage editing? The answer is that the compiler can't. The linkage editor ends up trying to match names (conceptually) like this:

```
int_printf_vargs ?== printf
```

Clearly, there has to be some way to turn off mangling when you want to reference plain C function names (such as *all* the standard library functions) in separately compiled modules. Of course, there is a way. To see what it is, use the Microsoft C/C++ editor to look at some of the standard C header files in the \include directory. The method of turning off function mangling is called *alternate linkage specification*. If, for example, you examine the stdlib.h header supplied with Microsoft C/C++, you will see declarations structured something like this:

```
/*      stdlib.h      */

#ifdef __cplusplus
extern "C" {
```

```
#endif


    ... Function declarations go here.

    ... Since function names declared here are known
    ... NOT to be mangled, the linkage editor will be
    ... able to find them when linking in plain C
    ... modules.


#ifdef __cplusplus
}
#endif
```

The general syntax for specifying alternate linkage for single declarations is fairly simple:

```
extern "C" double get_area( double circum );
extern "C" double get_circum( double area );
```

You also can specify alternate linkage for a whole group of declarations at once by surrounding them with curly braces, just as you would for a compound C statement:

```
extern "C" {
  double get_area( double circum );
  double get_circum( double area );
}
```

In most cases, you will use the extern "C" linkage specifier in your own header files. Linkage specifiers are not restricted to header files, however. From time to time, you may need to use the single-declaration form of the specifier directly within a program source-code file. As with all things C, some rules govern the use of linkage specifiers:

- ■ *"C++" is the default linkage and is always required to be present in every C++ compiler.* This rule simply means that function mangling is *on* by default in a C++ program.

- ■ *You cannot invent your own linkage strings.* From the point of view of the compiler designer, the value of the "C" and "C++" linkage strings is somewhat arbitrary; The compiler doesn't care what strings are used. Once they are set in place (by the designer), they are fixed: If you try to invent a string unknown to the compiler, an error results.

- ■ *Linkage specifiers can appear only at file scope.* You cannot write a linkage specifier locally, within a function, like this:

```
int dosumpin( int arg1 )
{
```

```
extern "C" double sumpinelse( double ); // ILLEGAL !!
...
}
```

Although you can use the extern keyword within a function body to declare ordinary linkage elsewhere within the source file, use of the
alternate linkage specifier is strictly illegal within a function body. This
restriction is used in C++ to avoid requiring compilers to incorporate
multiple linkages in different scopes.

■ *Linkage specifications do not create a new scope.* You may recall that a
block statement, enclosed in curly braces, creates a local scope in both C
and C++. Despite the similarities to block statement syntax, the compound form of the linkage specifier—extern "C" {...}—is not a block
statement and does not create a local scope.

■ *Linkage specifications are transmitted to inner scopes.* This rule means that
a linkage specification applied to a class applies to all nonmember functions and data objects declared within the class. Moreover, a linkage
specification applied to a function applies to functions and objects declared (not defined!) within the contained function.

■ *Multiple declarations for the same function, both with and without explicit
linkage specification, can exist in the same source file.* If this occurs, you
must write the declaration with explicit linkage specification first, followed by the declaration without any linkage specification. You can use
this feature to *phase in* a new C++ version of a function while still maintaining an older, plain C version. The declarations for two such functions
are packaged in this way:

```
extern "C" void dosumpin( int ); // Declare old version

void routeold( int arg )
{
        // Establish external linkage to outer declaration
        // to old dosumpin()
    extern void dosumpin( int );

        // Now call the old version
    dosumpin( arg );
}

// -------- Now set up new C++ version --------
// The new version provides return status information

int dosumpin( int );  // C++ version

...
```

```
void main()
{
  int i;

  routeold( 2 );     // Call the old C version
  i = dosumpin( 2 ); // Get return info from new version
}
```

■ *You can write a linkage specifier for an entire #include file.* Usually, you
write linkage specifiers for various declarations inside header files. If you
do not want to modify the contents of a header file, however, you can
declare alternate linkage for the whole header:

```
extern "C" {
  #include "myheader"
}
```

■ *Only one of a group of overloaded functions can have "C" linkage.* It requires only a moment's thought to figure this one out. Overloading is the
"reason for being" for function mangling. If you turn it off for more than
one overloaded function, you end up with two different functions having
exactly the same name—resulting in the expected compiler error.

■ *Functions and objects declared within a linkage specification act as if they
were explicitly declared* extern, *unless they were explicitly declared* static.
You can naturally assume that declarations surrounded by a linkage
specification are found in another source module—hence, the assumption of extern linkage. You may recall, however, that the static keyword forces internal linkage. Therefore, even though you can declare an
object or function static within the {} of a linkage specification, the linkage specification is effectively ignored for those static objects or functions.

Overloading Operators with C++

Operators are a critically important part of the C and C++ languages. Operators
give you the power and flexibility to manipulate data in an astonishing number
of ways, as you saw in Chapter 2.

The introduction of user-defined types, or classes, in C++ raises new issues
about the operator set. Specifically, if it is the programmer's responsibility to
define the behavior of a new type, as well as its data content, how are C operators affected by the new environment? You must define how the operator set
works with your new classes. This process is called *operator overloading*. It is
similar to function overloading because a single operator can now have

different significance for different objects. Furthermore, if you do not overload a particular operator for a class, it cannot be used with objects of that class. It's all up to you. In this section, you learn how to overload C operators for your classes.

Understanding Operator Overloading

You can, and indeed must, overload an operator before it can be used with objects of your just-invented new class. This does not mean, however, that you can invent new operators of your own. You can overload only a subset of the existing C++ operator set. Most of the C++ operators (which are in themselves a superset of the plain C operators) can be overloaded. Table 14.2 shows which C++ operators you can overload.

Table 14.2. C++ operators that can be overloaded.

New	Delete							
+	-	*	/	%	^	&	¦	~
!	=	<	>	+=	-=	*=	/=	%=
^=	&=	¦=	<<	>>	<<=	>>=	==	!=
<=	>=	&&	¦¦	++	—	,	->*	->
( )	[ ]							

Four of the operators in Table 14.2 have both binary and unary forms, depending on where in an expression they are used. These are the addition or positive (+), subtraction or negative (-), multiplication or dereference (*), and the AND or address-of (&) operators.

Two of the operators shown in Table 14.2—the increment (++) and decrement (--) operators—can be used in either a prefix (++*object*) or postfix (*object*++) position. Notice carefully that even though you can overload these operators to accept many different types of arguments, you must distinguish between their prefix and postfix use. You can overload the ++ operator in Microsoft C/C++ in the following way:

```
#include <iostream.h>

class A {
```

```
public:
  int data;
  A& operator++();     // Prefix increment
  A& operator++(int)   // Postfix increment
}

A& A::operator++()
{
  ++data;
  return *this;
}

A& A::operator++(int)
{
  data++;
  return *this;
}
```

In the preceding code fragment, the postfix increment operator is distinguished from the prefix operator by adding a single `int` argument to the postfix operator definition. You implement a decrement much as you do an increment—just add the `int` argument to the postfix decrement operator's definition.

Four C++ operators and two preprocessing operators cannot be overloaded. These operators are shown in Table 14.3.

Table 14.3. C++ operators that cannot be overloaded.

Operator	Description
.	Structure or class member access operator
.*	Pointer to member operator
::	Scope resolution operator
?:	Conditional (ternary) operator
#	Preprocessing operator
##	Preprocessing string concatenation operator

The class member (`.`), pointer to member (`.*`), and scope resolution (`::`) operators all have predefined meanings that would be difficult or impossible to change dynamically. These operators are therefore excluded from the list of overloadable operators. The C++ designers simply felt that the conditional or ternary (?:) operator was not worth the effort of overloading. Finally, over-loading preprocessing operators is a practical impossibility, as they are not used during the actual compilation process.

Because the pointer to class member operator (.*) is rarely seen, and almost never explained, this operator is shown in action in Listing 14.5.

Listing 14.5. ptrmbr.cpp. A program that uses a pointer to a class member.

```
1   #include <iostream.h>
2
3   class A {
4     int value;
5   public:
6     A( int );
7     void display( A& arg );
8   };
9
10  A::A( int which )
11  {
12    switch ( which ) {
13      case 1 : value = 1;
14              break;
15      case 2 : value = 2;
16              break;
17      case 3 : value = 3;
18              break;
19      default: value = 1;
20              break;
21    }
22  }
23
24  void A::display( A& arg )
25  {
26    int A::* type;
27    type = &A::value;
28
29    cout << arg.*type << "\r\n";
30  }
31
32  void main()
33  {
34    A x = 3;   // type 3
```

```
35
36    x.display( x );
37  }
```

The use of the pointer to member operator in Listing 14.5 is admittedly somewhat contrived. Still, it illustrates the syntax required and the procedure used
to bring the parts together. The `.*` operator is put to work in the `A::display()`
function found in lines 24 through 30.

The first thing to understand is how the pointer to member variable is itself
declared (see line 25). The declaration has three parts:

- *The type of the member pointed to.* This is not the type of the pointer variable, but the type of the data object or function pointed to. In the program in Listing 14.5, the type is `int` because that is the type of `A::value`.

- *The pointer to member declarator.* In the construction

  `classname::*`

  the name that follows identifies a pointer to member. Remember that the
  purpose, for the moment, is to declare a pointer variable although it
  is not an ordinary pointer.

- *The pointer to member identifier.* This is just the name of the pointer to
  the member object. In Listing 14.5, the name of the pointer variable is
  `type`.

To put the pointer to member to use, you need some way to initialize the
pointer to member variable. The method for doing this is found in line 27. The
expression `&A::value` takes the address of the member object. The following
syntax is the general form for taking the address of a class member:

`&classname::membername`

Its construction is not really surprising. The address-of operator (&) does just
what a C programmer would expect, and the fully qualified name of the member object is required to prevent ambiguous references.

You must also dereference the pointer to member to access the object to
which it points. The syntax for doing this is a little different from that in plain
C (see line 29 of Listing 14.5). You use the following general form:

`objectname.*ptr_to_member_name`

When dereferenced, as shown in line 29, the pointer to member refers to an
ordinary member object. It is then an *object locator,* used in the same way as
for dereferencing ordinary pointers. As an object locator, it can be used as
either an lvalue (left side of assignment) or rvalue (right side of assignment).

There are some additional considerations when you write overloaded operator
functions. Table 14.4 shows characteristics of various kinds of overloaded

operator functions. These characteristics pertain to class inheritance, virtual overloaded operator functions, return types, function accessibility, and default generation.

Table 14.4. Characteristics of the overloaded operator functions.

C++ Operator	Can Be Inherited	Can Be Virtual	Can Have Return Type	Member or Friend	Generated by Default
()	yes	yes	yes	member	no
[]	yes	yes	yes	member	no
->	yes	yes	yes	member	no
op=()	no	yes	yes	member	memberwise
new	yes	no	void*	static member	no
delete	yes	no	void	static member	no
other ops	yes	yes	yes	either	no

The first six entries in Table 14.4 give the characteristics of user-defined functions for special operators; the last entry gives the characteristics for all remaining operators.

Of the operators shown in Table 14.4, the assignment operator is unique. It cannot be inherited; all the others can. It is the only operator for which the compiler generates a default overloaded function. If you do not declare an overloaded assignment-operator function, the compiler generates one that copies the class object, member by member.

Although restrictions on operator function linkage are not shown directly in Table 14.4, some restrictions are implied. The first four operators—(), [], ->, and = —must be *nonstatic* member functions. The new and delete operators must be static functions; they are assumed to be static even if you don't code the static keyword in the function declaration. The static storage class for new and delete is dictated by the fact that these two operators, apart from all the others, must already exist *before* the class object has been completely constructed and initialized. The rest of the operators can be either static or nonstatic, and either member or friend functions.

All the operator functions in Table 14.4 can be declared also as virtual functions, with the exception of the class new and delete operators (that is, not global new and delete). The class new and delete operators have the additional requirement that the return types shown in the table are mandatory.

Declaring Overloaded Operator Functions

Before jumping directly into examples of overloading operators, you should pause and take stock of what will be required of you (what you should already know) and what you want to accomplish. This section covers some fairly complicated ground. If you aren't adequately prepared to approach the subject of overloading operators, your time will not be well spent.

Setting the Stage for Operator Functions

You should already have a clear idea of what a member function is, what the C++ operators (the ordinary ones) do, and how functions pass and return values. Most important, you should have a strong grasp of C++ references, how to form them, and what they do. Remember that references bind to objects, not addresses (even though addresses are at work behind the scenes).

While learning C++, or just trying to explain it to other programmers, several important questions must be answered for the person learning to overload operators:

- *How do you declare overloaded operator functions?* Without a knowledge of the fundamental syntax involved and its significance, operator over-loading becomes a hopeless muddle in the mind of the would-be C++ practitioner. The syntax is fairly simple, but it is rather strange looking.

- *What arguments are passed to operator functions?* How many arguments can an overloaded operator function accept? Is the number different for friend and member functions? Should the arguments be objects, pointers, or references—and how do you know when to choose each of these? As you can see, this particular discussion is important, as well as a source of potential confusion.

- *Should you return objects or references?* Does it make any difference whether you return objects or references? What if you are returning a *class* object? How is efficiency of execution affected? Do you need to know how the C++ compiler parses expressions? This topic is important also. Miss the boat here, and you find yourself wondering what happened (with no hope of finding out).

- *When should you use friend functions, and when should you use member functions?* Does the choice make any real difference? Using friend functions in the right places can affect program performance. There are also some wrong places to use friend functions.

- *How do you handle cast operators?* Yes, you can even overload cast operators in C++. This topic has not yet been raised, so you first need to know about basic syntax, return types, linkage—the works.

Understanding Overloaded Operator Function Syntax

Answers to all of the preceding questions, beginning with the first, are provided in this section and the next several sections. Listing 14.6 contains a program that illustrates how to overload operators.

Listing 14.6. $avings.cpp. A program that overloads the ! and = operators.

```
1   #include <stdio.h>
2   #include <stdlib.h>
3   #include <string.h>
4
5   class savings {
6     double total;
7   public:
8     savings() { total = 0.0; }        // CONSTRUCTOR FUNCTIONS
9     savings( double amt ) { total = amt; }
10    savings( int amt ) { total = (double)amt; }
11    savings( long amt ) { total = (double)amt; }
12    double operator!();               // REPORT FUNCTION
13    savings& operator=( savings& );   // ASSIGNMENT OPERATORS
14    savings& operator=( double );
15    savings& operator=( int );
16    savings& operator=( long );
17  };
18
19  double savings::operator!()
20  {
21    return total;
22  }
23
24  savings& savings::operator=( savings& otheracct )
25  {
26    total = otheracct.total; // notice ref to other savings object
27    return *this;            // notice return of reference type
28  }
29
30  savings& savings::operator=( double amt )
31  {
32    total = amt;
33    return *this;
34  }
```

```
35
36   savings& savings::operator=( int amt )
37   {
38     total = (double)amt;
39     return *this;
40   }
41
42   savings& savings::operator=( long amt )
43   {
44     total = (double)amt;
45     return *this;
46   }
47
48   void main()
49   {
50     savings account1( 100.01 );
51     savings account2, account3;  // using default constr., no ()
52
53                    // the following syntax requires the return of
54                    // a reference from assign op
55     account3 = account2 = account1;
56     printf( "The savings account now has $%10.2lf dollars\n",
57               !account3 );
58   }
```

Listing 14.6 shows constructor functions and operators overloaded in such a way as to allow the creation or manipulation of a savings object with double, integer, long, or other savings objects. Because you are already familiar with constructor functions, turn immediately to the operator functions. The declarations for the overloaded operator functions are found in lines 12 through 16. Here is the general form of the declaration:

returntype operator@(*arg*$_{opt}$);

In this declaration, operator is a keyword to be coded exactly as you see it here, and @ represents the particular operator you are overloading. The argument arg is required only for binary operators.

The *returntype* that you specify for an overloaded operator function depends on what you want the operator to do. Line 12, for example, shows that savings::operator!() returns a double, indicating the amount of money in the savings account. This particular operator function is, in fact, a good example of the flexibility allowed in defining operator behavior for a class. Because the NOT function usually associated with the ! operator has little significance for the savings class, that operator has been borrowed to report a value.

Notice, however, such flexibility does not mean that you can take liberties with the normal syntax for an operator, any more than you can invent new operators. You can see, for example, in line 57 of Listing 14.6 that the operator is written in the usual manner:

```
!account3
```

`account3` is a `savings` class instance object.

Looking again at the syntax for the declaration of an overloaded operator, notice next that the `operator` keyword is required in the declaration. Although you may substitute a particular operator for the @ in the syntax form, you must code some legitimate operator in that position.

Specifying Arguments for Overloaded Operator Functions

Now consider the significance of the optional argument shown in the syntax form. What does it mean? Are other arguments available? The `savings::operator!()` declaration has no arguments, whereas each of the `savings::operator=( arg )` declarations in lines 13 through 16 of Listing 14.6 has one argument.

To understand what arguments are made available to operator functions, you need to recall what happens to *any* member function when it is called. (The use of friends for operator functions, which is slightly different, is discussed later in this section.) The significant point is that a member function *always* has the `this` pointer as its implicit first or only argument. How this affects the implementation of `savings::operator( savings& )`, for example, is shown in Figure 14.4.

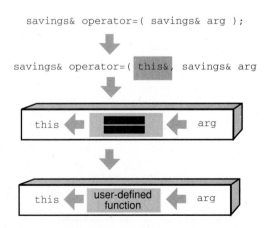

As shown in Figure 14.4, an `operator=()` function with one argument coded actually has two arguments: The object on the left side of the assignment is pointed to by `this`, and the object on the right side of the assignment is described by the coded argument (a reference to a `savings` class object in Figure 14.4). Because of this arrangement, the function definition for this particular assignment overload is coded like this:

```
savings& savings::operator=( savings& otheracct )
{
  total = otheracct.total; // Notice ref to other object
  return *this;            // Notice return of ref. type
}
```

Within the function body, the operand on the left is located by the current member variable total. The operand on the right is located by the class object passed as an argument to the function, so that access to the operand requires the qualified name `otheracct.total`.

Specifying a Return Type for an Operator Function

The returned value is important also. The comments near the end of Listing 14.6 indicate that the syntax of the statement in line 55 requires the assignment-operator overloaded functions to return a reference rather than an object. You can see in lines 27, 33, 39, and 45 that this is precisely what the functions do. The syntax of multiple assignment (a = b = c), however, does not strictly require returning a reference. You could, if you wanted, return an object by value. So why return a reference?

Look closely at what reference the `operator=()` functions return: It is a reference to the object pointed to by `this`. Thus, only an object locator (the reference, which is a disguised pointer) for the operand on the left is needed, and the object referred to already exists. The reference to the left-side operand then becomes the right-side argument in the next assignment operator to the left. That is, returning a reference in such a case is very efficient.

Consider the alternative of returning an object by value. The following code fragment shows how you would have to recode the `savings` class to return objects by value from the operator overload functions:

```
class savings {   // POOR METHOD FOR OVERLOADING =
  ...
public:
  savings operator=( savings );
  ...
};
...
```

```
savings savings::operator( savings& otheracct )
{
  total = otheracct.total; // still a reference!
  return *this;            // Return whole object
}
```

The most obvious thing about this new version of the savings class is that now the whole object must be copied onto the stack and returned to be used in further evaluating the expression a = b. Moving whole objects, particularly large ones, on and off the stack can be expensive both in stack space and execution time.

With multiple assignments in one expression, however, you can still leave the *argument* defined as a reference. Even though a rightmost assignment returns an object, remember that *references bind to objects*. Therefore, in an expression of the form a = b, b can be either a value or a reference because either one is an object locator. All this is just another way of saying that references can be viewed as merely providing an alternative name for an *object*.

Notice one final point about the operator=() functions for the savings class: They are member functions, not friend functions. This requirement was shown in Table 14.4. Overloaded operator functions must be nonstatic member functions.

Now consider overloaded functions for the +=, -=, and other compound assignment operators. These functions should be coded with references for return values, even though the compound assignment operator only modifies an existing object. You might think that for such expressions as

```
savings account;
...
account += 256.65;
```

it is perfectly acceptable to write the following void return type:

```
void savings operator+=( double );
```

After all, the account object is simply updated, and that is the end of the matter. Right? Wrong! Suppose you used a void return type as shown, and you then write something such as this:

```
printf( "After deposits, you have $%10.2lf dollars.\n",
        !(account += 256.64) );
```

What happens? As you may recall, the %10.2lf conversion specifier means printf() expects a double for its first argument after the format string. If void is the return type, the preceding line does not compile. If it does compile, you will find that a void is not the same as a double. If, however, you declared operator+=() to return a reference to a savings object, the expression !(account += 256.64) is correctly evaluated in the following manner:

1. First, the interior expression `account += 256.64` is evaluated. That is, the compiler generates code to call `operator+=(double)`, which in turn results in a reference to a savings object.

2. Next, the `!` operator (which is overloaded) is applied to the resulting reference to a savings object. This operator, remember, returns a `double`—which is just what the `printf()` function expects.

Overloading Operators with Friend Functions

There are all sorts of instances, however, in which it is preferable to use friend functions—for example, when you use compound assignment operators (+=, - =, and so on). Only the simple assignment operator must be a member and cannot be inherited. Compound assignment operators can be friends, and they can be inherited.

Why use friends to overload operators? There are various reasons in various contexts for using friend functions. The reason in the context of operator overload functions is *flexibility*. That is, friend functions allow you to specify arguments for *both* the left- and right-side operands of an operator, so that user-defined conversions can be applied to both operands.

Member operator functions, however, expect only one argument and assume that the left operand is `*this`. Thus, the left operand cannot be converted in this case and must be an lvalue. The significance of this restriction for object behavior is discussed in detail in Chapter 18, "Turbo Vision." In the meantime, use friend functions wherever you can.

Before examining some examples of friend functions that overload operators for the `savings` class, consider how using friend functions affects the argument list structure (the signature). The main thing affecting the design of friend operator functions is that friend functions are not in the scope of the class for which they are declared. That is, *there is no `this` pointer supplied automatically.*

How, then, does a friend operator function know what the current object is? It doesn't, unless you tell it. The implied first operator in Figure 14.4 (shown earlier) cannot be implied in a friend function—the operator must be explicit. The general form for declaring friend operator functions is this:

```
friend returntype operator@( arg ,arg_opt );
```

The first argument corresponds to the left-side operand of the operator, and the second argument corresponds to the right-side operand of the operator. Overloaded friend functions for binary operators always require *two* arguments because of the missing `this` pointer. Friend functions and unary operators are covered in the next section.

You can further expand the savings class by adding operator functions for the subtraction (-) and compound subtraction (-=) operators. This precise pair of operators shows that the different effects of the return types can be highlighted. Here are the declarations and functions for these operators:

```
class savings {
  ...
public:
  friend& savings operator-=( savings&, savings& );
  friend& savings operator-=( savings&, double );
  friend savings operator-( savings&, savings& );
  friend savings operator-( savings&, double );
};
...
savings& operator-=( savings& curr, savings& other )
{
  curr.total -= other.total; // Use global -=
  return curr;               // Return ref to left-side op
}


savings& operator-=( savings& curr, double amt )
{
  curr.total -= amt;         // Use global -=
  return curr;               // Return ref to left-side op
}


savings operator-( savings& curr, savings& other )
{
  savings TEMP;  // Declare a local temporary object

  TEMP = curr;    // Hold left-side operand
  TEMP -= other; // Cheat -- use overloaded -=
  return TEMP;    // Tricky, huh?
}
savings operator-( savings& curr, double amt )
{
  savings TEMP;  // Declare a local temporary object

  TEMP = curr;    // Hold left-side operand
  TEMP -= amt;    // Cheat -- use other overloaded -=
  return TEMP;    // Tricky, huh?
}
```

All four of the preceding overloaded operator functions are friends. There is no reason at all *not* to make them friends, and the goal of efficient objects is a good reason to make them friends. Notice, the function names are *not* qualified by the `savings::` syntax. That syntax does not apply to friend functions.

After you have examined the friend operator functions in the preceding code fragment, note the arguments and the return types. Did you notice that wherever a class object is an argument, a reference to it is coded? A good rule of thumb is this: *Always* use a reference to a class object in the argument list.

That rule is important for two reasons. First, as you learned earlier, you can call the operator function (by writing an expression with the particular operator) with either objects or references to an object with impunity—either choice works because references bind to objects. Second, and vastly important, remember that if you pass the argument by value, you can *modify only the copy of it on the stack*—you cannot reach the original object (just as in ordinary C, right?). This restriction might cause problems that are hard to debug.

When passing *ordinary objects* to operator functions, however, you may not want to use references. For anything less than structures, you can pass ordinary objects by value almost as efficiently. They don't require too much stack space or execution time, and they may even save execution time because no disguised pointer is processing for them. In the preceding code fragment, for example, `double` objects are passed by value.

The return types for the new `savings` operator functions are even more interesting. Both versions of the `operator-=()` function still return references, for all the reasons stated earlier. In the case of the `-=` operator, returning a reference is useful for two additional reasons. First, the left-side operand (first argument) is modified, and the returned value or object locator should reflect that modification. Second, returning a reference permits efficient behavior (fast execution times) of the class object and flexible use of the operator (remember the `printf()` example earlier).

The `operator-()` functions, however, return by *value*. Not only that, but you have little choice in the matter. If you think about it for a moment, you realize a return by value is required because an expression such as a - b yields a result that is not stored in either a or b. Both simple assignment and compound assignment modify the value of the left-side operand, which is where the result is stored. This is not the case for ordinary arithmetic and shift operators. Where, then, do you put the result? You put it in a temporary variable and then pass a copy of it back to the compiler-generated code that is evaluating the parsed expression. Whew!

Now look, one line at a time, at the code for the `operator-()` function (the one with the `double` second argument). The first thing you see is the declaration of a `savings` object within the friend function:

```
savings operator-( savings& curr, double amt )
{
    savings TEMP;   // Declare a local temporary object
```

```
    TEMP = curr;    // Hold left-side operand
    TEMP -= amt;    // Cheat -- use other overloaded -=
    return TEMP;    // Tricky, huh?
}
```

Won't this cause a recursive creation of savings objects? No, it won't. First, this function is a friend function and not part of the savings scope. Second, even if this were a member function, it still would not cause recursive creation of objects because it is not in the *constructor* function. The TEMP object, then, is a legitimate auto object that happens to have type savings.

The next line of code in the operator-() function places the value of the left-side operand (first argument) in the TEMP object. The value of the left-side operand can now be used without disturbing the contents of the original object. Furthermore, the overloaded assignment operator operator=(double) is the means of carrying out the transfer.

Next, the just-defined operator-=(double) function is used to subtract the right-side operand from the TEMP object. TEMP now has a value equal to *leftoperand - rightoperand*.

Finally, the TEMP object is returned by value. Wait! Won't that constitute a reference to a vanishing local variable? Not at all. The return value is only a *copy* of TEMP, and that copy will survive the destruction of TEMP when it goes out of scope.

In summary, use the following criteria in deciding whether to use references or values for return types for the arithmetic and shift operators:

■ *If the operator is to modify the left-side operand, return a reference to the left-side operand.* This rule does not apply to unary operators, as shown in the next section.

■ *Otherwise, create a local object of the class for use as a temporary variable, modify the temporary copy, and return it by value.* Neither the left- nor the right-side operand is modified this way, and returning by value prevents passing back a pointer (disguised or otherwise) to an out-of-scope and nonexistent auto object. This rule *does* apply to unary operators.

Defining Cast Operator Functions

Recall that five questions were presented earlier in this chapter. Four of these questions have now been covered. The fifth question is, how do you handle user-defined cast operators for class objects? For an answer, consider once again the example of the savings object. Provided here, for brevity, is the cast operator function for a cast to type long. This cast might not be useful in the real world because it truncates fractional parts, but the code aptly illustrates how to set up the class for user-defined casts:

```
class savings {
  ...
public:
  ...
  operator long(); // no return type, no arguments
};
...
savings::operator long()
{
  return (long)total; // Use global (long) cast
}
```

A user-defined conversion (cast) of this kind is quite simple. You just specify the targeted type name as the operator, and be sure to return that type. Within the conversion function in the preceding code fragment, the global cast to long is used (that is, an ordinary cast). Of course, for other conceivable conversions—savings to string (char *), for example—considerably more code may be required.

Notice that a user-defined conversion function cannot have a return type in the declaration part, even though the return verb is used to pass back a value of the desired type. The operator function name (a cast *is* an operator) already identifies the type. Notice also that user-defined cast operator functions must be *member* functions. They are clearly associated closely with their class—so that friend functions are not permitted.

Nor can a user-defined function have any explicit arguments. Only the implicit and ever-present this can be used by the function. This makes sense: What else would you want to convert, except an object of the class containing the conversion function?

Overloading Binary and Unary Operators

Binary operators, such as addition or subtraction, are characterized by having two operands: the left- and right-side operands mentioned previously. Overloaded operator functions are called, as needed, when the compiler-generated code for evaluating expressions that involve class objects is executed. The compiler-generated code passes arguments to the overloaded functions—arguments that correspond to the operands being used at that point in the evaluation.

The first argument, which may be the implicitly present this pointer, corresponds to the left-side operand being evaluated. The second argument, which is always explicitly coded in the function declaration (except for cast functions), corresponds to the right-side operand.

This manner of supplying function arguments for corresponding operands leads naturally to the syntax you must use to declare the operator functions for binary operators, depending on whether a member function or friend function is used. The following rules apply:

■ *Overloaded functions for binary operators, implemented as member functions, require one explicit argument.* The `this` pointer is implicitly supplied to member functions as the first or only argument. The implicit `this` pointer therefore corresponds to the left-side operand of a binary operator. The explicitly supplied argument is the right-side operand.

■ *Overloaded functions for binary operators, implemented as friend functions, require two explicit arguments.* Because friend functions are not in the scope of the class that declares them as friends, there is no `this` argument. Two explicit arguments are required, corresponding to the left- and right-side operands of a binary operator.

Similar considerations apply to unary operators although, of course, unary operators have by definition only one operand. The following rules apply to arguments for overloaded unary operators:

■ *Overloaded functions for unary operators, when implemented as member functions, require zero explicit arguments, except for the increment and decrement postfic operators, as explained previously.* The `this` pointer is still, as always, implicitly supplied so that no other arguments are necessary.

■ *Overloaded functions for unary operators, when implemented as friend functions, require one explicit argument.* Because friend functions are not in the scope of the class declaring them as friends, an argument is required to locate the only operand of a unary operator.

In the preceding section, you learned that you should implement functions for unary operators by using a locally declared temporary class object in order to avoid modifying the contents of the current operand. Is that always true? It is true in all but two cases, and then only if you return a class object or a reference to a class object from the function. Consider the sample expressions shown with each unary operator in Table 14.5.

Table 14.5. Unary operators with sample expressions.

Operator	Operator Name	Sample Expression(s)
+	Unary +	`a = +b;`
-	Unary –	`a = -b;`

Operator	Operator Name	Sample Expression(s)
*	Pointer declarator,	`char *text;`
	dereference	`a = *b;`
&	Address-of	`a = &b;`
~	One's complement	`a = ~b;`
!	Logical NOT	`a = !b;`
++	Increment	`++a; a++;`
--	Decrement	`--a; a--;`

For each of the unary operators shown in Table 14.5, except the increment and decrement operators, you do *not* want the action of the operator to change the value or state of its operand. You do want the operator to return a desired value, *based on* the original state of the operand. You would not want the address-of operator, for example, to replace an object's *value* with a *pointer*. With the ++ and -- operators, however, you do want to replace the original object's value.

What about using temporary local class objects in unary operator functions? The following code fragment shows two overloads for the unary - operator for the savings class:

```
                   // member functions, unary operator,
                   // take zero arguments
savings savings::operator-()
{
  savings TEMP;

  TEMP = *this;        // Get a copy of operand
  TEMP.total *= -1.0;  // Negate internal value
  return TEMP;         // and return by value
}

double savings::operator-()
{
  return -total;       // Don't need TEMP here
}
```

The operator-() function returning double in this code fragment obviously needs no help from a temporary variable. There is no danger of modifying anything permanently. The operator-() function returning savings does need that help, though, because there is no way to get a *whole object*, with its member data negated, into a position to be returned without a temporary object.

The `operator-()` function could have modified `this->total` (by writing `total *= -1.0`). Then, however, there would be no way to set `total` back to its original state after returning. Such a modification would surely cause unexpected results later in the program.

Overloading the Subscript and Function Call Operators

Two additional operators can be overloaded that have not yet been discussed. These are the *subscript operator,* `[]`, and the *function call operator,* `()`. Both are considered binary operators, and in most ways are handled in a normal manner. Because they have sufficiently interesting characteristics, however, these operators are covered separately in this section.

Notice that overloaded functions for both `[]` and `()` must be nonstatic member functions. Friends are not allowed in these cases.

Using an Overloaded Subscript Operator

You can define a class for which the array subscript operator function, `operator[]()`, is overloaded. Thus, you can treat objects of that class as arrays, even if the member data in such an object is not actually an array. Still, the most helpful way to think of such a class is as a means of encapsulating and protecting a normal array, and of building extra function into array objects.

Listing 14.7 shows a program, array.cpp, which illustrates the use of `operator[]()`. This program appears also in Que's *Using C*, but is repeated here because of the combination of interesting elements the program brings together. array.cpp shows you how to overload the subscript operator so that an individual array element can be used as an lvalue, how to declare and use a constructor function that has a variable argument list, how to write a copy constructor function, and how to implement a nifty little algorithm to reverse the order of array elements in place. This program also returns your attention to a whole, working C++ program that does something useful, thus reminding you of how all the pieces come together.

Listing 14.7. array.cpp. A program that illustrates `operator[]()` overloaded functions.

```
1   #include <stdlib.h>
2   #include <stdio.h>
3   #include <stdarg.h>
```

```
 4  #include <string.h>
 5
 6  class array {
 7    int value;
 8    int numelem;
 9    int *elem;
10    char *name;
11  public:
12    array( char *, ... );
13    array( array & );
14    ~array( void );
15    void *operator new( unsigned );
16    void operator delete( void * );
17    int &operator[](int);
18    void reverse( void );
19    void display( void );
20    int sum( void );
21    void newname( char * );
22  };
23
24  array::array( char *sname, ... ) // variadic declaration
25  {
26    va_list ap;
27    int work;
28     value = 0;                  // sum starts at zero
29    numelem = 0;
30    name = new char[strlen(name)+1];
31    strcpy( name, sname );  // init name string
32    va_start( ap, sname );  // Just count them this time
33    while ( 0 <= (work = va_arg( ap, int ) ) ) ++numelem;
34    va_end( ap );
35    if ( numelem > 0 )      // If there were any elements
36    elem = new int[numelem];
37     va_start( ap, sname);    // now load the array
38    for ( work=0; work<numelem; ++work )
39      elem[work] = va_arg( ap, int );
40    va_end( ap );
41  }
42
43  array::array( array &copy )    // copy constructor
44  {
45    int i;
46
```

Listing 14.7. Continued.

```
47    value = copy.value;    // ref op makes -> op unnecessary
48    numelem = copy.numelem;
49    name = new char[strlen(copy.name)+1];
50    strcpy( name, copy.name );    // init name string
51    elem = new int[copy.numelem];
52    for ( i=0; i<copy.numelem; ++i )
53      elem[i] = copy.elem[i];
54  }
55
56  array::~array( void )
57  {
58    delete elem;
59    delete name;
60  }
61
62  void *array::operator new( size_t size )
63  {
64    return ::new unsigned char[size];
65  }
66
67  void array::operator delete( void *objptr )
68  {
69    ::delete objptr;
70  }
71
72  int &array::operator[]( int n )
73  {
74                            // Returning a reference ensures
75                            // that the [] op can be used on
76                            // either side of the = operator
77    if ( n<0 || n >= numelem ) return elem[0];
78    return elem[n];
79  }
80
81  void array::reverse( void )
82  {
83    int a, b;
84    a = 0;
85    b = numelem - 1;
86    while ( b > a ) {
87      elem[a]^=elem[b];
```

```
88       elem[b]^=elem[a];
89       elem[a]^=elem[b];
90       ++a; --b;
91     }
92   }
93
94   void array::display( void )
95   {
96     int i;
97      for ( i=0; i<numelem; ++i ) {
98       printf( "%s[%d]=%d ", name, i, elem[i] );
99      }
100    printf( "\n" );
101  }
102
103  int array::sum( void )
104  {
105    int i;
106
107    value = 0;
108    for ( i=0; i<numelem; ++i ) value += elem[i];
109    return value;
110  }
111
112  void array::newname( char *n )
113  {
114    delete name;                    // Deallocate old name
115    name = new char[strlen(n)+1];   // Allocate new name
116    strcpy( name, n );              // Copy it in
117  }
118
119  main() {
120                   // Define an object on the stack
121    array x( "X", 1,2,3,4,5,6,7,8,9,0,-1 );
122
123    x.display(); // Send various messages to object
124    printf( "The sum of X's elements is %d\n", x.sum() );
125    x.reverse();
126    x.display();
127    x[0] = 99;   // Use the overloaded [] operator
128    x[1] = 101;  // You couldn't do this if op[]()
129    x[2] = x[1]; // returned other than int&
```

Listing 14.7. Continued.

```
130     x.display();
131
132     array y = x; // Use the copy constructor
133     y.newname( "Y" );
134     y.display();
135   }
```

The `int& array::operator[]( int )` declaration for the overloaded function appears in line 17 of Listing 14.7. Nothing is particularly unusual about the declaration. The argument for the function is required to be `int`, which is in keeping with the normal type of an array subscript.

There is nothing strange about the `operator[]()` function body. Its purpose is to return the *array[argument]* element, but the function body does go a little further (in the pursuit of encapsulation and protection) by checking the subscript value for correct range. If the subscript is out of range, it returns the zero element instead of aborting the program or trying to fetch the wrong data. This feature alone makes constructing an `array` class worthwhile.

Now pay special attention to the return type of `array::operator[]()`. It returns a *reference* to an integer. Why is this important? Even if you returned an `int` by value, an expression such as

```
a = arr[0]; // syntactically same as a = constant int
```

still executes correctly. What if the reference to an array element appeared on the *left* side of the assignment (as it does in lines 127 through 129)?

You need to go back to C theory to understand what happens then. The rule is that an lvalue—an *object locator*—must appear on the left side of an assignment. Is that beginning to sound familiar? A reference can be an object locator (lvalue). An integer value returned from a function, however, cannot be an lvalue. Therefore, because the return type for `array::operator[]()` is a reference, an expression such as

```
x[1] = 101;   // See line 128
```

modifies the value of `array::x.elem[1]` instead of producing a compile-time error. (`array::elem` is actually a pointer to `int`; see line 9. Remember, however, that pointer and subscript notations are equivalent.) Once again, the correct use of references is crucial to the smooth functioning of the class.

The nondefault constructor for the `array` class is found in lines 24 through 41 of Listing 14.7. Although writing a constructor function with a variable argument list may at first seem peculiar, nothing prevents it, as long as you control the arguments correctly. In the case of the `array` class, you are allowed to create an `array` object with as many or as few elements in the argument list as you want. Notice that the object declaration in line 121 specifies -1 as the last argument to fence off the argument list. By watching for that value, the constructor can first count the elements (line 33) and then initialize the array (lines 38 through 39). You might want to expand the class's capabilities by providing another constructor that accepts a single integer argument specifying the number of elements for which to allocate space.

The code for reversing the current element order is found in the `array::reverse()` member function (lines 81 through 92). This function uses the expedient of a `while` loop that accesses elements from the front and back of the array at the same time, and uses exclusive ORs to exchange their values with no temporary storage. You can exchange any two variables by using three successive exclusive ORs, as shown in these statements:

```
a ^= b;   // step 1
b ^= a;   // step 2
a ^= b;   // step 3
```

The order of the successive statements and the order of the operands within each statement are required to perform this trick.

Handling multidimensional arrays with the subscript operator, `[]`, is a problem. Remember that an overloaded function can accept only one argument (for member functions) or two arguments (for friend functions). In either case, the required syntax for the function limits the right-side operand to just one argument. Thus, there is no legal way to define a class so that `obj[]...[]` can be defined. In the next section, you learn how to get around this problem, using overloaded function call operators.

Using an Overloaded Function Call Operator

Overloading the function call operator, `()`, for a class enables you to access a class object with a minimum of coding. The general form for declaring an overloaded function call operator is this:

```
returntype operator()( args );
```

Once you have overloaded the function call operator for a class, you can call a member function "behind the scenes." Notice, for example, the following code fragment:

```
class A {
  ...
  char describe[80];
public:
  ...
```

```
A& operator()( char *arg ) {
  strcpy( describe, arg );
  cout << arg;
}
void main()
{
  A myobj;
  ...
  myobj( "A new description string." );
}
```

In this code you can set a new member value for the class A object myobj with a function call syntax, using only the object name. That is, the member function call syntax, myobj.`function`(...), is not needed when the proper function call overload has been defined.

Overloading the function call operator enables you to do more than just simplify the syntax of the member function call. You can use the feature to expand the functionality of the class as well. In the preceding section, for example, you saw how to use the function call operator to permit the implementation of multidimensional arrays.

You can approach the task of encapsulating a multidimensional array in several ways, using function call operator overloads. The obvious method is to define the class with member data that is a fixed-size multidimensional array. That is relatively easy and differs little from the array.cpp program shown in Listing 14.8.

Another alternative is to use the added functionality of default function arguments, plus algorithms to simulate multidimensionality based on a physically one-dimensional array. Using these techniques, you can define a class that has from one to three dimensions, with each dimension permitting any number of elements to be stored. The program marray.cpp, shown in Listing 14.8, demonstrates such a class.

Listing 14.8. marray.cpp. A program that uses function call overloading to provide multidimensional array capability.

```
1   #include <iostream.h>
2   #include <stdlib.h>
3   #include <stdio.h>
4   #include <stdarg.h>
5   #include <string.h>
6
7   class marray {
8     int vecsize[3]; // size of each dimension, can be 0
```

```
 9    int numelem;
10    int mux1, mux2;
11    int* elem;
12  public:
13    marray( int = 0, int = 0, int = 0 );
14    ~marray();
15    int& operator()( int = -1, int = -1, int = -1 );
16  };
17
18  marray::marray( int a, int b, int c )
19  {
20    if ( !a ) a = 1; // Make sure at least 1 elem exists;
21    numelem = a;
22    if ( b ) numelem *= b;
23    if ( c ) numelem *= c;
24    elem = new int[numelem];
25    vecsize[0] = a;
26    vecsize[1] = b;
27    vecsize[2] = c;
28    mux1 = a;          // multipliers to linearize subscript
29    mux2 = mux1 * b;
30  }
31
32  marray::~marray()
33  {
34    delete elem;
35  }
36
37  int& marray::operator()( int a, int b, int c )
38  {
39                    // If any subscript == -1, display array
40    if ( a == -1 || b == -1 || c == -1 ) {
41      int i, j, k;
42      for( i=0; i<vecsize[0]; ++i ) {
43        for( j=0; j<vecsize[1]; ++j ) {
44          for( k=0; k<vecsize[2]; ++k ) {
45            cout
46            << elem[ i + j*mux1 + k*mux2 ]
47            << "   " ;
48          }
49          cout << "\r\n";
50        }
```

Listing 14.8. Continued.

```
51          cout << "\r\n";
52        }
53      return elem[0]; // dummy return after display
54    }
55                    // Otherwise, return ref to indicated elem
56    if ( a >= vecsize[0] || b >= vecsize[1] || c >= vecsize[2] )
57      return elem[0];
58    else
59      return elem[ a + b*mux1 + c*mux2 ] ;
60  }
61
62  void main()
63  {
64    marray x( 3, 3, 3 );   // three dim, 2 each dim
65
66    int i, j, k, p = 1;    // init element values
67    for( i=0; i<3; ++i ) {
68      for( j=0; j<3; ++j ) {
69        for( k=0; k<3; ++k ) {
70          x( i, j, k ) = p++;  // Here it is !
71        }
72      }
73    }
74
75    x();                    // Show it off
76  }
```

In line 8 of Listing 14.8, the integer array vecsize[3] is declared as member
data for the class. The idea is to permit the construction of an array that has
one, two, or three dimensions, with the elements for each dimension being
considered a vector (one-dimensional array). The values of vecsize elements
contain the number of elements each vector can hold.

Furthermore, all but the first vectors can contain zero elements, allowing the
class to avoid allocating space for an array of maximum size when you want
fewer than three dimensions.

The member variables mux1 and mux2 are scaling variables for use in simulat-
ing multidimensionality over the physically one-dimensional data area. The
goal here is to mimic normal C usage in which all the elements for the
rightmost subscript are stored contiguously. Figure 14.5 illustrates how
physical storage layout compares to subscript usage.

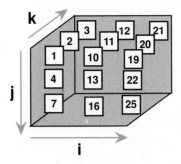

Figure 14.5.

Elements are stored so that contiguous elements exhaust the rightmost subscript first.

Figure 14.5 shows that a three-dimensional array, using subscripts i, j, and k, can be conceived of as a series of "planes" of elements numbered by subscript k. Each plane is composed of i columns and j rows of elements, or i * j elements.

Notice that to get to the first element of the second row, first plane, you must skip over exactly i elements. To get to the first element on the second plane, you must skip over i * j elements (over the whole first plane). Hence, the muxn variables are precomputed in the constructor function in lines 28 through 29 of Listing 14.8 in just this manner.

The multiplier values computed in the constructor functions are used later, in lines 46 and 59, to allow quicker calculation of the one-dimensional equivalent subscript number during access of the array.

The meat of the program in Listing 14.8 is almost anticlimactic. All the real work of setting up the array and the means of access, as for a multidimensional array, has already been done (including the reference return type). Accessing an element of the array, as in line 70, is marvelously simple. The only difference between line 70 and ordinary C-style multidimensional subscripting is that the function call operator is used rather than subscript brackets.

You may want to study Listing 14.8 in more detail. Look more closely at the way in which default function arguments are used, for example, to reduce the number of overloaded functions required and to tell the constructor how many dimensions are needed (and their sizes).

Exercises

The following exercises give you practice in overloading member and non-member functions, and in using both member and friend functions to overload C operators for use with your class objects:

1. Devise a class that does something you find interesting, overloading at least one of its member functions. You might, for example, write a parts class and provide an overloaded parts::update() function. The update() function might accept a string argument for updating the part description, a long to update the part number, an int to update the part count, and a double to update per-item cost of a part.

2. Modify the code for the lib class (discussed in Chapter 13, "Programming with Classes") to support the compound addition operator. That is, write the lib::operator+=() function so that an expression such as

```
lib A, B;
...
A += B;
```

results in all the members from B being added to the library A. This project is not as easy as it might seem, so be careful—and keep a backup copy of the original code!

3. Expand the operator functions defined for the savings class. Be sure to include both binary and unary operators. Pay close attention to the need for friends of member functions, argument number and types, and return types (if any). Experiment with the class and see what you can make it do. For example, why not overload the & operator to cause a savings object to store itself on disk? (Hint: Store only member data, and in a format you want. Don't try to write the object as a whole to a file.) Use the ¦ operator to reload from a disk file.

4. Invent a class that does something you are interested in, giving it a full, robust set of operator functions.

Summary

C++ overloaded functions and operators provide much of the same power and flexibility for C++ classes that the original operators provide for plain C data objects. The great difference is that you must define in C++ what a class member function or overloaded operator does. The plain C operators, of course, are built-in and have a fixed significance. This chapter presents most of the syntax and theory you need for harnessing overloaded functions and operators. The following points highlight the discussion:

■ *You learned the basic concepts of overloading.* When you write overloaded functions, you are providing your class with multiple versions of the function or operator. The compiler matches a call to an overloaded function (or operator, for that matter) to the correct function definition. To make the match, the compiler examines both the *return type* and the *signature* (that is, the argument list) of the function. You can vary the signature, or the signature and return type, but not just the return type of an overloaded function.

■ *You can overload any kind of function and most of the operators.* You can have several versions of member functions, friend functions, or non-member functions. If you have used an older C++ compiler in the past, remember that the `overload` keyword formerly required for nonmember functions is now obsolete.

■ *Type-safe linkage is a standard feature in current C++ compilers and is implemented through function mangling.* Function mangling is performed for all function names, by default, and consists of forming a unique internal identifier from the name, signature, and return type. If you need to include plain C standard functions (which is almost always the case), you can turn off function name mangling by using the `extern "C" {...}` linkage specifier.

■ *Overloaded operator functions have special requirements and restrictions placed on them.* Some operator functions must be members; others can be friends of the class. Some operator functions can return whatever type you want; others require a specific return type. Cast operator functions cannot specify any return type at all. The number of arguments for operator functions depends on whether the operator being overloaded is binary or unary. Finally, whether you can use references for argument and return types, as well as where you use such references, is an important consideration in designing overloaded operator functions.

Using C++ Constructors and Destructors

C ++ constructor and destructor functions are central to the implementation of user-defined types (classes). The `malloc()` and `calloc()` functions can acquire heap storage equal to the correct size of a class object, but these functions do nothing about initializing the member data or establishing linkage with the member functions of a class object. Furthermore, you may want to associate working memory with the object that is outside the boundaries of the class object, but the standard library's memory allocation routines can do nothing about that. Finally, a corresponding cleanup activity must take place when a class object is destroyed (by going out of scope or being deleted), but the standard library functions can't help there either.

All these initialization and termination activities for class objects are relegated to the constructor and destructor functions for a class. A *constructor* function declared for a class is automatically invoked when an object of that class is created. A *destructor* function declared for a class is automatically invoked when an object of that class is destroyed (for example, when a local object goes out of scope and is removed from the system stack). Under certain circumstances, you can call these functions directly. These functions are so important to the operation of the class that the compiler generates default functions for you, should you not declare any. Compiler-generated constructor and destructor functions have the `public` attribute.

A compiler-generated default constructor is sufficient to make a chunk of storage into a true class object, but is otherwise relatively useless, except for the simplest of classes (classes declared with `struct` perhaps). The default action of a compiler-generated constructor is to initialize member data to zero values or null pointers (linkage to member functions was accomplished invisibly at compile time).

A compiler-generated destructor is comparably simple: The `delete` operator is used to free the object's storage. That action is sufficient if the constructor has not acquired memory areas outside the boundaries of the object.

Your constructors and destructors may need to do many more things than the compiler-generated default versions are capable of doing. This chapter covers many of the advanced uses of constructors and destructors, as well as other related topics.

Specifically, you learn how to declare constructors and destructors and how to overload constructor functions. You learn when and why to call constructor and destructor functions, including how to make direct calls to these functions.

This chapter also shows you how to write initializer lists for constructor functions. The method you use is a convenient carry-over from plain C's method of writing initializers for aggregate objects, and it proves vital later when you learn how to derive classes. You learn not only how to write copy constructors but also how to recognize when you need them. They are needed more frequently than you might expect in real-world classes.

Finally, this chapter shows you how to use the global `new` and `delete` operators and how to use these operators overloaded by class. For these tasks, you need an understanding of C++'s free store. You see also how to overload the global `new` and `delete` operators.

Understanding Constructor and Destructor Calls

To understand how and when constructor and destructor functions are called, you must know and understand the rules for declaring these functions. You must know also how these functions are used for objects having different scopes and storage classes. This section covers these topics.

Declaring Constructors and Destructors

Constructor and destructor functions, like all other functions, must be declared and defined before they can be used. The declarations and definitions must also conform to certain rules that are unique to constructor and destructor functions. Both kinds of functions should be declared in the public part of the class declaration.

Declaring Constructor Functions

You declare and define constructor functions according to the following rules:

- *A constructor function must have the same name as the class for which the function is declared.* That is, class A {...} must have a constructor function A(), if you declare one at all. The purpose of a constructor function is to turn a chunk of raw memory into a class object. The constructor function body does not need to allocate space for the object: the space already exists by the time the constructor function is invoked. A constructor function is implicitly invoked when a class object is declared (that is, when a class object is created).

- *A constructor function cannot have a return type.* The Microsoft C/C++ compiler, like all other C++ compilers, generates its own special (and invisible) return type for a constructor function. You must write the declaration without a return type, as in the following example:

```
class A {
...
public:


...
A( args opt );   // Declare a constructor function
...
};
```

You can define a constructor function inline, but you should do this only when the function is short and simple. When the definition appears out-of-line, it is written in the usual manner for out-of-line member functions, except for the return type. The preceding declaration would require this corresponding definition:

```
A::A( args opt )
{
    ... // Function body goes here
}
```

- *Because a constructor function can have arguments, overloading is permitted.* If the function has a distinguishable signature, the compiler has no difficulty in mangling the function name. Overloading is useful if there are several different combinations of initial data types you want to use in creating an object of a class.

One special case of constructor overloading should be mentioned: using a constructor to convert data types. Such a constructor implementation is called *conversion by constructor* and can be quite handy. It is a special alternative to overloading cast operators, as discussed in the preceding chapter.

Conversion by constructor requires you to code a constructor function which either accepts a single argument or specifies enough default arguments so that the constructor can be invoked with just one argument. For example, to specify conversion from `int` to `class A`, you need to declare at least the following constructor:

```
class A {
  ...
public:
  A( int );  // constructor for conversion from int
};
```

Assuming the constructor function definition appears somewhere in your program, you can then create `class A` objects by conversion from `int`:

```
void main()
{
  int a;
  ...
  A obj1( a ); // This is the first form of call
  A obj2 = a;  // This is an entirely equivalent form of call
}
```

Notice that a conversion constructor differs from the copy constructor described later in this list, although the assignment operator can invoke the constructor as shown in the preceding code fragment because a whole object is not copied to another. Constructor conversion of type creates a new object, even if the argument's type is a different class. The objects handled by copy constructors have the same class.

■ *A constructor function can have default arguments.* You have already seen this feature in some of the sample code in previous chapters. Remember that the argument default values appear in the *declaration* of the constructor function, not in the definition. The syntax looks like this:

```
class A {
  ...
public:

  ...
  A( int = 1, int = 2, int = 3 );
  ...
};
  ...
A::A( int arg1, int arg2, int arg3 )
{
  ...
}
```

Having default arguments is not exactly the same as having no arguments (having no arguments defines a default constructor, not default arguments). The difference between no arguments and default arguments is most notably apparent in the way you declare objects of the class:

```
A obj;  // the form used with NO arguments, default constr.
A obj();            // declaration allowing default values
A obj( 1, 2, 3 );   // functionally same as second object
```

A quick summary is in order here. First, if you are going to declare objects with aggregate initializer lists, such as

```
struct twoclass { int a; int b; };
...
twoclass classobj = { 1, 2 };
```

the class cannot contain a constructor at all. Second, if you are going to declare arrays of class objects, as in

```
class myclass { ... };
...
myclass bunch[20];
```

you must use a default constructor (because you have no way to specify an argument list for each element). In this case, default can mean either a constructor with no arguments or a constructor with all default arguments. Either way, the constructor can be called without specifying arguments. This means if you code any constructor at all, you should provide a default (the compiler does not generate one if you write any constructors).

Third, other constructors can have whatever arguments you want, with or without default values. This final point has some rather strange variations when you are using class inheritance (deriving classes), but that discussion is deferred until Chapter 17, "Using C++ Derived Classes."

■ *You cannot take the address of a constructor function.* You can take the address of an ordinary member function and call the function through the pointer to member operator. Forming a pointer to a member function is similar to forming a pointer to a member data object (see the sample program shown in Listing 14.5 in Chapter 14, "Using Overloaded Functions and Operators in C++"). The following short program (which compiles and runs) illustrates the technique:

```
#include <iostream.h>  // a strange hello program

class A {
public:
  void display();
};
```

```
void A::display()
{
   cout << "Hello, there!\r\n";
}

void main()
{
   void (A::*dptr)();   // pointer to member function
   A *thing = new A;    // pointer to class object

   dptr = &A::display;
   (thing->*dptr)();
}
```

Although ordinary member functions can be handled through pointers, it is illegal and impossible to take the address of a constructor function. Notice that a pointer to a member function is internally similar to a near pointer. A pointer to a member function (or object) is recorded only in terms of its offset from the beginning of the class object; thus, the pointer can be used with more than one object of the class.

■ *A constructor function cannot be declared* static, const, *or* volatile. A constructor function must be a nonstatic member function because constructor functions cannot exist apart from particular objects. (Remember that static member functions can exist apart from specific objects and can be called before any object exists.) The other two specifiers also clearly do not apply to constructors. However, you can define const or volatile objects that also happen to have constructors.

■ *A constructor function cannot be inherited.* It is unique to its class. If a constructor could be inherited, a number of problems would result, including accidental failure to initialize derived class objects, and invisible changes made to the meaning of copy constructors. Why would these problems occur? When a derived class object is initialized, the base class constructor is invoked first, and then the derived class constructor is invoked. If constructors could be inherited, you could accidentally create a derived class that had no explicit constructor.

■ *When a class declaration contains member objects that are themselves objects of other classes, the member objects' constructors are executed before the constructor for the containing object.* Consider, for example, how the constructors for classes A and B in the following code fragment are used:

```
class A { ... };
class B {
   ...
   A workobj;
```

```
public:
   ...
};
...
B visibleobj; // Create B object with default constructor
```

When the `class B visibleobj` is created (by being declared), A's constructor is executed first on behalf of `workobj`, and only then is B's constructor function body executed.

■ *A copy constructor, like a default constructor, can be compiler-generated.* The copy constructor for a class is the special case in which the argument is a reference to an object of the same class. Consider this example:

```
class A {
   ...
   int var;
public;
   ...
   A( A& );
};
...
A:A( A& other )
{
   var = other.var; // just for an example
}
```

The copy constructor's single argument must be a reference to an object of the same class. This requirement is necessary because passing an object by value implies creating a copy of the argument to place on the stack. Creating that copy invokes the copy constructor, however, which creates another copy, and so on, causing infinite recursion of the copy constructor function.

Copy constructors are useful when you want to create a new object with reference to an existing object, as in the following code fragment:

```
void main()
{
   A obj1;
   A obj2 = obj1;  // obj2 is a copy of obj1
}
```

A copy constructor is generated for you only if you do not declare one yourself. If a memberwise copy of the object is acceptable, a compiler-generated copy constructor is sufficient. If the object has special requirements, such as maintaining a block of memory outside the boundaries of the object itself, you should write your own copy constructor.

■ *A* union *can declare a class in C++, but an* object *of a class having construc-*
tors cannot be a member of a union. This rule exists because unions are
viewed as overlays of the same area of storage. That is, a union can
contain many different members, but they all occupy the same area of
storage—only one member is active at a time. There can be no guarantee, therefore, that the member which happens to be a class object will
be active at a given time. There is also no guarantee its constructor
function will actually be called.

■ *Class member functions can be called from within a constructor function,*
and class member objects can be referenced from within a constructor func-
tion. The rationale used by previous compilers was simple: A constructor
function differs from all others in that a constructor takes a chunk of raw
memory—not a complete class object—and transforms the raw memory
into a working class object. Microsoft C/C++ and other recent C++ compilers now consider this usage obsolete because you can overload the new
and delete operators on a per class basis. Thus, there is never a time, in
the constructor function, when this is not valid. For a detailed discussion
of overloading the new and delete operators with class objects, see the
section "Overloading operator new() and operator delete()" later in this
chapter.

Declaring Destructor Functions

The rules for destructor functions are similar to those for constructor functions. You declare and define destructor functions according to the following
rules:

■ *A destructor function has the same name as its class, except the name is*
prepended with the tilde (~). That is, you declare a destructor in the following manner:

```
class A {
   ...
public:
   ...
   A();   // constructor for A
   ~A();  // destructor for A
};
```

The destructor function may be inline. If it is out-of-line, you write the
function definition in this way:

```
A::~A()
{
   ... // destructor function body
}
```

The destructor function's purpose is the opposite of that of the constructor function: the destructor transforms a class object into a chunk of raw data. In other words, the destructor "deinitializes" an object. The destructor function body does not need to explicitly free storage occupied by the class object itself, but may need to free storage that a member function acquired outside the class object's boundaries.

■ *A destructor function cannot have a return type.* Just as for a constructor function, the compiler generates its own internal type for a destructor function. You are not allowed to code a return type.

■ *Unlike a constructor function, a destructor function cannot have arguments.* Because a destructor has no arguments and thus no signature for function mangling, you cannot overload a destructor. The question of default arguments, of course, is not applicable to destructor functions.

■ *You cannot take the address of a destructor function.* You have no need to access a destructor function through a pointer because the function is used only to destroy a class object.

■ *A destructor function must be a nonstatic member function of its class.* That is, a destructor cannot be declared to be `const`, `volatile`, or `static`. Like a constructor function, though, a destructor function can be defined for classes that have `const` or `volatile` objects.

■ *A destructor function cannot be inherited.* Here the same problems exist for destructors as for constructors. If a destructor could be inherited, the correct destructor might not be executed.

■ *A destructor function can be a `virtual` function.* You may recall that the virtual-function facility is a kind of pass-through mechanism guaranteeing the correct version of a function (that is, the one belonging to the derived class) is executed. Thus, virtual destructors are permitted. In fact, declaring destructor functions `virtual` when deriving classes is often a good idea.

■ *When a class declaration contains member objects that are themselves objects of other classes, the body of the containing class's destructor is executed before the destructors for the contained objects.* Consider, for example, how the destructors for classes A and B in the following code fragment are used:

```
class A { ... };
class B {
   ...
   A workobj;
public:
   ...
   ~B();
```

```
};
...
B* visibleobj = new B;  // Create a B object
...
delete visibleobj;      // Now destroy it
```

When the class B visibleobj is destroyed (in this case, by being deleted), B's destructor is executed first, and only then is A's destructor invoked on behalf of workobj. The order of execution is exactly opposite that of constructor function execution.

■ *A union can declare a class in C++, but an object of a class having destructors cannot be a member of a union.* The reasons for this rule are the same as those for constructor functions: There can be no guarantee the destructor function is actually executed.

■ *Class member functions can be called from within a destructor function, and class member objects can be referenced from within a destructor function.* There is, of course, no question the this pointer already exists at the time a destructor function is invoked for an object. Thus, calls to member functions, as well as references to member data, are possible.

You now have before you all the rules that constrain the use of constructor and destructor functions. The rest of this chapter shows you what constructors and destructors can do, and presents some important related topics.

Using Constructor Initializers

You have already seen how a class with no constructor can have objects initialized by an aggregate initializer list. In other words, you can declare a class that can be initialized in this manner:

```
#include <stdlib.h>
#include <stdio.h>

struct A {          // struct means all members public
  int a, b;         // There is no constructor, either
  void display();
  void operator()();  // overload function call () op
};


void A::display()
{
  printf( "a = %d, b = %d\n", a, b );
}
```

```
void A::operator()() // Define function call operator
{
  display();
}

main()
{
  A obj1 = { 16, 64 };            // initializer list

  obj1();    // Use overloaded function call operator
}
```

You can go beyond the aggregate initializer list form, however, by providing a *constructor* initializer list directly in the definition for the constructor function. Using a constructor initializer list, you can have both an initializer list (although not an aggregate style list) and any constructor functions you want. Constructor initializer lists can be important later on, when you build constructors for derived classes. The following short program shows how to write a constructor initializer list:

```
#include <stdlib.h>
#include <stdio.h>

class A {
  int a, b;
public:
  A(int, int);
  void display();
  void operator()();  // Overload function call () op
};

          // Define initializer list for constructor

A::A( int i = 0, int j = 0 ) : a(i), b(j) {}

void A::display()
{
  printf( "a = %d, b = %d\n", a, b );
}

void A::operator()() // Define function call operator
{
  display();
}
```

```
main()
{
  A obj1;              // Take advantage of default args
  A obj2( 16, 64 );        //Use init list for this one

  obj1();     // Use overloaded function call operator
  obj2();                  // to display object values
}
```

You should be aware of several differences between the preceding program's constructor function and ordinary constructor functions. First, you should notice the syntax of the constructor function definition:

```
class::class( args ) : initlist { functionbody }
```

The punctuation must be coded as shown in this line. You must include comma separators between items in the initializer list, but not following the last item. The colon (:) that follows the declaration part and precedes the initializer list is always required, as is the list itself.

Next, you should understand that the default arguments shown in the preceding short program have nothing to do with the initializer list specifically. If the default arguments were not specified, the only thing that would happen is the compiler would produce an error message saying that no constructor function could be matched to the declaration A obj1; in main(). Notice, too, that in this short program the default argument values are supplied in the declaration part of the function definition, not in the function prototype declaration. Default arguments can appear in either place.

The syntax of each item in the initializer list is important also. The syntax determines how class members are matched with their initializing values:

```
memberobject( expression ), ...
memberobject( argument ), ...
```

As shown here, the most general form of an item in an initializer list consists of a member object to be initialized, followed by an expression within parentheses. You do not have to supply an item in the list for every member data object: Some of the objects can be initialized by code in the constructor function body. In other words, the number of items in the initializer list does not have to match the number of member data objects in the class.

The expression within the parentheses of an item in an initializer list can be just that—an expression. It can be one of the constructor's function arguments, but it doesn't have to be. You can use an expression containing any names that are currently in scope and visible.

You may have noticed in the preceding short program that the function body for the constructor function is null, composed only of opening and closing curly braces ({}). This is perfectly legal. This particular program has no need for any further logic because the initializer list takes care of setting up all the member data objects. The function can just as well have any code in it that is legal for ordinary constructors.

As noted before, the availability of constructor initializer lists proves extremely useful when deriving classes from other classes. One instance of class derivation requires the use of constructor initializers: building one class from another class by *composition*—that is, including objects of one class in another class.

There is only one problem with including an object of another class in the declaration for the current class. A member data object that is also a class object cannot be declared with an argument list for the constructor function. A class member class object is therefore normally constrained to using a default constructor. The following code fragment, for instance, is illegal:

```
class A { ... };

class B {
  A myobj( 22, 33 );  // ILLEGAL, args not permitted!
  ...
};
```

Because a member object cannot have an argument list, you might be wondering whether you can incorporate a class object as member data and also provide constructor arguments for the member object. You can—by using the constructor initializer list. The following short program illustrates the technique:

```
#include <iostream.h>

class X {
  int value;
public:
  X( int arg = 37 ) { value = arg; }
  void show() { cout << value << "\r\n"; }
};

class Y {
  int value;
  X obj1;     // can't have arguments here!
public:
  Y( int arg, int oarg ) :  value(arg), obj1(oarg) {}
  void show() {
    cout << value << "\r\n";
    obj1.show();
  }
};
```

```
void main()
{
  Y myobj( 37, 64 );

  myobj.show();
}
```

In this program, class Y is built by declaring, among other things, a class X member object. Notice that the object declaration X obj1 has no argument list, conforming to the rule. An argument, however, is still going to be passed to the X(int) constructor (the *nondefault* constructor). The argument can be passed to the X constructor because the Y constructor has an initializer list containing the initializer item obj1(oarg). The combination of class object declaration and constructor initializer is the functional equivalent of the following declaration:

```
X obj1 = oarg;
```

You should recognize the form of the preceding line of code: an X constructor accepts one argument, and a corresponding object declaration provides an integer value. Therefore, the X constructor is a *conversion constructor,* as described earlier in the chapter.

This example clarifies the reason for the constructor initializer list's syntax: The syntax is constructed precisely so that class objects can be used as class members, while still allowing contained objects to be initialized with a nondefault constructor.

When Are Constructor Functions Called?

Generally, constructor functions for a class are invoked when an object declaration of that class is encountered during execution. That is, constructor functions are executed as they are encountered at runtime. This sounds simple enough (although there are special considerations for base and derived class constructors, as discussed in Chapter 17), but you should know exactly when and under what circumstances constructors are called. With that knowledge, you can perhaps avoid stumbling into a dark pit while writing one of your C++ programs.

This section, then, shows how and when constructors are called for local objects, global objects, arbitrary objects, unnamed objects, and temporary objects. Also provided are a few comments about how and when copy constructors and constructors for arrays of class objects are called, as well as comments about causing recursion (possibly infinite recursion) during execution of a constructor function.

In normal programming practice for both C and C++, you should avoid the use of global variables or objects, preferring local objects whenever possible. You can declare a class object locally (with block scope) just as you can declare ordinary data types. A constructor for a local object is not called until the object declaration is reached during execution within the block, as shown in Figure 15.1.

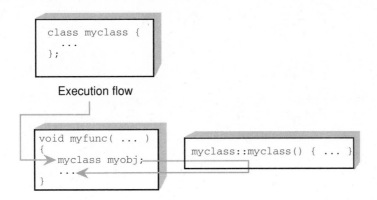

Figure 15.1.

A class constructor call for a locally declared object.

Recall that in C++ a local declaration for an object does not have to appear at the top of the block. Because such a declaration can appear anywhere within the block, a constructor call is also possible from anywhere within a block.

Unlike a local object, a global class object (one with file scope) must behave like an ordinary data type. That is, such an object must be initialized before the main() function executes. Thus, a constructor function can be called even before main(), as shown in Figure 15.2.

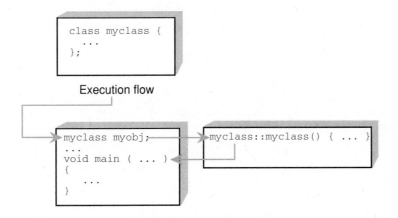

Figure 15.2.

A class constructor call for a globally declared object.

You should not be surprised that code is executed before main(). A good deal of program initialization has to be done before any function, including main(), can be called. Calling the constructors for global class objects is just a part of the start-up process.

An arbitrary class object (that is, one with arbitrary duration and created by the new operator) has its constructor called at whatever point in program execution the new operator is used to create the object. Normally, you use new to create the object directly in the declaration of a pointer to a class object. A typical sequence of declarations might look like this:

```
class A { ... };
...
void main()
{
  A* myobj = new A; // Declare pointer, create object,
                    // and call constructor
}
```

In the preceding code fragment, the class object created by new is an arbitrary duration object and exists physically on the free store. In contrast, the pointer to the object—the variable myobj—is a local variable existing on the system stack and within the scope of main(). The implication is that the pointer declaration and the creation of the class object do not have to appear in the same line of code. You can just as well write this:

```
class A { ... };
...
  A* myobj;          // Just declare the pointer
...
void main()
{
  myobj = new A;     // Create object and call constructor
}
```

This sequence of statements works, but the coding practice is not normal. The pointer declaration and object creation are often separated, but they are generally placed in the same scope—for example, both placed within main().

You can also cause a class's constructor to be called by explicitly invoking it. There is only one way to do this: you place the constructor call on the right side of an assignment statement. The syntax looks like this:

```
class A { ... };
...
A myobj = A( args );
```

In other words, the expression on the right consists of the class name (not an object name) followed by a parenthesized argument list. Notice, the parentheses are required in this kind of object declaration, even if the default constructor is used. A normal object declaration that uses the default constructor does not require empty parentheses (for example, A myobj;). The following short program demonstrates explicit calls and the required placement of parentheses:

```
#include <iostream.h>

class A {
  int value;
public:
  A( int arg = 0 ) : value( arg ) {} // two forms in one lick
  void dump() { cout << value << "\r\n"; }
};

void main()
{
  A obj1 = A();                       // Use default form
     // empty parentheses required for default constructor
  A obj2 = A( 37 );                   // Use argument form

  obj1.dump();
  obj2.dump();
}
```

An explicit call to a class's constructor function, such as one of the calls shown in the preceding short program, causes an *unnamed temporary object* to be created. The resulting object is then copied into the object being declared on the left side of the assignment statement. This process uses the copy constructor function if the objects are class objects, as they are in the preceding program.

Arrays of class objects present another variation on the theme of constructor calls. You have already learned that declaring an array of class objects causes the default constructor to be executed for the object in each array element. In what order are the constructor calls made? All arrays are created in an area of contiguous memory, in order of ascending memory address. That is, they are created in the order in which the constructors are called, because the call is made as each object is created.

Finally, consider a class object being declared as a member object in another class. At what time is the constructor for the included object called? Clearly, the constructor cannot be called before an object of the containing class is created. The constructor body for the included object, however, is executed before the constructor body for the containing class.

In the case of a constructor with an initializer list, you can easily see why the included object's constructor is executed first. Notice, for example, the following code fragment:

```
class A { ... };
 ...
```

```
class B {
...
  A someobj;   // included class object
public:
  B( int arg = 0 ) : someobj( arg ) { ... }
...
};
```

The initializer list item someobj(arg) causes the class A constructor to be invoked before the class B constructor function body is reached. In the preceding code fragment, the A class constructor is executed first only if the B class constructor contains a call to one of A's member functions or refers to A's public member data.

Even when there is no constructor initializer list, the compiler generates code that behaves as if the contained object's default constructor is physically called first.

Now consider a problem you might encounter when writing constructor functions—that of accidentally causing infinitely recursive constructor calls. You learned earlier that a copy constructor can accept as an argument only a reference to an object of its own class. The reason for this restriction is that passing an object to a copy constructor by value could cause just such infinite recursion. Is it possible to cause infinite recursion of a constructor function in some other way?

There certainly is a way to cause constructor recursion. The method consists of fooling the compiler into allowing you to create a new object of a class before the constructor gets through in the first place. Although the compiler can check the syntax of the copy constructor declaration, the compiler is not intelligent enough to interpret the significance of where you place object declarations. The following short program, for instance, causes infinite recursion of the constructor function (the program runs, but it costs you a system boot to see it):

```
// lockup.cpp will lock up your computer
#include <iostream.h>

class A {
  int value;
public:
  A() {
    A myobj;   // DANGER! Here is the culprit!

    value = 37;
    cout << value << "\r\n";
  }
};
```

```
void main()
{
  A someobj;  // Get it started
}
```

This program is appropriately named lockup.cpp—and that is precisely what it will do to your computer. Figure 15.3 shows the logic flow of a program with a constructor that locally declares an object of its own class.

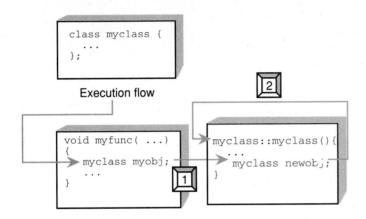

Execution flow

Figure 15.3.

The execution flow that results when a constructor function calls itself.

The cure, of course, is to observe the rule that you should never declare within a constructor function an object of the same class. At first, it might seem that the cure should be to modify the compiler to prevent such a declaration. To do that, however, you would need to eliminate the ability to declare an object of an incomplete type. In other words, you would no longer be able to declare objects in the following manner:

```
class A;  // Forward-declare class A
...
class B {
  A workobj; // Declare an A object here
...
};
...
class A {
  ... // Complete A's declaration now
};
```

Providing the ability to declare objects of an incomplete type (known as forward-declaration), as shown in the preceding code fragment, may seem needlessly complex. Forward-declaration is, in fact, a valuable feature in the design of complex classes. You can, for example, declare two classes that refer to each other.

Most frequently, one class refers to another class in order to declare the first class (or specific member functions of the first class) as friends of the second class. The code sequence looks like this:

```
class A;  // forward-declaration
class B {
  friend class A; // Declare whole class a friend
  ...
};


class A {  // Complete declaration for A
  ...      // All A members can refer to B members
};
```

A more subtle way in which classes can refer to one another is for both classes to declare as a friend a function that accepts arguments of *both* classes. A common operator function is typical here. Class A and class B might both declare a friend function that sums an A object and a B object, returning a simple integer, for example, like this:

```
class A;  // Forward-declare this one

class B {
  ...
  friend int operator+( A&, B& );
  ...
};

class A {  // Complete A class declaration
  ...
  friend int operator+( A&, B& );
  ...
};
...
int operator+( A& aobj, B& bobj )
{
  // Sum numbers somehow here
  // and return an int
}
```

You should exercise caution, though, when designing mutually referential classes. Just as declaring a constructor that contains an object declaration of its own class can cause infinite recursion, mutually referential classes can cause an infinite loop. For example, the following short program compiles and runs, but only stops running when memory is exhausted:

```
#include <iostream.h>

class A;

class B {
  int value;
  A *aobj;
public:
  B();
  void show();
};

class A {          // Finish A's declaration first
  int value;
  B *bobj;
public:
  A();
  void show();
};

// Member function definitions can be in any order,
// since there is now a declaration for everything

A::A()
{
  value = 37;
  bobj = new B;
}

void A::show() {
  cout << value << "\r\n";
}

B::B()
{
  value = 37;
  aobj = new A;
}

void B::show() {
  cout << value << "\r\n";
}
```

```
void main()
{
  A testobj;        // This causes recursion again

  testobj.show();  // Execution never gets here
}
```

The declaration `A testobj;` in function `main()` gets the ball rolling by invoking the default constructor `A::A()`. That constructor function, however, creates a B class object with operator `new`, invoking the B class constructor. The B class constructor also creates an A class object, and recursion inescapably begins.

When Are Destructor Functions Called?

As noted earlier, destructor functions perform the inverse task of constructor functions: destructors turn class objects into raw chunks of memory. Destructors are also the mirror images of constructors in that destructors are called whenever a class object is destroyed.

For *locally declared* class objects, the containing scope terminates when the current block is exited. The current block may be just a block statement, or the block may be a function body. In the latter case, the class object goes out of scope—and is destroyed—when the function returns to its caller. Calling the destructor for a local object is illustrated in Figure 15.4.

Figure 15.4.

The destructor for a local object is called when the containing scope terminates (at the end of the block or when the function returns).

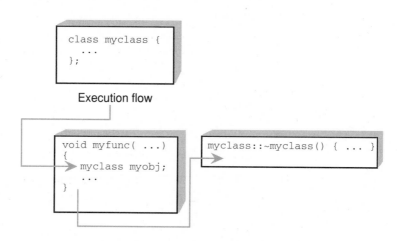

Figure 15.4 shows that the destructor for a local object is automatically invoked after the return mechanism is executed (the `return` statement or end-of-block is encountered) but before any other scope is entered.

The destructor for a *global* class object is invoked when file scope terminates. This timing also applies to objects declared locally within a function or block but modified with the static keyword.

You can terminate file scope in three ways. First, you can let program execution "fall through" the bottom of the main() function. This method is functionally identical to the second method: terminating program execution by executing the exit() function. The exit() function can, of course, be executed from anywhere in your program. In both these methods of terminating file scope, the compiler-generated cleanup code (including the code to invoke destructors) can be executed.

The third method of stopping program execution is very dangerous for all objects, including class objects. This method consists of calling the abort() function. The method is dangerous because there is no guarantee any cleanup is done; the program may just stop execution immediately. Both ANSI C and C++ 2.1 standards allow a compiler to generate abort() code that essentially does nothing at all.

Microsoft C/C++ calls the internal routine _exit()—notice the leading underscore—with a return code of 3, and displays a message on the stderr stream that execution was abnormally terminated. The _exit() function does nothing except pass on the return code of 3 to DOS or to the parent process. _exit() does not close any open files, flush output buffers, or call any registered atexit() functions. Nor are destructor functions invoked. If your class objects require some sort of extra processing before being destroyed, you are in trouble.

Using the abort() function guarantees there will be *no* orderly cleanup of class objects because the execution path that involves calling registered atexit() functions is bypassed. Also, the atexit() registered functions are called before the destructors for any global or static class objects, as illustrated in Figure 15.5.

Destructor functions for arrays of class objects are handled in mirror-image fashion, compared to constructor calls for arrays. Although the constructors for an array of class objects are called in ascending order of memory address, the destructors for an array are called in the reverse order of the objects' creation. In other words, the destructors are called backwards.

You can cause the destructor functions for arbitrary duration objects (those created with new) to be executed whenever you want. You just use the delete operator, as shown in the following code fragment:

```
class X { ... };  // Declare a class
...
void main()
{
  X* anobj = new X; // Create arbitrary duration object
  ...               // Things happen here
```

```
      delete anobj;      // Kill it at your pleasure
      ...                // More things happen here
}
```

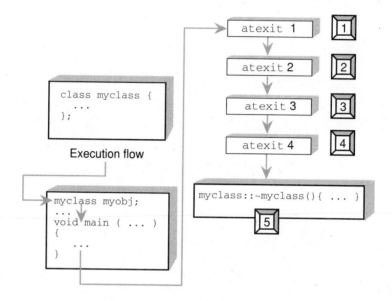

Figure 15.5.

Functions registered by **atexit()** are called before the destructors for global and static objects.

You can certainly create arrays of arbitrary objects and still `delete` them without regard to the current scope. The following code fragment does just that:

```
class X { ... };        // Declare a class
...
X* anobj = new X[22];   // Pointer to 22 X objects is global

void myfunc();          // Function declaration
...
void main()
{
  myfunc();             // Go execute myfunc()
}

void myfunc()           // Descend to a local scope
{
  delete anobj [22]     // Kill all 22 X objects
}
```

When you `delete` an array of arbitrary duration objects, you choose the timing, but you still follow the rules for calling destructors for arrays of objects. The destructors are called in reverse order of the objects' (the array elements') creation.

You can cause program recursion in a destructor function, too, just as in a constructor function. In the case of a destructor, however, the mechanism involves calling the `exit()` function from within the destructor function.

Specifically, `exit()` causes global and static objects to go out of scope, triggering their destructor functions (local objects are not destroyed in this case). If the destructor in which you call `exit()` is a global or static object, calling `exit()` causes the same destructor to be called again—destruction of the object is not yet complete. That leads again to the `exit()` call, and recursion established.

Finally, you can explicitly call the destructor function for an object. The following trivial program shows the syntax required for calling a destructor function directly:

```
#include <iostream.h>
#include <string.h>

class tool {
  char descr[41];
  int catlgnum;
public:
  tool( int = 0, char* = "" );
  ~tool() {}
  void tell();
};

tool::tool( int assigncat, char* name )
{
  strcpy( descr, name );
  catlgnum = assigncat;
}

void tool::tell()
{
  cout << "Tool number " << catlgnum << " is a "
       << descr << " device.\r\n";
}

void main()
{
  tool wrench( 1, "Turn nuts and bolts" );
```

```
    wrench.tell();
    wrench.tool::~tool();
}
```

This short program illustrates a couple of points about explicit destructor calls. First, although it is not apparent from just looking at this code, you must actually define a destructor function: The compiler-generated one will not do. Microsoft C/C++ does not recognize the destructor call unless you have defined a destructor. It can be an entirely empty function, like the one in the preceding program, but a defined destructor must be there.

Second, you must use the fully qualified name for the destructor function. In the preceding example, the class member operator (.) is used in the last line of main() to call the destructor. Had wrench been a pointer to a class object, you would have written the following:

```
wrench->tool::~tool();
```

The fully qualified class destructor function name, following the member name and operator, is always required. Otherwise, it would be possible to write expressions that confuse the one's complement operator (~) with the destructor name character (also ~).

You may recall from Chapter 11, "Using C++ Classes," that the program in Listing 11.6 used the lifo stack class to create a simple class object (on a lifo stack) at a specific memory address. (The technique was presented without much explanation at the time.) Later in the same program, an explicit destructor function call was used to remove the class object. That use, in fact, is one of the rare times you might need to call a destructor function directly. You might profitably return now to Chapter 11 and review Listing 11.6 with a more educated eye for what is going on there.

Overloading Constructor Functions

The constructor functions for a class clearly are an important part of the class's design. This section provides an expanded discussion of constructor design logistics.

Specifically, the section focuses on the issue of providing multiple constructors (overloading them) for a class. Also covered are some of the considerations that determine what logic must be put into the various kinds of constructors (that is, default and nondefault).

Writing a Default Constructor Function

If the process of constructing and initializing a class object is complex enough to require you to overload the constructor function in several different ways, you should provide your own version of the default constructor. This recommendation is especially true on three occasions:

- When the class object has special initialization requirements that go beyond what a compiler-generated constructor will do

- When you create class objects with the new operator or with arrays of class objects

- When you need to create an object at a particular memory location

What kinds of objects might have special initialization requirements? Almost any kind of object might have them. Think of the classes you can define as falling into one of three categories: object-like objects, value-like objects, and action-like objects. (Notice that no new technical terms are offered here, but descriptive phrases are provided.) Objects falling into any of these three categories could have special initialization requirements:

- *Object-like objects* include objects that control large amounts of data. These objects are focused more on data than behavior, although they do have a behavior. A large table of data that must be kept in main memory is an example of such an object. The dbllist class you saw earlier in this book is another example.

  Class objects belonging to the object-like category may require large amounts of memory for storing relatively extensive data, as in the case of the dbllist class. Any constructor for this class, including the default constructor, must be able to acquire such memory. Additionally, pointers to the acquired memory must be initialized—a null pointer won't do. Special attention must also be given to copy constructors for this category of objects because you usually do not want two objects to point to the same area of acquired memory.

- *Value-like objects* are objects whose significance centers on some particular arithmetic value such as a class describing complex number types. Value-like objects have important data content and behavior (such as the full range of arithmetic operations).

  Special initialization requirements for this category of objects are likely to include the setting of initial values for internal *state variables* associated with the object, and the controlling of the object's behavior.

- *Action-like objects* are objects whose most significant characteristic is what they do, not what they contain. You might design, for example, a command class that routes execution to the appropriate service function, based on a command string.

This category of objects is least likely to require special handling when a class object is created. However, each class has its own characteristics, and action-like objects may need starting values for state variables or other setup actions carried out.

The default constructors you provide for classes with objects either created by new or declared in arrays are important also. You can provide an initializer list to be passed to the constructor for an object created with new, as in the following short program:

```
#include <iostream.h>

class A {
  int value;
public:
  A() { value = 37; }
  A( int arg ) { value = arg; }
  void tell() { cout << value << "\r\n"; }
};

void main()
{
  A* aptr = new A ( 64 ); // Similar to A x( 64 );

  aptr->tell();
}
```

You more often use the new operator to specify only a type name, however. In the preceding short program, for example, aptr is usually initialized with this declaration:

```
A* aptr = new A;
```

If objects created with new have any of the special initialization requirements previously discussed, a default constructor is quite important. Creating arrays of objects presents a similar problem, but you do not have the flexibility of using a nondefault constructor for class objects created in arrays. Default constructors for objects declared in an array are essential.

Classes that are to have objects created at a particular place in memory (specific address) must receive the same design attention as classes that are created with new. In fact, placing an object at a specific memory location involves overloading the global new operator, as shown in the following program:

```
#include <iostream.h>

//
// Declare a simple class
//
```

```
class simple {
  int stuff;
public:
  simple( int arg = 16 ) { stuff = arg; }
  ~simple() {}                // Default destructor
  void showit() { cout << stuff << "\r\n"; }
};


//
// Overload global operator new()
//
void* operator new( size_t size, void *ptr )
{
  size = size; // Dummy statement avoids compiler warning
  return ptr;  // Here is what we are after
}


void main()
{
  void *fetch;              // Working pointer

                           // Get a block of memory using
                           // original global new
  fetch = (void *)( new unsigned char[ sizeof(simple) ] );

  simple* X;               // Pointer to simple object

  X = new(fetch) simple( 37 );   // Create object
  X->showit();
  X->simple::~simple();    // Explicitly delete object
  delete fetch;            // Release memory
}
```

As the preceding short program shows, you can overload global new (this subject is covered at the end of the chapter) and still use an initializer list to pass arguments to the constructor. Notice this line from the preceding program:

```
X = new(fetch) simple( 37 );   // Create object
```

You must still be careful to provide a way of handling special initialization requirements, however, even if initializers cannot be used. Every possible use of the object must be accounted for in actual practice. That is why the constructor in this short program is given default arguments—so that the constructor can be used as either a default or a nondefault constructor.

Writing Other Constructors

Providing your own version of a default constructor for a class instead of allowing the compiler to generate a constructor is important, but overloading the constructor in other ways is often equally important. There are three reasons (all discussed in earlier sections of this chapter) to provide a fairly rich set of overloaded constructor functions for a class:

- To avoid constructor argument conversions when performing the best-fit match

- To permit several different sets of constructor arguments to be used in creating class objects

- To provide for conversion of other types to the class's type by constructor conversion

There may be other reasons to provide a rich set of overloaded constructor functions, but these are probably the most important. There is, however, a tradeoff in declaring many overloaded constructor functions. On the one hand, a rich constructor set can contribute significantly to high-performance programs (by eliminating many instances of extra overhead). On the other hand, because each constructor function takes up code space, your program will be correspondingly longer. Generally, the extra code space is not overwhelming, and most programmers prefer high-performance code.

By designing your class and its constructor carefully and thoroughly, you can often eliminate much of the extra code space required by a rich constructor set. You can do this by isolating the initialization code that is common to all constructors and placing that code in its own separate function (perhaps in the private part of the class declaration). Each different constructor can then call the common initialization routine, and you won't have to repeat the code needlessly. A framework for such a class might look like this:

```
class A {
  ... // state variables, private data
  void common( int required_parm ) { ... } // common code
public:
  A()
  {
    common( arg );
    ... // other init code
  }
  A( char *descr )
  {
    common( arg );
    ... // other init code
  }
```

```
A( int arg, double darg )
{
  common( arg );
  ... // other init code
}
```

Occasionally, a programmer tries to use a direct constructor call in an effort to separate the common initialization code. That is, the programmer makes the mistake of packaging the common code as the basic constructor for the class. Notice this example:

```
#include <string.h>
#include <iostream.h>

class A {                                    // BAD CODE !!!
  int main_value;
  char descr[41];
public:
  A( int arg = 37 ) : main_value(arg) {
    strcpy( descr , "No description" );
  };
  A( char *text ) {
    A( 64 );        // Try to call this object's constructor
    strcpy( descr, text );
  }
  A( double arg ) {
    A( (int)arg );                    // Drop the ball again
    strcpy( descr, "It was a double" );
  }
  void blurb() {
    cout << "Value = " << main_value << "\r\n";
    cout << descr << "\r\n";
  }
};

void main()
{
  A obj( "Different text" );

  obj.blurb();
}
```

This program appears to have some fairly sophisticated code, on the surface. The code would be sophisticated—if it worked correctly. The program compiles without error and runs without blowing up. So what is wrong?

The second and third constructors call the first constructor directly, which is legal. The only thing that was forgotten in writing this program is that the syntax *class(args)* doesn't just call the constructor, but *first creates a temporary unnamed object.* Therefore, the second and third constructors are merely spinning their wheels uselessly by creating a temporary class object that is thrown away as soon as the statement is complete.

Thus, the object declaration in main() gives the appearance that it will invoke the second constructor, which will set main_value to 64, and then copy the argument string into descr. Although the string is indeed copied, if you run this program, the main_value for this object contains garbage. The value 64 is assigned, but it is assigned to the variable in a temporary class object that disappeared.

In summary, then, it is wise to separate common initialization code into a single (perhaps private) member function. However, don't try to get fancy by making that function a constructor. Your program compiles with no sign that anything is wrong, but it won't do what you expect it to do.

Deciding When You Need a Copy Constructor

The copy constructor is a special form of overloaded constructor function that you must consider when designing your classes. The problem with copy constructors is you often need them, but it is not always obvious *when* you need them. The following code fragment illustrates this point:

```
class X {
  int data;
public:
  X() { data = 64; }                  // Default constructor
  X( int arg ) { data = arg; }    // Conversion constructor
  X( X& other ) { data = other.data; }  // Copy constructor
};


void main()
{
  X obj1 = 2;     // Use conversion constructor

  X obj2 = obj1; // Obviously the copy constructor
  X obj3(obj2);   // Copy constructor but not obvious
}
```

What is going on in this program is quite clear—until the last line of main() is reached. The declaration of obj3 in that line uses the alternative form of declaring a class object with initialization from another class object. The syntax doesn't jump out at you and indicate that the copy constructor is going to be used. Because the constructor argument is a reference to another object of the same class, however, the copy constructor is in fact used. If you have allowed the compiler to generate the copy constructor, the result may not be what you want.

In deciding when you need a copy constructor, you should also consider initialization tasks. If any of the special initialization requirements mentioned earlier exist for a class, the compiler-generated copy constructor may not be adequate. Generally, it is best to provide a copy constructor yourself. If an object is then initialized by copying another object of the same class, there is no possibility of incorrect setup.

Using operator *new()* and operator *delete()*

In C++, the operators new and delete enable you to create dynamic objects of arbitrary duration. You can also use these operators to acquire memory for any kind of plain C object, much like allocating memory on the heap with malloc() and calloc().

Objects created with new reside on the *free store.* Objects on the free store are removed with the delete operator. In fact, Microsoft C/C++ uses the heap to implement the free store, but the differences in handling warrant treating the free store as a separate conceptual entity. Understanding the new and delete operators is central to the efficient use of C++'s free store.

This section shows you how to use and overload the new and delete operators. Stroustrup, the designer of C++, believed memory allocation was such an important part of C++ programming that the facilities for memory allocation were implemented as built-in operators rather than standard library routines. As a result, program execution of C++ programs that use these routines tends to be slightly faster, whereas program compilation with new and delete (rather than with the library functions) tends to be slower.

Using *new* and *delete* in General

You can use the new and delete operators to allocate space for any C data objects, not just to create class objects. The rules for using new to acquire space on the free store are quite simple:

■ *The new operator is a unary operator.* It has a single operand, positioned to its right. Notice this example:

```
int* data;
   ...
data = new int;
```

The operand for new can be, as you will soon discover, considerably more
complex than the one shown here.

■ *The operand for new is a type name.* Beginning C++ programmers can
easily be tempted to code an object for the new operand, when in fact it
should be a *type name.* The purpose of new is not to acquire, say, an
integer, but to allocate sufficient space for one. The following short program illustrates this point:

```
#include <iostream.h>

void main()
{
  int* value;       // pointer to an integer

  value = new int; // Allocate space on free store
  cout << value << "\r\n";;
  delete value;     // Destroy integer
}
```

■ *The new operator returns a pointer of the correct type.* Because the operand
must be a type name, new already knows what kind of pointer is required.
One of the nice features of new is that you don't have to cast the pointer
to the correct type, as you would when using malloc(), which always
returns a void pointer. Notice, new returns a *null pointer* if space cannot
be found on the free store.

■ *The new operator automatically calculates the size of the object for which
new is allocating memory.* This feature is also handy because you do not
have to use the sizeof() operator to compute the size required. The resulting code looks cleaner.

■ *You can use new to allocate space for more complex objects, such as arrays,
on the free store.* To use new to allocate memory for a string or an array,
simply write the type name and then the array size enclosed by the array
declarator ([ ]). The following short program demonstrates this use of
new:

```
#include <string.h>
#include <iostream.h>

void main()
{
```

```
char* str;            // pointer to a string

str = new char[41]; // Allocate array on free store
strcpy( str, "Here is another hello program.\r\n" );
cout << str;
delete str;           // Destroy string
}
```

Notice that when `new` allocates memory for an array, `new` returns only a pointer to the first element of the array. This is not a problem, however, because the plain C equivalence of pointers and subscripts also applies in C++.

■ *You can create multidimensional arrays of objects with `new`, but with some restrictions.* You can write multidimensional size declarators like this:

```
intptr = new int[2][2][2];
```

None of the array sizes can be omitted (that is, you cannot refer to an incomplete array type). All the dimensions except the first one must be constants. The first dimension can be any legitimate expression, such as the following:

```
int i = 2;
intptr = new int[i][2][2];
```

■ *References cannot be created with `new`.* A reference is an lvalue, but not strictly an object. Therefore, `new` cannot return a pointer to a reference— and `new` must return a pointer.

■ *Objects created with `new` are not automatically initialized to any value.* The contents of such an object are garbage, unless you do something about it. You can specify an initializer with `new`, but only for simple objects, not for arrays. Consider this example:

```
int* i = new int( 37 ); // Set int to 37
```

Using parentheses for the initializer enables you later to specify constructor arguments with `new`. (Surely you guessed that was coming.)

Objects created with `new` on the free store have *arbitrary duration*. (This point has been mentioned before in other contexts.) Arbitrary objects are neither precisely static nor global—they exist until you destroy them with `delete`. An important side effect of the nature of arbitrary duration objects is that C++ does not guarantee to automatically delete them at any time. You must take care of deleting them yourself. Failing to delete an object, however, is not usually considered an error but is wasteful and can lead to a shortage of storage later.

The rules for using the delete operator are also simple:

- *Like new, the delete operator is a unary operator.* delete works on an operand (or operands) to its right. You use the following general syntax for delete:

  ```
  ::opt delete pointer
  ::opt ]delete [size] pointer
  ```

  The preceding syntax forms incorporate an exception to the formatting rules that have been used throughout the book. The square brackets around the size token form the subscript operator and must be coded as shown here.

  Prefixing the scope resolution operator guarantees that the global operator delete is used. (You learn how to overload delete for a class in the following sections.) The pointer must be one that was returned by new, and the [size] declarator destroys an array of objects created with new. The following code fragment shows how to code each form of the syntax:

  ```
  double* x = new double; // Create and point to a simple double
  delete x;               // Kill the double
  ...
  int* i = new int[256];  // Create array of 256 ints
  delete [256] i;         // Kill the whole array
  ```

- *You use the delete operator only to free storage acquired by new.* Trying to delete memory allocated by malloc(), for example, is an error. Using delete 0, however, is guaranteed to be harmless. (In other words, you won't blow up your program by deleting a null pointer.)

- *You cannot delete a pointer to a constant.* Specifying a pointer to a constant with delete implies you are trying to destroy the constant object, and constants, by definition, cannot be modified.

As you can see, the rules for using new and delete with plain C data objects are simple. The process is uncluttered by constructor or destructor calls because they do not apply to ordinary data objects. Yet using new and delete with class objects is almost as easy, as discussed in the next section.

Dynamically Creating and Deleting Class Objects

You can use the new and delete operators to create and destroy class objects, and you can use these operators within constructor and destructor functions. To avoid infinite recursion, however, do not use new with the same class type as that of the constructor function containing it.

All the rules for using `new` and `delete` with ordinary data objects apply also to using these operators with class objects. You should notice some additional considerations, however. When using `new` to create class objects on the free store, observe the following points:

- *Using `new` with a class type causes a constructor for the class to be invoked.* This is the primary difference between using `new` with data types and with class types. If the class type alone is used, the class's default constructor is called. Notice the following code fragment:

```
class radio { ... };
...
radio* jambox = new radio; // Create object and call default
                           // constructor for class
```

  The `new` operator both allocates space on the free store for `jambox` and calls the `radio` class default constructor.

- *When class objects are created with `new`, the `new` initializer may be a list of arguments.* This list can be used as arguments for a constructor call. Arguments matching rules apply, so that you can control which overloaded constructor is invoked. Look at this example:

```
class twocon {
  ...
public:
   twocon ( int );
   twocon ( long, char * );
...
};
                              // Call second constructor
twocon* objptr = new twocon( 4L, "A string" );
```

- *When arrays of class objects are created with `new`, only the default constructor can be used.* This point has been mentioned before, but it should be repeated here. Declaring an array of class objects, either with `new` or in some other way, restricts constructor calls to the default version. Remember that because the default constructor can be a constructor with *all default arguments,* the constructor function can be called without arguments. The default constructor is called for each element of the array.

When you use `delete` to destroy class objects on the free store, be aware of these additional considerations:

- *When `delete` is applied to a class object on the free store, the object's destructor function is automatically invoked.* There can, of course, be only one version of the class destructor function because destructors cannot accept arguments.

■ *Do not use* delete *to destroy a class object created at a specific memory location with an overloaded* new. The reason for this restriction is that new didn't create the class object—you did. Even if you acquired the specific memory for the object with global new, the allocation was for a plain C object (such as an array of characters). The correct method of destroying a specifically placed object is to call the *destructor* directly and then separately release the storage occupied by the object.

■ *Using* delete *to destroy an array of class objects on the free store automatically invokes the destructor function for each array element.* The syntax for deleting an array of class objects is the same as for plain C objects:

```
class simple {
  char* str; // Point to string outside object
public:
  simple() { str = new char[41]; }
  ~simple() { delete str; }
};

void main()
{
  simple* sarray = new simple [16];   // Array of 16

  delete [16] sarray; // Call destructors for all 16
}
```

The form used for delete in the last line, above, specifies the size of the array: this form is an anachronism (an obsolete feature) that continues to be supported for compatibility with older C++ compilers. Microsoft C/C++ does not require the expression giving the array size, so you could code the last line in the preceding fragment in this way:

```
delete [] sarray; // Call destructors for all 16
```

As you can see, a considerable amount of programming power is inherent in the global new and delete operators. There are very few things related to the creation of class objects on the free store that you cannot do with these operators. Because there are some things you cannot do with new and delete, C++ allows you to overload them. Overloading new and delete is discussed in the remaining sections of this chapter.

Overloading operator *new()* and operator *delete()*

The new and delete operators discussed so far are an integral part of the C++ language. They are called the global new and delete operators, and they are available at any time. You can also provide `new` and `delete` operators unique to each of your classes. These operators are known as *user-defined* `new` and `delete` operators.

Because you already know how to overload operators for a class, it won't surprise you to learn that overloading either the global or the user-defined `new` and `delete` operators involves writing the overloaded function definition for the new version of the operator. Be aware that you take on extra responsibilities when you overload the `new` or `delete` operators. You should exercise extreme care in redefining these operators. Specifically, notice the following points:

■ *The use of operator* `new` *or operator* `delete` *in an expression causes the corresponding function to be called.* In other words, using operator `new` causes the function operator `new()` to be called, and using operator `delete` causes the operator `delete()` function to be called.

■ *A size argument having type* `size_t` *is the required first (or only) argument for every version of operator* `new()`. The operator `new()` function always returns a void pointer (`void*`). That is, you must at least define the function with the following declaration part:

```
void* operator new( size_t size ) { ... }
```

If you declare *only* the `size_t` argument for global `new`, you are not overloading the `new` operator—you are completely redefining it. The first argument must be a `size_t` type object, but you generally add other, optional arguments, as discussed later in this section.

■ *A void pointer* (`void*`) *is the required first argument for* `operator delete()`. The `operator delete()` function always returns `void` (nothing). That is, you must at least define the function with the following declaration part:

```
void operator delete( void* obj ) { ... }
```

Here `obj` is a pointer to the object being deleted. The `operator delete()` function can optionally have a second argument specifying the size of the object to be deleted:

```
void operator delete( void* obj, size_t size ) { ... }
```

You can use the optional argument for any purpose you want. It is not generally needed, but some circumstances may arise in which you need such an argument.

Overloading the Global Operators

You might want to overload the global operators `new` and `delete` for two reasons: to place a class object at a specific memory location (already mentioned briefly), or to take full control of free-store garbage collection and recovery from failures of new. Garbage collection and allocation-error recovery are discussed in Chapter 19, "Introduction to Microsoft C/C++ Windows Programming." Most of the important theory concerning overloading (or overriding) the new and delete operators, however, is presented in this section and is critical background for that later discussion.

You can create a class object at a particular memory location—for example, one you allocated with malloc()—because C++ recognizes the use of operator new with *placement syntax*. When you use placement syntax, you provide a pointer to the area in which the object is to be constructed. The global new operator with placement syntax looks like this:

$$::_{opt} new(locationptr) \; type \; [number]_{opt} \; (initializers)_{opt}$$

Notice in this syntax form that the prefix scope resolution operator, the array size declarator (which must be surrounded with subscript operator brackets, if used at all), and the list of initializers are all optional.

Earlier in the chapter, you saw a sample program in which a class object was constructed in place. That short program is repeated here for convenience. Because your primary concern (for the moment) is the construction of a single class object in place, the array size declarator has been left out temporarily. The following short program illustrates the technique required for constructing a class object at a particular location:

```
#include <iostream.h>

//
// Declare a simple class
//
class simple {
  int stuff;
public:
  simple( int arg = 16 ) { stuff = arg; }
  ~simple() {}                          // Default destructor
  void showit() { cout << stuff << "\r\n"; }
};


//
// Overload global operator new()
//
void* operator new( size_t size, void *ptr )
{
  size = size;  // Dummy statement avoids compiler warning
  return ptr;                // Here is what we are after
}
```

```
void main()
{
  void *fetch;                         // Working pointer

                      // Get a block of memory using
                            // original global new
  fetch = (void *)( new unsigned char[ sizeof(simple) ] );

  simple* X;                 // Pointer to simple object

  X = new(fetch) simple( 37 );              // Create object
  X->showit();
  X->simple::~simple();        // Explicitly delete object
  delete fetch;                          // Release memory
}
```

The catch to using new with placement syntax is that no corresponding function is available until you define one. You are therefore required to overload operator new().

In the preceding program, notice first how the global operator new() function is overloaded. The function accepts an object size and location pointer, in accordance with the rules outlined in the preceding section. One important consequence of this selection of arguments is that this function is indeed an overload of new, not a complete replacement for global operator new(). You can therefore use the original global new in the usual manner—as is done in main().

With the overloaded operator new() in place, constructing the class object in place is a straightforward procedure:

1. *Declare a void pointer that is used to locate the class object.* The pointer should be void* because that is the type which will be required for using the overloaded new operator and for releasing the acquired memory.

2. *Acquire the memory necessary to hold the object.* The memory you acquire at this point has nothing to do with classes (yet). You can use either a library function like malloc() or the original global new to allocate the memory. Notice how the sizeof() operator is used in the preceding sample program to ensure the correct amount of memory is allocated.

3. *Declare a pointer to a class object of the desired type.* Do not initialize the pointer yet; just declare it. (The constructor does the initialization.) In the preceding short program, the declaration amounted to simple* X, nothing more.

4. *Now use the overloaded new operator with placement syntax to construct the class object.* The first void pointer you declared is now used with new to cause the class constructor to build the object at the specified spot:

   ```
   X = new(fetch) simple( 37 );
   ```

Notice in this particular statement that an initializer value is also speci-fied. The action caused by this statement is the reason you did nothing earlier to initialize the class object pointer. `new` both invokes the con-structor and returns the pointer to the object here.

5. *Use the object however you want.* The resulting class object is a true class object and can be used accordingly. In the example here, one of the mem-ber functions is invoked.

6. *Call the destructor function explicitly.* There is no `delete` for the class ob-ject in this procedure. If you don't call the destructor explicitly, it is not called at all. If the object has special requirements (such as additional memory acquired within the constructor), you may want to leave a num-ber of loose ends dangling.

7. *Release the memory used to hold the object.* You can accomplish this step with a call to the standard library function `free()` or with global `delete`, as in the preceding program.

The procedure outlined represents a cookbook-style approach to constructing class objects at a precise location, but the procedure works—every time. Even though it is very simple, it is quite important. You will need it again later in this section.

You may have noticed in the preceding discussion that nothing was said about overloading `delete`. The reason is that no corresponding syntax exists for "in place `delete`." Is there any time when you need to overload `operator delete()`? Yes, there is—when you override (not just overload) `operator new()`.

Overriding the original global `operator new()` and `operator delete()` functions is a process fraught with danger; you can stumble into all kinds of deep, dark holes. Not least among your worries is the fact that overriding the global functions means that you accept the whole load for allocating memory on the free store—no other global routines except yours exist then. Although any decision to override these functions should be weighed carefully, there may be times (such as allocation recovery and garbage collection) when overriding is necessary. Therefore, you need to know the basic techniques for overriding `new` and `delete`, as well as the effects of overriding the global operators when you use them with *basic data types* and with *class objects*.

Consider first how overriding `new` and `delete` affects free store allocation for the basic data types. When you override the global functions, you must understand two things:

■ *Overriding the global functions defeats all the internal memory manage-ment schemes.* The `new` and `delete` functions supplied with the compiler perform tasks you don't notice on the surface, such as tracking the size, number, and type of memory allocations. All that is now up to you. Furthermore, you should not mix your `new` function with Microsoft C/C++'s `delete` function. Provide both functions so that you can release memory in a manner compatible with the way in which memory was acquired—for example, by using `malloc()` and `free()`.

■ *When you override `delete()`, you must specify one or two arguments.* You *must* declare your version of the function to accept a `void*` pointer to the memory to be released, and you *can* add an optional second argument specifying the size of the memory area. To override the Microsoft C/C++ global `delete`, you *must* use one of these forms:

```
void operator delete( void* );
```

or

```
void operator delete( void*, size_t )
```

If you fail to specify both arguments, you will define a function—one that is never used.

Because constructor calls are not an issue when you use your own global `new` and `delete`, the process of overriding the global operators is simple. One reason you might want to do this is to provide for preinitialization of the acquired memory (which original `new` doesn't do). The following short program illustrates this technique:

```
#include <stdlib.h>
#include <iostream.h>

void* operator new( size_t size )
{
  void* ptr;

  ptr = malloc( size );
  if ( !ptr ) return ptr;     // Return null if failed
  memset( ptr, '\0', size ); // Do init for user
  return ptr;                 // Return ptr by value
}

void operator delete( void *obj, size_t size )
{
  free( obj );
}

void main()
{
  char* str;
  str = new char[41];
  delete str;          // All works for plain C objects
}
```

Even though the plain C data type in the preceding code is actually a complex type (a string), only one call to your operator new() is made when this program is run. The size parameter passed to the function in this example is 41, which is the number of bytes indicated in the new array size declarator. The overridden delete function performs the necessary freeing of storage. Note two things about the size parameter passed to your global operator delete(): First, the size parameter is useless here; and second, its value is equal to the *size of the pointer argument,* not of the object pointed to.

Consider next the effects of overriding the global new and delete operators when you use them with class objects. Overriding these operators works well for creating class objects, as long as you don't define any arrays of class objects. The following short program shows no apparent differences between defining class objects and defining plain C objects:

```
#include <stdlib.h>
#include <iostream.h>

void* operator new( size_t size )
{
  void* ptr;

  ptr = malloc( size );
  if ( !ptr ) return ptr;       // Return null if failed
  memset( ptr, '\0', size ); // Do init for user
  return ptr;                   // Return ptr by value
}

void operator delete( void *obj, size_t size )
{
  free( obj );
}

class simple {
  int a, b, c, d, e;
public:
  simple() : a(37),b(37),c(37),d(37), e(37)
      { cout << "Hello!\r\n"; }
  ~simple() { cout << "Goodbye!\r\n"; }
};

void main()
{
  simple* oneobj = new simple;
  delete oneobj;  // All still OK for ONE class object
}
```

In the preceding short program, the expression `delete oneobj` causes the class destructor to be invoked, followed by the overridden version of `operator delete()`, just as it should be. Should you be so bold as to override global `new` and `delete`, and also attempt to create an array of class objects, you will find yourself in deep trouble.

Using operator `new` to construct an array of class objects always causes the global `new` function to be used. So far, so good, but that isn't all. Notice what happens when Microsoft C/C++ encounters the array size declarator with `new`, as shown here:

```
ptr = new classobj[num];
```

Microsoft C/C++ doesn't just call operator `new()`. Microsoft C/C++ first invokes a routine that creates storage-management information, and then invokes `new` and the appropriate constructors.

The tricky part is, even if you have overridden `new`, constructing an array of objects seems to proceed normally, including invoking your `new` routine to allocate the correct amount of contiguous memory for the array, and calling each constructor. When your program attempts to execute `delete [] ptr`, however, things go awry—quickly.

In such cases, the program usually doesn't blow up. It just invokes your global `delete` too many times, and with the wrong addresses. This happens because an internal routine is expecting to traverse the management information previously created, but it isn't there.

The management information is not there for a good reason: Microsoft C/C++, like all other C++ compilers, does not support creating vectors (arrays) of class objects when you override `new` and `delete`. As in the situation that exists when constructing class objects at a specific address, you should not use `delete` on an array of class objects created with *your* global `new` function. It's illegal.

You may be asking, can you use your `new` and `delete`, and still construct arrays of class objects at all? You certainly can, and the trick is to use the placement syntax for `new` again. Surprised? If you look back at the general syntax shown earlier, you can see that nothing stops you from using both a placement pointer and an array size declarator. The following short program shows you how to use both:

```
#include <iostream.h>

void* operator new( size_t size, void* where )
{
  size = size;
  return where;
}
```

```
class simple {
  int a, b, c;
public:
  simple() : a(37),b(37),c(37) { cout << "Hello!\r\n"; }
  ~simple() { cout << "Goodbye!\r\n"; }
};

void main()
{
  int i;
                    // Pointer to memory for array of objects
  void* oarray;


                            // Acquire memory independently
                            // for array of objects

  oarray = new unsigned char[ 10*sizeof(simple) ];

                        // Now create array of objects IN PLACE
                        // and invoke all constructors

  simple* bunch = new(oarray) simple[10];

                            // Be careful here, using
                            // pointer-subscript equivalence

  for ( i=0; i<10; ++i ) bunch[i].simple::~simple();

                            // Now "manually" get rid of
                            // object storage memory
  delete oarray;            // ::delete object memory
}
```

The procedure for constructing arrays of class objects with your global new overloaded function (but not delete) is nearly as simple as that for placement of class objects. You need to perform the following steps to construct an array of class objects with your new:

1. *Overload, but do not override, global new.* Providing a function definition to support the placement syntax (as is required) does not completely re-place global new. It only provides support for specific placement, nothing more.

2. *Set up the void* pointer that locates the array.* Do not initialize it yet.

3. *Acquire the memory for the whole array.* As before, you can use standard C library routines or `::new` for this purpose. Initialize the `void*` pointer with the result. Notice in the preceding program how the result of applying the `sizeof()` operator is multiplied by the number of elements in the proposed array.

4. *Declare a pointer to the class object, and initialize it with `new` by using both placement syntax and the array size declarator.* Because the placement syntax guarantees you have taken over storage management, the data otherwise created by internal routines is not required. The constructors for each class object are still properly called.

5. *After using the array of class objects, write a loop in which you directly call the destructor function for every class object in the array.* This step is similar to the direct destructor call for a single in-place class object.

6. *Use the correct method to release the block of memory holding the array.* Again, you can use either the library functions or global `delete`. `delete` will not be confused by the appearance of destroying a vector because you have not used an array size declarator. You are not destroying a vector, only a chunk of memory.

If you are getting the feeling that overloading and overriding global `new` and `delete` can be tricky business, and that there should be a better way to handle at least some of these rather sophisticated requirements, you are right. There will always be instances in which you need to use the techniques outlined in this section. There is a better way, however, to satisfy many of these needs without much of the confusion and difficulty: You can overload `new` and `delete` on a per-class basis. This topic is discussed in the final section.

Overloading the Operators for a Class

You can overload the `new` and `delete` operators for each class you define (if you want) by including as member functions the operator overload declarations. Fortunately, the syntax is identical to the syntax you have already seen in this chapter, with one exception. You cannot use the array size declarator with a class-specific user-defined `new` function. Arrays of objects (class and otherwise) are always allocated with global `new`, if `new` is in fact the means you use.

You do not need to make any modifications to the declarations or techniques you have already learned, except to the notation for declaring class member function definitions. This alteration is shown in the following short program:

```
#include <iostream.h>

class X {
  int a, b, c;
```

```
public:
  ~X();
  void* operator new( size_t size );  // static function
  void* operator new( size_t size, void* ptr );
  void operator delete( void* ptr );
};

  X::~X() { }

  void* X::operator new( size_t size )  // static function
  {
    void* ptr;
    cout << "Standard class new called.\r\n";
    ptr = (void*) ::new unsigned char[size];
    return ptr;
  }

  void* X::operator new( size_t size, void* ptr )
  {
    size = size;    // Look familiar?
    cout << "Placement class new called.\r\n";
    return ptr;
  }

  void X::operator delete( void* ptr )
  {
    cout << "Class delete called.\r\n";
    ::delete ptr;
  }

void main()
{
  X* obj1 = new X;
  delete obj1;

  X* obj2;
  void* buf = (void*) ::new unsigned char[ sizeof(X) ];
  obj2 = new(buf) X;
  obj2->X::~X();
  ::delete buf;
}
```

You should still observe the rule of thumb of providing class-specific `new` and `delete` overloaded functions in pairs. If you changed allocation methods by writing a `new` function, you should probably write also a corresponding `delete` function that releases acquired memory in the same way it was acquired.

Class-specific `new` and `delete` functions are always `static` member functions, even if you do not declare them with the `static` storage class specifier. This is true because `new` must be called before an object exists (there is no `this` pointer before the constructor is reached), and `delete` is called after the object has been destroyed. Notice that class-specific `delete` cannot be overloaded— you are allowed to declare only one `delete` function.

You can overload `new` however you want, as long as the first argument is always a `size_t` object size argument. For example, you may want to pass a flag parameter to a class-specific `new` function, as shown in the following code fragment:

```
#include <iostream.h>

class X {
  int a, b, c;
public:
  ...
  void* operator new( size_t size, int flag );
};
...
  void* X::operator new( size_t size, int flag )
  {
    void* ptr;
    cout << "Overloaded class new called.\r\n";
    cout << "Flag was " << flag << "\r\n";
    ptr = (void*) ::new unsigned char[size];
    return ptr;
  }
...

void main()
{
  X* obj1 = new(64) X;
  delete obj1;
}
```

In this code fragment, the `new` operator in `main()` has an initializer. This notation, called the *parenthesized form* of operator `new`, is nothing more than the function call method of invoking an overloaded `new`, passing it extra parameters. (The `size_t` parameter is implicit—do not write it directly into the function call.) When there are many overloaded new functions, the correct function is selected through best-fit signature matching, as for any other overloaded function.

Except in declarations of arrays of class objects, a class-specific new function is always called when an object of that class is created with new, if the class declares one. If the class does not declare an overloaded new function, the compiler resorts to the global new or delete function. Member functions of the class can use its overloaded new and delete by default, or they can use the scope resolution operator to access the global new and delete operators (::new and ::delete). In fact, the overloaded operators in the preceding examples resort to global new and delete to acquire and release memory.

Exercises

Because the exercises here are longer and more difficult than those for other chapters, only two exercises are provided.

1. Now you know how to overload just about everything in a C++ class. Design and write a class that is very rich in member functions, overloaded operators, and overloaded constructors (don't forget the copy constructor), and that can be created either with or without new and delete.

2. This exercise is much tougher than it might seem. Practice overloading new and delete. All but the very shortest code fragments in this chapter were compiled, run, and tested. To see how the code works, type in some of the code fragments and run them yourself. Then write some code of your own that performs the new and delete techniques presented.

Summary

In this chapter, you learned some important C++ programming techniques for using constructor and destructor functions. Before moving to the next chapter, review your grasp of these points:

■ *All C++ classes have constructor and destructor functions.* If you do not provide them, the compiler will generate default versions for you. You should understand how and when constructor functions are called.

■ *You learned the methods for overloading constructor functions, as well as the reason for overloading them.* Remember that a destructor function cannot be overloaded.

■ *The copy constructor is used when a class object is initialized by copying another object of the same class.* The compiler will also generate for you a default copy constructor that copies a class object on a member-for-member basis. If your class contains pointers to special areas outside the object, or other special requirements, you should write your own copy constructor, because only the pointers will be copied, not the data itself.

■ *You can both overload and override global `new` and `delete`.* You should understand especially when doing this can get you into deep trouble (some practice will help here).

■ *You learned how to provide extra parameters for a class-specific `new` function and how to pass the extra arguments to the function.* Remember that class `new` and `delete` are not used when an array of class objects is being created; the global versions are always used for this purpose.

Using C++ Streams

Following in the footsteps of its parent C language, C++ has no input/output facilities—no built-in facilities, that is. Like C, C++ has a standard I/O library, known as the C++ stream library, that can fulfill most of your needs for I/O immediately and can be extended easily.

Introducing C++ Streams

An experienced C programmer cannot avoid forming mental associations when he hears the term *C++ stream*. The C concept of handling I/O as a flowing stream of characters that move in and out of a program is inescapable. This association is partly fortunate and partly misleading.

C and C++ streams have many similarities, including the idea of a stream of characters flowing in and out of a program. This basic concept is indeed behind both the C and the C++ I/O libraries. C and C++ streams have many startling differences, too, which you must see and understand clearly. The most radical difference is the syntax C++ streams use to get the job done.

With Microsoft C/C++, you can use both C and C++ streams in the same program. The type-safe linkage feature of the compiler permits this without confusing the compiler about which library routine is to be used. Which library you should use at any point is another matter. That decision may be based on personal taste or on a real need.

Much of the C++ literature you see today touts the C++ stream library as a simpler and thus more efficient way to handle I/O. That may have been true with earlier compilers, when C++ streams were much more primitive and therefore simpler to use. Some other examples of C++ literature treat the subject in a more considered and accurate manner, referring to the *improved flexibility and elegance* of C++ streams.

What, then, is the truth about Microsoft C/C++ streams? First, the Microsoft C/C++ implementation of streams is compatible with the existing standards of practice. That is why programs written with Microsoft C/C++ streams should almost always be portable to other conforming compilers.

Second, C++ has several predefined standard streams that correspond to the plain C standard streams. Using the standard C++ streams for ordinary console I/O is quite easy, and the programmer's job, therefore, is easier at that level. The standard C++ streams are handy for quick console I/O, which is why you have seen them frequently in the sample code of preceding chapters. These standard C++ streams are still handy, even when you begin to use some of their more advanced features.

Third, some of the more advanced features for manipulating the stream state and the data format can get pretty esoteric in C++. Some of these features may actually take more code to implement I/O procedures in your programs. Really sophisticated I/O programming requires relatively more knowledge of class internals than with standard C I/O.

Are C++ streams worth the effort of learning a whole new approach to I/O? Yes, they are. Your initial reaction to C++ streams might be that they are unnecessary because the standard C library functions are available and you already know how to use them. If nothing else is true, however, C++ streams are an integral part of the C++ environment. They can be quite helpful, and you may not be able to read someone else's code if you don't learn about them.

Comparing C++ Streams to Standard Streams

Certain behind-the-scenes activities involved in I/O programming do not change, whether you are using standard C library functions or C++ streams. You are already accustomed to the standard C facilities for I/O: a file buffer for holding data; a FILE object, which is a structure holding important information about the stream (including the location of the buffer area); and the constellation of library routines that use the file buffer and the FILE object to perform I/O.

All these facilities are present in C++ streams as well; it may take just a little getting used to before you recognize them as such. C++, naturally enough, uses class objects both to implement and to encapsulate I/O support facilities, as well as to add more sophistication to them.

A C++ `streambuf` class object is the parallel facility to the ordinary C buffer. A `streambuf` object does more than hold data. It also provides logic for moving characters in and out of the buffer (including a parallel function to `ungetc()`), for flushing the buffer, and for disk file stream buffers, for opening and closing the file.

The `ios` class is the parallel to the `FILE` object of plain C. No objects of the `ios` class are ever created, however; it is used as a base class from which to derive input and output classes that do have objects. The purpose of the `ios` class is to contain information about the state of the stream, including any error data, and to contain a pointer to the associated `streambuf` object for the stream. Figure 16.1 illustrates the nature of these two low-level classes.

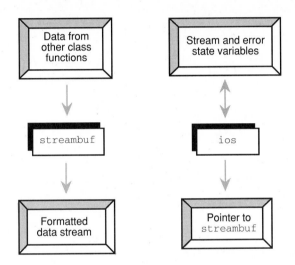

Figure 16.1.

The **streambuf** class controls the data buffer and drives character I/O. The **ios** class provides stream status and error information.

Just as for standard C I/O, some distinction between the input and output processes must be made in C++ stream classes. Microsoft C/C++ makes this distinction by deriving two new classes from the `ios` class (see Chapter 17, "Using C++ Derived Classes," for more details). These two new classes are the `istream` class (for input) and the `ostream` class (for output). Furthermore, facilities for performing both input and output on the same stream are provided by deriving the `iostream` class from both `istream` and `ostream`, using multiple inheritance. Figure 16.2 shows a schematic of the derivation of these classes.

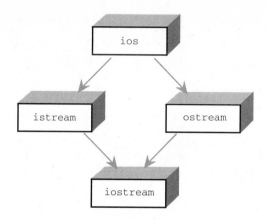

The Microsoft C/C++ header file iostream.h contains the declarations for all the classes mentioned so far, and it is the only header you need to include for simple console I/O. (Format conversion and manipulation are covered in the section "Using C++ Stream Manipulators" later in this chapter.) iostream.h contains declarations also for the four predefined C++ standard streams (cin, cout, cerr, and clog). The standard streams are class *objects* with type istream or ostream, as appropriate. Figure 16.3 illustrates the standard C++ streams.

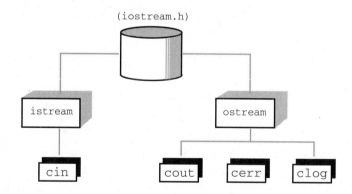

In fact, Microsoft C/C++ takes the process one step further. A class istream_withassign is derived from istream, and ostream_withassign is derived from ostream. The withassign classes provide copy constructors and over-loaded assignment operators for class objects. The standard streams are objects of the withassign classes, but it is more convenient to speak of the istream and ostream classes (as long as you know what is meant).

The Microsoft C/C++ standard streams perform tasks that are nearly parallel to those of the plain C standard streams. Thus, there is a natural correspondence between the C++ standard streams and the plain C streams. Table 16.1 summarizes the functional correspondence of C++ streams, C streams, and DOS handles.

Table 16.1. Standard C++ streams, C streams, and DOS handles.

C++ Stream	C Stream	DOS Handle Used by Plain C `stdio`
cin	stdin	0
cout	stdout	1
cerr	stderr	2
clog		
	stdaux	3
	stdprn	4

The `cin` and `cout` streams are line buffered, as are the counterpart `stdin` and `stdout`. The `cerr` stream is line buffered, whereas ANSI C requires `stderr` to be unbuffered. The `clog` stream is a fully buffered version of `cerr` and has no direct counterpart among the plain C standard streams. For general programming purposes, you likely will use `cerr` instead of `clog`.

Using C++ Streams for Standard I/O

To use the `cin`, `cout`, `cerr`, and `clog` streams in your programs, you do not need to declare any stream objects. These standard stream objects are already declared in the iostream.h header file. Just #include the header near the beginning of your program, and begin using the streams, as shown here:

```
#include <iostream.h>
...
cout << "Hello,there!\r\n" ;
```

You have already seen the `cout` stream used many times in the sample programs and code fragments in this book, although without explanation. The standard input stream, `cin`, is used in a similar way:

```
#include <iostream.h>
...
char c;
cin >> c; // Get a character from stdin
```

Obviously, the stream classes have overloaded the << and >> operators for use with stream objects. The overloaded shift-left operator (<<) is called the *output stream inserter* because it inserts data into the outflowing data stream. Similarly, the overloaded shift-right operator (>>) is called the *input stream extractor* because it extracts data from an inflowing data stream and brings it into the program's data areas. Figure 16.4 illustrates how the overloaded << operator function declaration corresponds to the operator's use with cout.

Figure 16.4.

The relationship between the << inserter operator and the overloaded operator<<() function declaration.

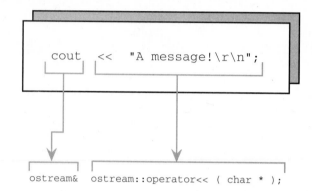

If the stream classes were defined so that only one data item at a time could be inserted or extracted, as shown in the preceding code fragments, the C++ stream would not be very useful. Fortunately, the stream classes are defined so that you can cascade, or *chain*, several insertions or extractions in one statement. See the following example:

```
#include <iostream.h>
...
int a, b, c;
cin >> a >> b >> c; // Extract/input 3 data values
cout << a << b << c; // Now insert/output them
```

In this code fragment, the cin stream is reading your keystrokes from the keyboard (ignoring whitespace), converting the character data to integers, and placing the results in the three variables. Furthermore, cin is preserving the order of appearance of variables and data. That is, it places the first integer you type in a, the second in b, and the third in c. It handles the inserted or extracted items in order, *from left to right,* just as you would intuitively expect.

The cout stream performs the companion output (insertion) of the three variables, also from left to right. In the preceding code fragment, only variable names are inserted or extracted. cout also allows you to insert any expression, constant, or variable identifier into the stream, as long as the type is supported by the class. For example, you might use the following code:

```
#include <iostream.h>
int a;
...
a = 16
cout << "The answer is " << a << "\r\n";
```

In this fragment, `cout` produces output on the screen with the following appearance:

```
The answer is 16
```

The supported data types for `cout` are shown in Table 16.2.

Table 16.2. `cout` data types.

Type	Signed	Unsigned	Default Display Format
int	Yes	Yes	Decimal integer
short	Yes	Yes	Decimal integer
long	Yes	Yes	Decimal integer
char	Yes	Yes	Text character
float	N.A.	N.A.	Fixed point, 6 digits Precision, rounded
double	N.A.	N.A.	Fixed point, 6 digits Precision, rounded
long double	N.A.	N.A.	Fixed point, 6 digits Precision, rounded
char*	N.A.	N.A.	Text string
void*	N.A.	N.A.	Pointer value, as either an *offset* or *segment:offset* pair

Notice in the preceding code fragment how the inserter operator (<<) is used between the items. Because each inserter sends just one value, a statement such as the following is in error:

```
cout << "The answer is " a "\r\n";  // WRONG
```

Notice also that to cause the output string to perform the carriage-return and line-feed action, you need to terminate the insertion sequence with "\r\n". This looks strange if you are accustomed to using only "\n" to terminate a string—for example, a printf() format string. However, cout does not provide (in this particular usage) translation of the newline character to the carriage-return/line-feed characters.

For both cin and cout, control of whitespace is basically up to you. The cout stream has a default field width of zero, meaning that as much space as is needed to represent the output is used, but no whitespace is inserted automatically between items. Therefore, if the integers in the preceding fragment had values of 1, 2, and 3, and you write

```
cout << a << b << c;
```

the resulting output appears as

```
123
```

even though the source code statement is nicely spaced for easy reading. Similarly, the statement

```
cin << a << b << c;
```

works just as well for all the following formats of keyboard input except the last format listed here:

```
1 2 3           // This is fine
1    2    3      // and so is this
1[tab]2[tab]3   // Tabs are whitespace, too
123             // wrong, no separation
```

The last input line would provide only a value of 123 for the variable a, and cin would continue to wait for the rest of the values to be entered. cin is a lot like scanf() in that respect; that is, you can type each value on a separate line, pressing Enter after each value.

cin is unlike scanf() in that you cannot include literals in the sequence of extractors and expect to have them exactly skipped over; cin by default skips over whitespace, but that is all. The following statement, for example, would yield quite unexpected results:

```
cin >> "A=" >> a;
```

In this line of code, you have fooled cin into expecting to receive a pointer to the constant string (which is invalid anyway), followed by an integer value. It just doesn't work out right.

The cin stream expects to read input character data for the various types in a format compatible with the way you write constants in a source program, with some slight exceptions. Table 16.3 shows the extractor types cin can accept. Notice, Table 16.3 has no entry for the void* type. Even if you could type a pointer value, what would it point to?

Table 16.3. The input data types for `cin`.

Type	Signed	Unsigned	Default Display Format
`int`	Yes	Yes	Source integer constant
`short`	Yes	Yes	Source integer constant
`long`	Yes	Yes	Source integer constant
`char`	Yes	Yes	Text character
`float`	N.A.	N.A.	Floating-point constant
`double`	N.A.	N.A.	Floating-point constant
`long double`	N.A.	N.A.	Floating-point constant
`char*`	N.A.	N.A.	Text string (not a line)

You must observe some constraints in typing data for `cin`. The most notable constraint is that you cannot use type suffixes as you can in your program's source code. That is, if `cin` is expecting a `long` integer as input, you cannot respond with the character 123L. Note the following example:

```
long k;
...
cin >> k;   // You type 123, not 123L
```

Specifying the `char*` type may not work the way you expect, either. Suppose you write the following declaration and statement:

```
char str[41];   // a place to hold a string
...
cin >> str;   // Read a string
cout << str;   // Write it back out
```

This code fragment makes it look as if you can type a whole string of characters, press Enter, and see the entire string displayed. That's not so, however. `cin` skips whitespace, but it also stops gathering characters for the expected type when whitespace is encountered again. For the preceding code fragment, if you type

```
hello, there!
```

`cout` in turn displays exactly what `cin` extracted. In this case, the result is

```
hello,
```

and nothing more.

You will have some problems if you expect to control each character of whitespace with cin and cout. Inserters and extractors, taken by themselves, don't quite measure up to the task. For that reason, the stream classes provide member functions (as opposed to overloaded operators) that can deal with whitespace one character at a time, or a whole line at a time. There are functions for handling pure binary data, too. Table 16.4 shows the istream and ostream member functions for handling all characters, whole strings, and binary data. cin and cout are only two specific class objects that can use the member functions. You can declare your own stream objects, including file streams, which can also access those member functions.

Table 16.4. Stream class member functions for special I/O.

Standard Stream	Function Prototype
istream	istream& get(char*, int, char='\n');
istream	istream& read(char*, int);
istream	istream& getline(char*, int, char='\n');
istream	istream& get(char&);
istream	int get();
istream	int peek();
istream	istream& putback(char);
istream	istream& ignore(int=1, int=EOF);
ostream	ostream& put(char);
ostream	ostream& write(const char*, int);

Table 16.4 does not show the signed and unsigned type modifiers for each char type, yet overloaded versions of each applicable function with these modifiers do exist. Of course, any of these functions can fail—by reaching an end-of-file (EOF) condition, if nothing else. Handling EOF and error conditions is covered in the next section. The functions in Table 16.4 operate in the following ways:

■ istream& get(char*, int, char='\n');

This version of the get() function reads characters into the char* buffer until it has either read int − 1 characters or encountered the terminating character (newline by default). Notice the following code sequence:

```
#include <iostream.h>
#include <iomanip.h>
```

```
char str[41];
...
istream.get( str, 40, '\n' );
```

For this code sequence, you could type the string a b c and press Enter, with the whitespace (or even binary characters) preserved. That is, the resulting string internally would have the following format:

```
a   b   c\0
```

This means the terminating character is not read in, but the null character is inserted to complete the string.

■ `istream& read( char*, int );`

The `read()` function operates similarly to `get()`, except no terminating character is recognized. Exactly `int` characters will be read, and they may consist of ordinary characters, whitespace characters, or binary characters. Note the following example:

```
#include <iostream.h>
#include <iomanip.h>

  char str[41];
...
  cin.read( str, 40 );
```

This code sequence reads 40 characters into `str`. If you press Ctrl-C for one of those characters, the internal character value would be 0x03. This function is more useful when used with file streams.

■ `istream& getline( char*, int, char='\n' );`

The `getline()` function operates just like the `get()` function for a string, except the terminating character is read in before the `'\0'` character is appended. Notice this code sequence:

```
#include <iostream.h>
#include <iomanip.h>

  char str[41];
...
  cin.getline( str, 40, '\n' );
```

When you use the preceding code to input the typed characters a b c followed by a press of Enter, the result is the following internal sequence of characters:

```
a b c\n\0
```

The `getline()` member function can be useful for either the `cin` standard stream or a file stream (`fstream`) being read in text mode.

■ `istream& get( char& );`

This is the single-character version of the `get()` function. This function can be used to input any ordinary, whitespace, or binary character. Note the following example:

```
char C;
...
cin.get( C );
```

You can use the single-character `get()` function with standard or file stream objects. Its primary purpose is to retrieve binary data. Notice that you can mix text and binary input in a stream by using a code sequence like this:

```
char c;
...
cin >> c; // Use the extractor to skip whitespace first
cin.get( c ); // Now get ANY second character
```

■ `int get();`

Like the single-character `get()`, this version of `get()` reads almost any character, but returns an integer rather than a reference to an `istream`. Furthermore, when the `cin` stream uses this version of `get()`, the function waits for you to press Enter before returning the character to the stream, and also interprets a Ctrl-C character as a system Break action. (This is not true for `fstreams` associated with disk files.) The normal use of the function looks like this:

```
char C;
...
C = cin.get();
```

■ `int peek();`

You can use the `peek()` member function to get a look ahead at the next character in the `streambuf` without actually extracting it. This function may seem to have little use with `cin` (and is more useful with file streams), but `peek()` can be used to good effect with standard input. Consider, for example, the following short program:

```
#include <iostream.h>
#include <iomanip.h>

void main()
{
```

```
   char c;

   cin >> c;
   cout << "First character was " << c << "\r\n";
   c = cin.peek();
   cout << "Next character will be " << c << "\r\n";
}
```

Obviously, peek() expects that there is more than one character waiting in streambuf. The statement

```
cin >> c;
```

however, appears to allow only one character to be input at the keyboard. The catch is that any invocation of cin allows you to type as much as you want, until you press Enter—the characters will be stored in streambuf and extracted as needed. If in response to the preceding program, for example, you type the characters abc and then press Enter, the program produces the following display:

```
First character was a
Next character will be b
```

What if you type only the single character a and immediately press Enter? What does peek() report then? The first message reports the character a, but the second message contains only the constant part of the string. What, then, is in c after the call to peek()? The answer is determined by the fact that peek(), like get(), retrieves binary data. The variable c simply contains the newline character '\n'.

■ istream& putback(char);

You can push a character back into streambuf (unextract it, so to speak) with putback() if the program logic decides that the time wasn't really right for extracting it. You might rewrite the preceding short program in the following equivalent way:

```
#include <iostream.h>
#include <iomanip.h>

void main()
{
   char c;

   cin >> c;
   cout << "First character was " << c << "\r\n";
   cin.get( c );
```

```
...  // Logic decides to unget the character here

   cin.putback( c );
}
```

You will probably use the `putback()` function, like the `peek()` function, in applications for scanning and parsing text (such as in a compiler or interpreter). This might be useful if you wanted to read all numeric data until you reach an alphabetic character. You could put back the alphabetic character and retrieve it later with an alphabetic input routine.

■ `istream& ignore( int=1, int=EOF );`

The `ignore()` function skips over the next `int` characters in `streambuf`. This is a binary mode function, and it is stopped only by an EOF condition if there aren't enough characters in the buffer to complete the operation. Suppose, for example, you have a program that ignores the first six characters from `streambuf`, as shown here:

```
#include <iostream.h>
#include <iomanip.h>

void main()
{
  char str[41];

  cin.ignore( 6 );
  cin.get( str, 40 ); // Use default fence character
  cout << str << "\r\n";
}
```

Run this program and type

```
hello there
```

and then press Enter. The `ignore()` function skips over six of the input characters, including the blank between the words. The resulting output consists only of the string `there`.

■ `ostream& put( char );`

The stream `put(char)` function is the mirror image of the stream `get(char)` function: `put(char)` inserts a binary character into `streambuf` (the character can also be text or whitespace). You can use this function with standard streams or file streams, as you can many of the other member functions. The use of `put(char)` looks like this:

```
#include <iostream.h>
#include <iomanip.h>

void main()
{
  char c

  cout.put( c );
}
```

■ ostream& write(const char*, int);

Stream write() inserts exactly the stated number of characters from the char* buffer into streambuf. Although you can use write() with standard streams, it is most useful for file streams, as is stream read(). Notice that write() does not take into account or transform newline characters or other text characters. You use write() in this way:

```
#include <iostream.h>
#include <iomanip.h>

void main()
{
  char buffer[256];

  cout.write( buffer, 256 ); // Insert all 256 characters
}
```

You should understand that inserters, extractors, and the stream member functions can be used with files (fstreams). Many of the member functions, in fact, find their greatest usefulness when applied to fstreams. The use of fstreams is covered later in this chapter, in the section "Using C++ File I/O Streams."

A few final points should be made about the nature of the << and >> stream operators. There aren't many deep pits you can stumble into, but there are definitely some things you ought to think about concerning these operators (especially when you begin to overload them yourself a little later).

First, remember that you cannot invent new operators for overloading in a class. For stream implementation, the existing shift operators are used. Second, be aware that you cannot change the predefined precedence and associativity of an operator when overloading it. A couple of questions are important here. Why are the shift operators used? And what difference does operator precedence and associativity make to the various stream classes?

The shift operators are used for two reasons. The first reason is that they have *relatively low precedence in the operator set*. This means the number of instances in which you must use grouping parentheses is reduced to a minimum. It would be inconvenient to be forced continually to resort to parentheses to keep insertion and extraction expressions straight. For example, consider what would happen if the addition operator had lower precedence than the shift-inserter-extractor operators. You would have to write expressions like this:

```
cout << "The value is " << ( a + b );
```

In fact, you would always have to write expressions like this. Stream manipulation could become quite messy if you used many complex expressions.

Just three operators, which you can use intermingled with inserters and extractors, have lower precedence than the shift operators. These three operators are the AND (&), the exclusive or XOR (^), and the inclusive or OR (¦) bitwise operators. When one of these operators appears in an insertion or extraction, you must use grouping parentheses in this manner:

```
cout << "The value is " << ( a & b ); // You MUST do this
```

If you fail to use grouping parentheses in such an expression, you receive the compiler error message `'<<' : bad right operand`.

The second reason for using the shift operators for overloading as inserters and extractors is the shift operators are *left associative*. That is, operands are associated with the operators from left to right. It is this fact that allows insertions and extractions to be chained together, while still preserving the order of the data values. Notice, for example, the statement

```
cout << a << b;
```

which is interpreted as calls to the `operator <<` function as

```
( cout.operator << (a) ).operator << (b);
```

In other words, the `cout` object and the variable `a` are operated on first, returning a reference to an `ostream`. Then the resulting reference to an `ostream` and the variable `b` are then operated on. The point, of course, is the expression was interpreted left to right—the variable `a` was sent (inserted into a `streambuf`), followed by the variable `b`.

Handling C++ Stream Errors

When the application of an overloaded stream operator or a stream member function fails, the stream is placed in an *error state*. The `ios` class declaration contains a protected variable `ios::state`, which has type `int`. An error state is indicated by setting a particular bit in `ios::state`. (Remember, `ios` is a base class for all streams, so its members are available to all streams.)

When a stream is placed in an error state, you must do something about it before attempting to insert or extract data from that stream. Two problems then face the C++ stream programmer: determining when an error state exists and correcting the problem. This section shows you how to handle both these tasks.

Detecting C++ Stream Error States

The possible error states that can be recorded for a stream are named in a public enumeration called ios::io_state. The enumerators (that is, the members of the enumeration list) are often called status "bits," even though they are integer values in the enumeration. ios::io_state enumerators are in fact integer bit *masks*, which can be used to test or set specific bits within the integer variable ios::state. What all this means becomes more apparent when you see the io_state enumeration itself:

```
class ios {
public:
  enum io_state {
    goodbit = 0x00;  // No bits means no error
    eofbit  = 0x01;  // End of file was reached
    failbit = 0x02;  // Previous insertion/extraction failed
    badbit  = 0x04;  // Last requested operation was invalid
  };
...
};
```

Because io_state is a public declaration, you can refer to the enumerators anywhere in your program by writing the enumerator name with scope resolution to the ios class. Thus, you can write statements like this:

```
int eofmask;
...
eofmask = ios::eofbit;
```

You have cause to use io_state enumerator names in detecting stream errors. The question is how to use them. You might be tempted, for example, to write code like the following fragment:

```
#include <iostream.h>
#include <iomanip.h>

void main()
{
  if ( cin.ios::state & ios::eofbit )
    cout << "Standard input is at EOF.\r\n";
}
```

This fragment looks good on the surface, and it would correctly test the value of the io_state end-of-file flag—if only the code would compile! It does not compile correctly because ios::state is a protected variable: It can be accessed only by members and friends of ios, and by members and friends of classes derived from ios, but not by any other functions. Figure 16.5 shows the results of trying to compile the preceding code.

Figure 16.5.

Accessing the **io_state** bit flags directly is illegal.

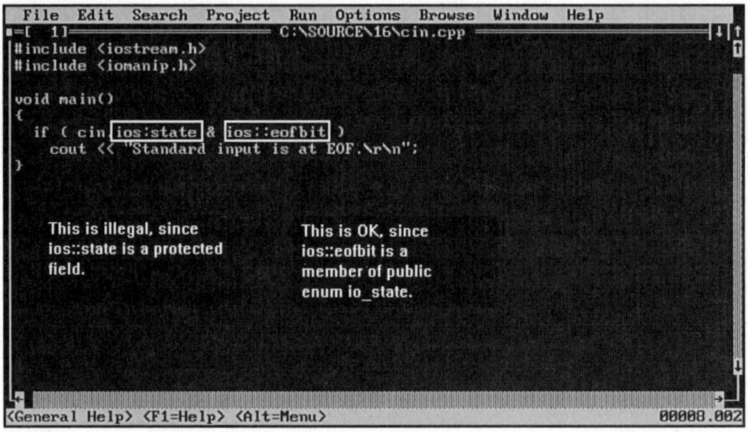

Well, how do you test the error status of a stream? There are several methods—including an overloaded operator, a type conversion (cast) function, and several member functions—that you can use to test the error state of a stream.

The overloaded operator and cast functions that can be used are all the more elegant because they are simple and sophisticated at the same time. You can overload the NOT (!) operator and the void* cast operator so that a class object identifier can be used directly in a Boolean expression. Examine the following code fragment to see how this is done:

```
class A {
public:
      operator void* () { return this; }
  int operator!() { return 1; }
};

void main()
{
  A a;

  if ( a ) cout << "Oops!\r\n"; // Needs void* cast
  cout << !a << "\r\n";         // operator!()
}
```

The preceding code fragment simplifies the issue by arbitrarily always returning a nonzero integer or void pointer (representing a true condition). The comments in the code fragment indicate which operator function is needed to allow the statement to compile and work properly. The reference to the object a, incidentally, works because signature matching can convert the object reference to a `void*` pointer. The workings of the `operator!()` function are more familiar.

The `ios` class declares and makes available to its derived classes just such operator functions. The `ios` operator functions perform in the following ways:

■ `ios::operator void*()` returns a null pointer if there has been an error, and a nonnull pointer if no error has occurred. This operator function therefore provides *normal* Boolean logic for error testing.

■ `ios::operator!()` returns a nonzero integer (a true indication) if there has been an error, and a zero integer (a false indication) if no error has occurred. This operator function therefore provides *inverted* Boolean logic for error testing.

Thus, you can easily write a functional replacement for the DOS TYPE.COM program by using the stream name in a Boolean expression, as shown in the following code:

```
#include <fstream.h>

void main()
{
  ifstream tfile( "fstream.cpp" );
  unsigned char c;

  while ( tfile.get( c ) ) cout.put( c );
}
```

This is a complete and functional program! It certainly illustrates how simple you can make file I/O when you use C++ streams. Remember that the `get(char)` function returns a reference to the stream object, so the conditional expression in the `while` statement is using the `void*` cast operator to test the stream state.

You can also use the `operator!()` implementation to test for stream errors directly, rather than to test for good I/O. For example, you can write the following code:

```
#include <iostream.h>
#include <string.h>
...
```

```
char str[] = "Here is a message\r\n";
cout.write( str, strlen( str ) );
if ( !cout )
  cerr << "Uh, oh! I/O problem!\r\n";
```

`ios::operator void*()` and `ios::operator!()` provide a slick, easy way to test for stream errors. What they don't do is tell you exactly what the error is. The stream classes also provide member functions for more detailed error reporting and correcting—a subject that is discussed next.

Using the Stream State Member Functions

Six member functions are declared in the `ios` class (thus making them available to all derived stream classes), which provide more precise error analysis and control of the error state flags. These functions are summarized in Table 16.5.

Table 16.5. Stream state member functions for analyzing and correcting stream I/O errors.

Function	Description
`int rdstate()`	Returns the value of `ios::state` flags vector
`int eof()`	Returns true if `ios::eofbit` is on
`int fail()`	Returns true if `ios::failbit` or `ios::badbit` is on
`int bad()`	Returns true if `ios::badbit` is on
`int good()`	Returns true if no bits are on
`void clear(int f=0)`	Sets io_state bits to f

In the preceding section, you saw how not to access the `ios::state` bits. Using the `rdstate()` and `clear()` functions, you can access the bits correctly. With these functions, you can test the error flags yourself, as well as do something about the error. The following code fragment shows one way of performing this task:

```
#include <iostream.h>
#include <iomanip.h>

void main()
{
  int statflags;
  ...
  statflags = cin.rdstate(); // Get all the error bits
  if ( statflags & ios::badbit ) {  // Test invalid operation
    cout << "Invalid I/O request, error reset.\r\n";
    cin.clear( 0 );  // Set all flags off
  }
  else {
    cerr << "Can't handle that error. Terminating.\r\n";
    abort();
  }
}
```

The preceding code sequence, however, shows how to do the task the hard way. To accomplish the same thing, you can use a more profitable combination of the overloaded operators (discussed in the preceding section) with the eof(), fail(), bad(), and good() functions. Using these functions, you could rewrite the preceding code fragment much more cleanly, like this:

```
#include <iostream.h>
#include <iomanip.h>

void main()
{
  ...
  if ( !cin ) {           // Go handle some error
    if ( cin.bad() ) {  // Test invalid operation
      cout << "Invalid I/O request, error reset.\r\n";
      cin.clear( 0 );   // Set all flags off
    }
    else {
      cerr << "Can't handle that error. Terminating.\r\n";
      abort();
    }
  }
}
```

Controlling Data Formats with C++ Streams

C programmers have long considered the `printf()` group of functions (if not the `scanf()` group) just about the handiest thing since sliced bread. The `printf()` function is capable of complex formatting of output data, and `printf()` can do it in the approved, concise C manner (some might read that as cryptic).

There is no doubt that `printf()`—and yes, `scanf()` too—is a powerful and flexible I/O tool. In the C++ stream examples you have seen so far, there has been nothing comparable to the facilities present in `printf()` for precise control of data formatting. The capability is there, however, and in this section you learn how to use C++ streams to format data in just about any way you want.

Using Inserters and Extractors for Built-In Types

Certain formatting conventions are assumed as defaults by the built-in stream inserter and extractor functions. These default values do not require the inclusion of another header file—iostream.h remains for the moment the only one you need. The conversion base, field width, fill character, and floating-point precision have default values as noted in the following list:

- *The* conversion base *is the number system that displays the data.* This value defaults to 10, which means that the decimal number system is used. If you change the conversion base (and you will soon learn how), it stays changed and does not revert back to the default after a stream is used.

- *The* field width *is most useful for formatting output data.* A typical instance in which output field width is needed is a report featuring columnar data. You can, however, set the field width for input operations, although some caution is needed. Suppose you type the string of characters abcdefg as input to the following code fragment:

```
#include <iostream.h>
#include <iomanip.h>

void main()
{
  int wide;
  char a[10], b[10];
```

```
    wide = cin.width(3);
    cin >> a >> b;
    cout << a << ' ' << b << "\r\n";
}
```

The resulting output is split into these two pieces:

```
ab cdefg
```

Notice that the `width()` function specifies a three-byte field width, yet only the first two characters appear before the space. This happens because room is needed for the trailing `'\0'` character in order to terminate the first string. Deliberately setting the width for input numbers can be even trickier. For instance, the following code fragment might make you think you can type a single sequence of four digits and have `cin` split it into two numbers:

```
int wide;
int a, b;

wide = cin.width(2);
cin >> a >> b;
cout << a << ' ' << b << "\r\n";
```

`cin` does not work that way, however. `cin` reads numeric characters until it receives a nonnumeric character for each of the two variables. The width specification of two bytes has no effect on the operation whatsoever.

The most important thing to remember about setting the output (inserter) field width is that it is set back to the default size after one insertion. The default width is 0, which means that `cout` uses as many output characters as needed to represent the entire value.

■ *When fields have a specified width, output that is less than the field width is padded with the* fill character. By default, the fill character is a space, but may be changed by calling the `fill()` function. For example,

```
cout.fill('*');
```

sets the fill character to an asterisk.

■ *The* floating-point precision *used by a stream defaults to the same as that used by* `printf()`. That is, there are six significant digits in the fraction part of the floating-point number, with the rightmost digit rounded rather than truncated. The precision also stays changed if you modify it.

In the `ios` base class, six member functions are defined for controlling the conversion base, field width, fill character, and precision. Three of these functions just report the current values; the other three functions first report current values and then change the values. Table 16.6 shows these six format-control functions.

Table 16.6. The six format-control member functions in `ios`.

Function Prototype	Action Taken
`int ios::width()`	Reports field width only
`int ios::width( int )`	Reports and changes field width (once)
`char ios::fill()`	Reports the fill character only
`char ios::fill( char )`	Reports and changes the fill character
`int ios::precision()`	Reports precision only
`int ios::precision( int )`	Reports and changes precision

The following short program illustrates the use (with the `cout` stream) of all six of the stream member functions shown in Table 16.6. Study the program carefully to see how the combination of values affects the appearance of the resulting output. In fact, it is a good idea to go ahead and type this short program into the Microsoft C/C++ editor, compile the program, and run it so that you can see exactly what happens. Here is the program:

```
#include <iostream.h>
#include <iomanip.h>

void main()
{
  int wide, precise;
  char filler;

  // Just report the formatting values

  wide = cout.width();
  precise = cout.precision();
  filler = cout.fill();

  cout << "Default width is " << wide << " bytes.\r\n";
  cout << "Default precision is " << precise << " digits.\r\n";
  cout << "Default fill char is '" << filler << "'.\r\n";

  // This time, change them, saving old values

  wide = cout.width(10);
  precise = cout.precision(3);
  filler = cout.fill('.');
```

```
// Observe the results of these two lines carefully

cout << 37 << 3.1415926 << "\r\n";
cout << 37 << setw(10) << 3.1415926 << "\r\n";
}
```

C++ streams can control a number of other formatting features as well. You control these features by setting bits in the formatting flags variable. This field is similar to the error-status flag variable, except that it is a long rather than an integer. Because the formatting flags variable also has the protected access attribute, you cannot directly access the variable.

There is, however, a public enumeration containing all the possible mask values for the formatting flags. Table 16.7 summarizes the formatting bit masks. The table shows the enumerator names as you would refer to them in your code.

Table 16.7. Formatting flags bit masks from `ios` enumeration.

Enumerator Name	Hex Mask Value	Action When Bit Is On
ios::skipws	0x0001	Skips whitespace for input
ios::left	0x0002	Left-justifies output
ios::right	0x0004	Right-justifies output
ios::internal	0x0008	Pads after sign or base indicator
ios::dec	0x0010	Decimal display conversion
ios::oct	0x0020	Octal display conversion
ios::hex	0x0040	Hexadecimal conversion
ios::showbase	0x0080	Forces display of base indicator
ios::showpoint	0x0100	Forces use of decimal point (floats)
ios::uppercase	0x0200	Hex display is uppercase
ios::showpos	0x0400	Adds plus sign to positive integers
ios::scientific	0x0800	Engineering notation (1.2345E2)
ios::fixed	0x1000	Fixed-point notation (123.45)
ios::unitbuf	0x2000	Flushes all streams after insertion
ios::stdio	0x4000	Flushes stdout and stderr after insertion

As indicated in Table 16.7, turning on a mask bit in the formatting flags variable causes the corresponding formatting convention to be used.

Before moving on to a discussion of the ios class member functions that affect the formatting flags, you should know that the ios class declaration contains three constant longs, allowing you to select only a *part* of the whole set of formatting flags. Table 16.8 shows these constant variables (again, as you should refer to them in your code), together with an indication of which groups of flag bits the variables select. A little patience is necessary here; Table 16.8 makes better sense when you see the format-control member functions.

Table 16.8. ios **class constants for selecting flag groups.**

Variable Name of Flag Group	Flag Bits Selected
ios:basefield	Dec, oct, and hex conversion flags
ios::adjustfield	Left and right justification, internal padding
ios::floatfield	Scientific and fixed-point notation flags

Now that you have before you all the formatting flag names and flag-group names, notice the ios member functions that control the formatting flags. These functions are shown in Table 16.9.

Table 16.9. ios **class member functions that control the formatting flags.**

Function Name and Return Type	Action
long ios::flags( )	Reports all only
long ios::flags(*long flags*)	Reports all, sets all
long ios::setf(*long group, long bits*)	Reports all, sets group
long ios::setf(*long flags*)	Reports all, sets masked
long ios::unsetf(*long flags*)	Reports all, clears masked

Table 16.9 shows that, except for the unsetf() function, the stream flags control functions appear in pairs that report only, and report and set flags, respectively. The flags(*long flags*) function is the most dangerous because it does not merge in flags—it replaces the flags variable wholesale. When you

use this function, you must be careful not to disturb the settings of flags you do not mean to modify. For example, to use the `flags(long flags)` function to set the `ios::hex` flag on, you must write code like this:

```
#include <iostream.h>

void main()
{
  ostream console( 2 ); // Send to stdout
  long hold_flags;

  hold_flags = console.flags();

  console.flags((hold_flags ^ ios::dec)
                    ¦ ios::hex ¦ ios::showbase);

  console << console.flags() << "\r\n";
}
```

In this short program, `ostream` console is defined to avoid modifying the flags for `cout`. Notice that the first action here is to use the report-only `flags()` function to get the bit settings for all the flags before any modifications are made. The result is placed in the variable `hold_flags`, which is in turn used to develop the new bit settings.

The manner in which you manipulate the bits shown in the preceding short program is also important. You must first turn off any conflicting bits (the `ios::dec` flag here), using the XOR (^) operator. You must also turn on the new bits, using the OR (¦) operator. You must take complete control of flag values when using the `flags()` functions. These functions enable you to do anything at all to the flag values—even if it is wrong. Finally, the last line of the preceding short program hex-dumps the new flag settings.

The `setf()` and `unsetf()` functions provide a much safer way to change formatting flag settings because these functions don't just overlay the entire flags variable. Instead, these functions deal only with the flags that are turned on in the *mask*, which forms an argument to the functions. For example, to turn off the `dec` flag and to turn on the `hex` and `showbase` flags, you can write the following (much simpler) code sequence:

```
#include <iostream.h>

void main()
{
  ostream console( 2 ); // Send to stdout

  console setf( ios::hex ); // Just do it!
}
```

There are two reasons why setf() (either version) and unsetf() are much safer than the flags() functions: setf() and unsetf() won't enable you to set conflicting flags, and you can set only one flag at a time. The next code fragment illustrates this feature by setting the fixed flag and then immediately setting the scientific flag. The intervening hex dumps of the flags field show that no conflicts developed:

```
ostream console( 2 ); // Send to stdout
...
  console.setf( ios::showbase );
  console.setf( ios::hex, ios::basefield );
...
  console.setf( ios::fixed, ios::floatfield );
  console << console.flags() << "\r\n";
  console.setf( ios::scientific, ios::floatfield );
  console << console.flags() << "\r\n";
```

The preceding code fragment also shows you how to use the flag-group name fields listed in Table 16.8 when you call setf(). The first parameter to this version of setf() is the bit name, which you have already seen. The second parameter is the flag-group field name from Table 16.8. This form of setf() allows only flag bits indicated by the group name to be manipulated.

The primary use of the unsetf(long flags) function is to return a flag bit to its default setting (by clearing it), as shown here:

```
ostream console( 2 ); // Send to stdout
...
  console.unsetf( ios::showbase ); // Clear showbase
```

Because the setf() functions do not allow conflicting values to be set, unsetf() is not frequently required, although some instances require it.

Overloading the << and >> Operators

Because the purpose of C++ is to deal with class objects, the stream classes would hardly be complete or useful without some means of performing I/O on your own class objects. Input or output of a class object is achieved by overloading the << operator or the >> operator.

The question that immediately arises about overloading these operators concerns the fact that a class, once it is completely defined, can be neither added to nor subtracted from. In other words, you cannot add new member functions to a complete class declaration. How, then, can you overload the << and >> operators?

Only one option remains: You can overload only the global versions of the shift operators. This may sound dangerous, but it really isn't, given the presence of type-safe linkage with full function signature matching. If you correctly define the overloaded functions, there is no danger of impeding the normal use of the shift operators.

Another issue you must consider is the determination of exactly what part of a class object participates in the I/O activity. If, for example, you are writing your widget class to standard output, is it meaningful to send the entire object, including function pointer and member data used strictly for internal purposes? It probably is not.

Generally, you arrange I/O for class objects so that only significant member data participate in the I/O. This rule is also the secret of reading and writing class objects on disk files for permanent storage. You must go to the trouble of setting up I/O for the class object so that only those parts which should be read or written are included. If you stop to think about it, that is exactly what is done in the program pds.cpp in Chapter 13, "Accessing C++ Objects"—a lib *file* is the significant data part of a lib *object*.

The best way to see how all these points come together in a program is to write one. A sample program therefore is developed here, which performs stream I/O on a class object one step at a time. First, you must take care of housekeeping matters, including the #include directives and the class declaration itself:

```
#include <iostream.h>
#include <iomanip.h>

class widget {
  int size;
  double price;
public:
  widget() { size = 0; price = 1.00; }
  void setsize( int s ) { size =s; }
  void setprice( double p ) { price = p; }
  int getsize() { return size; }
  double getprice() { return price; }
};
```

These lines of code include the iostream.h header, which is always required, and the iomanip.h header. iomanip.h is required because the program later uses the setw() stream manipulator to set the output field width temporarily. (Manipulators, which are function-like operators, are described in the next section.)

The class declared in the preceding lines of code is that catchall friend, the widget. It is used here because the most useful of all widgets, the doodad, will be declared as a class object. Notice that the widget class has member functions for setting and reporting the private data member values. These member functions are necessary because the operator functions that are about to be overloaded are not members of the class, and therefore do not have access to private members.

The next order of business, therefore, is to overload the << and >> global operators so that they can recognize a widget parameter and return the appropriate stream type. This task is accomplished in the following lines of code:

```
istream& operator>>( istream& instr, widget& thing )
{
  int size;        // local versions of these
  double price;

  cout << "Enter a size from 0 to 10, "
          "a blank, and a price "
          "from 1.00 to 100.00.\r\n";
  instr >> size >> price;
  thing.setsize( size );        // And now do it
  thing.setprice( price );
  return instr;
}


ostream& operator<<( ostream& outstr, widget& thing )
{
  outstr << "This widget's size and price are: ";
  outstr << "Size "
          << thing.getsize()
          << " and price $"
          << setprecision(2)
          << thing.getprice()
          << "\r\n";
  return outstr;
}
```

You can see how the input stream operator>>() function first inputs and holds the data values, and then uses the widget class access member functions to set the private data values. The output stream operator<<() does its work in a similar manner, except that the private data reporting functions can be referenced directly in the stream expression (because they return basic types).

Notice especially how the function arguments and return types are set up for the operator functions. The first argument is a *reference* to a stream of the proper type, and the second argument is a *reference* to a class object of the proper type. Both operator functions return their respective stream types.

That's all there is to it. The only task that's left is to use the overloaded operator functions with a widget class object. The following main() function declares a widget class doodad (what else would it be?), and then uses the overloaded stream operators with the cin and cout streams to input and output a doodad:

```
void main()
{
  widget doodad;  // A  doodad is a widget, naturally

  cin >> doodad;  // Input a doodad
  cout << doodad; // and display a doodad
}
```

The process of learning C++ is a complex and sometimes long one. It is often easy to focus on a new subject so completely that you momentarily forget other useful things you have already learned. Learning C++ streams is complicated, so be careful to keep knowledge already gained fresh in your mind.

You already know, for example, about friend functions, including the fact that they can be used to overload class operators. But did you think of applying that knowledge here? It can noticeably increase the efficiency of overloading the inserter and extractor operators. Here is the complete short sample program for overloading << and >>, implemented this time with friend functions:

```
#include <iostream.h>
#include <iomanip.h>

class widget {
  int size;
  double price;
public:
  widget() { size = 0; price = 1.00; }
  friend istream& operator>>( istream&, widget& );
  friend ostream& operator<<( ostream&, widget& );
};

istream& operator>>( istream& instr, widget& thing )
{
```

```
  cout << "Enter a size from 0 to 10, "
          "a blank, and a price "
          "from 1.00 to 100.00.\r\n";
  instr >> thing.size >> thing.price;
  return instr;
}


ostream& operator<<( ostream& outstr, widget& thing )
{
  outstr << "This widget's size and price are: ";
  outstr << "Size "
          << thing.size
          << " and price $"
          << setprecision(2)
          << thing.price
          << "\r\n";
  return outstr;
}


void main()
{
  widget doodad;   // A doodad is a widget, naturally

  cin >> doodad;   // Input a doodad
  cout << doodad; // and display a doodad
}
```

In this version of the program, the overloaded operator functions are still
declared at file scope (they are global functions, not class member functions),
but because they are now friends of the class, they can access private member
data directly. Therefore, it is possible to eliminate four class member
functions and to simplify the coding for the operator functions.

Using C++ Stream Manipulators

The stream member functions provide a powerful method of controlling errors
and formatting. So far, however, you have seen only two operators for performing I/O with streams: the inserter operator <<, and the extractor operator
>>. Wouldn't it be nice if there were additional operators that you could use
directly in stream I/O expressions like

```
stream << (do formatting) << ... ;
```

and that could perform nearly all the format-control tasks of the member functions? It would be nice, indeed. Fortunately, such operators do exist. They are called *manipulators*, and they have a function-like syntax. This section introduces you to the C++ manipulators and shows you how to define manipulators of your own.

Understanding C++ Manipulators

To say that the C++ manipulators have a function-like syntax simply means that some of them (not all) can have arguments. For example, corresponding to the now familiar `ios::width()` member function is a `setw()` manipulator. The following code fragment shows you how to set output field width, both by using stream member functions and by using the `setw()` manipulator:

```
cout.width( 10 );   // Set output field width to 10
cout << 37;         // output 37 in 10-position field
...
cout << setw(10) << 37; // Do it in one expression
```

Stream manipulators come in two varieties: those with arguments and those without arguments. Stream manipulators without arguments are already declared in iostream.h. You do not need to do anything more than include that header to use those manipulators. The hex manipulator, for example, performs the same task as the `ios::setf( ios::hex )` function call, as shown here:

```
cout << hex << 37; // Displays hex 25
```

Stream manipulators with arguments are more properly called *parameterized manipulators*. The declarations for the parameterized manipulators are very complex and reside in their own header file. To use parameterized manipulators, you must therefore include the header file iomanip.h in any program that uses these manipulators.

Operator associativity has a bearing on how you must write stream manipulators, just as it does on evaluating the results of insertions and extractions. Manipulators also associate from left to right, so that you must write a manipulator *before* (to the left of) any variables you want the manipulator to affect. Note this example:

```
cout << 16 << hex;  // ERROR! hex manip does nothing
cout << hex << 16;  // hex format for integer 16 and
                    // following expressions
```

The beauty of manipulators is their simplicity and ease of use in stream expressions.

Using Manipulators To Change States and Attributes

The principal task of stream manipulators is to modify a stream's formatting bit states and attributes (and thus the stream's behavior), and to do so by being included directly in a stream I/O expression. For this purpose, there are seven nonparameterized manipulators and six parameterized manipulators. The manipulators supplied by Microsoft C/C++ cover a wide range of I/O formatting possibilities but, as you will see, not all possibilities.

The seven nonparameterized manipulators are shown in Table 16.10. Three of these manipulators are used for setting the formatting flags, whereas the remaining four manipulators produce a direct effect on the stream. Notice in Table 16.10 that some of the manipulators apply to both istreams and ostreams, and others apply only to one of these.

Table 16.10. The simple stream manipulators.

Manipulator	Use	Description
dec	outstream << dec instream >> dec	Uses decimal conversion base
hex	outstream << hex instream >> hex	Uses hex conversion base
oct	outstream << oct instream >> oct	Uses octal conversion base
ws	instream >> ws	Eats whitespace ("sink" operator)
endl	outstream << endl	Inserts newline char, flush
ends	outstream << ends	Inserts string null '\0', flush
flush	outstream << flush	Flushes all data to output device

The hex, dec, and oct manipulators do the same job as the corresponding ios::setf() function call. This is very good when applied to output streams, but these manipulators can sometimes be dangerous when applied to input streams. Suppose you have written the following statements in your program:

```
int a;
...
cin >> hex >> a;
```

That looks simple enough, right? It isn't as simple as it looks, unfortunately—because it doesn't work for the hex digits *A* through *F*. Suppose you type the hex number FF (decimal 255), for example. What would the value of the integer a be after the last statement in the preceding code fragment? Microsoft C/C++ invariably interprets that input as the number 85 (decimal value). Here is how Microsoft C/C++ arrives at that result:

1. The first F is encountered in the cin stream (it doesn't matter whether F is uppercase). Because hex conversion is in progress, cin knows that this is a valid hex number.

2. Because the variable a that is being built is an integer, the first digit (which, remember, has decimal value 15) is scaled to the decimal digit range by subtracting 10 from it:

   ```
   15 - 10 = 5; partial result = 50 hex = 80 decimal
   ```

3. The second digit is encountered in the input stream and treated to the same scaling process as the first digit, leaving a second digit of 5.

4. The partial results are added—80 + 5—to yield the final answer, which is decimal 85.

It is important to be aware that the preceding process does not produce an error state. You cannot detect the error by means of the stream's state flags. For this reason, you might be well advised to consider *always* performing numeric input in the decimal base. If you must allow the user to type hex characters, you can read them as a string and perform the numeric conversion internally, using program logic.

Octal conversions work better because the allowed range of octal digits is completely within the range of decimal digits. For *either* conversion, cin can detect digits outside the conversion range (more than hex *F* or octal *7*). You can detect range problems with the methods you have already learned. When inputting numbers other than decimal numbers, you should include some sort of error-detection method, such as the following:

```
unsigned int j = 1;

if ( cin >> oct >> j ) {}
  else cout << "Error on input." << endl;
cout << j << endl;
```

With code like this in place, you will be informed should you accidentally enter an invalid number. Also note the use of endl, an ostream function that is equivalent to '\n\r' for generating a newline-return action in the output.

All the parameterized manipulators require some numeric value so that their appearance in the stream expression is meaningful. The parameterized manipulators are shown in Table 16.11.

Table 16.11. The parameterized stream manipulators.

Manipulator	Use	Description
resetiosflags(*n*)	`outstream << resetiosflags( long )` `instream >> resetiosflags( long )`	Clears the format flags named by *long* parameter.
setiosflags(*n*)	`outstream << setiosflags( long )` `instream >> setiosflags( long )`	Sets the format flags named by *long* parameter.
setfill(*n*)	`outstream << setfill( int )`	Sets fill char to *int* (can be char const). Does not apply to input.
setprecision(*n*)	`outstream << setprecision( int )`	Sets floating-point precision to *int* digits.
setw(*n*)	`outstream << setw( int )` `instream >> setw( int )`	Sets field width to *int* bytes. For input, only meaningful with characters/strings.

The nice thing about manipulators is that they can appear directly and conveniently in stream I/O expressions.

Finally, as if all these features do not provide enough flexibility for you, you can define your own nonparameterized manipulator functions. They can do whatever you want them to do, as long as you observe the following conventions in writing your own functions:

■ For manipulators that will have a direct effect on stream behavior, accept an argument that is a reference to the stream type, and return a reference to the stream type.

■ For manipulators that will affect flags only (in other words, that don't insert or extract data), accept an argument that is a reference to an `ios` class object, and return a reference to that same `ios` class object.

For example, you could write a function for a finish manipulator:

```
ostream& finish( ostream& ostr )
{
  ostr << endl << "The end." << endl;
  return ostr;
}
...
cout << finish;
```

On a more useful level, the program in Listing 16.1 provides some nonparameterized manipulators of both kinds mentioned previously. These manipulators provide handy functions not found among the predefined manipulators. Listing 16.1 shows you how to set up such manipulators.

Listing 16.1. manip.cpp. A program that includes user-defined stream manipulators.

```
1   #include <fstream.h>
2   #include <iostream.h>
3   #include <iomanip.h>
4   #include <conio.h>
5   #include <graph.h>
6   ostream& eject( ostream& ostr )
7   {
8     _clearscreen( _GCLEARSCREEN );
9     _settextposition( 1, 1 );
10    return ostr;
11  }
12
13  ios& engineering( ios& iosobj )
14  {
15    iosobj.setf( ios::scientific, ios::floatfield );
16    return iosobj;
17  }
18
19  ios& fixpoint( ios& iosobj )
20  {
21    iosobj.setf( ios::fixed, ios::floatfield );
22    return iosobj;
23  }
24
25  ios& indicatebase( ios& iosobj )
26  {
27    iosobj.setf( ios::showbase );
28    return iosobj;
29  }
30
31  void main()
32  {
33    char ch;
34
35    cout << "This here is some text." << endl;
36    ch = getch();
```

Listing 16.1. Continued.

```
37    cout << eject << "This here is some more text." << endl;
38    ch = getch();
39
40    cout << hex << indicatebase << 37 << endl;
41    cout << engineering << 3.1415926 << endl;
42    cout << fixpoint << 3.1415926 << endl;
43  }
```

The first thing you should notice about Listing 16.1 is how the user-defined manipulators are used in lines 35 through 42. The new manipulators are used immediately in the ostream expressions, as are any other manipulators or inserters. Furthermore, those manipulators whose definitions require references to ios class objects do not require any cast expressions or unusual support when used in the stream expressions (see lines 40 through 42).

The inclusion of the iomanip.h header in line 3 of Listing 16.1 is not strictly necessary because the program uses no parameterized manipulators. Then why is it there? It's there simply because it is a good practice always to include the iostream.h and iomanip.h headers in programs that will use C++ stream I/O. Including them doesn't hurt anything and could prevent puzzling linker errors caused by the absence of one of these headers.

You can also define your own parameterized manipulators if you are willing to spend a little more attention on implementation details. To write user-defined parameterized manipulators, observe the following procedure:

1. *Be certain that iomanip.h is included in the source file.* You will get nothing but compiler errors if you forget this header. The importance of iomanip.h for user-defined parameterized manipulators is explained shortly.

2. *Write any necessary support functions.* The manipulator functions themselves may need to call support functions, or a support function may need to be called before the manipulator is used. An instance of the second case is shown in the next sample program.

3. *Define the parameterized manipulator functions.* Observe the following requirements when you design the manipulator functions:

   A. *The return type must be a reference to the appropriate stream type.* For example, when you write a manipulator function that will be applied to an ostream, the return type must be ostream&.

   B. *The first argument type must be a reference to the appropriate stream type.* For example, when you write a manipulator function that will be applied to an istream, the declaration part will now begin to appear as istream& funcname(istream& istr, ...).

    C. *The second, and last, argument must be either a long or an* int. *The* declarations in iomanip.h provide support for only two arguments, the second of which is restricted to `long` or `int` types, as are found in the predefined parameterized manipulators shown in Table 16.11.

4. *Write an applicator declaration for each user-defined parameterized manipulator.* The iomanih header provides class declarations that can be used to apply your manipulator function to a selected stream type. An applicator declaration is actually the declaration of a class object, with a constructor argument that is a pointer to your function. Exactly how you write an applicator declaration is explained in the discussion of the next sample program.

If the previous procedure seems confusing, the best way to understand it is to see it in action. The program manipprm.cpp in Listing 16.2 shows you how to write the code for each step in the procedure.

Listing 16.2. manipprm.cpp. A program with user-defined parameterized manipulators implemented through applicators.

```
1   #include <iostream.h>
2   #include <iomanip.h>
3   #include <conio.h>
4   #include <graph.h>
5   // ---------------------------------------------------
6   //            You already know about this one
7   // ---------------------------------------------------
8
9   ostream& eject( ostream& ostr )
10  {
11    _clearscreen( _GCLEARSCREEN );
12    _settextposition( 1, 1 );
13    return ostr;
14  }
15
16  // ---------------------------------------------------
17  // definexy() builds a long from x, y screen coordinates
18  // so that manipulator can accept one parameter
19  // ---------------------------------------------------
20
21  long definexy( int x = 1, int y = 1 )
22  {
23    return ( (long)x << 16 ) + y;
24  }
```

Listing 16.2. Continued.

```
25
26  // ----------------------------------------------------------
27  // Enumerators define handy names for left or right
28  // adjustment flags for ostream. The values match those
29  // in the iostream.h declaration for ios::left, ios::right
30  // ----------------------------------------------------------
31
32  enum { adjleft = 2, adjright = 4 };
33
34  // ----------------------------------------------------------
35  // Manipulator sa() function definition. Notice that it has
36  // one more argument than operator<<() overload function.
37  // ----------------------------------------------------------
38
39  ostream& setadjust( ostream& ostr, int edge )
40  {
41    ostr.setf( edge, ios::adjustfield );
42    return ostr;
43  }
44
45  // ----------------------------------------------------------
46  // Manipulator goxy() function defintion. The parameter
47  // should be a long developed by definexy().
48  // ----------------------------------------------------------
49
50  ostream& positionxy( ostream& ostr, long position )
51  {
52    _settextposition( position & 0x0000FFFFL, position >> 16 );
53    return ostr;
54  }
55
56  // ----------------------------------------------------------
57  // Applicator declarations for the sa() and goxy()
58  // parameterized manipulator functions. Generic
59  // applicator classes for longs and ints are declared in
60  // iomanip.h.
61  //
62  //
63  //
64  // ----------------------------------------------------------
```

```
65
66   OAPP(int) sa(setadjust);
67   OAPP(long) goxy( positionxy );
68
69   // ----------------------------------------------------------
70   //                  Now put all that to use.
71   // ----------------------------------------------------------
72
73   void main()
74   {
75     long screenloc;
76
77     cout << eject << sa(adjleft) << setw(20)
78          << 16 << 32 << 64 << endl;
79
80     screenloc = definexy( 24, 12 );
81     cout << goxy(screenloc)
82          << "Take a look at this message!"
83          << endl;
84   }
```

The program in Listing 16.2 defines and uses two parameterized manipulators: sa(), for setting left or right output alignment of fields; and goxy(), for positioning the cursor on the screen. Of these two manipulators, goxy() is the most complicated, following every step of the procedure previously outlined for writing parameterized manipulators. Its implementation is discussed here in detail; feel free to analyze sa() on your own.

When you consider the steps necessary to implement the manipulator goxy(), you will quickly see that it cannot be implemented directly because cursor positioning requires two integer arguments. Remember that the manipulator function can have only one int or long as the second argument. The solution is just as obvious as the problem: write a support function that converts the cursor position into a single long value to be used as the manipulator's parameter. That task is carried out by the definexy() function, shown in lines 21 through 24 of Listing 16.2. The x-coordinate is shifted to the high-order bytes of the long, and the y-coordinate is placed in the low-order bytes (by adding it to the result). You must call this function before using the goxy() parameterized manipulator.

The manipulator function is defined next, in lines 50 through 54. positionxy() is defined for an ostream because little else is meaningful; and the function's second argument is a long, which will contain the long cursor address variable. The function body does little more than separate the x and y components of the desired cursor address once more and, using the results, invoke the Microsoft C/C++ _settextposition() function.

So far, the program has only disconnected parts, none of which affects stream operation. It is the applicator declaration, in line 67, that ties them all together. Look closely at that line again:

```
OAPP(long) goxy( positionxy );
```

This line of code declares a class object named goxy, which has type _OAPP_long. OAPP() is a macro defined in iomanip.h, which, when fully expanded and applied inside iomanip.h, automatically creates a class definition with the name _OAPP_long.

The constructor for this created class accepts an argument that is a pointer to a function of the specific type outlined in the previous procedure. Now the applicator object goxy can be used as a manipulator in a stream expression, because the object has been initialized with the address of the function to be called when the goxy() manipulator appears.

The program in Listing 16.2 uses only an ostream applicator. You can create an istream applicator using IAPP(). For either ostream or the istream, you use OAPP() or IAPP() to create parameterized manipulators for either int or long.

How does the applicator actually work? In other words, how does its presence cause the desired action to take place when the user-defined manipulator appears in a stream expression? Although it is not necessary for you to know how this is done, it is an interesting application of C++ class technology, and it certainly won't hurt to remove the mystery. The goxy() parameterized manipulator function is invoked when the manipulator is used, in the following four steps:

1. The OAPP() macro creates a class that defines a member function that overloads the () function call operator. Thus, when a stream expression such as

   ```
   cout << goxy( loc ) << ... ;
   ```

   is encountered, the _OAPP_long operator()() function is invoked.

2. The _OAPP long operator()() function creates an _OAMANIP_long class object, passing to its constructor the function address (positionxy, in this case) and the long parameter value. When the _OAMANIP_long constructor has finished its work, _OAPP long operator()() returns that _OMANIP_long class temporary object by value.

3. The stream operator << is now applied. That is, the stream operator is applied to the result of evaluating goxy(arg). The result, you may recall, was a temporary _OMANIP_long object. This part of the stream expression evaluation causes the omanip_long operator<<() function to be called.

4. The _OAMANIP long operator<<() function is nothing more than a globally overloaded << operator, which you have already seen in this chapter. operator<<() is declared as a friend function and does nothing other than invoke the user-defined manipulator function—which is positionxy(long) in Listing 16.2.

The information just described comes from an inspection of the iomanip.h header file produced this information. If you need a really detailed understanding of how to design parameterized manipulators of your own, you need to do the same thing. But be prepared to spend some time doing detective work. The declarations in iomanip.h are written with macros. The result is a very cryptic mess, typical of the old-style C code that was noted for its compactness but not its readability.

Using C++ File I/O Streams

Most of this chapter has dealt with standard streams, which perform I/O on the system console (screen and keyboard). That is as it should be, not because file streams are unimportant, but because standard streams are the easiest and therefore the best introduction to a strange new world.

By now, you are familiar with inserters, extractors, overloaded stream operators, simple manipulators, parameterized manipulators, and user-defined manipulators of all flavors (see how much you have learned in just one chapter?). It is time to apply stream concepts to files and to expand your working knowledge of streams in general.

Just as the istream, ostream, iostream, and streambuf classes are fundamental to standard stream I/O, file I/O has its own unique set of classes. Table 16.13 shows the stream classes associated with file I/O and how they are derived.

Table 16.13. Stream classes for file I/O support.

Stream Class	Derived From
filebuf	streambuf
fstreambase	ios
ifstream	fstreambase, istream
ofstream	fstreambase, ostream
fstream	fstreambase, iostream

As you can see from the table, the manner in which the file stream classes are derived is an excellent clue as to how they are used. Because the parallels to standard streams are in fact so exact (just about everything you have already learned applies directly to file streams), you will concentrate on mainly the new features that appear in file streams, as well as focusing on fstream objects.

To use file streams, you must include the fstream.h header in your program. Then, naturally, you must declare fstream objects with which you want to perform input or output. You can declare an fstream object in three ways:

■ *You can declare an* fstream *object without constructor initializers at all.* Using this form of declaration, you get a valid fstream, but it isn't connected to any particular file. You will have to open the file explicitly, later in the program. This is the simplest declaration, and it looks like this:

```
please indent following code
fstream myfile; // Declare the stream, worry later
```

■ *You can declare an* fstream *object with an integer constructor initializer.* The integer initializer must be a valid DOS handle for a file that is already open. This form of the declarator is most appropriate for defining an fstream for use with one of the predefined DOS handles, as shown here:

```
please indent following code
ofstream sysprint(4);  // Connect to the system printer PRN
```

Notice that this declaration is explicitly for an output file stream with class ofstream. To use this feature with a disk file (fstream), you must open the file yourself, using the Microsoft C/C++ open() or sopen() function, and use the resulting DOS handle to declare the stream, as shown in the following short program:

```
please indent following code
#include <fstream.h>
#include <iostream.h>
#include <stdlib.h>
#include <io.h>
#include <fcntl.h>
#include <sys\stat.h>

void main()
{
  int handle;

  if ( -1 == ( handle = open( "fstream.cpp", O_RDONLY ) ) ) {
    cerr << "Error opening input file." << endl;
    abort();
  }

  fstream infile( handle );  // Declare with existing handle
  if ( !infile ) {
    cerr << "Error declaring fstream." << endl;
    abort();
  }
```

```
  char ch;
  while ( infile.get(ch) ) cout << ch;
  close( handle );
}
```

As you can see, using this method for anything but the predefined DOS handles is a good deal of trouble, especially when `fstream` constructors exist that do all the work for you.

■ *You can declare an `fstream` object with a file-name string and open-mode constructor initializers.* For disk files, this is perhaps the best way to declare the `fstream` object. The preceding short program can be considerably simplified with the following syntax, while retaining all of its utility:

```
please indent following code
#include <fstream.h>
#include <iostream.h>
#include <stdlib.h>

void main()
{
            // Declare with file-name string and open mode

  fstream infile( "fstream.cpp", ios::in );
  if ( !infile ) {
    cerr << "Error declaring fstream." << endl;
    abort();
  }

  char ch;
  while ( infile.get(ch) ) cout << ch;
}
```

If you choose to use the first method of declaring an `fstream` object—using the default constructor—you will have to open the stream explicitly, as just mentioned, in order to supply a file name and connect the stream to a physical file. Here is the code sequence for performing this task (using the lifo.cpp source file shown in Chapter 11, "Using C++ Classes"):

```
#include <fstream.h>
#include <iostream.h>
#include <stdlib.h>

void main()
{
```

```
    fstream infile;

    infile.open( "lifo.cpp", ios::in, filebuf::openprot );
    if ( !infile ) {
      cerr << "Error opening stream." << endl;
      abort();
    }

    char ch;
    while ( infile.get(ch) ) cout << ch;
}
```

The `fstream` member function `open()` has an argument list much like that of the third constructor's argument list. The function prototype for the `open()` function is this:

```
void fstream::open( const char* name, int mode,
                    int prot = filebuf::openprot );
```

Only the third parameter—the file-protection mask—has a default value. This parameter is the easiest one to discuss because the default value is the only possible value at this time. You may as well let it default and go about your other business.

The second parameter of the `fstream::open()` function is known as the *open mode*. The open mode should be one of the `ios::open_mode` enumerators shown in Table 16.14 (or several ORed together, as discussed shortly).

Table 16.14. `fstream` **open-mode enumerator names and uses.**

Enumerator Name	Description of Use in `fstream::open( )`
`ios::in`	Opens for input (default for `ifstream`)
`ios::out`	Opens for output (default for `ofstream`)
`ios::app`	Opens in append mode: writes at end-of-file
`ios::ate`	Opens and then seeks to EOF
`ios::trunc`	Creates file, or trunc to 0 length if exist
`ios::nocreate`	Does not create if no file exists (fails if no file exists)
`ios::noreplace`	Does not trunc to 0 length if file exists (fails if file exists)
`ios::binary`	Opens in explicit binary mode

The open-mode enumerators obviously correspond largely with the plain C `fopen()` mode strings. Just as you can combine mode-string characters with `fopen()`, you can combine open-mode enumerators by ORing them together. Because some of the open-mode enumerators differ from `fopen()` mode strings, be cautious when specifying an open mode for `fstream::open()`.

The `ios::in` and `ios::out` open modes open the `fstream` for input and output operations, respectively. As with their plain C counterparts, the open modes can be combined to allow update (combined reads and writes) processing on an `fstream`. The following code fragment illustrates this:

```
fstream iofile( "mydata.dat", ios::in ¦ ios::out );


        // or opening the stream later ...

fstream iofile;
...
iofile.open( "mydata.dat", ios::in ¦ ios::out );
if ( !iofile ) { // do something about it
}
```

Notice that using the `ios::out` open mode alone truncates the length of an existing file to zero bytes, effectively overwriting the file.

When you use the `ios::app` mode, you should observe the same caveat that applies to plain C files opened in append mode. Write operations always occur at the end-of-file position, no matter what other open modes you may specify. You can open an `fstream` for both input-mode and append-mode writes in this way:

```
file inandapp( "weird.fil", ios::in ¦ ios::app );
```

You can both read the file normally and perform repositioning operations within it. But write operations still always occur at the end of the file. Including append mode in the open operation prevents truncating an existing output file to zero length and overwriting the file.

Using the `ios::ate` open mode (open, then position to EOF) actually performs the operation that novice C programmers are tempted to think append mode accomplishes (but doesn't). Using the at-end mode does not disturb the stream's capability to write elsewhere in the file; at-end mode only performs the often-useful task of opening the file in some other mode or modes, and automatically performing the repositioning operation. Notice, for example, the following code fragment:

```
char* fname[] = "todays.dat";
fstream iofile( fname, ios::in ¦ ios::out ¦ ios::ate );
```

This code opens the file named *todays.dat* ready to write new transaction data at the end of the file, but leaves it still able to update other records in the file, as well.

`ios::nocreate` and `ios::noreplace` are an interesting pair of open modes that do not have direct parallels in plain C open mode strings. With `ios::nocreate`, opening an output file should fail if the file does not already exist. In contrast, with `ios::noreplace`, opening an output file should fail if the file does already exist, unless either `ios::app` or `ios::ate` is also specified.

An `fstream` is opened in text mode by default. You must specify the `ios::binary` open mode in order to process a file in true binary mode. If you do not use this open mode, the file will be subject to having the end-of-line characters (carriage return and linefeed) transformed into a newline character, even if you do not use the formatted stream inserters and extractors.

Reading and Writing *fstream* Files

Reading and writing `fstream` files are carried out much the same as for the standard streams. However, you won't have much occasion to use simple inserters and extractors with `fstream` files. You will usually process an `fstream` with the `get()`, `put()`, `read()`, and `write()` functions, as shown in the following code fragment:

```
#include <fstream.h>
#include <iostream.h>
#include <stdlib.h>

void main()
{
  fstream infile;
  char hold[255];

  infile.open( "lifo.cpp", ios::in, filebuf::openprot );
  if ( !infile ) {
    cerr << "Error opening stream." << endl;
    abort();
  }

  while ( infile.getline( hold, 256 ) ) cout << hold;
}
```

One of the significant reasons for this practice is that extractors, for example, don't detect an end-of-file condition properly in an `fstream`. Suppose you write the last line of the preceding code fragment like this:

```
char ch;
while ( infile << ch ) cout << ch;
```

Although this line would work perfectly with `cin`, the program loops infinitely, continuously sending the closing brace (`}`) of the lifo.cpp source file to the display. This condition exists because the extractor operator sends the last valid character it encountered when it can retrieve no more from the `streambuf`.

In those cases in which you have opened the stream in binary mode, you will be reading and writing whole records at a time. You can accomplish these tasks with the `read()` and `write()` functions described earlier in this chapter. The following short program illustrates the method:

```
#include <fstream.h>
#include <iostream.h>

char names[4][20] = { // an array of fixed-size records
  "Washington",
  "Lincoln",
  "Jefferson",
  "Adams",
};

void main()
{
  int i;
  fstream namefile;

  namefile.open( "names.dat", ios::out );
  for ( i=0; i<4; ++i ) namefile.write( names[i], 20 );
  namefile.close();

  char hold[20];
  namefile.open( "names.dat", ios::in );
  for ( i=0; i<4; ++i ) {
    namefile.read( hold, 20 );
    cout << hold << endl;
  }
  namefile.close();
}
```

In binary mode, there is little logistical difference between processing an `fstream` and processing a plain C file with `fread()` and `fwrite()`.

File Positioning with C++ Streams

To process an `fstream` in update mode, you must be able to reposition the read and write locations within the file. The `fstream seekg()`, `seekp()`, `tellg()`, and `tellp()` member functions, as well as the `typedef streampos`, are available to assist you in this task.

The `tellg()` and `tellp()` member functions report the current read and write locations in the file, respectively. These functions return a type `streampos` result, and neither function requires arguments. You can report the current "get" or read position, for example, like this:

```
fstream iofile;
streampos currget;
...
currget = iofile.tellg();
```

The variable `currget` now contains the position of the next read operation, recorded as an offset from the beginning of the file. Later in the program, you can reposition back to this same location in the file, using `currget` as an argument for the `seekg()` member function, in the following manner:

```
iofile.seekg( currget, ios::beg );
```

As this line of code indicates, the `ios class` declaration contains an enumeration of seek directions named `seek_dir`. Table 16.15 shows the seek direction enumerator names and their significance.

Table 16.15. `ios::seek_dir` **enumerators.**

Seek Direction Enumerator	Meaning
`ios::beg`	Seeks relative to file beginning
`ios::cur`	Seeks relative to current position
`ios::end`	Seeks relative to end-of-file

The `seekg()` and `seekp()` member functions reposition the file's current read and write locations, respectively. Both functions return nothing and take two arguments. The first argument is the number of bytes to reposition in the file, relative to the location given by the second argument. This offset value can be negative, if such a value does not locate the current position before the beginning of the file (for obvious reasons). The second argument specifies a location within the file, using one of the seek direction enumerators shown in Table 16.15.

Armed with this information, you can rewrite the earlier `namefile` program to update the second and fourth names. That short program looks like this after rewriting:

```
#include <fstream.h>
#include <iostream.h>
#include <stdlib.h>

char names[4][20] = {
  "Washington",
  "Lincoln",
  "Jefferson",
  "Adams",
};

char newnames[2][20] = {
  "Roosevelt",
  "Wilson",
};

void main()
{
  int i;
  char hold[20];
  fstream namefile;

  // Open for update but trunc first and rewrite

  namefile.open( "names.dat", ios::in | ios::out | ios::trunc );
  for ( i=0; i<4; ++i ) namefile.write( names[i], 20 );

  // Now change the second and fourth names

  namefile.seekp( 20, ios::beg );
  namefile.write( newnames[0], 20 );
  namefile.seekp( -20, ios::end );
  namefile.write( newnames[1], 20 );
```

```
// Position to beginning of file and read it all

namefile.seekg( 0, ios::beg );
for ( i=0; i<4; ++i ) {
  namefile.read( hold, 20 );
  cout << hold << endl;
}
namefile.close();
}
```

Although C++ streams may seem intimidating when you first approach them, you can now see how they can make life easier for the C++ I/O programmer. This statement is especially true in programs that do complicated, direct-access, binary file I/O.

Exercises

The knowledge you have gained in this chapter will evaporate quickly if you do not put it to use. Use the following exercise in C++ stream manipulation to reinforce that knowledge—and do not hesitate to write C++ stream programs of your own devising.

1. Write a program that uses the `cin` and `cout` streams. Include such features as chained inserters and extractors, manipulators, and overloaded `operator<<()` and `operator>>()` functions.

2. Write another program that is a "file filter" program. Use only `cin` and `cout` streams with the `get()` and `put()` functions, or with the `read()` and `write()` functions to copy one file into another in strict binary mode. This arrangement requires the program's users to indicate which files to copy to and from by using command-line redirection.

3. You can declare a file stream and supply the DOS handle you want associated with it as a constructor argument. For example, you could define a `cprn` standard printer output file stream, as in the following code:

```
#include <iostream.h>
#include <fstream.h>

void main()
{
  ofstream cprn(4);  // stream to send output to printer

  cprn << "The number is " << 37 << "\r\n";
}
```

The standard DOS handle for the COM1 communications port is 3. Define an `fstream` capable of input and output, and write a simple communications and keyboard loop.

4. Use the stream member functions and manipulators to create a formatted report with multiple columns. You might want to use the `dir` class from Chapter 12, "Creating C++ Objects," as a source of input data. You will have to set up a Microsoft C/C++ project file for this program, including your program's name, dir.cpp, and dbllist.cpp.

5. Define an `fstream` object for an input/output file. Read the file in binary mode, retrieving data records from it (read them into a `struct`, for example). Transform the input data in some way and update the records in place.

Summary

C++ stream classes are richly functional, providing nearly all the I/O capability you are likely to need in your programs. Streams also provide all this functionality with type-safe linkage, so that such errors as the one in the following code fragment, which uses `printf()`, are not possible (or at least very difficult to engineer):

```
#include <stdio.h>
#include <stdlib.h>

void main()
{
  int a = 1;
  char msg[] = "The value of a is: ";

  printf( "%s%d\n", a, msg );  //BACKWARD ARGS
}
```

The compiler does not interpret the format string—that is done only at run time by the `printf()` library function. Therefore, plain C can have no way of knowing that the arguments are specified backward here. The program compiles completely free of errors but produces garbage at run time.

The corresponding C++ stream implementation is much more difficult to foul up, as you can see from the following line of code:

```
cout << msg << a << endl;
```

The drawback to C++ streams is that their internals are complex and difficult to learn—yet you must have at least some familiarity with stream internals to control and use them effectively. At the beginning of this chapter, you were advised to learn about C++ streams so that you could read another programmer's C++ code. By now, you may have other (and better) reasons for wanting to learn C++ streams.

In this chapter, you were presented with a mind-boggling assortment of new facts and techniques. Before you continue with the next chapter, be sure that you have learned the following important points:

- *The basic stream I/O mechanism consists of the overloaded shift operators << and >>, called an inserter and an extractor, respectively.* Inserters are used for putting data into output streams, and extractors are used for taking data from input streams.

- *Inserters and extractors can handle all the built-in types.* You can use all the usual C data types in C++ stream expressions, with no extra preparation required.

- *The stream operators can be overloaded to support input and output of user-defined data types.* Overloading the << and >> operators at file scope allows you to extend easily the I/O capabilities of C++ streams to handle I/O for your class objects.

- *You can detect and correct C++ stream errors, using the stream state member functions and operators.* The overloaded NOT (!) operator and void* cast operator enable you to use Boolean expressions to detect the existence of an error condition. With the rdstate() and clear() member functions, you can analyze the error and, in most cases, clear it as well.

- *The ios class members control formatting attributes.* You can set the formatting flags, as well as the width, precision, and fill character, by using the ios class member functions. Calls to stream member functions are not part of a stream I/O expression.

- *Manipulators control formatting state and behavior.* Manipulators can be either simple or parameterized, and can either set formatting flags or have an immediate effect on stream I/O. Manipulators do appear directly in stream I/O expressions.

- *You can define your own simple manipulators.* You can write your own manipulator functions to control formatting states or to perform special I/O tasks. The function name becomes the manipulator name. Manipulator must have specifically required return types and arguments.

■ *You can define your own parameterized manipulators.* User-defined parameterized manipulators are considerably more complex than simple manipulators. Defining parameterized manipulators requires an understanding of generic classes, applicator declarations, and the Microsoft C/C++ implementation of iomanip.h. The applicator class object name becomes the manipulator name, and the name of the implementation function can be anything you want.

■ *File streams support direct-access (random read-write) operations.* You can reposition a file, update it, and process it in true binary mode by using the file stream classes.

Using C++ Derived Classes

A good working definition of an object-oriented programming system (OOPS) is that it is a programming system that supports three features: abstract data typing, type derivation, and polymorphism. Earlier chapters have already covered abstract data typing—C++ classes—in some detail. This chapter introduces type derivation and polymorphism.

In C++, type derivation most often means *class derivation,* the process of deriving new classes from old ones. Class derivation is also sometimes referred to as *class inheritance* because the derived class (the new class) inherits many of its properties from its parent, or base class (the old class).

To a lesser degree, you can create new classes from old ones by grouping the old ones together as members of the new class. This process is called *code reuse by composition,* or just *composition.* Because composition is simpler than true derivation, this chapter covers class composition first.

Reusing Code Without Inheritance

Programmers are often told (constantly, in fact), "If it ain't broke, don't fix it!" Software doesn't "break" itself. Programmers break it when they unnecessarily meddle with code that already works. Modifying code to reuse it is an efficient way to "break" working software.

The controlling principle of both composition and derivation, then, is to reuse existing code wherever appropriate, *with little or no modification if possible,* to create new code that has more functionality than the original code. The resulting software isn't necessarily safer than the original (the new code uses the original code, after all); the new code is just more functional.

Class composition is a way of creating new classes without modifying existing code at all. Class derivation is a way of creating new classes with minimal modifications, and with improved isolation and control of the changed parts. Much of the discussion in this chapter is devoted to access and ambiguity control in composing and deriving classes. These are the programming activities that present the greatest opportunity for confusion.

Understanding Code Reusability

You may not have considered that, simply because you are a C programmer, you are already familiar with the concept of code reuse. You reuse code quite naturally and easily each time you use one of the predefined C library functions. These functions (which may be standard C functions or a vendor's extension to the language) are already compiled and placed in the library files you loaded when you installed your compiler. When you declare one of the predefined header files, you have also directed the linkage editor to include the appropriate module from one of Microsoft C/C++'s LIB files, as shown in Figure 17.1.

Figure 17.1.

Reusing code by including library functions.

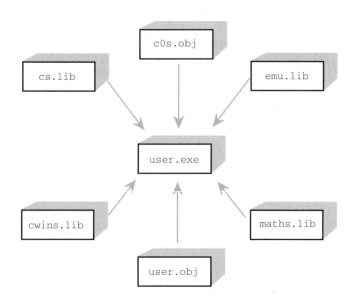

In plain C, you can write a function or a group of functions just once and then use it (from object modules or libraries) repeatedly. That is an efficient way to go about building programs. After a function or module has been written, however, you can reuse it only in its *original form*. What that function or module does is not flexible and cannot be changed (except by recoding the function, of course).

C++ classes give you not only the same efficiencies of reuse but also the capability of using the class in different, flexible ways—all without having to recode the classes. That is what class composition and class derivation are all about.

Reusing Code by Composition

Reusing class code without the benefit of class derivation (in other words, without class inheritance) is called *class composition*. Class composition is one of the two major ways that C++ programmers can take advantage of *encapsulation,* which isolates and protects code that already works.

Class composition is the simplest way of reusing class code, involving only the declaration within a class of an object of another class. Figure 17.2 illustrates this concept.

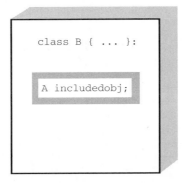

Figure 17.2.

Reusing code by composing classes.

Remember that a class declaration is just that—a user-defined type declaration. Therefore, an object of class B declared within class A is just a declaration until you create a class A object. The following short program demonstrates what this means:

```
#include <iomanip.h>

class A {
public:
```

```
  void display() {
    cout << "This is a class A object." << endl;
  }
};

class B {
  A compose;
public:
  void display() {
    compose.display();   // Call A::display
  }
  void unique() {
    cout << "This belongs to class B." << endl;
  }
};

void main()
{
  B testobj; // declare a composite class object

  testobj.unique();      // Use the unique member function
  testobj.display();     // Do it another way
}
```

In the preceding short program, class A is completely declared before being referred to in class B. Then class B is declared, with an included class A object. The main() function contains a class B object declaration, creating the class B object.

Note that the complete declaration of a contained (enclosed) class is necessary before an object of that class can be used either to compose or to derive another class. Forward declaration only of the enclosed class results in compile-time errors because the compiler does not yet know the size or contents of the enclosed class. For example, the following code fragment does not compile correctly:

```
class A;   // Name the enclosed class
...
class B {
  A compose;  // fatal error
  ...
};
```

You may recall that forward declaration of a class name is sufficient to designate the named class as a friend of the later class, because a friend declaration does not require the compiler to know anything about the size of the friend's type.

In the preceding short program, the compiler is allowed to generate the constructor functions. You should remember, however, that the constructor for class B is executed first, and then the class A object is instantiated (by executing its constructor).

You should remember also that only the *default* constructor (one with no arguments or all default arguments) can be called for a class object that is declared within another class. In other words, you can't declare an *enclosed* class object with constructor function arguments. Why does this restriction exist? The answer is that it is not really a restriction. As mentioned in the preceding paragraph, the enclosed object is not instantiated until the enclosing class declaration is used to create an object. Until then, everything remains just a user-defined type (class) declaration.

You may recall from the discussion of constructor functions in Chapter 15 that there is a way around this apparent restriction. You can use *constructor initializers* in the enclosing class's constructor function definition to pass arguments to the enclosed class object's constructor function. You can rewrite the previous short program by using constructor initializers in the following manner:

```
#include <iostream.h>
#include <iomanip.h>

class A {
  int stuff;
public:
  A( int anum = 0 ) {  // Here is the constructor
    stuff = anum;
  }
  void display() {
    cout << "This is a class A object with value "
         << stuff << endl;
  }
};

class B {
  A compose;
public:
  B( int bnum = 37 ) : compose( bnum ) {} // Make the end run!!
  void display() {
```

```
    compose.display();
  }
  void unique() {
    cout << "This belongs to class B." << endl;
  }
};

void main()
{
  B testobj( 64 ); // Call constructor with args

  testobj.unique();      // Call the member functions
  testobj.display();
}
```

In the preceding short program, the class A constructor is defined so that the only argument has a default value, qualifying the constructor as a default constructor. The class A object compose is declared exactly as before, with no arguments in the constructor call.

The class B constructor differs from the previous version, however, in that it now has a constructor initializer list that passes the B constructor's argument on to the A constructor—by way of the class A *object* compose.

Class scope and access control rules do not change just because an object of a class is declared within another class. In the preceding short programs, for example, class B functions have no special access to private data in class A. The following code fragment, for instance, does not compile because B attempts to access private data in A:

```
class A { ... };
class B {
  A compose;
public:
  B( int bnum = 37 ) : compose( bnum ) {}
  void display() {
    compose.display();
    compose.stuff = 0;  // ERROR: access violation
  }
  ...
};
```

In all the preceding examples of code, therefore, class B is a user of class A objects, just like any other nonclass function would be. A class B composite object, then, includes all the functionality of class A, plus its own added functionality, with no modifications having been made to class A code.

Using Single Base Classes

You can create new classes from old ones also by deriving them. The new class being created is called the *derived class,* and the one from which it is derived is called the *base class.* The entire process is accordingly called *class derivation.*

There is a distinct parent-child relationship between base classes and derived classes. In fact, members of the base class are said to be *inherited* by the derived class, so you can accurately refer to derivation as *class inheritance.* When there is only one base class, *single inheritance* takes place. (This chapter later covers multiple base classes and multiple inheritance.) How class members are inherited and what this means for scope and access issues are the subjects of this section, which contains some fairly extensive sample programs.

Understanding Inheritance

Class derivation is much like class composition in that the result of derivation is a combination of the members and capabilities of more than one class. Class derivation is more like class *concatenation* than class *enclosure,* however. Figure 17.3 illustrates what this means.

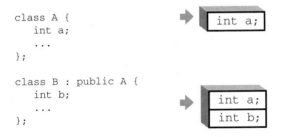

Figure 17.3.

Members from both base class declarations and derived class declarations are found in a derived class.

As Figure 17.3 shows, an object of a derived class can be viewed as a concatenated collection of *sub*objects, consisting of a base class object plus a subobject containing members declared only in the derived class.

Most similarities between composite and derived classes vanish at this point, however. Scope and access issues are largely different for derived classes. In particular, a derived class does not declare a base class object within its own declaration.

Declaring Base Classes and Derived Classes

How, then, are derived classes declared? The syntax required for deriving a class is reminiscent of that of a constructor initializer list. The simplest form for deriving a class from a base class is this:

```
class base { ... };
...
class derived : base { ... };
```

As was true of composite classes, a class that is merely named (not yet fully declared) cannot be used as a base class. The reasons for this restriction are exactly the same as for composite classes: To put the subobject types together, size information is required, and that information is not yet available when a forward declaration has been used.

It is important to understand that private members of the base class remain private: They are inaccessible even to the member functions of the derived class, and certainly not to nonmember functions. The only way available for circumventing this restriction is to declare `friend` functions explicitly within the base class, which, as you recall, can access private data and function members. The derived class can use only such `friend` functions to access private base class members.

Furthermore, *all* base class members are considered `private` members of the derived class if only the syntax explained so far is used. That is, nonmember functions can access the derived class in the normal ways, but they *cannot access any base class member.* Base class members become `private` derived class members by default. If you want to allow nonmember functions to access `public` base class members through the derived class, you must use an access specifier in declaring the derived class:

```
class base { ... };
...
class derived : public base { ... };
```

The access specifiers available are `public`, `private`, and `protected`. The base class access specifiers have the following effects on access to base class members through the derived class:

■ *Declaring a base class* `public`

The `public` access specifier causes the `public` members of the base class to become `public` members of the derived class, causes `protected` members of the base class to become `protected` members of the derived class, and leaves the `private` members of the base class `private`.

■ *Declaring a base class* protected

The protected access specifier causes public members of the base class to become protected members of the derived class, causes protected members of the base class to become private members of the derived class, and leaves private base class members inaccessible to all except the base class.

■ *Declaring a base class* private

The private access specifier causes both the public and protected members of the base class to become private members of the derived class. private members of the base class are, as always, private to the base class.

In most cases, you will want to make the public members of the base class public in the derived class as well (although this is by no means always true). Suppose that you rewrite the preceding short programs with the A and B classes using derivation. You can see the base class access specifier in action in the following new code:

```cpp
#include <iostream.h>
#include <iomanip.h>

class A {
public:
  void display() {
    cout << "This is a class A object." << endl;
  }
};

class B : public A {
public:
  void display() {
    cout << "This is a class B object." << endl;
  }
  void unique() {
    cout << "This belongs only to class B." << endl;
  }
};

void main()
{
  B testobj; // Declare a derived class object

  testobj.unique();       // Use the unique member function
```

```
      testobj.display();      // Do it one way
      testobj.A::display();   // Do it the other way

      A* otherobj = new B;    // Declare a B, cast it to A
      otherobj->display();    // and get A message
}
```

In this version of the workhorse demonstration program, class B is derived from class A, using the `public` access specifier. The `main()` function then defines a derived class object, `testobj`, and calls member functions in three different ways, as shown here:

```
testobj.unique();       // Use the unique member function
testobj.display();      // Do it one way
testobj.A::display();   // Do it the other way
```

The first two of these member function calls refer to members of the derived (B) class and work exactly as you would expect them to. The third function call, however, is able to access a member function of the base class directly because the base class was declared `public`. In fact, the only reason that the scope resolution operator is required at all in this third function call is that the function name is duplicated in each class. That raises the next issue for discussion.

Assuming that a particular base class member is accessible to a derived class (or perhaps even to nonmember functions), you must consider what happens when there is an overlap of names in the derived class. In other words, if there are members in both base and derived classes with exactly the same name (and the same signature if the member is a function), how does the compiler sort out which member is to be used?

In case of an exact overlap of this kind, the compiler assumes that the derived class's member name hides that of the base class. Therefore, the derived class's member is accessed, unless the scope resolution operator is used to construct a fully qualified member name, as it was in the preceding example.

The occurrence of name overlap in base and derived classes does not mean that ambiguous names exist—the hiding mechanism ensures that there is no ambiguity. Moreover, even if the overlap appears to occur for two member functions that have different signatures, this does not mean that the function is overloaded. There are merely two distinct functions, one belonging to each class.

Conversion member functions of a class (user-defined cast operators) are a somewhat special case when you consider name hiding under derivation. Conversion functions don't specify a return type and cannot have arguments (they are unary operators). Consequently, a conversion function in a derived class will not hide a conversion function in the base class unless they have identical target types. Note the following example:

```
class A {
  int var_a;
public:
  operator int() { return var_a; }
...
};

class B : public A {
  int var_b;
public:
  operator int() { return var_b; }  // Hide A operator int()
...
};
```

In this code fragment, because the type converted to in both base and derived classes is the same, the derived class's operator `int()` function hides the base class version. In contrast, you can accidentally introduce ambiguities into the code if the target types of the conversion functions do not match, but can be confused. The following code fragment illustrates this problem:

```
class A {
  int var_a;
public:
  operator int() { return var_a; }
...
};

class B : public A {
  int var_b;
public:
  operator void*() { return (void*)&var_b; }
...
};
```

With conversion functions defined as in this code fragment, the compiler won't know what to do with the following piece of code:

```
B obj_b;    // derived class object
...
if ( obj_b ) ... // Both void* and int can be tested here
```

In this case, a `void` pointer can be tested for null and an integer can be tested for zero with equal validity. The compiler therefore won't know which conversion function to pick. This circumstance is not as farfetched as you might think. You may recall that the `void*` conversion was used with stream classes to allow for testing the stream state easily. Such conversions are quite useful, and you may encounter this problem.

Now return your attention to the preceding complete short program. The last two lines in the `main()` function illustrate another interesting and important fact: A pointer to a derived class can be converted to a pointer to its base class if the base class is both accessible and unambiguous. Here are the two lines of code again:

```
A* otherobj = new B;    // Declare a B, cast it to A
otherobj->display();    // and get A message
```

The first of these lines creates a derived class object on the free store, returns its pointer, and implicitly converts the pointer to a pointer to the base (A) class. There is no problem so far; however, what if you now call the `display()` function again? Which version of `display()` will be invoked? The A class function will be invoked. Why this is the case is easy to understand if you recall the subobject structure of the derived class object. The pointer is merely adjusted to point to the base class subobject.

Conversion in the reverse direction—*from* pointer to base class object *to* pointer to derived class object—is another matter. If the compiler allowed conversions such as the following one, there would be trouble sooner or later:

```
A* baseobj = new A;
B* deriveptr = (A*)baseobj;  // ERROR: direction illegal
```

Although it is true that all derived class objects contain a base class subobject, it is not always true that a base class object is a subobject of anything. It is entirely possible to use a base class both to define objects directly and to use it as a base for deriving another class. A pointer to a base class object can therefore point only to a base class object; such a conversion, then, would lead to a type mismatch. The conversion is therefore illegal according to the C++ ANSI base document.

Microsoft designed its C++ compiler on the assumption that Microsoft C/C++ programmers know what they are doing. Thus, although Microsoft C/C++ will indeed catch and flag a blunder such as the implicit cast attempt

```
B* deriveptr = new A; // ERROR: Cannot assign A* to B*
```

the compiler will nevertheless allow the earlier code fragment to compile unmolested. The Microsoft C/C++ compiler allows a cast from base to derived class pointer type especially to permit the recasting of a class pointer to its original type. In other words, you can cast from derived class pointer to base class pointer and then back to derived class pointer. Note the following example:

```
A* baseptr;
B* deriveptr = new B;
B* derive2;
...
```

```
baseptr = (A*)deriveptr;  //Cast to a base pointer
derive2 = (B*)baseptr;    //  and back to a derived pointer
```

Now consider another point. Because casting a pointer to a derived class object into a pointer to a base class object is more than just a syntactical convenience—a pointer to a subobject results—then casting first to a base class pointer and then to some other type (such as char*) may not yield the pointer value you are expecting. Consider the following code fragment, for example, in which the class A and B objects are also used:

```
B* ptr = new B;            // pointer to derived class object
char* p1;                  // working pointers to base
char* p2;                  // and derived subobject locations
...
p1 = (char*)((A*)ptr);     // Convert to base*, then char*
p2 = (char*)ptr;           // Convert straight to char*
if ( p1 == p2 ) ...        // Condition may fail
```

This code fragment results in two pointers to char*, but their contents are probably different. In other words, casting to a base pointer and then casting to another type again (for example, char*) does not necessarily yield a pointer to the complete derived object. Both p1 and p2 do have type char*, but one points to the base class subobject and the other points to the complete derived object. The further conversion to char* does not change the address value of the pointer; however, the conversion to base pointer did change that value.

The reason that the resulting pointer contents are *probably* different is that there is no guarantee as to the order of appearance of the subobjects in a derived class object. The base class subobject might be placed first, in which case the preceding pointer comparison would in fact succeed. The base class subobject may not be first, however, in which case the comparison would fail.

Finally, consider what can and cannot be inherited. You have already learned how access specifiers control a derived class's accessibility to base class members, but the present topic goes beyond that. Some members of the base class cannot be inherited at all, although most can be inherited.

Restrictions on the inheritance of overloaded operators in a base class are the easiest to deal with. Except the operator=() (the assignment operator), all the operators that can be overloaded can be inherited. The assignment operator cannot be inherited because its action depends entirely on the specific structure of the class object: The structure of a base class object is not the same as the structure of a derived class object.

You must exercise some care in designing assignment operators for base and derived classes. If you do not code any assignment operator functions, recall that the compiler will generate one that performs a bitwise copy of the source object. That works fine, whether the object has base or derived type; everything gets copied one way or another.

Because the assignment operator is not inherited, however, you will most likely design base and derived classes, each of which has its own assignment operator function. Although such functions are present in the base class declaration, however, they are not necessarily used when a derived class object's operator=() is invoked. To illustrate this point, suppose that you have coded a base class in this way:

```
#include <iostream.h>
#include <iomanip.h>

class A {
  int a1, a2;
public:
  A( int v1 = 32, int v2 = 64 ) {  // base constructor
    a1 = v1;
    a2 = v2;
  }
  A& operator=( A& otherobj ) {        // Assign op here
    a1 = otherobj.a1;
    a2 = otherobj.a2;
    return *this;
  }
  void display() {
    cout << "Base class values are "
         << a1 << ' ' << a2 << endl;
  }
};
```

Everything seems fine so far: The base class has a valid operator=() function that will serve well for objects of class A. Now suppose that you write a class derived from this one. You might, for example, write the following code:

```
class B : public A {
  int b1, b2;
public:         // Derived constructor uses ctor-initializer
                // with base CLASS name to pass ctor args
  B( int v1 = 0, int v2 = 0, int v3 = 37, int v4 = 57 )
                                   : A( v1, v2 ) {
    b1 = v3;
    b2 = v4;
  }
  B& operator=( B& otherobj ) {        // Assign op here
    b1 = otherobj.b1;
    b2 = otherobj.b2;
    return *this;     // A class data not taken care of
  }
```

```
  void display() {
    A::display();
    cout << "Derived class values are "
         << b1 << ' ' << b2 << endl;
  }
};
```

This code fragment also looks good on the surface. The problem with it is that invoking the assignment operator for a class B object does nothing to provide for copying the base class subobject's member data—so it doesn't get copied. Therefore, when the `main()` function shown next copies one derived class object into another, base class members are displayed as unchanged:

```
void main()
{
  B obj1;
  B obj2( 1, 2, 3, 4 );

  obj1 = obj2;                  // Use the assign operator
  obj1.display();               // Base class member still 0, 0
}
```

Such an accidental failure to copy all members in both the base and derived class subobjects is called a *slicing copy operation,* which is a particularly dangerous trap when you are using class derivation. To get the base class member data updated during the assignment operation, you have to do something explicit about it. In this sample code, you would need to modify the class B (derived) declaration in the following manner:

```
class B : public A {
  int b1, b2;
public:        // Derived constructor uses ctor-initializer
               // with base CLASS name to pass ctor args
  B( int v1 = 0, int v2 = 0, int v3 = 37, int v4 = 57 )
                                    : A( v1, v2 ) {
    b1 = v3;
    b2 = v4;
  }
  B& operator=( B& otherobj ) {         // Assign op here
    A *temp;                            // Provide base pointer

    b1 = otherobj.b1;
    b2 = otherobj.b2;
    temp = (A*)this;           // Convert to base pointers
    *temp = otherobj;              // Invoke base class op=()
    return *this;    // all members, base and derived copied
```

```
  }
  void display() {
    A::display();
    cout << "Derived class values are "
         << b1 << ' ' << b2 << endl;
  }
};
```

In other words, the solution is to use the explicit conversion to a base pointer on the this pointer, and then to force the use of the base class's assignment operator function. Notice that in the expression

```
*temp = otherobj;
```

the left-side operand is a base class object and the right-side operand is a derived class object. This usage is permissible, as long as the base class is public. If it doesn't suit you to use this odd-looking construction, you can alternatively form base class pointers to both sending and receiving objects. Note the following example:

```
A *temp1, *temp2;  // base class pointers
...
temp1 = (A*)this;   // receiving object
temp2 = (A*)&otherobj; // sending object - notice adrs op
...
*temp1 = *temp2;
```

The list of member functions that cannot be inherited is a little more extensive. The following functions cannot be inherited:

- *Constructor functions.* Constructor functions depend on the internal structure of class objects, as do assignment operator functions. Constructor functions are thus not inherited.

- *Destructor functions.* Destructor functions are not inherited for the same reason that constructors are not inherited. Destructor functions can, however, be *virtual* functions, which is even better than inheritance (for destructors). Virtual destructor functions are discussed a little later in this chapter.

- *Friend functions.* Friend functions are not inherited simply as a protective measure against accidental access violations. If friend functions were inherited, you could derive a class from a private base class and still have access to all base class members, private and otherwise.

Using Virtual Functions

Earlier in this chapter, you learned that a pointer to a derived class object can be converted to a pointer to a base class object. That feature of C++ is quite useful but can cause some problems. Specifically, if both the base class and the derived class declare a function with the same name and signature, the pointer manipulations just alluded to can cause the wrong copy of the function to be executed. C++ virtual functions can help avoid this sort of problem.

Using Late Binding and Virtual Functions

The virtual function mechanism can be viewed as a *pass-through* mechanism intended to guarantee execution of the correct copy of identical functions appearing in both a base and a derived class. Consider, for example, what happens when you *don't* use virtual functions in the following short program:

```
#include <iostream.h>
#include <iomanip.h>

class A {
public:
  void hello() { cout << "My name is A." << endl; }
};

class B : public A {
public:
  void hello() { cout << "My name is B." << endl; }
};

void main()
{
  B* obj = new B; // Create derived object
  A* ptr;         // base pointer

  obj->hello();
  ptr = (A*)obj;  // Convert to base pointer type
  ptr->hello();
}
```

This short program produces a `hello()` from *each* class—a different message from each class:

```
My name is B.
My name is A.
```

The operation of the function is similar to the slicing copies you dealt with earlier. Then, not everything got copied when the assignment operator was invoked. Now, you may not be getting the function you actually wanted to call. Declaring the class A `hello()` member function *virtual*, however, guarantees that the derived class's copy will be executed—no matter how the object is accessed. The following rewrite of this short program adds the `virtual` keyword and fixes the problem:

```cpp
#include <iostream.h>
#include <iomanip.h>

class A {
public:           // Look at the difference in hello()
  virtual void hello() { cout << "My name is A." << endl; }
};

class B : public A {
public:
  void hello() { cout << "My name is B." << endl; }
};

void main()
{
  B* obj = new B; // Create derived object
  A* ptr;         // base pointer

  obj->hello();
  ptr = (A*)obj;  // Convert to base pointer type
  ptr->hello();
}
```

Here the base class function has been declared virtual. This means that if there is a derived class function by the same name and signature, the derived class's copy will be selected to execute. That is exactly what happens, producing the following (correct) output:

```
My name is B.
My name is B.
```

Now that the `hello()` function is declared `virtual` in the base class, the derived class function is said to *override* the base class function. Therefore, the same copy of `hello()` is called whether through a pointer with the derived class type or with the base class type. Note that if the derived class's function differs in signature, the virtual function mechanism is bypassed: The derived class function hides the base class function (it can still be accessed with the scope resolution operator).

Thus, a virtual function can be defined as a function that *depends only on the type of object for which it is called,* rather than on the type of reference or pointer used to make the function call. Selection of the correct copy of one of several identically typed functions is called *late,* or *dynamic, binding.* In other words, until it is determined at run time, it is not necessary to know precisely which derived class type the function call belongs to.

This important feature of C++ is useful in defining interfaces to an object, the precise nature of which may not be completely known in a given context. If the interface is defined with virtual functions and the base class interface is known, all is well—a function call binds to the correct version no matter what.

The classic example is the `shape` base class from which is derived specific `shape` classes (`square`, `circle`, `line`, and so on). The `shape` base class has a `draw()` virtual function that is overridden in each derived class to satisfy specific drawing requirements. If a pointer to a derived class `shape` object has been passed to a function that does not know which particular shape it has received, it can still `draw()` the object with some confidence in the results because that function (presumably) knows of the base class drawing interface.

From another point of view, the virtual function mechanism supplies the capability to call diverse functions through the same interface. This characteristic is called *polymorphism* (from Greek, meaning "many shapes"), and is used to give a single name to actions (or member functions) that are shared across all the classes in an object hierarchy. The `draw()` function of the `shape` base class described in the previous paragraph, for example, is implemented in each derived class as needed. Polymorphism is considered by many to be the essence of object-oriented programming (as opposed to object-based programming).

Of course, there are some rules for the use of virtual functions. As you develop your base and derived classes by using virtual functions, be aware of the following points:

- *A virtual function must be a nonstatic member function of a class.* The point of virtual functions is membership (and selecting which class type to bind). A virtual function cannot be `static` either. Binding for a virtual function depends on object type, so the function cannot be disassociated from particular objects of its class by being declared `static`.

- *An overriding function of a virtual function is itself virtual.* In other words, the overriding function does not have to be explicitly declared virtual, because it is associated with a virtual function. You can declare an overriding function `virtual` if you want, but it is not necessary.

- *You can define a virtual function in a base class, but not in any derived class.* If there is no overriding function in the derived class, the base class function will be called. You might find yourself declaring base class functions virtual without overriding functions during program development, in anticipation of later interfaces being added.

- *The scope resolution operator defeats the virtual function mechanism.* Because the scope resolution operator is aimed at "manually" selecting the class type to bind in a base class and derived class hierarchy, the virtual function mechanism does not apply.

- *A virtual function can be declared a friend by another class.* You learn how to arrange this bit of esoterica immediately following this list.

- *A virtual function in a base class must be either defined by the base class or declared to be a pure virtual function.* This rule means that you can't just write a function prototype for a virtual function in the base class, providing a function body only for overriding functions. The reason is that the base class copy might actually be called. The significance of this rule is slightly different if the function is a pure virtual function. That subject is covered later in this chapter, in the discussion of abstract classes.

You can declare a virtual function in one class to be a `friend` of another class, as mentioned in the preceding list. Although you probably won't see or use this technique often, a simple example is provided here. Note the following short program that declares a virtual function `friend` in another class:

```
#include <iostream.h>
#include <iomanip.h>

class C;

class A {
public:
  virtual void report( C& );
};

class B : public A {
public:
  void report( C& );
};
```

```
class C {  // not a derived class, but declares friend
  int c_data;
public:
  friend virtual void A::report( C& );
  friend         void B::report( C& );
  C() { c_data = 37; }
};

void A::report( C& cobj) {
  cout << "Nothing happening here." << endl;
}

void B::report( C& cobj ) {
  cout << cobj.c_data << endl;
}

void main()
{
  B bobj;    // derived class object
  C cobj;    // accessed by B friends
  A* ptr = (A*)&bobj; // but get base pointer

  ptr->report( cobj );
}
```

Notice carefully in this short program how the declarations and function definitions are arranged. The order is not accidental: It is designed to prevent "You haven't declared that yet!" messages.

You should notice also that class C declares both the base and derived class report() functions as friends. This is necessary because *friends are not inherited.* In other words, declaring the base class virtual function as a friend does not mean that the derived class virtual function is also a friend. In fact, it is not strictly necessary to declare the base class report() function a friend in this example; in other circumstances, however, the base class might be used to create an object directly, requiring the friend declaration. The declaration is included here to highlight this point.

The virtual function *pass-through* mechanism works in this example as expected. In this short program, the base class virtual friend function is not used; the derived class virtual function is used. As you can see, in the last line of main(), the derived class virtual function can still be accessed through a base class pointer, causing the overriding function to be invoked. Because that function is a friend of class C, C's private data can be accessed by it.

Using Scope Resolution To Control Member Function Access

You learned in the preceding section that the scope resolution operator can be used to call a base class copy of a virtual function, but that this circumvents the virtual function mechanism. Scope resolution can be used also in a hierarchy of derived classes to select which copy of a redefined function is to be used in a function call (or which version of a hidden variable is to be accessed).

That a hierarchy of derived classes can exist implies, of course, that a derived class can act as a base class for yet another derived class. For example, you can build a hierarchy of classes A, B, and C:

```
class A { ... };
class B : public A { ... };
class C : public B { ... };
```

Each class in the hierarchy depends on the previous class to form its base class. This arrangement of derived classes introduces the notion of *direct* bases and *indirect* bases for derived classes. In the preceding code fragment, for example, A is the direct base for B and B is the direct base for C, but A is an indirect base for C. The concatenation of subobjects in a hierarchy of derived classes is similar to that for single inheritance with one base class. Pointer casts to base classes are also the same, except that here a class C object pointer could be cast to either a B* or A* base class pointer. Virtual functions "cascade" down through the hierarchy, too, as long as there are properly formed overriding functions.

Note, however, that a hierarchy of derived classes is not multiple inheritance. Each derived class here has only one direct base. Multiple inheritance (discussed in the next section) involves defining multiple direct bases for a single derived class.

Returning now to the discussion of scope resolution, consider what happens when you have a hierarchy of derived classes, each of which redefines an identically typed function in its base class, as shown here:

```
class A { public: void func(); };
class B : public A { public: void func(); };
class C : public B { public: void func(); };
...
C someobj;
...
someobj.func();
```

In this code fragment, the class C object someobj seems to have no recourse but to use the class C copy of func(). The scope resolution operator can get you around this problem. With a fully qualified member function name, specifying the class whose copy you want to use is the solution:

```
someobj.B::func();  // Use class B copy
```

The scope resolution operator can be useful also in resolving ambiguous references in complicated derivations. The topic of the next section discusses when such complications are most likely to arise.

Using Multiple Base Classes

You are not restricted to using a single base class when you derive a new class. You can write a base list containing any number of direct base classes for the derived class. Deriving a class in this way is called *multiple inheritance,* or *class derivation with multiple base classes.*

Most of the knowledge you have just acquired in learning about single inheritance can be applied directly to multiple inheritance. There will, of course, be other considerations that arise for the first time when you are deriving classes with multiple base classes. One of the most important of these new considerations is the avoidance of ambiguous references, which are created more easily when you use multiple base classes rather than single base classes.

Deriving from More Than One Base Class

Suppose that you want to derive class C from classes A and B, making both base classes public (all the access specifiers still apply in the same ways you have just learned). The class declarations look like this:

```
class A { ... };
class B { ... };
class C : public A, public B { ... };
```

Thus, class C inherits public and protected members from both A and B: Subobjects are constructed by the compiler just as they are for single inheritance, but the resulting class object now has three, rather than two, subobjects. Classes derived from multiple bases always have, by definition, proportionately more subobjects than classes derived from single bases. Figure 17.4 illustrates the subobject construction for the preceding code fragment.

Figure 17.4.

Multiple bases mean multiple subobjects and the possibility of more than one valid cast to a base pointer type.

```
class A { ... };
class B { .. };
class C: public A, public B { ... };
```

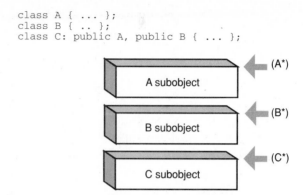

Figure 17.4 indicates also that conversion of derived class pointers to base class pointers is possible, as it is for classes derived from single bases. As you can see, however, there are more valid base class pointers to which you can convert when you are deriving from multiple base classes than when you are deriving from single bases.

The principles of virtual function declarations apply in multiple inheritance in the same way as they do in single inheritance. No matter which base class pointer is used to access the derived class object, a virtual function still correctly overrides any progenitor functions above it in the hierarchy.

You can also use hierarchies of derived classes, one or more of which have multiple base classes. For example, you can write the following:

```
class A { ... };
class B : public A { ... };
class C { ... };
class D : public C { ... };
class E : public B, public D { ... };
```

Because the preceding derivation has no redundancy of base classes, there will be five subobjects in a class E derived class object. It is possible, however, to introduce a redundant (or possibly redundant) copy of a base class, if it is an indirect base class of a derived class more than once. Figure 17.5 illustrates how this can occur.

Notice carefully in Figure 17.5 that no base class appears as the direct base for a derived class more than once: That is illegal. It is hardly possible, however, to outlaw the appearance of a class more than once as an indirect ancestor, because complicated derivations can conceivably make it impossible to proceed if such classes are not allowed. You might find yourself in a "you can't get there from here" design dilemma.

```
class common {...};

class A : public common {...};

class B : public common {...};

class C: public A, public B {...};
```

Figure 17.5.

A base class can be an
indirect base for a derived
class more than once;
however, its presence
increases the number of
subobjects present.

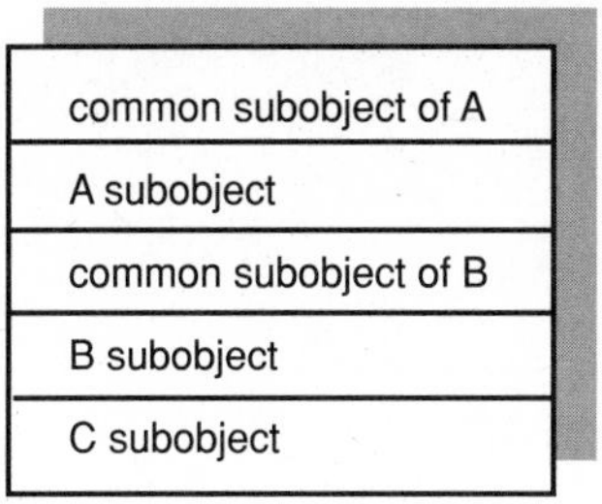

| common subobject of A |
| A subobject |
| common subobject of B |
| B subobject |
| C subobject |

Having a class appear as an indirect base more than once does not necessarily introduce ambiguous names into the derived class. Suppose that classes B and C are both derived from class A, and that class D is derived from both classes B and C. Suppose further that class A has a member integer named counter. Now, because there are two class A subobjects in the resulting derived class, is it possible to use one of the counter member objects—or for that matter, to unambiguously reference either? It *is* possible, and you can do it with the scope resolution operator. The code looks something like this:

```
class A {
public:
  int counter;
  ...
};
class B : public A { ... };
class C : public A { ... };
class D : public B, public C {
public:
  void report{
    cout << B::counter << endl; // Use A subobject of B
    cout << C::counter << endl; // Use A subobject of C
  }
};
```

Casts to base pointers can be especially tricky when a given class appears more than once as an indirect base class of a derived class. With the preceding code fragment in mind, the following casts to a base pointer (from a pointer to class D) are illegal because they are ambiguous:

```
D* d_ptr = new D;
...
A* a_ptr = d_ptr;  // Implicit cast is ambiguous - which A?
a_ptr = (A*)d_ptr; // Explicit cast is still ambiguous
```

In neither case in this code fragment is it possible for the compiler to sort out which class A subobject is meant. Is it the one belonging to B or the one belonging to C? There is no way to determine the answer.

That dilemma does not prevent you from accessing an A class subobject from the preceding example; however, you have to approach it the correct way. For example, you can write this:

```
A* a_ptr = (A*)(B*)d_ptr  // Point to B's A subobject
d_ptr = (D*)(C*)a_ptr     // Point to D containing C's A
```

Problems with ambiguous references probably will plague you more often concerning member names than concerning class names. There is a much greater likelihood that two base classes contributing to a derived class will contain identical member names (or member names that can be confused by the compiler) than that class names will conflict. Consider, for example, the following short program:

```
class A {
public:
  int a;
  int (A::* f1)();  // Notice how the pointer is declared
  int f2() { return 0; }
  int f3() { return 0; }
};

class B {
public:
  int a;
  int f1() { return 0; }
  int f2() { return 0; }
};

class C : public A, public B { };

void main()
{
  C c_obj;
```

```
  c_obj.f1 = f2;     // ERROR: f1 ambiguous and f2 undefined
  c_obj.a = 2;       // ERROR: A::a or B::a?
  c_obj.f2();        // ERROR A::f2 or B::f2?
  c_obj.f3();        // OK, not ambiguous

//
// Here is the correct way to do it:
//
  c_obj.A::f1 = A::f2;
  c_obj.B::a = 2;
  c_obj.A::f2();v
}
```

Once more, the scope resolution operator is the answer to the problem. If you use the scope resolution operator and the name of the appropriate base class, all ambiguities disappear.

Notice in the preceding short program that the member name ambiguities arise because the base classes are "siblings." If B had been derived from A (in a hierarchy, that is), the member identifier in the derived class would *dominate* the same identifier in the base class. You should understand that *dominance* is not the same thing as overloading, nor is it the same thing as overriding (which virtual functions do). There are conceptual similarities among the three terms—dominate, overload, and override—but they are different ideas that apply to different contexts.

Declaring and Using Virtual Base Classes

You have just seen the effects of designing a derived class for which an indirect base class was specified more than once. Because there are circumstances in which the repeated subobjects for that common base class are necessary, you need to know how to work with virtual base classes.

In most cases, you will find that allowing a repeated indirect base to cause the construction of multiple subobjects is wasteful—only one such subobject is usually needed. There is a way to control such repetition of subobjects for a common indirect base class. You can declare virtual base classes and cause the construction of the derived class to contain only one unique subobject for each *parent* class. Here is a sample of the syntax required to create and use virtual base classes:

```
class A { ... };
class B : public virtual A { ... };
class C : public virtual A { ... };
class D : public B, public C { ... };
```

Without virtual base classes, an object of the derived class D would consist of five subobjects (counting the extra class A subobject). Using virtual base classes, there will be only four subobjects. Furthermore, there will be no possible ambiguities involved in casting to the common indirect base class. Note also that because the virtual keyword is used here with the *derived class declaration,* the "virtualness" of a base class is a characteristic of this kind of derivation, not something inherent in a base class itself.

When you are not using virtual base classes, you can cast a derived class object pointer to a base class pointer, and you can cast it back again into a derived class pointer (as shown earlier). Using virtual base classes, however, you *can* cast from a derived class to a virtual base class, but you *cannot* cast from a virtual base class to a derived class. To allow this maneuver would require the compiler to develop lists of pointers to enclosing objects—in effect, converting from one kind of memory layout to another on the fly.

Finally, you can define virtual functions within virtual base classes. Doing this has the interesting result of enabling you to arrange virtual functions and base pointers so that sibling base class subobjects can communicate with one another. Again, assume that both classes B and C are derived from the virtual base class A; derived class D is derived from B and C. Here is a short program in which the C subobject acquires information from the B subobject:

```
#include <iostream.h>

class A {
  int a_val;
public:
  A() { a_val = 0; }
  virtual int b() { return a_val; }
  virtual int c() { return a_val; }
};

class B : public virtual A {
  int b_val;
public:
  B() { b_val = 16; }
  virtual int b() { return b_val; }
};

class C : public virtual A {
  int c_val;
public:
  C() { c_val = 64; }
  virtual int c() { return c_val; }
```

```
};

class D : public B, public C { };

void main()
{
  D* d_obj = new D;    // Declare derived object
  C* c_obj = d_obj;    // cast to C base pointer
                       // Now call C path, get value from B path
  cout << c_obj->b() << endl;
}
```

When you run the preceding program, it appears that you are reaching the desired virtual function by entering through the C class "path"—and indeed you are. However, the arrangement of the virtual base class and virtual functions guarantees that you will actually execute the B::b() function. The value returned and displayed is therefore 16, as you should expect.

If that is not enough flexibility to suit your needs for building derived classes, there are abstract classes and pure virtual functions available for you. These are discussed next.

Deriving Classes from Abstract Classes

The *abstract* class defines a concept or generalized type. An abstract class can be used *only* as a base class for another, derived, class. A few special rules apply to abstract classes:

■ *An abstract class must have at least one pure virtual function.* Pure virtual functions are what give abstract classes their distinctive character. These functions are discussed in the section following this list.

■ *An abstract class cannot be used as an argument type, a function return type, the type of an explicit conversion, or the type of an object.* In other words, if tree is an abstract class, all of the following statements are illegal:

```
tree oak;                  // tree cannot be object type
tree func();              // tree cannot be function return type
int numleaves(tree);      // tree cannot be argument type
someptr = (tree*)otherptr; // cannot be used in explicit cvt
```

■ *You can declare a pointer or reference to an abstract class.* The following statements are acceptable:

```
class oak : public tree{ ... };
...
oak* mytree = new oak;
tree* treeptr = mytree;
```

Because the essence of abstract classes is the pure virtual function, I discuss it first.

Understanding Pure Virtual Functions

Aside from being unavailable for creating objects, all abstract classes have one common characteristic: Each has at least one pure virtual function. The formal definition of a *pure virtual function* is that it possesses the pure specifier, as shown here:

```
virtual type functionname( args ) = 0;
```

It is true that this is a peculiar syntax. However, the point of abstract classes, and hence virtual functions, is that they define a concept rather than an object. This syntax suggests that (normally) a pure virtual function is a pathway to other, concrete, member functions that serve real objects.

Implementing Pure Virtual Functions

You can always understand a strange concept more easily if you see it in action. The following short program defines the abstract class tree that was mentioned earlier:

```
#include <iostream.h>
#include <string.h>

class tree {     // Declare an abstract TREE type
  char treehdr[30];
public:
  tree() { strcpy( treehdr, "This tree has no type." ); }
  virtual void saytree() = 0;   // <== pure virtual specifier
};

class oak : public tree {  // Here is a class for a real tree
  char treehdr[30];
```

```
public:
  oak() { strcpy( treehdr, "This tree is an oak." ); }
  void saytree() {                 // <== NO pure virtual spec.
    cout << treehdr << endl;
  }
};

void main()
{
  oak yardtree;  // Declare particular tree object

  yardtree.saytree();
}
```

The class tree is used here just to define the concept of a tree. A real tree, an oak in this case, has more specific attributes that the abstract class by definition cannot know about.

Pure virtual functions are inherited as pure virtual functions. Somewhere along the line, however, there has to be a function body for the function, or else it could never do anything useful. This implies that a pure virtual function can have a function body. Note that a pure virtual function in an abstract class doesn't need to have a function definition unless you intend to call it directly by using the scope resolution operator to locate it. The following rewrite of the preceding program shows how to call a pure virtual function in an abstract class:

```
#include <iostream.h>
#include <string.h>

class tree {
  char treehdr[30];
public:
  tree() { strcpy( treehdr, "This tree has no type." ); }
  virtual void saytree() = 0 {  // <== pure virtual specifier
    cout << treehdr << endl;
  }
};

class oak : public tree {
  char treehdr[30];
public:
  oak() { strcpy( treehdr, "This tree is an oak." ); }
  void saytree() {                 // <== NO pure virtual spec.
```

```
    cout << treehdr << endl;
  }
};

void main()
{
  oak yardtree;   // Declare particular tree object

  yardtree.saytree();
  yardtree.tree::saytree();
}
```

This version of the program produces two messages: One message identifies the derived object as an oak, and the second message calls the pure virtual function in the abstract class. The saytree() function in the abstract class promptly demonstrates that it has no knowledge of specific trees.

Using Constructors and Destructors with Inheritance

As you might imagine, the use of constructor and destructor functions in derived classes—particularly the more complicated ones—is more complex than in simple classes.

This section discusses the differences involved in designing constructors and destructors for derived classes, and wraps up the chapter as well.

Initialization Code Is Not Inherited

Initialization code (as well as deinitialization code) is not inherited. You now have enough background in deriving C++ classes to understand why this is true.

Although a derived class eventually acts as the type for a single unified object, a derived class consists of a number of subobject classes. Each of these classes (except for abstract classes) can also stand as the type definition for objects directly, as well as contribute to the structure of a derived class object. Thus, each base class has its own distinct initialization requirements.

The implication, of course, is not only that all classes coming together in a derived class have their own constructors and destructors, but also that all these initialization functions are executed. That may sound like a trivial deduction, but you would be surprised at the trouble you can buy for yourself by forgetting it even momentarily.

Understanding the Order of Constructor and Destructor Calls with Inheritance

Because all the constructors for base and derived classes are executed when an object of the derived class is created, it may be important to the design of your derived class to understand their order of execution. Usually, certain things must happen in a certain order. Here is the order of constructor calls made when a derived class object is created:

1. *All virtual base class constructors are executed first.* If there are multiple virtual base classes, their constructors are executed in the order in which they were declared.

2. *All nonvirtual base class constructors are executed next.* The dependency of nonvirtual base classes on their virtual parents is obvious. If there are multiple nonvirtual base classes, their constructors are executed in the order in which they were declared.

3. *The derived class constructor, or the only constructor when there is no hierarchy, is executed last.* There can be, by definition, only one of these in a hierarchy. That does not mean that there can be only one hierarchy, of course.

The order of destructor function calls made when an object is destroyed is simple: The order is exactly the reverse of the order of constructor function calls.

Using Virtual Destructor Functions

Constructor and destructor functions cannot be inherited, nor can a constructor function be a virtual function. A destructor function *can* be virtual, however, and it is often a good idea to make a destructor function virtual.

To understand why this is advisable, recall the earlier discussion of the slicing copy operation that can result when you are defining an assignment operator for a derived class. If a base pointer is used to access a derived class object and the assignment operator function is accessed through the base pointer path, not all members of the derived class will be copied. You learned how to get around that (and when to do so).

Something similar can happen to your destructor functions in a hierarchy of derived classes—a destructor can fail to be executed under the right circumstances. When can this happen? It is not uncommon when you have created a derived class object with new, placing the resulting pointer in a base class pointer, and then calling delete to destroy the object. Suppose that you have defined a tree base class and derived an oak class from it. The oak class constructor further acquires free memory outside the object to hold an array of leafdata. Now consider what happens in the following short program:

```
#include <iostream.h>
#include <string.h>

class tree {
  char treehdr[30];
public:
  tree() { strcpy( treehdr, "This tree has no type." ); }
  ~tree() { cout << "Bye, bye!" << endl; }
  virtual void saytree() = 0 {  // <== pure virtual specifier
    cout << treehdr << endl;
  }
};

class oak : public tree {
  char treehdr[30];
  int* leafdata;              // pointer to fairly large array
public:
  oak() {
    strcpy( treehdr, "This tree is an oak." );
    leafdata = new int[1000];
  }
  ~oak() {               // Derived destructor is virtual, too
    cout << "Releasing leaf storage." << endl;
    delete leafdata;
  }
  void saytree() {                // <== NO pure virtual spec.
    cout << treehdr << endl;
  }
};

void main()
{
  tree* yardtree = new oak;  // Look at this one carefully!
```

```
    yardtree->saytree();
    delete yardtree;
}
```

When this program runs, you receive only the Bye, bye! message from the base class destructor. The oak destructor is not executed. This means that the 1,000-integer array leafdata allocated by the oak constructor is still in free store. If you allow the derived class destructor to be bypassed often in the same program, you will soon exhaust free store altogether. You can correct this problem by adding the virtual keyword to the ~tree() destructor function, as shown here:

```
#include <iostream.h>
#include <string.h>

class tree {
  char treehdr[30];
public:
  tree() { strcpy( treehdr, "This tree has no type." ); }
  virtual ~tree() { cout << "Bye, bye!" << endl; }
  virtual void saytree() = 0 {   // <== pure virtual specifier
    cout << treehdr << endl;
  }
};

class oak : public tree {
  char treehdr[30];
  int* leafdata;              // pointer to fairly large array
public:
  oak() {
    strcpy( treehdr, "This tree is an oak." );
    leafdata = new int[1000];
  }
  ~oak() {                // Derived destructor is virtual, too
    cout << "Releasing leaf storage." << endl;
    delete leafdata;
  }
  void saytree() {                   // <== NO pure virtual spec.
    cout << treehdr << endl;
  }
};

void main()
{
```

```
tree* yardtree = new oak;   // Look at this one carefully!

yardtree->saytree();
delete yardtree;
}
```

When this version of the program runs, you receive three messages on the system display:

```
This tree is an oak.
Releasing leaf storage.
Bye, bye!
```

You should draw two conclusions from this demonstration. First, because the destructor function names for the base class and derived classes are not the same (but the technique still works), the destructor of a class derived from a class with a virtual destructor is *always* virtual. The function names don't matter here.

Second, you should notice that messages from both destructors appeared, although all access was through a base class pointer. They appeared in the correct order, too. Because the base constructor was called first, the base class *destructor* was called last.

Exercises

Derived classes are the essence of C++ object-oriented programming. The following exercises give you a chance to create and manipulate C++ derived classes:

1. Pick a simple type of object and write a class for it. Then reuse the object first by composition with another class and then by deriving another class from it.

2. Create a hierarchy of derived classes, each having a single base class (in other words, do not use multiple inheritance). Create an object of the derived class, using new, to get a pointer to it. Experiment with casting the derived class pointer to the various base class pointer types. Look carefully for such behavior as the slicing copy, which was discussed in this chapter.

3. Create another hierarchy of derived classes, this time using multiple base classes. Perform the same experiments on this class that you did in the preceding exercise.

4. Prove to yourself that virtual functions actually do what they are advertised to do. You can use pointer casts to test execution paths into the

derived class objects you create. You can do the same thing with virtual base classes, by using the `sizeof` operator to measure the size of the resulting objects compared to those created without virtual base classes. Hint: Member functions don't contribute to the size of a class object, so be sure to include member data objects in all classes for this test.

Summary

Class derivation and virtual functions (through which C++ implements its brand of polymorphism) are considered by most C++ programmers to be the essence of object-oriented programming. These features of the C++ language also supply some of its most powerful features. This chapter covered the following important points:

- ■ *C++ class code can be reused by class composition and by class derivation.* Class composition involves declaring an object of one class within another class. Composition allows code reuse with no modifications to existing code. Class derivation involves telling the compiler to create a new class that is just like the old class, with a few changes. Class derivation allows code reuse with stringently controlled changes to existing code.

- ■ *A derived class can be defined with only one base class.* Derivation using only one base class is also called *single inheritance.* Single inheritance allows the construction of hierarchies of derived classes, as long as every derived class has only one base.

- ■ *A derived class can be defined with multiple base classes.* Derivation using multiple base classes is also called *multiple inheritance.* You can build hierarchies of derived classes with multiple base classes.

- ■ *Virtual functions guarantee selection of the correct member function when identical function types appear under derivation.* The virtual function facility will select the correct member function for execution even when a pointer to a derived class object is cast to a pointer to a base class object. The ability to select among multiple functions at run time based on execution context is called *polymorphism* (also called *late binding*).

- ■ *Virtual base classes eliminate duplicate base class subobjects.* Using virtual base classes does more than reduce the size of derived class objects: It also helps to eliminate possible ambiguity and confusion.

- ■ *Abstract classes are used to define concepts rather than objects.* An abstract class must have at least one pure virtual function. Although you can never use an abstract class to create a class object directly, you can directly call a pure virtual function defined within an abstract class (assuming that the pure virtual function has a function body).

■ *Class initialization code requires special handling under derivation.* Class constructors and destructors are called in a specific, predictable order under derivation that may affect the way you design your classes. It is very important to remember that initialization code is not inherited. You can, however, define virtual destructor functions. It is often wise to do so.

If you don't feel comfortable yet with single inheritance and multiple inheritance, virtual functions and virtual base classes, abstract classes and pure virtual functions, and object construction and destruction under derivation, don't feel bad—these are tough subjects. By all means, go back and review if you need to, but don't let this part of C++ get by you.

Object Control and Performance Issues

This chapter wraps up the discussion of Microsoft C/C++ object-oriented programming by considering a collection of miscellaneous topics related to C++. These topics are of interest to all C++ programmers; however, some are difficult to group logically in other chapters. This chapter discusses the following:

- *User-defined type conversions.* Type conversions have been mentioned in other contexts in this book. This chapter reviews conversion methods and looks more closely at user-defined conversion functions implemented as class typecast operators.

- *Generic classes and class abstraction.* You used generic classes when you wrote parameterized C++ stream manipulators (see Chapter 16, "Using C++ Streams"). Now you will see how the techniques for using generic classes work so that you can design and use your own generic classes.

- *Class object performance and friend functions.* You can use friend functions to increase object performance as well as class flexibility. Now you find out why this is so. You also learn when to use friend functions to increase performance.

- *Use of the Source Browser function.* The source Browser function is a built-in feature of the PWB that can help you locate functions and symbol definitions, and help you understand the structure of your program.

The following sections occasionally mention the quad sample class. The quad class implements higher-precision integers by using an array of two long int variables (plus two more for work and overflow area). The complete source file listings for the quad class and its test driver program are in Appendix D. Some of the code from the quad class source files is repeated here as needed.

User-Defined Type Conversions

Without the capability to convert other types to a class type, C++ would not be a very useful language. A moment's reflection on the plain C programs you write show you that implicit and explicit conversions are used frequently in normal code. The same is true of programming with classes.

The two primary types of class-related conversion techniques were mentioned in previous chapters without focusing on the conversion processes themselves. You can convert other types to a class type in two ways: by using class constructor functions and by writing user-defined conversion functions (overloaded cast operator functions).

Using Constructors to Convert Types

When you declare a class object, you usually expect to be able to provide initialization data for that object at the same time. You already know about writing object declarations with constructor function arguments. It is possible to write constructors that accept argument lists containing many parameters. In the special case in which a constructor function accepts a single argument, the constructor is said to specify a conversion from the argument type to the class type.

In addition to the default and copy constructors, the quad class contains two constructors that convert their arguments to the class type. The declarations in the header file (quadword.hpp) for those constructors are

```
quad( long );
quad( int );
```

These declarations enable you to declare quad objects with a constructor type conversion like this:

```
int a;
long b;
...
quad qobj1( a );
quad qobj2( b );
```

These declarations are simple C++ code: There is nothing here that you have not already seen. Another syntax that is not so obvious, however, is equivalent to the preceding code fragment. You can also write the following:

```
int a;
long b;
...
quad qobj1 = a;
quad qobj2 = b;
```

Although the assignment operator is used in this code fragment, an over-loaded operator=() function is not invoked. Instead, the constructor function is called immediately, as though you had specified the first form of declaration, because the last two lines are object declarations.

Even if the class has what seems to be an applicable operator=() function, it will never be used for an object declaration that invokes constructor type conversion. The quad class does have an assignment operator function, de-clared as follows:

```
quad& operator=( char* );
```

Nevertheless, the following short program misuses the class constructor and assignment functions and does not compile:

```
#include <stdlib.h>
#include <stdio.h>

#include "quadword.hpp"

void main()
{
  quad X = "Hello!";

  printf( "%s\n", (char*)X );
}
```

If you try to compile this short program, you get an error message stating that the compiler cannot find a matching declaration for the called function quad::quad(char*). No such constructor function exists, and there is no search for any other function.

Conceptually, the assignment of a string to a quad class object is very much a conversion task. You may find the conversion of a string to a numeric quantity interesting; look at this code for the operator=() member function for the quad class:

```
quad& quad::operator=( char *s )
{
  int neg, i;
  if ( *s == '-' ) {
    neg = 1; s++;
  }
  else neg = 0;
  *this = 0;
  while ( *s ) {
    *this = *this * 10;      // Shift previous result left
    *this += (int)( *s++ - '0' ); // next partial product
  }
  if ( neg ) {          // Simulate 2's complement negation
    vdata[0] = ~vdata[0];
    vdata[1] = ~vdata[1];
    *this += 1;
  }
  return *this;
}
```

This function operates by stepping through the source string one character at a time and subtracting an ASCII '0' character from each input character. The subtraction converts each digit from a display character to a signed char. Then as the previously developed result is shifted left out of the way, the new digit is simply added to the accumulating result. Finally, if the program detects a minus sign at the beginning of a string, it negates the result using two's complement logic.

Although assignment operators do perform a conversion task, you should remember that assignment syntax does not cause the compiler to convert constant or data types at compile time: Your assignment operator function does it at runtime.

Overloading Typecast Operators

Other than using conversion by constructor function, you can convert other data types to your class type only by writing assignment operator functions (or explicit conversion functions—you could declare an inttoquad(int) function, for example). But, how can you convert your class type to another data type? Neither conversion technique discussed in the preceding section addresses that question.

Converting an object from your class type to another data type (including another class type) is a job for a user-defined conversion function, more descriptively called a *user-defined cast operator function.* The following short program shows the basic method of defining a class cast operator function:

```cpp
#include <iostream.h>

class A {
  int dat;
public:
  A( int num = 0 ) : dat( num ) {}
  operator int() { return dat; }
};

class X {
  int dat;
public:
  X( int num = 0 ) : dat( num ) {}
  operator int() { return dat; }     // castop to int
  operator A() {                     // castop to class A
    A temp = dat;
    return temp;
  }
};

void main()
{
  X stuff = 37;
  A more = 0;

  int hold;

  hold = (int)stuff;
  cout << hold << endl;

  more = (A)stuff;        // convert X::stuff to A::more
  hold = (int)more;       // convert A::more to int
  cout << hold << endl;
}
```

As the preceding short program demonstrates, cast operator functions are declared using the following syntax:

operator *typename* *$_{opt}$();

You can convert your class object to another object type as specified by *typename*, or to a pointer to *typename*. The preceding short program illustrates also that a cast operator function must return an object of the specified type (or a pointer to such an object if the indirection operator was used).

User-defined cast operator functions have these additional requirements and characteristics:

- *Cast operator functions must be nonstatic member functions.* These functions cannot be friend functions, nor can they be declared static.

- *The target type of the conversion cannot be an enumeration or a `typedef` name.* The reason for this restriction is obvious: Because enumerations and `typedef`s are not objects, you cannot return one from the conversion function.

- *You cannot specify a return type.* The type of the object to be returned is given by the target type name, and thus cannot be specified again.

- *You cannot declare arguments for a cast operator function.* Function arguments for a conversion function are irrelevant. It is assumed that the function is dealing with `*this` as input. No other inputs are allowed because a cast operator is considered a unary operator acting on your class object.

- *User-defined cast expressions can be used anywhere an ordinary cast is syntactically allowed.* If you have defined the greater-than operator (>) for your class, for example, you can write an expression like this:

```
class X { ... };
...
X a, b;
...
int biggest = ( a > b ) ? a : b;   // Pick the "largest"
```

- *Cast operator functions are inherited, and they can be virtual functions.* Nothing prevents the inheritance of a cast operator function, because by definition it deals only with data members from its own subobject type. Allowing cast operator functions to be virtual makes even more sense because cast operator functions depend on being bound to the correct subobject type.

- *User-defined cast operator functions are invoked implicitly if the conversion is not ambiguous and if the containing expression requires such a conversion.* Your cast operators are not "second-class citizens": They are invoked implicitly if expression syntax requires it, exactly as is done for basic (predefined) C types when conversion is indicated.

- *Only one cast operator function can be implicitly applied to a class object.* Plain C numeric types may undergo both conversion and promotion during expression evaluation; however, your cast operator functions are not repetitively applied to a class object. This rule does not mean that the result of your cast operator function cannot be converted or promoted again. If you cast a class X object to int, for example, the resulting int still can be promoted to long if the expression containing it requires such promotion. Furthermore, this rule does not prevent you from explicitly casting several times in one expression. For example, suppose that you have declared classes A, B, and C, and created a C object. Then, if you have written all the required cast operator functions, you could write:

```
C cobj;
...
A aobj = (A)(B)cobj;
```

■ *Cast operator functions cannot be overloaded.* If there is neither return type nor signature (as is the case here), a mangled function name cannot be developed, and overloading is impossible.

■ *A cast operator function in a derived class hides a cast operator function in its base class only if the target type is exactly the same.* This characteristic was mentioned and explained in Chapter 17, "Using C++ Derived Classes," but it is repeated here for completeness.

Cast operators can be designed in imaginative and useful ways. You have seen cast operator functions used to report errors in class states (the void* cast in stream, extended memory, and swap buffer classes). The most common and important use of cast operator functions, however, is changing data formats for input or output. For an example of this use of a cast operator function, look at this code for casting a quad class object to a string just before outputting a very long number:

```
static char outstr[81];
...
quad::operator char*()
{
  int neg, i;
  char *s, *p;
  quad VA = *this;

  s = outstr;
  if ( VA.vdata[1] & 0x80000000L ) {
    neg = 1;
    VA.vdata[0] = ~VA.vdata[0];
    VA.vdata[1] = ~VA.vdata[1];
    VA += 1;
  }
  else neg = 0;
  while( 1 ) {
    VA -= 10;
```

```
     if ( VA.vdata[1] & 0x80000000L ) break; // done
     VA += 10;
     *s++ = '0' + (int)( VA % 10 );
     VA = VA / 10;
  }
  VA += 10;                      // fixup from loop
  if ( (int)VA > 0 ) *s++ = (int)VA + '0';
  if ( neg ) *s++ = '-';
  *s = '\0'; // Terminate the string
  s = outstr;
  p = s + strlen( s ) - 1;
  while ( p > s ) {  // Reverse the string
    *s ^= *p; *p ^= *s; *s++ ^= *p--;
  }
  return outstr;
}
```

The technique for converting a quad number to a string is simple in concept: Continuously divide the number by 10, and take the remainder as the next output digit. When the number becomes less than 10, that is the last digit; no further division is needed. Because this process develops the output string backward, you must reverse the string as the last step.

Using Generic Classes

In Chapter 16, you read about stream applicator classes and learned about parameterized types for stream manipulators. That's quite a mouthful, and the implementation of such things is equally complicated. Still, the techniques briefly described in Chapter 16 are important as a foundation for future language developments. This section discusses the more general theory behind parameterized types.

The applicator classes in Chapter 16 were instances of control abstraction put into practice. The sample code in this chapter primarily involves type abstraction. What are these things, and how do you put them into your programs? How do they relate to parameterized types? Before you can answer these questions, you must begin to shift your thinking toward the realm of abstract, generalized program design.

Understanding Abstraction and Generic Class Design

When you were reading about parameterized manipulators for stream classes, you were learning how to devise a generalized approach to writing stream manipulators. There are only a handful of stream classes, but you can endlessly create parameterized manipulators.

The particular approach chosen in Chapter 16 for implementing parameterized manipulators seemed complicated, but that was due to the indirection of references required by generalizing the process. Parameterized manipulators of all kinds have much in common, differing from one another in internal details but not in syntax. In other words, manipulators involve classes that are only trivial variations on a single theme.

This situation means that you can generalize the method of implementing a set of similar facilities. You can best understand the idea of generalizing your code by thinking about generalized types, particularly class types. Class code that can be applied to a variety of different (but closely related) data types is said to be *generic*. The process of designing and writing generic classes is called *type abstraction*.

You have already started moving toward generic classes by using class derivation and virtual functions. With a little more thought and effort, you can further generalize your classes without using any new techniques. You can do it by carefully designing a base class, such as a class for maintaining lists, and then creating trivial derivations from the generalized (but not yet generic) base class. Listing 18.1 shows a LIST base class and the derivation of a LIST_String class. To simplify the example, the LIST base class provides member functions only for adding, deleting, and extracting list elements. The responsibility for displaying the list is shifted to the derived classes (LIST_String here).

Listing 18.1. genlist.cpp. A generalized LIST base class.

```
1   #include <string.h>
2   #include <iostream.h>
3
4   class LIST {
5     void* (*PtrList)[16]; // pointer to array of pointers
6     int Item;
7   public:
8     LIST() {
9       Item = -1;
```

Listing 18.1. Continued.

```
10       PtrList = (void* (*)[16] ) new (void*)[16];
11    }
12    virtual ~LIST() { delete PtrList; }
13    virtual void Add( void* Elem, size_t Size ) {
14      ++Item;
15      if ( Item == 16 ) return;
16      (*PtrList)[Item] = new char[Size];
17      memmove( (*PtrList)[Item], Elem, Size );
18    }
19    virtual void Delete() {
20      if ( Item < 0 ) return;
21      delete (*PtrList)[Item];
22      --Item;
23    }
24   void* GetItem( int Elem = 0 ) {
25     if ( Elem > Item ¦¦ Elem < 0 )
26       return NULL;
27     else return (*PtrList)[Elem];
28   }
29 };
30
31 typedef char* String; // typedefs for use in names
32 typedef int   Int;
33
34 size_t Size_String( String argument ) {
35   return strlen( argument ) + 1;
36 }
37 void Show_String( String argument ) {
38   cout << argument << endl;
39 }
40
41
42 class LIST_String : public LIST {
43   size_t (*ObjSize)(String);
44   void   (*Show)(String);
45 public:
46   LIST_String() {
47     ObjSize = Size_String;
48     Show = Show_String;
49   }
```

```
50    ~LIST_String();
51    void Add( String arg ) {
52      LIST::Add( (void*)arg, ObjSize( arg ) );
53    }
54    void Delete() {
55      LIST::Delete();
56    }
57    void Display();
58  };
59
60  LIST_String::~LIST_String() {  // out-of-line because of loop
61    while ( GetItem(0) ) Delete();
62  }
63
64  void LIST_String::Display() {  // out-of-line because of loop
65    int i = 0;
66
67    while ( GetItem(i) ) {
68      Show( (String)GetItem(i) );
69      ++i;
70    }
71  }
72
73  void main()
74  {
75    int i;
76    LIST_String X;
77
78    for ( i=0; i<16; ++i ) X.Add( "Hello" );
79    X.Display();
80  }
```

Both the LIST base class and the derived LIST_String classes in Listing 18.1 have features dictated by the design decision to generalize the base class to allow simple derivation of other types. Most notably, a void pointer in the base class is used to locate a list of pointers outside the object's boundaries. Each of these pointers in turn locates an unspecified data area that will be dynamically acquired.

Using void pointers in this manner allows a fair degree of generalization. The trade-off, however, is some added complexity in forming expressions dealing with pointers. In line 5, the base pointer for the list is written like this:

```
void* (*PtrList)[16]; // pointer to array of pointers
```

because the higher operator precedence of the subscript operator (`[]`) would otherwise have forced the interpretation of the expression as *array of 16 void pointers to pointer* rather than *pointer to array of 16 pointers*. Similarly, you have to use a peculiar pointer cast to get the pointer value returned from `new` to cooperate with your syntax, as follows (see line 10):

```
PtrList = (void* (*)[16] ) new (void*)[16];
```

Because `PtrList` has type `void*(*)[16]`, you must use parentheses to access a single pointer in the list. Because the resulting expression, `(*PtrList)[Item]`, refers to a pointer, you may be tempted to refer to a data area by writing `*(*PtrList)[Item]`. However, that expression is illegal: You cannot dereference a `void` pointer. You would first have to cast the pointer extracted from the list to another type (`int*`, for example).

Next, notice the arrangement of virtual functions in the base and derived classes in Listing 18.1. The `Add()` and `Delete()` base class member functions are made virtual to allow for future development of the classes into something more significant than sample code. The virtual destructors are quite important, however.

You can see in lines 60 through 62 that the derived class has the responsibility of stepping down the list and releasing memory for the data areas. The base class destructor (line 12) releases the array storage pointed to by `PtrList`. This arrangement allows the base class to remain as small and generalized as possible, but it places another burden on the class designer: Both the base and derived class destructors must execute, and they must execute in the correct order. The virtual destructors guarantee the correct execution of the destructor code.

Now reflect for a moment on the usefulness of writing generalized classes in this manner. Is it useful? Yes, but only in a restricted way. A generalized base class is good as far as it goes, but it requires that you design and code trivial derivations individually, for every type of list (in this case) you want to implement. Furthermore, it does not smooth the path of another programmer who may need to derive classes from the generalized base; that programmer will have to know something about the internal logistics required by the base class, and will have to spend time developing his or her own classes, as well.

It would be nice if you could write a single line of code, and specify a type parameter (sound familiar?), which automatically generates the desired type of class. It would be nice if also you could create objects of the new class without having to know internal naming schemes or structures. You can do both of these by writing generic classes and providing `declare()` and `implement()` macros for them. Generic classes are the subject of the next section.

Building Generic Classes

A generic class enables you to declare a parameterized type that generates a specific class declaration from the generic class. In the examples in this chapter, you develop a generic class named LIST, which you can use to declare specific classes such as LIST_String and LIST_Int by writing a single line of code (a macro call).

Building generic classes revolves around the ingenious use of the predefined token-pasting macros in the generic.h header. At this point, do not stop to inspect that header: Read a little further first, to get the outlines of the techniques required for building generic classes. The entire facility is founded on some powerful macros and can be confusing (because of the name indirection involved) if you begin by looking at implementation details. This chapter builds the details of those macros slowly, as you move through the discussion. You are introduced to three levels of concepts in this section:

- *How to use existing generic classes.* If you do not know what you want to do, understanding how you should go about it is difficult. Seeing generic classes in action is therefore the first order of business.

- *Writing the generic class itself.* A generic class is written as a single (large) function-like macro. Creating a generic class is simple (except for difficulties introduced by name indirection in the macros themselves) when you understand that one macro is at the bottom of it all.

- *Writing support macros and functions.* Some type-dependent activities require special handling (consider the difference between determining the length of a string and obtaining the size of an integer). Furthermore, because the generic class macro does not supply all the required user interfaces, you must write a few macros.

These three stages of developing concepts may remind you of the procedures in Chapter 16 for writing parameterized stream types. You do much the same thing in this chapter, using the same generic class facilities.

Look first, then, at Listing 18.2 to see how the LIST generic class is used in action. This program uses the generic class to declare and then use both LIST_String and LIST_Int classes. Note how easy it is to declare and implement a specific class using a generic base class. All the hard work is hidden at this level.

Listing 18.2. genlist2.cpp. Test drive the generic LIST class implementation.

```
1   #include "genlist.hpp"
2
3   // ------------------------------------------------------------
4   // The following macros declare classes for strings and ints.
5   // The declare macros generate more macros with the syntax
6   //   LISTdeclare(type)
7   // matching your own declaration macro in GENLIST.HPP.
8   // Notice that these macros must be used at file scope.
9   // ------------------------------------------------------------
10
11  declare(LIST, String)
12  declare(LIST, Int)
13
14  void main()
15  {
16    int i;
17    char Message[] = "Hello";
18
19
20    // ------------------------------------------------------------
21    // Now implement (instantiate) a LIST of strings.
22    // ------------------------------------------------------------
23
24    implement(LIST, String) X;  // Do it once for strings.
25
26    for ( i=0; i<16; ++i ) X.Add( Message );
27    X.Display();
28
29    implement(LIST, Int) I;     // Do it again for integers.
30
31    for ( i=0; i<16; ++i ) I.Add( i );
32    I.Display();
33  }
```

Two classes are declared in lines 11 and 12, one for a list of strings and one for a list of integers. The parameterized nature of the declarations is apparent. Both declarations depend on the LIST generic class. The comments bear important messages: The most important is that you should use the declare() macro only in file scope. This is because the macro generates a class declaration, which is illegal in block scope (inside main(), for example).

The comments indicate also that the declare() macro generates another macro before final expansion. The declare() macro is defined in generic.h; in this case it generates a token LISTdeclare(String), which is a macro you must define. The LISTdeclare(type) macro defines the generic class. You will see how to code it shortly.

The implement() macro is used to define a class object of the desired target type. It too is defined in generic.h and generates another token, LISTimplement(type). You must write a macro definition for this second name, as well. Because the implement() macro is used to instantiate an object, it can be used in block scope.

One of the main purposes of generic classes is to automate the production of trivial derivations from a base class. In these examples, the base class is BASELIST (renamed from the first version to avoid difficulties in naming macros). The BASELIST class is similar to the original LIST base class in Listing 18.1. In addition, the pointer manipulations in BASELIST are simplified (the macro construction has enough complexity for this example). BASELIST is shown in Listing 18.3.

Listing 18.3. listbase.hpp. The header containing the BASELIST base class.

```
1   #ifndef LISTBASE
2   #define LISTBASE
3
4   // ----------------------------------------------------------
5   // Base LIST class; not used alone
6   // ----------------------------------------------------------
7
8   class BASELIST {
9     char* PtrList[16];
10    int Item;
11  public:
12    BASELIST() {
13      int i;
14      Item = -1;
15    }
16    virtual ~BASELIST() {}
17    virtual void Add( char* Elem, size_t Size ) {
18      ++Item;
19      if ( Item == 16 ) return;
20      PtrList[Item] = new char[Size];
21      memmove( PtrList[Item], Elem, Size );
22    }
```

Listing 18.3. Continued.

```
23    virtual void Delete() {
24      if ( Item < 0 ) return;
25      delete PtrList[Item];
26      --Item;
27    }
28    char* GetItem( int Elem = 0 ) {
29      if ( Elem > Item ¦¦ Elem < 0 )
30        return NULL;
31      else return PtrList[Elem];
32    }
33  };
34
35  #endif
```

The BASELIST class is now contained in a header file to permit multiple uses of the LIST generic class code without introducing multiple declarations of the BASELIST class. Otherwise, it is essentially the same as before. Pointers to the unspecified data areas for list items now have type char*. This was done to simplify and speed debugging. Debugging a program heavily populated with macros is often necessary and difficult. Be prepared.

Now the fun can begin. The generic LIST class must be defined, according to the second step of development. This is done by coding a LISTdeclare() function-like macro. The generic class macro definition, together with support macros, is shown in Listing 18.4.

Listing 18.4. genlist.hpp. The header file for the generic LIST class implementation.

```
1   #ifndef GENLIST
2   #define GENLIST
3
4   #include <string.h>
5   #include <iostream.h>
6
7   // -----------------------------------------------------------
8   // Be sure to include generic.h.
9   // And do not forget LISTBASE.
10  // -----------------------------------------------------------
11
```

```
12  #include <generic.h>
13  #include "listbase.hpp"
14
15  // -----------------------------------------------------------
16  // Typedefs and helper macros for the generic LIST classes
17  // -----------------------------------------------------------
18
19  typedef char* String;
20  typedef int   Int;
21
22  #define Size_String(arg) strlen( arg ) + 1
23  #define Show_String(arg) cout << (String)arg << endl
24  #define AdrsOf_String(arg) (char*)arg
25
26  #define Size_Int(arg) sizeof(arg)
27  #define Show_Int(arg) cout << *(Int*)arg << endl
28  #define AdrsOf_Int(arg) (char*)&arg
29
30  // -----------------------------------------------------------
31  // Macros for developing specific names from generic names
32  // -----------------------------------------------------------
33
34  #define SIZE(type) _Paste2(Size_, type)
35  #define SHOW(type) _Paste2(Show_, type)
36  #define LIST(type) _Paste2(LIST_, type)
37  #define ADRS(type) _Paste2(AdrsOf_, type)
38
39  // -----------------------------------------------------------
40  // Declare macro for generic LIST classes.
41  // -----------------------------------------------------------
42
43  #define LISTdeclare(type)                          \
44  class LIST(type) : public BASELIST {               \
45  public:                                            \
46    ~LIST(type)();                                   \
47    void Add( type arg ) {                           \
48      BASELIST::Add( ADRS(type)(arg), SIZE(type)(arg) );  \
49    }                                                \
50    void Delete() {                                  \
51      BASELIST::Delete();                            \
52    }                                                \
53    void Display();                                  \
```

Listing 18.4. Continued.

```
54   };                                              \
55                                                   \
56   LIST(type)::~LIST(type)() {                     \
57     while ( GetItem(0) ) Delete();                \
58   }                                               \
59                                                   \
60   void LIST(type)::Display() {                    \
61     int i = 0;                                    \
62                                                   \
63     while ( GetItem(i) ) {                        \
64       SHOW(type)(GetItem(i));                     \
65       ++i;                                        \
66     }                                             \
67   }
68
69   #define LISTimplement(type) _Paste2(LIST_, type)
70
71   #endif
```

The generic LIST class macro is defined in lines 43 through 67 of Listing 18.4.
Again, the entire generic class definition is one macro. That is why the
backslash continuation character (\) is used on all lines of the macro except
the last line.

Line 43 is the prototype part of the macro declaration. It consists of a preprocessing token composed of the generic class name (LIST) and the declare
constant token, followed by the formal argument in parentheses. The formal
argument is named type because during macro invocation the argument will be
a type name. (typedef was used to define String in this file to simplify the
handling of the char* type.) The discussion of Listing 18.2 mentioned that the
declare() macro is expanded into another macro: LISTdeclare(type) is that
macro. Figure 18.1 shows the progressive expansion of the declare() macro
into a usable class declaration in your program.

The LISTdeclare() macro contains the class declaration body, but there are
support macros wherever a type-dependent name is required. How are specific names built from generic ones in the generic class definition macro? You
use the _Pastex macros defined in generic.h to write the support macros, and
build them from the type name argument pasted to the generic class name.

Four support macros are used for this purpose in genlist.hpp in Listing 18.4:
the SIZE, SHOW, LIST, and ADRS macros, in lines 34 through 37. The LIST support
macro is used only to construct the specific derived class name. Thus, coding
a declare(LIST,String) macro invocation expands line 44 to LIST_String.

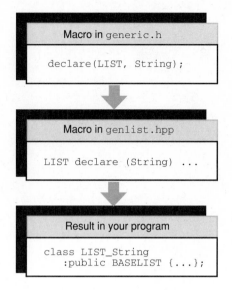

Figure 18.1.

Expansion of the **declare()** macro when declaring a specific class using generic class definitions.

The remaining three support macros in this first group deal with type-dependent operations. For example, the SIZE(String) macro call expands to an expression using the strlen() function (see line 22), and the SIZE(Int) macro call expands to an expression using the sizeof operator (see line 26).

In looking at these first four support macros, you can see clearly how name indirection is compounded when you are building generic classes. The SHOW(String) macro call used in line 64, for example, expands to another macro name, Show_String, which is defined in line 23 (that expansion performs the display operation). The Show_String macro is one of a group of similar macros in lines 22 through 28 that form the next layer of support macros to be expanded. The generic LIST class definition does not use this second group of macros directly but are invoked as a result of expanding a macro from the first group, or layer.

The proliferation of name indirection in layers of macros can be confusing, but such indirection is necessary to build abstract type definitions. This is particularly true because some degree of control abstraction is required to achieve generality. To see why, look at the generic LIST(type)::Display() member function implementation:

```
60  void LIST(type)::Display() {                    \
61    int i = 0;                                    \
62                                                   \
63    while ( GetItem(i) ) {                         \
64      SHOW(type)(GetItem(i));                      \
65      ++i;                                         \
66    }                                              \
67  }
```

Notice that line 64 uses the SHOW(type) macro in the LISTdeclare() macro to generate the correct output statements. The only indication that a type dependency might be in this function is the use of the formal argument type. Why go to such lengths to avoid type-specific code in the generic class? In other words, why not rewrite line 64 as follows to simplify the output statements:

```
SHOW(type)((type*)GetItem(i));
```

You should avoid the temptation to perform the pointer cast to the correct type at this point in the code. The reason is that if you do not move type-dependent code outside the generic class and into the support macros and functions (in other words, abstract the control functions for the class), you may lose control of the internal interfaces to the generic class.

Specifically, you can define several Show_type macros for the LIST generic class. Because of the way this class is designed, all these macros expect to receive a void pointer to the object they will display, and to cast the pointer to the correct type for themselves. If the Display() function has already performed the cast (and possibly even dereferenced the pointer), there is no common protocol for invoking a Show_type macro. That is not much of a problem in the simple LIST class presented here, but code for production is often much more complicated.

Alternatively, you could write the necessary macro logic directly into the LISTdeclare() macro for all possible types (you should either do it or not, but be consistent—macro debugging can be tough). The drawback to this approach is that you will have to perform some fancy footwork with #if conditional logic, and that will require more #define support macros. You are already dealing with a complicated macro structure. Why make it worse?

Thus, it is better to abstract type-dependent statements or declarations into support macros. It will make your life easier, even if you must write a few more lines of code. Moreover, macros are generally the best method of dealing with abstracted logic. There are two reasons for using macros rather than functions in a generic class definition wherever possible: to simplify the resulting compilable code, and to increase the performance of the final product.

As a rule of thumb, try to design your macros so that the resulting compilable code is as simple as possible. Otherwise, you may lose control of the coding process. For example, the Show_type macros could have been implemented as functions rather than as macros. In that case, the SHOW(type) macros would have been expanded into functions rather than inline code. That is fine for displaying data, because the output does not depend on the location of the data to be displayed. The ADRS(type) macros are a different story, however.

Consider what happens if you define the ADRS(type) macros to expand into function calls. You pass a copy of the argument to the support function, which takes the argument's address at its stack location rather than at its original location, and returns the erroneous address to the caller. Trying to use an `auto` variable after its owner function has gone out of scope is a classic error. You won't get away with it in the `LIST` generic class because the `PtrList` array assumes that it is pointing to objects that stay put long enough to use them.

Designing `ADRS(type)` to expand to a support macro has the opposite and accurate effect. The resulting compilable code will contain the proper reference to the argument name substituted for the macro call. Not only does this design work much better, it also localizes the code to the class member function that uses it. You must keep in mind the difference between preprocessing time and compile time. Although several macros are used in this example, dispersed throughout the generic class definition, the final result is one line of inline code to be compiled.

That last comment leads to the second reason for using support macros rather than support functions. Inline statements run faster (sometimes much faster) than function calls. You will often find that type-dependent statements, which must be abstracted from the generic code, require only trivial support functions consisting of one or two lines of code in the function body. Repetitive calls to trivial functions greatly increase runtime overhead, and there is no point in deliberately designing an inefficient program.

The last support macro to discuss in this section is the `LISTimplement(type)` macro. Just as generic.h for `declare()` has a macro definition that expands into a macro call of `LISTdeclare(type)` (in the example), generic.h has an `implement()` macro. The `implement()` macro similarly expands into a macro call for `LISTimplement(type)` (again using the example's name), and you must define this last macro. Thus, when users of your `LIST` generic class want to create a `LIST` of integers named `ilist`, they can simply write:

```
implement(LIST, Int) ilist;
```

The macro definition in generic.h expands this macro call into another macro call, resulting in this statement:

```
LISTimplement(Int) ilist;
```

Finally, the macro definition in genlist.hpp expands the new macro call into compilable code:

```
LIST_Int ilist;  // This statement creates a LIST_Int object
```

These macro manipulations make using generic classes seem like going around the block just to get next door. The complexity of the macros is probably the major drawback of using generic classes. Automating the derivation of repetitive and similar classes from a common base is not nearly as advanced as it could be, given more compiler support. Yet the macro preprocessing facility can get you a long way down the road to automation: The task of abstracting type-specific logic and names from the class declaration will remain for the programmer, even with more advanced compiler support.

Generic classes do serve a purpose, however, and can make life easier for the users of these classes, if not for their designers. Generic classes provide support for parameterized typing and help you avoid coding multiple trivial derivations. Perhaps most important, generic classes are all you have until later releases of C++ provide true parameterized types in the form of class templates. One of the reasons this discussion has been presented is to prepare you for the discussion of class templates later in this chapter. In the meantime, to use your generic classes, users need to know only how to use the `declare()` and `implement()` macros, the generic class name, and the interfaces to the classes you provide (that is, the callable functions and their arguments).

Controlling Object Behavior and Performance

You can wander into many dark corners while writing C++ programs unless you take the time to reflect on the significance of the programming tools you are using—how they affect expression evaluation, how they use storage, and what resources they use to get their assigned tasks done. This section explores issues that deal with class object behavior and performance. The issues discussed here are an example of the kind of thinking you need to do when you design and write C++ programs.

Using Friend Functions to Boost Efficiency

Friend functions are an important part of your toolkit for crafting C++ programs, and you should understand what they will and will not do for your programs.

You can use friend functions to increase the efficiency (speed) of your class objects. It is easy to imagine that defining a class support function as a friend rather than as a member could increase the class's efficiency simply because it reduces the class object's size. If that were the case, you could pass objects by value on the stack, for example, with less overhead in the movement of data.

But that is not the case. Because neither friend functions nor member functions are physically part of a Microsoft C/C++ class object, defining a function as a friend makes little difference in object size. You can use CodeView to see that there is no difference internally in the number of machine instructions required to access a class object for friends and members. Figure 18.2 proves this point. The figure shows the assembler code used to access a single object, once by a friend and once by a member. The instruction streams are almost identical.

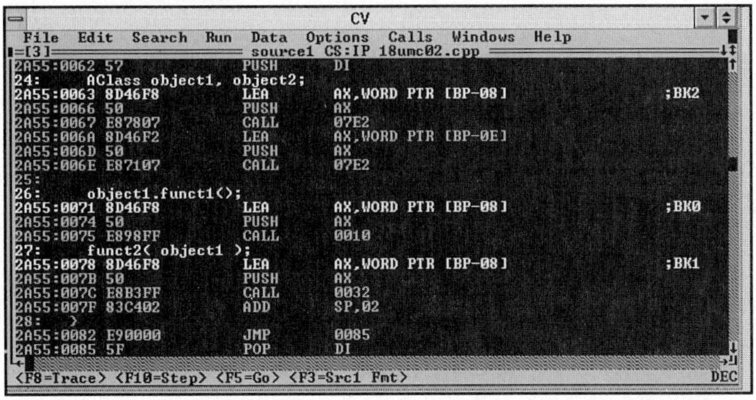

```
                                 CV                          ▼ ⬍
  File  Edit  Search  Run  Data  Options  Calls  Windows  Help
 =[3]=========================== source1 CS:IP 18umc02.cpp ===========⬍‡
 2A55:0062 57            PUSH     DI                                    ⬆
 24:     AClass object1, object2;
 2A55:0063 8D46F8        LEA      AX,WORD PTR [BP-08]              ;BK2
 2A55:0066 50            PUSH     AX
 2A55:0067 E87807        CALL     07E2
 2A55:006A 8D46F2        LEA      AX,WORD PTR [BP-0E]
 2A55:006D 50            PUSH     AX
 2A55:006E E87107        CALL     07E2
 25:
 26:     object1.funct1();
 2A55:0071 8D46F8        LEA      AX,WORD PTR [BP-08]              ;BK0
 2A55:0074 50            PUSH     AX
 2A55:0075 E898FF        CALL     0010
 27:     funct2( object1 );
 2A55:0078 8D46F8        LEA      AX,WORD PTR [BP-08]              ;BK1
 2A55:007B 50            PUSH     AX
 2A55:007C E8B3FF        CALL     0032
 2A55:007F 83C402        ADD      SP,02
 28:     }
 2A55:0082 E90000        JMP      0085
 2A55:0085 5F            POP      DI                                    ⬇
 <F8=Trace> <F10=Step> <F5=Go> <F3=Src1 Fmt>                      DEC
```

Figure 18.2.

Machine instructions required by friends of a class to access its objects are almost the same as the instructions required by members.

So what can friend functions do to increase performance? Perhaps the most important aspect of using friends for performance is that they have access to all class members, including private ones. Thus, a friend function can be used as an interface to a class object in a direct manner. One such friend function might replace several otherwise required member functions designed to provide a generalized user interface. You should use friends when you are tempted to write a global function as part of the programming interface to your class objects.

When you use friend functions (where possible) to provide programming interfaces to your classes, you reduce the number of function calls. Function calls can be surprisingly expensive in processing time, especially when you make them frequently. Reducing their number almost always leads to noticeable increases in the performance of your code.

Using the *static* Storage Class to Avoid Repetitive Instantiation

This section deals with another aspect of evaluating expressions that contain class objects: the need for temporary objects, and the effect this has on class performance (in terms of speed rather than syntax). To understand why you might need a temporary object during expression evaluation, think of an operator as something that has inputs (its operands), and an output (the resulting object or value). The catch is that the output of an operator may or may not be one of the inputs.

This view of an operator as something that has a target destination (an output) leads to a conceptual grouping of all the operators your class will use: Some operators have a unary effect, whereas some have a binary effect. An operator in either category can use either a member function or a friend function (except assignment, which requires a nonstatic member function), depending on the syntactical flexibility you require. The unary or binary effect of an operator has a bearing on both the operator's return type and its need for an internal temporary holding object, as follows:

■ *Operators with a unary effect produce a result that replaces the value of the left operand object.* For example, in an expression such as ++i, the value of i is incremented and put back into i. Operator functions with a unary effect typically return a reference to the modified operand (usually *this) after modifying its value. Further, these operator functions usually do not require the use of a temporary class object in the operator function body, because they modify the operand contents. Other operators in this class include unary plus and minus, and the compound assignment operators (for example, += and -=). Simple assignment is also in this category because the operator function modifies its left operand; however, the operator function must be a member function rather than a friend, because the left operand must be an lvalue.

■ *Operators with a binary effect produce a result that must not modify either operand.* This category of operators includes the remainder of the true binary operators. The addition operator, for example, must not modify either operand, but rather should return a value that can be used to further parse the complete expression containing it. Further, because the result must be held somewhere, operators with a binary effect typically require an internal temporary class object.

Creating local class objects to hold temporary results, as was done in the two preceding programs, takes time. When complex expressions are evaluated, your class's operator functions are called more often (operator functions are often the hardest-working functions in a class), so the time required for instantiating (creating) local temporaries can be high. Overhead devoted to temporary object control can be so time-consuming that some method usually is needed to control the amount of overhead time. One method is to assign a static storage class to internal temporary class objects.

A simple experiment will give you some idea of how much overhead you can save by declaring temporaries as static. A static object is created once, and then it is left alone. Listing 18.5 was designed to invoke the addition operator function frequently (it performs multiplication by repeated addition, which is not the usual method). The program in Listing 18.5 assigns the static attribute to temporary class objects. You may want to enter this program in the Programmer's WorkBench and compile and run it now to see what happens.

Listing 18.5. tempvar.cpp. Using the static storage class to prevent the unnecessary creation of temporary objects.

```cpp
1   #include <iostream.h>
2   #include <time.h>
3
4   class Int1 {
5     long value;
6   public:
7    Int1( long newval = 0 ) { value = newval; }
8    Int1& operator=( Int1& other ) {
9      value = other.value;
10     return *this;
11   }
12   Int1  operator+( Int1& rightop );
13   Int1  operator*( Int1& rightop );
14  };
15
16  Int1 Int1::operator+( Int1& rightop )
17  {
18    static Int1 SUM(0);
19
20    SUM.value = value + rightop.value;
21    return SUM;
22  }
23
24  Int1 Int1::operator*( Int1& rightop )
25  {
26    long i;
27    static Int1 ACCUM(0);
28
29    for ( i=0; i<rightop.value; ++i )
30      ACCUM = ACCUM + *this;
31    return ACCUM;
32  }
33
34  void main()
35  {
36    Int1 a(0), b(2), c(100000);
37
38    clock_t time0, time1;
39    double seconds;
```

Listing 18.5. Continued.

```
40
41    time0 = clock();
42    a = b * c;
43    time1 = clock();
44    seconds = (double)(time1-time0) / (double)CLK_TCK;
45    cout << seconds
46         << " seconds elapsed." << endl;
47  }
```

When the program in Listing 18.5 runs, it requires 2.7 seconds to complete the long-winded multiplication on a 386DX running at 25 MHz (normal methods of multiplying numbers would run with normal speeds). To see how much time is required to build auto class local temporaries, just remove the static key-word, and recompile and rerun the program. Building the temporaries now requires 2.802 seconds, a 37.8 percent increase in execution time.

There is a trade-off to using static class temporary objects: They increase the memory requirements of your program. In the preceding sample program, the cost in memory is not high. Because the quad class presented in Appendix D has many more temporary objects, the cost is higher. Even with the quad class, however, the cost is not too high, but it is something you should consider when you design class operator functions.

So far, the execution speed of the tempvar.cpp program has been improved by almost 40 percent, just by using the static storage class with temporary variables. Can you do better? Yes, you can, by using references.

Using References and Pointers

When the temporary object used in the previous operator+() functions was an auto class object, the object had to be returned by value: Other methods would not work (or even compile with Microsoft C/C++). Returning a result by value in this way means that intermediate results (such as an accumulating total) during the evaluation of an expression are copied back and forth to the stack. Intermediate results reside on the stack when temporary holding objects are auto.

In the next step (Listing 18.5), the temporary object was made static. That improved performance considerably for the example class, primarily because temporary object creation is mostly eliminated in the operator function. That step eliminated many free store allocations and constructor function calls.

As long as the temporary objects are static (so that they will not go away), and you understand completely what you are doing, you can go one step further: You can return results by reference so that intermediate values are not copied to the stack. Listing 18.6 shows the example program rewritten to do this.

Listing 18.6. tempvar2.cpp. Returning a temporary value by reference from an operator function.

```
1   #include <iostream.h>
2   #include <time.h>
3
4   class Int1 {
5     long value;
6   public:
7    Int1( long newval = 0 ) { value = newval; }
8    Int1& operator=( Int1& other ) {
9      value = other.value;
10     return *this;
11   }
12   Int1&  operator+( Int1& rightop );
13   Int1&  operator*( Int1& rightop );
14  };
15
16  Int1& Int1::operator+( Int1& rightop )
17  {
18    static Int1 SUM(0);
19
20    SUM.value = value + rightop.value;
21    return SUM;
22  }
23
24  Int1& Int1::operator*( Int1& rightop )
25  {
26    long i;
27    static Int1 ACCUM(0);
28
29    ACCUM.value = 0;
30    for ( i=0; i<rightop.value; ++i )
31      ACCUM = ACCUM + *this;
32    return ACCUM;
33  }
34
```

Listing 18.6. Continued.

```
35  void main()
36  {
37    Int1 a(0), b(2), c(100000);
38
39    clock_t time0, time1;
40    double seconds;
41
42    time0 = clock();
43    a = b * c;
44    time1 = clock();
45    seconds = (double)(time1-time0) / (double)CLK_TCK;
46    cout << seconds
47         << " seconds elapsed." << endl;
48  }
```

The use of references as the return type from the operator+() function elimi-nates much copying of objects to and from the stack. How much does it eliminate? The previous version of the program ran in about 2.03 seconds; this version runs in about 1.76 seconds. You have increased the speed of the operator+() function by another 14 percent.

You must be very careful when you return operator function values by refer-ence. Intermediate values are no longer on the stack; they are now in the static temporary variable for that operator. You must take care to ensure that the intermediate value is not destroyed accidentally. This is not as difficult to arrange as it might seem. Line 20 in Listing 18.6, for example, makes it look as though the previous value of SUM is being destroyed, but does not actually do so. Consider what happens when an expression such as a+b+c is evaluated.

First, the subexpression a+b is evaluated, using the operator+() function. The intermediate result is stored in SUM, and a reference to SUM is returned. That reference becomes the left operand in another call to operator+(), and c becomes the right operand. Thus, the operator+() function statement

```
SUM.value = value + rightop.value;
```

is, on this second pass through the function, equivalent to this statement:

```
SUM.value = SUM.value + rightop.value;
```

This statement is exactly what is needed to preserve the intermediate result and continue to accumulate the total value.

So far, you have been provided with a workable, high-performance operator+() function that can handle a chain of additions (a+b+c+...) without upsetting intermediate values. But how will using reference return types and static temporaries affect more complicated expressions such as a=b+c*c*c+b? First, the operator*() function must be reworked into something fitting for the real world, because it was deliberately rigged to take a long time. The following code fragment is the rewritten function:

```
Int1& Int1::operator*( Int1& rightop )
{
  long i;
  static Int1 ACCUM(0);

  ACCUM.value = value * rightop.value;
  return ACCUM;
}
```

Replace lines 24 through 33 of Listing 18.6 with the preceding lines. If you now compile and run the tempvar2.cpp program under CodeView, you discover two things. The a=b+c*c*c+b expression evaluates to the correct answer, and intermediate results are distributed among the temporary objects to which they belong.

That is, additive intermediate results reside in SUM, and multiplicative intermediate results reside in ACCUM. You need to do nothing further to the operator functions to make them work correctly in arbitrarily complex expression evaluations (assuming that you provided any other necessary operator functions).

Using Inline Functions to Eliminate Function Calls

In the tempvarx.cpp programs developed in this chapter, you may have noticed that the assignment operator function definition is written directly into the class declaration. When you write a member function definition in this way, it is implicitly considered to be an inline function. You can also explicitly request that a function body be expanded inline at the point where the function is called (something like a macro expansion) by using the inline keyword just before the function's return type specification.

If a function is expanded inline, all the overhead of a function call is eliminated. That could save considerable execution time for a function called frequently. The price, however, is a larger code segment in your program, particularly if the inline function is called in many different places.

Using inline functions involves some problems. You should write only the most trivial (very short) functions as inline functions because of the severe restrictions on the kinds of statements that can be in an inline function. For example, in the preceding examples, you cannot use the inline keyword with the operator+() function because static variables cannot be declared in an inline function.

Finally, Microsoft C/C++ regards the `inline` keyword as merely a suggestion, much as it does the `register` keyword. Even if you do explicitly declare a function `inline`, it may not be compiled as one. The `inline` keyword is recognized in only C++ programs; you can use the `inline` keyword in C (or C++) to accomplish the same goal with any function.

Is there anything more you can do to improve the performance of these operator classes? You can do one more thing, but it will help performance only very slightly. Because the temporary objects are declared static anyway, you might consider moving their declarations outside the member function body. In other words, make the temporary object a global object.

There are enough objections to this maneuver that it is probably not worthwhile. One objection is that now you must be sure that you do not attempt to declare (for other purposes) another class object with the same name. The temporary object is no longer protected or hidden by the class scope. Second, the internal integrity of the class has been compromised because the temporary object is now global. Any nonmember (or member) function can manipulate the temporary object, and destroy the validity of intermediate results.

Finally, because the object is static, it is created only once per program execution. Eliminating one constructor function call results in only a slight improvement in performance. If you are desperate to tune up your operator functions, however, you may still want to resort to this last-ditch option.

Using the Source Browser

Microsoft C/C+ 7.0 provides a *source browser,* a tool to help you locate your program's functions and variables, which is similar to but much more powerful and convenient to use than the **F**ind command. The browser shows you where your symbols are defined or used within your program source files. The browser also gives you views of your program in terms of which functions call other functions. For C++ programs, the browser can show you how your classes are related through derivation, and show which class is derived from other classes and a list of all class members, including those that are inherited.

You can always use the **S**earch menu's **F**ind command to locate a particular function or variable definition or use. The **F**ind command finds every occurrence of a symbol, however, including both its definition and where it is referenced. If, as in most programs, the symbol you are searching for is referenced in many locations, the **F**ind command stops at every line containing the symbol, and it may take a while to locate the symbol's definition.

The Browser, on the other hand, can jump directly to each function or variable definition. In conjunction with the compiler and a utility program named *bscmake,* the browser produces a separate index into your program so that you can quickly locate every symbol definition and reference.

To use the Browser, you must create first a browser database. To create the browser database, open your source program or project file. Assume that you've opened the array.cpp program from Chapter 14. Next, choose **B**rowse Options... from the **O**ptions menu. This step displays the Browse Options dialog box shown in Figure 18.3.

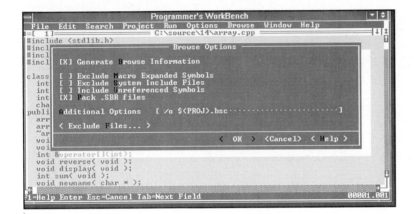

Figure 18.3.

The Browse Options dialog box.

Use the mouse or space bar to turn on the Generate **B**rowse Information checkbox item. By default, the browser database will include system definitions brought into your program from #include files. To disable inclusion of these symbols, select Exclude **S**ystem Include Files. You can use the Include **U**nreferenced Symbols item to help you locate functions and variables not used anywhere in your program. You can use this feature to reduce the total code and data memory requirements of your program.

To build the browser database, compile your program. Choose **R**ebuild All from the **P**roject menu. NMAKE automatically constructs the browser database. For array.cpp, this step produces a browser database file named array.bsc and a temporary file named array.sbr. If you are building a project, each source file in the project produces a corresponding .sbr file.

NOTE The .bsc file contains the source browser database for your application. The .sbr file is a temporary file used to hold information about each module. The .sbr files can be quite large. According to Microsoft, a typical .sbr file is approximately half the size of a preprocessed C source file. A preprocessed file has had all comments removed, but also includes #included header files.

For C++ applications, however, the .sbr files can easily grow to anywhere from 2 to 20 times larger than the original source file!

The .sbr files contain all symbols and their data types, including all those brought in from #include files, plus line numbers and other information.

The browser database file, ending in .bsc, is the union of all data contained in the .sbr files for the project. When the database is built, the .sbr data is moved into the .bsc database, and the original .sbr file's filesize is reset to 0. The date and time stamp on the .sbr file is used subsequently by the Make process to prevent rebuilding a database unless the data has changed. Because the date and time stamp of the .sbr file is useful to NMAKE, you may want to avoid deleting the sbr. files, even when they are zero length.

After the database has been constructed, put the browser to work using the **B**rowse menu of the PWB, shown in Figure 18.4.

Figure 18.4.

The PWB's **B**rowse menu.

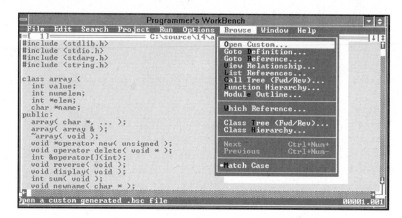

To locate a symbol's definition point, select Goto **D**efinition.... This step displays the screen shown in Figure 18.5. Scan through the Names list box to locate the symbol you want. The symbol's definition location is shown on the right. To go to the source line on which the symbol is defined, double-click the mouse on the symbol name or the location. This action returns you to the editor, with the cursor at the beginning of the line on which the symbol's definition is located.

To find where a symbol is used in your program, choose the Goto **R**eference... browse function. The Goto Reference dialog box is nearly identical to the Goto Definition dialog box: The difference is that this dialog box locates in your program's source files each point where the desired symbol is referenced (see Figure 18.6).

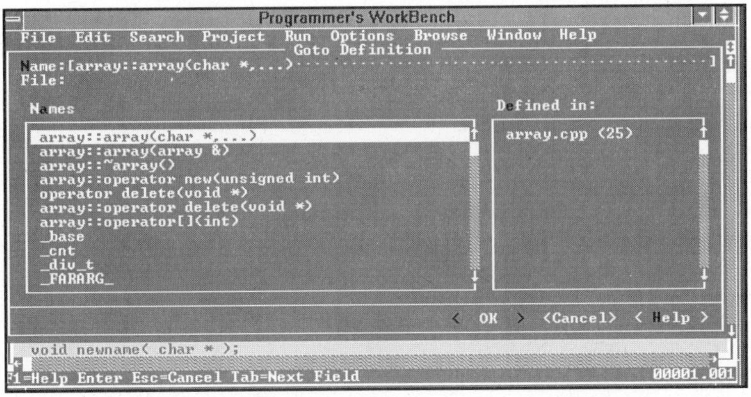

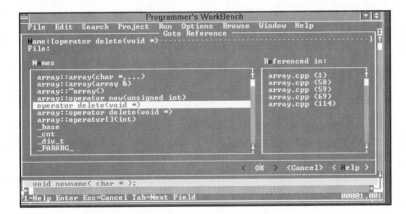

Figure 18.5.

The Goto **D**efinition... option of the browser lets you locate a symbol's definition. By finding the symbol in the **Na**mes list and reading the definition location beneath the **De**fined in: heading.

Figure 18.6.

The Goto **R**eference option locates each line on which a symbol is used inside your program.

Finding Unreferenced Symbols

To locate a function or variable not referenced in your program, you have to check the Include Unreferenced Symbols box on the Browse Options dialog box and rebuild your application (if this option was not selected already before the preceding build).

Next, select the **L**ist References... option from the **B**rowse menu. This action displays a dialog box. Be sure to select the options to show **F**unctions and **V**ariables, and then choose < OK >. The Browser displays a list of each function or variable, with a list of calling points to the right. Any variable or function that has no calling points listed is a symbol that is unreferenced in your program. This often happens in large programs, when through the course of program development you change your data and function requirements. Without a tool like the Browser, it's easy to lose track of code, and data items may no longer be needed.

Using the Call Tree

The Call Tree function displays information regarding which function calls other functions, or which function is called by other functions. When you select **C**all Tree, the PWB displays a Display Tree dialog box (not shown here). The dialog contains two list boxes, a Modules list box and a Functions list box. Use the Modules list box to choose a particular source module. As you scroll through the Modules list box, the Functions list displays all functions defined in that source module. Select a function and then choose < OK >. Figure 18.7 shows the browser output window with each function (or member function) name displayed. Indented under each function name is a list of all functions called from inside that function. In this format, the Browser is displaying a forward Call Tree.

In the *reverse* calling tree mode, you can select an individual function and see a list of all functions that call it. To select the reverse Call Tree, check the Reverse Tree box in the Display Tree dialog. Figure 18.7 shows a reverse tree for the strcpy function. Figure 18.8 shows that strcpy is called by the array constructor and the newname member function. Each of these, in turn, is called solely from the main function.

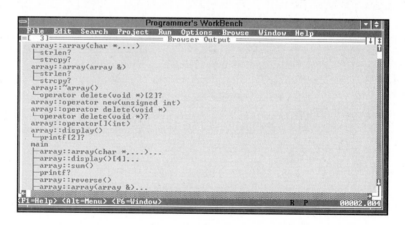

Use the Module Outline... option to display a list of all symbols defined in your program (see Figure 18.9). You can choose to show any combination of functions, variables, types, macros, or classes by selecting the appropriate checkboxes at the right side of the dialog box.

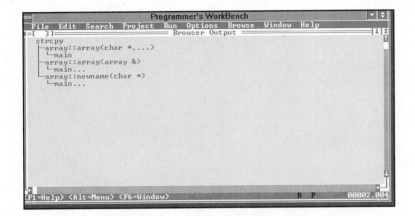

Figure 18.8.

The Call Tree showing a list of all functions that call a specific function, shown here as **strcpy**. This is called a reverse Call Tree.

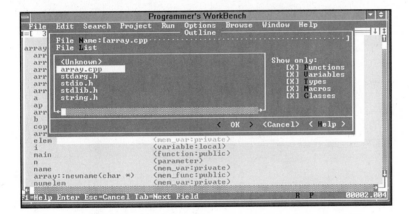

Figure 18.9.

The Module Outline dialog is used to produce a display of all symbols defined in your program.

For C++ object-oriented programming, the browser provides an indispensable feature: a class hierarchy display showing how your classes are derived from other classes, and which members are available to a given class. As you progress in object-oriented programming, the number of classes you create increases. As you derive new classes from existing classes and then derive new classes from your derived classes, it becomes difficult to determine how many members your new class may have, let alone remember the attributes of the base classes from which the class was derived.

To see a class derivation, select Class **H**ierarchy... from the browse menu. This step displays the large dialog box shown in Figures 18.10 and 18.11, displaying a class hierarchy of the derive2.cpp program from Chapter 17. Choose a class by entering its name in the Class **N**ame field or by selecting the class from the **C**lasses: list box. For example, to determine the members of class A, choose A from the **C**lasses: list box. The **B**ase Classes list box shows which classes class A is derived from. The box is empty if A is the root class. The **D**erived Classes list shows which classes, if any, are derived from this class.

Figure 18.10.

For class A, the **D**erived Classes list shows that B is the only derived class. The members of A are shown in the **M**embers: list box.

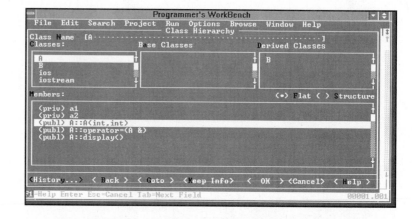

Figure 18.11.

For class B, the class hierarchy shows that A is the base class and that B's members include all the members of A.

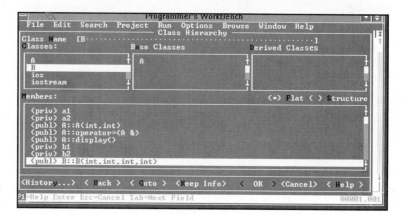

Exercises

The following exercises help you polish your understanding of class type conversions, generic classes, and methods for tuning the performance of class operator functions:

1. Design and write a class that has a distinctive numeric data element. Write conversion functions for the class that can cast a class object to various other numeric types, and to char* as well.

2. Add other data types to the LIST generic class. When you have added two or three other types, design your own generic class. For example, you could redesign the lifo generalized stack class into a true generic class. Remember that the original lifo class can handle different object types simultaneously; your generic class objects handle only one type each.

3. Design and write a class that is rich in operator functions. Use CodeView to examine and experiment with the various combinations of return types, auto and static temporary objects, and so on. It will be difficult to become accustomed to writing workable operator functions until you invest time in this activity.

Summary

This chapter contains a miscellany of C++-related topics that are of great importance to all C++ programmers. The chapter covered the following topics:

- *User-defined conversion functions.* User-defined cast operators are more important to a full-featured class than you might at first expect. Cast operator functions are distinctive in that they allow neither return types nor function arguments.

- *Generic classes.* Generic classes provide a means for you to abstract both data structure and control logic. Currently, generic classes are implemented with the macro preprocessor. This can be troublesome, but sometimes generic classes are worthwhile.

- *C++ class object performance and syntax issues.* Friend functions can be used to provide greater power and flexibility for your class designs, and for many class operator function definitions. Friend functions contribute nothing to object execution speed, however. Object execution speed is greatly influenced by your choice of operator function return types and the storage class of internal temporary objects.

- *The Source Browser provides a convenient tool for locating function and variable definitions and references.* In conjunction with C++ classes, the Browser displays object derivation hierarchies and lists of class members. These features of the Browser make it an indispensable tool for object-oriented programming.

This chapter concludes the discussion of C++ and object-oriented programming. Part III introduces you to developing Microsoft Windows-compatible applications.

PART III

Using Microsoft C/C++ with Windows

OUTLINE

19 Introduction to Microsoft C/C++
    Windows Programming
20 Designing Windows Applications
21 Writing Windows Applications
    with Microsoft C/C++

Introduction to Microsoft C/C++ Windows Programming

This chapter discusses using the Microsoft C/C++ compiler package to create Microsoft Windows-compatible applications. With Microsoft C/C++ 7.0, Microsoft has provided a Windows-aware set of C and C++ language-development tools. Now, you can conveniently develop Windows applications from within Windows.

Developing Windows applications is a complex undertaking. If you previously have developed windowing software using *event-driven* techniques, you will find the concepts of Windows familiar. On the other hand, if your experience is primarily in the development of traditional DOS applications, you will find Windows to be quite peculiar. Whether you like it or not, sooner or later (and preferably sooner) you will need to learn to program in Windows. You should move into this area of C programming unless you are content with writing code for only one of the currently important environments.

Is it worth the effort to learn a new programming regime just to write Windows applications? That question sounds similar to the question asked about learning C++. It is definitely worth the effort to learn how to write Windows applications, now that the tools for doing so have become so readily available. The reasons that learning Windows programming is worthwhile are much the same as they were for learning C++. You get added power and flexibility. With the Windows graphical user interface (GUI), the appearance of your programs makes a quantum leap forward. Even more, you will find that using a GUI such as Windows adds unexpected functionality to your programs as a side effect.

The remainder of this book introduces Windows programming using the Microsoft C/C++ 7.0 compiler and tools. The discussion is directed at Windows users. If you are not a Windows user, you can easily remedy that. Windows 3.1 is not expensive, and you need only a little practice to become a fairly proficient Windows user. *The example Windows programs and techniques presented in this book will also work with Windows 3.0.*

Because Windows programming is an extensive and sometimes complicated subject, this chapter presents a only a brief tour of the subject. This tour, however, may kindle your interest in further study of Windows programming. For additional study, you may want to consult Tim Farrell and Runnoe Connally's *Programming in Windows 3.1* (Second Edition, Que, 1992) or James McCord's *Windows 3.1 Programmer's Reference* (Que, 1992). The Microsoft Quick Help system, included in the Microsoft C/C++ 7.0 package, provides detailed information about each of the Windows applications programming interface functions.

Understanding the Windows Programming Environment

Microsoft C/C++ 7.0 provides three separate approaches to creating Windows-compatible applications. These methods are as follows:

- *Use the QuickWin library to compile DOS-like C or C++ programs that run and display their output within a Microsoft Windows window.* QuickWin programs are not true Windows programs; however, they do enable you to run your programs within a resizeable window and provide limited access to features of Windows, such as on-line help. QuickWin programs have important limitations, such as prohibition from using the regular graphics library and certain standard C functions.

- *Create a true Windows application using the Windows application programming interface.* The Windows API is a C language-compatible object-oriented interface. Because C is not itself an object-oriented language, Windows supports object programming through the use of message passing. This support adds to the complexity of Windows programming, but it gives your application access to Windows pull-down menus, dialog boxes, and the Windows multitasking environment.

- *Write Windows applications using the Microsoft Foundation Classes.* Microsoft provides an object-oriented interface to Windows using a class library. This class library enables you to use C++ features to clarify the complexity of Windows programming.

Use of the QuickWin library and the Windows API are described in this book. To learn more about Windows programming using the Microsoft Foundation Classes, consult "Windows Programming with the Microsoft Foundation Classes" in the *Microsoft C/C++ Class Libraries User's Guide*. In the Class Libraries User's Guide, Microsoft provides a detailed tutorial in the use of its class library interface to Windows. Microsoft recommends, however, that you first become familiar with traditional Windows programming, which is the topic of the next three chapters in this book.

Understanding the QuickWin Library

The easiest way to create a "Windows-aware" program is to compile your existing DOS applications with the QuickWin library. QuickWin lets you convert many DOS applications into a form in which they can be executed within a text-only window. Your applications operate just like any other DOS text mode application, except that their `printf()` output is displayed within a window.

QuickWin provides several advantages over running your DOS application within a DOS window box. As a QuickWin application, your DOS application runs within a true Microsoft Windows window that can be moved around the screen or resized. QuickWin applications also have access to traditional Windows features such as the About box and scrollable output windows. Figure 19.1 shows the order.c program from Chapter 1, renamed winorder.c, running as a sample QuickWin application.

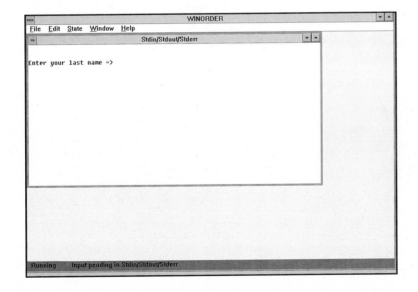

Figure 19.1.

A sample QuickWin application.

Using enhanced features of the QuickWin libraries, your DOS program can also create and manage multiple windows, directing its output to whichever window it needs. As an added benefit, QuickWin can add scroll bars to the output windows, and give your users a way to look back at information that has scrolled off the "screen" of your DOS application.

QuickWin Limitations

Before you begin to use QuickWin, you must be aware of several important limitations. DOS programs compiled as QuickWin applications must not use any graphics functions, the _getch() or _getche() functions, serial communications, or a mouse, and they must not run in Windows real mode.

Because of these limitations, QuickWin may not be an ideal solution for you. QuickWin may be used as a tool for quickly creating simple programs, however, without the bother of writing a true Windows application.

Compiling the order.c Program

Listing 19.1 is a slightly modified version of the order.c program presented in Chapter 1. The only modification was to remove the #include <graph.h> statement and all references to _clearscreen(). This modification was necessary because none of the graphics functions can be used in a QuickWin-compatible program.

Listing 19.1. winorder.c, a slightly modified version of order.c, is used to demonstrate a QuickWin application.

```
1   /* WINORDER.C  An illustration of the basic parts of a
2      C program. Modified for use with QuickWin */
3
4   #include <stdio.h>
5   #include <stdlib.h>
6
7
8   float calc_sub_total( int quantity, float price );
9   float calc_tax( float sub_total );
10
11  main()
```

```
12  {
13    char name[30];
14    char product[30];
15    int quantity;
16    float price;
17    float sub_total;
18    float tax;
19
20
21    printf( "\n\nEnter your last name => " );
22    scanf( "%s", name );
23    printf( "\n\nEnter the name of the product => " );
24    scanf( "%s", product );
25    printf( "\n\n Enter the quantity and price => " );
26    scanf( "%d %f", &quantity, &price );
27
28    sub_total = calc_sub_total( quantity, price );
29    tax = calc_tax( sub_total );
30
31
32    printf( "\n\nOrder Information\n\n" );
33    printf( "Name: %s\n", name );
34    printf( "Product ordered: %s\n\n", product );
35    printf( "Quantity ordered: %d\n\n", quantity );
36    printf( "Price per unit: $%3.2f\n", price );
37    printf( "Sub total:      $%3.2f\n", sub_total );
38    printf( "Tax:            $%3.2f\n", tax );
39    printf( "Total:          $%3.2f\n", ( sub_total + tax ) );
40  }
41
42  float calc_sub_total( int quantity, float price )
43  {
44    float sub_total;
45
46    sub_total = price * quantity;
47    return sub_total;
48  }
49
50  float calc_tax( float sub_total )
51  {
52    const float tax_rate = 0.06;
53
```

Listing 19.1. Continued.

```
54    float tax;
55
56    tax = sub_total * tax_rate;
57    return tax;
58  }
```

To compile winorder.c in the PWB, you must select the Project **T**emplate... item from the **O**ptions menu and select **S**et Project Template... from the submenu. Then choose the Windows QuickWin EXE template. To locate the Windows QuickWin EXE selection, you must scroll through the list box titled Project **T**emplates with Runtime Support. This choice tells the compiler to use the QuickWin library in conjunction with this program.

To compile winorder.c using the cl compiler, specify the /Mq command-line switch.

Depending on your application, you may need to create a .DEF definition file. .DEF files are described later in this chapter and in Chapters 20 and 21. By default, QuickWin uses the CL.DEF file in the \C700\BIN directory (assuming that this is where your compiler and other binary files were installed). CL.DEF sets a default HEAPSIZE of 1,024 bytes and a default STACKSIZE of 8,096 bytes. If your application requires different values for these settings, copy CL.DEF to a new .DEF file and edit the values used for HEAPSIZE and STACKSIZE. Then, use the project feature of the PWB and add to the project both your application's source files and the new .DEF file. The Linker will use the .DEF file when it constructs your executable .EXE file.

The Microsoft documentation incorrectly states that if you are running the PWB from within Windows, you should not attempt to run your program from the PWB. However, Microsoft has verified that this statement is incorrect. You will have no trouble launching QuickWin applications from inside the PWB when the PWB is running from within Windows. Just remember to launch the WX Server program before entering the PWB (or switch to the Program Manager from the PWB application and launch the WX Server). The WX Server must be running in order to execute a Windows application from the PWB.

Each QuickWin application is provided with one window labeled StdIn/StdOut/ StdErr. All input and output (I/O) performed to the standard streams stdin, stdout, or stderr appear in this window. If alternate windows are needed, you can create them for your program's output (see the section "Multiple Windows" later in this chapter).

Running a QuickWin Application

When a QuickWin application is running, its main, or client, window displays the usual control menu box and your application's program name as the window title. A predefined standard menu bar with **F**ile, **E**dit, **S**tate, **W**indow, and **H**elp menus is also provided.

The **F**ile menu bar selection has only one command: **E**xit. **E**xit terminates your application and closes all associated windows.

Use the **E**dit menu to select text from your QuickWin application's window for copying to the clipboard. Unlike standard Windows applications, if you are using the keyboard to make your selection, you must first choose the **M**ark command. Then you can press the Shift key and simultaneously use the arrow keys to select an area of text. If you use a mouse, you can instead drag the mouse over the selection area. (If you are using the mouse, it's not necessary to select **M**ark, although it will cause no harm if you do select **M**ark first.)

You can use the **E**dit function even while your program is running; however, QuickWin automatically suspends your application's execution until you finish your clipboard operation. Choose **C**opy to copy the selected area to the Windows clipboard.

The **S**tate pull-down menu has two functions: **P**ause and **R**esume. During program execution, selecting **P**ause stops your application temporarily. Selecting **R**esume restarts the program.

Use the **W**indows functions to arrange your application windows in tiled or cascaded format. If your QuickWin application uses multiple windows, you can select and make active any of the individual windows by choosing the window from this menu.

The **H**elp menu provides access to help information about the QuickWin system. You cannot use this **H**elp item to provide help information about your program. The **A**bout selection on this menu, however, can be programmed by your application to provide a custom text message. Using the **A**bout item is described in the child.c sample program later in this chapter.

Using the Special Features of QuickWin

QuickWin offers much more than merely executing your DOS applications inside a Window. Through special functions provided by QuickWin, your converted DOS application can create, display, and use multiple child windows for output and input. QuickWin can provide a scroll buffer to retain data that has scrolled off the top of a window by adding scroll bars to your output window. These scroll bars then can be used to review the DOS program's output that has moved off the "screen."

Always keep in mind that whereas QuickWin provides much Windows-like functionality, your program can never be a true Windows application, nor can it access any of the Windows application programming interface features. To create a true Windows program, you must write programs using the Windows API or the Microsoft Foundation Classes.

Although QuickWin does not require it, in good QuickWin programming practice you should periodically call the QuickWin function _wyield() during CPU-intensive computations inside your application. Windows is a multi-tasking environment. When QuickWin is running your DOS application, it occasionally tries to give other tasks a chance to run. In some situations it may not be able to let the other tasks run. If Windows runs slowly (or more slowly than normal) while your application is executing, or if using the menu bar features of your application is difficult, place calls to _wyield() inside your program's loops. Because the _wyield() function has no arguments and a void return value, you should insert it as a statement wherever it might be needed. The use of _wyield() ensures that other Windows applications and features are given adequate processing time.

Adding Multiple Windows

QuickWin provides two approaches to adding multiple windows to your DOS application. Listing 19.2 illustrates the technique of using stream access functions that permit you to create and access each window in a manner similar to a file stream. These features "open" and access windows using file-like access functions.

Listing 19.2. child.c demonstrates the creation and use of multiple child windows.

```
1   /* CHILD.C - Demonstrates creating and using child Windows
2              from a QuickWin application.
3   */
4
5   #include <stdio.h>
6   #include <io.h>
7
8   void main(void)
9   {
10
11      /* Define structures for holding window title and info. */
12      struct _wopeninfo window1 = { _QWINVER, "Window 1", 2048 };
```

```
13    struct _wopeninfo window2 = {_QWINVER, "Window 2", 2048 };
14
15    /* Define two file pointers for accessing child windows.*/
16    FILE * pWindow1;
17    FILE * pWindow2;
18    char yourname[80];
19    int result;
20
21    result =_wabout("CHILD.C Demonstrates use of child windows in QuickWin");
22
23    /* Open the two windows, NULL selects default values for size/location.*/
24    pWindow1 = _fwopen( &window1, NULL, "w+" );
25    pWindow2 = _fwopen( &window2, NULL, "w+" );
26
27    fprintf( pWindow1, "This is Window 1\n" );
28    fprintf( pWindow2, "This is Window 2\n" );
29
30    result = _wsetfocus( fileno( pWindow1 ));
31    fprintf( pWindow1, "Enter your name: " );
32    rewind( pWindow1 );
33    fscanf( pWindow1, "%s", yourname );
34
35    result = _wsetfocus( fileno( pWindow2 ));
36    fprintf( pWindow2, "\nIn Window 1, you entered the name: %s\n", yourname );
37    fprintf( pWindow2, "Press x <Enter> to continue." );
38    rewind( pWindow1 );
39    fscanf( pWindow2, "%s", yourname );
40
41    result = _wsetfocus( fileno( pWindow1 ));
42    fprintf( pWindow1, "This output appears back in Window 1\n" );
43    fprintf( pWindow1, "Press x <Enter> to continue." );
44    rewind( pWindow1 );
45    fscanf( pWindow1, "%s", yourname );
46
47    _fclose( pWindow1 );
48    _fclose( pWindow2 );
49
50  }
```

Child windows are created and accessed just like streams. You use the
_fwopen() function to open a window and associate the window with a file
pointer. Lines 24 and 25 show how this is done. _fwopen() has three parameters: The first is a struct _wopeninfo that specifies both the window title and
the size of a scroll buffer, if any. _wopeninfo is defined as follows:

```
struct _wopeninfo {
  unsigned int _version;
  const char _far * _title;
  long _wbufsize;
};
```

You should assign the Windows version number to _version; this version
number is available in a predefined constant symbol _QWINVER. The Microsoft
documentation incorrectly states that you should use the _WINVER symbol;
however, no _WINVER symbol is defined for use with QuickWin.

The default _wbufsize is 2,048 bytes. When the window cannot display the
amount of data specified in _wbufsize, scroll bars will be added to the window.
The use of scroll bars is explained in the next program example.

The second parameter to _fwopen(), set to NULL in child.c, can be used to set an
initial window size and location. (If either the first or second parameter is set
to NULL, QuickWin substitutes default values). To set an initial window size or
location, you should first define a struct _wsizeinfo variable and initialize its
fields to appropriate values. Then, pass the filled-in structure as the second
parameter to _fwopen(). _wsizeinfo is defined by QuickWin as follows:

```
struct _wsizeinfo {
  unsigned int _version; /* Set to _QWINVER */
  unsigned int _type;    /* See text */
  unsigned int _x;       /* Upper-left x coordinate */
  unsigned int _y;       /* Upper-left y coordinate */
  unsigned int _h;       /* Window height */
  unsigned int _w;       /* Window width */
};
```

To minimize the window, set _type to _WINSIZEMIN. To maximize the window,
set _type to _WINSIZEMAX. To set the window size and location according to the
values in _x, _y, _h, and _w, set _type to _WINSIZECHAR.

The third parameter is the usual file mode argument, which may be r, w, r+, or
w+, with either t (for text) or b (for binary) appended to the mode string.

_fwopen() returns a pointer to a FILE structure. This return value must be
saved so that it can be used in subsequent fprintf() and fscanf() function
calls. To print data to a window, call fprintf(), using the appropriate file
pointer to select the window that should receive the output (see lines 27
and 28).

Because windows can overlap, you should ensure that your *active* window is the one on top. To make a window active, call _wsetfocus(). Line 30 provides an example of making the first window the active window. If the selected window is invisible or obscured, _wsetfocus() will cause the window to be placed in front of all the other windows. To determine which window is currently on top, call _wgetfocus(). It has no parameters and returns the active window's handle.

To input a value from a window, use fscanf(), as shown in line 33. It is very important that you call rewind() (see line 32) when switching from output to input or from input to output. You must call rewind() to reset the stream when switching from fprintf() to fscanf() and vice versa.

To close a window, use the normal _fclose() or _fcloseall() functions. If you want, it's acceptable to skip calling _fclose(), because the program's normal termination handles window closing automatically.

Another Approach to Creating Child Windows

If you want to perform low-level I/O to a child window, you may alternately use the _wopen() function to create the child window and then use the standard _read() or _write() functions for I/O. _wopen() is similar to _fwopen() in that its first parameter is a pointer to a _wopeninfo structure, and the second parameter is a pointer to a _wsizeinfo structure. The third argument, however, is an integer having one of the manifest constant values _O_BINARY, _O_RDONLY, _O_RDWR, _O_TEXT, or _O_WRONLY.

When _wopen() successfully creates a child window, it returns a handle that is used to access the window. You should use the standard C _read() and _write() functions to perform I/O, using the handle returned by _wopen() as the first parameter to either function.

If you use _wopen() to create a child window, use _wclose() to close it. _wclose() has two arguments. The first argument is the handle to the window, and the second is choosing how the window should be disposed:

```
int _wclose( int wfh, int persist );
```

The persist argument can be set to either _WINNOPERSIST, in which case the window is erased, or _WINPERSIST. For the _WINPERSIST setting, the window becomes deactivated but you can still select text. Use the **E**dit pull-down menu and copy values to the clipboard. Use the control menu to close the window when you are finished examining the output.

Exiting from a Window

In addition to the `persist` argument of `_wclose()`, you may also change the application's exit behavior at any time, by calling the `_wsetexit()` function. The only argument to `_wsetexit()` is one of these constants: `_WINEXITPROMPT`, `_WINEXITNOPERSIST`, or `_WINEXITPERSIST`.

`_WINEXITNOPERSIST` and `_WINEXITPERSIST` work like the `_WINNOPERSIST` and `_WINPERSIST` constants described in the preceding section, except that they apply to all the active windows your application is currently using. If you have three windows displayed at program exit and you have selected `_WINEXITPERSIST`, all three windows remain on-screen at the conclusion of your program. Use the control menu box to close and erase your application's windows.

`_WINEXITPROMPT` causes QuickWin to prompt the user at program exit, asking whether the windows should be erased or should remain on-screen.

Using the About Box

Line 21 makes a call to `_wabout()`. This function assigns to the About function a character string that is accessible from the About... item on the Help menu. The string parameter can be as much as 256 characters long. If you do not call `wabout()`, QuickWin substitutes a default message.

Controlling a Window's Size and Location

You have already seen how a `_wsizeinfo` structure can be used to set initial window size and location. After the window has been created, you can determine its current size by calling `_wgetsize()`, where `_wgetsize()` is defined as

```
int _wgetsize( int wfh, int reqtype, struct _wsizeinfo *wsize);
```

`wfh` is the window's handle returned by the `_wopen()` function or by calling `fileno( filepointer )`, where `filepointer` is the file associated with the window.

`reqtype` should be either `_WINCURREQ` to return the window's current size, or `_WINMAXREQ` to return the maximum size. If you set `wfh` to `_WINFRAMEHAND`, you can use `_wgetsize()` to return information about the main or client window.

Use `_wsetsize()` to change a window's size or location. `_wsetsize()`'s function prototype is

```
int _wsetsize( int wfh, struct _wsizeinfo *wsize );
```

Initialize the appropriate values in _wsize and then set wfh to the handle of the desired window.

Adding Scroll Bars to a Child Window

Adding scroll bars to a child window is easy. When the window is opened, set the _wopeninfo's _wbufsize parameter to the desired size, in bytes, of the scroll buffer. If the window cannot display all the characters in the scroll buffer, QuickWin automatically places scroll bars on the window. See Listing 19.3 for an example of a program that uses a scroll bar. You can set the scroll buffer to a larger or smaller value.

Listing 19.3. scroll.c. A simple program using a scroll buffer for its output.

```
1    /* SCROLL.C - Demonstrates use of scroll bars in a QuickWin application
2    */
3
4    #include <stdio.h>
5    #include <io.h>
6
7    void main(void)
8    {
9       struct _wopeninfo window1 = { _QWINVER, "Demo of scrolling window", 8192 };
10
11      /* Define two file pointers for accessing child windows. */
12      FILE * pWindow;
13      char inputvalue[80];
14      int result, i;
15
16      result =_wabout("SCROLL.C Demonstrates use of scrolling windows in QuickWin");
17
18      pWindow = _fwopen( &window1, NULL, "w+" );
19
20      for (i=0; i<200; i++){
21        fprintf( pWindow, "This is line %d of the scrolled window\n", i );
22      }
23
24      fprintf( pWindow, "Press x <Enter> when ready to quit. " );
```

Listing 19.3. Continued.

```
25    rewind( pWindow );
26    fscanf( pWindow, "%s", inputvalue );
27
28    fclose( pWindow );
29
30  }
```

To learn a window's current maximum scroll buffer size, call _wgetscreenbuf(), passing the window's parameter as its only argument. To change the scroll buffer size, you can call _wsetcreenbuf() like this:

```
result = _wsetscreenbuf( fileno( pWindow ), 10000 );
```

This example changes the scroll buffer for pWindow to 10,000 bytes in size. _wsetscreenbuf() returns 0 if the size was changed successfully, and −1 if the change was unsuccessful.

Accessing Menu Bar Functions

Using the _wmenuclick() function, your application can activate several of the menu bar functions. By setting _wmenuclick()'s only argument to one of the following constants, you can programmatically request the following features:

_WINTILE	Tiles all applications windows
_WINCASCADE	Cascades all windows
_WINARRANGE	Arranges any icons
_WINSTATBAR	Toggles the visibility of the status bar

Programming in the Windows Applications Programming Interface

To create a Windows application, your program must have a Windows-compatible structure and must call routines in the Windows API. The API provides hundreds of functions, giving you access to all the capabilities of Windows applications, including pull-down menus, dialog boxes, graphics, printing, and other functions. Before examining the API functions, you must first gain an understanding of the Windows multitasking environment and how it affects the structure of your programs.

Understanding the Windows Multitasking Environment

If you have read the previous parts of this book, you know something about dealing with objects. Thus, the object-oriented nature of Windows programming will not cause you grief when you are learning Windows programming. Rather, the multitasking environment—and the programming style it requires—may at first perplex you.

Don't be put off if multitasking programming stumps you momentarily. Multitasking, whether on PCs or mainframes, has always confused programmers, at least temporarily. With a little patience and persistence, you will rapidly overcome the hurdles to a new way of perceiving the art of programming.

Windows handles its guest applications in different ways. DOS applications running under Windows often cannot be preempted, thereby defeating the multitasking scheme of the environment. True Windows applications, however—those using the Windows interfaces and protocols as they should—can run at the same time as other Windows applications. With true Windows applications, many programs can be running (and not just waiting to be swapped into memory) at the same time. The Task List dialog box of the Program Manager illustrates this point, as shown in Figure 19.2.

As you can see in Figure 19.2, Windows can load and run several native applications at one time. Other applications may be running even though the main window for only one application program is visible. In Figure 19.2, for example, only the Program Manager has a window visible on-screen. You can tell that other applications are present because their icons appear at the bottom of the screen. The Terminal application, however, very easily could be processing data from the communications ports in background mode, although only its icon is visible at the moment.

What kind of structural program changes does the multitasking environment require? The answer revolves around the requirement that your program now must be designed to coexist with other active programs. For your program to exist cooperatively with Windows, a few things *must* be in your program, and other things *can* be in your program. Typically, you will write four kinds of functions in your Windows C programs: the main Windows interface function, the main window procedure (still a C function), other Windows-oriented functions, and simple helper functions. The significance of these four kinds of functions follows:

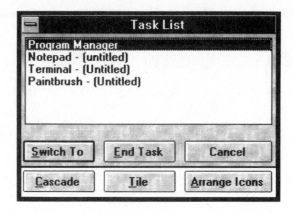

Program Manager   Notepad - (untitled)

Terminal - (Untitled)   Paintbrush - (Untitled)

■ *The main Windows interface function is required, and must be named*
   WinMain(). WinMain() is similar to the ordinary C function main(), in that it
   is required to get things rolling—it is the main entry point for the program (note that a Windows program does not have a main() function).
   The WinMain() function does three crucially important things:

   1. WinMain() registers the window class for the application's main
      window. This statement means simply that the WinMain() func-
      tion tells Windows what the characteristics of the main window
      will be (the name of the window procedure function, what icon
      to use to represent the application when its window is mini-
      mized, background color, what menu to use, and other things).

   2. WinMain() creates the application's main window. WinMain() is-
      sues the CreateWindow() Windows function calls to create the
      main window for the application, and to display it on-screen.
      Function arguments to CreateWindow() include the application's
      Windows name, the caption text for the window, and the
      window's style, initial position, and menu name.

   3. WinMain() contains the application's main message loop. The
      main message loop gets commands and data input from Win-
      dows and sends requests for certain services to Windows. The

principal Windows function call in the main message loop is the `GetMessage()` function call, which requests and receives data and commands from Windows. When your program calls `GetMessage()`, Windows may decide to momentarily execute another application's program: This is the primary vehicle for implementing the Windows multitasking scheme. The main message loop is discussed in detail in the section "Setting Up the Main Message Loop" in Chapter 21, "Writing Windows Applications with Microsoft C/C++."

■ *The main window procedure is also required, and usually is named* `WndProc()`. The `WinMain()` message loop indirectly invokes the main window procedure, but never calls it directly. The main window procedure processes and acts on Windows commands and messages received by the main message loop.

To understand this strange state of affairs, remember that Windows was given the name of the main window procedure when your program registered the window class. When the main message loop gets a message from Windows, it performs any necessary translation of the message, and then dispatches the message back to Windows. Only at this point does Windows finally invoke the main window procedure, passing to it the message (data or commands) for action.

■ *Other Windows-oriented functions may be required, depending on which Windows features you use.* Some functions are required only if you use certain features of the Windows environment. Creating, displaying, and handling a dialog box, for example, requires the use of a dialog function, the name of which is made known to Windows (it too will be called directly by Windows, rather than your program). In this and the next two chapters, you develop a sample application program called FCWIN that uses several dialog boxes.

■ *Simple helper functions may be needed to complement your program's work. Simple* helper functions means non-Windows functions; they might be quite complex, depending on what your program does.

You will learn how to code these four kinds of functions in your Windows program as you develop the sample application code in Chapters 20 and 21. For now, think about the fact that you soon will be programming in a new environment, and what that might mean. You need to see, at least briefly, a number of new concepts and tools before you tackle the program code for FCWIN.

Windows Is an Object-Oriented Environment

Having already taken on the task of learning C++ object-oriented programming, you will avoid the double culture shock of encountering the object-oriented system and multitasking for the first time.

Windows is decidedly an object-oriented system, and Windows programming is definitely a form of object-oriented programming. You probably can think of one object that is present in the Windows environment: the window. A Windows window is handled very much like a C++ object. It has a user-defined type (remember registering the window class?), instances of the class (objects) are created at runtime (`CreateWindow()`), and you handle objects by sending messages to them (with `GetMessage()` and `DispatchMessage()` functions). It all sounds familiar, doesn't it?

A window type object is not the only object type in Windows. There are many more, some of which are indicated in Figure 19.3.

Figure 19.3.

Windows deals with objects (such as windows) and operates by routing messages among them.

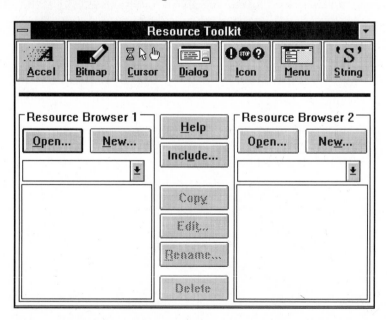

Windows programs routinely deal with such objects as bit maps, cursors, dialog boxes, icons, menus, and string resources. Most of these objects are easy to understand—you deal with them regularly in the Programmer's WorkBench, for example. Other resources, such as keyboard accelerators (tables defining application hot keys), may be familiar in concept, but are implemented in new ways. That is all part of the fun of learning to write Windows applications: New toys are everywhere!

To briefly illustrate the concepts mentioned so far, the easy.c program is presented here. This program, the Windows equivalent of the ubiquitous *hello, world* introductory C program, does nothing but create a main window, with text for the caption bar and text in the client area of the window. All text lines are centered in the client area of the window. The appearance of the easy.c window is shown in Figure 19.4.

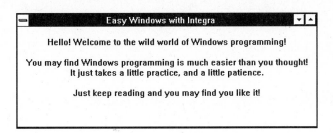

Figure 19.4.

The easy.c window, with caption bar and text in the client area.

The interesting thing about easy.c is that you can drag its window around the screen and size it to any proportion you want (within limits), and the text in the client area stays centered. How is this accomplished? Putting the easy.c Windows application together requires three source files, plus a project file, because the PWB is used to build the program. The project file is the easiest to build. You just open a new project and insert the following files:

```
easy.c
easy.def
```

Before compiling the easy.c program, read through the section titled "Compiling and Linking Windows Applications" that follows this section.

The nature of the easy.def file will become clear in just a moment. The easy.h header file is also simple; it consists of one line:

```
#define szAppName "EasyC"
```

The szAppName macro defines a string containing the application name used to identify the application to Windows when the main window is created. You should #include the easy.h header at the beginning of the easy.c application program. Later, when you write a longer and more complex application, the application header file will contain several macros (manifest constants) used to identify menu items and window components. Thus, although the easy.h header is ridiculously simple, the application header plays a serious role in the construction of a serious Windows application.

Now turn your attention to the easy.def file. Its contents are shown in Listing 19.4.

Listing 19.4. easy.def. The module-definition file for easy.c.

```
1  NAME         EasyC
2  DESCRIPTION  'First Windows application for UMC'
3  STUB         'WINSTUB.EXE'
4  CODE         PRELOAD MOVEABLE DISCARDABLE
5  DATA         PRELOAD MOVEABLE MULTIPLE
6  HEAPSIZE     8192
7  STACKSIZE    8192
8  EXPORTS      WndProc
```

The first thing you should know about .DEF files is that they are called *module-definition files.* A module-definition file describes to the Microsoft Linker the program's attributes and some resources it will need, so that the .EXE module can be set up properly for the Windows environment. For this project, type the .DEF file exactly as you see it in Listing 19.4.

The significance of the individual statements in the module-definition file are explained in detail in Chapters 20 and 21, when you learn about the development of a much larger project. Notice, however, that the EXPORTS statement names a function called WndProc (which will be the main window function for easy.c). This is how you tell the linker which functions can be called by Windows system code from outside your program.

The source code for easy.c is shown in Listing 19.5. As you look through the program listing, notice that the WinMain() function and a main window procedure function named WndProc() are present, but the third and fourth categories of functions are not necessary in this short program.

Listing 19.5. easy.c. The Windows application program for the EASY window.

```
1  #include <string.h>
2  #include <windows.h> /* Declarations for Windows */
3  #include "easy.h"     /* Declarations for EASY.C */
4
5  char *HelloMsgs[] = {
6    "Hello! Welcome to the wild world of Windows programming!",
7    " ",
8    "You may find Windows programming is much "
         "easier than you thought!",
```

```
 9    "It just takes a little practice, and a little patience.",
10    " ",
11    "Just keep reading and you may find you like it!",
12  };
13
14  long FAR PASCAL WndProc (HWND, unsigned, WORD, LONG) ;
15
16  int PASCAL WinMain(HANDLE hInstance, HANDLE hPrevInstance,
17              LPSTR lpszCmdLine, int nCmdShow )
18  {
19      WNDCLASS    wndClass;
20      MSG         msg;
21      HWND    hWnd;
22
23      /*
24       * Register window class style if first
25       * instance of this program.
26       */
27      if ( !hPrevInstance )
28      {
29       wndClass.style         =CS_HREDRAW | CS_VREDRAW ;
30       wndClass.lpfnWndProc   =WndProc;
31       wndClass.cbClsExtra    =0;
32       wndClass.cbWndExtra    =0;
33       wndClass.hInstance     =hInstance;
34       wndClass.hIcon         =LoadIcon(NULL,
35                                        IDI_APPLICATION);
36       wndClass.hCursor       =LoadCursor(NULL,IDC_ARROW );
37       wndClass.hbrBackground=GetStockObject(WHITE_BRUSH );
38       wndClass.lpszMenuName =NULL;
39       wndClass.lpszClassName=szAppName;
40
41      if (!RegisterClass(&wndClass))
42       return FALSE;
43      }
44
45      hWnd = CreateWindow(szAppName,
46                      "Easy Windows with Integra",
47              WS_OVERLAPPEDWINDOW,
48              CW_USEDEFAULT,
49              CW_USEDEFAULT,
50              CW_USEDEFAULT,
```

Listing 19.5. Continued.

```
51                  CW_USEDEFAULT,
52                       NULL,
53                       NULL,
54                       hInstance,
55                       NULL);
56
57     ShowWindow(hWnd, nCmdShow);
58     UpdateWindow(hWnd);
59
60     while (GetMessage(&msg, NULL, 0, 0))
61     {
62         TranslateMessage(&msg );
63      DispatchMessage(&msg );
64     }
65     return msg.wParam;
66  }
67
68  long FAR PASCAL WndProc (HWND hWnd, unsigned Message,
69                  WORD wParam, LONG lParam)
70  {
71    static HANDLE hDc;
72    PAINTSTRUCT ps;
73    int LineWidth, LineSpace, xPos;
74    int i;
75    TEXTMETRIC TextMetric;
76    LONG dwExtent;
77    RECT rect;
78
79    switch(Message)
80    {
81
82      case WM_PAINT:
83        hDc = BeginPaint( hWnd, &ps );
84        GetTextMetrics( hDc, &TextMetric );
85        LineSpace = TextMetric.tmHeight
86                  + TextMetric.tmExternalLeading;
87        GetClientRect( hWnd, &rect );
88        LineWidth = rect.right - rect.left + 1;
89        for ( i=0; i<6; ++i ) {
90          dwExtent = GetTextExtent( hDc, HelloMsgs[i],
```

```
 91                       strlen( HelloMsgs[i] ) );
 92             xPos = ( LineWidth - LOWORD( dwExtent ) ) / 2;
 93             TextOut( hDc, xPos, (i+1)*LineSpace,
 94                      (LPSTR)HelloMsgs[i], strlen(HelloMsgs[i]) );
 95           }
 96         EndPaint( hWnd, &ps );
 97         return 0;
 98
 99
100      case WM_DESTROY:
101            PostQuitMessage(0);
102            return 0;
103      }
104      return DefWindowProc(hWnd,Message,wParam,lParam);
105    }
106
```

Lines 1 through 14 of Listing 19.5 contain necessary preliminary statements. Notice that windows.h and easy.h are #included in lines 2 and 3. Other material in these lines includes the array of pointers to the message strings that will be painted on the client area of the window, and a function prototype for the WndProc() main window procedure's function.

The required WinMain() function is found in lines 16 through 66 of Listing 19.5. As mentioned, WinMain() does three important things: It registers the main window class, creates and displays the main window, and contains the main message loop.

In lines 29 through 43, you can see the process of registering the window class, which consists of assigning values to members of a window class structure (which has type WNDCLASS and is declared in windows.h) and calling the RegisterClass() Windows function. RegisterClass() is only one of hundreds of functions residing in Windows (not in your code) that constitute the programming interface to the Windows environment. As long as you remember to declare #include <windows.h>, all these Windows functions and facilities are available without other preparatory action.

Registering the window class does not cause anything to happen on the system display, however. To create and display the window, you must use the CreateWindow() function, as seen in lines 45 through 58. CreateWindow() uses the szAppName macro declared in the easy.h header (line 45), and you can write the window caption text directly into the function call as a constant string (line 46).

Even after the CreateWindow() function has been called, the main window still exists only as an area of memory in Windows. To force the window to appear on the system screen, call the ShowWindow() function (line 57). To invoke the user code that paints the contents of the window's client area, call the UpdateWindow() function (line 58).

The main message loop (lines 60 through 65) is in the WinMain() function. It drives the entire application—without the main message loop, no Windows messages are received or dispatched. The main message loop is the indirect interface between Windows and your main window procedure. Chapter 21 covers the main message loop in more detail, but the following lists its three basic components:

- *The while loop controlled by the GetMessage() Windows function.* GetMessage() retrieves the next Windows message from your application's input message queue (by asking Windows to return it), and gives Windows the opportunity to select another application for execution (by simply giving control to Windows momentarily).

- *The TranslateMessage() Windows function call in the while loop.* The TranslateMessage() function call is important for handling keyboard input, especially if you want your program to handle ANSI multibyte characters. This function translates keyboard scan and character codes into ANSI-standard character codes (which may be ASCII single-byte characters on English-based systems).

- *The DispatchMessage() Windows function call.* This function call passes the message—ready for dispatching—back to Windows. *Dispatching* is the process of routing the message to the window to which it belongs. In easy.c, for example, there is only one active window (the main window), and its window procedure function is WndProc(). Windows therefore passes the message to WndProc() for handling and action.

The most important thing to remember about the main message loop is that you do not call a window procedure yourself. You let Windows route messages to the correct window, by simply giving the message back to Windows through DispatchMessage(). It is important to understand this idea, especially when you progress to writing applications that use multiple windows.

Next, look at the main window procedure's function, WndProc(). Its code is found in lines 68 through 105. Remember that the main window procedure can have any valid name. In easy.c, the main window procedure name is identified during window class registration (line 30 of Listing 19.5) as WndProc.

The main window procedure for easy.c handles two Windows messages: WM_PAINT and WM_DESTROY (both declared in windows.h). The names of these messages clearly show what they are, but not when they might be generated.

The WM_PAINT message is received whenever the UpdateWindow() function is called, the window is moved, or the window is resized (by a Windows user). The code that handles the WM_PAINT message (see lines 82 through 97) has the primary responsibility of keeping the client area of the window painted correctly under all circumstances. This short piece of code (just 16 lines) clearly illustrates why there is a steep learning curve associated with Windows programming; the code contains seven calls to Windows functions. That number is more than you might expect, when the objective is to put lines of text in the client area, centered in the window. The seven Windows functions and their uses are as follows:

- *BeginPaint() establishes the device context for the window.* Establishing a device context for the window display (or printer, or other device or resource) is similar to invoking the constructor for a C++ class object. It tells Windows what you are about to do, and where you are about to do it.

- *GetTextMetrics() acquires information about the font being used in the current device context.* easy.c needs this information in order to compute the height of a line of text. Remember that all window I/O is graphics I/O—one of the main reasons for the existence of Windows. The pixel-based dimensions of the text and window must be converted to text-based dimensions to keep track of the current text location.

- *GetClientRect() acquires information from Windows about the size (in pixels) of the client area of the Window.* This action is necessary because you want to center every line of text in the client area. The only way to do that is to count pixels (especially because the default font for Windows 3.1 is a variable-pitch font).

- *GetTextExtent() determines the line length, in pixels, of a line of text.* The line length is used with the client-area dimensions to compute the starting horizontal position for each line of centered text.

- *LOWORD() extracts the low-order word from a double word object.* This function-like macro is used to extract the horizontal dimensions of the current line of text from the double word (DWORD) returned by GetTextExtent().

- *TextOut() paints the line of text in the client area in the desired location.* Using arguments computed by the previous logic and function calls, TextOut() positions the current text line in the client area.

- *EndPaint() releases the device context and tells Windows that the window is now valid.* BeginPaint() and EndPaint() must always be used in pairs, to begin and end the painting process.

It might seem that seven Windows calls is excessive for putting text on-screen, but there is a good reason for the added complexity. The simplicity of the easy.c sample program is misleading in this case. More overhead is required in order to control a window than to display a string using puts(). The overhead is both necessary and acceptable, however, because Windows programs typically do much more than plain DOS-based programs, and do it much more attractively (with graphics, windows, dialogs, and so on).

The processing required for the WM_DESTROY message is simple compared to the preceding code. Windows sends the WM_DESTROY message to the window procedure when the user pulls down the system menu in the window and selects Close. Because you cannot exit() a Windows program to end it, the code for handling WM_DESTROY sends back to Windows a message indicating that the program is finished, using the PostQuitMessage() Windows function call. Windows then sends that message to the main message loop in WinMain(). This causes the GetMessage() function to return a NULL value, which ends the while loop, and ends the program also.

Finally, look at line 104 of Listing 19.5. This line of code calls the DefWindowProc() Windows function if all case statements for processing the message fail (fall through). As the function name indicates, the DefWindowProc() call invokes the Windows default window procedure for any messages that your window did not process. You should always code this function call as the last line in the main window procedure.

Compiling and Linking Windows Applications

This section explores using the PWB and the command-line compiler, cl, to build Windows applications. Also included is an explanation of how to build the easy.c Windows executable file.

The compiler's job in building a Windows application program is only slightly different from building plain C or C++ modules in that Windows programs must have special entry and exit code inserted for each function call. The PWB and the cl compiler both provide options to enable compilation of Windows programs. Once these options are set, the compiler generates appropriate entry and exit code.

The linker's job in building a Windows application is very different, however. A new set of runtime code (object modules and runtime libraries) is involved in building a Windows application program. The linker now must access different libraries to provide Windows-oriented initialization and runtime library code. For a small-model Windows application program, for example, the SLIBCEW runtime library is used. The original initialization modules and runtime libraries are still available for plain DOS projects.

If you are developing applications for Windows, you will likely prefer to use the PWB as a Windows-launched application. In this mode, you can edit, compile, and execute your Windows applications all from within the PWB. If you selected the Windows development option when you installed Microsoft C/C++ 7.0, a Microsoft C/C++ 7.0 group was created automatically. To run the PWB, double-click the Programmer's WorkBench icon.

If you choose to use the command-line compiler, cl, you will need to either compile and link your programs in a Windows-launched DOS box or develop them outside of Windows entirely. In the latter case, you then must start Windows each time you want to test your application.

Using the PWB to Compile and Link a Windows Application

This section assumes that you will be accessing the PWB from within the Windows environment. Open the Microsoft C/C++ 7.0 program group (if it is not already visible). Launch the program named *WX Server* by double-clicking its icon. The WX Server program is a "helper" program that lets the PWB execute your Windows application. The WX Server must be present if you want to execute your program after compiling it from within the PWB. When the WX Server is running, it will be displayed only as an icon on your Windows desktop. If you forget to launch the WX Server, the PWB will be incapable of running your program.

You are now ready to launch the PWB by double-clicking the Programmer's WorkBench icon from the Microsoft C/C++ 7.0 group. To compile a Windows program using the PWB, you must prepare a project file. To compile the easy.c program, Select New Project... from the Project menu. Create a new make file named easy.mak. To this project file, add easy.c and easy.def.

Next, you must tell the compiler that it will be creating a Windows application. Do this by selecting **S**et Project Template... from the **O**ptions menu. Select C language runtime support (or C++ if you want to use C++ features in your program). Under the Project Templates heading, page down through the list box to find Windows EXE. With Windows EXE highlighted, select the < OK > button. This selection completes the setup of the PWB for compiling Windows applications.

If your program uses *resource files* (described in the section "Preparing Resource Files" later in this chapter), you should also add the appropriate .RES files to your project file. Because the easy.c program does not use any external resources, this step is not required to compile and link easy.c.

Using the *cl* Command-Line Compiler

You can compile and link a Windows application using the cl compiler and the Microsoft Linker from the DOS command line. For all Windows applications, you must include the command-line switches /GA and /GEf. In Microsoft C 6.0, the /Gw switch was used to enable Windows applications support. Although the /Gw switch still is supported in Microsoft C/C++ 7.0, Microsoft recommends that you discontinue using /Gw and begin using the /GA /GEf switch combination.

Use cl to compile (but not link) your object modules by typing

```
cl /c /GA /GEf easy.c
```

where easy.c is the name of the program to be compiled. Remember that the /c switch compiles but does not link your program.

To link your program, you have to run the Linker directly, like this:

```
link easy, /align:16, NUL, /nod slibcew libw, easy.def
```

In this line, easy refers to easy.obj produced by the compiler, and easy.def is the appropriate definitions file. Note that you must include the appropriate Windows library file (slibcew is for the small model, mlibcew is for the medium model, and so on).

For all but the smallest applications, you will want to create a make file for use with the NMAKE utility program. See Chapter 5, "Building, Compiling, and Testing Microsoft C/C++ Programs," for instructions on creating your own make files.

If you try to compile and link in one step using cl, you will encounter problems when the linker attempts to access the EXPORTS statement in the .DEF file. The reason is that cl calls link with the /NOIGNORECASE option, and this is incompatible with linking the Windows application.

Using The Resource Compiler

If your program uses external resources (and most Windows programs do), the project building process will invoke the resource compiler (RC) to compile a resource script file to produce the .RES resource file (a binary format file). The RC file also is invoked in the process to combine the .RES file with the .EXE file built by the linker to produce the completed Windows .EXE file. Because the easy.c program has no resource file, the invocation of RC is not needed for that application.

Preparing Resource Files

Because a Windows application is object-oriented, it uses a number of resources to accomplish certain tasks in the Windows environment. A Windows resource is both a thing and an actor (that is, a thing that can act on itself).

This sounds much like C++ class objects, and Windows resources are much like class objects. A Windows menu, for instance, is a thing that displays options the user can choose in the window, and it can report to its owner program what the selected option was.

Windows resources include such things as memory, the display, the keyboard, and the system printer, menus, icons, bit maps, strings, keyboard accelerators (hot-key definitions), and others. To introduce you to the world of Windows resources in a concrete context, the remainder of this chapter describes the kinds of resources needed by a fairly lengthy Windows program called FCWIN (its project name), which is developed in detail in Chapters 20 and 21.

Creating Resources

FCWIN is a financial calculator program that does a number of interesting and useful things with money calculations. FCWIN uses a Windows menu to detect the user's choices, and dialog boxes to input data and display results. The dialog boxes use such resources as edit boxes, static text, group boxes, list boxes, and pushbuttons. The system printer will be used, and you can use an icon (a dollar bill—what else?) to add FCWIN to a Program Manager group.

Resources are created in a variety of ways, depending on the resource. Most resources can be created using a *resource script* file. A resource script contains a textual description of resources, such as pull-down menus, dialog boxes, and so on. You will use a resource script file to describe pull-down menus.

Other resources can be created and edited using a resource editor, which is a special program, similar to a painting program, for literally drawing the resource on the screen. When the resource definition has been completed, the resource editor saves and converts the resource into the necessary script or binary file format.

Microsoft provides several resource-editor programs with Microsoft C/C++ 7.0: the dialog editor for creating dialog boxes, the image editor for creating and editing icons, and the font editor for editing or creating new text fonts.

Because Windows resources all have standardized formats, you may also use Windows development tools provided by other companies to create and edit your resources. For example, you can use the Whitewater Resource Toolkit or Borland's Resource WorkShop. Some of the tools provided by other companies have additional features not included in the Microsoft tools set. As you progress in your Windows development experience, you may want to investigate the use of these other tools.

You will learn more about the Microsoft resource editors in just a moment in the sections "Creating and Editing Dialog Boxes" and "Creating and Editing Icons."

Resources Needed by the fcwin.c Sample Program

You may have surmised already that a single .RES file can contain a number of different resources. That is the case with fcwin.res. The fcwin.res file contains 16 resources: 1 icon, 1 menu, and 14 dialog boxes (14 types of financial calculations are supported).

Each resource in an .RES file has associated with it a *resource name,* an identifier by which it is known to Windows. Table 19.1 lists all the resources used by FCWIN, along with their names, types, and uses.

Table 19.1. FCWIN resources and names.

Resource Name	Type Resource	Description
FCICON	Icon	The dollar bill icon for the application.
FCMENU	Menu	The menu for the application, including the main menu bar and pull-down entries.
FCEFFCON	Dialog box	Dialog, effective interest rate with continuous compounding.
FCEFFPER	Dialog box	Dialog, effective interest rate with periodic compounding.
FCFVANN	Dialog box	Dialog, future value of an annuity.
FCFVSIN	Dialog box	Dialog, future value of a single amount.
FCLOANDA	Dialog box	Dialog, mortgage-loan data entry.
FCMKUPCO	Dialog box	Dialog, markup over cost.
FCMKUPPR	Dialog box	Dialog, markup over price.
FCMORTLS	Dialog box	Dialog, display amortization schedule in a scrollable list box.
FCMORTPR	Dialog box	Dialog, set up and send amortization schedule to system printer.
FCPAYOUT	Dialog box	Dialog, display loan payout analysis.
FCPCTCG	Dialog box	Dialog, percent change in amount.
FCPCTTO	Dialog box	Dialog, percent of total amount.

Resource Name	Type Resource	Description
FCPVANN	Dialog box	Dialog, present value of an annuity.
FCPVSIN	Dialog box	Dialog, present value of stated amount.

This chapter doesn't show you a sample of every resource used by FCWIN, but it does present an example of each significant type of resource use. (The binary format fcwin.res file is included on the program disk offered at the back of this book. The resource script format—.RC file format—for all the FCWIN resources is presented in Appendix E.)

Creating and Editing Menus

Before you look at the next figure, think about the structure of a Windows menu. The menu bar across the top of the client area contains a list of items, each of which is itself a pull-down menu.

The first item on the menu bar of the FCWIN application, for instance, is *General Business*. Clicking this item displays a pull-down menu containing four more items (in a drop-down format). With that in mind, now look at how this menu structure is defined as a menu resource script file in Listing 19.6.

Listing 19.6. fcmenu.rc. Resource script for the FCWIN menu.

```
1    FCMENU   MENU PRELOAD MOVEABLE PURE DISCARDABLE
2    BEGIN
3      POPUP "General &Business"
4      BEGIN
5        MenuItem   "Percent Ch&ange", IDM_PCTCHANGE
6        MenuItem   "Percent &Total", IDM_PCTTOTAL
7        MenuItem   "Markup Over &Cost", IDM_MKUPCOST
8        MenuItem   "Markup Over &Price", IDM_MKUPPRICE
9      END
10     POPUP "&Interest Rates"
11     BEGIN
12       MenuItem   "Effective &Periodic Rate", IDM_EFFPER
13       MenuItem   "Effective &Continuous Rate", IDM_EFFCONT
14     END
15     POPUP "&Actuarial Functions"
16     BEGIN
```

Listing 19.6. Continued.

```
17      MenuItem  "Future Value, Single Deposit", IDM_FVSINGLE
18      MenuItem  "Present Value, Single Deposit", IDM_PVSINGLE
19      MenuItem  "Future Value,  Regular Deposits", IDM_FVREGULAR
20      MenuItem  "Present Value, Regular Deposits", IDM_PVREGULAR
21    END
22    POPUP "&Loan Amortization"
23    BEGIN
24      MenuItem  "&Input Loan Data", IDM_LOANDATA
25      MenuItem  "Payout &Analysis", IDM_PAYOUT
26      MenuItem  "&Display Amortization Table", IDM_DISPAMORT
27      MenuItem  "&Print Amortization Table", IDM_PRNTAMORT
28    END
29    POPUP "&Help"
30    BEGIN
31      MenuItem  "Percent Change", HLP_PCTCHANGE
32      MenuItem  "Percent Total", HLP_PCTTOTAL
33      MenuItem  "Markup Percent of Cost", HLP_MKUPCOST
34      MenuItem  "Markup Percent of Price", HLP_MKUPPRICE
35      MenuItem  "Effective Rate, Periodic", HLP_EFFPER
36      MenuItem  "Effective Rate, Continuous", HLP_EFFCONT
37      MenuItem  "Future Value, Single Payment", HLP_FVSINGLE
38      MenuItem  "Present Value, Single Payment", HLP_PVSINGLE
39      MenuItem  "Future Value, Regular Deposits", HLP_FVREGULAR
40      MenuItem  "Present Value, Regular Deposits", HLP_PVREGULAR
41      MenuItem  "Input Loan Data", HLP_LOANDATA
42      MenuItem  "Payout Analysis", HLP_PAYOUT
43      MenuItem  "Display Amortization Table", HLP_DISPAMORT
44      MenuItem  "Print Amortization Table", HLP_PRNTAMORT
45      MenuItem  " ", 0
46    END
47  END
```

You can see in Listing 19.6 all the menu items and the constant values for the selectable items. The constants IDM_PCTCHANGE, IDM_PCTTOTAL, and so on, are defined in the fcwin.h header file (see Table 19.2 in the following section). To make the listing easier to follow, all you need to know is that each menu item is numbered consecutively beginning from 1. So IDM_PCTCHANGE is set to 1, IDM_PCTTOTAL is set to 2, and so on.

At this point, you do not need to concern yourself with most of the content of line 1 except that the first item, FCMENU, names this resource, and MENU identifies the type of resource that follows.

Each pull-down menu item is identified with the special keyword POPUP, followed by the menu bar label used for the pull-down menu. The first menu bar selection is *General Business*, followed by *Interest Rates*, and so on. The & symbol indicates that the immediately following letter should be a highlighted hot key. For the first pull-down, the & symbol appears before the letter *B* in *Business.* When the program is executing, you can drop down the first menu by pressing Alt-B.

Beneath each pull-down menu label is a nested BEGIN-END pair. Inside the BEGIN-END is the keyword MenuItem followed by the text of the menu item, followed by a macro name. The macro is a substitution for an ordinal number (1, 2, 3, and so on) and is the value that Windows sends to your program when the particular menu item is selected. All the macro symbols are defined in fcwin.h (see Table 19.2 in the following section).

When a user clicks the mouse on the menu bar, Windows simply pops up the associated submenu. If a user then clicks an item from that menu, Windows reports that to your program. It does so by sending a WM_COMMAND message to WndProc() (the main window procedure), and supplying a function argument that has the same value as the ordinal value of the menu item (for example, IDM_PCTTOTAL). You use a switch statement, similar to those in Listing 19.5, to interpret which menu item was selected.

Creating and Editing Dialog Boxes

Dialog boxes are the meat and potatoes of FCWIN. All the work is accomplished in a dialog box, whatever financial calculation is being performed. The reason for this approach is simple—it is the easiest way to get into some sophisticated Windows programming.

Although you can define dialogs using a resource script, you will probably choose not to. Instead, you use the Dialog Editor provided with the Microsoft C/C++ package. Appendix E presents listings of all of FCWIN's resource script files.

It is easy to pack much function into a simple-looking dialog box. For example, look at Figure 19.5, which shows the Calculate Percent Change dialog box being edited in the Dialog Editor.

The Calculate Percent Change dialog has two edit boxes into which the user types the old and new amounts to be used in the computation. Each box is assigned a number. The Old_Value field is associated with the number *101* (see the line labelled Symbol: near the top of Figure 19.5), and the New_Value field is associated with the number *102* (not shown). The last box (number 103) is an edit box; however, attributes have been assigned to it such that it cannot be tabbed to or typed into. It is used strictly for displaying results. The edit boxes (and other items in the dialog box, too) are called *controls,* and the numbers shown with them are their ordinal values—like the values for menu items you just read about.

Figure 19.5.

The Calculate Percent Change dialog box combines input fields, output fields, and pushbuttons.

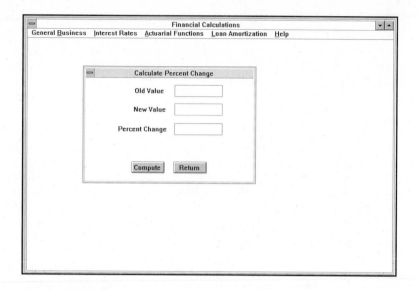

The nice thing about dialog boxes is shown in FCWIN: The application program can control the entire dialog box by simply watching for a WM_COMMAND message with an argument corresponding to the Compute pushbutton (value 105). When that message is detected, the dialog function (explained in Chapters 20 and 21) just has to read the text in the edit controls, convert the input data to numeric values, compute, and place the answer in the Percent Change edit control (103). Similarly, when the Return pushbutton is detected (value 104), the dialog can end.

It should be obvious that controlling menus and dialog boxes involves many ordinal values. The application program must know about all these values to control processing logic. This requirement could result in a serious logistical problem without some means of keeping track of all these numbers. The means of keeping track of these numbers is the application header file.

You may recall that the application header for the easy.c program was almost empty, but you were warned that larger programs utilize the header heavily. FCWIN is one of those larger programs (although it is still not very complicated). One of the first tasks in designing FCWIN was deciding which ordinal values would signify a particular control. The resulting value assignments are shown in Table 19.2. The assignment of values is made by means of a #define object-like macro; the table shows macro names and corresponding values. Using the macro names rather than ordinal values in the program's source code makes it possible for the programmer to keep up with what is happening (rather than getting completely lost).

Table 19.2. Ordinal-value assignments used by FCWIN.

Control Macro Name	Ordinal Value Assigned
IDM_PCTCHANGE	1
IDM_PCTTOTAL	2
IDM_MKUPCOST	3
IDM_MKUPPRICE	4
IDM_EFFPER	5
IDM_EFFCONT	6
IDM_FVSINGLE	7
IDM_PVSINGLE	8
IDM_FVREGULAR	9
IDM_PVREGULAR	10
IDM_LOANDATA	11
IDM_PAYOUT	12
IDM_DISPAMORT	13
IDM_PRNTAMORT	14
HLP_PCTCHANGE	15
HLP_PCTTOTAL	16
HLP_MKUPCOST	17
HLP_MKUPPRICE	18
HLP_EFFPER	19
HLP_EFFCONT	20
HLP_FVSINGLE	21
HLP_PVSINGLE	22
HLP_FVREGULAR	23
HLP_PVREGULAR	24
HLP_LOANDATA	25
HLP_PAYOUT	26
HLP_DISPAMORT	27
HLP_PRNTAMORT	28

continues

Table 19.2. Continued.

Control Macro Name	Ordinal Value Assigned
FCWIN_OLD	101
FCWIN_NEW	102
FCWIN_ANS	103
FCWIN_RETURN	104
FCWIN_COMPUTE	105
FCWIN_APR	106
FCWIN_AMT	107
FCWIN_YEARS	108
FCWIN_FREQ	109
FCWIN_LISTBOX	110
FCWIN_LEVELPAY	111
FCWIN_INTPAY	112
FCWIN_TOTPAY	113
FCWIN_BALLOON	114
FCWIN_START	115
FCWIN_CANCEL	116

You already know about the ordinal values assigned to menu-selection items. But why are the values for edit boxes assigned beginning with 101? These values are just standard default values. You can start the numbering sequence from some other value if you want. Note that the values assigned to controls in different dialogs can be reused: The values 101 through 105 almost always are used in all 14 dialog boxes for FCWIN.

The ordinal values for static text, such as the heading Old_Value, are assigned beginning with 200; in Table 19.2, there are no macros for these items. This is because a control must have an ordinal value, but these values are not needed for FCWIN. Therefore, these values were conveniently separated from values that are actually used.

To use the Dialog Editor, double-click its icon in the Microsoft C/C++ 7.0 group under the Program Manager. When the Dialog Editor is running, you can open an existing resource file, or you can create a new dialog, using the **O**pen command from the **F**ile menu or the **N**ew command from the **F**ile menu, respectively.

If you select **New**, you see the screen shown in Figure 19.6. The Dialog Editor presents a sample dialog for you to begin editing. An icon bar containing an array of editing tools appears at the right side of the Dialog Editor window.

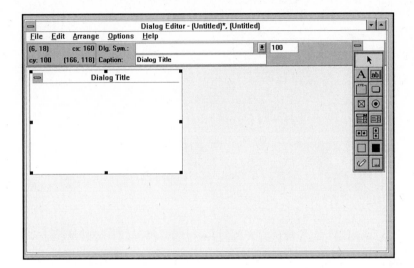

Figure 19.6.

The Dialog Editor.

To move the sample dialog to a new location on-screen, move the mouse pointer to the title area of the dialog (where it displays *Dialog Title*), and while you press down the mouse button, drag the dialog box to a new location within the edit window. To resize the sample dialog, click and drag any of the eight handles on the sides or corners of the dialog.

To change the dialog box's caption, move the mouse pointer to the Caption: field shown near the top of the screen and type a new heading for the dialog box.

Adding typical dialog controls is easy. To add a textual label, click the mouse on the letter *A* shown in the tools box. Then position the mouse on the location where you want your label to appear and click the mouse button. This step deposits a text box on-screen. Most likely, you will have to change the size of the default text box. Grab the handles surrounding the text and adjust the box size as needed. Type your new text in the Text field at the top of the screen (see Figure 19.7).

By selecting the appropriate control from the tools box, you can add all types of dialog box controls to your dialogs. Each dialog box can be assigned both a #define constant and an ordinal value, used to identify the control. Type the #define constant in the Symbol field, and its ordinal value in the small field to the right of the Symbol field. You can edit the symbol values using the Symbols... option from the **Edit** menu.

Figure 19.7.

Adding a text label to a
dialog.

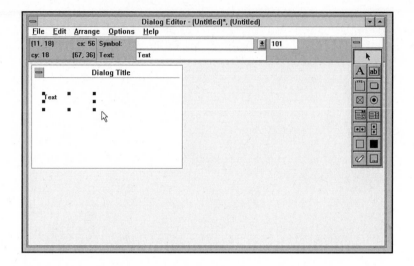

When you save the dialog resource, the Dialog Editor automatically creates a
.RES file, a .DLG file containing a resource script equivalent to the dialog you
have drawn, and an .h file containing the #define symbols you have defined
for the dialog. By using #define symbols in your source code, you can easily
match the controls and their control values as passed to your application from
Windows.

Some dialogs, such as the Mortgage Loan Data Entry dialog, do not display
answers; they just collect input data. Figure 19.8 shows this dialog box while
being edited. The figure also shows how to assign the control attributes just
mentioned.

Figure 19.8.

The Mortgage Loan Data
dialog box has only input
fields and one pushbutton.

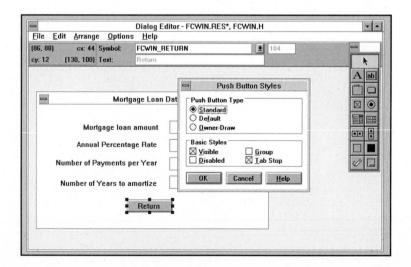

To edit the attributes for a control or text label, first select the control or label by clicking the mouse over the control. If you double-click or choose Styles from the Edit menu, a dialog will be displayed, with a list of style or attribute information you can select for the specific control or label.

FCWIN uses another powerful window control, the list box. Figure 19.9 shows the Loan Amortization Schedule dialog's list box being edited.

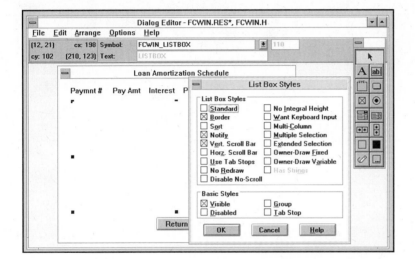

Figure 19.9.

The Loan Amortization Schedule dialog box has a Windows list box as its most important feature.

If you look at the program listing for fcwin.c (see Listing 20.2 in Chapter 20), you can see how the text strings are added to the list box. You can also see how little effort is required to control a list box's scrolling display. (No effort is required: Windows does it all!)

The visual effect of a list box is pleasing, making it an attractive feature for users of your program. Figure 19.10 shows the list box just edited, as FCWIN runs.

Creating and Editing Icons

The FCWIN program uses a dollar bill icon (fcicon.ico) created with the Image Editor. Figure 19.11 shows the icon editor with FCICON loaded and ready to be edited.

Figure 19.10.

The Loan Amortization Schedule dialog box in action, displaying a Windows list box.

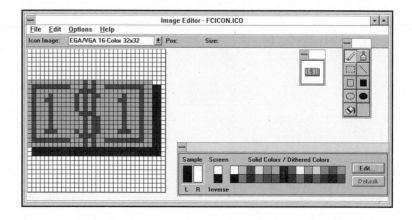

Paymnt #	Pay Amt	Interest	Principal	Balance
81	438.78	395.82	42.96	47455.73
82	438.78	395.46	43.32	47412.41
83	438.78	395.10	43.68	47368.72
84	438.78	394.73	44.04	47324.68
85	438.78	394.37	44.41	47280.26
86	438.78	394.00	44.78	47235.48
87	438.78	393.62	45.15	47190.32
88	438.78	393.25	45.53	47144.79
89	438.78	392.87	45.91	47098.88
90	438.78	392.49	46.29	47052.58
91	438.78	392.10	46.68	47005.90
92	438.78	391.71	47.06	46958.83

Figure 19.11.

Using the Image Editor to create the dollar bill icon for FCWIN.

An icon is simple to create. From the File menu, choose New. This choice displays a Resource Type dialog box. Check the Icon radio button and choose OK to display a selection of Target devices. You probably will want to choose the *EGA/VGA 16-Color 32x32* icon image. Finally, you see a grid similar to that shown in Figure 19.11.

To draw, select the pencil tool and draw the icon by dragging the pencil. You can also click individual pixels to set them to the current drawing color. What you see is what you get. Use the color selections to change the color of the drawing pencil.

To draw a box or circle, select the appropriate drawing tool. You can even fill in an enclosed region using the paint bucket tool. Just make sure that you "spill the bucket" within an area that is enclosed. Otherwise, the paint will smear over the entire icon drawing area.

Most of this chapter has been a whirlwind tour of the resources used by the FCWIN project. If you want to get better acquainted with the resource editing tools, there is only one good way to do so—go play with your new toy! The Windows graphical interfaces to the editors make the learning process easy and intuitive (which is the point of a GUI).

Compiling Resources Using the Resource Compiler

To use the resources and scripts, you must use the RC resource compiler program. The resource compiler performs two tasks: compiling the resource script file into a binary .RES resource file, and adding the .RES file to an .EXE file. Here you look at compiling the .RC file into a .RES file. Chapter 20 discusses the use of RC to append the resulting .RES file onto the executable file.

The resource script describes each of the resources to be incorporated into an application. Listing 19.7 contains the resource script for fcwin.c.

Listing 19.7. The fcwin.rc resource script file for the fcwin.c Windows program.

```
1   #include <windows.h>
2   #include "fcwin.h"
3
4   rcinclude fcmenu.rc
5
6   FCICON ICON fcicon.ico
7
8   rcinclude fceffcon.dlg
9   rcinclude fceffper.dlg
10  rcinclude fcfvann.dlg
11  rcinclude fcfvsin.dlg
12  rcinclude fcloanda.dlg
13  rcinclude fcmkupco.dlg
14  rcinclude fcmkuppr.dlg
15  rcinclude fcmortls.dlg
16  rcinclude fcmortpr.dlg
17  rcinclude fcpayout.dlg
18  rcinclude fcpctcg.dlg
19  rcinclude fcpctto.dlg
20  rcinclude fcpvann.dlg
21  rcinclude fcpvsin.dlg
```

Just like a C program, lines 1 and 2 `#include` the windows.h and fcwin.h header files. Both headers define certain symbols required by the various resource scripts. For example, the fcmenu.rc file uses the manifest constants `IDM_PCTTOTAL` and so forth, defined in fcmenu.rc. These contents provide the link between the pull-down menu item described in fcmenu.rc and the Windows message that sends the menu-selection number to the fcwin.c program code.

Line 4 uses the `rcinclude` statement to include the contents of fcmenu.rc in the resource script. `rcinclude` operates identically to `#include`, inserting in the current file the contents of another file. If you change `rcinclude` to `#include "fcmenu.rc"`, the script compiles the same as though you had used `rcinclude`. fcmenu.rc defines the pull-down menus used in the application.

Line 6 includes the icon resource. Note the syntax of the statement. `FCMENU` is the name of the resource, `MENU` is the type of the resource, and fcicon.ico is the name of the file containing the resource.

Each of the program's dialog scripts is included in lines 8 through 21. Remember that the Dialog Editor creates both a .RES file and a .DLG file. The .DLG file contains the textual description of the dialog and is the one that is needed for incorporation into your application's overall resource script. Appendix E presents listings of all .DLG files used in FCWIN.

To compile the fcwin.rc script file, type

```
rc -r fcwin.rc
```

At this stage, be sure to include the `-r` switch. This switch tells RC to compile fcwin.rc and create fcwin.res. Without the `-r` switch, RC appends the .RES file to fcwin.exe. You don't want to do that just yet! Creating the fcwin.exe program file isn't described until the next chapter.

Exercises

1. Use the Icon Editor to create an icon for easy.c (just Save **As** an .ICO file for now).

2. Use the easy.c source code as a skeleton for a program that paints your text in the client area of the window. Try writing the code so that only the first line of text is centered; left-justify the remainder. Here is a tip for positioning the left-justified lines: Assume a left margin of 40 pixels. This would require a `TextOut()` function like the following one:

```
TextOut( hDc, 40, (i+1)*LineSpace,
  (LPSTR)HelloMsgs[i], strlen(HelloMsgs[i]) );
```

You will need a project file to build the application's .EXE file, as described previously in this chapter. The project file should contain references to easy.c and easy.def. Before making the project, do not forget to set the Project **T**emplate... from the PWB **O**ptions menu correctly for a Windows application (the small memory model is fine for this exercise).

3. Use the Dialog Editor to practice creating dialogs. Add each of the control types, such as buttons, radio buttons, and list boxes. Create a group of radio buttons or checkboxes.

Summary

This chapter introduced you to a number of new ideas. Before you read the next chapter, be sure that you have grasped the following ideas:

■ *The Windows graphical user interface (GUI) is different from traditional DOS programming.* Windows is a multitasking, object-oriented environment. Your experiences as a C++ programmer should have helped prepare you for this new environment. Working with a GUI requires several important structural changes to your programs.

■ *There are two required functions in a Windows application program.* The first is the WinMain() function, and it must have that name. The second required function is the main window procedure. It usually is named WndProc(), but you can choose another name. You tell Windows about the main window procedure during window class registration.

■ *A Windows application program is driven by the main message loop.* The main message loop is the most critical part of your Windows program. It receives messages from Windows, translates them, and dispatches them. The main window procedure is reached only indirectly, through messages dispatched by the main message loop.

■ *The main window procedure handles and acts on all messages for the main window.* You saw in this chapter how the WM_PAINT and WM_DESTROY messages are used. In the next two chapters (developing FCWIN), you will see how you can use the WM_CREATE and WM_COMMAND messages. The WM_COMMAND message identifies selected menu items to your application program.

■ *If you are using the Programmer's WorkBench, you must be certain to select the Windows .EXE template.* If you choose to use the command-line compiler, use the /GA and /GEf switches to ensure that the compiler inserts Windows-compatible function entry and exit code.

■ *The Dialog Editor is one of the most important tools you will use when you create resources for Windows programs.* With the Dialog Editor you can draw dialog resources quickly and easily.

Designing Windows Applications

T he preceding chapter introduced you to the Dialog Editor and the creation and editing of various resources for use by Windows application programs. This chapter and the next guide you through the development of a Windows program written with Microsoft C/C++ using the Microsoft Windows applications programming interface (or API). First, however, you should understand the basic components of a Windows executable (.EXE) file, and how Windows uses directories in storing and running its applications programs. The text is directed at readers familiar with the operation and handling characteristics of Windows from a user's point of view.

Setting Up the Windows Application Environment

The Microsoft C/C++ 7.0 installation process installs the tools and libraries needed for creating Windows-compatible applications (assuming that you elected to have the Windows files installed during the installation process). When you run Windows, the C/C++ development tools appear in a C/C++ 7.0 Dev Tools group you can access with the Program Manager.

If you did not originally install the Windows development tools, you can do so now by running the SETUP program on Disk 1 of the Microsoft C/C++ disk set. Use the Custom Installation option to select installation of only the Windows features.

If you want to construct the helpmsg.dll dynamic-link library file described in Chapter 21, you have to install also the Windows DLL Libraries. Instructions for installing the Windows DLL Libraries are presented in the "Using Dynamic-Link Libraries" section in Chapter 21.

The WINSTUB.EXE Program

What happens if you try to run a Windows application program without using Windows to run it? For example, suppose that you change to the Windows directory and attempt to execute the Notepad program directly. You receive the following message:

```
This program requires Microsoft Windows.
```

To understand what happened, you must understand that a Windows executable file contains much more than a simple DOS program file. You can find out how much more by running the EXEHDR.EXE program in the \C700\BIN directory. EXEHDR produces the output shown in Listing 20.1. This program analyzes .EXE files and reports their structure and contents (for Windows programs as well as for DOS programs). Running EXEHDR against the NOTEPAD.EXE file in the Windows directory yields the following report:

Listing 20.1. Output produced by EXEHDR.

```
Microsoft (R) EXE File Header Utility Version 3.00
Copyright (C) Microsoft Corp 1985-1992. All rights reserved.


Module:                 NOTEPAD
Description:            Microsoft Windows Notepad
                          Application (c)1989
Data:                   NONSHARED
Initial CS:IP:          seg   1 offset 19d4
Initial SS:SP:          seg   8 offset 0000
Extra stack allocation: 1000 bytes
DGROUP:                 seg   8

no. type address  file  mem   flags
  1 CODE 000007a0 032fb 032fb PRELOAD, (movable), (discardable)
  2 CODE 00003e00 0057a 0057a PRELOAD, (movable), (discardable)
  3 CODE 00004c20 0079d 0079e (movable), (discardable)
  4 CODE 00005500 00240 00240 (movable), (discardable)
  5 CODE 00005770 0066a 0066a (movable), (discardable)
  6 CODE 00005ec0 005f6 005f6 (movable), (discardable)
```

```
  7 CODE 00006580 0014a 0014a (movable), (discardable)
  8 DATA 00004480 00738 00738 PRELOAD, (movable)


Exports:
ord seg offset name
   1   1  0541  NPWNDPROC exported
   9   5  040b  FNABOUT exported
  12   1  0a90  FNABORTPROC exported
  11   1  0afe  FNABORTDLGPROC exported
  10   6  00d6  DLGFNOPEN exported
  14   1  10f7  PAGESETUP exported
   3   3  0000  FNSAVEAS exported
   8   5  0000  FNFIND exported
  13   1  2864  DLGFNPRINTSETUP exported
```

Clearly, many kinds of information are recorded in a Windows program .EXE
file that are not found in a DOS .EXE file. One important new item—which is
not visible in the preceding report—is the Windows *stub*. The stub is an .EXE
program, but you connect it to your Windows application program. Its sole
function is to produce a message (such as the one shown previously) when
someone attempts to run the program without Windows, and then to return to
DOS. The stub is a required bit of protection present in all Windows programs.
Microsoft provides the necessary stub program in the file WINSTUB.EXE. This
program must be located in the same directory that contains the cl command-
line compiler. The Microsoft C/C++ installation procedures automatically
placed WINSTUB.EXE in the \C700\BIN directory (or in another directory
if you requested a different installation directory).

You don't have to name the stub .EXE file in the project or make file, but you
do have to name the stub .EXE file in the module-definition file, which you
create later in this chapter, in the "Creating a Module-Definition File" section.
Then when you NMAKE or build the complete application's .EXE file using the
PWB, the Resource Compiler (RC) is invoked to combine the stub .EXE with
your Windows program's .EXE file.

Windows Directory Usage

You use several disk directories when you develop Windows applications.
These directories and what can be placed in them are important. For this
discussion, assume that Microsoft C/C++ 7.0 is installed in the \C700\BIN
directory, and that Windows is in the \windows directory. The following
directories and subdirectories are used by your program and Windows at
runtime:

- **\SOURCE\FCWIN**

  This is the current directory (the one that contains your program's source and .EXE files). The current directory can be any directory you want. If your program has an associated DLL (dynamic-link library), it can reside in the current directory also, but it is not required to reside there. Establishing a current directory while running under Windows is discussed after this list.

- **\WINDOWS**

  This is the main Windows directory. You can place your application programs here, but you usually should not do so. If your program has an associated DLL, it can reside here if it is not in the same directory as your program's .EXE file. The name of this directory does not have to be windows; you can obtain its name at runtime by using the `GetWindowsDirectory()` Windows function.

- **\WINDOWS\SYSTEM**

  This is the Windows system subdirectory. It contains module files and DLL files that are basic components of Windows. You usually should not place your program's .EXE file here, although you might want to put an associated DLL in this directory. This subdirectory also can have a different name. You can obtain the name of the Windows system subdirectory at runtime by using the `GetSystemDirectory()` Windows function.

- **PATH=*directoryname***

  Both programs and DLLs can be placed in a directory named in the PATH environment variable. PATH is established before you start Windows.

- **A mapped network directory**

  If you are running Windows on a network, directories are available from the network. Windows can search these directories for programs and other resources.

When Windows looks for a program or resource, the directories in the preceding list are searched in the order shown.

Of all the directories listed, the current directory may not be set in concrete—it can vary for different applications. Additionally, when you start Windows, the \windows directory is the DOS current directory. So what is the current directory as far as your program is concerned?

The current directory for your program is whatever path you specified to execute the program. You specify a path when you execute a program by selecting the **R**un command from the Program Manager's **F**ile menu and typing the execution name as follows:

```
c:\source\fcwin\fcwin.exe
```

The current directory for FCWIN.EXE is now C:\SOURCE\FCWIN.

You do much the same thing when you install your program as a Program Item in a Program Manager group window. When you define the Program Item Properties of the item (your program), or when you create a .PIF file for the program, you still must type the execution path. In all cases, when Windows runs your program, the specified execution path becomes the current directory for the duration of the program—but only for that program. Any programs running concurrently probably will have a different current directory.

Learn by Doing: Designing fcwin.c

Enough preliminaries: It's time to write some Windows code with Microsoft C/C++. The sample code is a simple financial calculator that originally appeared in the book *Using C* (published by Que Corporation). The original financial calculator is recast into a Windows application that uses the graphical user interface (GUI) of Windows. The program has now become fcwin.c, and supports movable, sizable windows, with a complete pull-down menu system, 14 dialogs for the various calculations, and a dynamic printer-configuration dialog for spooled hard-copy output. The program also uses a DLL to support a complete help facility. Figure 20.1 shows a dialog box created by FCWIN.

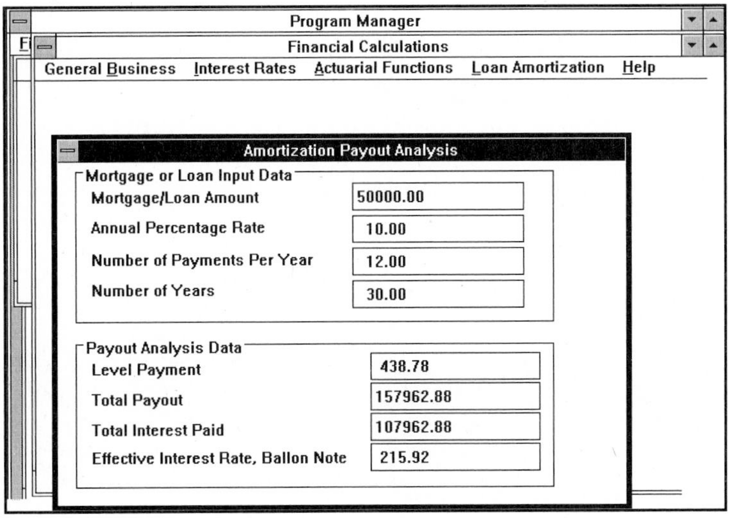

Figure 20.1.

FCWIN uses the Windows GUI to create a finished, attractive application.

Although fcwin.c is lengthy, this straightforward program uses a limited number of Windows resources, and can be compiled using the small memory model (but its size is about as large as you want a program to get with the small model). The remainder of this chapter and Chapter 21 examine the fcwin.c program, and look specifically at the following techniques:

■ *Building the main program file and its support files.* You probably are not surprised that more is required of a program (and its programmer) in the Windows environment. You must add Windows support material to the source file, and modify the compile-and-link procedure. The remainder of this chapter presents most of the source files for the application, and begins to explain their uses. Because there is much source code, the discussion of FCWIN is continued in Chapter 21. The help DLL source files also are presented and explained in Chapter 21.

■ *Writing the main message loop.* The main message loop, required in every Windows program, must be coded in a function named WinMain(). This function registers the window class (if this is the first execution instance of the program), creates the main window (the frame window), and then loops while dispatching messages it receives. Messages come from two sources: the window procedure you code or Windows itself.

■ *Writing the window procedure.* The window procedure handles messages received, and can send messages back to WinMain() and Windows. This function typically is named WndProc(), and performs such functions as creating dialogs and child windows and calling support functions.

■ *Setting up and writing dialog procedures.* A dialog invites user interaction, and is probably the easiest and quickest way to begin writing sophisticated Windows applications. A dialog procedure is a callback function, which means that the function is called by Windows rather than from your code. You will be shown how to set up this procedure, and how to utilize controls for the dialog (edit boxes, list boxes, static controls, and other things).

■ *Using a Windows printer device.* Learning how to establish a device context for a device prepares you for controlling the window display (or other devices, such as communications ports). You can apply much of what you learn here about using GDI (graphics device interface) calls directly to programming the window display.

■ *Building and using a DLL.* A dynamic-link library can enable resources (such as common functions and bit maps) to be shared among several programs running concurrently, without duplicating those resources. A DLL also can help you simplify a program and control its size. FCWIN uses a DLL to implement the display of all the help message boxes. This moves both the logic for this task and the text associated with it out of the fcwin.c module.

The source code for fcwin.c is presented in Listing 20.2. Much of what you see in Listing 20.2 will be confusing if this is your first exposure to Windows programming, but it will become less confusing as you continue to read. Just remember that the results of writing Windows programs can be more than satisfying—they can be spectacular.

When you look over Listing 20.2 you will notice several unusual or nonstandard symbols, such as PASCAL, BOOL, and FAR. These symbols are defined in the windows.h header file and are important to the correct compilation of your program. The FAR symbol is a synonym for the familiar __far keyword and ensures that far procedure calls are used when calling the associated functions.

The PASCAL keyword is a peculiar one to see inside a C program. When PASCAL precedes a function declaration, the PASCAL keyword requests the C compiler to emit function calls using the format traditionally used by Pascal programming language compilers. It is not particularly important (in the context of this book) that you understand the details of the differences in generated code for C versus PASCAL function calls, but you do need to know that this keyword is important when writing Windows applications.

BOOL is equivalent to an int data type, but indicates to you, the programmer, that this function returns a boolean result such as 0 for false and a nonzero value for true.

Listing 20.2. fcwin.c. A financial calculator program using the Windows 3.1 GUI.

```
 1   #include <stdio.h>
 2   #include <string.h>
 3   #include <stdlib.h>
 4   #include <stdarg.h>
 5   #include <math.h>
 6   #include <windows.h> /* Declarations for Windows */
 7   #include "fcwin.h"   /* Declarations for FCWIN   */
 8
 9
10   /* -------------------------------------------------- */
11   /*  Declare pointers to all the exported functions.    */
12   /*     These are the functions that Windows will call   */
13   /*     from outside FCWIN to support the main (frame)    */
14   /*     window with its menu  and the dialog functions.   */
15   /* -------------------------------------------------- */
16
17   long FAR PASCAL WndProc (HWND, unsigned, WORD, LONG) ;
18   BOOL FAR PASCAL PopupMsg( int );        /* DLL Function */
19   BOOL FAR PASCAL DoPctChg( HWND, unsigned, WORD, LONG );
20   BOOL FAR PASCAL DoPctTot( HWND, unsigned, WORD, LONG );
21   BOOL FAR PASCAL DoPayOut( HWND, unsigned, WORD, LONG );
22   BOOL FAR PASCAL DoMkupCo( HWND, unsigned, WORD, LONG );
```

Listing 20.2. Continued.

```
23  BOOL FAR PASCAL DoMkupPr( HWND, unsigned, WORD, LONG );
24  BOOL FAR PASCAL DoEffPer( HWND, unsigned, WORD, LONG );
25  BOOL FAR PASCAL DoEffCon( HWND, unsigned, WORD, LONG );
26  BOOL FAR PASCAL DoFvSin( HWND, unsigned, WORD, LONG );
27  BOOL FAR PASCAL DoPvSin( HWND, unsigned, WORD, LONG );
28  BOOL FAR PASCAL DoFvAnn( HWND, unsigned, WORD, LONG );
29  BOOL FAR PASCAL DoPvAnn( HWND, unsigned, WORD, LONG );
30  BOOL FAR PASCAL DoLoanDat( HWND, unsigned, WORD, LONG );
31  BOOL FAR PASCAL ListAmort( HWND, unsigned, WORD, LONG );
32  BOOL FAR PASCAL PrntAmort( HWND, unsigned, WORD, LONG );
33
34  /* ------------------------------------------------------ */
35  /*  Prototype declarations for FCWIN helper functions.    */
36  /*      These functions support pop-up message boxes for  */
37  /*      displaying help information, as well as           */
38  /*      financial computations.                           */
39  /* ------------------------------------------------------ */
40
41  void BuildTextMessage( char* szFormat, ... );
42  double SPFV( double apr, double freq, double periods );
43  double SPPV( double apr, double freq, double periods );
44  double USPV( double apr, double freq, double periods );
45  double USFV( double apr, double freq, double periods );
46
47  /* ------------------------------------------------------ */
48  /*  Declare global variables. Try to keep these to a      */
49  /*      minimum.                                          */
50  /* ------------------------------------------------------ */
51
52  char textmsg[256];
53  double apr = 10, years = 30, amt = 50000, freq = 12;
54  double levelpay, intpay, prinpay, numpay = 360, payno;
55  double bal, old, new, ans;
56  char instring[32];
57
58  /* ------------------------------------------------------ */
59  /*                                                        */
60  /*      CREATE FRAME WINDOW, DISPATCH WINDOWS MESSAGES    */
61  /*                                                        */
62  /*  WinMain() is required in every Windows program. It    */
63  /*      contains the main message loop. It is not         */
```

```
64  /*     exported; it is always assumed to be present.     */
65  /*                                                        */
66  /* ----------------------------------------------------- */
67
68  int PASCAL WinMain(HANDLE hInstance, HANDLE hPrevInstance,
69                  LPSTR lpszCmdLine, int nCmdShow )
70  {
71      WNDCLASS    wndClass;
72      MSG         msg;
73      HWND        hWnd;
74
75      /*
76       * Register window class style if first
77       * instance of this program.
78       */
79      if ( !hPrevInstance )
80      {
81          wndClass.style          =CS_HREDRAW | CS_VREDRAW ;
82          wndClass.lpfnWndProc    =WndProc;
83          wndClass.cbClsExtra     =0;
84          wndClass.cbWndExtra     =0;
85          wndClass.hInstance      =hInstance;
86          wndClass.hIcon          =LoadIcon(NULL,
87                                           "IDI_APPLICATION");
88          wndClass.hCursor        =LoadCursor(NULL,IDC_ARROW );
89          wndClass.hbrBackground=GetStockObject(WHITE_BRUSH );
90          wndClass.lpszMenuName ="FCMenu";
91          wndClass.lpszClassName=szAppName;
92
93      if (!RegisterClass(&wndClass))
94          return FALSE;
95      }
96
97      /*
98       * Create and display the window.
99       */
100     hWnd = CreateWindow(szAppName,
101                     "Financial Calculations",
102                     WS_OVERLAPPEDWINDOW,
103                     CW_USEDEFAULT,
104                     CW_USEDEFAULT,
105                     CW_USEDEFAULT,
```

Listing 20.2. Continued.

```
106                         CW_USEDEFAULT,
107                         NULL,
108                         NULL,
109                         hInstance,
110                         NULL);
111
112     ShowWindow(hWnd, nCmdShow);
113     UpdateWindow(hWnd);
114
115     while (GetMessage(&msg, NULL, 0, 0))
116     {
117         TranslateMessage(&msg );
118         DispatchMessage(&msg );
119     }
120     return msg.wParam;
121 }
122
123 /* ------------------------------------------------------- */
124 /*                                                         */
125 /*       PROCESS ALL MESSAGES FROM THE FRAME WINDOW        */
126 /*                                                         */
127 /*  WndProc() handles the processing of all messages       */
128 /*      dispatched by WinMain(). A pointer to this         */
129 /*      function was placed in the wndClass structure      */
130 /*      during registration of the frame window.           */
131 /*                                                         */
132 /* ------------------------------------------------------- */
133
134 long FAR PASCAL WndProc (HWND hWnd, unsigned Message,
135                         WORD wParam, LONG lParam)
136 {
137   static FARPROC lpfnDoPctChg;
138   static FARPROC lpfnDoPctTot;
139   static FARPROC lpfnDoMkupCo;
140   static FARPROC lpfnDoMkupPr;
141   static FARPROC lpfnDoEffPer;
142   static FARPROC lpfnDoEffCon;
143   static FARPROC lpfnDoFvSin;
144   static FARPROC lpfnDoPvSin;
145   static FARPROC lpfnDoFvAnn;
```

```
146    static FARPROC lpfnDoPvAnn;
147    static FARPROC lpfnDoLoanDat;
148    static FARPROC lpfnDoPayOut;
149    static FARPROC lpfnListAmort;
150    static FARPROC lpfnPrntAmort;
151    static HANDLE hInstance;
152
153    switch(Message)
154    {
155                /* ------------------------------------- */
156                /* Note which instance of FCWIN execution */
157                /* this is, and create instance chunks   */
158                /* (connect dialog procedures to instance).*/
159                /* Note that several copies of FCWIN      */
160                /* might be running at the same time.     */
161                /* ------------------------------------- */
162
163      case WM_CREATE:
164        hInstance = ((LPCREATESTRUCT) lParam)->hInstance;
165        lpfnDoPctChg =
166                MakeProcInstance( DoPctChg, hInstance );
167        lpfnDoPctTot =
168                MakeProcInstance( DoPctTot, hInstance );
169        lpfnDoMkupCo =
170                MakeProcInstance( DoMkupCo, hInstance );
171        lpfnDoMkupPr =
172                MakeProcInstance( DoMkupPr, hInstance );
173        lpfnDoEffPer =
174                MakeProcInstance( DoEffPer, hInstance );
175        lpfnDoEffCon =
176                MakeProcInstance( DoEffCon, hInstance );
177        lpfnDoFvSin =
178                MakeProcInstance( DoFvSin, hInstance );
179        lpfnDoPvSin =
180                MakeProcInstance( DoPvSin, hInstance );
181        lpfnDoFvAnn =
182                MakeProcInstance( DoFvAnn, hInstance );
183        lpfnDoPvAnn =
184                MakeProcInstance( DoPvAnn, hInstance );
185        lpfnDoLoanDat =
186                MakeProcInstance( DoLoanDat, hInstance );
187        lpfnDoPayOut =
```

Listing 20.2. Continued.

```
188              MakeProcInstance( DoPayOut, hInstance );
189          lpfnListAmort =
190              MakeProcInstance( ListAmort, hInstance );
191          lpfnPrntAmort =
192              MakeProcInstance( PrntAmort, hInstance );
193          return 0;
194
195                  /* ----------------------------------- */
196                  /* Process window commands. For FCWIN,  */
197                  /* this means noting which menu item    */
198                  /* was picked and starting the dialog   */
199                  /* for it. The case values shown here   */
200                  /* are declared in FCWIN.H.             */
201                  /* ----------------------------------- */
202
203      case WM_COMMAND:
204          switch( wParam ) {
205            case IDM_PCTCHANGE:
206                  if ( DialogBox( hInstance, "FCPCTCG",
207                              hWnd, lpfnDoPctChg ) )
208                    InvalidateRect( hWnd, NULL, TRUE );
209                  return 0;
210
211            case IDM_PCTTOTAL :
212                  if ( DialogBox( hInstance, "FCPCTTO",
213                              hWnd, lpfnDoPctTot ) )
214                    InvalidateRect( hWnd, NULL, TRUE );
215                  return 0;
216
217            case IDM_MKUPCOST :
218                  if ( DialogBox( hInstance, "FCMKUPCO",
219                              hWnd, lpfnDoMkupCo ) )
220                    InvalidateRect( hWnd, NULL, TRUE );
221                  return 0;
222
223            case IDM_MKUPPRICE :
224                  if ( DialogBox( hInstance, "FCMKUPPR",
225                              hWnd, lpfnDoMkupPr ) )
226                    InvalidateRect( hWnd, NULL, TRUE );
227                  return 0;
228
```

```
229        case IDM_EFFPER :
230             if ( DialogBox( hInstance, "FCEFFPER",
231                             hWnd, lpfnDoEffPer ) )
232               InvalidateRect( hWnd, NULL, TRUE );
233             return 0;
234
235        case IDM_EFFCONT :
236             if ( DialogBox( hInstance, "FCEFFCON",
237                             hWnd, lpfnDoEffCon ) )
238               InvalidateRect( hWnd, NULL, TRUE );
239             return 0;
240
241        case IDM_FVSINGLE :
242             if ( DialogBox( hInstance, "FCFVSIN",
243                             hWnd, lpfnDoFvSin ) )
244               InvalidateRect( hWnd, NULL, TRUE );
245             return 0;
246
247        case IDM_PVSINGLE :
248             if ( DialogBox( hInstance, "FCPVSIN",
249                             hWnd, lpfnDoPvSin ) )
250               InvalidateRect( hWnd, NULL, TRUE );
251             return 0;
252
253        case IDM_FVREGULAR :
254             if ( DialogBox( hInstance, "FCFVANN",
255                             hWnd, lpfnDoFvAnn ) )
256               InvalidateRect( hWnd, NULL, TRUE );
257             return 0;
258
259        case IDM_PVREGULAR :
260             if ( DialogBox( hInstance, "FCPVANN",
261                             hWnd, lpfnDoPvAnn ) )
262               InvalidateRect( hWnd, NULL, TRUE );
263             return 0;
264
265        case IDM_LOANDATA :
266             if ( DialogBox( hInstance, "FCLOANDA",
267                             hWnd, lpfnDoLoanDat ) )
268               InvalidateRect( hWnd, NULL, TRUE );
269             return 0;
270
```

Listing 20.2. Continued.

```
271          case IDM_PAYOUT:
272               if ( DialogBox( hInstance, "FCPAYOUT",
273               hWnd, lpfnDoPayOut ) )
274                  InvalidateRect( hWnd, NULL, TRUE );
275               return 0;
276
277          case IDM_DISPAMORT:
278               if ( DialogBox( hInstance, "FCMORTLS",
279                               hWnd, lpfnListAmort ) )
280                  InvalidateRect( hWnd, NULL, TRUE );
281               return 0;
282
283          case IDM_PRNTAMORT:
284               if ( DialogBox( hInstance, "FCMORTPR",
285                               hWnd, lpfnPrntAmort ) )
286                  InvalidateRect( hWnd, NULL, TRUE );
287               return 0;
288
289          case HLP_PCTCHANGE:
290           PopupMsg( HLP_PCTCHANGE - HLP_PCTCHANGE );
291           return 0;
292
293          case HLP_PCTTOTAL:
294           PopupMsg( HLP_PCTTOTAL - HLP_PCTCHANGE );
295           return 0;
296
297          case HLP_MKUPCOST:
298           PopupMsg( HLP_MKUPCOST - HLP_PCTCHANGE );
299           return 0;
300
301          case HLP_MKUPPRICE:
302           PopupMsg( HLP_MKUPPRICE - HLP_PCTCHANGE );
303           return 0;
304
305          case HLP_EFFPER:
306           PopupMsg( HLP_EFFPER - HLP_PCTCHANGE );
307           return 0;
308
309          case HLP_EFFCONT:
310           PopupMsg( HLP_EFFCONT - HLP_PCTCHANGE );
```

```
311            return 0;
312
313        case HLP_FVSINGLE:
314          PopupMsg( HLP_FVSINGLE - HLP_PCTCHANGE );
315          return 0;
316
317        case HLP_PVSINGLE:
318          PopupMsg( HLP_PVSINGLE - HLP_PCTCHANGE );
319          return 0;
320
321        case HLP_FVREGULAR:
322          PopupMsg( HLP_FVREGULAR - HLP_PCTCHANGE );
323          return 0;
324
325        case HLP_PVREGULAR:
326          PopupMsg( HLP_PVREGULAR - HLP_PCTCHANGE );
327          return 0;
328
329        case HLP_LOANDATA:
330          PopupMsg( HLP_LOANDATA - HLP_PCTCHANGE );
331          return 0;
332
333        case HLP_PAYOUT:
334          PopupMsg( HLP_PAYOUT - HLP_PCTCHANGE );
335          return 0;
336
337        case HLP_DISPAMORT:
338          PopupMsg( HLP_DISPAMORT - HLP_PCTCHANGE );
339          return 0;
340
341        case HLP_PRNTAMORT:
342          PopupMsg( HLP_PRNTAMORT - HLP_PCTCHANGE );
343          return 0;
344        }
345      break;
346
347   case WM_DESTROY:
348        PostQuitMessage(0);
349        return 0;
350   }
351   return DefWindowProc(hWnd,Message,wParam,lParam);
352 }
```

Listing 20.2. Continued.

```
353
354   /* ---------------------------------------------------- */
355   /*                                                      */
356   /*                 DIALOG PROCEDURES                    */
357   /*                                                      */
358   /* ---------------------------------------------------- */
359
360   BOOL FAR PASCAL DoPctChg( HWND hDlg, unsigned message,
361                             WORD wParam, LONG lParam)
362   {
363     switch ( message ) {
364
365       case WM_INITDIALOG:
366           SetFocus( GetDlgItem( hDlg, FCWIN_OLD ) );
367           return FALSE;
368
369       case WM_CLOSE:
370           EndDialog( hDlg, TRUE );
371           return TRUE;
372
373       case WM_COMMAND:
374         switch ( wParam ) {
375
376           case FCWIN_COMPUTE :
377               old = new = ans = 0.0;
378
379               GetDlgItemText( hDlg,FCWIN_OLD,instring,32 );
380               sscanf( instring, "%lf", &old );
381
382               GetDlgItemText( hDlg,FCWIN_NEW,instring,32 );
383               sscanf( instring, "%lf", &new );
384
385               if ( old != 0.0 )
386                 ans = ((new-old)/old)*100.0;
387               sprintf( instring, "%7.2f", ans );
388
389               SetDlgItemText( hDlg,FCWIN_ANS,instring );
390               SetFocus( GetDlgItem( hDlg,FCWIN_OLD ) );
391               return FALSE;
392
393           case FCWIN_RETURN:
```

```
394              EndDialog( hDlg, TRUE );
395              return TRUE;
396          }
397      break;
398      }
399    return FALSE;
400  }
401
402  BOOL FAR PASCAL DoPctTot( HWND hDlg, unsigned message,
403                            WORD wParam, LONG lParam)
404  {
405    switch ( message ) {
406
407      case WM_INITDIALOG:
408          SetFocus( GetDlgItem( hDlg, FCWIN_NEW ) );
409          return FALSE;
410
411      case WM_CLOSE:
412          EndDialog( hDlg, TRUE );
413          return TRUE;
414
415      case WM_COMMAND:
416        switch ( wParam ) {
417
418          case FCWIN_COMPUTE :
419              old = new = ans = 0.0;
420
421              GetDlgItemText( hDlg,FCWIN_NEW,instring,32 );
422              sscanf( instring, "%lf", &new );
423
424              GetDlgItemText( hDlg,FCWIN_OLD,instring,32 );
425              sscanf( instring, "%lf", &old );
426
427              if ( old != 0.0 )
428                ans = (new/old)*100.0;
429              sprintf( instring, "%7.2f", ans );
430
431              SetDlgItemText( hDlg, FCWIN_ANS, instring );
432              SetFocus( GetDlgItem( hDlg, FCWIN_NEW ) );
433              return FALSE;
434
435          case FCWIN_RETURN:
```

Listing 20.2. Continued.

```
436                 EndDialog( hDlg, TRUE );
437                 return TRUE;
438         }
439     break;
440     }
441   return FALSE;
442 }
443
444 BOOL FAR PASCAL DoMkupCo( HWND hDlg, unsigned message,
445                          WORD wParam, LONG lParam)
446 {
447   switch ( message ) {
448
449     case WM_INITDIALOG:
450         SetFocus( GetDlgItem( hDlg, FCWIN_OLD ) );
451         return FALSE;
452
453     case WM_CLOSE:
454         EndDialog( hDlg, TRUE );
455         return TRUE;
456
457     case WM_COMMAND:
458       switch ( wParam ) {
459
460         case FCWIN_COMPUTE :
461             old = new = ans = 0.0;
462
463             GetDlgItemText( hDlg,FCWIN_OLD,instring,32 );
464             sscanf( instring, "%lf", &old );
465
466             GetDlgItemText( hDlg,FCWIN_NEW,instring,32 );
467             sscanf( instring, "%lf", &new );
468
469             if ( new != 0.0 )
470               ans = ((old-new)/new)*100.0;
471             sprintf( instring, "%7.2f", ans );
472
473             SetDlgItemText( hDlg, FCWIN_ANS, instring );
474             SetFocus( GetDlgItem( hDlg, FCWIN_OLD ) );
475             return FALSE;
```

```
476
477        case FCWIN_RETURN:
478            EndDialog( hDlg, TRUE );
479            return TRUE;
480        }
481    break;
482    }
483    return FALSE;
484 }
485
486 BOOL FAR PASCAL DoMkupPr( HWND hDlg, unsigned message,
487                          WORD wParam, LONG lParam)
488 {
489    switch ( message ) {
490
491    case WM_INITDIALOG:
492        SetFocus( GetDlgItem( hDlg, FCWIN_OLD ) );
493        return FALSE;
494
495    case WM_CLOSE:
496        EndDialog( hDlg, TRUE );
497        return TRUE;
498
499    case WM_COMMAND:
500        switch ( wParam ) {
501
502        case FCWIN_COMPUTE :
503            old = new = ans = 0.0;
504
505            GetDlgItemText( hDlg,FCWIN_OLD,instring,32 );
506            sscanf( instring, "%lf", &old );
507
508            GetDlgItemText( hDlg,FCWIN_NEW,instring,32 );
509            sscanf( instring, "%lf", &new );
510
511            if ( new != 0.0 )
512                ans = ((old-new)/old)*100.0;
513            sprintf( instring, "%7.2f", ans );
514
515            SetDlgItemText( hDlg, FCWIN_ANS, instring );
516            SetFocus( GetDlgItem( hDlg, FCWIN_OLD ) );
517            return FALSE;
```

Listing 20.2. Continued.

```
518
519          case FCWIN_RETURN:
520                  EndDialog( hDlg, TRUE );
521                  return TRUE;
522          }
523      break;
524    }
525    return FALSE;
526  }
527
528  BOOL FAR PASCAL DoEffPer( HWND hDlg, unsigned message,
529                             WORD wParam, LONG lParam)
530  {
531    switch ( message ) {
532
533      case WM_INITDIALOG:
534          SetFocus( GetDlgItem( hDlg, FCWIN_APR ) );
535          return FALSE;
536
537      case WM_CLOSE:
538          EndDialog( hDlg, TRUE );
539          return TRUE;
540
541      case WM_COMMAND:
542        switch ( wParam ) {
543
544          case FCWIN_COMPUTE :
545              apr = freq = ans = 0.0;
546
547              GetDlgItemText( hDlg,FCWIN_APR,instring,32 );
548              sscanf( instring, "%lf", &apr );
549
550              GetDlgItemText( hDlg,FCWIN_FREQ,instring,32 );
551              sscanf( instring, "%lf", &freq );
552
553              if ( freq != 0.0 && apr != 0.0 )
554                ans = ( pow(1.0+apr/(100.0*freq),freq)-1 )
555                        * 100.0;
556              sprintf( instring, "%7.2f", ans );
557
```

```
558                SetDlgItemText( hDlg, FCWIN_ANS, instring );
559                SetFocus( GetDlgItem( hDlg, FCWIN_APR ) );
560                return FALSE;
561
562          case FCWIN_RETURN:
563                EndDialog( hDlg, TRUE );
564                return TRUE;
565        }
566      break;
567    }
568    return FALSE;
569 }
570
571 BOOL FAR PASCAL DoEffCon( HWND hDlg, unsigned message,
572                          WORD wParam, LONG lParam)
573 {
574    switch ( message ) {
575
576      case WM_INITDIALOG:
577            SetFocus( GetDlgItem( hDlg, FCWIN_APR ) );
578            return FALSE;
579
580      case WM_CLOSE:
581            EndDialog( hDlg, TRUE );
582            return TRUE;
583
584      case WM_COMMAND:
585        switch ( wParam ) {
586
587          case FCWIN_COMPUTE :
588                apr = ans = 0.0;
589
590                GetDlgItemText( hDlg,FCWIN_APR,instring,32 );
591                sscanf( instring, "%lf", &apr );
592
593                if ( apr != 0.0 )
594                  ans = ( exp(apr/100.0)-1 ) * 100.0;
595                sprintf( instring, "%7.2f", ans );
596
597                SetDlgItemText( hDlg, FCWIN_ANS, instring );
598                SetFocus( GetDlgItem( hDlg, FCWIN_APR ) );
599                return FALSE;
```

Listing 20.2. Continued.

```
600
601          case FCWIN_RETURN:
602                  EndDialog( hDlg, TRUE );
603                  return TRUE;
604          }
605      break;
606    }
607    return FALSE;
608  }
609
610  BOOL FAR PASCAL DoFvSin( HWND hDlg, unsigned message,
611                          WORD wParam, LONG lParam)
612  {
613    switch ( message ) {
614
615      case WM_INITDIALOG:
616              SetFocus( GetDlgItem( hDlg, FCWIN_AMT ) );
617              return FALSE;
618
619      case WM_CLOSE:
620              EndDialog( hDlg, TRUE );
621              return TRUE;
622
623      case WM_COMMAND:
624        switch ( wParam ) {
625
626          case FCWIN_COMPUTE :
627                  apr = amt = freq = numpay = ans = 0.0;
628
629                  GetDlgItemText( hDlg,FCWIN_AMT,instring,32 );
630                  sscanf( instring, "%lf", &amt );
631
632                  GetDlgItemText( hDlg,FCWIN_APR,instring,32 );
633                  sscanf( instring, "%lf", &apr );
634
635                  GetDlgItemText( hDlg,FCWIN_FREQ,instring,32 );
636                  sscanf( instring, "%lf", &freq );
637
638                  GetDlgItemText( hDlg,FCWIN_YEARS,instring,32 );
639                  sscanf( instring, "%lf", &years );
```

```
640
641              if ( apr != 0.0 && amt != 0.0
642                  && freq != 0.0 && years != 0.0 ) {
643                 numpay = freq * years;
644                 ans = amt * SPFV( apr, freq, numpay );
645              }
646              sprintf( instring, "%7.2f", ans );
647
648              SetDlgItemText( hDlg, FCWIN_ANS, instring );
649              SetFocus( GetDlgItem( hDlg, FCWIN_AMT ) );
650              return FALSE;
651
652          case FCWIN_RETURN:
653              EndDialog( hDlg, TRUE );
654              return TRUE;
655          }
656      break;
657      }
658    return FALSE;
659 }
660
661 BOOL FAR PASCAL DoPvSin( HWND hDlg, unsigned message,
662                    WORD wParam, LONG lParam)
663 {
664    switch ( message ) {
665
666      case WM_INITDIALOG:
667          SetFocus( GetDlgItem( hDlg, FCWIN_AMT ) );
668          return FALSE;
669
670      case WM_CLOSE:
671          EndDialog( hDlg, TRUE );
672          return TRUE;
673
674      case WM_COMMAND:
675        switch ( wParam ) {
676
677          case FCWIN_COMPUTE :
678              apr = amt = freq = numpay = ans = 0.0;
679
680              GetDlgItemText( hDlg,FCWIN_AMT,instring,32 );
681              sscanf( instring, "%lf", &amt );
```

Listing 20.2. Continued.

```
682
683                GetDlgItemText( hDlg,FCWIN_APR,instring,32 );
684                sscanf( instring, "%lf", &apr );
685
686                GetDlgItemText( hDlg,FCWIN_FREQ,instring,32 );
687                sscanf( instring, "%lf", &freq );
688
689                GetDlgItemText( hDlg,FCWIN_YEARS,instring,32 );
690                sscanf( instring, "%lf", &years );
691
692                if ( apr != 0.0 && amt != 0.0
693                    && freq != 0.0 && years != 0.0 ) {
694                  numpay = freq * years;
695                  ans = amt * SPPV( apr, freq, numpay );
696                }
697                sprintf( instring, "%7.2f", ans );
698
699                SetDlgItemText( hDlg, FCWIN_ANS, instring );
700                SetFocus( GetDlgItem( hDlg, FCWIN_AMT ) );
701                return FALSE;
702
703           case FCWIN_RETURN:
704                EndDialog( hDlg, TRUE );
705                return TRUE;
706         }
707       break;
708     }
709    return FALSE;
710 }
711
712 BOOL FAR PASCAL DoFvAnn( HWND hDlg, unsigned message,
713                     WORD wParam, LONG lParam)
714 {
715    switch ( message ) {
716
717      case WM_INITDIALOG:
718           SetFocus( GetDlgItem( hDlg, FCWIN_AMT ) );
719           return FALSE;
720
721      case WM_CLOSE:
722           EndDialog( hDlg, TRUE );
```

```
723            return TRUE;
724
725      case WM_COMMAND:
726        switch ( wParam ) {
727
728          case FCWIN_COMPUTE :
729                apr = amt = freq = numpay = ans = 0.0;
730
731                GetDlgItemText( hDlg,FCWIN_AMT,instring,32 );
732                sscanf( instring, "%lf", &amt );
733
734                GetDlgItemText( hDlg,FCWIN_APR,instring,32 );
735                sscanf( instring, "%lf", &apr );
736
737                GetDlgItemText( hDlg,FCWIN_FREQ,instring,32 );
738                sscanf( instring, "%lf", &freq );
739
740                GetDlgItemText( hDlg,FCWIN_YEARS,instring,32 );
741                sscanf( instring, "%lf", &years );
742
743                if ( apr != 0.0 && amt != 0.0
744                    && freq != 0.0 && years != 0.0 ) {
745                  numpay = freq * years;
746                  ans = amt * USFV( apr, freq, numpay );
747                }
748                sprintf( instring, "%7.2f", ans );
749
750                SetDlgItemText( hDlg, FCWIN_ANS, instring );
751                SetFocus( GetDlgItem( hDlg, FCWIN_AMT ) );
752                return FALSE;
753
754          case FCWIN_RETURN:
755                EndDialog( hDlg, TRUE );
756                return TRUE;
757        }
758      break;
759    }
760    return FALSE;
761 }
762
763 BOOL FAR PASCAL DoPvAnn( HWND hDlg, unsigned message,
764                    WORD wParam, LONG lParam)
```

Listing 20.2. Continued.

```
765  {
766    switch ( message ) {
767
768      case WM_INITDIALOG:
769          SetFocus( GetDlgItem( hDlg, FCWIN_AMT ) );
770          return FALSE;
771
772      case WM_CLOSE:
773          EndDialog( hDlg, TRUE );
774          return TRUE;
775
776      case WM_COMMAND:
777        switch ( wParam ) {
778
779          case FCWIN_COMPUTE :
780              apr = amt = freq = numpay = ans = 0.0;
781
782              GetDlgItemText( hDlg,FCWIN_AMT,instring,32 );
783              sscanf( instring, "%lf", &amt );
784
785              GetDlgItemText( hDlg,FCWIN_APR,instring,32 );
786              sscanf( instring, "%lf", &apr );
787
788              GetDlgItemText( hDlg,FCWIN_FREQ,instring,32 );
789              sscanf( instring, "%lf", &freq );
790
791              GetDlgItemText( hDlg,FCWIN_YEARS,instring,32 );
792              sscanf( instring, "%lf", &years );
793
794              if ( apr != 0.0 && amt != 0.0
795                  && freq != 0.0 && years != 0.0 ) {
796                numpay = freq * years;
797                ans = amt * USPV( apr, freq, numpay );
798              }
799              sprintf( instring, "%7.2f", ans );
800
801              SetDlgItemText( hDlg, FCWIN_ANS, instring );
802              SetFocus( GetDlgItem( hDlg, FCWIN_AMT ) );
803              return FALSE;
804
805          case FCWIN_RETURN:
```

```
806              EndDialog( hDlg, TRUE );
807              return TRUE;
808         }
809     break;
810     }
811   return FALSE;
812 }
813
814 BOOL FAR PASCAL DoLoanDat( HWND hDlg, unsigned message,
815                     WORD wParam, LONG lParam)
816 {
817   switch ( message ) {
818
819                 /*------------------------------------ */
820                 /*  Prime the edit control boxes with  */
821                 /*   initial values.                   */
822                 /*------------------------------------ */
823
824     case WM_INITDIALOG:
825         sprintf( instring, "%7.2f", amt );
826         SetDlgItemText( hDlg, FCWIN_AMT, instring );
827
828         sprintf( instring, "%7.2f", apr );
829         SetDlgItemText( hDlg, FCWIN_APR, instring );
830
831         sprintf( instring, "%7.2f", freq );
832         SetDlgItemText( hDlg, FCWIN_FREQ, instring );
833
834         sprintf( instring, "%7.2f", years );
835         SetDlgItemText( hDlg, FCWIN_YEARS, instring );
836
837         SetFocus( GetDlgItem( hDlg, FCWIN_AMT ) );
838         return FALSE;
839
840     case WM_CLOSE:
841         EndDialog( hDlg, TRUE );
842         return TRUE;
843
844     case WM_COMMAND:
845       switch ( wParam ) {
846
847         case FCWIN_RETURN :
```

Listing 20.2. Continued.

```
848              GetDlgItemText( hDlg, FCWIN_AMT, instring, 32 );
849              sscanf( instring, "%lf", &amt );
850
851              GetDlgItemText( hDlg, FCWIN_APR, instring, 32 );
852              sscanf( instring, "%lf", &apr );
853
854              GetDlgItemText( hDlg, FCWIN_FREQ, instring, 32 );
855              sscanf( instring, "%lf", &freq );
856
857              GetDlgItemText( hDlg, FCWIN_YEARS, instring, 32 );
858              sscanf( instring, "%lf", &years );
859
860              if ( apr != 0.0 && amt != 0.0
861                  && freq != 0.0 && years != 0.0 ) {
862                numpay = freq * years;
863              }
864
865              EndDialog( hDlg, TRUE );
866              return TRUE;
867          }
868      break;
869      }
870      return FALSE;
871  }
872
873  BOOL FAR PASCAL DoPayout( HWND hDlg, unsigned message,
874                            WORD wParam, LONG lParam)
875  {
876    switch ( message ) {
877
878      case WM_INITDIALOG:
879          levelpay = 1 / USPV( apr, freq, numpay ) * amt;
880
881          sprintf( instring, "%7.2f", amt );
882          SetDlgItemText( hDlg, FCWIN_AMT, instring );
883
884          sprintf( instring, "%7.2f", apr );
885          SetDlgItemText( hDlg, FCWIN_APR, instring );
886
887          sprintf( instring, "%7.2f", freq );
```

```
888          SetDlgItemText( hDlg, FCWIN_FREQ, instring );
889
890          sprintf( instring, "%7.2f", years );
891          SetDlgItemText( hDlg, FCWIN_YEARS, instring );
892
893          sprintf( instring, "%7.2f", levelpay );
894          SetDlgItemText( hDlg, FCWIN_LEVELPAY, instring );
895
896          sprintf( instring, "%7.2f", levelpay*numpay );
897          SetDlgItemText( hDlg, FCWIN_TOTPAY, instring );
898
899          sprintf( instring, "%7.2f", levelpay*numpay-amt );
900          SetDlgItemText( hDlg, FCWIN_INTPAY, instring );
901
902          sprintf( instring, "%7.2f",
903                    ((levelpay*numpay-amt)/amt)*100.0 );
904          SetDlgItemText( hDlg, FCWIN_BALLOON, instring );
905
906          return TRUE;
907
908      case WM_CLOSE:
909          EndDialog( hDlg, TRUE );
910          return TRUE;
911
912     }
913     return FALSE;
914  }
915
916  BOOL FAR PASCAL ListAmort( HWND hDlg, unsigned message,
917                             WORD wParam, LONG lParam )
918  {
919     HANDLE hWndCntrl;
920
921     switch ( message ) {
922
923      case WM_INITDIALOG:
924          hWndCntrl = GetDlgItem( hDlg, FCWIN_LISTBOX );
925
926          levelpay = 1 / USPV( apr, freq, numpay ) * amt;
927          payno = 0;
928
929          while ( payno < numpay ) {
```

Listing 20.2. Continued.

```
930                ++payno;
931                intpay = levelpay
932                        * USPV( apr, freq, numpay-payno+1.0 )
933                        * (apr/freq/100.0);
934                prinpay = levelpay - intpay;
935                bal = levelpay * USPV( apr, freq, numpay-payno );
936                BuildTextMessage( "%12d%12.2f%12.2f%12.2f%12.2f",
937                                  (int)payno, levelpay,
938                                  intpay, prinpay,
939                                  bal
940                                );
941                SendMessage( hWndCntrl, LB_ADDSTRING, NULL,
942                            (LONG)(LPSTR) textmsg );
943            }
944
945            SetFocus( GetDlgItem( hDlg, FCWIN_RETURN ) );
946            return FALSE;
947
948        case WM_CLOSE:
949            EndDialog( hDlg, TRUE );
950            return TRUE;
951
952        case WM_COMMAND:
953          switch ( wParam ) {
954
955            case FCWIN_RETURN  :
956                EndDialog( hDlg, TRUE );
957                return TRUE;
958          }
959        break;
960      }
961      return FALSE;
962  }
963
964  BOOL FAR PASCAL PrntAmort( HWND hDlg, unsigned message,
965                             WORD wParam, LONG lParam )
966  {
967
968                    /* ---------------------------------- */
969                    /* DeviceMode() not in windows.h file.  */
```

```
970                    /* Provide a typedef for the function.  */
971                    /* --------------------------------- */
972
973    typedef VOID (FAR PASCAL *DEVMODEPROC)(HWND,HANDLE,
974                                      LPSTR,LPSTR);
975
976    HDC hPr;           /* Device context handle for printer */
977
978    char szPrinter[80];        /* Device info from WIN.INI */
979    char szDriverFile[16];  /* Name of prt driver DLL file */
980
981    HANDLE hLibrary;      /* Handle for prt driver DLL file */
982    DEVMODEPROC lpfnDM;    /* Pointer to DeviceMode() proc */
983
984    LPSTR szPrintType;             /* Printer type string */
985    LPSTR szPrintDriver;    /* Printer driver name string */
986    LPSTR szPrintPort;          /* Printer port name string */
987
988    int LineSpace, LinesPerPage, CurrentLine, LineLength;
989
990    POINT PhysPageSize;
991    TEXTMETRIC TextMetric;
992
993    switch ( message ) {
994
995      case WM_INITDIALOG:
996          SetFocus( GetDlgItem( hDlg, FCWIN_START ) );
997          return FALSE;
998
999      case WM_CLOSE:
1000          EndDialog( hDlg, TRUE );
1001          return TRUE;
1002
1003      case WM_COMMAND:
1004        switch ( wParam ) {
1005
1006          case FCWIN_START :
1007
1008                    /* --------------------------------- */
1009                    /* Get the profile string for the    */
1010                    /* current printer and parse it.     */
1011                    /* --------------------------------- */
```

Listing 20.2. Continued.

```
1012
1013            GetProfileString( "windows", "device", ",,,",
1014                            szPrinter, 80 );
1015        if ( (szPrintType   = strtok( szPrinter, "," )) &&
1016             (szPrintDriver = strtok( NULL,      "," )) &&
1017             (szPrintPort   = strtok( NULL,      "," )))
1018
1019                /* ---------------------------------- */
1020                /* Create a device context for the    */
1021                /* printer.                           */
1022                /* ---------------------------------- */
1023
1024          hPr = CreateDC( (LPSTR)szPrintDriver,
1025                          (LPSTR)szPrintType,
1026                          (LPSTR)szPrintPort,
1027                          NULL );
1028        else {
1029          MessageBox( hDlg, "Unable to start printing.",
1030                      NULL, MB_OK | MB_ICONHAND );
1031          DeleteDC( hPr );
1032          EndDialog( hDlg, TRUE );
1033          return TRUE;
1034        }
1035
1036                /* ---------------------------------- */
1037                /* This code loads the driver file from */
1038                /* the DLL. Get the handle for the    */
1039                /* driver. Use the handle to get the  */
1040                /* address of its DeviceMode() function, */
1041                /* and invoke it using the pointer. This */
1042                /* code causes the printer             */
1043                /* initialization dialog to pop up.    */
1044                /* ---------------------------------- */
1045
1046        strcat( strcpy( szDriverFile, szPrintDriver ), ".DRV" );
1047        hLibrary = LoadLibrary( szDriverFile ); /* get DLL mod
*/
1048        if ( hLibrary < 32 ) {
1049          MessageBox( hDlg, "Can't locate the driver\n"
1050                      "file for this printer.",
1051                      NULL, MB_OK | MB_ICONHAND );
```

```
1052            DeleteDC( hPr );
1053            EndDialog( hDlg, TRUE );
1054            return TRUE;
1055        }
1056        lpfnDM = GetProcAddress( hLibrary, "DEVICEMODE" );
1057        (*lpfnDM)( hDlg, hLibrary, (LPSTR)szPrintType,
1058                (LPSTR)szPrintPort );
1059
1060            /* ----------------------------------- */
1061            /* Notify Print Manager that you are    */
1062            /* about to start spooling print using  */
1063            /* the STARTDOC Escape call.            */
1064            /* ----------------------------------- */
1065
1066        if ( Escape( hPr, STARTDOC, 11,
1067            "PrintAmort", 0L ) < 0 ) {
1068        MessageBox( hDlg, "Unable to start printing.",
1069                NULL, MB_OK | MB_ICONHAND );
1070        DeleteDC( hPr );
1071        EndDialog( hDlg, TRUE );
1072        return TRUE;
1073        }
1074
1075            /* ----------------------------------- */
1076            /* Now calculate printing area parameters */
1077            /* using the GetTextMetrics() function  */
1078            /* and the GETPHYSPAGESIZE Escape call. */
1079            /* ----------------------------------- */
1080
1081        GetTextMetrics( hPr, &TextMetric );
1082        LineSpace = TextMetric.tmHeight
1083                + TextMetric.tmExternalLeading;
1084        Escape( hPr, GETPHYSPAGESIZE, NULL, NULL,
1085                (LPSTR)&PhysPageSize);
1086        LinesPerPage = ( PhysPageSize.y / LineSpace ) - 6;
1087        CurrentLine = LinesPerPage + 1;
1088
1089        levelpay = 1 / USPV( apr, freq, numpay ) * amt;
1090        payno = 0;
1091
1092            /* ----------------------------------- */
1093            /* Finally, loop and use TextOut() to   */
```

Listing 20.2. Continued.

```
1094                    /* spool print.                        */
1095                    /* -------------------------------- */
1096
1097            while ( payno < numpay ) {
1098                if ( ++CurrentLine >= LinesPerPage ) {
1099                    Escape( hPr, NEWFRAME, 0, 0L, 0L );
1100                    CurrentLine = 0;
1101                    BuildTextMessage( "%s%s%s%s%s%s",
1102                                      "  Paymnt #  ",
1103                                      " Level Pay  ",
1104                                      "   Int Amt   ",
1105                                      "  Prin Amt   ",
1106                                      "  Balance   " );
1107                    TextOut( hPr, 0, CurrentLine*LineSpace,
1108                            (LPSTR)textmsg, strlen(textmsg) );
1109                    ++CurrentLine;
1110                    BuildTextMessage( "%s%s%s%s%s%s",
1111                                      "-----------",
1112                                      "-----------",
1113                                      "-----------",
1114                                      "-----------",
1115                                      "-----------" );
1116                    TextOut( hPr, 0, CurrentLine*LineSpace,
1117                            (LPSTR)textmsg, strlen(textmsg) );
1118                    ++CurrentLine;
1119                }
1120                ++payno;
1121                intpay = levelpay
1122                        * USPV( apr, freq, numpay-payno+1.0 )
1123                        * (apr/freq/100.0);
1124                prinpay = levelpay - intpay;
1125                bal = levelpay * USPV( apr, freq, numpay-payno );
1126                BuildTextMessage( "%12d%12.2f%12.2f%12.2f%12.2f",
1127                                  (int)payno, levelpay,
1128                                  intpay, prinpay,
1129                                  bal
1130                                );
1131                TextOut( hPr, 0, CurrentLine*LineSpace,
1132                        (LPSTR)textmsg, strlen(textmsg) );
1133            }
1134
```

```
1135              Escape( hPr, NEWFRAME, 0, 0L, 0L );
1136              Escape( hPr, ENDDOC, 0, 0L, 0L );
1137              FreeLibrary( hLibrary );
1138              DeleteDC( hPr );
1139              EndDialog( hDlg, TRUE );
1140              return TRUE;
1141
1142          case FCWIN_CANCEL :
1143              EndDialog( hDlg, TRUE );
1144              return TRUE;
1145        }
1146      break;
1147    }
1148    return FALSE;
1149 }
1150 /* ------------------------------------------------------ */
1151 /*                                                        */
1152 /*              HELPER ROUTINES FOLLOW                    */
1153 /*                                                        */
1154 /* ------------------------------------------------------ */
1155
1156 void BuildTextMessage( char* szFormat, ... )
1157 {
1158    va_list ap;
1159
1160    va_start( ap, szFormat );
1161    vsprintf( textmsg, szFormat, ap );
1162    va_end( ap );
1163 }
1164
1165 double SPFV( double apr, double freq, double periods )
1166 {
1167    return( pow(1.0+(apr/freq)/100.0,periods) );
1168 }
1169
1170
1171 double SPPV( double apr, double freq, double periods )
1172 {
1173    return( 1.0 / SPFV(apr,freq,periods) );
1174 }
1175
1176 double USPV( double apr, double freq, double periods )
```

Listing 20.2. Continued.

```
1177  {
1178     return( ( 1.0 - 1.0
1179                 / SPFV(apr,freq,periods))
1180                 / (apr/freq/100.0) );
1181  }
1182
1183  double USFV( double apr, double freq, double periods )
1184  {
1185     return( ( SPFV(apr,freq,periods)- 1.0) / (apr/freq/100.0) );
1186  }
1187
```

Creating Source Files for Windows Applications

A graphical user interface such as Windows is a complicated environment because you can do so much *with* it and *in* it. This fact is highlighted by the contrast between the original finance.c program and the Windows version, fcwin.c. Both programs do similar things; however, fcwin.c provides the user with a more pleasant appearance, more flexibility and utility in handling the windows (for editing, display, and so on), and greatly enhanced printing capability. All this is true just because FCWIN (referring to it by the project name) exists in a GUI.

The original text-based finance.c program consisted of a single source file capable of being compiled immediately and directly. But FCWIN consists of three ASCII text source files and a binary Windows resource file that all must be compiled, linked, and combined—in addition to the DLL file that must be produced to support the help facility (the original finance.c program had no help facility).

Thus, much of the design of FCWIN must focus on the program's interface to the Windows environment. This section explains these design considerations. The discussion assumes that you have read the description of the fcwin.res resource file and its components in Chapter 19.

Understanding the Windows 3.1 Programming Environment

A number of elements must come together correctly to create a Windows executable program file for even the simplest application program, such as FCWIN. Figure 20.2 shows the components that create the finished FCWIN application.

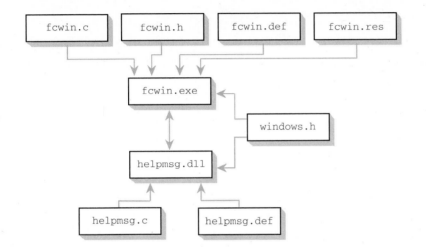

Figure 20.2.

Source files, support files, and finished executable files for FCWIN.

Figure 20.2 includes the fcwin.res resource file (containing menus, dialog boxes, and icons). If necessary, refer to Chapter 19 for a discussion of resource files, and fcwin.res in particular.

The main file is a standard C file, fcwin.c. The fcwin.c file, shown in Listing 20.2, contains the logic that drives the entire application. The main source file cannot function without the module-definition (.DEF) file; however, the main source file does not use the module-definition file directly.

The main file does use the fcwin.h application header file, in that the program #includes the header and depends on constant values #defined there. The main file uses the resource (.RES) file directly, in that it refers to objects located in the resource file by resource name. (A resource name is recorded in the .RES file with each resource object.)

The manner in which the main source file depends on the contents of its support files is discussed in the remainder of this chapter. Chapter 21 explains the logical structure of the main program file, and discusses the construction and use of the help DLL.

Creating a Module-Definition File

The module-definition file describes for the compiler and linker the relationship of the main source file to the Windows environment. Listing 20.3 is the module-definition file for FCWIN.

Listing 20.3. fcwin.def, the FCWIN module-definition file.

```
 1  NAME          FCCalcs
 2  DESCRIPTION   'Sample Windows application for UMC'
 3  STUB          'WINSTUB.EXE'
 4  EXETYPE       WINDOWS
 5  CODE          PRELOAD MOVEABLE DISCARDABLE
 6  DATA          PRELOAD MOVEABLE MULTIPLE
 7  HEAPSIZE      8192
 8  STACKSIZE     8192
 9  EXPORTS       WndProc
10          DoPctChg
11          DoPctTot
12          DoMkupCo
13          DoMkupPr
14          DoEffPer
15          DoEffCon
16          DoFvSin
17          DoPvSin
18          DoFvAnn
19          DoPvAnn
20          DoLoanDat
21          DoPayOut
22          ListAmort
23          PrntAmort
24  IMPORTS     HELPMSG.PopupMsg
```

The tokens coded in all uppercase are reserved words, and should be written as you see them here. The NAME statement (in line 1) both defines the associated source file as a Windows application program and identifies the application to Windows. A program module must have a NAME statement, but the NAME field does not have to be the same as the program name.

The statements in lines 2 through 8 provide a description of the program module plus important information about how the module can be handled by Windows. Notice that the stub program is named here (in line 4). Lines 5 and 6 tell Windows that both code and data should be preloaded when starting the application, and that they can be moved in memory during execution. Program code can even be thrown away and reloaded during execution (the code is discardable). If multiple instances of the application are running concurrently, line 6 also tells Windows that each instance has its own data segment. Finally, notice that you can control the heap and stack size for the program (lines 7 and 8).

The EXPORTS statement (lines 9 through 23) identifies for Windows the functions in the main source file that Windows can call outside your program. For FCWIN, these functions include the WndProc() window procedure and the dialog procedures (functions called to control a dialog). FCWIN has 14 dialogs, one for each kind of financial computation.

The IMPORTS statement in line 24 identifies the PopupMsg() function, which resides in the HELPMSG.DLL file. This declaration tells Windows where to locate the function when PopupMsg() is called. Building the DLL is discussed at the end of Chapter 21.

Designing the Program's Header File

The next step is coding the application program's header file, fcwin.h. The application header is used by only the main source file. An application header usually contains a macro defining the application name (used to register the window class) and *manifest constants* used by the program. The manifest constants correspond to the ordinal (integer) values of display windows and their controls that send messages to your program. The fcwin.h header is shown in Listing 20.4.

Listing 20.4. fcwin.h. The FCWIN header file for the Windows environment.

```
 1   #define szAppName "FinancialCalcs"
 2
 3   #define IDM_PCTCHANGE    1
 4   #define IDM_PCTTOTAL     2
 5   #define IDM_MKUPCOST     3
 6   #define IDM_MKUPPRICE    4
 7   #define IDM_EFFPER       5
 8   #define IDM_EFFCONT      6
 9   #define IDM_FVSINGLE     7
10   #define IDM_PVSINGLE     8
11   #define IDM_FVREGULAR    9
12   #define IDM_PVREGULAR   10
13   #define IDM_LOANDATA    11
```

Listing 20.4. Continued.

```
14   #define IDM_PAYOUT       12
15   #define IDM_DISPAMORT     13
16   #define IDM_PRNTAMORT     14
17
18   #define HLP_PCTCHANGE     15
19   #define HLP_PCTTOTAL      16
20   #define HLP_MKUPCOST      17
21   #define HLP_MKUPPRICE     18
22   #define HLP_EFFPER        19
23   #define HLP_EFFCONT       20
24   #define HLP_FVSINGLE      21
25   #define HLP_PVSINGLE      22
26   #define HLP_FVREGULAR     23
27   #define HLP_PVREGULAR     24
28   #define HLP_LOANDATA      25
29   #define HLP_PAYOUT        26
30   #define HLP_DISPAMORT     27
31   #define HLP_PRNTAMORT     28
32
33   #define FCWIN_OLD         101
34   #define FCWIN_NEW         102
35   #define FCWIN_ANS         103
36   #define FCWIN_RETURN      104
37   #define FCWIN_COMPUTE     105
38   #define FCWIN_APR         106
39   #define FCWIN_AMT         107
40   #define FCWIN_YEARS       108
41   #define FCWIN_FREQ        109
42   #define FCWIN_LISTBOX     110
43   #define FCWIN_LEVELPAY    111
44   #define FCWIN_INTPAY      112
45   #define FCWIN_TOTPAY      113
46   #define FCWIN_BALLOON     114
47   #define FCWIN_START       115
48   #define FCWIN_CANCEL      116
```

Line 1 in Listing 20.4 defines a constant string containing the application name. The application name could have been declared directly in the main source file, but this place is better (in other words, more visible).

Manifest constants of various sorts make up the rest of the FCWIN header. The macro name IDM_PCTCHANGE (line 3), for example, defines the ordinal value of the menu-selection item for the Percent Change calculation. When a user clicks the Percent Change menu item, Windows sends a Windows message command (WM_COMMAND) to your window procedure (WndProc()) using that value as a subparameter. It is much easier to refer to the message ID by name rather than by the ordinal number. These manifest constants are associated with the menu item based on their usage in the fcmenu.rc file.

The object-like macros in lines 33 through 48 serve a different purpose. These macros define ordinal values associated with window controls, such as edit boxes, list boxes, and pushbuttons. The FCWIN_COMPUTE macro, for example, is assigned an ordinal value of 105. Defining these constants is one of the most tedious parts of Windows programming because you must be sure that the value matches the one you assigned to any Compute pushbutton in a dialog box. Control IDs are passed to the appropriate dialog procedure and acted on there, in a manner similar to the processing performed in the window procedure for the parent window.

Before compiling the program, be sure that your header is included in the main source file, together with the Windows header, as follows:

```
#include <windows.h>
#include "fcwin.h"
```

If you do not include both of these header files, the compile will fail miserably.

Creating a Project File for FCWIN

The application's project file is the first of two keys to building a Windows program, as opposed to building just a C program. Using the PWB, open a new project and add to it the three files fcwin.c, fcwin.def, and fcwin.res. When you are prompted, be sure to specify C runtime support and the Windows EXE template. Otherwise, the correct entry and exit code will not be compiled for the program's functions.

Having created a project file, select either **B**uild or **R**ebuild all from the **Pr**oject menu. The FCWIN Windows application is built in the following steps:

- *Compilation of the source code to object code proceeds normally.* The only visible difference between this and a normal C compilation is the presence of the windows.h header with its (large) collection of prototypes and declarations. (Remember, however, that internally the entry and exit code generated is now specifically for Windows).

- *The linker takes notice of the requested Windows environment.* At this point, things begin to happen differently from a normal C program build. First, the program needs different initialization code. Second, because the entry and exit code normally wrapped around the library functions won't do either, you need the Windows versions of the libraries (SLIBCEW.LIB for the small model, plus LIBW).

■ *Finally, the Resource Compiler builds the completed application .EXE file.* Although the output from the preceding step is an .EXE file, it lacks the Windows stub and the resources (menus, icons, dialog boxes, and more) your program uses. All these things are packaged in the Windows executable file. Clearly, the result is not a normal DOS .EXE file.

You can take full control of the application-building process if you want. You can use the command compiler and linker, or you can write an NMAKE file to compile and link your Windows application program. Considering the convenience of the Windows development tools provided by the combination of the Microsoft C/C++ PWB and the Windows-based Dialog Editor, it is difficult to conceive of circumstances that would force you to abandon the convenience of the Programmer's WorkBench.

Now you know everything there is to know about building a basic Windows application with Microsoft C/C++ 7.0, except how to write the code (and a few other variations and details). Constructing the logic for a Windows program is covered in the next chapter.

Exercises

Because Chapters 20 and 21 are tightly coupled, the practice exercises for this chapter are deferred until the end of Chapter 21.

Summary

This chapter gave you an introduction to the source files required to build a Windows application program, and a basic knowledge of the environment in which your application program will operate. You were introduced to the following topics:

■ *Using the WINSTUB.EXE executable file, and how to understand the Windows directory structure.*

■ *How to design and write the supporting source files for your Windows program.* These files include the module-definition (.DEF) file, your program's header (.H) file, and the binary resource definition (.RES) file.

■ *How the compiler and linker use the support files to tailor your program to the Windows environment.*

This is not a good place to end the discussion; because all the pieces are not in place yet, stopping here would leave many questions unanswered. Continue by reading Chapter 21 to see how your Windows program does its work in the Windows environment.

Writing Windows Applications with Microsoft C/C++

In Chapter 20, you learned how to design and write the necessary source files for a Windows application program, and you learned about the environment in which the program operates. This chapter is an extension of the same subject. It discusses the program logic required to interface your program with the Windows environment. The application used to illustrate these techniques is still FCWIN, the financial calculator program.

The program listing for fcwin.c (refer to Listing 20.2) is mentioned frequently in this chapter. In many places, portions of the code are repeated, retaining the original line numbers from Listing 20.2. You may want to glance occasionally at the entire source file for a sense of context and continuity.

Designing Windows Interfaces

You *must* write a number of things into your Windows program, and many more things *can* be written into your Windows program. Necessary tasks include registering the window class, creating the main window, setting up the main message loop, and providing a window procedure to handle incoming messages. Some optional features used by FCWIN include establishing dialog boxes, controlling dialogs by using callback functions, by using message boxes, establishing a device context for the printer device, producing a report, and using a DLL module to provide a help facility. This section deals with these topics.

Just as there must be a `main()` function in a plain C or C++ program, a Windows application program has a required function that is the primary entry point. In the Windows environment, this required function is `WinMain()`, and it must have that name. Furthermore, because the `WinMain()` function is called by Windows from outside your program, it must be exported. For the FCWIN application, the export is performed by writing the EXPORTS statement in the .DEF file, as follows:

```
EXPORTS      WinMain
             ... ( other exports )
```

Any function that will be called by Windows management modules from outside your program must be exported—just add the function names to the EXPORTS list in the .DEF file. Such functions are termed *callback functions* because they are called from elsewhere in the environment.

The `WinMain()` function is where you write the code that drives the entire application. In this function you must register the window class, create the main window, and establish the main message loop. These topics are discussed in this section.

Registering the Window Class

Before you can create a window for FCWIN, you must tell Windows something about the attributes of the window. This action, called *registering the window class,* is performed in the `WinMain()` function (or in a function that `WinMain()` can call). In addition to registering the window class, you must make the program aware of which instance (in other words, which execution) of the application owns the class: A window class has to be registered only once, no matter how many concurrent copies are running. The following lines of code excerpted from Listing 20.2 show how to register the window class:

```
68   int PASCAL WinMain(HANDLE hInstance, HANDLE hPrevInstance,
69                      LPSTR lpszCmdLine, int nCmdShow )
70   {
71        WNDCLASS    wndClass;
...
79        if ( !hPrevInstance )
80        {
81            wndClass.style       =CS_HREDRAW | CS_VREDRAW ;
82            wndClass.lpfnWndProc  =WndProc;
```

```
83              wndClass.cbClsExtra    =0;
84              wndClass.cbWndExtra    =0;
85              wndClass.hInstance     =hInstance;
86              wndClass.hIcon         =LoadIcon(NULL,
87                                            "IDI_APPLICATION");
88              wndClass.hCursor       =LoadCursor(NULL,IDC_ARROW );
89              wndClass.hbrBackground=GetStockObject(WHITE_BRUSH );
90              wndClass.lpszMenuName ="FCMenu";
91              wndClass.lpszClassName=szAppName;
92
93      if (!RegisterClass(&wndClass))
94          return FALSE;
...
121     }
```

The concept of *instance* is an important one in the Windows environment
because several copies of the same program can be running at the same time.
You must take care to register the window class only once, as shown in the
preceding code fragment. Notice that WinMain() accepts the hInstance and
hPrevInstance arguments. The class has to be registered only if there is no
previous instance (no other copy running yet—this one is the first). If there
are no other instances, hPrevInstance is zero.

The window class is built in a structure with type WNDCLASS. Ten member-data
items must be filled in by the program, as follows:

■ wndClass.style = CS_HREDRAW ¦ CS_VREDRAW;

Assigning these attributes to the window's style tells Windows to redraw
the window automatically if it is moved or resized by the user.

■ wndClass.lpfnWndProc = WndProc;

This member variable informs Windows which function you will provide for the window procedure that interprets and acts on Windows
messages.

■ wndClass.cbClsExtra=0;

The cbClsExtra member tells Windows how many extra bytes to allocate
for this class structure. FCWIN needs none.

■ wndClass.cbWndExtra=0;

The cbWndExtra member tells Windows how many extra bytes to allocate
for all windows created with this class. FCWIN needs none.

■ wndClass.hInstance=hInstance;

This member informs Windows which instance of FCWIN owns the window class (*this* one does—sounds much like the C++ this pointer,
doesn't it?).

■ `wndClass.hIcon=LoadIcon(NULL, "IDI_APPLICATION");`

The `hIcon` member specifies which icon is used if the application's window is minimized by a user. `IDI_APPLICATION` specifies the built-in application icon.

■ `wndClass.hCursor=LoadCursor(NULL,IDC_ARROW );`

`hCursor` specifies the cursor to use with the application. It is the normal mouse arrow cursor for FCWIN.

■ `wndClass.hbrBackground=GetStockObject(WHITE_BRUSH );`

The `GetStockObject( WHITE_BRUSH )` Windows function causes the background for FCWIN to be painted white.

■ `wndClass.lpszMenuName="FCMenu";`

You must specify the menu to be used with FCWIN. The string given here, `"FCMenu"`, must match the resource name of the menu shown in the fcmenu.rc resource script file and stored eventually in the FCWIN.RES file.

■ `wndClass.lpszClassName=szAppName;`

Finally, tell Windows the application's name. Remember that `szAppname` is a C macro in the fcwin.h header (line 1) and is equated to the `"FinancialCalcs"` string.

You use the `RegisterClass()` Windows function to register the window class (see lines 93 and 94 of Listing 20.2). If the class cannot be registered, the program returns a `FALSE` value and ends the application.

After registering the window class, you must tell Windows to create the window. You do this with the `CreateWindow()` function, shown in lines 73 through 110 of Listing 20.2:

```
73      HWND          hWnd;
74

...
100     hWnd = CreateWindow(szAppName,
101                   "Financial Calculations",
102                   WS_OVERLAPPEDWINDOW,
103                   CW_USEDEFAULT,
104                   CW_USEDEFAULT,
105                   CW_USEDEFAULT,
106                   CW_USEDEFAULT,
107                   NULL,
108                   NULL,
109                   hInstance,
110                   NULL);
```

Line 73 declares a window handle (a unique integer that identifies this particular window, corresponding to *this* particular instance of program execution—using the word *this* in much the same sense as the C++ *this). The call to CreateWindow() in lines 100 through 110 tells Windows how to go about initializing the window.

The first argument to the function is the application name string, followed by a string used as the window's title text. The next argument tells Windows that this is an overlapped window, meaning that it can be covered partially or wholly by another window, and must be refreshed if that occurs.

Next, four consecutive arguments specify CW_USEDEFAULT. This means that Windows is to build the FCWIN window with default values for the horizontal position, vertical position, window width, and window height, respectively.

The first NULL argument specifies that FCWIN's main window has no parent window (it is a parent window). The next NULL argument indicates that there is no override menu; the one given in the window class structure should be used.

Creating a window does not necessarily mean that it is visible yet on-screen. You should use the ShowWindow() function as soon as possible after creating the window to display it (line 112):

```
112     ShowWindow(hWnd, nCmdShow);
113     UpdateWindow(hWnd);
```

The UpdateWindow() function call in line 113 tells Windows that all or part of the window's client area is invalid, and that the WM_PAINT message should be issued to the window procedure.

Usually, the WM_PAINT message is very important for applications that paint information in the client area. FCWIN does not process this message in WndProc() because the application uses dialog boxes for everything—it does not matter whether the client area becomes invalid, because there is nothing in it.

Setting Up the Main Message Loop

Your windows program does not interact directly with the screen, keyboard, printer, or any other device. Windows does all that, and puts the results in an application message queue (in a device-independent manner). Messages from this queue are popped off and sent to your application's program for processing. Processing these messages is the business of the main message loop. Figure 21.1 compares the flow of execution in your program to the flow of message and data traffic from Windows to your program.

Figure 21.1.

Messages and data flow from Windows queues to your program, while your program's message loop continuously checks the message queues and dispatches messages to `WndProc()`.

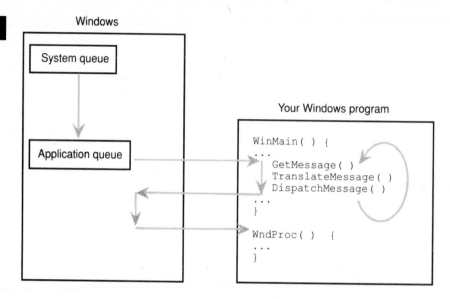

Although the arrangement depicted in Figure 21.1 may seem awkward at first, it allows Windows to multitask several applications at the same time. It seems to your program as though the `WinMain()` procedure is the only one ever executed: `WinMain()` does not directly call any other function in the program. `WinMain()` indirectly invokes the `WndProc()` window procedure, but it must do so by dispatching messages to `WndProc()` through Windows. At this point, Windows has the opportunity to interleave the execution of other application programs. The following discussion looks in more detail at how this is done.

The main message loop for FCWIN is simple, and is found in lines 115 through 120, as follows:

```
115       while (GetMessage(&msg, NULL, 0, 0))
116       {
117           TranslateMessage(&msg );
118           DispatchMessage(&msg );
119       }
120       return msg.wParam;
```

The `GetMessage()` returns a non-NULL value for every message except the quit message (you see how to generate a quit message in the following section). When `GetMessage()` gets a quit message, the loop ends and the application is finished. Note that a return value has been placed in `msg.wParam` by the quit procedure, and should be returned from the `WinMain()`.

The `TranslateMessage()` Windows function passes along many messages as they are, but also translates keyboard scan codes and character codes into ANSI character values. (An ANSI character can be an ANSI multibyte or wide character or an ASCII character.) If your program expects to receive keyboard input from the user, as FCWIN does, this function call should be present. Finally, DispatchMessage() sends the message to the appropriate window procedure. FCWIN uses the WndProc() main window procedure and a number of dialog procedures (a *dialog* is itself a special kind of child window), all of which must receive their messages at the proper time.

Writing the *WndProc()* Function

The WinMain() function is made known to Windows by exporting it in the .DEF file (see line 9 of Listing 20.3). The *window procedure* (the function that receives and interprets all your program's messages from Windows), however, is identified by the lpfnWndProc member of the window class structure at registration time. After the window class has been registered, the window procedure is invoked each time the DispatchMessage() function is called in the main message loop. Note that, a little later in program execution, it may be a dialog function that is dispatched—Windows keeps up with what part of your program is active at any given time, and forwards the dispatched message to the correct function. A Windows program can have several existing windows and dialogs at the same time.

The window procedure for FCWIN is in lines 134 through 352 of Listing 20.2. This procedure processes the messages received from the main message loop, and performs whatever action is indicated. The following partial listing of the FCWIN window procedure illustrates its generally required form:

```
134  long FAR PASCAL WndProc (HWND hWnd, unsigned Message,
135                          WORD wParam, LONG lParam)
136  {
...
151    static HANDLE hInstance;
152
153    switch(Message)
154    {
...
162
163    case WM_CREATE:
...                        /* Perform setup tasks
193      return 0;
...
203    case WM_COMMAND:
204         switch( wParam ) {
205           case IDM_PCTCHANGE:
206               if ( DialogBox( hInstance, "FCPCTCG",
207                              hWnd, lpfnDoPctChg ) )
```

```
208                       InvalidateRect( hWnd, NULL, TRUE );
209                    return 0;
...
344         }
345         break;
346
347     case WM_DESTROY:
348         PostQuitMessage(0);
349         return 0;
350     }
351     return DefWindowProc(hWnd,Message,wParam,lParam);
352 }
```

As you can see, WndProc() processes the WM_CREATE, WM_COMMAND, and WM_DESTROY messages. There are many more possible messages, but FCWIN needs only these three.

The WM_CREATE message is the first message received by the window procedure, and should be used to perform any final initialization tasks. FCWIN, for example, uses the WM_CREATE message as a signal that it is time to set up all the pointers to the dialog procedure functions.

A WM_COMMAND message is received each time the user clicks a menu item. When this happens, the wParam argument contains the ordinal value of the menu's control item. All the macro names for the ordinal values become very handy here. Without such names, determining whether the case statements are coded correctly would be very difficult.

The third and final Windows message processed by WndProc() is the WM_DESTROY message. Windows sends this message when a user pulls down the window's system menu (using the button in the top left corner of the main window frame) and clicks **C**lose. When this happens, the WndProc() code uses the PostQuitMessage() Windows function to send the quit message (WM_QUIT) to the main message loop, as mentioned previously.

If all the case statements fail, WndProc() must pass along an unprocessed message to the default handlers in Windows. This is done by returning the value received from the DefWinProc() function (the default window procedure).

Setting Up Callback Functions for Dialogs

As mentioned, FCWIN does not use the client area of the main window directly to display information. All data input and display is handled by dialogs because this is a good way to produce a sophisticated display quickly.

To use a dialog, your program must have available the dialog resources necessary to control the screen. These resources, described in Chapter 20, were created using the Dialog Editor. Each dialog resource contains controls (edit boxes, list boxes, and static text), each of which is associated with an ordinal value. Defining control IDs is a good place to use macros to define these ordinal values, as was done in the fcwin.h file. Without the macros, it would be difficult to keep track of which numbers indicate which controls.

In the main source file, you must set up and then control the dialog functions. You must provide Windows with pointers to the dialog functions (they are callback functions, and will be called by Windows from outside your program); you must create the dialog at the right moment; and you must provide the code for controlling and ending the dialog.

Creating Dialog Functions

Before your program can create a dialog, Windows must be informed of the location of the dialog procedure (function) that will control it. Therefore, the first step is to declare far pointers to the dialog functions. This is done in the WndProc() function, as follows:

```
134  long FAR PASCAL WndProc (HWND hWnd, unsigned Message,
135                                 WORD wParam, LONG lParam)
136  {
137     static FARPROC lpfnDoPctChg;
138     static FARPROC lpfnDoPctTot;
139     static FARPROC lpfnDoMkupCo;
140     static FARPROC lpfnDoMkupPr;
...  /* Other declarations */
352  }
```

Note two important things about these pointer declarations. First, be sure to declare them with the static storage class specifier (or perhaps make them global variables) so that the compiler will locate them in the data segment of the program. If you allow them to be compiled as auto variables, they will be destroyed before a dialog can be started. Second, always use the FARPROC Windows type name to declare the pointers to functions. The strange-looking prefix lpfn *(long pointer to function)* used with function names to form a pointer name is not required, but it is common practice to use it.

The next task is to initialize the pointers to the dialog functions. You use the MakeProcInstance() Windows function, as follows:

```
163        case WM_CREATE:
164          hInstance = ((LPCREATESTRUCT) lParam)->hInstance;
165          lpfnDoPctChg =
166                  MakeProcInstance( DoPctChg, hInstance );
```

Notice in line 163 that the WndProc() function does not automatically know which instance of the application it is serving at the moment. This must be determined by extracting the instance handle from the lParam argument of the WndProc() function (shown in line 164). The resulting instance handle, hInstance, is in turn used as an argument to MakeProcInstance(), which returns the address of the current copy of the dialog procedure.

Now only the creation of the dialog remains. This is not done until a user clicks the corresponding menu item. At that time, the DialogBox() Windows function is given arguments for the instance and function pointer, and is called to create the dialog:

```
203    case WM_COMMAND:
204        switch( wParam ) {
205          case IDM_PCTCHANGE:
206              if ( DialogBox( hInstance, "FCPCTCG",
207                              hWnd, lpfnDoPctChg ) )
208                  InvalidateRect( hWnd, NULL, TRUE );
209              return 0;
```

The DialogBox() function uses the second parameter as the name of the desired dialog resource. This resource name is used to access and display the correct dialog for this menu item. When the dialog returns to WndProc() immediately after the DialogBox() call, the dialog has run to completion (controlled by the dialog procedure described next). The call to the InvalidateRect() Windows function informs Windows that the screen area occupied by the dialog box is now invalid and needs repainting.

Controlling the Dialog

When Windows invokes the dialog procedure in response to the CreateDialog() call, it passes several parameters to the dialog. These parameters include a window handle for the dialog box (which is, after all, a special child window), a Windows message, and two more parameters, only one of which is used by FCWIN. Here is the dialog function for the Percent Change dialog:

```
360  BOOL FAR PASCAL DoPctChg( HWND hDlg, unsigned message,
361                            WORD wParam, LONG lParam)
362  {
363    switch ( message ) {
364
365      case WM_INITDIALOG:
366          SetFocus( GetDlgItem( hDlg, FCWIN_OLD ) );
367          return FALSE;
```

```
368
369      case WM_CLOSE:
370            EndDialog( hDlg, TRUE );
371            return TRUE;
372
373      case WM_COMMAND:
374        switch ( wParam ) {
375
376          case FCWIN_COMPUTE :
377                old = new = ans = 0.0;
378
379                GetDlgItemText( hDlg,FCWIN_OLD,instring,32 );
380                sscanf( instring, "%lf", &old );
381
382                GetDlgItemText( hDlg,FCWIN_NEW,instring,32 );
383                sscanf( instring, "%lf", &new );
384
385                if ( old != 0.0 )
386                  ans = ((new-old)/old)*100.0;
387                sprintf( instring, "%7.2f", ans );
388
389                SetDlgItemText( hDlg,FCWIN_ANS,instring );
390                SetFocus( GetDlgItem( hDlg,FCWIN_OLD ) );
391                return FALSE;
392
393          case FCWIN_RETURN:
394                EndDialog( hDlg, TRUE );
395                return TRUE;
396        }
397      break;
398      }
399      return FALSE;
400  }
```

The first parameter a dialog procedure receives is a window handle, here named hDlg. This window handle is not for the main window; it is only for the dialog box (child window). This handle is used in several Windows function calls: to set the input focus to a particular control (item) in the dialog box, to get text from a dialog control, to place text in a dialog control, and to end the dialog.

A dialog does not receive a WM_CREATE message from Windows. Instead, it receives a WM_INITDIALOG message. The DoPctChg() dialog function sets the input focus to the top edit box in the dialog at this time (see lines 365 through 371).

The WM_CLOSE Windows message is received when a user has clicked Close in the dialog box's system menu. This signals the dialog function that the dialog should be ended using the EndDialog() Windows function (see lines 369 through 371).

When a WM_COMMAND message is received, the third function argument, wParam, contains the ordinal value of the dialog control that the user clicked. Notice that DoPctChg() has to detect only the FCWIN_COMPUTE control (which indicates that the user clicked the Compute pushbutton). When the FCWIN_COMPUTE control ID has been detected, you can use the GetDlgItemText() Windows function to retrieve text from the various edit boxes and the SetDlgItemText() Windows function to send text to the output control box.

Using *MessageBox()* for Pop-Up Help and Error Messages

There is another, even quicker way to get display information on-screen. You can use the MessageBox() Windows function to display text in a message box that has at least one built-in pushbutton (which you do not have to control), an optional window caption (a message box is a window), and an optional icon, such as the exclamation point, hand, or stop sign. The following code fragment, from the printer dialog function of fcwin.c in Listing 20.2, shows how to use a message box to produce an error message:

```
1024              hPr = CreateDC( (LPSTR)szPrintDriver,
1025                             (LPSTR)szPrintType,
1026                             (LPSTR)szPrintPort,
1027                             NULL );
1028         else {
1029           MessageBox( hDlg, "Unable to start printing.",
1030                       NULL, MB_OK | MB_ICONHAND );
1031           DeleteDC( hPr );
1032           EndDialog( hDlg, TRUE );
1033           return TRUE;
1034         }
```

In this code fragment, MessageBox() is used to display an error message when the function fails to correctly create the printer device context (which is explained in the section "Spooling Hard Copy to the Windows Print Manager" later in this chapter). The first argument must be either a window handle (hDlg is the dialog's window handle) or NULL if the message box does not have to be associated with a particular window.

The second argument for the MessageBox() function is a pointer to a string containing the message text (it can be a string literal here, as in most C code). The third argument, if present, is another pointer to a string containing caption text for the message box. This sample does not use a caption; however, you see how to supply that parameter in the discussion of the PopupMsg() help function for FCWIN in the section "Using Dynamic-Link Libraries" later in this chapter.

The fourth argument is an integer containing bit flags that tell the MessageBox() procedure what kind of icon to use (if any) and which pushbuttons to use. The icon and pushbutton flags should be identified using only the Windows macro names. The two kinds of flags should be ORed together, as shown in the preceding code fragment.

You can use the following macro names for the icon type: MB_ICONHAND, MB_ICONINFORMATION, MB_ICONEXCLAMATION, MB_ICONSTOP, or MB_ICONQUESTION. This flag has no default value: If you do not supply one, there will be no icon in the message box.

Several pushbutton macros have fairly self-explanatory names. These macros include MB_OK, MB_OKCANCEL, MB_YESNO, MB_YESNOCANCEL, MB_RETRYCANCEL, and MB_ABORTRETRYIGNORE. The macro name tells you what label will appear on the pushbutton. This value has a default: It is MB_OK. Because you can specify only one of these macro names, the message box can have three buttons at most (if you specify MB_ABORTRETRYCANCEL or MB_YESNOCANCEL).

How can you tell which pushbutton was activated? A return value from the MessageBox() call was not used in the preceding code fragment, but MessageBox() does return one of six ordinal values. The following code fragment shows you how to use the return value from MessageBox():

```
switch( MessageBox( /* parms */ ) {
case IDOK:      /* Do something about OK status */
        break;
case IDCANCEL:  /* Do something about canceling task */
        break;
case IDYES:     /* Do something about YES answer */
        break;
case IDNO:      /* Do something about NO answer */
        break;
case IDABORT:   /* Do something about aborting the task */
        break;
case IDRETRY:   /* Do something about retrying */
        break;
}
```

You see another use of the MessageBox() function in the discussion of the PopupMsg() DLL module later in this chapter, in the section "Using Dynamic-Link Libraries."

Spooling Hard Copy to the Windows Print Manager

FCWIN can generate all kinds of useful financial information, including complete amortization schedules for your home loan. What good is an amortization schedule, however, if you cannot print and keep it? Because amortization information has limited usefulness without print capability, FCWIN has a dialog for spooling output hard copy to the Windows Print Manager (the normal method under Windows).

The PrntAmort() dialog procedure is the most complicated function in the FCWIN application. Therefore, the majority of its code will be discussed in sections. Lines 964 through 992 in Listing 20.2 are shown next, and contain the dialog function's declaration part and variable declarations, as follows:

```
964   BOOL FAR PASCAL PrntAmort( HWND hDlg, unsigned message,
965                          WORD wParam, LONG lParam )
966   {
967
968                  /* -------------------------------------- */
969                  /* DeviceMode() is not in windows.h file. */
970                  /* Provide a typedef for the function.    */
971                  /* -------------------------------------- */
972
973       typedef VOID (FAR PASCAL *DEVMODEPROC)(HWND,HANDLE,
974                                       LPSTR,LPSTR);
975
976       HDC hPr;          /* device-context handle for printer */
977
978       char szPrinter[80];      /* device info from WIN.INI */
979       char szDriverFile[16];   /* name of prt driver DLL file */
980
981       HANDLE hLibrary;     /* handle for prt driver DLL file */
982       DEVMODEPROC lpfnDM;      /* pointer to DeviceMode() proc */
983
984       LPSTR szPrintType;             /* printer type string */
985       LPSTR szPrintDriver;      /* printer driver name string */
986       LPSTR szPrintPort;           /* printer port name string */
987
988       int LineSpace, LinesPerPage, CurrentLine, LineLength;
989
990       POINT PhysPageSize;
991       TEXTMETRIC TextMetric;
992
```

The typedef in the preceding code fragment is present because the printer driver's DeviceMode() function is called later, and there is no prototype for it in windows.h. The meaning and use of the other variables follow:

■ HDC hPr;   /* device context handle for printer */

As with most things in Windows, you must establish a context to use a facility, and you must have a handle for that context. hPr stores the printer device context for the dialog. The context is deleted at the end of the dialog. You could compare creating a context to opening a file in plain C.

■ char szPrinter[80];   /* device info from WIN.INI */

szPrinter holds the unparsed printer-profile text string. This profile string is acquired from the WIN.INI Windows file using the GetProfileString() Windows function.

■ char szDriverFile[16];   /* name of prt driver DLL file */

This string holds the name of the printer driver DLL file, after the .DRV file extension has been concatenated to it.

■ HANDLE hLibrary;   /* handle for prt driver DLL file */

Because a DLL file is a Windows resource, like everything else, it will have a handle. The DLL handle is stored in the hLibrary variable in this application.

■ DEVMODEPROC lpfnDM;   /* pointer to DeviceMode() proc */

lpfnDM is a far pointer to a function that will contain the address of the printer driver's DeviceMode() function. The DeviceMode() function pops up a printer-configuration dialog box, the contents of which depend on the type of printer attached to the system.

■ LPSTR szPrintType;   /* printer type string */

The szPrintType string contains a descriptive name for the system printer, such as "Epson 24 Pin". It is used in creating the printer device context.

■ LPSTR szPrintDriver;   /* printer driver name string */

After parsing the profile string, the szPrintDriver string holds the text string name of the printer driver module library (DLL). The printer that this dialog was tested on, for example, was an Epson LQ-800, so the driver filename is EPSON24. This string will also be used in creating the device context.

■ LPSTR szPrintPort;   /* printer port name string */

This string is the third parameter used to create the printer device context. It contains the name of the printer port, such as "LPT1:".

■ `int LineSpace, LinesPerPage, CurrentLine, LineLength;`

These integer variables contain the results of the text-dimensioning calculations performed to fit the output text on the printer page.

■ `POINT PhysPageSize;`

The GETPHYSPAGESIZE escape call (described shortly) returns an object with type POINT. A POINT object contains two integers that reflect the number of horizontal and vertical printer pixels on a page.

■ `TEXTMETRIC TextMetric;`

The TextMetric variable (a structure) contains detailed information about the dimensions of characters in the current font selected in the printer information context (which FCWIN does not attempt to change).

Normal start-up code for the dialog function appears next, and there is nothing unusual about it. The start-up code is as follows:

```
993     switch ( message ) {
994
995       case WM_INITDIALOG:
996           SetFocus( GetDlgItem( hDlg, FCWIN_START ) );
997           return FALSE;
998
999       case WM_CLOSE:
1000          EndDialog( hDlg, TRUE );
1001          return TRUE;
1002
1003      case WM_COMMAND:
1004        switch ( wParam ) {
1005
1006          case FCWIN_START :
1007
```

Now the real fun begins. The goal is to set up the printer context for whatever printer is attached to the system on which FCWIN is running at the time. This task involves getting the profile string for the printer from Windows, parsing it, and creating the device context. The device context handle will be needed later for sending text to the printer device. Here is the code for this activity:

```
1008                    /* --------------------------------- */
1009                    /* Get the profile string for the    */
1010                    /* current printer and parse it.     */
1011                    /* --------------------------------- */
1012
1013          GetProfileString( "windows", "device", ",,,",
```

```
1014                        szPrinter, 80 );
1015          if ( (szPrintType  = strtok( szPrinter, "," )) &&
1016               (szPrintDriver = strtok( NULL,      "," )) &&
1017               (szPrintPort   = strtok( NULL,      "," )))
1018
1019              /* ---------------------------------- */
1020              /* Create a device context for the    */
1021              /* printer.                           */
1022              /* ---------------------------------- */
1023
1024          hPr = CreateDC( (LPSTR)szPrintDriver,
1025                          (LPSTR)szPrintType,
1026                          (LPSTR)szPrintPort,
1027                          NULL );
1028          else {
1029            MessageBox( hDlg, "Unable to start printing.",
1030                        NULL, MB_OK | MB_ICONHAND );
1031            DeleteDC( hPr );
1032            EndDialog( hDlg, TRUE );
1033            return TRUE;
1034          }
1035
```

The GetProfileString() Windows function call in the preceding code fragment gets the printer profile string from the WIN.INI file and places it in szPrinter. The ordinary strtok() C library function then is used to parse the profile string into its component parts. Lines 1024 through 1027 call the CreateDC() Windows function to create the device context (once more, this is similar to opening a DOS file in C) and place the resulting device context handle in the hPr variable.

After the printer type, driver, and output port are established, the printer driver must be found and loaded (it is a DLL library). In addition, the address of the driver's DeviceMode() printer-setup dialog function is extracted, and then DeviceMode() is called using the resulting pointer to function. The following code accomplishes this action:

```
1036              /* ---------------------------------- */
1037              /* This code loads the driver file from */
1038              /* the DLL. Get the handle for the    */
1039              /* driver. Use the handle to get the  */
1040              /* address of its DeviceMode() function, */
1041              /* and invoke it using the pointer. This */
1042              /* code causes the printer             */
1043              /* initialization dialog to pop up.    */
1044              /* ---------------------------------- */
```

```
1045
1046            strcat( strcpy( szDriverFile, szPrintDriver ), ".DRV" );
1047            hLibrary = LoadLibrary( szDriverFile );
1048            if ( hLibrary < 32 ) {
1049              MessageBox( hDlg, "Can't locate the driver\n"
1050                          "file for this printer.",
1051                             NULL, MB_OK | MB_ICONHAND );
1052              DeleteDC( hPr );
1053              EndDialog( hDlg, TRUE );
1054              return TRUE;
1055            }
1056            lpfnDM = GetProcAddress( hLibrary, "DEVICEMODE" );
1057            (*lpfnDM)( hDlg, hLibrary, (LPSTR)szPrintType,
1058                       (LPSTR)szPrintPort );
1059
```

Line 1046 in the preceding code fragment builds the driver library filename, complete with the .DRV file extension. Line 1047 calls the LoadLibrary() Windows function to load the printer driver DLL and place the resulting handle in the hLibrary variable. (Nothing else is done with the library yet.) The hLibrary handle then is used in line 1056 as a parameter for the GetProcAddress() Windows function to determine the address of the DeviceMode() printer driver function. Last, lines 1057 and 1058 show how the far pointer to the lpfnDM function is used to call the DeviceMode() function.

Using the printer driver's built-in DeviceMode() function lends a nice touch to the application, one for which you do not have to write explicit code. The DeviceMode() function starts a dialog for printer setup, using a dialog screen like the one shown in Figure 21.2.

Now you can inform Windows that you are about to start sending output to the printer device context. Use the Escape() Windows function for this purpose, passing the hPr device context handle (see line 1024) and the STARTDOC flag as parameters to the function. The only complication here is detecting any errors resulting from the function call and displaying a message box notifying the user that a problem occurred. Here is the StartDOC escape sequence:

```
1060                    /* --------------------------------- */
1061                    /* Notify the Print Manager that you   */
1062                    /* are about to start spooling print   */
1063                    /* using the STARTDOC Escape call.     */
1064                    /* --------------------------------- */
1065
1066            if ( Escape( hPr, STARTDOC, 11,
1067                 "PrintAmort", 0L ) < 0 ) {
1068              MessageBox( hDlg, "Unable to start printing.",
```

```
1069                        NULL, MB_OK ¦ MB_ICONHAND );
1070              DeleteDC( hPr );
1071              EndDialog( hDlg, TRUE );
1072              return TRUE;
1073          }
1074
```

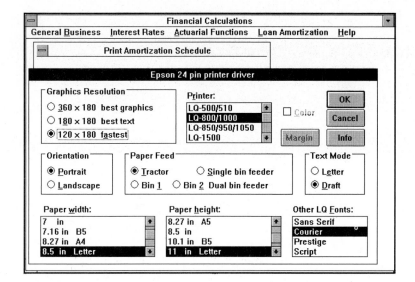

Figure 21.2.

The `DeviceMode()` dialog screen for an Epson 24-pin printer.

Unlike DOS printer services, which view everything as a character stream, Windows views the printer as a graphics device similar to the system display—the printer is an integral part of the Windows GUI. Thus, a printer page is thought of as a graphics frame in much the same way as a window is perceived. Approaching printing tasks from this new perspective adds responsibilities to the programmer's workload.

Specifically, it is up to you (that is, the application program) to determine what can fit on a page, how it will be displayed (displaying printer graphics is nearly as easy as displaying printer text with Windows), and when to clear the current frame (printer page) to receive the next image. The printer dialog's next task, therefore, is to determine the size and characteristics of the printer page. The printer dialog can accomplish this by using the GETPHYSPAGESIZE escape sequence to determine the printer page size in printer pixels, and the GetTextMetrics() Windows function to determine the dimensions of the current font's characters, also in printer pixels (FCWIN allows the printer's built-in text font to be used). From all this information, you can determine the number of text lines that will fit on one page, as follows:

```
1075              /* ---------------------------------------- */
1076              /* Now calculate the printing area parameters */
1077              /* using the GetTextMetrics() function and    */
1078              /* the GETPHYSPAGESIZE Escape call.           */
1079              /* ---------------------------------------- */
1080
1081         GetTextMetrics( hPr, &TextMetric );
1082         LineSpace = TextMetric.tmHeight
1083                    + TextMetric.tmExternalLeading;
1084         Escape( hPr, GETPHYSPAGESIZE, NULL, NULL,
1085                    (LPSTR)&PhysPageSize);
1086         LinesPerPage = ( PhysPageSize.y / LineSpace ) - 6;
1087         CurrentLine = LinesPerPage + 1;
1088
```

Notice especially in line 1086 that FCWIN does not allow the `LinesPerPage` variable to be as large as the theoretical maximum. Six lines are subtracted from the maximum to prevent printing down to the bottom perforation of the page. (Another reason for preventing this, besides aesthetics, will become clear shortly.)

Finally, the printer dialog function is ready to send the amortization schedule to the printer device. A `while` loop is used to do this:

```
1089         levelpay = 1 / USPV( apr, freq, numpay ) * amt;
1090         payno = 0;
1091
1092              /* ---------------------------------------- */
1093              /* Finally, loop and use TextOut() to    */
1094              /* spool print.                          */
1095              /* ---------------------------------------- */
1096
1097         while ( payno < numpay ) {
1098          if ( ++CurrentLine >= LinesPerPage ) {
1099            Escape( hPr, NEWFRAME, 0, 0L, 0L );
1100            CurrentLine = 0;
1101            BuildTextMessage( "%s%s%s%s%s%s",
1102                                  "  Paymnt #  ",
1103                                  " Level Pay ",
1104                                  "  Int Amt  ",
1105                                  " Prin Amt  ",
1106                                  "  Balance  " );
1107            TextOut( hPr, 0, CurrentLine*LineSpace,
1108                    (LPSTR)textmsg, strlen(textmsg) );
```

```
1109                    ++CurrentLine;
1110                    BuildTextMessage( "%s%s%s%s%s%s",
1111                                       "-----------",
1112                                       "-----------",
1113                                       "-----------",
1114                                       "-----------",
1115                                       "-----------" );
1116                  TextOut( hPr, 0, CurrentLine*LineSpace,
1117                            (LPSTR)textmsg, strlen(textmsg) );
1118                    ++CurrentLine;
1119                }
1120            ++payno;
1121            intpay = levelpay
1122                    * USPV( apr, freq, numpay-payno+1.0 )
1123                    * (apr/freq/100.0);
1124            prinpay = levelpay - intpay;
1125            bal = levelpay * USPV( apr, freq, numpay-payno );
1126            BuildTextMessage( "%12d%12.2f%12.2f%12.2f%12.2f",
1127                               (int)payno, levelpay,
1128                               intpay, prinpay,
1129                               bal
1130                             );
1131          TextOut( hPr, 0, CurrentLine*LineSpace,
1132                    (LPSTR)textmsg, strlen(textmsg) );
1133        }
1134
1135        Escape( hPr, NEWFRAME, 0, 0L, 0L );
1136        Escape( hPr, ENDDOC, 0, 0L, 0L );
1137        FreeLibrary( hLibrary );
1138        DeleteDC( hPr );
1139        EndDialog( hDlg, TRUE );
1140        return TRUE;
1141
```

Lines 1098 through 1119 of the preceding fragment of fcwin.c detect page breaks and format and print a header line for the report. The page is physically ejected by the NEWFRAME escape sequence, as seen in line 1099. The use of this escape sequence in the printer device context is important enough to discuss in more detail.

The NEWFRAME escape sequence is the same escape sequence you must use to clear a graphics frame (such as the client area of the main window) when painting in a display window. The behavior of this escape sequence in the printer device context is the other reason for not allowing printing to continue to the physical bottom of the page. If you allow this condition to occur, a strange thing happens when the Windows Print Manager sends the spooled print to the real device: It not only physically ejects the page, but also sends your page eject after it has automatically ejected the page, leaving a blank sheet of paper in the middle of your report. Furthermore, it skips the data that goes with that page. Therefore, you should avoid the physical bottom of a printer page.

The TextOut() Windows function is used to send print to the Print Manager. Note that the BuildTextMessage() function is not a Windows function: It is a helper function written to facilitate the construction of strings that are sent to displays and printers by the dialog functions. The code for BuildTextMessage() appears in Listing 20.2, beginning in line 1156.

When the entire amortization schedule is printed, execution falls out the bottom of the while loop. A final NEWFRAME escape sequence ejects the last page, and the ENDDOC escape sequence notifies Windows that printing is complete. Because the printer driver DLL was loaded earlier, the FreeLibarary() Windows function releases it (line 1137), and the DeleteDC() Windows function deletes the printer device context.

Using Dynamic-Link Libraries

Windows dynamic-link libraries are very useful. They can contain code (functions), bit maps, icons, or just about anything else you want. The objects in a DLL reside in a file outside your main program, which helps save lines of code. FCWIN implements all the help dialogs using the PopupMsg() DLL module, as shown here:

```
289             case HLP_PCTCHANGE:
290             PopupMsg( HLP_PCTCHANGE - HLP_PCTCHANGE );
291             return 0;
```

In this section, you learn how to implement a simple function, the PopupMsg() function, in a DLL file named HELPMSG.DLL. This DLL and function are used in FCWIN to implement the help facility.

NOTE To install the Windows DLL support libraries, you should have used the Custom Installation option of the Microsoft C/C++ SETUP program. If you did not choose to have the DLL support libraries installed originally, you have to install them now.

To install the DLL libraries, insert Disk 1 of the Microsoft C/C++ disk set and run the SETUP program again. Select Build Additional Libraries and then Windows. Select the memory models you need (for the example in this chapter, the compact model), and check the Windows DLL libraries option. The SETUP program may have other items selected by default, such as Windows .EXE libraries. You can disable this option if all you need to install is the DLL support libraries.

Understanding DLLs

A DLL is a library, but it is not like a DOS LIB file. A DLL can contain executable code and must be written in a source file, compiled, and linked much like your application's main source file.

Although a DLL file can have any file extension, using the DLL extension makes the DLL file implicitly available to your program. In other words, you won't have to use the LoadLibrary() function as FCWIN did to get to the printer driver's DLL. You still must let the linker know, however, that your program will be using a DLL module. You can do this with the IMPORTS statement in your main program's .DEF file. The last line of the FCWIN.DEF file (see Listing 21.3 later in this chapter), for example, contains the following statement:

```
IMPORTS         HELPMSG.PopupMsg
```

This IMPORTS statement tells the linker that the PopupMsg() function in the HELPMSG.DLL file will be used by the program.

In the main source file, you should also provide a function prototype of the function that will be imported, as seen in line 18 of Listing 20.2:

```
BOOL FAR PASCAL PopupMsg( int );        /* DLL function */
```

By now, you may be asking why, if a DLL module is not linked to the application until the application is running, the linker program needs to know about the DLL. What happens when the linker sees a reference to PopupMsg(), for example? It cannot generate a simple function call sequence because the function never will be in a predictable memory location at runtime.

The linker uses supplied code to generate Windows calls to get the address of the DLL module and call it. At this stage, the DLL module is identified only by the familiar ordinal value assigned to it when the DLL was compiled and linked.

How does the linker know the function's ordinal value? The linker can get this value by examining the HELPMSG.LIB import library (in this instance), which was generated when helpmsg.c was compiled and linked.

You should know about a few other oddities concerning DLLs. First, when an executable DLL module is called from the main program (as PopupMsg() will be), the called DLL function is considered logically part of the main application. The DLL program therefore uses the calling program's stack, even though the DLL is not part of the calling program. A DLL module has no stack of its own.

Second, a DLL can access data segment variables using only far pointers. The DLL's stack and data segment never can be in the same segment of memory, because a DLL module has no stack of its own. Therefore, a DLL's data segment is allocated separately, in another segment of memory, and requires far pointers to be accessed. By selecting the compact memory model to compile a DLL, the compiler makes pointers to the data segment use the far form. Other much more complicated problems arise because of this situation, but they are beyond the scope of this book. For now, you can write DLL functions like the PopupMsg() function (presented in the next section) with little trouble. Just don't try to get fancy until you know a good deal more about DLL internals.

Writing a DLL Application

Because a DLL is a Windows file (potentially containing executable code), you should begin construction of the DLL by writing a module-definition file for it. The helpmsg.def file for use with FCWIN is shown in Listing 21.1.

Listing 21.1. helpmsg.def. The module-definition file for the HELPMSG DLL.

```
1   LIBRARY      HELPMSG
2   DESCRIPTION  'Sample DLL Module Def file'
3   EXETYPE      WINDOWS
4   CODE             PRELOAD MOVEABLE DISCARDABLE
5   DATA             PRELOAD MOVEABLE SINGLE
6   HEAPSIZE     4096
7   EXPORTS      PopupMsg
```

The first thing to notice about the helpmsg.def file is that, although there is a HEAPSIZE statement, there is no STACKSIZE statement. Again, A DLL module has no stack of its own.

The second thing to notice is the LIBRARY statement in line 1. This identifies the module-definition file as belonging to a DLL rather than to a Windows program. This statement is required, and causes all sorts of confusion if you accidentally code a NAME statement instead.

Notice also the EXETYPE statement in line 3. This statement is present because the default target environment is OS/2 rather than Windows.

At this stage of development, all the facilities necessary for your main program and the DLL function to recognize each other are present, in the form of the IMPORTS and EXPORTS statements in the respective .DEF files. Figure 21.3 illustrates this state of affairs.

Figure 21.3.

IMPORTS and EXPORTS statements for the FCWIN and HELPMSG source files.

Writing the source code for helpmsg.c is simplicity itself. The code for this file, including the PopupMsg() function, is shown in Listing 21.2. Note that the window.h file must be included in this source file, just as it was in the main source file for fcwin.c. Also note the use of the keyword __export before the definition of PopupMsg(). Microsoft C/C++ requires that __export be placed in front of the identifier so that it will be sure to include the needed DLL export information in the executable.

Listing 21.2. helpmsg.c. C source code that will compile and link to helpmsg.dll.

```
1    #include <windows.h>
2
3    #define NUMMSG 14
4
5    struct {
6      char* caption;
7      char* body;
8    } Messages [] = {
9      "General Business/Percent Change",
10         "Percent change calculates the\n"
11         "difference between the new amount\n"
12         "and the old amount as a percentage\n"
13         "of the old amount.",
14     "General Business/Percent of Total",
15         "Percent of total calculates the\n"
16         "partial amount as a percentage of\n"
17         "the total amount.",
18     "General Business/Markup Over Cost",
19         "Markup over cost calculates the\n"
20         "difference between the price and\n"
21         "the cost as a percentage of the cost.",
22     "General Business/Markup Over Price",
23         "Markup over price calculates the\n"
24         "difference between the price and\n"
25         "the cost as a percentage of the price.",
26     "InterestRates/Effective Periodic Rate",
27         "Effective periodic rate calculates\n"
```

Listing 21.2. Continued.

```
28          "the effective interest rate with\n"
29          "periodic compounding of an APR, when\n"
30          "all interest is reinvested.",
31      "InterestRates/Effective Continuous Rate",
32          "Effective continuous rate calculates\n"
33          "the effective interest rate with\n"
34          "continuous compounding of an APR, when\n"
35          "all interest is reinvested.",
36      "Actuarial/Future Value Single Amount",
37          "Future value of a single amount calculates\n"
38          "the future value of a single deposit given\n"
39          "the initial amount, an APR, compounding\n"
40          "frequency, and the number of years.",
41      "Actuarial/Present Value Single Amount",
42          "Present value of a single amount calculates\n"
43          "the lump sum deposit you would have to\n"
44          "make now to grow to the requested amount\n"
45          "over the given time.",
46      "Actuarial/Future Value Regular Deposits",
47          "Future value of regular deposits (i.e.,\n"
48          "of an annuity) calculates the future total\n"
49          "value of a series of deposits of the reques-\n"
50          "ted amount over the given time.",
51      "Actuarial/Present Value Regular Deposits",
52          "Present value of regular deposits (i.e.,\n"
53          "of an annuity) calculates the equivalent\n"
54          "lump sum deposit you must make now to grow\n"
55          "to the same value as a series of deposits.",
56      "Amortization/Loan Data Entry",
57          "Enter the loan amount, percentage rate,\n"
58          "payment frequency, and number of years.\n"
59          "If you close the dialog without clicking\n"
60          "Return, no changes are made to variables.",
61      "Amortization/Payout Analysis",
62          "Payout analysis displays the level pay-\n"
63          "ment required, total dollars repaid, total\n"
64          "interest paid, and the eff. interest % for a\n"
65          "balloon note (the real cost of the loan).",
66      "Amortization/Display Amortization Sched",
67          "The complete amortization schedule for the\n"
```

```
68          "loan is displayed in a scrollable listbox.\n"
69
70      "Amortization/Print Amortization Sched",
71          "The complete amortization schedule for the\n"
72          "loan is sent to the Windows Print Manager.\n"
73          "A setup dialog box is displayed first, to\n"
74          "allow you to configure the printer.",
75      };
76
77
78      int FAR PASCAL LibMain( HANDLE hInstance, WORD wDataSeg,
79                                  WORD wHeapSize, LPSTR lpszCmdLine )
80      {
81        if ( wHeapSize > 0 ) UnlockData( 0 );
82        return 1;
83      }
84
85      BOOL FAR PASCAL __export PopupMsg( int msgnum )
86      {
87        if ( msgnum >= NUMMSG ) return FALSE;
88        MessageBox( NULL, (LPSTR)(Messages[msgnum].body),
89                    (LPSTR)(Messages[msgnum].caption),
90                    MB_ICONINFORMATION ¦ MB_OK  );
91        return TRUE;
92      }
```

As you can see in Listing 21.2, most of the source file is taken up by the array of structures containing caption and message text. The large amount of this material was the primary reason to move it out of fcwin.c and locate it elsewhere, but in a manner still easily accessible to the program. A DLL is made to order for that kind of task.

Lines 78 through 83 contain the only required function in a DLL. There must be a LibMain() function in a DLL, just as there must be a WinMain() function in a Windows program, or a main() function in an ordinary C or C++ program. In the simple version of a DLL that FCWIN uses, it is necessary only to verify that a local heap is available, to call UnlockData() to tell Windows that the DLL's data segment now can be moved if necessary, and to return a TRUE (nonzero) value.

Locating the bulk of the help messages in the DLL is a good design decision. First, because the DLL can be shared by more than one copy of the application, the error message text has to be loaded into memory only once, which reduces overhead. If all the help messages had been defined in fcwin.c, each instance of the application would load a fresh copy of all that text. Second, this arrangement allows Windows to move the data in memory, or swap it out to disk if necessary, to streamline multitasking operations. This arrangement makes FCWIN a more courteous "guest" of the system, capable of coexisting efficiently with other applications.

The use of the array of structures to access the help and caption text (lines 85 through 92) is ordinary, but there is something new in the way that the MessageBox() function is used (lines 88 through 91). Notice that the first argument for MessageBox() is not a window or dialog handle, as it was in fcwin.c when this function was used to display error messages. Unless you supply a window handle, PopupMsg() is not aware of which instance of FCWIN invoked it.

You do not have to know a particular handle to use MessageBox(). You can simply code NULL for the first argument, as was done here, so that the message box is not associated with any instance or window. The message box pops up in the middle of the screen instead of aligning with a window boundary, but that does not hurt a thing for our purposes.

Before you compile and link a DLL source file using the PWB, be sure to select the Windows DLL template, using the Project Templates selection from the Options menu. You must do this so that the correct Entry/Exit code for the DLL functions can be used, and also so that the import librarian can be invoked during the link edit process. You must also use the C Language Options... selection from the Options menu to choose the Compact memory model.

The function of the import librarian is to generate the HELPMSG.LIB file, in addition to the .EXE file. This file is used by the linkage editor when it processes fcwin.c to obtain the ordinal value of the PopupMsg() function mentioned previously.

Exercises

This chapter demonstrated the potential power of a fully developed Windows program. Although FCWIN is a simple sample program—much of its length is due to the large number of dialogs it supports—it does some interesting and useful things in a pleasing format.

This chapter has enough information to help you write some interesting, although simple, Windows programs, but much had to be omitted. You still have before you the majority of the learning curve required for full-fledged Windows programming.

1. Use the menu you created in Chapter 20 for easy.c to enable a user to start a dialog. In the dialog, display in the dialog box a static text message

of your own choosing. Hint: You will have to use the Dialog Editor to create the dialog box and to identify the static text control. Do not forget to provide the necessary #defines in easy.h.

2. Modify the FCWIN program by adding one or more items to any of the pull-down menus. Have each of your new items display a dialog box. The item names and the contents of the dialog boxes can be of your own choosing. Experiment with the Dialog Editor to incorporate additional dialog controls into your application.

3. Using the sample code in easy.c (Listing 19.5) as a model, incorporate a WM_PAINT message handler into fcwin.c. Use your WM_PAINT message handler to display text on the application's main window area.

4. Consult other references on Windows programming, such as Que's *Programming in Windows 3.1*. Also read "The Microsoft Foundation Class Library Tutorial" in the *Microsoft C/C++ Class Libraries User's Guide*.

5. The Microsoft C/C++ documentation set does not include details about the Windows Applications Programming Interface. Instead, use the Index command in the PWB's Help menu to locate the Windows API entry. Use the online help to learn more about the many functions, messages, and other features of the Windows programming interface.

Summary and Conclusion

This is quite a chapter. Although it is impossible to get a complete working knowledge of programming Windows applications from the whirlwind tour of the subject presented in this part of the book, perhaps this chapter has whet your appetite for the subject. The new Microsoft C/C++ 7.0 compiler and associated tools provide access to the world of powerful, multitasking, graphically based applications in the Windows environment.

This chapter has given you just a taste of what you can do by writing Windows applications with Microsoft C/C++. Although getting to the Windows support functions is more difficult than it is in ordinary C or C++ programs, it is well worth the effort.

To learn about the Microsoft Foundation Class library and how it can provide you with an object-oriented Windows programming interface, consult the *Microsoft C/C++ Class Libraries User's Guide*. In particular, see the section titled "Windows Programming with the Microsoft Foundation Classes."

This chapter introduced the following topics:

■ *How to set up the Windows interfaces for your program.* This activity includes registering the window class and starting the main message loop, creating the main window, and setting up linkage between Windows and your program's callback functions. In the fcwin.c sample program, you learned how to create and control dialogs with their callback functions.

■ *How to use message boxes to display pop-up information, such as help information and error messages.*

■ *How to write and use a dynamic-link library (DLL).* The DLL is a central feature of the Windows programming environment. This powerful feature permits the construction of large application programs with maximum efficiency.

There is much more to Windows programming. If you have read this entire book, you certainly have covered a lot of ground. If you mastered all the information presented here, you should be able to write C++ programs that will astonish your friends.

Exciting and important things are going on in the world of C and C++ programming, including the recent open-access policy of Microsoft concerning Windows. All these things require greater programming expertise, utilizing all the new tools and working in the new environments. If this book has helped prepare you for the future of Microsoft C and C++ programming, it has accomplished what it was intended to do.

ASCII Charts

The original ASCII character set is composed of a 7-bit code, to avoid turning on the high-order bit. The resulting possible decimal integer values for the ASCII character set are 0 through 127. If a byte is treated as an unsigned char, an additional 128 characters (decimal values 128 through 255) can be used. These characters, together with the original ASCII values, are called the IBM extended ASCII character set. This appendix shows the original codes and their corresponding characters, as implemented on an IBM PC or compatible, and the second group of 128 characters (the extended characters).

Char	Value	Char	Value	Char	Value	Char	Value
0	null	11	♂	22	–	33	!
1	☺	12	♀	23	↕	34	"
2	●	13	♪	24	↑	35	#
3	♥	14	♪♪	25	↓	36	$
4	◆	15	☼	26	→	37	%
5	♣	16	►	27	←	38	&
6	♠	17	◄	28	∟	39	'
7	●	18	↕	29	↔	40	(
8	◘	19	‼	30	▲	41	)
9	○	20	¶	31	▼	42	*
10	◙	21	§	32		43	+

Char	Value	Char	Value	Char	Value	Char	Value
44	,	73	I	102	f	131	â
45	-	74	J	103	g	132	ä
46	.	75	K	104	h	133	à
47	/	76	L	105	i	134	á
48	0	77	M	106	j	135	ç
49	1	78	N	107	k	136	ê
50	2	79	O	108	l	137	ë
51	3	80	P	109	m	138	è
52	4	81	Q	110	n	139	ï
53	5	82	R	111	o	140	î
54	6	83	S	112	p	141	ì
55	7	84	T	113	q	142	Ä
56	8	85	U	114	r	143	Å
57	9	86	V	115	s	144	É
58	:	87	W	116	t	145	æ
59	;	88	X	117	u	146	Æ
60	<	89	Y	118	v	147	ô
61	=	90	Z	119	w	148	ö
62	>	91	[	120	x	149	ò
63	?	92	\	121	y	150	û
64	@	93	]	122	z	151	ù
65	A	94	^	123	{	152	ÿ
66	B	95	–	124	¦	153	Ö
67	C	96	'	125	}	154	Ü
68	D	97	a	126	~	155	¢
69	E	98	b	127	Δ	156	£
70	F	99	c	128	Ç	157	¥
71	G	100	d	129	ü	158	P$_t$
72	H	101	e	130	é	159	ƒ

Char	Value	Char	Value	Char	Value	Char	Value
160	á	184	╕	208	╨	232	Φ
161	í	185	╣	209	╤	233	θ
162	ó	186	║	210	╥	234	Ω
163	ú	187	╗	211	╙	235	δ
164	ñ	188	╝	212	╚	236	∞
165	Ñ	189	╜	213	╒	237	ø
166	ª	190	╛	214	╓	238	∈
167	º	191	┐	215	╫	239	∩
168	¿	192	└	216	╪	240	≡
169	┌	193	┴	217	┘	241	±
170	┐	194	┬	218	┌	242	≥
171	1/2	195	├	219	█	243	≤
172	1/4	196	─	220	▄	244	⌠
173	¡	197	+	221	▌	245	⌡
174	«	198	╞	222	▐	246	÷
175	»	199	╟	223	▀	247	≈
176	░	200	╚	224	*a*	248	°
177	▒	201	╔	225	β	249	•
178	▓	202	╩	226	Γ	250	·
179	│	203	╦	227	π	251	√
180	┤	204	╠	228	Σ	252	η
181	╡	205	=	229	σ	253	²
182	╢	206	╬	230	μ	254	■
183	╖	207	╧	231	τ	255	

Details on Using *printf()* and *scanf()*

C hapter 6, "Using the Microsoft C/C++ I/O Function Library," explained how to use the printf() and scanf() families of functions, but there wasn't enough room in the chapter to show all the format string options that can be used with these two functions. This appendix is a brief listing of those format string options. The first part covers the printf() functions, and the second part covers the scanf() functions.

printf()

The printf() format string specifiers have the folowing form:

% *flags*_{opt} *width*_{opt}.*precision*_{opt} F¦N¦h¦l¦L_{opt} *type*

The percent sign (%) is a required part of the format specifier. The percent sign signals the printf() function that the information following it is a conversion specification.

The optional flags specify how the displayed data will be presented. Only one flag at a time can be used. Table B.1 explains each of the flags.

Table B.1. Optional flag characters defined for use with `printf()`.

Flag	Meaning
-	Left justification. The result is aligned on the left; the right is padded with blanks if needed. If the - flag is not used, `printf()` right-justifies by default. (When right-justified, the left side is padded with blanks or zeros as appropriate.)
+	Specifies that signed conversion will begin with a plus sign (+) or minus sign (-).
blank	Tells `printf()` to begin nonnegative values with a blank character. Negative values are preceded with a minus sign (-).
#	This character signals that the argument will be converted using an alternate form, as follows:

Conversion Character	Alternate Conversion
c, s, d, i, u	The # flag has no effect on these conversion characters.
0	Prefixes a 0 to a nonzero argument.
x, X	Prefixes 0x or 0X to the argument.
e, E, f	Forces the floating point number to display a decimal point.
g, G	This works the same as e or E execpt any trailing zeros are not removed.

The optional `width` specification sets the minimum field width. Table B.2 lists ways in which the `width` argument can be specified.

Table B.2. `printf()` optional width specifiers.

Width Specifier	Effect of Specifier
n	Causes at least n number of characters to be printed. If n characters are not available, the result is padded with blanks.
0n	Causes at least n number of characters to be printed. If n characters are not available, the result is padded with zeros.

The optional precision is noted by the precision specification. In general, the precision specifies how many digits are displayed for integer values or how many fractional digits are displayed for floating point values. The beginning decimal point (.) in the precision specification option is mandatory even if the width is not specified. If both the width and precision are used in a conversion specifier, there cannot be any whitespace between them (for example, %6 .2 is wrong, use %6.2). Table B.3 shows how the precision specification is used.

Table B.3. Optional precision specifiers.

Precision Specification	Effect of Specifier
.n	Prints n number of decimal places. When the value being displayed is larger than n, the type of the value determines whether the displayed value is truncated or rounded, as shown in the next table.
.0	For floating point numbers of type e, E, and f, the fractional portion is suppressed. For integer type values i, d, o, u, and x, precision is set to default values.
none	Sets default precision values. For integer type values, precision is 1. For floating point values, precision is 6. For g and G type values, all significant digits are displayed. With string types, all characters to the first NULL value are printed. There is no default for character type values.

The type of the value being displayed determines what effect the precision specification will have. Table B.4 shows how the precision specification affects each of the basic data types.

Table B.4. The effect of precision specifiers on different data types.

Data Type	Effect of Precision Specification (.n)
d, i, o, u, x, X	At least n digits are displayed. If the value does not contain enough digits to display, the display value is padded to the left with zeros. If the output value is larger than n, there is no truncation or rounding.
e, E, f	At least n fractional characters are displayed. The last digit to be displayed is rounded.

continues

Table B.4. Continued.

Data Type	Effect of Precision Specification (.n)
g, G	At most, n significant digits are printed.
s	No more than n characters are printed.
c	The precision specification has no effect on character data.

The input-size modifiers, [F¦N¦h¦l¦L], tell printf() what type of pointer or argument is in the argument list. Table B.5 documents the type of value associated with each of the input-size modifiers.

Table B.5. Optional input-size modifier characters.

Input-Size Modifer	Type of Argument
F	far pointer
N	near pointer
h	short int
l	long int or double floating point
L	long double

The last part of a conversion specification is the type specification, which tells printf() the data type of the information being displayed. Table B.6 lists each type specification and the data type associated with the specification.

Table B.6. Data type specifiers.

Type Specification	Data Type
d, i	Signed int
o	Unsigned octal int
u	Unsigned int
x	Unsigned hexadecimal int using abcdef
X	Unsigned hexadecimal int using ABCDEF

Type Specification	Data Type
e	Signed floating point with exponent e
E	Signed floating point with exponent E
f	Signed floating point in format *dddd.dddd*
g	Signed floating point in f or e format, whichever is more compact
G	Same as g format except using G for e exponent
c	char
s	string
n	Copies the number of characters output so far to the matching integer parameter
p	far pointer to void
	Prints the address pointed to by the parameter value in the form *xxxx.yyyy*. If %Np is given, then outputs the *yyyy* segment value only.

Inside the formatting string, you may place special escape characters to output characters that would not normally be allowed within a quoted string. Table B.7 describes these escape characters. These special characters are entered into a string using the backslash (\) as a preface character. For instance, to print a newline character, write \n. To print a backslash character, write \\. A word to the wise: the use of \ can cause problems when working with DOS path specifications. For instance, if you want to print the string constant C:\WINDOWS\SYSTEM, type **C:\\WINDOWS\\SYSTEM**.

Table B.7. Escape characters recognized in printf() format strings.

Characters	Description	Characters	Description
\a	Alert (bell)	\?	Literal question mark
\b	Backspace	\'	Single quotation mark
\f	Form feed	\"	Double quotation mark
\n	Newline	\\	Backslash
\r	Carriage return	\ddd	ASCII character in octal notation
\t	Horizontal tab		
\v	Vertical tab	\xdd	ASCII character in hex notation

scanf()

The scanf() family of functions is used to input data. Like printf(), the scanf() functions have a format string and an argument list. The format of the conversion specifiers in the format string is

% *opt *width*~opt~ F¦N~opt~ h¦l¦L~opt~ *type*

The percent character (%) tells scanf() that it is about to encounter a conversion specification. The percent character is a required part of every conversion specification you include.

The asterisk (*) is an optional modifier that suppresses the assignment of the next input field. Although this assignment suppression option looks like a pointer operator, it isn't.

The optional width value tells scanf() the maximum number of characters to read. When scanf() reads an input field, it reads as many characters as possible for the data type being converted, up to the number specified by width.

The input-size modifiers determine how scanf() interprets the address associated with a conversion specification. Table B.8 shows the effect of the input-size modifiers.

Table B.8. scanf() **input-size modifiers.**

Input-Size Modifer	Effect
F	Tells scanf() that a far pointer argument is associated with the current conversion specification.
N	Tells scanf() that a near pointer argument is associated with the current conversion specification.

The argument-type modifiers indicate how input data will be converted. Table B.9 lists the modifiers and their effects. If a type of conversion specifier is not listed with an argument-type modifier, the modifier has no effect on that conversion specifier.

Table B.9. scanf() argument type modifiers.

Argument Type Modifer	Effect
h	With d, i, o, u, and x data types, the input data is converted to a short int and stored in a short type data object.
l	For the d, i, o, u, and i data types, the input is converted to a long int and stored in a long type data object. For the e, f, and g types, the input is converted to a double and stored in a double type object.
L	The L format works with e, f, and g conversion specification types. The input value is converted to a long double and stored in a double type data object.

The type is a character that indicates the data type of the information that scanf() is reading. Table B.10 shows the type specification and the data type for each of the characters.

Table B.10. scanf() data type specifiers.

Type Specifier	Data Type
d	Decimal integer; pointer to int
D	Decimal integer; pointer to long
o	Octal integer; pointer to int
O	Octal integer, pointer to long
i	Decimal, octal, or hex; pointer to int
l	Decimal, octal, or hex; pointer to long
u	Unsigned decimal integer; pointer to unsigned int
U	Unsigned decimal integer; pointer to unsigned long
x	Hexadecimal integer; pointer to int
X	Hexadecimal integer; pointer to long
e, E, f, g, G	Floating point; pointer to float
c	Character; pointer to char
s	String; pointer to array of char

Details on Using _exec...() and _spawn...()

T he _exec...() and _spawn...() functions are used to run child processes. A *child process* is an executable program that is started from inside another executable program.

The _exec...() and _spawn...() families contain several functions. Each function in each family performs the same basic task, but each function works somewhat differently. This appendix lists each function and its distinctive features.

The _exec...() family of functions consists of the following functions:

```
int _execl( char *cmdname, char *arg0, *arg1, ..., *argn, NULL );
int _execle( char *cmdname, char *arg0, *arg1, ..., *argn, NULL,
             char **env );

int _execlp( char *cmdname, char *arg0, *arg1, ..., *argn, NULL );
int _execlpe( char *cmdname, char *arg0, *arg1, ..., *argn, NULL,
              char **env );

int _execv( char *cmdname, char *argv[] );
int _execve( char *cmdname, char *argv[], char **envp );

int _execvp( char *cmdname, char *argv[] );
int _execv( char *cmdname, char *argv[], char **envp );
```

Each of the functions in the _exec...() family is made by appending the letters l, p, e, and v to exec. Table C.1 lists the purpose of each of these suffixes.

Table C.1. Suffix characters used with the _exec...() functions.

_exec...() Suffix	Purpose
l	Causes the argument pointers $arg0$, $arg1$, etc., to be passed as separate arguments. Use the l suffix when you already know how many arguments you will have to pass. Either this option or the v option is required.
v	Causes the argument pointers $arg0$, $arg1$, etc., to be passed to the child process as an array of pointers. Use the v option when you have a variable number of arguments to pass to the child process. Either this option or the l option is required.
p	Tells _exec...() to search for the child process in the directories listed in the DOS path command.
e	The _exec...() functions with the e option can send a new envp argument to the child process.

The cmdname argument in the _exec...() function call is the filename of the child process being started. The argn parameters are arguments passed to the child process. On the _exec...() functions that support it, env is a list of new environment settings that can be used by the child process.

The _exec...() functions must pass at least one argument to the child process. If you do not supply an argument, a copy of the cmdname argument is passed to the child process.

If the _exec...() function is successfully called, the function is unable to return a value. If _exec...() fails, however, a value of –1 is returned and the errno variable is set. Table C.2 lists the values that can be placed in errno if _exec...() fails.

Table C.2. Error codes returned by failed _exec...() calls.

errno Value	Meaning
E2BIG	The argument list was too long.
EACCES	Permission was denied—the file is locked or shared.
EMFILE	Too many files are open.
ENOENT	Either the pathname or filename was not found.
ENOEXEC	There was an exec format error.
ENOMEM	Not enough memory is left.

The _spawn...() family of functions is also used to start one executable program from within another. The functions in the _spawn...() family are:

```
int _spawnl( int mode, char *cmdname, char *arg0, arg1, ..., argn,
        NULL );
int _spawnle( int mode, char *cmdname, char *arg0, arg1, ..., argn,
        NULL, char *envp[] );

int _spawnlp( int mode, char *cmdname, char *arg0, arg1, ..., argn,
        NULL );
int _spawnlpe( int mode, char *cmdname, char *arg0, arg1, ..., argn,
        NULL, char *envp[] );

int _spawnv( int mode, char *cmdname, char *argv[] );
int _spawnve( int mode, char *cmdname, char *argv[], char *envp[] );

int _spawnvp( int mode, char *cmdname, char *argv[] );
int _spawnvpe( int mode, char *cmdname, char *argv[], char *envp[] );
```

cmdname specifies the name of the file that will be executed as the spawned process. If no filename extension is provided, the _spawn...() function first will look for a .COM file, then an .EXE file, and then a .BAT file, in that order. The mode argument determines what happens to the parent process after the spawn...() function is called. Table C.3 lists the possible values that can be used for the mode command:

Table C.3. The mode argument values for use with _spawn...().

Argument	Effect
P_WAIT	Forces the parent process to wait until the child process has completed execution.
P_OVERLAY	Overlays the child process in the memory area formerly occupied by the parent process.

Arguments are passed to the spawned process using pointers to character strings. Depending on the _spawn...() function used, pointers to each argument are used (as in _spawnl, _spawnle, _spawnlp, or _spawnlpe) or an array of pointers is used (_spawnv, _spawnve, _spawnvp, or _spawnvpe). You must pass at least one argument: either *arg0* or *argv[0]*. Typically, you should set this argument to the name of the program (equivalent to the *cmdname* argument).

Each of the functions in the _spawn...() family is made by appending the letters l, p, e, and v to _spawn. Table C.4 lists the purpose of each suffix.

Table C.4. Suffix characters used with the _spawn...() functions.

spawn...() Suffix	Purpose
l	Causes the argument pointers, *arg0*, *arg1*, etc., to be passed as separate arguments. Use the l suffix when you already know how many arguments you will have to pass. Either this option or the v option is required.
v	Causes the argument pointers, *arg0*, *arg1*, etc., to be passed to the child process as an array of pointers. Use the v option when you have a variable number of arguments to pass to the child process. Either this option or the l option is required.
p	Tells _spawn...() to search for the child process in the directories listed in the DOS path command.
e	The _spawn...() functions with the e option can send a new *env* argument to the child process.

If the _spawn...() function completes successfully, the exit status of the child process is returned. Normally, the exit status is 0. If _spawn...() is unsuccessful, a value of –1 is returned and errno is set. Table C.5 lists the values _spawn...() can store in errno:

Table C.5. Possible error codes returned if _spawn...() fails.

errno Value	Meaning
E2BIG	The argument list was too long.
EINVAL	An invalid argument was used.
ENOENT	The path or file name was not found.
ENOEXEC	An exec format error occurred.
ENOMEM	There was not enough memory.

Program Listings for the quad Class

The quad class is similar to the vli (Very Large Integer) class presented in *Using C* (Que, 1990). The quad class is in fact a conversion of the vli class. The conversion is straightforward, but it is tedious and not trivial. (One reason for presenting the complete listings was to avoid conversion issues.) If you do not have a copy of *Using C* and want to compare the two classes with an eye toward making your own conversions, you should do two things before you make any such attempt. First, understand thoroughly the physical formats used by the 80x86 CPU for storing data. Second, understand completely the arithmetic principles involved in performing multiplication and division by emulating hardware shift registers.

The quadword.hpp header file is shown in Listing D.1. Note that the operators with binary effect (see Chapter 18, "Object Control and Performance Issues") return by value rather than by reference in this version.

Listing D.1. quadword.hpp. Header file for the quad class source file quadword.cpp.

```
1   #include <stdlib.h>
2   #include <stdio.h>
3   #include <string.h>
4
5   class quad {
6     unsigned long vdata[4];
```

Listing D.1. Continued.

```
7    int quadoflow;
8    int quaduflow;
9  public:
10    quad();
11    quad( quad & );
12    quad( long );
13    quad( int );
14    quad& operator=( quad& );
15    quad& operator=( long );
16    quad& operator=( int );
17    quad& operator=( char* );
18    operator long();
19    operator int();
20    operator char*();
21    friend quad operator+(  quad&, quad& );
22    friend quad operator+( quad&, long );
23    friend quad operator+( quad&, int );
24    friend quad &operator+=( quad&, quad& );
25    friend quad &operator+=( quad&, long );
26    friend quad &operator+=( quad&, int );
27    friend quad operator-( quad&, quad& );
28    friend quad operator-( quad&, long );
29    friend quad operator-( quad&, int );
30    friend quad &operator-=( quad&, quad& );
31    friend quad &operator-=( quad&, long );
32    friend quad &operator-=( quad&, int );
33    friend void shiftleft( quad& );
34    friend void shiftright(quad& );
35    friend quad operator<<( quad&, int );
36    friend quad operator>>( quad&, int );
37    friend quad operator*( quad&, quad& );
38    friend quad operator*( quad&, long );
39    friend quad operator*( quad&, int );
40    friend quad operator/( quad&, quad& );
41    friend quad operator/( quad&, long );
42    friend quad operator/( quad&, int );
43    friend quad operator%( quad&, int );
44  };
```

The quad class member functions are shown in Listing D.2. Note that in this version, internal temporary quad objects are not static. Creating and destroying multiple temporary objects during the evaluation of an expression involving quad class objects can be expensive. You may want to try using the class as-is and also after making temporary objects static and changing the return type to a reference. The difference in execution speed can be considerable.

Listing D.2. quadword.cpp. Member functions for the quad class.

```
 1   #include "quadword.hpp"
 2
 3   static char outstr[81];
 4
 5   quad::quad()
 6   {
 7     int i;
 8
 9     for ( i=0; i<4; ++i ) vdata[i] = 0;
10     quadoflow = 0;
11     quaduflow = 0;
12   }
13
14   quad::quad( quad &old )
15   {
16     int i;
17
18     for ( i=0; i<4; ++i ) vdata[i] = old.vdata[i];
19     quadoflow = old.quadoflow;
20     quaduflow = old.quaduflow;
21   }
22
23   quad::quad( long value )
24   {
25     int i;
26
27     memset( (void *)vdata, 0, 16 );
28     vdata[0] = value;
29     if ( vdata[1] & 0x80000000L )
30       vdata[1]=0xFFFFFFFFL;
31     quadoflow = 0;
32     quaduflow = 0;
33   }
```

Listing D.2. Continued.

```
34
35  quad::quad( int value )
36  {
37    int i;
38
39    memset( (void *)vdata, 0, 16 );
40    vdata[0] = value;
41    if ( vdata[0] & 0x80000000L )
42      vdata[1]=0xFFFFFFFFL;
43    quadoflow = 0;
44    quaduflow = 0;
45  }
46
47  quad& quad::operator=( quad& other )
48  {
49    int i;
50
51    memmove( (void *)vdata, (void *)other.vdata, 16 );
52    quadoflow = other.quadoflow;
53    quaduflow = other.quaduflow;
54    return *this;
55  }
56
57  quad& quad::operator=( long value )
58  {
59    int i;
60
61    memset( (void *)vdata, 0, 16 );
62    vdata[0] = value;
63    if ( vdata[1] & 0x80000000L )
64      vdata[1]=0xFFFFFFFFL;
65    quadoflow = 0;
66    quaduflow = 0;
67    return *this;
68  }
69
70  quad& quad::operator=( int value )
71  {
72    int i;
73
```

```
74    memset( (void *)vdata, 0, 16 );
75    vdata[0] = value;
76    if ( vdata[1] & 0x80000000L )
77      vdata[1]=0xFFFFFFFFL;
78    quadoflow = 0;
79    quaduflow = 0;
80    return *this;
81  }
82
83  quad& quad::operator=( char *s )
84  {
85    int neg, i;
86    if ( *s == '-' ) {
87      neg = 1; s++;
88    }
89    else neg = 0;
90    *this = 0;
91    while ( *s ) {
92      *this = *this * 10;
93      *this += (int)( *s++ - '0' );
94    }
95    if ( neg ) {
96      vdata[0] = ~vdata[0];
97      vdata[1] = ~vdata[1];
98      *this += 1;
99    }
100   return *this;
101 }
102
103 quad::operator long()
104 {
105   return *(long *)vdata;
106 }
107
108 quad::operator int()
109 {
110   return *(int *)vdata;
111 }
112
113 quad::operator char*()
114 {
115   int neg, i;
```

Listing D.2. Continued.

```
116   char *s, *p;
117   quad VA = *this;
118
119   s = outstr;
120   if ( VA.vdata[1] & 0x80000000L ) {
121     neg = 1;
122     VA.vdata[0] = ~VA.vdata[0];
123     VA.vdata[1] = ~VA.vdata[1];
124     VA += 1;
125   }
126   else neg = 0;
127   while( 1 ) {
128     VA -= 10;
129     if ( VA.vdata[1] & 0x80000000L ) break; // done
130     VA += 10;
131     *s++ = '0' + (int)( VA % 10 );
132     VA = VA / 10;
133   }
134   VA += 10;              // fixup from loop
135   if ( (int)VA > 0 ) *s++ = (int)VA + '0';
136   if ( neg ) *s++ = '-';
137   *s = '\0'; // terminate the string
138   s = outstr;
139   p = s + strlen( s ) - 1;
140   while ( p > s ) {  // reverse string
141     *s ^= *p; *p ^= *s; *s++ ^= *p--;
142   }
143   return outstr;
144 }
145
146 quad operator+( quad& a, quad& addend )
147 {
148   unsigned int* ADD1 = (unsigned int*)a.vdata;
149   unsigned int* ADD2 = (unsigned int*)addend.vdata;
150   unsigned long x, y;
151   unsigned carry = 0;
152   int i;
153   quad SUM;
154   unsigned int* ANS = (unsigned int*)SUM.vdata;
155
```

```
156    SUM = 0;
157    for ( i=0; i<4; ++i ) {
158      x = ADD1[i]; y=ADD2[i];
159      x += y + carry;            // add with carry
160      ANS[i] = x & 0x0000FFFF;      // store partial result
161      carry = (unsigned)( x >> 16 ); // save the carry
162    }
163    if ( carry ) SUM.quadoflow = 1; else SUM.quadoflow = 0;
164    return SUM;
165 }
166
167 quad operator+( quad& a, long addend )
168 {
169   quad SUML;
170
171   SUML = addend;
172   return a + SUML;
173 }
174
175 quad operator+( quad& a, int addend )
176 {
177   quad SUMI;
178
179   SUMI = addend;
180   return a + SUMI;
181 }
182
183 quad& operator+=( quad& a, quad& addend )
184 {        // compound assign needs assign back to this
185   return a = a + addend;
186 }
187
188 quad& operator+=( quad& a, long addend )
189 {
190   return a = a + addend;
191 }
192
193 quad& operator+=( quad& a, int addend )
194 {
195   return a = a + addend;
196 }
197
```

Listing D.2. Continued.

```
198   quad operator-( quad& a, quad& subt )
199   {
200     int i;
201     quad DIFF;
202
203     for ( i=0; i<2; ++i ) subt.vdata[i] = ~subt.vdata[i];
204     subt += 1;
205     DIFF = a + subt;    // perform subtraction
206     for ( i=0; i<2; ++i ) subt.vdata[i] = ~subt.vdata[i];
207     subt += 1;
208     return DIFF;
209   }
210
211   quad operator-( quad& a, long subt )
212   {
213     quad DIFFL;
214
215     DIFFL = subt;
216     return a - DIFFL;
217   }
218
219   quad operator-( quad& a, int subt )
220   {
221     quad DIFFI;
222
223     DIFFI = subt;
224     return a - DIFFI;
225   }
226
227   quad& operator-=( quad& a, quad& subt )
228   {
229     int i;
230
231     for ( i=0; i<2; ++i ) subt.vdata[i] = ~subt.vdata[i];
232     subt += 1;
233     a = a + subt;          // perform subtraction
234     for ( i=0; i<2; ++i ) subt.vdata[i] = ~subt.vdata[i];
235     subt += 1;
236     return a;
237   }
```

```
238
239   quad& operator-=( quad& a, long subt )
240   {
241     return a = a - subt;
242   }
243
244   quad& operator-=( quad& a, int subt )
245   {
246     return a = a - subt;
247   }
248
249   void shiftleft( quad& a )
250   {
251     int i, carry;
252
253     for ( i=3; i>=0; --i ) {
254       if ( a.vdata[i] & 0x80000000L ) carry = 1;
255       else carry = 0;
256       a.vdata[i] <<= 1;
257       if ( i < 3 ) a.vdata[i+1] |= carry;
258     }
259   }
260
261   void shiftright( quad& a )
262   {
263     int i;
264     unsigned long carry;
265
266     for ( i=0; i<4; ++i ) {
267       if ( a.vdata[i] & 0x00000001L ) carry = 0x80000000L;
268       else carry = 0;
269       a.vdata[i] >>= 1;
270       if ( i > 0 ) a.vdata[i-1] |= carry;
271     }
272   }
273
274   quad operator<<( quad& a, int dist )
275   {
276     int numbytes, numbits, i;
277     char *s;
278     quad SLEFT;
279
```

Listing D.2. Continued.

```
280    SLEFT = a;
281    dist =  ( dist > 128 ) ? 128 : dist;
282    numbytes = dist / 8; numbits = dist % 8 ;
283    s = (char *)SLEFT.vdata;
284    if ( numbytes < 16 && numbytes > 0 )
285      memmove( &s[numbytes], &s[0],
286            16 - numbytes );
287    for ( i=0; i<numbytes; ++i ) s[i] = 0;
288    for ( i=0; i<numbits; ++i ) shiftleft( SLEFT );
289    return SLEFT;
290  }
291
292  quad operator>>( quad& a, int dist )
293  {
294    int numbytes, numbits, i;
295    char *s;
296    quad SRIGHT;
297
298    SRIGHT = a;
299    dist =  ( dist > 128 ) ? 128 : dist;
300    numbytes = dist / 8; numbits = dist % 8 ;
301    s = (char *)SRIGHT.vdata;
302    if ( numbytes < 16 && numbytes > 0 )
303      memmove( &s[0], &s[numbytes],
304            16 - numbytes );
305    for ( i=16-numbytes; i<16; ++i ) s[i] = 0;
306    for ( i=0; i<numbits; ++i ) shiftright( SRIGHT );
307    return SRIGHT;
308  }
309
310  quad operator *( quad& a, quad& mcand )
311  {
312    unsigned char mask;
313    unsigned char *m1;
314    int loop, inloop;
315    quad MUX;
316
317    MUX = 0; // init running total
318    m1 = (unsigned char *)a.vdata;
319    for ( loop=7; loop>=0; --loop )
```

```
320      if ( m1[loop] != 0 ) break; //skip leading 0's
321    if ( loop < 0 ) return MUX;
322    for ( ; loop>=0; --loop ) { // process every byte
323      mask = 0x80;
324      for ( inloop=0; inloop<8; ++inloop ) {    // every bit
325        if ( m1[loop] & mask ) MUX += mcand;
326        mask >>= 1;              // shift mask for next bit
327        shiftleft( MUX );           // adjust running sum
328      }
329    }
330    shiftright( MUX ); // put last shift back
331    return MUX;
332 }

334 quad operator *( quad& a, long mcand )
335 {
336    quad MUXL;
337
338    MUXL = mcand;
339    return MUXL * a;
340 }

342 quad operator *( quad& a, int mcand )
343 {
344    quad MUXI;
345
346    MUXI = mcand;
347    return MUXI * a;
348 }

350 quad operator/( quad& a, quad& div )
351 {
352    int i, aneg = 0, bneg = 0;
353    quad DIVIDEND;
354    quad DIVISOR;
355    quad FRAG;
356
357    DIVIDEND = a;            // get a working copy of dividend
358    DIVISOR = div;          // get a working copy of divisor
359    DIVISOR -= 1;
360    if ( DIVISOR.vdata[1] & 0x80000000L ) // it was 0
361      return DIVIDEND;
```

Listing D.2. Continued.

```
362    DIVISOR += 1;
363    if ( DIVIDEND.vdata[1] & 0x80000000L ) { // any negatives?
364      aneg = 1;                    // dividend was negative
365      for (i=0;i<2;++i) DIVIDEND.vdata[i]=~DIVIDEND.vdata[i];
366      DIVIDEND += 1;
367    }
368    if ( DIVISOR.vdata[1] & 0x80000000L ) {
369      bneg = 1;                    // divisor was negative
370      for (i=0;i<2;++i) DIVISOR.vdata[i]=~DIVISOR.vdata[i];
371      DIVISOR += 1;
372    }
373
374    for ( i=0; i<64; i+=32 ) { // skip 0's in dividend
375      if ( DIVIDEND.vdata[1] != 0 )
376        break;
377      else DIVIDEND = DIVIDEND << 32;
378    }
379    if ( i == 64 ) return DIVIDEND;       // dividend was zero
380
381           // the gyrations with FRAG are necessary
382           // to allow arithmetic with the high order
383           // part of DIVIDEND
384
385    for ( ; i<64; ++i ) {                // do division
386      shiftleft( DIVIDEND );    // shift dividend left one bit
387      memmove( (void *)&FRAG.vdata[0],  // set up subtraction
388           (void *)&DIVIDEND.vdata[2], 8 );
389      FRAG -= DIVISOR;                // trial subtraction
390      if ( FRAG.vdata[1] & 0x80000000L ) FRAG += DIVISOR;
391      else DIVIDEND.vdata[0] |= 0x00000001L;  // quotient bit
392      memmove( (void *)&DIVIDEND.vdata[2],     // restore it
393           (void *)&FRAG.vdata[0], 8 );
394    }
395
396    if ( aneg ^ bneg ) {        // make it negative if necessary
397      DIVIDEND.vdata[0]=~DIVIDEND.vdata[0];
398      DIVIDEND.vdata[1]=~DIVIDEND.vdata[1];
399      DIVIDEND += 1;
400    }
401    return DIVIDEND;
402  }
```

```
403
404   quad operator/( quad& a, long div )
405   {
406     quad DIVL;
407
408     DIVL = div;
409     return a / DIVL;
410   }
411
412   quad operator/( quad& a, int div )
413   {
414     quad DIVI;
415
416     DIVI = div;
417     return a / DIVI;
418   }
419
420   quad operator%( quad& a, int div )
421   {
422     int i;
423     quad MODULUS, FRAG;
424
425     MODULUS = div;
426     MODULUS = a / MODULUS;
427            // use this memmove to do the 128-bit
428            // shift quickly
429     memmove( (void *)&FRAG.vdata[0],
430       (void *)&MODULUS.vdata[2], 8 );
431     return FRAG;
432   }
```

Finally, Listing D.3 shows a test driver program for the quad class.

Listing D.3. testquad.cpp. Test drive the quad class functions.

```
1   #include <conio.h>
2   #include "quadword.hpp"
3
4   void main()
5   {
6     quad X, Y, Z;
```

Listing D.3. Continued.

```
 7
 8    X = 2; Y = 3; Z = 4;
 9    X = ( X * Y - Z ) / 2;
10    printf( "%ld\n", (long)X );
11    X = "-999999999";
12    printf( "%s\n", (char *)X );
13    X = ( X / 2 ) * 3;
14    printf( "%s\n", (char *)X );
15  }
```

If you want to use the quad class for serious purposes, you must make temporaries static and use references wherever possible. You may also want to use other internal methods for performing the arithmetic to achieve good execution speeds. You might, for example, want to familiarize yourself with the 80x87 coprocessor and use its high-speed integer arithmetic capabilities.

Complete Listings of FCWIN Resources

In Chapters 19 through 21, the FCWIN financial calculator application for Windows was developed in some detail. However, complete details on the Windows resources used by FCWIN were not presented there. For those of you who do not wish to obtain the FCWIN.RES binary file from the program disk, the resources are provided here in resource *script* format. You can type them all into their respective files using the PWB or another text editor. Be careful, however, not to make any keystroke errors while typing.

The only resource which cannot be described in a resource script file is the application icon. It is therefore shown in Figure E.1, so you can duplicate it with the Image Editor.

The FCWIN menu structure drives the entire application. Its structure is shown in Listing E.1.

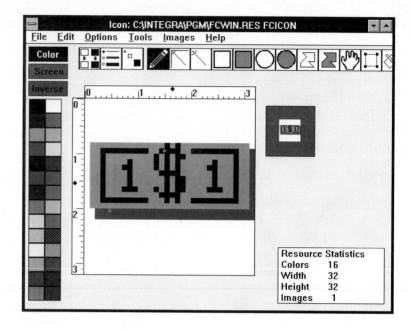

Listing E.1. fcwin.rc. The resource script for FCWIN.

```
#include <windows.h>
#include "fcwin.h"

rcinclude fcmenu.rc

FCICON ICON fcicon.ico

rcinclude fceffcon.dlg
rcinclude fceffper.dlg
rcinclude fcfvann.dlg
rcinclude fcfvsin.dlg
rcinclude fcloanda.dlg
rcinclude fcmkupco.dlg
rcinclude fcmkuppr.dlg
rcinclude fcmortls.dlg
rcinclude fcmortpr.dlg
rcinclude fcpayout.dlg
rcinclude fcpctcg.dlg
rcinclude fcpctto.dlg
rcinclude fcpvann.dlg
rcinclude fcpvsin.dlg
```

Listing E.2. fcmenu.rc. The menu resource script for FCWIN.

```
2FCMENU   MENU PRELOAD MOVEABLE PURE DISCARDABLE
BEGIN
  POPUP "General &Business"
  BEGIN
    MenuItem   "Percent Ch&ange", IDM_PCTCHANGE
    MenuItem   "Percent &Total", IDM_PCTTOTAL
    MenuItem   "Markup Over &Cost", IDM_MKUPCOST
    MenuItem   "Markup Over &Price", IDM_MKUPPRICE
  END
  POPUP "&Interest Rates"
  BEGIN
    MenuItem   "Effective &Periodic Rate", IDM_EFFPER
    MenuItem   "Effective &Continuous Rate", IDM_EFFCONT
  END
  POPUP "&Actuarial Functions"
  BEGIN
    MenuItem   "Future Value, Single Deposit", IDM_FVSINGLE
    MenuItem   "Present Value, Single Deposit", IDM_PVSINGLE
    MenuItem   "Future Value,  Regular Deposits", IDM_FVREGULAR
    MenuItem   "Present Value, Regular Deposits", IDM_PVREGULAR
  END
  POPUP "&Loan Amortization"
  BEGIN
    MenuItem   "&Input Loan Data", IDM_LOANDATA
    MenuItem   "Payout &Analysis", IDM_PAYOUT
    MenuItem   "&Display Amortization Table", IDM_DISPAMORT
    MenuItem   "&Print Amortization Table", IDM_PRNTAMORT
  END
  POPUP "&Help"
  BEGIN
    MenuItem   "Percent Change", HLP_PCTCHANGE
    MenuItem   "PerCent Total", HLP_PCTTOTAL
    MenuItem   "Markup Percent of Cost", HLP_MKUPCOST
    MenuItem   "Markup Percent of Price", HLP_MKUPPRICE
    MenuItem   "Effective Rate, Periodic", HLP_EFFPER
    MenuItem   "Effective Rate, Continuous", HLP_EFFCONT
    MenuItem   "Future Value, Single Payment", HLP_FVSINGLE
    MenuItem   "Present Value, Single Payment", HLP_PVSINGLE
    MenuItem   "Future Value, Regular Deposits", HLP_FVREGULAR
    MenuItem   "Present Value, Regular Deosits", HLP_PVREGULAR
    MenuItem   "Input Loan Data", HLP_LOANDATA
```

Listing E.2. Continued.

```
    MenuItem  "Payout Analysis", HLP_PAYOUT
    MenuItem  "Display Amortization Table", HLP_DISPAMORT
    MenuItem  "Print Amortization Table", HLP_PRNTAMORT
    MenuItem  " ", 0
  END
END
```

Listing E.3. fceffcon.dlg. Dialog resource script for Effective Rate, Continuous Compounding.

```
FCEFFCON DIALOG DISCARDABLE LOADONCALL PURE MOVEABLE 34,43,188,81
STYLE WS_POPUP ¦ WS_CAPTION ¦ WS_SYSMENU ¦ 0x80L
CAPTION "Effective Rate, Continuous Compounding"
BEGIN
    CONTROL "" 106, "EDIT", WS_CHILD ¦ WS_VISIBLE ¦ WS_BORDER ¦
                        WS_TABSTOP, 111, 17, 54, 12
    CONTROL "" 103, "EDIT", WS_CHILD ¦ WS_VISIBLE ¦ WS_DISABLED ¦
                        WS_BORDER, 111, 37, 54, 12
    CONTROL "Return" 104, "BUTTON", WS_CHILD ¦ WS_VISIBLE ¦
                        WS_TABSTOP, 101, 59, 40, 12
    CONTROL "Compute" 105, "BUTTON", WS_CHILD ¦ WS_VISIBLE ¦
                        WS_TABSTOP, 42, 59, 40, 12
    CONTROL "Annual Percentage Rate" 200, "STATIC", WS_CHILD ¦
                        WS_VISIBLE ¦ 0x2L, 11, 18, 84, 12
    CONTROL "Effective Periodic Rate" 201, "STATIC", WS_CHILD ¦
                        WS_VISIBLE ¦ 0x2L, 11, 37, 84, 12
END
```

Listing E.4. fceffper.dlg. Dialog resource script for Effective Interest, Periodic Compounding.

```
FCEFFPER DIALOG DISCARDABLE LOADONCALL PURE MOVEABLE 44, 45,
        177, 106
STYLE WS_POPUP ¦ WS_CAPTION ¦ WS_SYSMENU ¦ 0x80L
CAPTION "Effective Interest, Periodic Compounding"
BEGIN
    CONTROL "" 106, "EDIT", WS_CHILD ¦ WS_VISIBLE ¦ WS_BORDER ¦
                        WS_TABSTOP, 111, 16, 54, 12
```

```
CONTROL "" 109, "EDIT", WS_CHILD ¦ WS_VISIBLE ¦ WS_BORDER ¦
                    WS_TABSTOP, 111, 35, 54, 12
CONTROL "" 103, "EDIT", WS_CHILD ¦ WS_VISIBLE ¦ WS_DISABLED ¦
                    WS_BORDER, 111, 53, 54, 12
CONTROL "Return" 104, "BUTTON", WS_CHILD ¦ WS_VISIBLE ¦
                    WS_TABSTOP, 99, 86, 40, 12
CONTROL "Compute" 105, "BUTTON", WS_CHILD ¦ WS_VISIBLE ¦
                    WS_TABSTOP, 40, 86, 40, 12
CONTROL "Annual Percentage Rate" 200, "STATIC", WS_CHILD ¦
                    WS_VISIBLE ¦ 0x2L, 11, 18, 84, 12
CONTROL "# Compounding Periods" 201, "STATIC", WS_CHILD ¦
                    WS_VISIBLE ¦ 0x2L, 11, 36, 84, 12
CONTROL "Effective Periodic Rate" 202, "STATIC", WS_CHILD ¦
                    WS_VISIBLE ¦ 0x2L, 11, 54, 84, 12

END
```

Listing E.5. fcfvann.dlg. Dialog resource script for Future Value of Regular Deposits.

```
2FCFVANN DIALOG DISCARDABLE LOADONCALL PURE MOVEABLE 10, 35,
        235, 138
STYLE WS_POPUP ¦ WS_CAPTION ¦ WS_SYSMENU ¦ 0x80L
CAPTION "Future Value of Regular Deposits"
BEGIN
  CONTROL "" 107, "EDIT", WS_CHILD ¦ WS_VISIBLE ¦ WS_BORDER ¦
                    WS_TABSTOP, 127, 15, 65, 12
  CONTROL "" 106, "EDIT", WS_CHILD ¦ WS_VISIBLE ¦ WS_BORDER ¦
                    WS_TABSTOP, 127, 32, 65, 12
  CONTROL "" 109, "EDIT", WS_CHILD ¦ WS_VISIBLE ¦ WS_BORDER ¦
                    WS_TABSTOP, 127, 49, 65, 12
  CONTROL "" 108, "EDIT", WS_CHILD ¦ WS_VISIBLE ¦ WS_BORDER ¦
                    WS_TABSTOP, 127, 66, 65, 12
  CONTROL "" 103, "EDIT", WS_CHILD ¦ WS_VISIBLE ¦ WS_DISABLED ¦
                    WS_BORDER, 127, 83, 65, 12
  CONTROL "Compute" 105, "BUTTON", WS_CHILD ¦ WS_VISIBLE ¦
                    WS_TABSTOP, 66, 111, 44, 12
  CONTROL "Return" 104, "BUTTON", WS_CHILD ¦ WS_VISIBLE ¦
                    WS_TABSTOP, 123, 111, 44, 12
  CONTROL "Regular deposit amount?" 200, "STATIC", WS_CHILD ¦
                    WS_VISIBLE ¦ 0x2L, 18, 16, 98, 9
```

Listing E.5. Continued.

```
CONTROL "Annual Percentage Rate" 201, "STATIC", WS_CHILD ¦
                    WS_VISIBLE ¦ 0x2L, 33, 33, 82, 8
CONTROL "Number of Payments per Year" 202, "STATIC", WS_CHILD ¦
                    WS_VISIBLE ¦ 0x2L, 15, 50, 100, 9
CONTROL "Number of Years" 203, "STATIC", WS_CHILD ¦ WS_VISIBLE ¦
                    0x2L, 52, 69, 63, 9
CONTROL "Future Value of Deposits" 204, "STATIC", WS_CHILD ¦
                    WS_VISIBLE ¦ 0x2L, 30, 87, 85, 8
END
```

Listing E.6. fcfvsin.dlg. Dialog resource script for Future Value of a Single Amount.

```
FCFVSIN DIALOG DISCARDABLE LOADONCALL PURE MOVEABLE 10, 35,
                    235, 138
STYLE WS_POPUP ¦ WS_CAPTION ¦ WS_SYSMENU ¦ 0x80L
CAPTION "Future Value of a Single Amount"
BEGIN
    CONTROL "" 107, "EDIT", WS_CHILD ¦ WS_VISIBLE ¦ WS_BORDER ¦
                    WS_TABSTOP, 127, 15, 65, 12
    CONTROL "" 106, "EDIT", WS_CHILD ¦ WS_VISIBLE ¦ WS_BORDER ¦
                    WS_TABSTOP, 127, 32, 65, 12
    CONTROL "" 109, "EDIT", WS_CHILD ¦ WS_VISIBLE ¦ WS_BORDER ¦
                    WS_TABSTOP, 127, 49, 65, 12
    CONTROL "" 108, "EDIT", WS_CHILD ¦ WS_VISIBLE ¦ WS_BORDER ¦
                    WS_TABSTOP, 127, 66, 65, 12
    CONTROL "" 103, "EDIT", WS_CHILD ¦ WS_VISIBLE ¦ WS_DISABLED ¦
                    WS_BORDER, 127, 83, 65, 12
    CONTROL "Compute" 105, "BUTTON", WS_CHILD ¦ WS_VISIBLE ¦
                    WS_TABSTOP, 66, 111, 44, 12
    CONTROL "Return" 104, "BUTTON", WS_CHILD ¦ WS_VISIBLE ¦
                    WS_TABSTOP, 123, 111, 44, 12
    CONTROL "FV of what amount?" 200, "STATIC", WS_CHILD ¦
                    WS_VISIBLE ¦ 0x2L, 39, 17, 77, 8
    CONTROL "Annual Percentage Rate" 201, "STATIC", WS_CHILD ¦
                    WS_VISIBLE ¦ 0x2L, 33, 33, 82, 8
    CONTROL "Number of Payments per Year" 202, "STATIC", WS_CHILD ¦
                    WS_VISIBLE ¦ 0x2L, 15, 50, 100, 9
```

```
    CONTROL "Number of Years" 203, "STATIC", WS_CHILD ¦ WS_VISIBLE ¦
                    0x2L, 52, 69, 63, 9
    CONTROL "Future Value of Amount" 204, "STATIC", WS_CHILD ¦
                    WS_VISIBLE ¦ 0x2L, 30, 87, 85, 8
END
```

Listing E.7. fcloanda.dlg. Dialog resource script for Mortgage Loan Data Entry.

```
FCLOANDA DIALOG DISCARDABLE LOADONCALL PURE MOVEABLE 10, 35,
                220, 113
STYLE WS_POPUP ¦ WS_CAPTION ¦ WS_SYSMENU ¦ 0x80L
CAPTION "Mortgage Loan Data Entry"
BEGIN
    CONTROL "" 107, "EDIT", WS_CHILD ¦ WS_VISIBLE ¦ WS_BORDER ¦
                    WS_TABSTOP, 127, 15, 65, 12
    CONTROL "" 106, "EDIT", WS_CHILD ¦ WS_VISIBLE ¦ WS_BORDER ¦
                    WS_TABSTOP, 127, 32, 65, 12
    CONTROL "" 109, "EDIT", WS_CHILD ¦ WS_VISIBLE ¦ WS_BORDER ¦
                    WS_TABSTOP, 127, 49, 65, 12
    CONTROL "" 108, "EDIT", WS_CHILD ¦ WS_VISIBLE ¦ WS_BORDER ¦
                    WS_TABSTOP, 127, 66, 65, 12
    CONTROL "Return" 104, "BUTTON", WS_CHILD ¦ WS_VISIBLE ¦
                    WS_TABSTOP, 86, 88, 44, 12
    CONTROL "Mortgage loan amount" 200, "STATIC", WS_CHILD ¦
                    WS_VISIBLE ¦ 0x2L, 39, 17, 77, 8
    CONTROL "Annual Percentage Rate" 201, "STATIC", WS_CHILD ¦
                    WS_VISIBLE ¦ 0x2L, 33, 33, 82, 8
    CONTROL "Number of Payments per Year" 202, "STATIC", WS_CHILD ¦
                    WS_VISIBLE ¦ 0x2L, 15, 50, 100, 9
    CONTROL "Number of Years to amortize" 203, "STATIC", WS_CHILD ¦
                    WS_VISIBLE ¦ 0x2L, 4, 69, 111, 9
END
```

Listing E.8. fcmkupco.dlg. Dialog resource script for Markup Over Cost.

```
FCMKUPCO DIALOG DISCARDABLE LOADONCALL PURE MOVEABLE 43, 48,
                193, 118
STYLE WS_POPUP ¦ WS_CAPTION ¦ WS_SYSMENU ¦ 0x80L
```

Listing E.8. Continued.

```
CAPTION "Markup Over Cost"
BEGIN
  CONTROL "" 101, "EDIT", WS_CHILD | WS_VISIBLE | WS_BORDER |
                      WS_TABSTOP, 107, 8, 66, 12
  CONTROL "" 102, "EDIT", WS_CHILD | WS_VISIBLE | WS_BORDER |
                      WS_TABSTOP, 107, 38, 66, 12
  CONTROL "" 103, "EDIT", WS_CHILD | WS_VISIBLE | WS_DISABLED |
                      WS_BORDER, 107, 66, 66, 12
  CONTROL "Return" 104, "BUTTON", WS_CHILD | WS_VISIBLE |
                      WS_TABSTOP, 101, 91, 40, 12
  CONTROL "Compute" 105, "BUTTON", WS_CHILD | WS_VISIBLE |
                      WS_TABSTOP, 40, 91, 44, 12
  CONTROL "Price of Item" 200, "STATIC", WS_CHILD | WS_VISIBLE |
                      0x2L, 6, 10, 83, 12
  CONTROL "Cost of Item" 201, "STATIC", WS_CHILD | WS_VISIBLE |
                      0x2L, 6, 39, 83, 12
  CONTROL "Markup % of Cost" 202, "STATIC", WS_CHILD | WS_VISIBLE |
                      0x2L, 6, 67, 83, 12
END
```

Listing E.9. fcmkuppr.dlg. Dialog resource script for Markup Over Price.

```
FCMKUPPR DIALOG DISCARDABLE LOADONCALL PURE MOVEABLE 47, 44,
                195, 114
STYLE WS_POPUP | WS_CAPTION | WS_SYSMENU | 0x80L
CAPTION "Markup Over Price"
BEGIN
  CONTROL "" 101, "EDIT", WS_CHILD | WS_VISIBLE | WS_BORDER |
                      WS_TABSTOP, 109, 14, 64, 12
  CONTROL "" 102, "EDIT", WS_CHILD | WS_VISIBLE | WS_BORDER |
                      WS_TABSTOP, 109, 38, 64, 12
  CONTROL "" 103, "EDIT", WS_CHILD | WS_VISIBLE | WS_DISABLED |
                      WS_BORDER, 109, 64, 64, 12
  CONTROL "Return" 104, "BUTTON", WS_CHILD | WS_VISIBLE |
                      WS_TABSTOP, 109, 87, 40, 12
  CONTROL "Compute" 105, "BUTTON", WS_CHILD | WS_VISIBLE |
                      WS_TABSTOP, 50, 87, 40, 12
  CONTROL "Price of Item" 200, "STATIC", WS_CHILD | WS_VISIBLE |
                      0x2L, 9, 14, 82, 12
```

```
   CONTROL "Cost of Item" 201, "STATIC", WS_CHILD ¦ WS_VISIBLE ¦
                     0x2L, 9, 40, 82, 12
   CONTROL "Markup % of Price" 202, "STATIC", WS_CHILD ¦
                     WS_VISIBLE ¦ 0x2L, 9, 65, 82, 12
END
```

Listing E.10. fcmortls.dlg. Dialog resource script for Loan Amortization Schedule (displayed in a list box).

```
FCMORTLS DIALOG DISCARDABLE LOADONCALL PURE MOVEABLE 29, 31,
              222, 149
STYLE WS_POPUP ¦ WS_CAPTION ¦ WS_SYSMENU ¦ 0x80L
CAPTION "Loan Amortization Schedule"
BEGIN
   CONTROL "Return" 104, "BUTTON", WS_CHILD ¦ WS_VISIBLE ¦
        WS_TABSTOP, 92, 128, 40, 12
   CONTROL "LISTBOX" 110, "LISTBOX", WS_CHILD ¦ WS_VISIBLE ¦
        WS_BORDER ¦ WS_VSCROLL ¦ 0x41L, 12, 21, 198, 102
   CONTROL "Paymnt #     Pay Amt    Interest   Principal  Balance"
        200, "STATIC", WS_CHILD ¦ WS_VISIBLE, 10, 7, 187, 10
END
```

Listing E.11. fcmortpr.dlg. Dialog resource script for Print Amortization Schedule.

```
FCMORTPR DIALOG DISCARDABLE LOADONCALL PURE MOVEABLE 58, 37,
              193, 80
STYLE WS_POPUP ¦ WS_CAPTION ¦ WS_SYSMENU ¦ 0x80L
CAPTION "Print Amortization Schedule"
BEGIN
   CONTROL "Start" 115, "BUTTON", WS_CHILD ¦ WS_VISIBLE ¦
                     WS_TABSTOP, 111, 54, 36, 12
   CONTROL "Cancel" 116, "BUTTON", WS_CHILD ¦ WS_VISIBLE ¦
                     WS_TABSTOP, 46, 54, 36, 12
   CONTROL "Printing the amortization schedule for the current loan"
        200, "STATIC", WS_CHILD ¦ WS_VISIBLE, 10, 9, 177, 9
   CONTROL "data. Click Start to begin printing, and click Cancel"
        201, "STATIC", WS_CHILD ¦ WS_VISIBLE, 10, 17, 177, 9
   CONTROL "to change your mind." 202, "STATIC", WS_CHILD ¦
                     WS_VISIBLE, 10, 25, 177, 9
END
```

Listing E.12. fcpayout.dlg. Dialog resource script for Amortization Payout Analysis.

```
FCPAYOUT DIALOG DISCARDABLE LOADONCALL PURE MOVEABLE 10, 35,
                252, 149
STYLE WS_POPUP ¦ WS_CAPTION ¦ WS_SYSMENU ¦ 0x80L
CAPTION "Amortization Payout Analysis"
BEGIN
  CONTROL "Mortgage/Loan Amount" 200, "STATIC", WS_CHILD ¦
                WS_VISIBLE, 15, 11, 78, 9
  CONTROL "Annual Percentage Rate" 201, "STATIC", WS_CHILD ¦
                WS_VISIBLE, 15, 24, 79, 9
  CONTROL "Number of Payments Per Year" 202, "STATIC", WS_CHILD ¦
                WS_VISIBLE, 15, 38, 101, 9
  CONTROL "Number of Years" 203, "STATIC", WS_CHILD ¦ WS_VISIBLE,
                15, 51, 58, 9
  CONTROL "Level Payment" 204, "STATIC", WS_CHILD ¦ WS_VISIBLE,
                15, 85, 50, 9
  CONTROL "Total Payout" 205, "STATIC", WS_CHILD ¦ WS_VISIBLE,
                15, 98, 43, 9
  CONTROL "Total Interest Paid" 206, "STATIC", WS_CHILD ¦
                WS_VISIBLE, 15, 111, 62, 8
  CONTROL "Effective Interest Rate, Ballon Note" 207, "STATIC",
                WS_CHILD ¦ WS_VISIBLE, 15, 123, 117, 9
  CONTROL "" 107, "EDIT", WS_CHILD ¦ WS_VISIBLE ¦ WS_DISABLED ¦
                WS_BORDER ¦ 0x2L, 131, 9, 76, 12
  CONTROL "" 106, "EDIT", WS_CHILD ¦ WS_VISIBLE ¦ WS_DISABLED ¦
                WS_BORDER ¦ 0x2L, 131, 23, 76, 12
  CONTROL "" 109, "EDIT", WS_CHILD ¦ WS_VISIBLE ¦ WS_DISABLED ¦
                WS_BORDER ¦ 0x2L, 131, 37, 76, 12
  CONTROL "" 108, "EDIT", WS_CHILD ¦ WS_VISIBLE ¦ WS_DISABLED ¦
                WS_BORDER ¦ 0x2L, 131, 51, 76, 12
  CONTROL "Mortgage or Loan Input Data" 208, "BUTTON", WS_CHILD ¦
                WS_VISIBLE ¦ 0x7L, 8, 0, 212, 69
  CONTROL "" 111, "EDIT", WS_CHILD ¦ WS_VISIBLE ¦ WS_DISABLED ¦
                WS_BORDER ¦ 0x2L, 139, 82, 75, 12
  CONTROL "" 113, "EDIT", WS_CHILD ¦ WS_VISIBLE ¦ WS_DISABLED ¦
                WS_BORDER ¦ 0x2L, 139, 95, 75, 12
  CONTROL "" 112, "EDIT", WS_CHILD ¦ WS_VISIBLE ¦ WS_DISABLED ¦
                WS_BORDER ¦ 0x2L, 139, 108, 75, 12
```

```
    CONTROL "" 114, "EDIT", WS_CHILD ¦ WS_VISIBLE ¦ WS_DISABLED ¦
                    WS_BORDER ¦ 0x2L, 139, 121, 75, 12
    CONTROL "Payout Analysis Data" 209, "BUTTON", WS_CHILD ¦
                    WS_VISIBLE ¦ 0x7L, 8, 74, 212, 66
END
```

Listing E.13. fcpctcg.dlg. Dialog resource script for Calculate Percent Change.

```
FCPCTCG DIALOG DISCARDABLE LOADONCALL PURE MOVEABLE 60, 40,
            177, 105
STYLE WS_POPUP ¦ WS_VISIBLE ¦ WS_CAPTION ¦ WS_SYSMENU ¦ 0xC0L
CAPTION "Calculate Percent Change"
BEGIN
    CONTROL "Compute" 105, "BUTTON", WS_CHILD ¦ WS_VISIBLE ¦
                    WS_TABSTOP, 49, 85, 35, 12
    CONTROL "Return" 104, "BUTTON", WS_CHILD ¦ WS_VISIBLE ¦
                    WS_TABSTOP, 93, 85, 35, 12
    CONTROL "" 101, "EDIT", WS_CHILD ¦ WS_VISIBLE ¦ WS_BORDER ¦
                    WS_TABSTOP ¦ 0x82L, 94, 7, 50, 12
    CONTROL "" 102, "EDIT", WS_CHILD ¦ WS_VISIBLE ¦ WS_BORDER ¦
                    WS_TABSTOP ¦ 0x82L, 94, 26, 50, 12
    CONTROL "Old Value" 200, "STATIC", WS_CHILD ¦ WS_VISIBLE ¦
                    0x2L, 10, 9, 73, 12
    CONTROL "New Value" 201, "STATIC", WS_CHILD ¦ WS_VISIBLE ¦
                    0x2L, 12, 28, 73, 12
    CONTROL "Percent Change" 202, "STATIC", WS_CHILD ¦ WS_VISIBLE ¦
                    0x2L, 13, 48, 73, 12
    CONTROL "" 103, "EDIT", WS_CHILD ¦ WS_VISIBLE ¦ WS_DISABLED ¦
                    WS_BORDER ¦ 0x2L, 94, 46, 50, 12
END
```

Listing E.14. fcpctto.dlg. Dialog resource script for Percent of Total.

```
FCPCTTO DIALOG DISCARDABLE LOADONCALL PURE MOVEABLE 44, 49,
            173, 108
STYLE WS_POPUP ¦ WS_CAPTION ¦ WS_SYSMENU ¦ 0x80L
CAPTION "Percent of Total"
BEGIN
```

Listing E.14. Continued.

```
    CONTROL "Partial Amount" 200, "STATIC", WS_CHILD | WS_VISIBLE |
                            0x2L, 17, 14, 52, 12
    CONTROL "Percent Total =" 202, "STATIC", WS_CHILD | WS_VISIBLE |
                            0x2L, 17, 56, 52, 12
    CONTROL "Total Amount" 201, "STATIC", WS_CHILD | WS_VISIBLE |
                            0x2L, 17, 36, 52, 12
    CONTROL "" 102, "EDIT", WS_CHILD | WS_VISIBLE | WS_BORDER |
                        WS_TABSTOP | 0x82L, 95, 12, 56, 12
    CONTROL "" 101, "EDIT", WS_CHILD | WS_VISIBLE | WS_BORDER |
                        WS_TABSTOP | 0x82L, 95, 33, 56, 12
    CONTROL "" 103, "EDIT", WS_CHILD | WS_VISIBLE | WS_DISABLED |
                        WS_BORDER | 0x2L, 95, 54, 56, 12
    CONTROL "Compute" 105, "BUTTON", WS_CHILD | WS_VISIBLE |
                        WS_TABSTOP, 38, 87, 44, 12
    CONTROL "Return" 104, "BUTTON", WS_CHILD | WS_VISIBLE |
                        WS_TABSTOP, 92, 87, 40, 12
END
```

Listing E.15. fcpvann.dlg. Dialog resource script for Present Value of Regular Deposits.

```
FCPVANN DIALOG DISCARDABLE LOADONCALL PURE MOVEABLE 10, 35,
            235, 138
STYLE WS_POPUP | WS_CAPTION | WS_SYSMENU | 0x80L
CAPTION "Present Value of Regular Deposits"
BEGIN
  CONTROL "" 107, "EDIT", WS_CHILD | WS_VISIBLE | WS_BORDER |
                      WS_TABSTOP, 127, 15, 65, 12
  CONTROL "" 106, "EDIT", WS_CHILD | WS_VISIBLE | WS_BORDER |
                      WS_TABSTOP, 127, 32, 65, 12
  CONTROL "" 109, "EDIT", WS_CHILD | WS_VISIBLE | WS_BORDER |
                      WS_TABSTOP, 127, 49, 65, 12
  CONTROL "" 108, "EDIT", WS_CHILD | WS_VISIBLE | WS_BORDER |
                      WS_TABSTOP, 127, 66, 65, 12
  CONTROL "" 103, "EDIT", WS_CHILD | WS_VISIBLE | WS_DISABLED |
                      WS_BORDER, 127, 83, 65, 12
  CONTROL "Compute" 105, "BUTTON", WS_CHILD | WS_VISIBLE |
                      WS_TABSTOP, 66, 111, 44, 12
```

```
    CONTROL "Return" 104, "BUTTON", WS_CHILD ¦ WS_VISIBLE ¦
                        WS_TABSTOP, 123, 111, 44, 12
    CONTROL "Regular deposit amount?" 200, "STATIC", WS_CHILD ¦
                        WS_VISIBLE ¦ 0x2L, 16, 17, 100, 8
    CONTROL "Annual Percentage Rate" 201, "STATIC", WS_CHILD ¦
                        WS_VISIBLE ¦ 0x2L, 33, 33, 82, 8
    CONTROL "Number of Payments per Year" 202, "STATIC", WS_CHILD ¦
                        WS_VISIBLE ¦ 0x2L, 15, 50, 100, 9
    CONTROL "Number of Years" 203, "STATIC", WS_CHILD ¦ WS_VISIBLE ¦
                        0x2L, 52, 69, 63, 9
    CONTROL "Present Value of Deposits" 204, "STATIC", WS_CHILD ¦
                        WS_VISIBLE ¦ 0x2L, 30, 87, 85, 8

END
```

Listing E.16. fcpvsin.dlg. Dialog resource script for Present Value of a Single Amount.

```
FCPVSIN DIALOG DISCARDABLE LOADONCALL PURE MOVEABLE 10, 35,
            220, 136
STYLE WS_POPUP ¦ WS_CAPTION ¦ WS_SYSMENU ¦ 0x80L
CAPTION "Present Value of a Single Amount"
BEGIN
    CONTROL "" 107, "EDIT", WS_CHILD ¦ WS_VISIBLE ¦ WS_BORDER ¦
                        WS_TABSTOP, 129, 17, 65, 12
    CONTROL "" 106, "EDIT", WS_CHILD ¦ WS_VISIBLE ¦ WS_BORDER ¦
                        WS_TABSTOP, 129, 34, 65, 12
    CONTROL "" 109, "EDIT", WS_CHILD ¦ WS_VISIBLE ¦ WS_BORDER ¦
                        WS_TABSTOP, 129, 51, 65, 12
    CONTROL "" 108, "EDIT", WS_CHILD ¦ WS_VISIBLE ¦ WS_BORDER ¦
                        WS_TABSTOP, 129, 68, 65, 12
    CONTROL "" 103, "EDIT", WS_CHILD ¦ WS_VISIBLE ¦ WS_DISABLED ¦
                        WS_BORDER, 129, 85, 65, 12
    CONTROL "Compute" 105, "BUTTON", WS_CHILD ¦ WS_VISIBLE ¦
                        WS_TABSTOP, 64, 113, 44, 12
    CONTROL "Return" 104, "BUTTON", WS_CHILD ¦ WS_VISIBLE ¦
                        WS_TABSTOP, 121, 113, 44, 12
    CONTROL "PV of what amount?" 200, "STATIC", WS_CHILD ¦
                        WS_VISIBLE ¦ 0x2L, 41, 19, 77, 8
    CONTROL "Annual Percentage Rate" 201, "STATIC", WS_CHILD ¦
                        WS_VISIBLE ¦ 0x2L, 35, 35, 82, 8
```

Listing E.16. Continued.

```
CONTROL "Number of Payments per Year" 202, "STATIC", WS_CHILD ¦
                    WS_VISIBLE ¦ 0x2L, 17, 52, 100, 9
CONTROL "Number of Years" 203, "STATIC", WS_CHILD ¦ WS_VISIBLE ¦
                    0x2L, 54, 71, 63, 9
CONTROL "Present Value of Amount" 204, "STATIC", WS_CHILD ¦
                    WS_VISIBLE ¦ 0x2L, 32, 89, 85, 8
END
```

Symbols

- - (decrement) unary operator, 82
! (NOT) (reverse true or false
condition of expressions), 65, 82,
229, 680
!= (operator)
not equal to relational, 65, 83
not equal NMAKE Expression,
229
$avings.cpp program, 586-587
% (remainder) NMAKE Expression
operator, 229
& (operator), 829
address-of unary, 82, 147, 549
ampersand, 52, 114
AND, 678
bitwise AND NMAKE Expression,
83, 229
reference, 454
&& (operator)
AND both expressions are true, 65
logical AND NMAKE Expression,
83, 229
&= (bitwise AND) binary assignment,
83
( ) parentheses, 114, 229
" " (quotation marks), 92, 216
(string concatenation) operator,
95
(string literal) operator, 95

% (operator)
modulus binary mathematical, 82
percent sign, 244
%= (remainder) binary assignment,
83
¦ (bitwise OR) operator, 83, 229, 678
, (left to right forced evaluation)
operator, 84
* (operator)
multiplication binary
mathematical, 82
indirection, 147
*= (product) binary assignment, 83
+ (addition) binary mathematical
operator, 82
++ (increment) unary operator, 82
+= (sum) binary assignment
operator, 82
- (subtraction) binary mathematical
operator, 82, 229
-= (difference) binary assignment, 83
- > (operators)
indirect component selection, 83
structure pointer, 168, 439, 488,
523
- >* (dereference pointer to class
member), 84
. (operators)
direct component selection, 83
structure member, 166, 438, 523
. * (dereference pointer to class
member), 84

... (ellipsis), 24

/ (division) binary mathematical operator, 82, 229

/= (quotient) binary assignment, 83

:: (scope access/resolution) class member operator, 84, 447, 508, 520

; (semicolon), 426

< (less than) relational operator, 65, 83, 229

<< (shift-left) operator, 83, 668

<= (less than or equal to) relational operator, 65, 83, 229

=() (assignment operator), 731

= (assignment) binary operator, 82

== (equal to) relational operator, 65, 83, 229

> (greater than) relational operator, 65, 83, 229

> = (greater than or equal to) relational operator, 83

>> (shift-right) operator, 83, 229, 668

[ ] (subsript) operator, 768

\ (backslash), 90, 492

\n (new-line character), 236

^ (operators)
  bitwise exclusive OR NMAKE Expression, 229
  XOR operator, 83, 678

^= (operators)
  bitwise XOR binary assignment, 83
  exclusive-OR-and-assign compound, 150

_ (underscore), 111

{ } (braces), 66, 104

¦= (bitwise OR) binary assignment, 83, 229

¦¦ (logical OR) operator, 65, 83, 229

~ (operators)
  tilde, 434
  bitwise complement unary operator, 82, 229

*(operators)
  indirection unary, 82
  multiplication NMAKE Expression, 229

+ (addition) NMAKE Experssion operator, 229

- (minus) unary operator, 82

<< and >> stream operators, 670-677

@ (at), 225

16-bit microprocessor, 278

20-bit address bus, 278-279

2's-complement, 167

386MAX memory management utility, 19

386MAX.SYS device driver, 19

4-bit shift to left, 278

80286 microprocessor, 280

80386-protected mode, 19

80x86 interrupts, 391-398

80x87 Calls Floating-Point Library option, 405

A

a?b:c (if a then b; else c) conditional operator, 84

abort() function, 128

About command, 803

abstract class, 747-750
  pointers, 748
  reference, 748

abstraction type, 765

access specifiers, 445

accessing
  arguments, 130
  array elements, 156-159
  base class members, 726-728
  C++ featuress, 412
  class, 418
    members, 522
    objects, 422-425
  CodeView debugger, 25
  data, 144
  data objects, 439
  file parts, 259
  functions
    in other source files, 212-213
    project-management, 208-209
  local variables, 77-78

member functions, class objects, 553-555

memory, 278-279, 284

menu bar, 810

menus, 21-22

nested classes, 510

objects, 211, 548

pointers, 159

Programmer's WorkBench (PWB)
  menu system, 21-22
  windows, 22-25

source files, 212

stack class member functions, 432

structure members, 166, 439

union members, 168

values in objects, 152

variables, 122, 145

windows, 22-25

acquireblk() member function, 544

action buttons, 25

action-like objects, 637

activating
  action buttons, 25
  p-code (packed code) options, 406
  windows, 807

active
  pages, 346
  windows, 23

Add Watch... command, 366

Add() base class member
  function, 768

<Add/Delete> button, 210

adding
  files
    C source, 38
    member, 544
    source, 208
  pointers, 154
  virtual keywords, 753
  watches, 366

<Additional Global Options...>
  command, 30

<Additional Release Options...>
  command, 31

addmem() function, 544

address bus, 278
  20-bit, 278-279

address-of operator (&), 147, 152, 549

addresses
  functions
    constructor, 615
    destructor, 619
  memory, 279
  offset, 278
  segment, 278, 282
  storing functions, 174
  string, passing, 160

addressing, indirect, 145-147

ADRS(type) macros, 776

aggregate initializer list, 621

aggregate types, 142, 155

All Windows option, 23

ALLOC macro, 432

allocating
  last-in-first-out (lifo) stacks, 443
  memory, 78
    bytes, 178
    dynamically, 178-184
    in arrays, 143
    objects, 178
  memory for variables, 121
  virtual memory block, 304-307

Alt key (move to menu bar)
  keyboard shortcut, 21

Alt key-window *n* (access window)
  keyboard shortcut, 23

Alt-2 (display watch window)
  keyboard shortcut, 367

Alt-7 (select register) keyboard
  shortcut, 368

Alt-9 (Command) keyboard
  shortcut, 364

alternate linkage specification, 576-579

American Standard Code for
  Information Interchange (ASCII), 75

ampersand (&), 52, 114

analyzing stream I/O errors, 682-683

AND (&) operator, 678
Animate command, 363
Annotated C++ Reference Manual, The, 411
append() function, 488, 491
applications
DOS, 12
FCWIN financial calculator, 947-959
QuickWin, 803
Windows, 12, 797-798
compiling, 823
creating, 798
linking, 823
source files, 876-881
Windows-launched DOS, 19
arbitrary-duration class objects, 464-478, 479, 480, 481, 645
_arc() function, 335
arcs, 339
arguments, 43
accessing, 130
function-like macros, 95-96
functions
constructor, 453, 614
destructor, 619
matching, 564-565
print() function, 96,244
in function prototypes, 109
last fixed, 247
lists, 96, 244
memory address, 113
mode, 129, 253
numbers, 109
P_OVERLAY, 129
P_WAIT argument, 129
passing to functions, 111-115
by reference, 112-114
by value, 111-112
pointers, 113, 132
types, 109
variable list, 242
arithmetic
operations, 86, 154
types, 140
array.cpp program, 598-602

arrays
allocating, dynamically, 143, 183-184
declarations, 142-143, 156
dimensions, 142-143
elements, 156-159
identifiers, 156
index, 157
initializier lists, 158
memory, 142
multidimensional, 141, 157
objects, 557-559
size values, 141
"stepping through" with pointers, 151
subscripts, 156, 183-184
types, 140-142, 156
ASCII (American Standard Code for Information Interchange), 75
__asm keyword, 387-391
asm statement, 81
assembly language, 386-391
<Assign> action command, 26
assigning
class objects, 462-464
memory addresses, 179
mnemonic identifiers to integer values, 143
assignment operators [=()], 731-732
assignments, 149
at-end mode, 709
atexit() function, 127
atof() function, 55
atoi() function, 55-57
attribute bytes, 313
auto duration, 121-122
auto specifier, 462
automatic duration, 78
autovariable errors, 357

B

backslash (\), 90, 492
backup disks, 11
bad() function, 683

base classes, 512-514, 725-734
  assignment operators, 731-732
  constructors, 751
  derivation, 741-745
  inheriting, 731
  members, 726-728,733
  multiple, 741-745
  pointers, 730
  updating, 733
  virtual
    declaring, 745
    executing, 751
based pointer, 283
.BAT batch files, 373-374
`BeginPaint()` function, 821
BIN directory, 19
binary
  file-access mode, 259
  operators, 82, 595-598
  streams, 235-236
bit-fields, 153, 167
bitmapped fonts, 347
bits
  4-bit shift, 278
  masks, 679
  modifying values, 279
  states, 696
blocks
  data, 525, 543
  free, 525
  header, 525
  reading, 543
  scopes, 119-120
`blurb()` member function, 513-514
`BOOL` keyword, 847
Boolean
  expression, 680
  logic, 681
  parameter, 27
braces ({}), 66, 81, 426
break statement, 71, 81, 125
breakpoints
  location, 368
  modifying, 369
  setting, 363, 368-369
  status, 368

Browse Options dialog box, 787
browser databases
  building, 787
  creating, 787
bscmake utility, 786
buffered devices, 233
buffers
  C, 665
  file, 257-259
  I/O, 233
  input, 233
  locations, 260
  output, 233
  scroll, 810
  sizes, 260
bugs
  errors, 356
  locating, 357
  see also errors
Build command, 219
Build function, 32
Build Libraries option, 15
Build Operation Complete dialog
  box, 360
Build Options option, 29
building
  browser databases, 787
  generic classes, 769-778
`BuildTextMessage()` function, 906
bundling
  data, 415
  methods, 415
buses
  address, 278-279
  data, 278
buttons
  <Add / Delete>, 210
  <Clear All>, 367
  <Debug> action, 360
  <Save List>, 210
  <View>, 219
bypassing derived class
  destructors, 753
bytes, 179
  allocating, 178
  attribute, 313
  high-order, 86

C

C Compiler Options, 290
C Compiler Options dialog box, 30
C program, 412
  buffers, 665
  comments, 415
  compiling, 39
  creating, 36-49
  global declarations, 40-41
  main() function, 42-43
  operator set, 81-85, 357
  preprocessor directives
    #define, 38-40
    #include, 38-39
  sample, 36-37
  user-defined functions, 43
  writing, 43-45
C Programmer's Toolkit, 465
C Run-Time Customization dialog
  box, 16
C scope, 517-520
C source files
  adding, 38
  locating, 39
  writing, 62
C streams, 667
  inheritance mechanism, 412
C++ Compiler Options, 290
C++ program, 412
  arbitrary objects, 464
  classes, 422-445
  comments, 415
  compiler, 412
  compiling, 798
  data formats, 684-690
  derived types, 413-414
  file input/output (I/O) streams,
    705-714
  files, 712-714
    implementing, 664
    input/output (I/O), 667-674,
    705-714
  objects, 461-500, 523
  operators, 580-581
  scope rules, 423, 517-520

stream error states, 678-683
stream manipulators, 694-705
streambuf class object, 665
streams, 663-678
trivial conversions, 565
C/C++ 7.0 File Groups dialog box, 15
\C700 (Microsoft C/C++ default
  installation), 13-14
Calculate Percent Change dialog
  box, 835
calculating data objects, 178
Call Tree function, 790-792
callback functions, 886, 892-896
calling
  functions, 170, 563-564
    class member, 618
    constructor, 624-632
    destructor, 632-636, 620
  pointers, 170-175
calloc() function, 178-179
calls, function, 41
captions,dialog boxes, 838
carriage-return/line-feed
  characters, 236
case-sensitive compiler, 33
Cast operator functions, 88, 594-595,
  761-763
casting return values in
  functions, 118
central processing unit (CPU), 283,
  368
CGA, *see* Color Graphics Array
chains, 544
char ios::fill() function, 686
character arrays, *see* strings
character (char) data type, 75, 85,
  89, 115,119
characters, 140, 915
  carriage-return/line-feed, 236
  classifying, 105
  constants, 92
  conversion specification, 131
  displaying, 312
  in macros, 91
  inputting, 248-253

lowercase, converting to
  uppercase, 57
non-whitespace, 243
outputting, 248-252
reading, 50,248
sign, 56
single, 50
strings, 162-163
`streambuf`
  extracting from, 675
  inserting, 676-677
  returning to, 675
string of digit, 56
whitespace, 56,62, 243
writing, 53-54, 248-249
check boxes, 25
checking
  conditions, 69
  streams, 272
child processes, 129, 927-931
child windows, 804-806
  creating, 807-810
  scrolls bars, 809-810
`cin` stream, 671
cinsdel (Morse code) pratice
  program, 199
`cinsert()` function, 162-163
circles, 336
circuit traces, 278
`cl` (command-line) compiler,
  822-824
`cl` command-line switches, 34-35
class object identifier, *see* Boolean
  expression
class-key, 426
class-name, 426
classes, 411
  abstract, 747-750
  accessing, 418
  base, 512-514, 725-734
    declaring, 726-734
    multiple, 741-745
    pointer, 730
  codes, 432
  composition, 721-724
  creating, 719, 725-734

data objects, 427, 510-512,
  570-572
declarations, 415, 425-429, 463,
  721-722, 725
derived, 512-514, 719, 725-734,
  747-748, 791
designing, 765-768
dir, 491-497
empty, 427
functions
  constructor, 433-434
  declaring, 523-524
  destructor, 434
  member, 445-455, 510-512
  names, 429
generic, 764-778
inheritance, 719, 725
`istream` (input), 665
keywords, 426
last-in-first-out (LIFO), 430-438
LIST, 772
members, 422-425
  operator, 524
  syntax, 447
names, 429, 508-510, 518-522
nested, 428
objects, 411, 523, 553-555
  arbitrary, 464
  block scope, 462
  converting, 762
  creating, 412, 646-648
  defining, 464-481
  deleting, 481
  derived, 751
  destroying, 420, 647-648
  duration, 462
  global (`static`), 491-500
  initializing, 420, 433-434,
    500-504
  inputting, 690-691
  lifo (last-in-first-out), 442
  local (`auto`), 483-491
  members, 418
  outputting, 690-691
  passing, 552
  size, 455-456, 464

storage, 462-464
unnamed, 429
ostream (output), 665
pointer operator, 524
quad, 758, 933-946
scopes, 425, 519
shape, 515
static storage, 779-782
unnamed, 427
structs, 417-421
types, 413, 760
window, 886-889
classification functions, 105
classifying characters, 105
<Clear All> button, 367
clear() function, 682
clearerr() function, 273
clearing
files, I/O errors, 273-274
screens, 108, 345
stream indicators, 273
_clearscreen() function, 108, 172, 345
_clearscreen() statement, 48
clipping boundary, 333
close box, 22
Close command, 22
close() function, 261
closing
files, 256
windows, 22, 807
code segment (CS) register, 284
codes
blocks, 68
deinitialization, 750-751
initialization, 750-751
reusing, 719-724
CodeView debugger utility, 12
accessing, 25
command mode, 364-366
compatibility, 31, 356
data, viewing, 366-368
executing, 358-360
linking, 25
programs, 360-364
watches, 366

color
background, 315-317, 321, 326
editing, 28
foreground, 315-317, 321, 326-327
modifying, 317
palettes, 324-325
Color Graphics Array (CGA), 325
Enhanced Graphics Adapter, 328-329
text
displaying, 108, 317-318
selecting, 315-317
Color Graphics Array (CGA), 324
color palettes
high-resolution mode, 325-327
low-resolution mode, 325
Colors dialog box, 28
Colors... option, 28-29
.COM executable files
creating, 293-295
limits, 293-295
combining
addresses
offset, 279
segment, 279
libraries, 18
memory models, libraries, 18
Command (CodeView utility) mode, 364-366
command lines, 225
compiler (cl), 33, 46, 822-824, 404
switches, 33-35
COMMAND.COM, 129
commands
About, 803
Add Watch..., 366
<Additional Global Options...>, 30
<Additional Release Options...>, 31
Animate, 363
<Assign> action, 26
Build, 219
Close, 22
Compile File, 221
Copy, 803

<Delete>, 27
Delete Watch..., 367
DOS, 129
DOS COPY, 372
Edit Breakpoints, 369
Execute, 220
Exit, 803
F5=Step (CodeView utility), 362
F8=Trace (CodeView utility), 362
Find, 24, 786
Go, 361
Language Options..., 290
Mark, 803
New, 45
New Project, 208
NMAKE, 222
Open, 24, 208
Open Module, 367
Open Source..., 368
<Optimizations...>, 31
Options, 25
Program Arguments, 221
Rebuild All, 787
Run, 844
<Save...>, 27
selecting, 21-22
Set Breakpoints, 368
<Set Color>, 29
<Set Switch>, 27
Step, 363
<Switch Help>, 27
<Unassign>, 27
zoom, 23
comments whitespace
characters, 62
Common User Access (CUA), 26
Compact memory models, 16-17,
289, 297
comparing
files, 221
logical comparisons
with pointer, 284
strings, 53, 117
values, 65
comparisons
converting from void
pointers, 149

converting to void
pointers, 149
Compile File command, 220-221
compilers
case-sensitive, 33
command-line (cl), 822-824
resource compiler (RC), 824, 839
compiling
class codes, 432
header files, 35
Programmer's WorkBench
(PWB), 32, 219-220
programs, 32-48
C, 39
C++, 798
complex, 220-221
DOS-like C, 798
order.c, 800-802
overlay, 303
with inline assembly
statements, 386
project files, 219
quick compiler, 35
resources, 839
source files, 63
Windows applications, 822-824
complex programs
compiling, 220-221
executing, 220-221
expressions, 79
composition, 719, 721-724
compound statements, 81
concatenating strings, 160-161
concealing internal data, 416
conditional
compilation directives, 216-218
expressions
converting from void
pointers, 149
converting to void
pointers, 149
if statement, 64-65
inclusion directives, 216-218
switch statement, 64-65
conditions
checking, 69
evaluating, 65-66

configuring
  Microsoft C/C++, 25-32
  Programmer's WorkBench
  (PWB), 26
  Windows Application
  Environment, 841-842
constants
  character, 92
  ios class, 688
  manifest, 879
  symbolic, 315
  values, 90
constructor functions, 420, 433-434,
  451, 611, 616, 723, 734
  arguments, 453
  calling, 624-632
  class objects, 501-503
  converting types, 613, 758-760
  copying, 454, 642-643
  declaring, 434, 452, 612-618
  overloading, 636, 640-642
  virtual, 752-753
  writing default, 637-639
constructor initializers, 620-624, 723
  default, 723
  derived class, 751
  scopes, 522
continue statement, 81, 125
controlling
  ambiguities with scope
    resolution operator, 512-516
  buffers, 257-259
  data formats, 684-690
  drawing functions, 341-345
  header files, 218
  memory addresses, 442
  program complexity, 446
  screens, 346
  type conversions, 85-89
  windows
    location, 808-809
    size, 808-809
controls, 835
conversions
  base, 6684
  by constructor, 613

C++ trivial, 565
functions, 105, 729
specification characters, 131
specifiers, 55,243-244
type, user-defined, 758-764
converting
  class objects, 762
  class types, 760
  data, 105
  integer types, 86
  pointers
    to base class, 730
    to derived class, 730-731
  programs to machine-language
    instructions, 62-63
  quad numbers to strings, 764
  source files, 62
coordinates, 333-334
  graphics, 331
  screen, 318
  text-mode, 331
Copy command, 803
copy constructor, 454, 503, 617-618,
  642-643
copying
  members
    base classes, 733
    derived classes, 733
  string contents, 160-161
correcting stream I/O errors,
  682-683
counting profiling mode, 381
cout stream, 669
coverage profiling mode, 381
cprintf() function, 245
CPU, see central processing unit
create() function, 488
CreateDC() Windows function, 901
CreateWindow() function, 812-819,
  888-889
creating
  browser databases, 787
  C program, 36-49
  child windows, 807-810

classes, 719, 725-734
    base, 731-732
    derived, 731-732, 751
    generic, 211, 769-777
    last-in-first-out (LIFO), 430-438
    objects, 646
dialog boxes, 829, 837-839
dialog procedures, 846
disk backups, 11
doubly-linked list, 488, 491
executable programs, 61-72
files
    .COM executable, 293-295
    executable, 29
    FCWIN project, 881-882
    header, 214-215, 879-881
    module definition, 878-879
    programs, 62-63, 846
    project, 208-210, 881-883
    source, 61, 876
    temporary, 256
functions, 108-115
    declarations, 109
    definitions, 110
    prototypes, 109
icons, 839
macros
    function-like, 89-97
    object-like, 89-97
menus, 827-829
objects, 211
overlay programs, 297-304
Programmer's WorkBench
    (PWB), 208-210
resources, 825
structures, 164-167
Windows applications, 798
CS (code segment) register, 284, 389
cscanf() function, 243
Ctrl-F4 (close message window)
  keyboard shortcut, 220
Ctrl-V (insert/overstrike type modes
  toggle) keyboard shortcut, 26
CUA, *see* Common User Access
cube() function, 111

current directory, 844
Current Keys list box, 27
cursor, 322
Custom Installation option, 15-16
customizing
    keystrokes, 25
    Microsoft C/C++ 7.0, 14
CW (Morse code) practice program
    source code, 189-198

D

data
    accessing, 144
    blocks, 525, 543
    bundling, 415
    bus, 278
    converting, 105
    cout stream, 669
    errors, 356
    extracting, 668
    formatting, 684-690
    inputting, 49-53, 231-237, 243
    internal, concealing, 416
    locating, 282
    loss, preventing, 255
    members, 464
    moving, 105
    object-like macros, 89
    objects, 411
        accessing, 439
        complex, 140
        declaring, 75
        functions, 118-119
        groups, 156
        printing, multibyte, 155
    outputting, 53-55, 231-233, 237,
      244
    partitioned (pds), 545
    reading, 242
    selecting, 147-148
    size, calculating, 178
    sorting, 268
    storing, 232-233, 280-281
        in structures, 164-165

streams, 234-235, 253, 664
types, 72-79, 103
  character (char), 85, 89,115, 119
  character data, 74-75
  declaring, 72
  defining in functions, 115-118
  double, 115
  floating-point numbers, 73-74, 89, 119
  integer value (int), 72-73, 85, 89, 119 85,115
  modifying, 140
  print() function specifiers, 922-923
  scanf() function specifiers, 925
  segment (DS) register, 284, 692
  using constructor to convert, 613
  updating, 733
  values, 692
  viewing CodeView utility, 366-368
  writing to file, 261
Data menu, 366-367
databases, 787
date, 221
dbllist() constructor function, 489
~dbllist() destructor function, 489
deactivating p-code (packed code) options, 406
deallocating memory, 177, 180-183
<Debug> action button, 360
debugging
  code, 31
  CodeView utility programs, 360-363
dec manipulator, 696
declaration lists parameter, 104
declarations
  arrays, 142-143, 156
  class, 415-417, 422-445, 463, 721-722, 726-734, 745, 761
  data objects, 75
  floating-point numbers, 74
  fstream objects, 706-708

functions, 39-41
  constructor, 434, 613-618
  destructor, 612, 618-620
  friend, 568
  in classes, 523-524
  in structures, 523-524
  member, 449-450, 565-567
  nonmember, 573-574
  operator, 587-588
  pointers, 152, 170-171, 557-559
global variable, 42
header files, 214-215
integer data types, 72
interrupt handler functions, 397-398
multiple variables, 74
objects, 211, 557-559
source files, 214
statement, 81
structure type, 164-166
variable, 39
  floating-point, 73-74
  integer, 72
  parameter declaration class, 748
virtual functions, 738-739
declare() macro, 770-771
default constructor function, 434, 637-639, 723
Default Installation option, 16
#define preprocessor directive, 38-40, 89
definexy() function, 703
defining
  arbitrary-duration class objects, 464-481
  C++ objects, 461-500
  class objects
    global (static), 491-500
    local (auto), 482-491
  code blocks, 68
  constant values, 90
  data types in functions, 115-118
  functions, 42
    at beginning of program, 109
    disadvantages, 109-110

member, 446-447, 510-512
virtual, 746
macros
function-like, 93-97
in make files, 227
object-like, 89-93
new types, 414
objects, 211, 429
parameterized manipulators, 700
static data members, 464
strings for macros, 92
definition points, locating, 788
definitions
function, 41-42
header files, 215
macro, 39
DefWindowProc() function, 822
DefWinProc() Windows function, 892
deinitialization code, 750-751
<Delete> command, 27
Delete Watch dialog box, 367
Delete Watch... command, 367
Delete() base class member
function, 768
delete() operator, 643-646
creating and destroying class
objects, 646
deleting class objects with,
647-648
overloading, 648-649
deleting
class objects, 481
files
contents, 69
from disk drive, 256
member, 545
watches, 366
delmem() function, 545
dependent relationship statement,
224-225
dereferencing pointers, 149, 152
derived class, 512-514, 719, 791
assignment operators, 726-734
characteristics, 515
classes, 725-734, 751
constructor, executing, 751

destructor, bypassing, 753
hierarchy, 740-741
members, 733
multiple, 741-745
pointers, 730-731
derived types, 140-142, 413-414
deriving classes, 747-748
describing
objects, 140-141
variables, 140
designing
Enhanced Graphics Adapter
(EGA), 330
fcwin.c program, 845-847
header files, 879
destroying class objects, 420, 646
destructor functions, 420, 434, 451,
454, 611, 734, 754
calling, 632-636
declaring, 612, 618-620
virtual, 751-753
detecting
C++ stream error states, 679-681
file I/O errors, 272-273
determining
errors, 273
files
length, 271
location, 269-270
linkage in variables, 122-123
pointer types, 142
structure objects, 166
device context handle, 900-901
device drivers, 19
device-independent programs, 49
DeviceMode() function, 899-902
devices
buffered, 233
interactive, 232
permanent, 232
printer, 846
diagnostic functions, 105
dialog boxes, 24
Browse Options, 787
Build Operation Complete, 360
C Compiler Options, 30

C Run-Time Customization, 16
C/C++ 7.0 File Groups, 15
Calculate Percent Change, 835
captions, 838
Colors, 28
creating, 829, 835-838
Delete Watch, 367
Display Tree, 790
editing, 829, 837-839
Editor Settings, 27
File Groups, 15
Goto Definition, 788
Goto Reference, 788
Key Assignments, 26
Link Options, 46
moving, 838
New Project, 209
Save, 45
Set Breakpoint, 369
Dialog Editor, 838
dialog procedures, 846
DialogBox() Windows function, 894
dialogs, callback functions for,
 892-896
dimensions, arrays, 142-143
dir class, 491-497
direct files
 input/output (I/O), 259-268
 reading, 261-268
 writing, 261-268
directives
 conditional compilation, 216-218
 #elif, 217
 #else, 217
 #endif, 217
 !if, 227
 #if, 217
 make file, embedding, 227
directories
 BIN, 19
 \C700 (Microsoft C/C++ default
  installation), 13-14
 current, 844
 library, 544
 root, 254
 specifiers, 257

Windows, 843-845
Windows 3.1, 843-844
directory-control functions, 105
disks
 backups, 11
 drives, 256
 hard, 232, 395
 heads, 395
 Microsoft Source Profiler, 12
 source files, 208
 space requirements, 12
dispatching, 820
DispatchMessage() function, 814,
 820, 891
Display Tree dialog box, 790
displaying
 active windows, 23
 Boolean parameter, 27
 characters, 312
 class name, 510
 colors, 108
 files input/output (I/O) errors,
  273-274
 resolutions, 323
 text in color, 317-318
 variables, 508
 viewing region, 333
dividing functions, 188-207
DLLs (dynamic-link libraries), 846,
 907
do statement, 81
do-while loop, 69
DoPctChg() dialog function, 895-896
DOS
 applications
  box, 19
  SETUP program, 12-14
  Windows-launched, 19
 commands, 129
  COPY, 372
 DISKCOPY disk backups, 11
 environmental variables, 26
 executing, 129
 interrupts, 393
 Microsoft C/C++ 7.0 compiler, 19
 programs, 798

`_dos_findfirst()` function, 492
`_dos_findnext()` function, 492
`_dos_getvect()` function, 398
`_dos...()` functions, 398
double data types, 115
doubly-linked list, 488, 491, 525
dragging windows, 815
`draw()` member function, 516
`draw()` virtual function, 737
drawing
    arcs, 339
    circles, 336
    ellipses, 336
    functions, 334-339
    lines, 338-343
    objects, 339-340
        filled, 339-343
    pies, 338
    polygons, 339
drivers, loading, 901-902
DS (data segment) register, 284, 389
duration
    auto, 121-122
    static, 121-122
    variables, 121-122
dynamic allocation of memory,
    175-184
dynamic link libraries (DLLs), 846,
    906-912
dynamic memory, 176-184
dynamic overlay swapping, 296

E

Edit Breakpoints command, 369
Edit function, 803
Edit menu, 803
editing
    colors, 28
    dialog boxes, 829, 837-839
    DOS environment variables, 26
    icons, 839
    menus, 827-829
    programs, 32-35
    values, 367

Editor Settings dialog box, 27
Editor Settings option, 27
EGA, *see* Enhanced Graphics
    Adapter
eight-bit data bus, 278
elements, 482-483
`#elif` directive, 217
`_ellipse()` function, 327, 335, 339
ellipsis (...), 24, 336
Ellis, Margaret A., 411
`#else` directive, 217
`else` statement, 81
embedding, 228-229
Emulation Calls Floating-Point
    Library option, 405
encapsulation, 415-417, 721
end-of-file indicator (EOF), 261, 273
`EndDialog()` Windows function, 896
`#endif` directive, 217
`EndPaint()` function, 821
`ends` manipulator, 696
Enhanced Graphics Adapter (EGA),
    324, 328-330
enumeration integer type, 143
enumerations, 140
`eof()` function, 683
errors, 219
    autovariable, 357
    C++ streams, 678-683
    determining, 273
    indicators, 273
    locating, 357
    loop counter, 358
    messages, 896-897
    printing to standard error
        device, 273
    programming, 357-358
    states, 679-681
ES register, 389
escape characters, 923
escape sequences, 905-906
`Escape()` Windows function, 902
evaluating conditions, 65-66
event-driven, 797
exclusive-OR-and-assign compound
    operator (^=), 150

.EXE executable files, 293
_exec...() function, 128, 927-929
exec...() function, 128, 928
executable programs, 61-72
Execute command, 220
executing
   child processes, 927-931
   CodeView utility, 358-360
   constructors, 503
     copy, 503
     derived class, 751
     nonvirtual, 751
   DOS commands, 129
   functions
     constructor, 6116
     destructor, 619-620
   Microsoft C/C++ 7.0 compiler, 19
   multiple statements, 66
   preprocessing directives, 63
   programs, 43
     complex, 220-221
     from top of loop, 125-126
     oversized, 295-296
     Programmer's WorkBench
      (PWB), 219-220
     with CodeView utility, 360-363
   SETUP program, 12-13
   virtual base class constructors,
    751
exercising keyboard class, 572-573
EXETYPE statement, 908
Exit command, 803
exit() function, 126-127
exiting
   loops, 71
   Programmer's WorkBench
    (PWB), 220
   statements, 71
   windows, 808
expanding macros, 92
explicit rules dependent
  relationship, 224-225
explict type conversion, 88
EXPORTS statement, 879
expressions, 79-85
   complex, 79

operands, 79
operators, 79
punctuators, 79
simple, 79
size-constant, 156
values, 80
extern keyword, 210-212, 463
external
   functions, 212-213
   linkage, 122
   references, 210-213
extracting
   characters from streambuf, 675
   data, 668
extractmem() function, 545

F

F5=Go keystroke command, 361
F5=Step (CodeView utility)
  command, 362
F6 (next menu) keyboard shortcut,
  23
F8=Trace (CodeView utility)
  command, 362
fail() function, 683
FAR keyword, 847
far pointer, 284-287
Fast Alternate Math/FPa Floating-
  Point Library option, 405
_fclose() function, 807
fclose() function, 235, 255
_fcloseall() function, 807
fcloseall() function, 256
FCWIN financial calculator
  application, 947-959
   designing, 845-847
   header file, 879
   menu, 947
   module-definition file, 878
   project files, 881-882
   resources and names, 826
FCWIN_COMPUTE macro, 881
feof() function, 70, 272
ferror() function, 273

`fflush()` function, 259
`fgetc()` function, 248
`fgetchar()` function, 248-250
`fgetpos()` function, 269
`fgets()` function, 248, 251
field width, 684
File Groups dialog box, 15
File menu, 803
file records, 259
file scope, 119, 519
file-access mode, 259
file-positioning functions, 268-272
`filebuf` stream class, 705
files
  accessing, 259
  .BAT batch, 373-374
  beginning, 260
  buffers, 257-259
  C source, 38, 62
  closing, 256
  .COM executable, 293-295
  comparing, 221
  creating, 256
  data
    storing, 232
    writing to, 261
  deleting, 69, 256
  direct
    reading, 261-268
    writing, 261-268
  end of, 272
  .EXE executable, 293
  executable
    creating, 29
    p-code, 29
  extensions, 907
  FCWIN project, 881-882
  `fstream`
    reading, 710-712
    writing, 710-712
  header
    creating, 214-215, 879-881
    designing, 879
    keynew.hpp, 568-569
    user-supplied, 215-216

input/output (I/O)
  errors, 273-274
  functions, 259-268
  length, 271
  library, 543
  listing, 224-225
  locating, 39, 260, 269-270
  member, 544-545
  module definitions (.DEF),
    299-303, 816, 878-879
  opening, 253-255
  origin, 260
  positioning, 270-272, 712-714
  program, 846
  project, 208-210, 219, 881-883
  README, 17
  rebuilding, 221
  recompiling, 221
  renaming, 257
  resource, 823-825
  source, 31-32, 62, 188-208
    compiling, 63
    creating, 61, 876-881
files position indicator, 270
fill character, 685
`fill()` function, 685
Find command, 24, 786
fixed argument, 247
fixed disk heads, parking, 395
flags register, 283
Floating-Point Library Options
  Inline Emulation, 405
floating-point numbers
  data type, 73-74, 89, 119
  declaring, 74
  precision, 685
  variable, 88
`_floodfill()` function, 339
flush manipulator, 696
fonts
  active, 351
  bitmapped, 347
  Microsoft Windows, 351
  modifying, 348-349
  storing, 351
  stroked, 347

fopen() function, 70, 253-255
for statement, 81, 114
for() loop, 40, 70-71, 125
format strings, 52, 131
    print() function, 244, 919
    scanf() function, 242
format-control member function, 686-687
format-conversion functions, 55-58
formatting
    data, 55
    flags, 687-688
forming pointer to member function, 615-616
fprintf() function, 245, 806
fputc() function, 248, 250
fputchar() function, 248
fputs() function, 248, 251
fragmenting heaps, 180
fread() function, 261-263, 543
free block, 525
free chain, 525
free store, 438, 643-648
free() function, 180-181
freeing virtual memory space, 308
FreeLibarary() Windows function, 906
freopen() function, 255
friend functions, 455-457, 522, 734, 778-779
    declaring, 568
    keynew, 570-572
    overloading, 568-573
    overloading operators with, 591-594
friend keyword, 568
fscanf() function, 243, 806-807
fseek() function, 271-272, 543
fsetpos() function, 270
fstream
    files
        reading, 710-712
        writing, 710-712
    objects, declaring, 706-708

open-mode enumerator names and uses, 708-709
    stream class, 705
ftell() function, 269-270, 526
function arguments
    matching, 564-565
    scope, 522
function call operators, 603-607
function calls, 41-42, 103, 523
function declarations, 39-40, 109-110
function mangling, 575-579
function prototypes
    contents
        arguments, 109
        function name, 109
    converting from void, pointers, 149
    converting to void, pointers, 149
    creating, 109
    scopes, 120
    see also function declarations
function scope, 119-519
function types, 140
function-like macros
    arguments, 95-96
    creating, 89-97
    defining, 93-97
    replacement-lists, 95
functions, 42, 101
    abort(), 128
    accessing, 212-213
    acquireblk(), 544
    Add() base class member, 768
    addmem(), 544
    addresses, storing, 174
    append(), 488, 491
    _arc(), 335
    arguments, 43
        passing, 111-115
        passing by reference, 112-114
        passing by value, 111-112
    atexit(), 127
    atof(), 55
    atoi(), 55-57
    bad(), 683
    BeginPaint(), 821

blurb(), 513-514
braces ({}), 104
Build, 32
BuildTextMessage(), 906
Call Tree, 790-792
callback, 886
calling, 170-175, 272, 563-564
calloc(), 178-179
cast operator, 594-595, 761-763
char ios::fill(), 686
character I/O, 248-253
cinsert(), 162-163
classification, 105
clear(), 682
clearerr(), 273
_clearscreen(), 108, 172, 345
close, 261
compiling without return
   statements, 104
completion status, indicating,
   104
constructor, 420, 433-434, 451,
   501-503, 611, 734
      arguments, 453
      calling, 624-632
      converting type, 758-760
      declaring, 612-618
      default, 452
      overloaded, 640-642
      overloading, 636
conversion, 105, 729
cprintf(), 245
create(), 488
CreateWindow(), 812-814, 819
creating, 108-115
cscanf(), 243
cube(), 111
data objects, 118-119
data types, defining, 115-118
dbllist() constructor, 489
~dbllist() destructor, 489
declaring
      with void types, 105
      within classes, 523-524
      within structures, 523-524
default constructor, 637-639

definexy(), 703
defining, 42
      at beginning of program, 109
      disadvantages, 109-110
DefWindowProc(), 822
Delete() base class member, 768
delmem(), 545
destructor, 420, 434, 451, 454,
   611, 734, 754
      calling, 632-636
      declaring, 612-620
DeviceMode(), 899-902
diagnostic, 105
direct file I/O, 259-268
directory-control, 105
DispatchMessage(), 814, 820
dividing, 188-207
DoPctChg(), 895-896
_dos_findfirst(), 492
_dos_findnext(), 492
_dos_getvect(), 398
_dos...(), 398
draw() member, 516
draw() virtual, 737
drawing, 334-339
Edit, 803
_ellipse(), 327, 335, 339
EndPaint(), 821
eof(), 683
_exec...(), 927-929
exec...(), 128
exit(), 126-127
external, 212-213
extractmem(), 545
fail(), 683
_fclose(), 807
fclose(), 235, 255
_fcloseall(), 807
fcloseall(), 256
feof(), 70, 272
ferror(), 273
fflush(), 259
fgetc(), 248
fgetchar(), 248-250
fgetpos(), 269
fgets(), 248, 251

file-positioning, 268-272
fill(), 685
_floodfill(), 339
fopen(), 70, 253-255
format-control member, 686-687
format-conversion, 55-58
fprintf(), 245, 806
fputc(), 248-250
fputchar(), 248
fputs(), 248, 251
fread(), 261-263, 543
free(), 180-181
freopen(), 255
friend, 455-457, 522, 734, 778-779
   declaring, 568
   keynew, 570-572
   overloading, 568-573
   overloading operators with,
     591-594
fscanf(), 243, 806-807
fseek(), 271-272, 543
fsetpos(), 270
ftell(), 269-270, 526
function definition, 42
_fwopen(), 806-807
fwrite(), 261-264
get(), 672-674, 710
get...(), 49-51
_getbkcolor(), 321
getbutton(), 480
getc(), 273
getc() get, 50
getche(), 75
getche() get, 50
GetClientRect(), 821
getcurrent() member, 493
_getcurrentposition( ), 341
_getfillmask(), 341
_getfontinfo(), 351-352
_getgtextextent(), 352
_getgtextvector(), 352
getline(), 673
getline() member, 674
_getlinestyle(), 341
GetMessage(), 813-814, 820
getnext() member, 493

getnextblk(), 544
getprev() member, 493
getprevblk(), 544
gets() get, 50
GetSystemDirectory() Windows,
  844
_gettextcolor(), 321
GetTextExtent(), 821
GetTextMetrics(), 821
_gettextposition(), 322
_gettextwindow(), 322
_getvideoconfig(), 321-323
GetWindowsDirectory() Windows,
  844
_getwritemode(), 341
global, displaying, 508
gohead() member, 489-491
gonext() member, 489-493
good(), 683
goprev() member, 489, 493
gotail(), 489-491
graphics, 105
graphics-mode text-output,
  348-349
hello(), 736-737
I/O, 105, 237-241
ignore(), 676
including in overlay units, 296
increment(), 391
inheriting, 734
initok(), 468
inlines, 785-786
input, 49-53
input stream operator>>(), 692
insert() member, 488, 491
int bad() stream state
  member, 682
int eof() stream state
  member, 682
int fail() stream state
  member, 682
int good() stream state, 682
int ios::precision(), 686
int ios::width(), 686
int rdstate() stream state
  member, 682

int(), 729
int86(), 393-394
int86x(), 393
intdos(), 393-396
intdosx(), 393
interface, 106
inttoquad(int), 760
ios::width() member, 695
_kbhit(), 247
keyboard insert, cinsdel (Morse code) practice program, 199
keynew, class member, 570-572
kill() member, 488-491
LibMain(), 911
library, 49-58, 101-108
libseek(), 544
libtell(), 544
lifo member, 435
_lineto(), 335
list, displaying, 367
listdir(), 544
listmem(), 545
locating, 787
long ios::flags(), 688
long ios::setf(), 688
long ios::setf(long flags), 688
long ios::unsetf(long flags), 688
long_name(), 117
loop_count(), 112-114
LOWORD(), 821
lpfn (long pointer to function) prefix, 893
main(), 42-43, 101-105, 362
malloc(), 179
manipulation, 106
math, 106
mem, 106
member, 414, 778
    overloading, 561-567
    writing, 445-455
members, 449-450
menu(), 363
miscellaneous, 106
_moveto(), 341
names, 103, 110

navigate() member, 497
nonmember, overloading, 573-574
nonstatic member, 762
_OAMANIP ong operator<<(), 704
_OAPP long operator()(), 704
open(), 706-708
operator, 585, 694
    specifying return type for, 589-591
operator!(), 681
operator+(), 782-784
operator=(), 732, 759
output, 53-55
output stream operator<<(), 692
_outtext(), 317, 320
overlaying, 298
overloaded operator
    characteristics, 584
    declaring, 587-588
    specifying arguments, 588-589
overloading, 429
Pause, 803
peek(), 676
peekA(), 455
perror(), 273
_pie(), 335, 339
pointers, returning, 116
_polygon(), 335, 339
pop() member, 432
PopupMsg(), 879, 906-912
positionxy(), 703
pow(), 88
print(), 244-247, 919-923
printf(), 54-55, 245, 684
printf() output, 237
PrntAmort(), 898-901
process-control, 106
product(), 42
project-management, accessing, 208-209
purgeblk(), 543
purgedir(), 543
push() member, 432
put(), 710
put...(), 53-54

put_msg(), 42
putback(), 675-676
putc() put, 53
putchar(), 378
puts() put, 53
qsort(), 267
rdstate(), 682
_read(), 807
read(), 673, 710
readn(), 544
realloc(), 180
_rectangle(), 335, 339
RegisterClass(), 819
_registerfonts(), 349
registering, 128
releaseblk() member, 544
_remappalette(), 328-329
remove(), 256-257
rename(), 257
report(), 739
report-only flags(), 689
reset() member, 497
Resume, 803
return statements, 104
return types, 103
    specifying, 117
    void, 111
return values, casting, 118
rewind(), 270
saytree(), 750
scanf(), 49-53, 241-244, 684, 924
scanf() input, 237
seekg(), 712
seekp(), 712
SEGMENTS, 299
separating into files, 212-213
_setbkcolor(), 316, 326
setbuf(), 257-258
_setcolor(), 317
_setfillmask(), 341
setfillmask(), 343-345
_setfont(), 351
_setfont() function, 349-350
_setlinestyle( ), 341-343
_settextcolor(), 108, 315-316
_settextposition(), 703

_settextwindow(), 318-320
setvbuf(), 258
_setvideomode(), 312-315
_setvieworg(), 331-332
_setviewport( ), 332-333
_setvisualpage(), 346
_setwritemode(), 341
showclass(), 421
ShowWindow(), 820
size() member, 514
sopen(), 706
_spawn...(), 929-930
spawn...(), 128-130
sprintf(), 245
sscanf(), 243
Standard, 105, 106
strcat(), 160-162
strcmp() (string-comparison), 53
strcpy(), 160
stream class member, 672
strerror(), 273
strlen(), 160-162, 775
strtok(), 901
sum(), 40, 134
sum_it(), 119
system(), 128-129
tellg(), 712
tellp(), 712
text-window, 106
TextOut(), 821
time and date, 106
tmpnam(), 256
toupper(), 57-58, 115
TranslateMessage(), 820
TranslateMessage() Windows, 820
~tree() destructor, 753
unload(), 545
unsetf(), 688
UpdateWindow(), 820
user-defined, 43, 102, 108-115
user-defined cast operator,
    761-763
va_...(), 131-135
va_arg(), 132 -135
va_end(), 132

va_start(), 132
values, 43, 111
    modifying, 112-113
    passing, 48
    returning, 104, 115-119
    storing, 104
    unreturned, 117-118
Variable argument list, 106
variables
    declaring, 104
    verifying, 41
vfprintf(), 245
_vheapinit(), 304-306
_vheapterm(), 308
virtual, 515, 584, 735-740
    constructor, 751-753
    defining, 746
    destructor, 751-753
    pure, 748-750
_vload(), 305
_vlock(), 305-308
_vmalloc(), 304
void clear(int f=0), 682
void types, 117-118
vprintf(), 245-247
vsprintf(), 245
_wabout(), 808
_wclose(), 807
_wgetfocus(), 807
_wgetscreenbuf(), 810
_wgetsize(), 808
width(), 685
Windows
    CreateDC(), 901
    CreateWindow(), 888-889
    DefWinProc(), 892
    DialogBox(), 894
    DispatchMessage(), 891
    EndDialog(), 896
    Escape(), 902
    FreeLibarary(), 906
    GetDlgItemText(), 896
    GetMessage(), 890
    GetProcAddress(), 902
    GetProfileString(), 899-902
    GetTextMetrics(), 903-904
    InvalidateRect(), 894
    LoadLibrary(), 902
    MakeProcInstance(), 893-894
    MessageBox(), 896-897, 912
    RegisterClass(), 888
    SetDlgItemText(), 896
    ShowWindow(), 889
    TextOut(), 906
    TranslateMessage(), 890-891
    UpdateWindow(), 889
    WinMain(), 886
    WndProc(), 891-892
WinMain(), 812-813, 819, 846
with default arguments, handling,
    573-574
with unused formal arguments,
    handling, 573-574
_wmenuclick(), 810
WndProc(), 813-820, 846
_wopen(), 807
_write(), 807
write(), 677, 710
writeblk(), 543
writen(), 544
_wsetexit(), 808
_wsetfocus(), 807
_wsetscreenbuf(), 810
_wsetsize(), 808
_wyield(), 804
functions declarations, prototypes,
    40
_fwopen() function, 806-807
fwrite() function, 261-264

G

generic classes, 764-778
    building, 769-778
    creating, 769-777
get() function, 672-674, 710
get...() functions, 49-51
_getbkcolor() function, 321
getbutton() function, 480
getc() function, 273
getc() get function, 50
getche() function, 75

getche() get function, 50
GetClientRect() function, 821
getcurrent() member function, 493
_getcurrentposition() function, 341
GetDlgItemText() Windows
function, 896
_getfillmask() function, 341
_getfontinfo() function, 351-352
_getgtextextent() function, 352
_getgtextvector() function, 352
getline() function, 673-674
_getlinestyle() function, 341
GetMessage() function, 813-814, 820
GetMessage() Windows function, 890
getnext() member function, 493
getnextblk() function, 544
getprev() member function, 493
getprevblk() function, 544
GetProcAddress() Windows function,
902
GetProfileString() Windows
function, 899-902
gets() get function, 50
GetSystemDirectory() Windows
function, 844
_gettextcolor() function, 321
GetTextExtent() function, 821
GetTextMetrics() function, 821
GetTextMetrics() Windows function,
903-904
_gettextposition() function, 322
_gettextwindow() function, 322
_getvideoconfig() function, 321-323
GetWindowsDirectory() Windows
function, 844
_getwritemode() function, 341
global class declaration, 463
global new and delete operators,
648-657
global (static) class objects,
491-500
global variables, 76
declarations, 40-42
disadvantages, 76
displaying, 508
static duration, 76

Go command, 361
gohead() member function, 489-491
gonext() member function, 489-493
good() function, 683
goprev() member function, 489, 493
gotail() function, 489-491
Goto Reference dialog box, 788
goto statement, 81, 124-125
goxy() parameterized manipulator,
703
graphical user interface (GUI), 845
graphics
color, 326
coordinates, 331
functions, 105
mode, 311, 323-330, 336
pages, 346
screens
clearing, 345
controlling, 346
text, 346-351
Graphics Libraries, installing, 15, 46
graphics-mode text-output
functions, 348-349
GUI, see graphical user interface

H

handles, 900-901
handling
functions
with default arguments,
573-574
with unused formal
arguments, 573-574
hard copy, spooling to Windows
Print Manager, 898-906
hard disks, see disks
hard drive, 12
header block, 525
header files, 107, 214
compiling, 35
conditional compilation
directives, 216
controlling, 218
creating, 214-215

declarations, 214-216
designing, 879
keynew.hpp, 568-569
macro definitions, 215
programs, 879-881
user-supplied, 215-216
headers, precompiled, 35
heaps
fragmenting, 180
memory, 177
hello() function, 736-737
Help menu, 803, 896-897
Hercules Monochrome, 324
hex manipulator, 696
hiding
class names, 508-509, 518
names, 728
high-order byte, values, 86
high-resolution mode, 325
Color Graphics Array (CGA)
palettes, 327
horizontal (x-axis) screen
coordinate, 318
Huge memory models, 18, 289, 297
huge pointer, 285

I

I/O buffers, 233
errors
data, 671
detecting, 272-273
displaying, 273-274
files, 272-273
functions, 105, 237-241
direct file, 259-268
programs, 663-678
icons
creating, 839
editing, 839
identifiers, 90-93, 156
Boolean expression, 680
mnemonic, assigning to integer
values, 143
!if directive, 227
#if directive, 217

if statement, 64-65, 81
if-else statements
nested, 66
writing, 67
ifstream stream class, 705
ignore() function, 676
implement() macros, 771, 777
implementing C++ streams, 664
implicit type conversion, 86-87
IMPORTS statement, 879, 907
improving ptest1, 378
in-use chain, 526
#include macro, 214
#include preprocessor directive,
38-39,107, 216
including header files, 215-216
incomplete types, 140-141
increment (postfix) operator (++),
71, 115, 151
increment() function, 391
incremental linking, 31
incrementing
pointer values, 115
variables, 71
indicating
data types, 103
end of files, 272
indirect addressing, 145-147
indirection operator (*), 114, 147,
152
inference rules, 224-226
inheritance
base class, 731
characters, 515
class, 719, 725
functions, 734
constructor, 616
destructor, 619
mechanism, 412
single, 725
initialization code, 750-751
initializer
constructor, 620-623, 723
lists, 157-158, 503-504
initializing
action-like objects, 637

class objects, 420, 433-434, 500, 504
  with constructor function, 501-503
function pointers, 171
graphics mode, 336
Microsoft Overlay Virtual Environment (MOVE), 297
object-like objects, 637
strings, 160-161
value-like objects, 637
virtual memory management system, 304
initok() function, 468
Inline 80x87 Floating-Point Library option, 405
inline assembly statements
  inserting, 387-391
  language, 386-391
  memory models, 387
  pointer sizes, 387
  programs, 386
Inline Emulation Floating-Point Library option, 405
inline functions, 785-786
inline member functions, 447-448
inputting
  characters, 248-252
  class objects, 690-691
  data, 49-50, 53, 231-233, 237, 243, 671
    sequence, 51-52
  data values, 692
  functions, 49-52
  stream extractor, 668
  stream operator>>() function, 692
  values, 807
Ins key (insert/overstrike type modes toggle) keyboard shortcut, 26
insert typing mode, 26
insert() member function, 488, 491
inserting
  characters into streambuf, 676-677
  function-like macros, 95

inline assembly statements into programs, 387-391
  strings, 162-163
installing
  386MAX.SYS device driver, 19
  Graphics Libraries, 15
  libraries, 15-17
  memory models, 16-19
  Microsoft C/C++ 7.0, 14
  Microsoft
    Source Profiler, 12-13
    Windows, 12
  Windows Targets, 16
instances, 887
instantiation, repetitive, 779-782
instruction pointer (IP) register, 397
int bad() stream state member function, 682
int eof() stream state member function, 682
int fail() stream state member function, 682
int good() stream state function, 682
int ios::precision() function, 686
int ios::width() function, 686
int rdstate() stream state member function, 682
int() function, 729
int86() function, 393-394
int86x() function, 393
intdos() function, 393-396
intdosx() function, 393
integer arguments, 41
integer (int) data type, 72, 89, 115, 119
  converting, 86
  enumeration, 143
  ranges, 73
  sizes, 73
integer values, 41
  menomic identifiers, 143
  pointers, 154
  _setvideomode() function, 315
integer variables, 72, 88
integral types, 140

Intel 80x86 microprocessors, 17
interactive devices, 232
Interface functions, 106
internal linkage, 122
interrupt handler functions, 396-403
interrupt service routine (ISR), 391
interrupt vector, 391
interrupts
    80x86, 393
    DOS, 393
    timer tick, 398-403
inttoquad (int) function, 760
InvalidateRect() Windows function, 894
ios class constants, 688
ios::width() member function, 695
IP (instruction pointer) register, 397
ISR, *see* interrupt service routine
istream (input) class, 665
iteration statement, 81

J-K

jump statement, 81

_kbhit() function, 247
Key Assignments dialog box, 26
Key Assignments... option, 26-27
keyboard class, testing and
  exercising, 572-573
keyboard shortcuts
  Alt key (move to menu bar), 21
  Alt key-window *n* (access
    window), 23
  Alt-2 (display watch window),
    367
  Alt-7 (select register), 368
  Alt-9 (Command), 364
  Ctrl-F4 (close message window),
    220
  Ctrl-V (insert/overstrike type
    modes toggle), 26
  customizing, 25
  F5=Go, 361
  F6 (next menu), 23

Ins key (insert/overstrike type
    modes toggle), 26
  QH (Quick Help), 33
  redefining, 26
keyboard-input, stredit.c (Morse
  code) practice program, 199-203
keynew class member functions,
  570-572
keynew friend functions, 570-572
keynew.hpp header file, 568-569
keywords
  __asm, 387-391
  BOOL, 847
  class, 426
  extern, 210-212, 463
  FAR, 847
  friend, 568
  PASCAL, 847
  private, 444-445
  protected, 444-445
  public, 444-445
  static, 462
  struct, 426
  typedef, 165
  union, 426
kill() member function, 488-491

L

labeled statements, 81
Language Options item, 404
Language Options option, 30-31
Language Options... command, 290
Large memory models, 18, 289, 297
last fixed argument, 247
last-in-first-out (LIFO), creating,
  430-438
last-in-first-out sequencing of
  objects, 430
LibMain() function, 911
libraries
  additional, specifying, 31
  combining memory models, 18
  installing, 15-17
  QuickWin, 798-800

library directory, reading, 544
library files, opening, 543
library functions, 49-58, 101-108
    header functions, 107
    including in programs, 106-108
    information, locating, 106
LIBRARY statement, 908
`libseek()` function, 544
`libtell()` function, 544
lifo class objects, 442
lifo member functions, 435
LIFO stacks, 430-438
    memory, 431
    pointers, 431
lines, drawing, 338, 342-343
`_lineto()` function, 335
Link Options dialog box, 46
LINK Options option, 31
linkage
    external, 122
    in variables, 122-123
    internal, 122
    none, 122
    specifications, 577-579
    type-safe, 575-579
linkers, 63
linking
    CodeView debugger, 25
    incremental, 31
    object modules, 223
    overlay programs, 303
    programs, 32-35, 46
    Windows applications, 822-824
list boxes, 839
    Current Keys, 27
    Macro/Function List, 26
    Runtime Support, 29
    Switch List, 27
    Unassigned Keys, 26
LIST class, 772
`listdir()` function, 544
listing
    elements, 483
    files, 224-225
Listing 1.1. begin.c, 36-37
Listing 1.2. order.c, 44

Listing 1.3. scandemo.c, 52
Listing 1.4. strtoint.c, 56
Listing 1.5. upperc.c, 58
Listing 2.1. swdemo.c, 67-68
Listing 2.2. fdump.c, 69-70
Listing 2.3. gvar.c, 76
Listing 2.4. lvar.c, 77-78
Listing 2.5. objmac.c, 91
Listing 3.1. blank.c, 102
Listing 3.2. txt_demo.c, 107
Listing 3.3. loopcnt.c, 112
Listing 3.4. loopref.c, 113
Listing 3.5. name_cmp.c, 116
Listing 3.6. term.c, 127
Listing 3.7. v_list1.c 132
Listing 3.8. v_list2.c, 134
Listing 4.1. p_intro.c, 146
Listing 4.2. exchange.c, 147
Listing 4.3. uitoh.c, 154
Listing 4.4. name.c, 161
Listing 4.5. car.c, 172
Listing 4.6. dyna.c, 181
Listing 4.7. newdyna.c, 183
Listing 5.1. cw.c, 189
Listing 5.2. cinsdel.c, 199
Listing 5.3. stredit.c, 199
Listing 5.4. utility.c, 203
Listing 5.5. stredit.h, 215
Listing 5.6. cinsdel.h, 218
Listing 6.1. fdata.c, 237
Listing 6.2. varprint.c, 246
Listing 6.3. A program that uses
    `fgetc()` and `fputc()`, 249
Listing 6.4. strio.c 252
Listing 6.5. dirio.c, 262
Listing 6.6. prtlab.c, 264
Listing 6.7. getpos.c, 269
Listing 7.1. farmem.c, 286
Listing 7.2. module1.c, 291
Listing 7.3. module2.c, 291
Listing 7.4. little.c, 293
Listing 7.5. ovrmain.c, 299
Listing 7.6. ovrmod1.c, 301
Listing 7.7. ovrmod2.c, 302
Listing 7.8. ovrmod3.c, 302
Listing 7.9. ovrmod4.c, 302

Listing 7.10.ovrmain.c, 303
Listing 7.11.vmem.c, 305
Listing 8.1. A demonstration of _setcolor() and _setbkcolor(), 317
Listing 8.2. A demonstration of _settextwindow(), 319
Listing 8.3. graph1.c, 335
Listing 8.4. graph2.c, 336
Listing 8.5. ssolid.c, 339-340
Listing 8.6. Example usage of _setfillmask(), 344
Listing 8.7. showtext.c, 348
Listing 9.1. ptest1.c, 372
Listing 9.2. The output produced by the lcount program, 374-375
Listing 9.3. ptest1.c, 376-377
Listing 9.4. ptest2.c, 378
Listing 9.5. Line timing analysis of ptest2, 379-380
Listing 10.1. inline.c, 387-388
Listing 10.2. fdpark.c, 394
Listing 10.3. calldos.c, 395-396
Listing 10.4. ticker.c, 399-402
Listing 11.1. structob.cpp, 418-421
Listing 11.2. access.cpp, 422
Listing 11.3. access2.cpp, 424
Listing 11.4. lifo.hpp, 432-433
Listing 11.5. lifo.cpp, 435-437
Listing 11.6. uselifo.cpp, 440-442
Listing 11.7. defarg.cpp, 449
Listing 11.8. constr.cpp, 451-452
Listing 12.1. msmouse.hpp, 466-468
Listing 12.2. msmouse.cpp, 468-473
Listing 12.3. usemouse.cpp, 474-480
Listing 12.4. dbllist.hpp, 482-483
Listing 12.5. dbllist.cpp, 484-487
Listing 12.6. usedbl.cpp, 489-491
Listing 12.7. dir.hpp, 491-492
Listing 12.8. dir.cpp, 493-497
Listing 12.9. usedir.cpp, 498-499
Listing 12.10. colorobj.cpp, 502-503
Listing 13.1. docu.cpp, 512-514
Listing 13.2. lib.hpp, 527-528
Listing 13.3. lib.cpp, 529-543
Listing 13.4. pds.cpp, 545

Listing 16.1. manip.cpp, 699
Listing 16.2. manipprm.cpp, 703
Listing 18.1. genlist.cpp, 765-767
Listing 18.2. genlist2.cpp, 770
Listing 18.3. listbase.hpp, 771
Listing 18.4. genlist.hpp, 772-774
Listing 18.5. tempvar.cpp, 781-782
Listing 18.6. tempvar2.cpp, 783-784
Listing 19.1. winorder.c, 800-802
Listing 19.2. child.c, 804-805
Listing 19.3. A simple program using a scroll buffer, 809-810
Listing 19.4. easy.def, 816
Listing 19.5. easy.c, 816-819
Listing 19.6. fcmenu.rc, 827-828
Listing 19.7. fcwin.rc , 839
Listing 20.1. Microsoft (R) EXE File Header Utility, 842-843
Listing 20.2. fcwin.c, 847-876
Listing 20.3. fcwin.def 878
Listing 20.4. fcwin.h, 879-880
Listing 21.1 helpmsg.def, 908
Listing 21.2 helpmsg.c, 909-911

listmem() function, 545
lists
    aggregate initializer, 621
    constructor initializer, 621-624
load modules, 63
loading
    printer drivers, 901-902
    text data into push buffer, 572
LoadLibrary() Windows function, 902
local (auto) class objects, 482-491
local scope, 78, 120, 519
local variables, 177
    accessing, 77-78
    testing, 521-522
locals window, 367
locating
    bugs, 357
    C source files, 39
    data, 282
    definition points, 788
    errors, 357

files, 39
  member, 545
functions, 787
library functions, 106
unreferenced symbols, 789
variables, 787
location of windows, controlling, 808-809
locators, object, 602
lockup.cpp program, 628-629
logic errors, 357
logic of programs, 64-72
long ios::flags(), 688
long ios::setf() function, 688
long ios::unsetf() function, 688
long_name() function, 117
loop counter errors, 358
loop structures, 125
loop-control statements, writing, 123-126
loop_count() function, 112-114
loops
  do-while, 69
  exiting, 71
  for(), 40, 71, 125
  main message, 820
    setting up, 889-891
    writing, 846
  postchecked, 69
  prechecked, 69
  programs, executing, 125-126
  while, 69-70
low-resolution mode, 325
lowercase characters, converting to uppercase, 57
LOWORD() function, 821
lpfn (long pointer to function) function prefix, 893

M

macro definitions, 38-39
  header files, 215
macros, 226-227
  ADRS, 776
  advantages, 90

ALLOC, 432
characters, 91
constant values, defining, 90
declare(), 770-771
defining in make files, 227
expanding, 92
FCWIN_COMPUTE, 881
function-like
  creating, 89-97
  defining, 93-97
identifiers, 90-93
implement(), 771, 777
#include, 214
names, replacing, 92
naming, 90
NMAKE set, 227
OAPP(), 704
object-like
  creating, 89-97
  defining, 89-93
_Pastex, 774
POP, 432
PUSH, 432
scanning, 92
SHOW(), 776
strings, 91
  defining, 92
  quotation marks, 92
support, 435
szAppName, 815
undefining, 93
va_end(), 247
va_start(), 247
main message loop, 820
  setting up, 889-891
  writing, 846
main() function, 42-43, 101, 362
  short, 102
  writing, 103-105
make files, 208
  command lines, 225
  embedding directives, 228-229
  inference rules, 226
  macros, 226-227
MakeProcInstance() Windows function, 893, 894

`malloc()` function, 179
mangling functions, 575-576
  turning off, 576-579
manifest constants, 879
manipulation functions, 106
manipulators
  C++ stream, 694-705
  dec, 696
  endl, 696
  ends, 696
  flush, 696
  hex, 696
  oct, 696
  parameterized, 695-700
  stream, 699
  ws, 696
Mark command, 803
marray.cpp program, 604-606
mask values, formatting flags, 687-688
masks, bit, 679
matching function arguments, 564-565
math functions, 106
Medium memory model, 17, 289, 297
member data, updating base class, 733
member files, 544-545
member functions, 414, 778
  class objects, accessing, 553-555
  compiling class, 446-447
  declarations, 449-450
  defaults, 449-450
  inline, writing, 447-448
  naming, 737
  overloaded, declaring, 565-567
  overloading, 561-565
  writing, 437-438
member objects
  accessing, 444-445
  visibility, 422-425
members
  accessing, nested classes, 510
  copying, 733
  data, static, 463-464

memory
  accessing, 284
  allocating, 78
    dynamically, 176-184
    in arrays, 143
  arrays, 142
  blocks, 142, 180
  bytes, 178-179
  deallocating, 177-183
  dynamic, 176-184
    free store, 438
  functions, 106
  graphics screens, pages, 346
  heaps, fragmenting, 180
  LIFO stacks, 431
  location
    accessing, 278
    swapping contents, 150
  objects, allocating, 178
  segments, 17
  variables, allocating, 121
  video, 313
  virtual
    allocating, 304-307
    freeing, 308
    locking in memory, 308
    terminating, 308
memory addresses, 141
  assigning to pointer variables, 179
  controlling, 442
  of argument, 113
  operands, returning, 152
  referencing, 283
  relocation, 145
  specifying, 313
  writing, 279
memory heap, 177
memory models, 14, 288-292
  Compact, 16-17, 289, 297
  Huge, 18, 289, 297
  inline assembly statements, 387
  installing, 16-19
  Large, 18, 289, 297
  libraries, combining, 18
  Medium, 17, 289, 297

mixed, programming, 290-292
  selecting, 17-19, 289-290
  Small, 17, 289, 297
  source codes, translating, 18
  Tiny, 17, 289, 297
memory-mapped screen I/O, 313
menu bar, accessing, 810
menu system, accessing
  Programmer's WorkBench (PWB),
  21-22
menu() function, 363
menus
  accessing, 21-22
  creating, 827-829
  Data, 366-367
  Edit, 803
  editing, 827-829
  FCWIN, 947
  File, 803
  Help, 803
  Options, 25
  Project, 32, 64, 219
  Run, 221
  Search, 24
  State, 803
merging source files, 214
MessageBox() Windows function,
  896-897, 912
messages
  pop-up help and error, creating,
  896-897
  WinMain(), 813
  WM_COMMAND, 892
  WM_CREATE, 892
  WM_DESTROY, 822, 892
  WM_PAINT, 820
methods, bundling, 415
microprocessors
  16-bit, 278
  80286, 280
  80386, 280
  80486, 280
  Intel 80x86, 17
microprocessors, *see* central
  processing unit
Microsoft C Compiler, warnings, 30

Microsoft C Run-Time Library
  Reference, 492
Microsoft C/C++
  configuring, 25-32
  disk space requirements, 12
  executing, 19
  installing, 12-14
Microsoft Linker, 303
Microsoft Mouse Programmer's
  Reference, 465
Microsoft Overlay Virtual
  Environment (MOVE), 295-297
Microsoft Profiler, 370-381
  PLIST program, 373
  PREP program, 373
  PROFILE program, 373
  starting, 372
Microsoft Source Profiler, installing,
  12-13
Microsoft Windows
  availability, 12
  fonts, 351
  installing, 12
  SETUP program, 12-14
minimizing
  class object size, 455-456
  windows, 806
miscellaneous functions, 106
mnemonic identifiers, assigning to
  integer values, 143
mode arguments, 129, 253
  values, 254
modes
  80386-protected, 19
  at-end, 709
  binary file-access, 259
  Command (CodeView utility),
  364-366
  graphics, 311, 323-330, 346-351
  insert, 26
  open, 708
  overstrike, 26
  profiling, 380-381
  quick compile, 35
  text, 311-313, 321
  video, 314-315

modifying
 breakpoint settings, 369
 color, 317
 data types, 140
 files, position, 270-272
 fonts, 348-349
 options, 14
 pointers, 286-288
 streams, bit states, 696
 values
  bits, 279
  in functions, 112-113
module definitions file (.DEF), 299, 303, 816
 creating, 878-879
modules
 object, linking, 223
 overlay, 297-298, 303
 with mixed memory models, 290-292
Morse code practice program, 208
mouse
 action buttons, activating, 25
 check boxes, on/off toggle, 25
 commands, selecting, 22
 windows
  accessing, 23
  resizing, 24
MOVE (Microsoft Overlay Virtual Environment), 295-297
_moveto() function, 341
moving
 data, 105
 dialog boxes, 838
MS-DOS Graphics Libraries option, 16
multiple
 inheritance, 515
 windows, 804-807
multitasking programming, 811-813

N

\n (the new-line character), 55
NAME statement, 878

names
 hiding, 728
 resource, 826
naming
 actions, 737
 destructor functions, 618-619
 functions, 110
 member functions, 737
navigate() member function, 497
near pointer, 283-284
nested classes, 428
 accessing memory, 510
nesting, #include directives, 216
new and delete operators
 for classes, overloading, 657-660
 global, 648
 user-defined, 649
new class, *see* derived class
New command, 45
new() operator
 acquiring space, 643-645
 creating and destroying class objects, 646
 creating class objects with, 647-648
 overloading, 648-649
New Project command, 208
New Project dialog box, 209
new types, defining, 414
new-line character (\n), 55, 236
NEWFRAME escape sequence, 905-906
NMAKE command, 222
NMAKE macros, 227
NMAKE options, 31-32
NMAKE utility, 221-224, 824
no linkage, 122
non-whitespace character, 243
nonmember functions, overloading, 573-574
nonstatic member functions, 762
 destructor function, 619
nonstatic operators, 584
nonvirtual base class constructors, executing, 751
nonzero (true) value, 431

normalized pointer, 285
NOT (!) operator, 680
null pointer, 644
   value, 431
NULL value, 154
numbers
   floating-point, 73-74
   quad, converting to strings, 764
   real, 73-74
   whole, 72

O

_OAMANIP ong operator<<()
 function, 704
_OAPP long operator()()
 function, 704
OAPP() macro, 704
   linking, 223
object types
   arithmetic, 140
   integral, 140
   scalar, 140
object-like macros
   creating, 89-97
   defining, 89-93
   replacing, 89
object-like objects, 637
object-oriented programming
 (OOP), 412, 814-816
objects
   accessing, 211, 548
   arrays, 557-559
   browser, 25
   C++, defining, 461-500
   class, 411
      converting, 762
      creating, 412
      deleting, 481
      global (static), 491-500
      initializing, 433-434, 500-504
      inputting, 690-691
      last-in-first-out (LIFO), 442
      local (auto), 482-491
      outputting, 690-691
      reducing, 464
      size, 455-456
   creating, 211
   data, 411
      accessing, 439
      multibyte, 155
      size, 178
   declaring, 211, 557-559
   defining, 211, 429
   describing, incomplete types, 141
   drawing, 339-340
   filled, 334, 339-343
   fstream, 706
   initializing
      action-like, 637
      object-like, 637
      value-like, 637
   locators, 583, 602
   member, accessing, 444-445
   memory
      addresses, 141
      allocating, 178
   modules, 63
   ordinary, passing to operator
    functions, 593
   pointing to, 141
   selecting, 147-148
   singleton, 426-427
   stacks, 430
   storing, 178
   unfilled, 334
   user-defined, placing outside
    main program, 417
   values, 141
      accessing, 152
      returning, 132
oct manipulator, 696
offset address, combining, with
 segment address, 278-279,282
offset values, 279
ofstream stream class, 705
old class, 512
Olivetti/AT&T 6300, 324
Open command, 24, 208
open mode, 708

Open Module command, 367
Open Source... command, 368
open() function, 706-708
opening
  files, 253-255
  library files, 543
operands, 79
  memory addresses, returning, 152
operator functions, 585
  cast, 594-595
  overloaded
    characteristics, 584
    declaring, 587-588
    specifying arguments, 588-589
  passing ordinary objects to, 593
  specifying return type for, 589-591
operator new(), 442
operator overloading, 583-589
operator!() function, 681
operator+() function, 782-784
operator=() function, 732, 759
operators, 79, 779-782
  ! and =, 586-587
  ++ (postfix increment), 151
  - > (structure pointer), 488
  -> (structure pointer), 168
  . (structure member), 166, 523
  ¦ (bitwise OR), 678
  << and >> (stream), 670-677, 692
  & address-of (&), 152, 549
  $ (AND), 678
  array subscript, 156
  =() (assignment), 731
  binary assignment, 82, 595-598
    %= (remainder), 83
    &= (bitwise AND), 83
    ^= (bitwise XOR), 83
    *= (product), 83
    + (assignment), 82
    += (sum), 82
    -= (difference), 83
    /= (quotient), 83
    <<= (bitwise left-shift), 83

    = (assignment), 82
    >>= (bitwise right-shift), 83
    ¦= (bitwise OR), 83
  binary mathematical
    % (modulus), 82
    * (multiplication), 82
    + (addition), 82
    - (subtraction), 82
    / (division), 82
  cast, 88
  class membes, 524
    ->* (dereference pointer to class member), 84
    .* (dereference pointer to class member), 84
    :: (scope access/resolution), 84
  class pointer, 524
  comma
    , (left to right forced evaluation), 84
  component selection
    -> (indirect), 83
    . (direct), 83
  conditional
    a?b:c (if a then b; else c), 84
  delete(), 643, 646
    creating and destroying class objects, 646-648
    overloading, 648-649
  equality
    != (not equal to), 83
    < (less than), 83
    <= (less than or equal to), 83
    == (equal to), 83
    > (greater than), 83
    >= (greaater than or equal to), 83
  ^= (exclusive-OR-and-assign compound), 150
  function call, 603-607
  global
    << and >>, 692
    overloading new and delete, 649-657
  increment, 71, 115

logical
   ! (NOT) (reverse true or false
   condition of expression), 65
   && (AND) (both expressions are
   true), 65, 83
   ¦¦ (OR) (yields true if either
   expression is true), 65, 83
new ( )
   creating and destroying class
   objects, 646-648
   overloading, 648-649
new and delete
   overloading for classes,
   657-660
NMAKE Expression
   ! (unary logical NOT), 229
   != (not equal), 229
   % (remainder), 229
   & (bitwise AND), 229
   && (logical AND), 229
   () (parentheses may group
   expression elements), 229
   ^ (bitwise exclusive OR), 229
   * (multiplication), 229
   + (addition), 229
   - (subtraction), 229
   - (unary negation), 229
   / (division), 229
   < (less than), 229
   << (left shift), 229
   == (exactly equal), 229
   <= (less than or equal), 229
   > (greater than), 229
   >= (greater than or equal), 229
   >> (right shift), 229
   ¦ (bitwise OR), 229
   ¦¦ (logical OR), 229
   ~ (unary bitwise complement),
   229
nonstatic, 584
! NOT !, 680
¦ OR ¦, 678
overloading, 579-583
   << and >>, 690-694
   with friend functions, 591-594
++ postfix increment, 151

precedence, 85
reference, 454, 549-551
relational
   != (not equal to), 65
   < (less than), 65
   <= (less than or equal to), 65
   == (equal to), 65
   > (greater than), 65
   >= (greater than or equal to),
   65
scope resolution, 437, 507-517
shift, precedence, 678
shift and bitwise
   & (bitwise AND), 83
   << (shift left), 83
   >> (shift right), 83
   ^ (bitwise XOR), 83
   ¦ (bitwise OR), 83
<< (shift-left), 668
>> (shift-right), 668
sizeof, 178
static, 584
string concatenation, 95
string literal, 95
-> (structure pointer), 523
[ ] (subscript), 598-603, 768
typecast, overloading, 760-764
unary
   -- (decrement), 82
   ! (not/logical negation), 82
   & (address), 82
   * (indirection), 82, 152
   + (plus), 82
   ++ (increment), 82
   - (minus), 82
   ~ (bitwise complement), 82
   & (address-of), 152
   overloading, 595-598
   sample expressions, 596
:: (unary scope), 520
user-defined cast for class
   objects, 594
void* cast, 680
^ (XOR), 678
<Optimizations...> command, 31

optimizing
    command-line compiler `cl`, 404
    programs, 370, 403-405
options
    All Windows, 23
    Build Libraries, 15
    Build Options, 29
    Colors..., 28-29
    Compile File, 220
    Custom Installation, 15-16
    Default Installation, 16
    Editor Settings, 27
    Floating-Point Library
        80x87 Calls, 405
        Emulation Calls, 405
        Fast Alternate Math/FPa, 405
        Inline 80x87, 405
        Inline Emulation, 405
    Key Assignments..., 27
    Language Options, 30-31
    LINK Options, 31
    modifying, 14
    MS-DOS Graphics Libraries, 16
    NMAKE, 31-32
    Project, 208
    Project Template, 406
    Rebuild All, 221
    Set Project Template, 29
    Window menu, 23
    Windows Targets
        .DLL Files, 16
        .EXE Files, 16
        QuickWin .EXE Files, 16
Options command, 25
Options menu, 25
    Build Options option, 29
    Colors... option, 28-29
    Editor Settings option, 27
    Key Assignments..., 26-27
    Language Options option, 30-31
    LINK Options option, 31
    NMAKE options, 31-32
    Set Project Template option, 29
`OR` (¦) operator, 678
order-of-appearance doubly-linked
  list, creating, 488

order.c Program, compiling, 800-802
ordered doubly-linked list, creating, 488
ordinal-value assignments used by FCWIN, 837
`ostream` (output) class, 665
output
    buffers, 233
    characters, 248-252
    class objects, 690-691
    data, 53-55, 231-233, 237, 244
    functions, 53-55
    stream inserter, 668
    `stream operator<<()` function, 692
`_outtext()` function, 317, 320
overlapping offset values, 279
overlay
    manager, 295-296
    modules, 303
    programs
        compiling, 303
        creating, 297-304
        linking, 303
    swapping, dynamic, 296
    units, 295-296
overlaying
    functions, 298
    modules, 297-298
overloading
    << and >> global operators, 692
    << and >> operators, 690-694
    binary operators, 595-598
    C++ operators, 580-581
    constructor function, 613, 636 640-642
    `delete()` operator, 648-649
    friend functions, 568-573
    functions, 429
    member functions, 561-565
    `new` operator, 648-649
    new and delete operators for classes, 657-660
    nonmember functions, 573-574
    operators, 579-589, 694
        function call, 603-607

subscript, [], 598-603
  with friend functions, 591-594
typecast operators, 760-764
unary operators, 595-598
overriding
  member objects access, 444-445
  operator delete(), 442
  operator new(), 442
overstrike type mode, 26

P

p-code (packed code) options, 29, 33, 406
P_OVERLAY argument, 129
P_WAIT argument, 129
padding, 167
pagesl, 346
palettes
  color, 324-325
  Color Graphics Array, 327
  Video Graphics Array, 327
paragraphs, 279
parameter declaration list, 104
parameterized stream
  manipulators, 695-697
    defining, 700
    goxy(), 703
    resetiosflags(n), 698
    sa(), 703
    setfill(n), 698
    setiosflags(n), 698
    setprecision(n), 698
    setw(n), 698
parameters, Boolean, 27
parentheses [()], 114
parenthesized form of operator new, 659
parsing text, 676
partitioned data (pds), 545
PASCAL keyword, 847
pass-through mechanism, 735
passing
  arguments
    to functions, 111-115
    to functions by reference, 112-114
    to functions by value, 111-112
  by value, 48
  ordinary objects to operator functions, 593
  pointers to arguments, 113
  string addresses, 160
_Pastex macros, 774
paths
  root directory, 254
  specifying, 844
Pause function, 803
pds (partitioned data), 545
peek() function, 674-676
peekA() function, 455
Percent Change dialog, 894-895
percent signs(%), 244
permanent devices, 232
perror() function, 273
_pie() function, 335, 339
pies, 338
pixels, 323
placement syntax, 650
pointers, 144-153, 555-556, 782-785
  arguments, 132
  arithmetic operations, 154
  array elements, 151, 159
  assignments, converting to void, 149
  based, 283
  casts, 154-155
  comparing, 284
  conditional expressions, converting to void, 149
  data, 144
  declaring, 152, 170-171, 557-559, 748
  dereferencing, 149-152
  far, 284-287
  functions, calling, 171
  huge, 285
  integer values, 154
  last-in-first-out (LIFO stacks), 431
  memory addresses, 141
  modifying, 286-288

near, 283-284
normalized, 285
operators, 152
passing to arguments, 113
reference types, 141
returning to strings, 116
sizes, 387
strings, 147-149
subtracting, 154
this, 438-442, 548-549
to member variable, 583
types, 140-142
values, 141
void, 444
points, locating, 788
_polygon() function, 335, 339
polygons, 339
polymorphism, 737
POP macro, 432
pop() function, 432
popping strings, 443
PopupMsg() function, 879, 906-912
positioning files with C++ streams, 712-714
positionxy() function, 703
postchecked loops, see do-while loops, 69
postfix increment operator (++), 151
pow() function, 88
pragma, 406
precedence of operators, 85, 678
prechecked loops, 69-70
precision specifiers, print() function, 921-922
precompiled headers, 35
preparing resource files, 824-825
preprocessor directives
    executing, 63
    #define, 40, 38-89
    #include, 38-39, 107
    scanning, 92
    #undef, 93
preventing data loss, 255
Print Manager, spooling hard copy to, 898-906

print() function, 244-247, 919-923
    characters
        escape, 923
        input-size modifier, 922
    data type specifiers, 922-923
    flags, 920
    format strings, 919
    precision specifiers, 921-922
    width specifiers, 920
printers
    devices, 846
    drivers, 901-902
printf() function, 54-55, 237, 245, 684
    format string, 244
    variable argument list, 244
printf() statement, 48, 96
printing
    data objects, 155
    errors, 273
    quotation marks, 96
private keyword, 444-445
PrntAmort() dialog function, 898-901
process-control functions, 106
product() function, 42
profiling modes
    counting, 381
    coverage, 381
    sampling, 381
    selecting, 380
    timing, 381
Program Arguments command, 221
Programmer's WorkBench (PWB), 12, 25, 823
    CodeView utility, 358-360
    configuring, 26
    exiting, 220
    files
        comparing, 221
        project, 208-210
        recompiling, 221
    menu system, 21-22
    practice exercises, 58
    programs
        compiling, 219-220
        executing, 32, 219-220

starting, 19-20
status bar system, 21
windows, 21-25
programming
errors, 357-358
functions, 42
memory models, mixed, 290-292
multitasking, 811-813
Windows 3.1, 798-807, 877
programming environments
Windows, 798-799
Windows 3.1, 877
Programming in Windows 3.1, 798
programs
$avings.cpp, 586-587
386MAX memory management
utility, 19
array.cpp, 598-602
C, 412
C++, 412
calling destructor functions,
635-636
child processes, 129
compiling, 32-48
Programmer's WorkBench
(PWB), 32, 219-220
with inline assembly
statements, 386
complex, 220-221, 446
constructor initializer list,
621-624
converting to machine-language
instructions, 62-63
creating, 62-63
debugging with CodeView utility,
360-363
demonstrating new () operator,
644-645
device-independent, 49
DOS commands, executing, 129
editing, 32-35
efficiency, 370-372
executing, 43, 61-72
from top of loop, 125-126
Programmer's WorkBench
(PWB), 32, 219-220

suspending, 247
with CodeView utility, 360-363
execution, changing flow, 126-130
explicit calls and required
placement of parentheses,
626-627
fcwin.c, designing, 845-847
files, 846
forming pointer to member
function, 615-616
header files, 879-881
inline assemlby statements,
387-391
input/output (I/O), 663-678
linking, 32-35, 46
lockup.cpp, 628-629
logic, 64-72
marray.cpp, 604-606
object-oriented, 814-816
optimizing, 370, 403-405
order.c, compiling, 800-802
overlay, 303
creating, 297-304
linking, 303
oversized, 295-296
profiling, 370-372
ptrmbr.cpp, 582-583
scanning, 92
separating into logical units, 47
SETUP, 12-14
stopping temporarily, 63, 129
strings.cpp, 566-567
stub, 843
terminating, 126-128
testnew.cpp, 572-573
viewing with CodeView utility,
364
Windows, see Windows
programs, 885
WINSTUB.EXE, 842-843
WX Server, 823
Project
menu, 32, 64, 219
option, 208
Template option, 29, 406

project files
  compiling, 219
  creating, 208-210, 881-882
    Programmer's WorkBench
      (PWB), 208-210
    FCWIN, 881-882
project-management functions,
  accessing, 208-209
`protected` keyword, 444-445
prototypes, 40
ptest1, improving, 378
ptrmbr.cpp program, 582-583
public access specifier, 726-728
`public` keyword, 444-445
punctuators, 79, 357
`pure virtual` function, 748-750
`purgeblk()` function, 543
`purgedir()` function, 543
push buffer, loading text
  data into, 572
PUSH macro, 432
`push()` member function, 432
`put()` function, 710
`put...()` functions, 53-54
`put_msg()` function, 42
`putback()` function, 675-676
`putc()` put function, 53
`putchar()` function, 378
`puts()` put function, 53
PWB, *see* Programmer's WorkBench

Q

QH (Quick Help) keyboard shortcut,
  33
`qsort()` function, 267
`quad` class, 758, 933-946
`quad` numbers, 764
quick compile mode, 35
QuickWin Library, 798-804
quotation marks (" "), 92, 96, 216
`_QWINVER` symbol, 806

R

radio buttons, 25, 359
RAM (random-access memory), 145
random-access (RAM) memory, 145
RC (resource compiler), 824, 839
`rdstate()` function, 682
`_read()` function, 807
`read()` function, 673, 710
read-only memory (ROM), 312
reading
  blocks, 543
  characters, 248
  data, 242
  files
    direct, 261-268
    `fstream`, 710-712
    member, 545
  library directory, 544
  single characters, 50
  source files, 62
  streams
    binary, 236
    text, 236
  strings, 50, 251-253
README file, 17
`readn()` function, 544
real numbers, 73-74
`realloc()` function, 180
Rebuild All command, 787
Rebuild All option, 221
rebuilding files, 221
recompiling
  Programmer's WorkBench (PWB)
    files, 221
  source files, 31-32
`_rectangle()` function, 335, 339
redefining
  derived types in C++, 413-414
  keyboard shortcuts, 26-27
redirecting streams, 255
reducing class objects size, 464
references, 602, 782-785
  abstract class, declaring, 748
  external, 210-213

operator (&), 454, 549-551
types, 141
using for return types, 594
referencing
functions
class member, 618
constructor, 618
destructor, 620
memory addresses, 283
variables, 366
register
functions, 128
specifiers, 462
variable, 153
RegisterClass() function, 819
RegisterClass() Windows
function, 888
_registerfonts() functions, 349
registers
CS, 389
data, 280-281
DS, 389
ES, 389
flags, 283
functions, 281-282
instruction pointer (IP), 397
segment, 390
segment address, 282
SS (stack segment), 282, 389
Registers window, 368
releasable executable, 29
releaseblk() member function, 544
_remappalette() function, 328-329
remove() function, 256-257
rename() function, 257
renaming files, 257
repetitive instantiation, 779-782
replacement-lists, 95-96
replacing macros, 89, 92
report() function, 739
report-only flags() function, 689
requirements for disk space, 12
reset() member function, 497

resetiosflags(n) parameterized
stream manipulator, 698
resize box, 24
resizing
allocated memory blocks, 180
windows, 24
resolutions, displaying, 323
resource compiler (RC), 824, 839
resource files, 823-825, 949-959
resources
compiling, 839
creating, 825
names, 826
Resume function, 803
return statements, 81
functions, completion status, 104
purposes, 104
values, 104
return types
destructor, 619
for arithmetic and shift
operators, 594
functions, 103, 117-108
operator, 589-591
void, 111
returning
characters to streambuf, 675
pointers to strings, 116
values from functions, 115-119
reusing code, 719-724
rewind() function, 270
ROM, *see* read-only memory
root
directory, 254
unit, 295
rules
reference operators, 551
virtual functions, 737-738
Run command, 844
Run menu, 221
running
chain, 544
QuickWin applications, 803
Runtime Support list box, 29

S

sa() parameterized manipulator, 703

sampling profiling mode, 381

\<Save...> command, 27

Save dialog box, 45

\<Save List> button, 210

saytree() function, 750

scalar types, 140

scanf() function, 49-53, 237, 241-244, 684, 924
  data types, 925
  format string, 242
  modifiers
    argument-type, 925
    input-size, 924
  variable argument list, 242

scanning
  macros, 92
  programs, 92
  text, 676

scopes, 120-121, 423-425, 462
  class, 519
  constructor initializers, 522
  file, 519
  function arguments, 519, 522
  local, 78, 519
  resolution operator (::), 437, 447, 507-517
  rules
    C, 517-520
    C++, 517-520

screens
  attributes, 322
  clearing, 108
  controlling, 346
  coordinates, 318
    x-axis (horizontal), 318
    y-axis (vertical), 318
  displaying, 345
  resolution, 323
  text-mode, 314
  user, 46

scroll bars, 23, 809-810

scroll buffer size, 810

scrolling windows, 23

Search menu, 24

seekg() function, 712

seekp() function, 712

segment
  addresses, 278-279, 282
  registers, 390

SEGMENTS function, 299

selecting
  color, 315-317, 326-327
  commands, 21-22
  memory models, 17-19, 289-290
  objects, 147-148
  profiling modes, 380
  video modes, 314-315

selection statement, 81

semicolons (;), 426

separating programs into logical units, 47

sequence input of data, 51-52

Set Breakpoint
  command, 368
  dialog box, 369

\<Set Color> command, 29

Set Project Template option, 29

\<Set Switch> command, 27

_setbkcolor() function, 316, 326

setbuf() function, 257-258

_setcolor() function, 317

SetDlgItemText() Windows function, 896

setfill(n) parameterized stream manipulators, 698

setfillmask() function, 341, 343-345

_setfont() function, 349-351

setiosflags(n) parameterized stream manipulators, 698

_setlinestyle() function, 341-343

setprecision(n) parameterized manipulator, 698

_settextcolor() function, 108, 315-316

_settextposition() function, 703

_settextwindow() function, 318-320

setting
    breakpoints, 368-369
    data values, 692
    error indicators, 273
SETUP program
    disk space requirements, 12
    executing, 12
    versions, 13-14
setvbuf() function, 258
_setvideomode() function, 312-315
_setvieworg() function, 331-332
_setviewport() function, 332-333
_setvisualpage() function, 346
setw(n) parameterized stream
  manipulator, 691, 698
_setwritemode() function, 341
shift-left operator (<<), 668
shift-right operator (>>), 668
SHOW(type) macro, 776
showclass() function, 421
ShowWindow() functions, 820, 889
sign bit, 167
sign character, 56
simple expressions, 79
single inheritance, 725
singleton objects, 426-427
size() member function, 514
size-constant expression, 156
sizeof operator, 178
sizing windows, 808-809, 815
slicing copy operation, 733
Small memory models, 17, 289, 297
sopen() function, 706
sorting data, 268
"source browser" utility, 20, 786-792
source codes
    CW program, 189-198
    errors, 30
    memory models, 18
source files
    adding to project files, 208
    contents, 188-207
    converting, 62
    creating, 61, 876-881
    data objects, 75
    declarations, 214

    functions, 212-213
    location on disk, 208
    multiple, 63, 188-207
    reading, 62
    recompiling, 31-32
    status, 31-32
    translating into object modules,
      63
    variables, 119, 122, 212
    Windows Applications, 876
space, acquiring with new ()
  operator, 643-645
space whitespace characters, 62
spawn...() function, 128-130,
  929-931
specifiers
    auto, 462
    conversion, 243-244
    directory, 257
    public access, 726-728
    register, 462
    static, 462
    storage class, 462
specifying
    additional libraries, 31
    arguments
      for overloaded operator
        functions, 588-589
    class member data objects, 427
    CodeView debugger, 31
    functions, 117
    linkage, 576-579
    memory
      addresses, 313
      objects, 178
    paths, 844
    return types, 589-591
    wildcards, for filenames, 226
spooling hard copy to Windows
  Print Manager, 898-906
sprintf() function, 245
SS (stack segment) register, 282,
  389
sscanf() function, 243
stack class member functions, 432
stack frame, 388

stack segment (SS) register, 282, 389

stacks, last-in-first-out (LIFO), 430-438, 443

standard
functions, 105-106
input/output (I/O), 667-674
streams, 664-667

starting
COMMAND.COM, 129
Microsoft Profiler, 372
Programmer's WorkBench (PWB), 19-20

State menu, 803

statements, 79-85
asm, 81
beginning, 80-81
break, 71, 125
calloc(), 179
_clearscreen(), 48
compound, 81
continue, 125
declaration, 81
do, 81
else, 81
ending, 80-81
EXETYPE, 908
exiting, 71
EXPORTS, 879
expressions, 81
for, 81, 114
goto, 124-125
grouping, 102
if, 64-65, 81
if-else, 66
IMPORTS, 879, 907
iteration
di, 81
do, 81
for, 81
while, 81
jump
break, 81
continue, 81
goto, 81
return, 81

labeled, 81
goto, 81
switch, 81
LIBRARY, 908
loop-control, 123-126
multiple, 66
NAME, 878
nested if-else, 66
printf(), 48, 96
return, 104
selection, 81
else, 81
if, 81
switch, 81
switch, 64-68, 81
while, 81

static
constructor functions, 616
data members, 463
duration, 76, 121-122
keyword, 462
operators, 584
specifiers, 462
storage class, 779-782

stdaux stream, 235
stderr stream, 235
stdin stream, 235
stdout stream, 235
stdprn stream, 235

Step command, 363

"stepping through"
arrays, 151
pointers, 147-149
strings, 147-148

stopping programs, 63

storage classes, 119-123
class objects, 462-464
duration, 119
linkage, 119
scope, 119
specifiers, 462

storing
2's-complement bit-fields, 167
data, 232-233
in structures, 164-165
often-used, 280-281

fonts, 351
function addresses, 174
objects, 178
strings, 159-163
variables, 430
strcat() function, 160-162
strcmp() (string-comparison)
   function, 53
strcpy() function, 160
stream argument, 50
stream classes
   fstream stream, 705
   fstreambase, 705
   functions, 672
   ifstream, 705
stream I/O errors
   analyzing, 682-683
   correcting, 682-683
stream manipulators, 696, 699
   arguments, 695
   C++, 694-705
   setw(), 691
streambuf characters
   extracting, 675
   inserting, 676-677
   objects, 665
   returning, 675
streams, 49, 231-233, 260
   binary, 235-236
   bit states, 696
   C++, 663-683, 705-714
   checking, 272
   cin, 671
   cout, 669
   data, 234-235, 253, 664
   indicators
      end-of-file, 273
      errors, 681
   redirecting, 255
   standard, 664-667
   status, 665
   stdaux, 235
   stderr, 235
   stdin, 235
   stdout, 235

stdprn, 235
text, 235-236
stredit.c program, 199-203
strerror() function, 273
string concatenation operator (##),
   95
string literal operator (#), 95
string of digit characters, 56
strings, 47, 156, 236
   ("stepping through")
      pointers, 147-149
   addresses, 160
   characters
      inserting, 162-163
      "stepping through", 147-148
   comparing, 53, 117
   concatenating, 160-161
   contents, 160-161
   converting to floating-point
      number, 55
   creating from quad numbers, 764
   defining, 92
   format, 52, 131
   in macros, 91
   initializing, 160-161
   literals, 159
   popping off stacks, 443
   reading, 50, 251-253
   storing, 159-163
   values, 56
   writing, 53-54, 251-253
strings.cpp program, 566-567
strlen() function, 160-162, 775
stroked fonts, 347
Stroustrup, Bjarne, 411
strtok() C library function, 901
struct keywords, 426
structs
   scopes, 425
   _wopeninfo struct, 806
   _wsizeinfo, 806
structures, 413, 418
   bit-fields, 164-167
   members, 439
   objects, 166
   operators,

member (.), 166, 438, 523
pointer (->), 168, 439, 488, 523
type declaration, 164-166
types, 156
WNDCLASS, 887
stub programs, 843
subscript bound, 141
subscript operator ([ ]), 598-603, 768
subtracting pointers, 154
sum() function, 40, 134
sum_it() function, 119
support macros, 435
suppressing virtual call
mechanism, 516
swapping
dynamic overlay, 296
memory locations, 150
<Switch Help> command, 27
Switch List list box, 27
switch statements, 64-68, 81, 125
switches, cl command-line, 34
symbolic constants, 315
symbols
_QWINVER, 806
unreferenced, 789
_WINVER, 806
syntactical convenience, 575
syntax
class declaration, 426-429
class member, 447
overloaded operator function,
586-588
placement, 650
system() function, 128-129
szAppName macro, 815

T

tab whitespace characters, 62
tellg() function, 712
tellp() function, 712
temporary files, 256
temporary unnamed objects, 642
terminating
programs, 126-128
semicolon, 426

value, 131
virtual memory, 308
testing
class membership, 520
constructor initializers, 522
errors, 681
function arguments, 522
keyboard class, 572-573
program efficiency, 370-372
variables, 521-522
testnew.cpp program, 572-573
text
boundaries, 322
colors, 315-318
graphics mode, 346-351
modes, 311-313, 321
parsing, 676
positioning, 320-322
scanning, 676
streams, 235-236
windows, 318-323
text-mode
color, 108
coordinates, 331
screens, 314
text-window functions, 106
TextOut() function, 821, 906
this pointer, 438-442, 548-549
tilde (~), 434
time and date functions, 106
timer tick interrupt, 398-403
timing profiling mode, 381
Tiny memory models, 17, 289, 297
title bar, 22
tmpnam() function, 256
tokens, 81
toupper() function, 57-58, 115
tracing, 358
transferring data, 232-235, 253
TranslateMessage() function, 820,
890-891
translating source codes, 18
~tree() destructor function, 753
truth tables, 98
type abstraction, 765
type casting, 88

type conversions, 86-88
  automatic, 86
  controlling, 85-89
  explicit, 88
  implicit, 86-87
  process, 86-87
  user-defined, 758-764
  with constructor functions,
    758-760
type name, 644
type-safe linkage, 575-579
typecast operators, 760-764
`typedef` keyword, 165
types, 221
  aggregate, 155
  array, 140-142, 156
  data, 72-79, 115
  derived, 140, 413
  function, 140
  incomplete, 140-141
  new, 414
  object, 140
  pointer, 140
  reference, 141
  structures, 156
  union, 167-170
  user-defined, 413
  void, 117-118
types, *see* class

U

unary operators, 82
  overloading, 595-598
  sample expressions, 596
  scope operator (::), 520
<Unassign> command, 27
Unassigned Keys list box, 26
`#undef` preprocessor directive, 93
undefining macros, 93
underscore (_), 111
union keywords, 426
union types, 167-170
unions, 167, declaring a class,
  618-620
unique name, 575

`unload()` function, 545
unnamed temporary object, 627
unreferenced symbols, 789
`unsetf()` function, 688
`UpdateWindow()` function, 820, 889
updating base classes, 733
uppercase chararacters, 57
Use Debug Options radio button,
  359
user screen, 46
user-defined
  cast operators, 594, 761-763
  functions, 43, 102, 108-115
  new and delete operators, 649
  objects, 417
  type conversions, 758-764
  types, 413
user-supplied header files, 215-216
Using C, 845
utilities
  bscmake, 786
  CodeView, 356
  NMAKE, 221-224, 824
  "source browser", 20
utility.c program, 203-206

V

`va_...()` functions, 131-135
`va_arg()` functions, 132, 135
`va_end()` function, 132, 247
`va_start()` function, 132, 247
value-like objects, 637
values, 141
  accessing in objects, 152
  bits, 279
  bytes, 86
  comparing, 65
  constant, 90
  data, 692
  editing, 367
  file position indicator, 270
  in expressions, 80
  in functions, 43, 111
  initializer lists, 158

inputting, 807
integer, 143
local variables, 367
mask, 687-688
modifying, 112-113
nonzero (true), 431
NULL, 154
null pointer, 431
passing to differents, 48
pointer, 115
returned, 41-43, 104, 115-119, 132
segment address, 282
storing, 104
string, 56
subscript bound, 141
unreturned, 117-118
using for return types
    for arithmetic and shift
        operators, 594
viewing, 366
variable argument list
    printf() function, 244
    scanf() function, 242
variables
    accessing, 122, 130, 145, 212
    argument lists, 130-136, 242
        functions, 106
        status, 131
        terminating values, 131
    attributes, 119
    availability, 121-122
    declarations, 39
        global, 42
        integer, 72
        parameters, 104
    describing, 140
    duration, 121-122
    floating-point, 73-74, 88
    global, 76, 508
    in source files, 119
    incrementing, 71
    integer, 88
    linkage, 122-123
    local, 77-78, 177, 367, 521-522
    locating, 120, 787
    memory, 121

multiple, 74
pointer, 115, 179, 583
referencing, 212, 366
register, 153
scopes, 120-121
temporary, 430
values, 113
verifying in functions, 41
visibility, 120-121
vertical (y-axis) screen
    coordinate, 318
Very Large Integer (vli), 933
vfprintf() function, 245
VGA (Video Graphics Array), 324,
    327
_vheapinit() function, 304-306
_vheapterm() function, 308
video
    adapter, 312
    memory, 313
    modes, 314-315
Video Graphics Array (VGA), 324,
    327
<View> button, 219
viewing
    class derivations, 791
    data, 366-368
    DOS environment variables, 26
    programs, 364
    region, 333
    values, 366
viewpoint, 331
virtual functions, 515, 584, 735-741
    call mechanism, 516
    constructor, 745, 751-753
    defining, 746
    destructor, 751-753, 619
    keyword, 753
    pass-through mechanism, 735,
        739
    pure, 748-750
    rules, 737-738
virtual memory
    blocks, 304-307
    locking in, 308
    management system, 304

mode, 280
space, 308
terminating, 308
visibility, 120-121
visual pages, 346
vli, *see* Very Large Integer
_vload() function, 305
_vlock() function, 305-308
_vmalloc() function, 304
void clear(int f=0) function, 682
void pointer, 444
void types, 111, 117-118
void* cast operator, 680
volatile constructor functions, 616
vprintf() function, 245-247
vsprintf() function, 245

W

_wabout() function, 808
warnings, 30, 219
watches, 366
_wclose() function, 807
_wgetfocus() function, 807
_wgetscreenbuf() function, 810
_wgetsize() function, 808
while loop, 69-70
while statement, 81
whitespace characters, 56, 62, 243
whole numbers, 72
width() function, 685
wildcards, specifying for
  filenames, 226
windows
  accessing, 22-25
  action buttons, 25
  activating, 807
  check boxes, 25
  child, 804-806
    creating, 807-810
    scroll bars, 809-810
  classes, 886-889
  closing, 22, 807
  displaying, 23

dragging, 815
exiting, 808
input boxes, 24
list boxes, 24
locals, 367
location, 808-809
minimizing, 806
moving, 23
multiple, 804-807
number, 23
radio buttons, 25
Registers, 368
resizing, 24
scroll bars, 23
size, 808-809, 815
text, 318-323
title bar, 22
zooming, 23
Windows 3.1, 841-842
  compiling, 822-824
  creating, 797-798
  directories, 843-845
  dynamic-link libraries (DLLs),
    906-912
  graphical user interface (GUI),
    845
  linking, 822-824
  menu option, 23
  printer devices, 846
  programming, 798-807, 877
  source files, 877-881
Windows 3.1 Programmer's
  Reference, 798
Windows programs, designing
  interfaces, 885-886
  callback functions, 892-895
  error messages, 896-897
  hard copy to Print Manager,
    898-906
  main message loop, 889-891
  pop-up help, 896-897
  window procedures, 891-892
  windows classes, 886-888
Windows Targets options, 16
Windows-launched DOS application,
  19

`WinMain()`
  function, 812-813, 819, 846
  message loop, 813
  Windows function, 886
WINSTUB.EXE Program, 842-843
`_WINVER` symbol, 806
`WM_COMMAND` Windows
  message, 892
`WM_CREATE` Windows
  message, 892
`WM_DESTROY` message, 822
`WM_DESTROY` Windows
  message, 892
`WM_PAINT` message, 820
`_wmenuclick()` function, 810
WNDCLASS structure type, 887
`WndProc()` function, 813, 816, 820,
  846, 891-892
`_wopen()` function, 807
`_wopeninfo` struct, 806
`write()` function, 677, 710, 807
`writeblk()` function, 543
`writen()` function, 544
writing
  C programs, 43-45, 62
  characters, 53-54, 248-249
  data
    blocks, 543
    to files, 261
  dynamic data libraries (DDLs),
    908-912
  files, 545
    direct, 261-268
    `fstream`, 710-712
  functions
    constructor, default 637-639
    inline member, 447-448
    `main()`, 102-105
    member, 437-438, 445-455
    user-defined, 110
    `WndProc()`, 891-892
  main message loop, 846
  memory address, 279

statements
  `if-else`, 67
  loop-control, 123-126
strings, 53-54, 251-253
`ws` manipulator, 696
`_wsetexit()` function, 808
`_wsetfocus()` function, 807
`_wsetscreenbuf()` function, 810
`_wsetsize()` function, 808
`_wsizeinfo` struct, 806
WX Server program, 823
`_wyield()` function, 804

X-Z

x-axis (horizontal) screen
  coordinate, 318
`XOR` (^) operator, 678

y-axis (vertical) screen coordinate,
  318

zero-origin array index, 157
zoom command, 23

Computer Books from Que Mean PC Performance!

Spreadsheets

1-2-3 Beyond the Basics	$24.95
1-2-3 for DOS Release 2.3 Quick Reference	$ 9.95
1-2-3 for DOS Release 2.3 QuickStart	$19.95
1-2-3 for DOS Release 3.1+ Quick Reference	$ 9.95
1-2-3 for DOS Release 3.1+ QuickStart	$19.95
1-2-3 for Windows Quick Reference	$ 9.95
1-2-3 for Windows QuickStart	$19.95
1-2-3 Personal Money Manager	$29.95
1-2-3 Power Macros	$39.95
1-2-3 Release 2.2 QueCards	$19.95
Easy 1-2-3	$19.95
Easy Excel	$19.95
Easy Quattro Pro	$19.95
Excel 3 for Windows QuickStart	$19.95
Excel for Windows Quick Reference	$ 9.95
Look Your Best with 1-2-3	$24.95
Quattro Pro 3 QuickStart	$19.95
Quattro Pro Quick Reference	$ 9.95
Using 1-2-3 for DOS Release 2.3, Special Edition	$29.95
Using 1-2-3 for Windows	$29.95
Using 1-2-3 for DOS Release 3.1+, Special Edition	$29.95
Using Excel 4 for Windows, Special Edition	$29.95
Using Quattro Pro 4, Special Edition	$27.95
Using Quattro Pro for Windows	$24.95
Using SuperCalc5, 2nd Edition	$29.95

Databases

dBASE III Plus Handbook, 2nd Edition	$24.95
dBASE IV 1.1 Qiuck Reference	$ 9.95
dBASE IV 1.1 QuickStart	$19.95
Introduction to Databases	$19.95
Paradox 3.5 Quick Reference	$ 9.95
Paradox Quick Reference, 2nd Edition	$ 9.95
Using AlphaFOUR	$24.95
Using Clipper, 3rd Edition	$29.95
Using DataEase	$24.95
Using dBASE IV	$29.95
Using FoxPro 2	$29.95
Using ORACLE	$29.95
Using Paradox 3.5, Special Edition	$29.95
Using Paradox for Windows	$26.95
Using Paradox, Special Edition	$29.95
Using PC-File	$24.95
Using R:BASE	$29.95

Business Applications

CheckFree Quick Reference	$ 9.95
Easy Quicken	$19.95
Microsoft Works Quick Reference	$ 9.95
Norton Utilities 6 Quick Reference	$ 9.95
PC Tools 7 Quick Reference	$ 9.95
Q&A 4 Database Techniques	$29.95
Q&A 4 Quick Reference	$ 9.95
Q&A 4 QuickStart	$19.95
Q&A 4 Que Cards	$19.95
Que's Computer User's Dictionary, 2nd Edition	$10.95
Que's Using Enable	$29.95
Quicken 5 Quick Reference	$ 9.95
SmartWare Tips, Tricks, and Traps, 2nd Edition	$26.95
Using DacEasy, 2nd Edition	$24.95
Using Microsoft Money	$19.95
Using Microsoft Works: IBM Version	$22.95
Using Microsoft Works for Windows, Special Edition	$24.95
Using MoneyCounts	$19.95
Using Pacioli 2000	$19.95
Using Norton Utilities 6	$24.95
Using PC Tools Deluxe 7	$24.95
Using PFS: First Choice	$22.95
Using PFS: WindowWorks	$24.95
Using Q&A 4	$27.95
Using Quicken 5	$19.95
Using Quicken for Windows	$19.95
Using Smart	$29.95
Using TimeLine	$24.95
Using TurboTax: 1992 Edition	$19.95

CAD

AutoCAD Quick Reference, 2nd Edition	$ 8.95
Using AutoCAD, 3rd Edition	$29.95

Word Processing

Easy WordPerfect	$19.95
Easy WordPerfect for Windows	$19.95
Look Your Best with WordPerfect 5.1	$24.95
Look Your Best with WordPerfect forWindows	$24.95
Microsoft Word Quick Reference	$ 9.95
Using Ami Pro	$24.95
Using LetterPerfect	$22.95
Using Microsoft Word 5.5: IBM Version, 2nd Edition	$24.95
Using MultiMate	$24.95
Using PC-Write	$22.95
Using Professional Write	$22.95
Using Professional Write Plus for Windows	$24.95
Using Word for Windows 2, Special Edition	$27.95
Using WordPerfect 5	$27.95
Using WordPerfect 5.1, Special Edition	$27.95
Using WordPerfect for Windows, Special Edition	$29.95
Using WordStar 7	$19.95
Using WordStar, 3rd Edition	$27.95
WordPerfect 5.1 Power Macros	$39.95
WordPerfect 5.1 QueCards	$19.95
WordPerfect 5.1 Quick Reference	$ 9.95
WordPerfect 5.1 QuickStart	$19.95
WordPerfect 5.1 Tips, Tricks, and Traps	$24.95
WordPerfect for Windows Power Pack	$39.95
WordPerfect for Windows Quick Reference	$ 9.95
WordPerfect for Windows Quick Start	$19.95
WordPerfect Power Pack	$39.95
WordPerfect Quick Reference	$ 9.95

Hardware/Systems

Batch File and Macros Quick Reference	$ 9.95
Computerizing Your Small Business	$19.95
DR DOS 6 Quick Reference	$ 9.95
Easy DOS	$19.95
Easy Windows	$19.95
Fastback Quick Reference	$ 8.95
Hard Disk Quick Reference	$ 8.95
Hard Disk Quick Reference, 1992 Edition	$ 9.95
Introduction to Hard Disk Management	$24.95
Introduction to Networking	$24.95
Introduction to PC Communications	$24.95
Introduction to Personal Computers, 2nd Edition	$19.95
Introduction to UNIX	$24.95
Laplink Quick Reference	$ 9.95
MS-DOS 5 Que Cards	$19.95
MS-DOS 5 Quick Reference	$ 9.95
MS-DOS 5 QuickStart	$19.95
MS-DOS Quick Reference	$ 8.95
MS-DOS QuickStart, 2nd Edition	$19.95
Networking Personal Computers, 3rd Edition	$24.95
Que's Computer Buyer's Guide, 1992 Edition	$14.95
Que's Guide to CompuServe	$12.95
Que's Guide to DataRecovery	$29.95
Que's Guide to XTree	$12.95
Que's MS-DOS User's Guide, Special Edition	$29.95
Que's PS/1 Book	$22.95
TurboCharging MS-DOS	$24.95
Upgrading and Repairing PCs	$29.95
Upgrading and Repairing PCs, 2nd Edition	$29.95
Upgrading to MS-DOS 5	$14.95
Using GeoWorks Pro	$24.95
Using Microsoft Windows 3, 2nd Edition	$24.95
Using MS-DOS 5	$24.95
Using Novell NetWare, 2nd Edition	$29.95
Using OS/2 2.0	$24.95
Using PC DOS, 3rd Edition	$27.95
Using Prodigy	$19.95
Using UNIX	$29.95
Using Windows 3.1	$26.95
Using Your Hard Disk	$29.95
Windows 3 Quick Reference	$ 8.95
Windows 3 QuickStart	$19.95
Windows 3.1 Quick Reference	$ 9.95
Windows 3.1 QuickStart	$19.95

Desktop Publishing/Graphics

CorelDRAW! Quick Reference	$ 8.95
Harvard Graphics 3 Quick Reference	$ 9.95
Harvard Graphics Quick Reference	$ 9.95
Que's Using Ventura Publisher	$29.95
Using DrawPerfect	$24.95
Using Freelance Plus	$24.95
Using Harvard Graphics 3	$29.95
Using Harvard Graphics for Windows	$24.95
Using Harvard Graphics, 2nd Edition	$24.95
Using Microsoft Publisher	$22.95
Using PageMaker 4 for Windows	$29.95
Using PFS: First Publisher, 2nd Edition	$24.95
Using PowerPoint	$24.95
Using Publish It!	$24.95

Macintosh/Apple II

Easy Macintosh	$19.95
HyperCard 2 QuickStart	$19.95
PageMaker 4 for the Mac Quick Reference	$ 9.95
The Big Mac Book, 2nd Edition	$29.95
The Little Mac Book	$12.95
QuarkXPress 3.1 Quick Reference	$ 9.95
Que's Big Mac Book, 3rd Edition	$29.95
Que's Little Mac Book, 2nd Edition	$12.95
Que's Mac Classic Book	$24.95
Que's Macintosh Multimedia Handbook	$24.95
System 7 Quick Reference	$ 9.95
Using 1-2-3 for the Mac	$24.95
Using AppleWorks, 3rd Edition	$24.95
Using Excel 3 for the Macintosh	$24.95
Using FileMaker Pro	$24.95
Using MacDraw Pro	$24.95
Using MacroMind Director	$29.95
Using MacWrite Pro	$24.95
Using Microsoft Word 5 for the Mac	$27.95
Using Microsoft Works: Macintosh Version, 2nd Edition	$24.95
Using Microsoft Works for the Mac	$24.95
Using PageMaker 4 for the Macintosh	$24.95
Using Quicken 3 for the Mac	$19.95
Using the Macintosh with System 7	$24.95
Using Word for the Mac, Special Edition	$24.95
Using WordPerfect 2 for the Mac	$24.95
Word for the Mac Quick Reference	$ 9.95

Programming/Technical

Borland C++ 3 By Example	$21.95
Borland C++ Programmer's Reference	$29.95
C By Example	$21.95
C Programmer's Toolkit, 2nd Edition	$39.95
Clipper Programmer's Reference	$29.95
DOS Programmer's Reference, 3rd Edition	$29.95
FoxPro Programmer's Reference	$29.95
Network Programming in C	$49.95
Paradox Programmer's Reference	$29.95
Programming in Windows 3.1	$39.95
QBasic By Example	$21.95
Turbo Pascal 6 By Example	$21.95
Turbo Pascal 6 Programmer's Reference	$29.95
UNIX Programmer's Reference	$29.95
UNIX Shell Commands Quick Reference	$ 8.95
Using Assembly Language, 2nd Edition	$29.95
Using Assembly Language, 3rd Edition	$29.95
Using BASIC	$24.95
Using Borland C++	$29.95
Using Borland C++ 3, 2nd Edition	$29.95
Using C	$29.95
Using Microsoft C	$29.95
Using QBasic	$24.95
Using QuickBASIC 4	$24.95
Using QuickC for Windows	$29.95
Using Turbo Pascal 6, 2nd Edition	$29.95
Using Turbo Pascal for Windows	$29.95
Using Visual Basic	$29.95
Visual Basic by Example	$21.95
Visual Basic Programmer's Reference	$29.95
Windows 3.1 Programmer's Reference	$39.95

For More Information,
Call Toll Free!
1-800-428-5331

All prices and titles subject to change without notice.
Non-U.S. prices may be higher. Printed in the U.S.A.

Personal computing is easy
when you're using Que!

Order Your Program Disk Today!

You can save yourself hours of tedious, error-prone typing by ordering the companion disk to *Using Microsoft C/C++ 7*. The disk contains source code for all complete programs and many of the other shorter samples in the book. You will get code that shows you how to use all the basic and advanced features of Microsoft C/C++ 7. Samples include code for graphics and screen control, MOVE overlay management, C Input/Output, and mixing C and assembly language. C++ samples include classes for stacks; linked-lists; Mouse control; virtual memory use; and samples of derived classes and virtual functions, overloaded operators, and C++ generic classes. Windows 3.1 sample programs include window procedures; dialog procedures; DLL modules; and a complete, working Windows financial calculator application.

Order by telephone for fastest service (overnight delivery is available at an additional charge). Disks are available in both $5\frac{1}{4}$" and $3\frac{1}{2}$" format. The cost is $14.95 per disk plus $1.50 for shipping and handling to U.S. addresses (outside the U.S. add $5.00). *Washington State residents must add 7.5% sales tax.* Allow 2 to 4 weeks for delivery.

To order by mail, complete the order form below and mail to:

Creative Concepts, Unltd.
430 N. Pine
Ellensburg, WA 98926
Hours: Tues-Fri 9-6, Sat-Sun 10-5, Pacific time

To order by telephone, have your credit card information ready and call

    1-800-942-2066 or 1-509-925-3585

To order by FAX, complete the order form below and FAX to

    1-509-925-1796

Using Microsoft C/C++ 7 Disk Order Form
Please *PRINT*

Product code # 101
Check desired disk size: $5\frac{1}{4}$" _____ $3\frac{1}{2}$" _____
Check payment method: Check _____   Money order _____

For credit card orders: Visa _____   MasterCard _____
Credit card # _____   Expiration: _____
Shipping preference: Regular UPS ($1.50) _____   UPS NextDay (extra charge) _____

Signature: _____

Name: _____

Street Address: _____

City: _____   State: _____   ZIP: _____

Telephone: _____

Free Catalog!

Mail us this registration form today, and we'll send you a free catalog featuring Que's complete line of best-selling books.

Name of Book _____

Name _____

Title _____

Phone ( ) _____

Company _____

Address _____

City _____

State _____ ZIP _____

Please check the appropriate answers:

1. Where did you buy your Que book?
   ☐ Bookstore (name: _____)
   ☐ Computer store (name: _____)
   ☐ Catalog (name: _____)
   ☐ Direct from Que
   ☐ Other: _____

2. How many computer books do you buy a year?
   ☐ 1 or less
   ☐ 2-5
   ☐ 6-10
   ☐ More than 10

3. How many Que books do you own?
   ☐ 1
   ☐ 2-5
   ☐ 6-10
   ☐ More than 10

4. How long have you been using this software?
   ☐ Less than 6 months
   ☐ 6 months to 1 year
   ☐ 1-3 years
   ☐ More than 3 years

5. What influenced your purchase of this Que book?
   ☐ Personal recommendation
   ☐ Advertisement
   ☐ In-store display
   ☐ Price
   ☐ Que catalog
   ☐ Que mailing
   ☐ Que's reputation
   ☐ Other: _____

6. How would you rate the overall content of the book?
   ☐ Very good
   ☐ Good
   ☐ Satisfactory
   ☐ Poor

7. What do you like *best* about this Que book?
   _____
   _____

8. What do you like *least* about this Que book?
   _____
   _____

9. Did you buy this book with your personal funds?
   ☐ Yes   ☐ No

10. Please feel free to list any other comments you may have about this Que book.
    _____
    _____
    _____

— **que** —

Order Your Que Books Today!

Name _____

Title _____

Company _____

City _____

State _____ ZIP _____

Phone No. ( ) _____

Method of Payment:

Check ☐   (Please enclose in envelope.)

Charge My: VISA ☐   MasterCard ☐

American Express ☐

Charge # _____

Expiration Date _____

Order No.	Title	Qty.	Price	Total

You can **FAX** your order to **1-317-573-2583**. Or call **1-800-428-5331, ext. ORDR** to order direct.

Please add $2.50 per title for shipping and handling.

Subtotal	
Shipping & Handling	
Total	

— **que** —

BUSINESS REPLY MAIL
First Class Permit No. 9918   Indianapolis, IN

Postage will be paid by addressee

11711 N. College
Carmel, IN 46032

BUSINESS REPLY MAIL
First Class Permit No. 9918   Indianapolis, IN

Postage will be paid by addressee

que®

11711 N. College
Carmel, IN 46032